Deterministic and Stochastic Optimal Control and Inverse Problems

Editors

Baasansuren Jadamba
Rochester Institute of Technology
Rochester, New York, USA

Akhtar A. Khan
Rochester Institute of Technology
Rochester, New York, USA

Stanisław Migórski
Faculty of Mathematics and Computer Science
Jagiellonian University, Krakow, Poland

Miguel Sama
National Distance Education University (UNED)
Madrid, Spain

T0144521

CRC Press
Taylor & Francis Group
Boca Raton London New York

CRC Press is an imprint of the
Taylor & Francis Group, an **informa** business
A SCIENCE PUBLISHERS BOOK

First edition published 2022
by CRC Press
6000 Broken Sound Parkway NW, Suite 300, Boca Raton, FL 33487-2742

and by CRC Press
4 Park Square, Milton Park, Abingdon, Oxon OX14 4RN

ISBN: 978-0-367-50630-8 (hbk)
ISBN: 978-0-367-50631-5 (pbk)
ISBN: 978-1-003-05057-5 (ebk)

DOI: 10.1201/9781003050575

Typeset in Times New Roman
by Radiant Productions

Dedicated to Zuhair Nashed on his 85th birthday

Preface

It is our immense pleasure and privilege to dedicate this volume to Professor Zuhair Nashed on the occasion of his 85th birthday. During the last almost six decades, Prof. Zuhair Nashed made fundamental contributions to strengthening various aspects of operator theory, functional analysis, numerical analysis, inverse and ill-posed problems, iterative methods, differentiability concepts, generalized inverses, variational inequalities, regularization techniques, integral equations, signal analysis, sampling theory, among others. Prof. Zuhair Nashed is the founding editor of the journal Numerical Functional Analysis and Optimization and the founding co-editor of the Journal of Integral Equations and Applications. He has published more than 150 papers in reputed journals. His original and widely cited research work remains a source of inspiration for several generations of aspirants and accomplished researchers alike. His unique scientific contributions and dynamic personality have well-deservedly made him a recipient of many accolades. The fascinating tribute by K. Atkinson and C. Groetsch "Zuhair Nashed. A biographical tribute. J. Integer Eq. Appl., 20: 153–160, 2008" provides details on his personal and professional accomplishments. Another beautiful tribute that offers insight into the life of Prof. Nashed is by J. Ding: A conversation with Zuhair Nashed (in Chinese). Math. Cult., 9: 41–57, 2018. To gauge Prof. Nashed's impact on international research, we wish to mention the tribute by Y. Wang and Y. Wei: Special Issue Research on Generalized Inverses in China, Numerical Functional Analysis and Optimization, 41: 1669–1671, 2020.

Inverse problems constitute a vital area of research that possesses a toolbox of powerful theoretical tools, efficient and reliable computational techniques, and applications to a wide array of real-world problems. During the last decades, inverse problems witnessed explosive growth, and many directions of research emerged. The primary object of this volume is to present, in a unified framework, some of the recent developments in deterministic and stochastic inverse problems. This subject enjoyed Prof. Zuhair Nashed's concentrated attention and benefited from his creativity. We anticipate this volume will give a glimpse of some of the commonly pursued research directions in inverse problems and related domains.

This volume is comprised of fifteen chapters. It begins with a contribution by A. Schlintl and B. Kaltenbacher, who study the Bayesian approach to inverse problems in an all-at-once framework. R. Filippozzi, J.C. Rabelo and A. Leitão propose a nonstationary iterated Tikhonov Kaczmarz method for obtaining stable approximate solutions to systems of ill-posed equations. X. Cheng, R. Gong and W. Han consider the numerical approximation of optimal control problems governed by a stationary Stokes hemivariational inequality. B. Hofmann, C. Hofmann, P. Mathé and R. Plato focus on some aspects of analytical developments of Tikhonov regularization for nonlinear ill-posed equations with smoothness promoting penalties. J. Gwinner develops a general framework for the inverse problem of parameter identification in variational inequalities of the second kind that treat the parameter linked to a bilinear form and a nonlinear non-smooth function. S. Zeng, J. Cen, S. Migórski and V.T. Nguyen investigate a generalized fuzzy variational-hemivariational inequality in an infinite-dimensional Banach space. M. Bongarti and I. Lasiecka study a boundary stabilization of a linearized version of the so-called Jordan–Moore–Gibson–Thompson (JMGT) equation. M. Sofonea and Y. Xiao study a new mathematical model (and associated control problem) that describes the quasistatic contact of a viscoelastic body with a deformable obstacle covered by a layer of viscous fluid. S. Pollock reviews some recent developments on the acceleration properties of the extrapolation technique know as Anderson acceleration. M.A. Mansour, M.A. Bahraoui and A.E. Bekkali consider approximate coincidence points for single-valued maps and approximate fixed points for Aubin continuous set-valued maps. A. Barbagallo, M. Ferrara and P. Mauro investigate a stochastic variational inequality that models the Cournot-Nash equilibrium principle with uncertainty. O. Chadli and R.N. Mohapatra develop an augmented Lagrangian framework for optimal control problems governed by mixed variational-hemi-variational inequalities. A. Aspri, L. Frischauf, Y. Korolev and O. Scherzer study a purely data-driven regularization method for inverse problems and devise a projection algorithm with respect to frames as a data-driven reconstruction procedure in inverse problems. The work of W. Freeden deals with the Antenna problem induced regularization and sampling strategies. B. Jadamba, A.A. Khan, Q.T. Kolt and M. Sama propose a new equation error approach for identifying a random parameter in the stochastic diffusion equation.

We firmly believe that the breadth and diversity of areas covered in this volume will make it of great interest to researchers in inverse problems, optimal control, variational inequalities, optimization problems, and areas that are enriched by their applications.

A final word of gratitude is due to the researchers who contributed to this volume with their excellent contributions. We are grateful to the referees of the chapters included and Vijay Primlani for his professionalism and patience.

March, 2021

Baasansuren Jadamba
Akhtar A. Khan
Stanisław Migórski
Miguel Sama

Contents

Contributors

Andrea Aspri
University of Pavia
Pavia, Italy

Adham El Bekkali
FST-Tanger, Abdelmalek Essaadi University
Morocco

Annamaria Barbagallo
University of Naples Federico II
Naples, Italy

Mohamed Amin Bahraoui
FST-Tanger, Abdelmalek Essaadi University
Morocco

Marcelo Bongarti
University of Memphis
Memphis, USA

Jinxia Cen
Southwest Petroleum University
Sichuan, China

Ouayl Chadli
Ibn Zohr University
Agadir, Morocco

Xiaoliang Cheng
Zhejiang University
Zhejiang, China

Massimiliano Ferrara
University Mediterranea of Reggio Calabria
Reggio Calabria, Italy

Rafaela Filippozzi
Federal University of St. Catarina
Florianopolis SC, Brazil

Willi Freeden
University of Kaiserslautern
Kaiserslautern, Germany

Leon Frischauf
University of Vienna
Vienna, Austria

Baasansuren Jadamba
Rochester Institute of Technology
Rochester, USA

Rongfang Gong
Nanjing University of Aeronautics and Astronautics
Jiangsu, China

Joachim Gwinner
Universität der Bundeswehr München
Neubiberg/Munich, Germany

Weimin Han
University of Iowa
Iowa, USA

Barbara Kaltenbacher
Alpen-Adria-Universität Klagenfurt
Klagenfurt, Austria

Akhtar A Khan
Rochester Institute of Technology
Rochester, USA

Quinn T Kolt
Rochester Institute of Technology
Rochester, USA

Yury Korolev
University of Cambridge
Cambridge, UK

Irena Lasiecka
University of Memphis
Memphis, USA

Antonio Leitao
Federal University of St. Catarina
Florianopolis SC, Brazil

Mohamed Ait Mansour
FP-SAFI, Cadi Ayyad University
Morocco

Paolo Mauro
University of Catania
Catania - Italy

Stanisław Migórski
Jagiellonian University in Krakow
Krakow, Poland

Ram N Mohapatra
University of Central Florida
Florida, USA

Van Thien Nguyen
FPT University
Hanoi, Vietnam

Sara Pollock
University of Florida
Gainesville, USA

Joel C Rabelo
Federal University of St. Catarina
Florianopolis SC, Brazil

Miguel Sama
Universidad Nacional de Educación a Distancia
Madrid, Spain

Anna Schlintl
Alpen-Adria-Universität Klagenfurt
Klagenfurt, Austria

Otmar Scherzer
University of Vienna and Johann Radon Institute for Computational and Applied Mathematics (RICAM)
Vienna and Linz, Austria

Shengda Zeng
Yulin Normal University
Guangxi, China

Bernd Hofmann
Chemnitz University of Technology, Chemnitz, Germany

Christopher Hofmann
Chemnitz University of Technology, Chemnitz, Germany

Peter Mathé
Weierstraß Institute for Applied Analysis and Stochastics, Berlin, Germany

Robert Plato
Universität Siegen, Siegen, Germany

Mircea Sofonea
University of Perpignan, Perpignan, France

Yi-bin Xiao
University of Electronic Science and Technology of China, Sichuan, PR China

Chapter 1

All-At-Once Formulation Meets the Bayesian Approach: A Study of Two Prototypical Linear Inverse Problems

Anna Schlintl and *Barbara Kaltenbacher**

2000 Mathematics Subject Classification. 35R30, 49N45, 65J22, 65M30.

1.1 Introduction

In a general setting, the model to work with in the Bayesian approach is given by

$$y^\delta = Gx + \delta\eta, \tag{1.1}$$

where G is the (linear) forward operator, mapping between Hilbert spaces X and Y, $\delta \geq 0$ describes the noise level, x is the unknown target and y^δ denotes the data, when η is a random variable describing the noise. We restrict our considerations to Gaussian noise, i.e., $\eta \sim \mathcal{N}(0,\Sigma)$. This equation can be transformed such that it results in a problem under Gaussian white noise given by

$$z^\delta = \Sigma^{-1}Gx + \delta\Sigma^{-1}\eta. \tag{1.2}$$

Alpen-Adria-Universität Klagenfurt, Klagenfurt, Austria.

* Corresponding author: Barbara.Kaltenbacher@aau.at

The prior distribution for x is chosen to be normal, i.e., $x \sim \mathcal{N}(0, \frac{\delta^2}{\alpha} C_0)$, with the noise level δ and a scaling parameter α. In that setting, much is known, especially that the posterior is also normally distributed with mean and covariance given by

$$x_\alpha^\delta = C_0^{1/2}(\alpha I + H)^{-1} B^* z^\delta, \tag{1.3}$$

$$C_\alpha^\delta = \delta^2 C_0^{1/2}(\alpha I + H)^{-1} C_0^{1/2}, \tag{1.4}$$

where $B = \Sigma^{-1/2} G C_0^{1/2}$ and $H = BB^*$, see, e.g., [3, 4, 12, 14, 20, 25, 8, 9, 1, 21]. Here and below the superscript * denotes the Hilbert space adjoint.

In equation (1.1) the inverse problem is given in its reduced form, i.e., the model

$$\mathbb{M}(u,x) = 0 \tag{1.5}$$

and the observation equation

$$\mathbb{O}(u) = y \tag{1.6}$$

with operators $\mathbb{M} : U \times X \to W' \times Y$, $\mathbb{O} : U \to Y$ mapping between Hilbert spaces U, X, W', Y, are combined through the parameter-to-state map S, which maps the parameter x to the state u and is determined by the identity

$$\mathbb{M}(S(x), x) = 0.$$

The problem then transforms to

$$G(x) := \mathbb{O}(S(x)) = y.$$

Contrary to the reduced approch, the all-at-once formulation combines the model (1.5) and the observation equation (1.6) in one system given by

$$\mathcal{G}(\mathbf{x}) = \mathcal{G}(u,x) = \begin{pmatrix} \mathbb{M}(u,x) \\ \mathbb{O}(u) \end{pmatrix} = \begin{pmatrix} 0 \\ y \end{pmatrix} = \mathbf{y}. \tag{1.7}$$

This approach has recently gained attention, see, e.g., ([5, 6, 13, 15, 16, 18, 22]). While these paper remain in a purely deterministic setting, it is the aim of this chapter to apply the Bayesian approach to the all-at once formulation. Incorporating a priori information not only on the parameter but also on the state is expected to potentially improve reconstructions. Moreover, considering possible perturbations in both model and observations, i.e., assuming $\mathbf{y}^\delta = \mathbf{y} + \delta \begin{pmatrix} \eta_1 \\ \eta_2 \end{pmatrix}$, allows to take into account not only noise in the data but also uncertainty in the model, which is relevant in many applications. Combinations to a posterior distribution obtained by Bayes' formula allows to quantify the resulting uncertainty in both state and parameter.

1.1.1 Examples

To illustrate the all-at-once setting for inverse problems, two examples of linear inverse problems for PDEs are given in this section. These examples will serve as prototypical showcases in the analytic and numerical considerations of the following sections. Here we will only sketch these examples; the function spaces and operator definitions will be made clear in the next section.

To avoid confusion with the space variable, we will rename the parameter θ here.

Example 1 *The first example is a linear inverse source problem where we aim to recover the source u from the model*

$$\begin{aligned} -\Delta u &= f+\theta && \text{in } \Omega \\ u &= 0 && \text{on } \partial\Omega \end{aligned} \tag{1.8}$$

with noisy observations y^δ given through the equation

$$y^\delta = \mathbb{O}u + \delta\eta \quad \in \Omega. \tag{1.9}$$

The problem can be reformulated in an all-at-once fashion resulting in

$$\mathbf{y}^\delta = \mathcal{G}\mathbf{x} + \delta\eta \Longleftrightarrow \begin{pmatrix} y_1^\delta(x) \\ y_2^\delta(x) \end{pmatrix} = \begin{pmatrix} -\Delta & -I \\ \mathbb{O} & 0 \end{pmatrix} \begin{pmatrix} u(x) \\ \theta(x) \end{pmatrix} + \delta \begin{pmatrix} \eta_1 \\ \eta_2 \end{pmatrix}, \tag{1.10}$$

where $\mathbf{y}$ is now a vector consisting of the known inhomogeneity term f and of the observation y, $\mathcal{G}$ is a block matrix operator, the target $\mathbf{x}$ is a vector of the state variable u and the source θ. Additionally, the noise consists of two components, where the possible perturbation in the system is modeled through η_1 and the error in the observation equation by η_2.

Inverse source problems with possibly more complicated elliptic operators in place of $-\Delta$ as well as restricted measurements $\mathbb{O}u$, arise in numerous applications. For example, with the Helmholtz equation in place of the Poisson equation as a model, the problem corresponds to the frequency domain formulation of reconstructing sound sources from measurements taken by a microphone array, see, e.g., [17, 24].

Example 2 *The second example of interest in this chapter is the backward heat equation. The ambition is to recover the initial temperature when measurements are only available at some point later in time. This means, contrary to the first example this problem is time dependent. We consider the model as*

$$\begin{aligned} \partial_t u - \Delta u &= f && \text{in } (0,T)\times\Omega \\ u &= 0 && \text{on } (0,T)\times\partial\Omega \\ u(0,x) &= \theta(x) && x\in\Omega. \end{aligned}$$

with given observation equation

$$y^\delta(x) = u(T,x) + \delta\eta \quad \text{in } \Omega.$$

To formulate the model and the observation equation in one system, some rewriting has to be carried out first. To symbolize the observation of $v(t,x)$ *in point* T, *we use the Dirac operator defined by* $\delta_T v(t,x) := v(T,x)$, *which maps the state to its value at the final time* T. *Further, we want to incorporate the initial condition into the state space, which we do by making the ansatz* $u(t,x) := \hat{u}(t,x) + \theta(x)$ *for some* $\hat{u}$ *contained in a linear space of functions vanishing at initial time. This (after skipping the hat) leads to the all-at-once formulation*

$$\mathbf{y}^\delta = \mathcal{G}\mathbf{x} + \delta\eta \iff \begin{pmatrix} y_1^\delta \\ y_2^\delta \end{pmatrix} = \begin{pmatrix} \partial_t - \Delta & -\underline{I}\Delta \\ \delta_T & \underline{I} \end{pmatrix} \begin{pmatrix} u \\ \theta \end{pmatrix} + \delta \begin{pmatrix} \eta_1 \\ \eta_2 \end{pmatrix}. \quad (1.11)$$

Here $y_1(t,x) = f(t,x)$, $y_2(x) = y(x)$ *and the operator* $\underline{I}$ *maps an only space-dependent function to a formally space and time dependent function by assigning* v *to the time-constant function* $t \mapsto v$.

A classical application that can be modeled by backwards diffusion is deconvolution of images. Further related application examples are the identification of airborne contaminants [2] and imaging with acoustic or elastic waves in the presence of strong attenuation, arising, e.g., in photoacoustic tomography [19].

The remainder of this chapter is organized as follows. In Section 1.2 we provide more details on appropriate function space settings for the two prototypical examples above. In particular, since the adjoint of $\mathcal{G}$ is required for the computation of the posterior mean and covariance (1.3), (1.4), but also for many other reconstruction methods, we will provide details on this. For both of these examples, the degree of ill-posedness, i.e., the decay rate of the eigenvalues of G^*G is well known in the reduced setting and the question arises whether this behaviour may change in the all-at-once formulation. We therefore investigate the eigenvalues of the operators $\mathcal{G}^*\mathcal{G}$ both analytically and numerically in Section 1.3. Section 1.4 is devoted to a convergence analysis of the Bayesian all-at-once approach, where we can heavily rely on existing literature, especially the results from [1, 21], that largely carry over to the all-at-once formulation; however, certain conditions need a different interpretation than in the reduced setting, which we do by means of the prototypical examples above. The important question of how to choose priors not only for the parameter but also for the state is discussed in Section 1.5. Finally, in Section 1.6, we provide some numerical results.

1.2 Function Space Setting and Computation of Adjoints

For the following theoretical and numerical considerations, the two examples given in Section 1.1.1 are stated more precisely in terms of functions spaces and their adjoint operators are computed in this section. To this end, we will restrict ourselves to full observations $(\mathbb{O}u)(x) = u(x)$, $x \in \Omega$, and vanishing inhomogeneity f, and employ the following notations. The superscript * denotes the Hilbert space adjoint $B^* : Z \to A$ of a linear operator $B : A \to Z$, whereas $B^\star : Z' \to A'$ denotes its Banach space adjoint, mapping between the dual spaces A', Z'. The Laplacian $-\Delta$ with homogeneous Dirichlet boundary conditions will be denoted by $\mathcal{A}$ both when acting from $H_0^1(\Omega)$ to its dual $H^{-1}(\Omega)$ and when acting from $H_0^1(\Omega) \cap H^2(\Omega)$ to $L^2(\Omega)$. In the context of the time dependent model of the backwards diffusion problem, we will denote by $C(0,T;H)$, $L^2(0,T;H)$, $H^1(0,T;H)$ or simply shorthand $C(H)$, $L^2(H)$, $H^1(H)$, the Bochner spaces of time dependent functions with values in the space H (which will typically be a space of x dependent functions). Moreover, to map elements of such a space H into formally time dependent functions, we will use the operator $\underline{I}$ defined by

$$\underline{I} : H \to L^2(0,T;H) \quad v \mapsto (t \mapsto v)$$

(which can as well be considered as an operator mapping into $C(0,T;H)$, or $H^1(0,T;H)$ or even $C^\infty(0,T;H)$), whose H-$L^2(0,T;H)$ Hilbert space adjoint is the averaging operator defined by

$$\underline{I}^* : L^2(0,T;H) \to H \quad z \mapsto \int_0^T z(t)\,dt\,.$$

Finally, by $(e^{-\mathcal{A}t})_{t>0}$ we denote the semigroup associated with the heat equation, cf., e.g., [10] and Subsection 1.5.4 below.

1.2.1 *Inverse Source Problem*

The all-at-once formulation of the inverse source problem, as given in (1.10) consists of the vector of functions $\mathbf{x}(x) = (u(x), \theta(x))^T$ and the block operator matrix

$$\mathcal{G} = \begin{pmatrix} \mathcal{A} & -I \\ I & 0 \end{pmatrix}, \tag{1.12}$$

which acts from the space $U \times X := H_0^1(\Omega) \cap H^2(\Omega) \times L^2(\Omega)$ to $W' \times Y := L^2(\Omega) \times L^2(\Omega)$. Here I denotes both the embedding of $H_0^1(\Omega) \cap H^2(\Omega)$ into $L^2(\Omega)$ and the identity on $L^2(\Omega)$. The scalar product on U for elements $u, v \in U$ is defined as

$$\langle v(x), u(x) \rangle_U := \int_\Omega \mathcal{A}v(x)\mathcal{A}u(x)\,\mathrm{dx}. \tag{1.13}$$

For functions $\mathbf{x_1}(x) = (u_1(x), \theta_1(x))$ and $\mathbf{x_2}(x) = (u_2(x), \theta_2(x)) \in U \times L^2(\Omega)$ it holds that

$$\langle \mathbf{x_1}, \mathbf{x_2} \rangle_{U \times L^2(\Omega)} = \int_\Omega [\mathcal{A}u_1(x)\mathcal{A}u_2(x) + \theta_1(x)\theta_2(x)] \text{ dx} . \tag{1.14}$$

Therefore, the adjoint $\mathcal{G}^*$ of $\mathcal{G}$ can be computed from

$$\langle \mathcal{G}\mathbf{x_1}, \mathbf{x_2} \rangle_{L^2 \times L^2} = \int_\Omega [(\mathcal{A}u_1 - \theta_1)u_2 + u_1\theta_2] \text{ dx} \tag{1.15}$$

$$= \int_\Omega \left[\mathcal{A}u_1 \mathcal{A}(\mathcal{A}^{-1}u_2 + \mathcal{A}^{-2}\theta_2) - \theta_1 u_2\right] \text{ dx} = (\mathbf{x}_1, \mathcal{G}^*\mathbf{x}_2)_{U \times L^2}, \tag{1.16}$$

resulting in

$$\mathcal{G}^* = \begin{pmatrix} \mathcal{A}^{-1} & \mathcal{A}^{-2} \\ -I & 0 \end{pmatrix}, \quad \mathcal{G}^*\mathcal{G} = \begin{pmatrix} I + \mathcal{A}^{-2} & -\mathcal{A}^{-1} \\ -\mathcal{A} & I \end{pmatrix}. \tag{1.17}$$

1.2.2 Backwards Heat Problem

The same analysis can be done for the backwards heat problem, although it is a bit trickier, due to time dependence. The operator of interest in the all-at-once formulation of the backwards heat equation is given by

$$\mathcal{G} = \begin{pmatrix} \partial_t + \mathcal{A} & \underline{I}\mathcal{A} \\ \delta_T & I \end{pmatrix}, \tag{1.18}$$

which is an operator from the space $U_0 \times X$ to $W' \times Y := L^2(H^{-1}(\Omega) \times L^2(\Omega)$ where $X = H_0^1(\Omega)$,

$$U_0 := \{w \in L^2(H_0^1(\Omega)) \cap H^1(H^{-1}(\Omega)) : w(0,x) = 0\},$$

which means, that the initial condition $(u + \underline{I}\theta)(0) = \theta$ is implicitly enforced through the function space we are using for u. The operator $\underline{I}\mathcal{A}$ maps the static parameter into a time-dependent function space, i.e., $\theta \mapsto (t \mapsto \mathcal{A}\theta)$, and I here denotes the embedding of $H_0^1(\Omega)$ into $L^2(\Omega)$. The scalar product on U_0 for all $v(t,x), u(t,x) \in U_0$ is given by

$$\langle v, u \rangle_{U_0} = \int_0^T \int_\Omega \left[\nabla v \nabla u + \nabla \mathcal{A}^{-1} v_t \nabla \mathcal{A}^{-1} u_t\right] \text{dx dt} + \int_\Omega v(T)u(T) \text{ dx} \tag{1.19}$$

$$= \int_0^T \int_\Omega \mathcal{A}^{-1/2}(\partial_t + \mathcal{A})v \mathcal{A}^{-1/2}(\partial_t + \mathcal{A})u \text{ dx dt} \tag{1.20}$$

$$= \int_0^T \int_\Omega v\left[\mathcal{A}u - \mathcal{A}^{-1}u_{tt}\right] \text{ dx dt} + \int_\Omega v(T)\left[u(T) + \mathcal{A}^{-1}u_t(T)\right] \text{ dx}. \tag{1.21}$$

The other scalar products of interest are those of $L^2(H^{-1})$ and of $H_0^1(\Omega)$:

$$\langle v,u\rangle_{L^2(H^{-1})} = \int_0^T \int_\Omega \nabla\mathcal{A}^{-1}v\cdot\nabla\mathcal{A}^{-1}u \,\mathrm{dx}\,\mathrm{dt}\,,\quad \langle v,u\rangle_{H_0^1} = \int_\Omega \nabla v\cdot\nabla u\,\mathrm{dx} \tag{1.22}$$

With the help of these scalar products the operator $\mathcal{G}^*$ will form as

$$\mathcal{G}^* = \begin{pmatrix} (\partial_t+\mathcal{A})^* & \delta_T^* \\ (\underline{I}\mathcal{A})^* & I^* \end{pmatrix},$$

where for some components of the operator a bit more investigation is needed. We start with computing the first operator $(\partial_t+\mathcal{A})^*$ with the help of the scalar product equation

$$\langle(\partial_t+\mathcal{A})u,v\rangle_{L^2(H^{-1})} = \langle u,(\partial_t+\mathcal{A})^*v\rangle_{U_0}, \tag{1.23}$$

where the left hand side computes as

$$\begin{aligned}\langle(\partial_t+\mathcal{A})u,v\rangle_{L^2(H^{-1})} &= \int_0^T\int_\Omega u(t,x)\left[\mathcal{A}^{-1}v_t+v\right](t,x)\,\mathrm{dx}\,\mathrm{dt}\\ &+\int_\Omega u(T,x)\mathcal{A}^{-1}v(T,x)\,\mathrm{dx}\end{aligned}$$

and the right hand side, with $(\partial_t+\mathcal{A})^*v =: z$ according to the identity (1.19) works out as

$$\begin{aligned}\langle u,(\partial_t+\mathcal{A})^*v\rangle_{U_0} &= \int_0^T\int_\Omega u(t,x)\left[\mathcal{A}z-\mathcal{A}^{-1}z_{tt}\right](t,x)\,\mathrm{dx}\,\mathrm{dt}\\ &+\int_\Omega u(T,x)[z(T,x)+\mathcal{A}^{-1}z_t(T,x)]\,\mathrm{dx}.\end{aligned}$$

Then, equation (1.23) leads to the system

$$\begin{aligned}\mathcal{A}^2z-z_{tt} &= \mathcal{A}v-v_t \qquad \text{in } (0,T)\\ \mathcal{A}z(T)+z_t(T) &= v(T)\end{aligned} \tag{1.24}$$

By factorizing $\mathcal{A}^2-\partial_{tt}=(\mathcal{A}-\partial_t)(\mathcal{A}+\partial_t)$ and from the fact that $z\in U_0$ the system in (1.24) results in

$$\begin{aligned}(\partial_t+\mathcal{A})z &= v \qquad \text{in } (0,T)\\ z(0) &= 0.\end{aligned}$$

Therefore the adjoint operator $(\partial_t+\mathcal{A})^*$ applied to v can be written as the solution of the heat equation using the variation of constants formula for the heat semigroup

$$((\partial_t+\mathcal{A})^*v)(t,x) = \int_0^t e^{-\mathcal{A}(t-s)}v(s,x)\,\mathrm{ds}.$$

The next operator computed is δ_T^*. We proceed as before with the scalar product equation

$$(\delta_T u, v)_{L^2(\Omega)} = (u, \delta_T^* v)_{U_0},$$

which, with rewriting $z = \delta_T^* v(x)$, due to (1.19) is equivalent to

$$\int_\Omega u(T,x)v(x)\,\mathrm{dx} = \int_0^T \int_\Omega u(t,x)[\mathcal{A}z - \mathcal{A}^{-1}z_{tt}](t,x)\,\mathrm{dx}\,\mathrm{dt} \tag{1.25}$$

$$+ \int_\Omega u(T,x)[z(T,x) + \mathcal{A}^{-1}z_t(T,x)]\,\mathrm{dx}. \tag{1.26}$$

Then, (1.25) leads to the system

$$\begin{aligned} (\partial_t - \mathcal{A})(\partial_t + \mathcal{A})z &= 0 \quad \text{in } (0,T) \\ (\partial_t + \mathcal{A})z(T) &= \mathcal{A}v. \end{aligned}$$

Again using the heat semigroup, the solution can be given as

$$(\delta_T^* v)(t,x) = \mathcal{A}\int_0^t e^{-\mathcal{A}(T+t-2s)}v(x)\,\mathrm{ds} = \tfrac{1}{2}[e^{-\mathcal{A}(T-t)} - e^{-\mathcal{A}(T+t)}]v(x).$$

The other two adjoint operators compute as

$$((\mathcal{A}\underline{I})^* u)(x) = \mathcal{A}^{-1}\int_0^T u(s,x)\,\mathrm{ds}, \quad (I^* v)(x) = (\mathcal{A}^{-1}v)(x).$$

Altogether, the adjoint operator $\mathcal{G}^*$ is given by

$$\mathcal{G}^* = \begin{pmatrix} \int_0^{\cdot} e^{-\mathcal{A}(\cdot-s)}.(s)\,\mathrm{ds} & \tfrac{1}{2}[e^{-\mathcal{A}(T-\cdot)} - e^{-\mathcal{A}(T+\cdot)}] \\ \mathcal{A}^{-1}\underline{I}^* & \mathcal{A}^{-1} \end{pmatrix},$$

and $\mathcal{G}^*\mathcal{G}$ is given by

$$\mathcal{G}^*\mathcal{G} = \begin{pmatrix} I + \tfrac{1}{2}[e^{-\mathcal{A}(T-\cdot)} - e^{-\mathcal{A}(T+\cdot)}]\delta_T & \underline{I} - e^{-\mathcal{A}\cdot} + \tfrac{1}{2}[e^{-\mathcal{A}(T-\cdot)} - e^{-\mathcal{A}(T+\cdot)}] \\ \underline{I}^* + 2\mathcal{A}^{-1}\delta_T & TI + \mathcal{A}^{-1} \end{pmatrix}.$$

1.3 Analysis of the Eigenvalues

In this section the eigenvalues of the all-at-once operators are analyzed in terms of the two prototypical examples. For the analysis, the adjoint operators from Section 1.2 will be used. Especially the operator $\mathcal{G}^*\mathcal{G}$ is of interest. As one might have already noticed, these operators do not look symmetric. However, they are indeed symmetric, but with respect to the specific inner product on $U \times L^2(\Omega)$ and $U_0 \times H_0^1(\Omega)$, respectively. Therefore, a transformation is applied first, to find a representation of the operator in an L^2-related inner product. It can be shown that this transformed operator leads to approximate eigenvalues of the true operator.

Lemma 1.3.1 *Let V and H be Hilbert spaces with $C : V \to V$ self-adjoint and compact and $\mathcal{T} : V \to H$ boundedly invertible with $\mathcal{T} \in L(V,H)$ and $\mathcal{T}^{-1} \in L(H,V)$. Then the operator $\tilde{C} := (\mathcal{T}^{-1})^* C \mathcal{T}^{-1} : H \to H$ is self-adjoint and compact and the eigenvalues λ_k of C and μ_k of $\tilde{C}$ decay at the same rate, more precisely it holds*

$$\frac{1}{\|\mathcal{T}^{-1}\|^2}\mu_k \leq \lambda_k \leq \|\mathcal{T}\|^2 \mu_k,$$

with $\lambda_1 \geq \lambda_2 \geq \cdots \geq 0, \mu_1 \geq \mu_2 \geq \cdots \geq 0$.

Proof. The proof is based on the Courant-Fischer Theorem, which we quote here for the convenience of the reader

> THEOREM (COURANT-FISCHER). Let $C : V \to V$ be a selfadjoint and compact operator. Then the eigenvalues of C fulfill
>
> $$\lambda_k = \max\{\min\{(Cx,x)_V : x \in S_k, \|x\| = 1\} : \dim(S_k) = k, S_k \text{ subspace of V}\}$$

Let

$$\begin{aligned}
\lambda_k &= \max\{\min\{(Cx,x)_V : x \in S_k, \|x\| = 1\} : \dim(S_k) = k, S_k \text{ subspace of } V\} = \\
&= \max_{\dim(S_k)=k} \min_{x \in S_k, \|x\|=1} (Cx,x)_V = \max_{\dim(S_k)=k} \min_{x \in S_k, \|x\|=1} ((\mathcal{T}^{-1})^* C \mathcal{T}^{-1} \mathcal{T}x, \mathcal{T}x)_V = \\
&= \max_{\dim(S_k)=k} \min_{x \in S_k, \hat{x}=\mathcal{T}x/\|\mathcal{T}x\|, \|x\|=1} (\tilde{C}\hat{x},\hat{x})_H \|\mathcal{T}x\|^2 \quad (\star).
\end{aligned}$$

Due to the fact that

$$\hat{x} = \frac{\mathcal{T}x}{\|\mathcal{T}x\|} \in \hat{S}_k = \mathcal{T}S_k,$$

and the dimension of S_k being k, due to regularity of $\mathcal{T}$, $\hat{S}_k$ is of dimension k as well. Therefore, taking the minimum over a superset and using $\|\mathcal{T}x\| \geq \frac{1}{\|\mathcal{T}^{-1}\|}\|x\|$ results in

$$(\star) \geq \frac{1}{\|\mathcal{T}^{-1}\|^2} \max_{\dim(\hat{S}_k)=k} \min_{\hat{x} \in \hat{S}_k, \|x\|=1} (\tilde{C}x,x)_H = \frac{1}{\|\mathcal{T}^{-1}\|^2}\mu_k.$$

Analogously it holds

$$\mu_k \geq \frac{1}{\|(\mathcal{T}^{-1})^{-1}\|^2}\lambda_k = \frac{1}{\|\mathcal{T}\|^2}\lambda_k.$$

◊

With the help of Lemma 1.3.1 we will transform the operator $\mathcal{G}^*\mathcal{G}$ both for the inverse source and backwards heat problem and then investigate in the computation of the eigenvalues of the resulting operators.

1.3.1 Inverse Source Problem

The operator $\mathcal{G}^*\mathcal{G}$ as stated in (1.17), will be transformed according to Lemma 1.3.1 with the operator $\mathcal{T} : U \times L^2(\Omega) \to L^2(\Omega) \times L^2(\Omega)$ given by

$$\mathcal{T} = \begin{pmatrix} \mathcal{A} & 0 \\ 0 & I \end{pmatrix},$$

which can be easily seen to be unitary in this setting of spaces, i.e., $(\mathcal{T}^{-1})^* = \mathcal{T}$, therefore $\mathcal{G}^*\mathcal{G}$ transforms to

$$\widetilde{\mathcal{G}^*\mathcal{G}} = (\mathcal{T}^{-1})^*\mathcal{G}^*\mathcal{G}\mathcal{T}^{-1} = \begin{pmatrix} \mathcal{A} & 0 \\ 0 & I \end{pmatrix}\begin{pmatrix} I+\mathcal{A}^{-2} & -\mathcal{A}^{-1} \\ -\mathcal{A} & I \end{pmatrix}\begin{pmatrix} \mathcal{A}^{-1} & 0 \\ 0 & I \end{pmatrix}$$
$$= \begin{pmatrix} I+\mathcal{A}^{-2} & -I \\ -I & I \end{pmatrix},$$

which is obviously a compact perturbation of $\overline{\mathcal{G}^*\mathcal{G}} = \begin{pmatrix} I & -I \\ -I & I \end{pmatrix}$ whose eigenvalues are 0 and 2 with eigenspaces $E_0 = \{(g,g)^T : g \in L^2(\Omega)\}$, $E_2 = \{(-g,g)^T : g \in L^2(\Omega)\}$, that actually span all of $L^2(\Omega)$, $E_0 \oplus E_2 = L^2(\Omega)$.

1.3.1.1 Analytic Computation of the Eigenvalues

The eigenvalues λ are computed both analytically and numerically. For the analytic computation the characteristic eigenvalue equation is considered

$$\begin{pmatrix} I+\mathcal{A}^{-2} & -I \\ -I & I \end{pmatrix}\begin{pmatrix} f \\ g \end{pmatrix} = \lambda\begin{pmatrix} f \\ g \end{pmatrix},$$

which leads to the system

$$(1-\lambda)f + \mathcal{A}^{-2}f - g = 0, \quad (1-\lambda)g - f = 0,$$

resulting in

$$\mathcal{A}^{-2}g = \frac{\lambda(2-\lambda)}{(1-\lambda)}g$$
$$f = (1-\lambda)g.$$

Therefore, let $\mu = \lambda\frac{2-\lambda}{1-\lambda}$ be an eigenvalue of $\mathcal{A}^{-2}$. Then λ solves the quadratic equation

$$\lambda^2 - \lambda(2+\mu) + \mu = 0,$$

resulting in the two solutions

$$\lambda_{1,2} = \frac{2+\mu}{2} \pm \sqrt{\frac{\mu^2}{4}+1} = 1 + \frac{\mu}{2} + \sqrt{1+\frac{\mu^2}{4}}, \quad \frac{\mu}{1+\frac{\mu}{2}+\sqrt{1+\frac{\mu^2}{4}}}.$$

As $\mu \to 0$, the solutions for $\lambda_{1,2}$ tend to 2 and 0, respectively. Therefore, the eigenvalues of $\widetilde{\mathcal{G}^*\mathcal{G}}$ accumulate at 0 and 2, at the same (basically linear) speed as $\mu \to 0$.

Thus, besides the singular values tending to zero at a linear rate, known from the reduced setting and reflecting the mild ill-posedness of the inverse source problem, we have another sequence tending to a positive value.

1.3.1.2 Numerical Computation of the Eigenvalues

The computation is done in python with the help of the finite element discretization in FEniCS and the eigensolver from SLEPc. The discretization is done on a unit square mesh with degree 1 Lagrange elements. To overcome the computation of $\mathcal{A}^{-2}$ the inverse operator $\widetilde{\mathcal{G}^*\mathcal{G}}^{-1} = \begin{pmatrix} \mathcal{A}^2 & \mathcal{A}^2 \\ \mathcal{A}^2 & \mathcal{A}^2+I \end{pmatrix}$ is used. The matrices resulting from the finite element discretization $u(x) \approx \sum_{i=1}^{n_{el}} u_i\phi_i(x)$ with the FE basis functions ϕ_i, and the coefficient vector $\underline{u} = (u_1,\ldots,u_{n_{el}})$, according to the identities

$$\mathcal{A}u = \lambda u \Leftrightarrow K\underline{u} = \lambda M\underline{u}, \quad \mathcal{A}^2 u = \lambda u \Leftrightarrow KM^{-1}K\underline{u} = \lambda M\underline{u},$$

are

$$\widetilde{\mathcal{G}^*\mathcal{G}_h}^{-1} = \begin{pmatrix} KM^{-1}K & KM^{-1}K \\ KM^{-1}K & KM^{-1}K+M \end{pmatrix}, \quad \mathcal{M} = \begin{pmatrix} M & 0 \\ 0 & M \end{pmatrix},$$

with M and K being the assembled mass and stiffness matrices according to

$$M_{i,j} = \int_\Omega \phi_i\phi_j, \tag{1.27}$$

$$K_{i,j} = \int_\Omega \nabla\phi_i \cdot \nabla\phi_j, \tag{1.28}$$

to state the eigenvalue equation as

$$\mathcal{M}\mathbf{x} = \lambda \widetilde{\mathcal{G}^*\mathcal{G}_h}^{-1}\mathbf{x},$$

with λ and $\mathbf{x}$ denoting the eigenvalue and eigenvector, respectively. Sampling of 500 eigenvalues leads then to the following visualized output as seen in Figure 1.1(a), the square root scaled plot in Figure 1.1(b) suggests quadratic decay, corresponding to the fact that $\lambda_{2,n} \sim \frac{\mu_n}{2} \sim \frac{C}{n^2}$ as the eigenvalues of the Laplacian on the 2-d unit square are given by $\mu_{j,k} = \frac{j^2+k^2}{4}$, $j,k \in \mathbb{N}$ and therefore, upon proper renumbering, decay linearly in n.

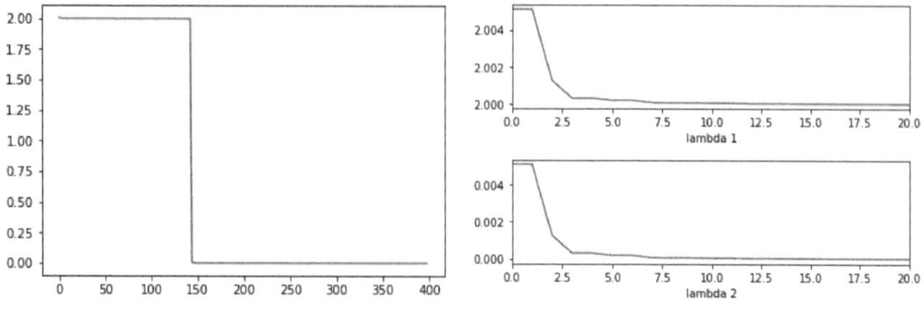

(a) Eigenvalues (b) Detailed plot

Figure 1.1: Numerical results for the eigenvalues of $\widetilde{\mathcal{G}^*\mathcal{G}}$ for the inverse source problem.

1.3.2 Backwards Heat Equation

The same analysis is done with the backwards heat equation. Here, the operator of interest is

$$\mathcal{G}^*\mathcal{G} = \begin{pmatrix} I + \mathcal{A}\int_0^t e^{-\mathcal{A}(T+t-2s)}\,.(s)\delta_T & I - e^{-\mathcal{A}t} + \mathcal{A}\int_0^t e^{-\mathcal{A}(T+t-2s)}\,.(s) \\ \underline{I}^* + 2\mathcal{A}^{-1}\delta_T & TI + \mathcal{A}^{-1} \end{pmatrix}. \tag{1.29}$$

The transformation from the space $U_0 \times H_0^1(\Omega)$ to the space $L^2(L^2(\Omega)) \times L^2(\Omega)$ is computed with Lemma 1.3.1 where the operator $\mathcal{T}$ for the transformation is given by

$$\mathcal{T} = \begin{pmatrix} \mathcal{A}^{-1/2}(\partial_t + \mathcal{A}) & 0 \\ 0 & \mathcal{A}^{1/2} \end{pmatrix}$$

and therefore,

$$\widetilde{\mathcal{G}^*\mathcal{G}} = (\mathcal{G}\mathcal{T}^{-1})^*\mathcal{G}\mathcal{T}^{-1}.$$

Here

$$\mathcal{T}^{-1}\begin{pmatrix} f \\ g \end{pmatrix} = \begin{pmatrix} u \\ \theta \end{pmatrix} \Leftrightarrow \begin{cases} (\partial_t + \mathcal{A})u = \mathcal{A}^{1/2}f \\ \theta = \mathcal{A}^{-1/2}g \end{cases}$$

and

$$\mathcal{G}\begin{pmatrix} u \\ \theta \end{pmatrix} = \begin{pmatrix} a \\ b \end{pmatrix} \Leftrightarrow \begin{cases} (\partial_t + \mathcal{A})u + \mathcal{A}\theta = a \\ u(T) + \theta = b \end{cases},$$

thus

$$\begin{cases} \mathcal{A}^{1/2}f(t) + \mathcal{A}^{1/2}g = a(t),\ t \in (0,T) \\ \int_0^T e^{-\mathcal{A}(T-t)}\mathcal{A}^{1/2}f(t)\,dt + \mathcal{A}^{-1/2}g = b \end{cases},$$

i.e.,

$$\mathcal{G}\mathcal{T}^{-1} = \begin{pmatrix} \mathcal{A}^{1/2} & \mathcal{A}^{1/2}\underline{I} \\ \int_0^T e^{-\mathcal{A}(T-s)}\mathcal{A}^{1/2}.(s)\,\mathrm{ds} & \mathcal{A}^{-1/2} \end{pmatrix}.$$

For computing the adjoint $(\mathcal{G}\mathcal{T}^{-1})^*$ we consider the identity

$$
\begin{aligned}
&\left\langle \mathcal{G}\mathcal{T}^{-1}\begin{pmatrix} f \\ g \end{pmatrix}, \begin{pmatrix} a \\ b \end{pmatrix}\right\rangle_{L^2(H^{-1})\times L^2} \\
&= \int_0^T \int_\Omega (f(t,x)+g(x))\mathcal{A}^{-1/2}a(t,x)\ \mathrm{dx\ dt} \\
&\quad + \int_\Omega \left(\int_0^T e^{-\mathcal{A}(T-s)}\mathcal{A}^{1/2}f(s,x)\ \mathrm{ds} + \mathcal{A}^{-1/2}g(x)\right) b(x)\ \mathrm{dx} \\
&= \int_0^T \int_\Omega f(t,x)\left(\mathcal{A}^{-1/2}a(t,x) + e^{-\mathcal{A}(T-t)}\mathcal{A}^{1/2}b\right)\ \mathrm{dx\ dt} \\
&\quad + \int_\Omega g(x)\mathcal{A}^{-1/2}\left(\int_0^T a(t,x)\ \mathrm{dt} + b\right)\ \mathrm{dx},
\end{aligned}
$$

which yields

$$
(\mathcal{G}\mathcal{T}^{-1})^* = \begin{pmatrix} \mathcal{A}^{-1/2} & e^{-\mathcal{A}(T-\cdot)}\mathcal{A}^{1/2} \\ \mathcal{A}^{-1/2}\underline{I}^* & \mathcal{A}^{-1/2} \end{pmatrix}.
$$

Therefore,

$$
\begin{aligned}
&\widetilde{\mathcal{G}^*\mathcal{G}} = (\mathcal{G}\mathcal{T}^{-1})^*\mathcal{G}\mathcal{T}^{-1} = \\
&= \begin{pmatrix} I + e^{-\mathcal{A}(T-\cdot)}\mathcal{A}^{1/2}\int_0^T e^{-\mathcal{A}(T-s)}\mathcal{A}^{1/2}.(s)\ \mathrm{ds} & \underline{I} + e^{-\mathcal{A}(T-\cdot)} \\ \underline{I}^* + \int_0^T e^{-\mathcal{A}(T-s)}.(s)\ \mathrm{ds} & TI + \mathcal{A}^{-1} \end{pmatrix}.
\end{aligned}
\tag{1.30}
$$

This shows that $\widetilde{\mathcal{G}^*\mathcal{G}}$ is a compact perturbation of the operator $\overline{\mathcal{G}^*\mathcal{G}} = \begin{pmatrix} I+D & \underline{I} \\ \underline{I}^* & TI \end{pmatrix}$, where $D = e^{-\mathcal{A}(T-\cdot)}\mathcal{A}^{1/2}\int_0^T e^{-\mathcal{A}(T-s)}\mathcal{A}^{1/2}.(s)\ \mathrm{ds}$. To see this, consider a system of eigenvalues γ_n and eigenfunctions ϕ_n of $\mathcal{A}$ and the estimate

$$
\begin{aligned}
&\|\int_0^T e^{-\mathcal{A}(T-s)}u(s)\ \mathrm{ds}\|_{\dot{H}^1(\Omega)} = \|\mathcal{A}^{1/2}\int_0^T e^{-\mathcal{A}(T-s)}u(s)\ \mathrm{ds}\|_{\dot{H}^1(\Omega)} \\
&= \left(\sum_{n=1}^\infty \gamma_n\left(\int_0^T e^{-\gamma_n(T-s)}\langle u(s),\phi_n\rangle_{L^2}\ \mathrm{ds}\right)^2\right)^{1/2} \\
&\leq \Big(\sum_{n=1}^\infty \int_0^T \langle u(s),\phi_n\rangle_{L^2}^2\ \mathrm{ds}\,\underbrace{\gamma_n\int_0^T e^{-2\gamma_n(T-s)}\ \mathrm{ds}}_{=\frac{1}{2}(1-e^{-2\gamma_n T})}\Big)^{1/2} \leq \frac{1}{\sqrt{2}}\|u\|_{L^2(L^2)},
\end{aligned}
$$

which together with compactness of the embedding $\dot{H}^1(\Omega) := \mathcal{D}(\mathcal{A}^{1/2}) \to L^2(\Omega)$, shows that the operator $\int_0^T e^{-\mathcal{A}(T-s)}.(s) : L^2(0,T;L^2(\Omega)) \to L^2(\Omega)$ is compact and so is its adjoint $e^{-\mathcal{A}(T-\cdot)} : L^2(\Omega) \to L^2(0,T;L^2(\Omega))$. However

$D : L^2(0,T;L^2(\Omega)) \to L^2(0,T;L^2(\Omega))$ is only bounded, as the following computation shows

$$
\begin{aligned}
&\|e^{-\mathcal{A}(T-\cdot)}\mathcal{A}^{1/2}\int_0^T e^{-\mathcal{A}(T-s)}\mathcal{A}^{1/2}u(s)\,\mathrm{ds}\|_{L^2}\\
&=\left(\int_0^T\sum_{n=1}^{\infty}\left(\gamma_n e^{-\gamma_n(T-t)}\int_0^T e^{-\gamma_n(T-s)}\langle u(s),\phi_n\rangle_{L^2}\,\mathrm{ds}\right)^2\mathrm{dt}\right)^{1/2}\\
&\le\left(\int_0^T\sum_{n=1}^{\infty}\gamma_n^2 e^{-2\gamma_n(T-t)}\int_0^T e^{-2\gamma_n(T-s)}\,ds\int_0^T\langle u(s),\phi_n\rangle_{L^2}^2\,\mathrm{ds}\,\mathrm{dt}\right)^{1/2}\\
&=\left(\sum_{n=1}^{\infty}\int_0^T\langle u(s),\phi_n\rangle_{L^2}^2\,\mathrm{ds}\left(\gamma_n e^{-2\gamma_n(T-t)}\,\mathrm{dt}\right)^2\right)^{1/2}\le\frac{1}{2}\|u\|_{L^2(L^2)}.
\end{aligned}
$$

1.3.2.1 Analytic Computation of the Eigenvalues

With that operator we now again state the eigenvalue equation

$$
\widetilde{\mathcal{G}^*\mathcal{G}}\begin{pmatrix} f \\ g \end{pmatrix}=\lambda\begin{pmatrix} f \\ g \end{pmatrix}, \tag{1.31}
$$

where we write $f(t)$ and g in terms of their generalized Fourier series with respect to the eigensystem $(\mu_n,\phi_n)_{n\in\mathbb{N}}\subseteq\mathbb{R}\times L^2(\Omega)$ of $\mathcal{A}^{-1}$

$$
f(t,x)=\sum_{n=1}^{\infty}f_n(t)\phi_n(x),\quad g(x)=\sum_{n=1}^{\infty}g_n\phi_n(x),
$$

with $f_n(t)=\langle f(t),\phi_n\rangle_{L^2(\Omega)}$, $g_n=\langle g,\phi_n\rangle_{L^2(\Omega)}$. Then, with (1.30), upon taking inner products with ϕ_n, equation (1.31) leads to the system

$$
\begin{aligned}
&(1-\lambda)f_n(t)+e^{-\frac{1}{\mu_n}(T-t)}\frac{1}{\mu_n}\int_0^T e^{-\frac{1}{\mu_n}(T-s)}f_n(s)\,\mathrm{ds}+(1+e^{-\frac{1}{\mu_n}(T-t)})g_n=0,\\
&\int_0^T f_n(s)\,\mathrm{ds}+\int_0^T e^{-\frac{1}{\mu_n}(T-s)}f_n(s)\,\mathrm{ds}+(T+\mu_n-\lambda)g_n=0,
\end{aligned}\tag{1.32}
$$

for all $n\in\mathbb{N}$ and $t\in(0,T)$. This has a nontrivial solution $(f_n,g_n)_{n\in\mathbb{N}}\in L^2(0,T,\ell^2)\times\ell^2$, if and only if there exists $m\in\mathbb{N}$ such that (1.32) holds for $n=m$ and $f_m\not\equiv 0$ or $g_m\neq 0$ (to see sufficiency, set all other components of $(f_n,g_n)_{n\in\mathbb{N}}$ to zero and they will trivially satisfy the linear system (1.32)). With the particular time dependent functions $b_0^m : t\mapsto 1$ and $b_1^m : t\mapsto e^{-\frac{1}{\mu_n}(T-t)}$ playing a role here, this is the case iff either

$$
\text{(a) } \lambda=1 \text{ and } \begin{cases} g_m b_0^m(t)+\left(\frac{1}{\mu_m}\int_0^T b_1^m(s)f_m(s)\,\mathrm{ds}+g_m\right)b_1^m(t)=0,\ t\in(0,T)\\ \int_0^T b_0^m(s)f_m(s)\,\mathrm{ds}+\int_0^T b_1^m(s)f_m(s)\,\mathrm{ds}+(T+\mu_m-\lambda)g_m=0\end{cases}
$$

or

$$\text{(b) } \lambda \neq 1 \text{ and } \begin{cases} f_m = a_m b_0^m + c_m b_1^m \text{ where} \\ a_m = \frac{1}{\lambda-1} g_m, \quad c_m = \frac{1}{\lambda-1}\left(\frac{1}{\mu_m}\int_0^T b_1^m(s) f_m(s)\, \mathrm{ds} + g_m\right) \\ \int_0^T b_0^m(s) f_m(s)\, \mathrm{ds} + \int_0^T b_1^m(s) f_m(s)\, \mathrm{ds} + (T+\mu_m-\lambda) g_m = 0 \end{cases}.$$

The first equation of case (a) $\lambda = 1$ due to linear independence of the functions b_0^m, b_1^m leads to the conditions $g_m = 0$ and $\frac{1}{\mu_m}\int_0^T b_1^m(s) f_m(s)\, \mathrm{ds} + g_m = 0$, that, combined with the second equation, yield the necessary and sufficient conditions

$$g_m = 0, \int_0^T b_1^m(s) f_m(s)\, \mathrm{ds} = 0 \text{ and } \int_0^T b_0^m(s) f_m(s)\, \mathrm{ds} = 0.$$

This corresponds to a unit eigenvalue with the infinite dimensional eigenspace E_1

$$\lambda_0 = 1, \quad E_1 = \mathrm{span}\{(x,t) \mapsto \psi(t)\phi_m(x) \ : \ \psi \in \{b_0^m, b_1^m\}^{\perp}, \ m \in \mathbb{N}\} \quad (1.33)$$

where $.^{\perp}$ denotes the $L^2(0,T)$ orthogonal complement.

In case (b) $\lambda_m \neq 1$ inserting the representation $f_m = a_m b_0^m + c_m b_1^m$ into the two equations involving f_m and $g_m = (\lambda-1)a_m$, we get the following system for a_m and b_m

$$\begin{aligned} c_m &= \frac{1}{\lambda-1}\frac{1}{\mu_m}\int_0^T b_1^m(s)(a_m b_0^m(s) + c_m b_1^m(s))\, \mathrm{ds} + a_m, \\ &\int_0^T b_0^m(s)(a_m b_0^m(s) + c_m b_1^m(s))\, \mathrm{ds} + \int_0^T b_1^m(s)(a_m b_0^m(s) + c_m b_1^m(s))\, \mathrm{ds} \\ &\quad + (T+\mu_m-\lambda)(\lambda-1) a_m = 0, \end{aligned}$$

which with the integrals $\int_0^T b_0^m(s)^2\, \mathrm{ds} = T$, $\int_0^T b_1^m(s)^2\, \mathrm{ds} = \frac{\mu_m}{2}(1-e^{-\frac{1}{\mu_m}2T})$, $\int_0^T b_0^m(s) b_1^m(s)\, \mathrm{ds} = \mu_m(1-e^{-\frac{1}{\mu_m}T})$ reads as

$$\begin{aligned} &\left((\lambda-1)+1-e^{-\frac{1}{\mu_m}T}\right)a_m + \left(-(\lambda-1)+\tfrac{1}{2}(1-e^{-\frac{1}{\mu_m}2T})\right)c_m = 0, \\ &\left(T+(T+\mu_m-\lambda)(\lambda-1)+\mu_m(1-e^{-\frac{1}{\mu_m}T})\right)a_m \\ &\quad + \mu_m(\tfrac{3}{2}-e^{-\frac{1}{\mu_m}T}-e^{-\frac{1}{\mu_m}2T})c_m = 0, \end{aligned}$$

i.e.,

$$\begin{aligned} &(\lambda - e^{-\frac{1}{\mu_m}T})a_m + (\tfrac{3}{2}-\lambda-\tfrac{1}{2}e^{-\frac{1}{\mu_m}2T}))c_m = 0, \\ &\left(-\lambda^2+\lambda(T+1+\mu_m)-\mu_m e^{-\frac{1}{\mu_m}T}\right)a_m + \mu_m(\tfrac{3}{2}-e^{-\frac{1}{\mu_m}T}-e^{-\frac{1}{\mu_m}2T})c_m = 0. \end{aligned}$$

Existence of a nontrivial solution a_m, c_m by setting the determinant of this system to zero is equivalent to the following cubic equation for λ

$$\lambda^3 - \lambda^2(T+\tfrac{5}{2}+\alpha_m) + \lambda\left(\tfrac{3}{2}(T+1)+\beta_m\right) = \mu_m e^{-\frac{1}{\mu_m}2T},$$

with $\alpha_m = \mu_m - \frac{1}{2}e^{-\frac{1}{\mu_m}T}$, $\beta_m = 2\mu_m e^{-\frac{1}{\mu_m}T} - \frac{1}{2}e^{-\frac{1}{\mu_m}2T}(T+1)$ whose solutions $\lambda^1_{\mu_m}$, $\lambda^2_{\mu_m}$, $\lambda^3_{\mu_m}$ will be the remaining (besides $\lambda_0 = 1$) eigenvalues of $\widetilde{\mathcal{G}^*\mathcal{G}}$. To investigate the asymptotics of the eigenvalues, in particular of $\lambda^1_{\mu_n}$, we consider another sequence of values, namely

$$\begin{aligned}
\bar{\lambda}_{1,m} &= 0 =: \bar{\lambda}_1, \\
\bar{\lambda}_{2,m} &= \frac{T+\frac{5}{2}+\alpha_m}{2} + \frac{\sqrt{(T-\frac{1}{2})^2+\alpha_m^2+(2T+5)\alpha_m-4\beta_m}}{2} \to \begin{cases} T+1 \text{ if } T \geq \frac{1}{2} \\ \frac{3}{2} \text{ if } T < \frac{1}{2} \end{cases} =: \bar{\lambda}_2, \\
\bar{\lambda}_{3,m} &= \frac{\frac{3}{2}(T+1)+\beta_m}{\bar{\lambda}_{2,m}} \to \begin{cases} \frac{3}{2} \text{ if } T \geq \frac{1}{2} \\ T+1 \text{ if } T < \frac{1}{2} \end{cases} =: \bar{\lambda}_3 .
\end{aligned}$$

(where the limits are to be understood as $m \to \infty$ and therewith $\mu_m \to 0$), so that the cubic equation for λ above can be written as

$$\lambda(\lambda - \bar{\lambda}_{2,m})(\lambda - \bar{\lambda}_{3,m}) = \mu_m e^{-\frac{1}{\mu_m}2T} . \tag{1.34}$$

Since $\lambda^i_{\mu_m}$ are roots of cubic polynomial whose coefficients converge to those of a cubic polynomial with the three single roots $\bar{\lambda}_1$, $\bar{\lambda}_2$, $\bar{\lambda}_3$, we also have the convergence

$$\lambda^i_{\mu_m} \to \bar{\lambda}_i \text{ as } m \to \infty , \; i \in \{1,2,3\} .$$

In particular this means that since $\bar{\lambda}_1 = 0 < \bar{\lambda}_2, \bar{\lambda}_3$ and from (1.34) we have

$$\lambda^1_{\mu_m} = \frac{\mu_m e^{-\frac{1}{\mu_m}2T}}{(\lambda^1_{\mu_m} - \bar{\lambda}_{2,m})(\lambda^1_{\mu_m} - \bar{\lambda}_{3,m})} ,$$

where the denominator on the right hand side is positive and bounded away from zero for m sufficiently large. Hence, there exists $m_0 \in \mathbb{N}$ such that for all $m \geq n_0$ we have $\lambda^1_{\mu_m} > 0$ (compatibly with the fact that $\lambda^1_{\mu_m}$ is an eigenvalue of the positive semidefinite operator $\widetilde{\mathcal{G}^*\mathcal{G}}$) and $\lambda^1_{\mu_m} = O(\mu_m e^{-\frac{1}{\mu_m}2T})$.

Thus, we here have, in addition to $\lambda_0 = 1$, three sequences of eigenvalues: One tending to zero at an exponential rate (like in the reduced setting) in according to the severe ill-posedness of the backwards diffusion problem, and two further sequences accumulating at the positive values $\frac{3}{2}$ and $T+1$.

1.3.2.2 Numerical Computation of the Eigenvalues

The computation is done in python similarly to the computation of the eigenvalues of the inverse source problem, relying on a finite element discretization of the Laplacian. To obtain the right matrices for representing the semigroup expressions appearing in the definition of $\widetilde{\mathcal{G}^*\mathcal{G}}$, we exemplarily consider the term $w(t) = \int_0^t e^{-(t-s)\mathcal{A}} f(s)\,ds$ for some $f \in L^2(L^2(\Omega))$, and make a semidiscretization in space with a finite element ansatz $f(t,x) \approx \sum_{i=1}^{n_{el}} f_i(t)\phi_i(x)$,

$w(t,x) \approx \sum_{i=1}^{n_{el}} w_i(t)\phi_i(x)$ with basis functions $\phi_1,\ldots,\phi_n$. Taking into account the fact that w solves

$$\begin{aligned} \partial_t w + \mathcal{A}w &= f & &\text{in } (0,T)\times\Omega \\ w &= 0 & &\text{on } (0,T)\times\partial\Omega \\ w(0,x) &= 0 & &x\in\Omega, \end{aligned}$$

i.e., inserting the above ansatz, and testing with FE shape functions ϕ_j, $j \in \{1,\ldots,n_{el}\}$, (a procedure known as Faedo-Galerkin approximation,) we end up with the system of ODEs

$$M\underline{\dot{w}}(t) + K\underline{w}(t) = M\underline{f}(t)\,, t\in(0,T)\,, \quad \underline{w}(0) = 0\,,$$

where M and K are FE mass and stiffness matrices according to (1.27), (1.28), which, in order to obtain symmetry with respect to the Euclidean inner product, we write as $M^{1/2}\underline{\dot{w}}(t) + M^{-1/2}KM^{-1/2}M^{1/2}\underline{w}(t) = M^{1/2}\underline{f}(t)$. Thus the coefficient vector function $\underline{w}(t) = (w_1(t),\ldots,w_{n_{el}}(t))^T$ is determined by the identity

$$M^{1/2}\underline{w}(t) = \int_0^t e^{-(t-s)A_h}M^{1/2}\underline{f}(s)\,,ds$$

with $A_h = M^{-1/2}KM^{-1/2}$.

Additional discretization in time is done by piecewise constant basis functions on a uniform partition $0 = t_0 < t_1 < \cdots < t_N = T$, $t_k = \frac{T}{N}j = \tau k$, of the time interval, i.e., $f_i(t) = \sum_{k=0}^{N} f_i^k \psi^k(t)$ with $\psi^0(t) = \chi_{[0,\tau/2)}$, $\psi^N(t) = \chi_{[T-\tau/2,T)}$, $\psi^k(t) = \chi_{[t_k-\tau/2,t_k+\tau/2)}$, $k = 1,\ldots,N-1$, so that with

$$f_h(t,x) = \sum_{k=0}^{N}\sum_{i=1}^{n_{el}} f_i^k\psi^k(t)\phi_i(x)\,, \quad g_h(x) = \sum_{i=1}^{n_{el}} g_i\phi_i(x)\,,$$

the discretized eigenvalue equation in variational form reads as

$$\left\langle \widetilde{\mathcal{G}^*\mathcal{G}}\begin{pmatrix} f_h \\ g_h \end{pmatrix}, \begin{pmatrix} \psi^\ell\phi_j \\ \phi_j \end{pmatrix}\right\rangle_{L^2(L^2)\times L^2} = \left\langle \begin{pmatrix} f_h \\ g_h \end{pmatrix}, \begin{pmatrix} \psi^\ell\phi_j \\ \phi_j \end{pmatrix}\right\rangle_{L^2(L^2)\times L^2}, \tag{1.35}$$

$$\forall \ell \in \{0,\ldots,N\}, j\in\{1,\ldots,n_{el}\}, \tag{1.36}$$

with $\widetilde{\mathcal{G}^*\mathcal{G}}$ as in (1.30), i.e., in matrix-vector form

$$\begin{pmatrix} \mathcal{M}+\mathcal{E} & (\mathcal{M}^1+\mathcal{E}^1)^T \\ \mathcal{M}^1+\mathcal{E}^1 & TM + M^{1/2}A_h^{-1}M^{1/2} \end{pmatrix}\begin{pmatrix} \underline{\underline{f}} \\ \underline{g} \end{pmatrix} = \lambda\begin{pmatrix} \mathcal{M} & 0 \\ 0 & M \end{pmatrix}\begin{pmatrix} \underline{\underline{f}} \\ \underline{g} \end{pmatrix},$$

with the matrices

$$\begin{aligned}
\mathcal{M} &= \tau\text{diag}(\tfrac{1}{2}M, M, \cdots, M, \tfrac{1}{2}M),\\
\mathcal{M}^1 &= \tau(\tfrac{1}{2}M, M, \cdots, M, \tfrac{1}{2}M),\\
\mathcal{E}_{\ell,k} &= \tau^2 M^{1/2} A_h e^{-A_h(2T-t_\ell-t_k)} M^{1/2},\\
\mathcal{E}_{0,k} &= \mathcal{E}_{k,0} = \tfrac{\tau^2}{2} M^{1/2} A_h e^{-A_h(2T-t_k)} M^{1/2}, \quad \mathcal{E}_{0,0} = \tfrac{\tau^2}{4} M^{1/2} A_h e^{-A_h 2T} M^{1/2},\\
\mathcal{E}_{N,k} &= \mathcal{E}_{k,N} = \tfrac{\tau^2}{2} M^{1/2} A_h e^{-A_h(T-t_k)} M^{1/2}, \quad \mathcal{E}_{N,N} = \tfrac{\tau^2}{4} M^{1/2} A_h M^{1/2},\\
\mathcal{E}^1 &= \tau(\tfrac{1}{2} M^{1/2} e^{-A_h T} M^{1/2}, \ldots, M^{1/2} e^{-A_h(T-t_k)} M^{1/2}, \ldots, \tfrac{1}{2} M)
\end{aligned}$$

for $\ell, k \in \{1, \ldots, N-1\}$. Here we have computed and approximated the time integrals in (1.35) as follows

$$\int_{t_k-\tau/2}^{t_k+\tau/2} \mathrm{ds} = \tau,$$

$$\int_{t_k-\tau/2}^{t_k+\tau/2} e^{-A_h(T-s)}\,\mathrm{ds} = A_h^{-1}\left(e^{A_h\tau/2} - e^{-A_h\tau/2}\right) e^{-A_h(T-t_k)} \approx \tau e^{-A_h(T-t_k)},$$

$$\int_{t_\ell-\tau/2}^{t_\ell+\tau/2} e^{-A_h(T-t)} A_h \int_{t_k-\tau/2}^{t_k+\tau/2} e^{-A_h(T-s)}\,\mathrm{ds}\,\mathrm{dt} = A_h^{-1}\left(e^{A_h\tau} - 2 + e^{-A_h\tau}\right) e^{-A_h(2T-t_\ell-t_k)}$$

$$\approx \tau^2 A_h e^{-A_h(2T-t_\ell-t_k)}.$$

To simplify the implementation we transform the eigenvalue equation by pre-multiplication with $\begin{pmatrix} \mathcal{M} & 0 \\ 0 & M \end{pmatrix}^{-\frac{1}{2}}$ and setting $\begin{pmatrix} \tilde{\underline{f}} \\ \tilde{\underline{g}} \end{pmatrix} = \begin{pmatrix} \mathcal{M} & 0 \\ 0 & M \end{pmatrix}^{\frac{1}{2}} \begin{pmatrix} \underline{f} \\ \underline{g} \end{pmatrix}$ which results in the following equation

$$\begin{pmatrix} \mathcal{I} + \tilde{\mathcal{E}} & (\mathcal{I}^1 + \tilde{\mathcal{E}}^1)^T \\ \mathcal{I}^1 + \tilde{\mathcal{E}}^1 & TI + A_h^{-1} \end{pmatrix} \begin{pmatrix} \tilde{\underline{f}} \\ \tilde{\underline{g}} \end{pmatrix} = \lambda \begin{pmatrix} \tilde{\underline{f}} \\ \tilde{\underline{g}} \end{pmatrix}, \tag{1.37}$$

with the matrices

$$\begin{aligned}
\mathcal{I} &= \text{diag}(I, \cdots, I),\\
\mathcal{I}^1 &= \sqrt{\tau}(\tfrac{1}{\sqrt{2}} I, I, \cdots, I, \tfrac{1}{\sqrt{2}} I),\\
\tilde{\mathcal{E}}_{\ell,k} &= \tau A_h e^{-A_h(2T-t_\ell-t_k)},\\
\tilde{\mathcal{E}}_{0,k} &= \tilde{\mathcal{E}}_{k,0} = \tfrac{\tau}{\sqrt{2}} A_h e^{-A_h(2T-t_k)}, \quad \tilde{\mathcal{E}}_{0,0} = \tfrac{\tau}{2} A_h e^{-A_h 2T},\\
\tilde{\mathcal{E}}_{N,k} &= \tilde{\mathcal{E}}_{k,N} = \tfrac{\tau}{\sqrt{2}} A_h e^{-A_h(T-t_k)}, \quad \tilde{\mathcal{E}}_{N,N} = \tfrac{\tau}{2} A_h,\\
\tilde{\mathcal{E}}_{0,N} &= \tilde{\mathcal{E}}_{N,0} = \tau A_h e^{-A_h},\\
\tilde{\mathcal{E}}^1 &= \sqrt{\tau}(\tfrac{1}{\sqrt{2}} e^{-A_h T}, \ldots, e^{-A_h(T-t_k)}, \ldots, \tfrac{1}{\sqrt{2}} I).
\end{aligned}$$

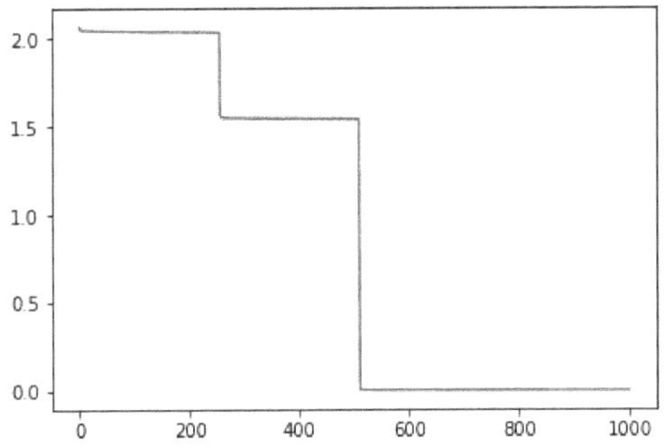

Figure 1.2: Eigenvalues of $\widetilde{\mathcal{G}^*\mathcal{G}}$ for backwards heat problem.

With that setting the eigenvalues are computed with the time interval $[0,T]$ with $T = 1$ discretized in the points $t_0 = 0, t_1 = 0.25, t_2 = 0.5, t_3 = 0.75, t_4 = T = 1$. Sampling of 700 eigenvalues leads to the following visualized output, which can be seen in Figure 1.2. The eigenvalues tend to zero, in three steps, which was also found in the analytic considerations.

1.4 Convergence Analysis

For the convergence analysis, the results in [1, 21] are extended to problems formulated in an all-at-once fashion, which can be done in a very straightforward fashion, so we keep this section short by more or less recalling the essential results from [1, 21].

The aim is to find out about the convergence of the posterior towards the true element $\mathbf{x}^*$ which generates the data $\mathbf{y}^\delta$. This is typically done by analyzing the squared posterior contraction, given by

$$\text{SPC} := \mathbb{E}^{\mathbf{x}^*}\mathbb{E}_\alpha^\delta \|\mathbf{x}^* - \mathbf{x}\|, \quad \alpha, \delta > 0, \tag{1.38}$$

where the outward expectation is taken with respect to the data generating function, which means with given $\mathbf{x}^*$, the distribution which generates the data $\mathbf{y}^\delta$. The inward expectation is taken with respect to the posterior distribution with given data $\mathbf{y}^\delta$ and chosen scaling parameter α. The squared posterior contraction can be decomposed into the squared bias, the estimation variance and the posterior spread, i.e.,

$$\text{SPC} = \|\mathbf{x}^* - \mathbb{E}^{\mathbf{x}^*}\mathbf{x}_\alpha^\delta\|^2 + \mathbb{E}^{\mathbf{x}^*}\|\mathbf{x}_\alpha^\delta - \mathbb{E}^{\mathbf{x}^*}\mathbf{x}_\alpha^\delta\|^2 + \text{tr}\,[\mathcal{C}_\alpha^\delta], \tag{1.39}$$

where $\mathbf{x}_\alpha^\delta$ and $\mathcal{C}_\alpha^\delta$ are denoting the posterior mean and covariance, respectively. It suffices to bound the bias $b_{\mathbf{x}^*}(\alpha) = \|\mathbf{x}^* - \mathbb{E}^{\mathbf{x}^*}\mathbf{x}_\alpha^\delta\|$ and the posterior spread $\text{tr}\,[\mathcal{C}_\alpha^\delta]$, as the estimation variance $\mathbb{E}^{\mathbf{x}^*}\|\mathbf{x}_\alpha^\delta - \mathbb{E}^{\mathbf{x}^*}\mathbf{x}_\alpha^\delta\|^2$ is always bounded by the posterior spread. To bound the posterior spread, it is shown that the necessary methods given in [1, 21] can be extended to block matrix operators. First, the concept of index functions is discussed.

Definition 1.4.1 *(index function) A function $\psi : (0,\infty) \to \mathbb{R}^+$ is called an index function if it is a continuous non-decreasing function with $\psi(0) = 0$.*

To be able to compare index functions the following partial ordering is defined.

Definition 1.4.2 *(partial ordering for index functions) Given two index functions g,h we write $g \prec h$ if the function $h(t)/g(t)$ is an index function (which means h tends to zero faster than g).*

In addition to ordering index function, also self-adjoint operators need to be partially ordered.

Definition 1.4.3 *(partial ordering for self-adjoint operators) Let $\mathcal{G}$ and $\mathcal{G}'$ be bounded self-adjoint operators in some Hilbert space $X \times Y$. We say that $\mathcal{G} \leq \mathcal{G}'$ if for all $\mathbf{x} \in X \times Y$ the inequality $\langle \mathcal{G}\mathbf{x}, \mathbf{x}\rangle \leq \langle \mathcal{G}'\mathbf{x}, \mathbf{x}\rangle$ holds.*

The last definition of interest states operator concavity for self-adjoint operators.

Definition 1.4.4 *Let $f : [0,a] \to \mathbb{R}^+$ be a continuous function. It is called operator concave if we have for any pair $\mathcal{G},\mathcal{H} \geq 0$ of self-adjoint operators with spectra in $[0,a]$*

$$f\left(\frac{\mathcal{G}+\mathcal{H}}{2}\right) \geq \frac{f(\mathcal{G})+f(\mathcal{H})}{2}.$$

The theorem stated below is the range inclusion theorem, which also holds for block operator matrices.

Theorem 1.4.5 *(Douglas' Range Inclusion Theorem; Theorem 1 in [23]) Let the operators $\mathcal{S},\mathcal{T} : X \times Y \to X \times Y$ be bounded and act between Hilbert spaces. Then the following statements are equivalent:*

1. *$\mathcal{R}(\mathcal{S}) \subset \mathcal{R}(\mathcal{T})$*
2. *$\mathcal{S}\mathcal{S}^* \leq C^2\mathcal{T}\mathcal{T}^*$, for some $C \geq 0$*
3. *there exists an bounded operator $\mathcal{R} : X \times Y \to X \times Y$ with $||\mathcal{R}|| \leq C$, such that $\mathcal{S} = \mathcal{T}\mathcal{R}$.*

Before continuing we introduce the functions

$$\Theta(t) = \Theta_\psi(t) := \sqrt{t}\psi(t), \quad t > 0, \quad s_\alpha(t) := \frac{\alpha}{\alpha+t}, \qquad \alpha > 0, \tag{1.40}$$

which will be needed in the further analysis. The main concept of the convergence analysis in [21] is the fulfillment of two assumptions, namely a link and a source condition, which will be given next. With these two assumptions one is able to bound the squared bias and the posterior spread, and therefore, the squared posterior contraction.

Assumption 1 *(link condition) There is an index function ψ, and there are constants $0 < \underline{m} \leq \overline{m} < \infty$ such that*

$$\underline{m}\|\psi(\mathcal{C}_0)\mathbf{x}\|_{W'\times Y} \leq \|\Sigma^{1/2}\mathcal{G}\mathbf{x}\|_{U\times X} \leq \overline{m}\|\psi(\mathcal{C}_0)\mathbf{x}\|_{W'\times Y}, \quad \mathbf{x} \in U \times X. \quad (1.41)$$

In addition, with the function Θ from (1.40) the function

$$f_0(s) := \left((\Theta^2)^{-1}(s)\right)^{-1/2}, \ s > 0,$$

has an operator concave square f_0^2.

For the following analysis we define

$$\varphi_0(t) := \sqrt{t}, \ t > 0 \quad (1.42)$$

and state the following proposition, which will allow us to bound the bias.

Proposition 1.4.6 *(Proposition 1 in [21]) Under Assumption 1 we have that $\mathcal{R}(\mathcal{C}_0^{1/2}) = \mathcal{R}(f_0(\mathcal{H}))$. Mainly we have that the operator $f_0(\mathcal{H})\varphi_0(\mathcal{C}_0)^{-1}$ is norm bounded by $\overline{m}$.*

As mentioned before, the second assumption of importance is a source condition, which will be stated next.

Assumption 2 *(source set) There is an index function φ such that*

$$\mathbf{x}^* \in \mathcal{S}_\varphi := \{\mathbf{x}, \quad \mathbf{x} = \varphi(\mathcal{C}_0)\mathbf{v}, \ \|\mathbf{v}\| \leq 1\}. \quad (1.43)$$

By using Proposition 1.4.6 we can bound the bias as

$$\begin{aligned} b_{\mathbf{x}^*}(\alpha) &\leq \tfrac{1}{\underline{m}}\|f_0(\mathcal{H})s_\alpha(\mathcal{H})\varphi_0(\mathcal{C}_0)^{-1}\varphi(\mathcal{C}_0)\| \\ &= \tfrac{1}{\underline{m}}\|s_\alpha(\mathcal{H})f_0(\mathcal{H})\varphi_0(\mathcal{C}_0)^{-1}\varphi(\mathcal{C}_0)\|. \end{aligned} \quad (1.44)$$

Now, with the assumptions made, one can give an upper bound for the squared bias.

Proposition 1.4.7 *(Proposition 3 in [21]) Suppose that either $\varphi_0 \prec \varphi \prec \theta$, and the function*

$$g^2(t) := \left(\frac{\varphi}{\varphi_0}\right)^2 \left(\left(\theta^2\right)^{-1}(t)\right), \quad t > 0,$$

is operator concave, or $1 \prec \varphi \prec \varphi_0$ and φ is operator concave. Under Assumptions 1 and 2 we have that

$$b_{\mathbf{x}^*}(\alpha) \leq \frac{\overline{m}}{\underline{m}}\|s_\alpha(\mathcal{H})\varphi(f_0^2(\mathcal{H}))\|. \quad (1.45)$$

With the help of Assumption 1, one can bound the posterior spread as stated in the next proposition.

Proposition 1.4.8 *(Proposition 6 in [21]) Under Assumption 1 we have that*

$$tr[C_{\alpha}^{\delta}] \leq \frac{\delta^2}{\underline{m}^2} tr[(\alpha+\mathcal{H})^{-1} f_0^2(\mathcal{H})]. \tag{1.46}$$

Under certain circumstances, see [21] and the references therein, we can rewrite the upper bound for the bias as

$$b_{\mathbf{x}^*}(\alpha) \leq \frac{\overline{m}}{\underline{m}} \varphi(f_0^2(\alpha)), \quad \alpha > 0, \tag{1.47}$$

using the fact that $s_\alpha(t)t \leq \alpha$, for $t, \alpha > 0$.

Combination of the results from Proposition 1.4.7 and 1.4.8 leads to a bound on the squared posterior contraction as stated in the following theorem.

Theorem 1.4.9 *(Theorem 3 in [21]) Supposed that Assumption 1 and Assumption 2 hold for some index functions ψ and φ and additionally, the assumptions in Proposition 1.4.7 and holds true, then*

$$SPC(\alpha,\delta) \leq \frac{1}{\underline{m}^2}\left(\overline{m}^2 ||s_\alpha(\mathcal{H})\varphi(f_0^2(\mathcal{H}))|| + \delta^2\ tr\left[(\alpha+\mathcal{H})^{-1} f_0^2(\mathcal{H})\right]\right), \ \alpha,\delta > 0. \tag{1.48}$$

Remark 1.4.9 If only the lower bound in (1.41) holds, with (1.44) and under a source condition one still obtains the estimate

$$\mathrm{SPC}(\alpha,\delta) = \frac{1}{\underline{m}^2}\left(||s_\alpha(\mathcal{H}) f_0(\mathcal{H}) \varphi_0(C_0)^{-1}\varphi(C_0)|| + \delta^2\ \mathrm{tr}\left[(\alpha+\mathcal{H})^{-1} f_0^2(\mathcal{H})\right]\right), \tag{1.49}$$

for $\alpha, \delta > 0$. ▮

1.4.1 Fulfillment of the Link Condition for the All-At-Once-Formulation

A straightforward example that always allows to fulfill the link condition, is as follows. Choosing the prior covariance to be given by

$$C_0 := \mathcal{G}^*\mathcal{G}, \tag{1.50}$$

and the link condition is always fulfilled by choosing the link function to be given by

$$\psi(t) := t^{1/2}. \tag{1.51}$$

Assume $\mathcal{G} : X \times Y \to S \times T$, then $\mathcal{G}^* : S \times T \to X \times Y$ and $\mathcal{G}^*\mathcal{G} : X \times Y \to X \times Y$ which yields

$$||\psi(\mathcal{G}^*\mathcal{G})\mathbf{x}||_{X\times Y} = ||\mathcal{G}\mathbf{x}||_{S\times T}, \quad \text{for all } \mathbf{x} \in X \times Y, \tag{1.52}$$

and the link condition is fulfilled. However, since $\mathcal{G}^*\mathcal{G}$ is ill-posed, (1.50) will not be a good regularizer, so we look at further possible choices for our two examples in the following Section 1.5.

In particular, for the backwards heat equation, the severe ill-posedness is prohibitive for (1.50). In the Section 1.5.2 below, we therefore derive a prior that is motivated by the link condition but much easier to handle than (1.50).

1.5 Choice of Joint Priors

1.5.1 Block Diagonal Priors Satisfying Unilateral Link Estimates

In this section, we investigate to which extent the link condition (1.41) can be satisfied by block diagonal operators $\psi(\mathcal{C}_0)$, as these are convenient for applying ψ^{-1} in order to obtain the prior covariance $\mathcal{C}_0$ itself again in block diagonal form, which in its turn is useful for numerical computations. For this purpose we again focus on our two prototypical examples from Sections 1.2.1 and 1.2.2. We will consider the upper and lower bound in (1.41) separately and, assuming that Σ is an isomorphism on Y, without loss of generality, set it to the identity, i.e., we will investigate fulfillment of

$$\|\psi(\mathcal{C}_0)\mathbf{x}\|_{U\times X} \leq \frac{1}{\underline{m}}\|\mathcal{G}\mathbf{x}\|_{W'\times Y} \text{ for all } \mathbf{x}=(u,\theta)\in U\times X, \tag{1.53}$$

$$\|\mathcal{G}\mathbf{x}\|_{W'\times Y} \leq \overline{m}\|\psi(\mathcal{C}_0)\mathbf{x}\|_{U\times X} \text{ for all } \mathbf{x}=(u,\theta)\in U\times X, \tag{1.54}$$

for $\psi(\mathcal{C}_0)$ of the form

$$\psi(\mathcal{C}_0)=\begin{pmatrix}\mathcal{B} & 0\\ 0 & \mathcal{D}\end{pmatrix}. \tag{1.55}$$

For the inverse source problem from Section 1.2.1 we have

$$\|\mathcal{G}(u,\theta)\|_{W'\times Y}=\|\mathcal{A}u-\theta\|_{L^2}+\|u\|_{L^2}$$

and

$$\|\psi(\mathcal{C}_0)(u,\theta)\|_{U\times X}=\|\mathcal{A}\mathcal{B}u\|_{L^2}+\|\mathcal{D}\theta\|_{L^2}$$

so setting θ and u to zero separately we get the following two necessary conditions

$$\begin{aligned}&\|\mathcal{A}u\|_{L^2}\leq\overline{m}\|\mathcal{A}\mathcal{B}u\|_{L^2} \text{ for all } u\in U=H_0^1(\Omega)\cap H^2(\Omega),\\ &\text{i.e., } \mathcal{B}:U\to U \text{ bijective with bounded inverse } \mathcal{B}^{-1}\end{aligned} \tag{1.56}$$

and

$$\begin{aligned}&\|\theta\|_{L^2}\leq\overline{m}\|\mathcal{D}\theta\|_{L^2} \text{ for all } \theta\in X=L^2(\Omega),\\ &\text{i.e., } \mathcal{D}:L^2(\Omega)\to L^2(\Omega) \text{ bijective with bounded inverse } \mathcal{D}^{-1}\end{aligned} \tag{1.57}$$

for (1.54). On the other hand, an easy application of the triangle inequality together with boundedness of $\mathcal{A}^{-1}: L^2(\Omega) \to L^2(\Omega)$ implies sufficiency of (1.56), (1.57) for (1.54).
The lower bound (1.53), with $\theta = \mathcal{A}u$ implies

$$\|\mathcal{A}\mathcal{B}u\|_{L^2} + \|\mathcal{D}\mathcal{A}u\|_{L^2} \leq \frac{1}{\underline{m}}\|u\|_{L^2} \text{ for all } u \in U = H_0^1(\Omega) \cap H^2(\Omega),$$

thus since $\|\mathcal{D}\mathcal{A}\|_{L^2 \to L^2} = \|\mathcal{A}\mathcal{D}^*\|_{L^2 \to L^2}$ we get the necessary conditions

$$\mathcal{B}: L^2(\Omega) \to H_0^1(\Omega) \cap H^2(\Omega) \text{ and } \mathcal{D}^*: L^2(\Omega) \to H_0^1(\Omega) \cap H^2(\Omega) \text{ bounded} \tag{1.58}$$

for (1.53). To see sufficiency of (1.58) together with boundedness of $\mathcal{D}$: $L^2(\Omega) \to L^2(\Omega)$ for (1.53), we set $f = \mathcal{A}u - \theta$ to obtain

$$\begin{aligned} \|\psi(\mathcal{C}_0)(u,\theta)\|_{U \times X} &= \|\mathcal{A}\mathcal{B}u\|_{L^2} + \|\mathcal{D}(\mathcal{A}u - f)\|_{L^2} \\ &\leq (\|\mathcal{B}\|_{L^2 \to H^2} + \|\mathcal{D}^*\|_{L^2 \to H^2})\|u\|_{L^2} + \|\mathcal{D}\|_{L^2 \to L^2})\|f\|_{L^2} \\ &\leq \frac{1}{\underline{m}}(\|f\|_{L^2} + \|u\|_{L^2}) = \frac{1}{\underline{m}}\|\mathcal{G}(u,\theta)\|_{W' \times Y} \end{aligned}$$

with $\underline{m} := \frac{1}{\max\{\|\mathcal{B}\|_{L^2 \to H^2} + \|\mathcal{D}^*\|_{L^2 \to H^2}, \|\mathcal{D}\|_{L^2 \to L^2}\}}$.
Unfortunately, conditions (1.56) and (1.58) are contradictory, so the full squared posterior contraction estimate (1.48) cannot be applied. Still, with, e.g., $\psi(\mathcal{C}_0) = \begin{pmatrix} \mathcal{A}^{-s} & 0 \\ 0 & \mathcal{A}^{-p} \end{pmatrix}$ and $s, p \geq 1$, which satisfies (1.53), we obtain (1.49).
For the backwards heat problem from Section 1.2.1 with

$$\|\mathcal{G}(u,\theta)\|_{W' \times Y} = \|\mathcal{A}^{-1/2}(\partial_t + \mathcal{A})u + \mathcal{A}^{1/2}\theta\|_{L^2(L^2)} + \|u(T) + \theta\|_{L^2}$$

and

$$\|\psi(\mathcal{C}_0)(u,\theta)\|_{U \times X} = \|\mathcal{A}^{-1/2}(\partial_t + \mathcal{A})\mathcal{B}u\|_{L^2(L^2)} + \|\mathcal{A}^{1/2}\mathcal{D}\theta\|_{L^2}$$

we see, by considering the two special cases $\theta = 0$ and $u = 0$, that a necessary condition for (1.54) is

$$\mathcal{B}^{-1}: U_0 \to U_0 \text{ and } \mathcal{D}^{-1}: H_0^1(\Omega) \to H_0^1(\Omega) \text{ bounded.} \tag{1.59}$$

Indeed, as can be seen by the triangle inequality and fact that that $\|u(T)\|_{L^2} \leq \|\mathcal{A}^{-1/2}(\partial_t + \mathcal{A})u\|_{L^2(L^2)}$ (cf. (1.19)) condition (1.59) is also sufficient for (1.54).
The lower bound (1.53) is again more challenging to obtain. With the particular choices $\theta = 0$ on one hand and $(\partial_t + \mathcal{A})u = -\mathcal{A}\theta$, i.e., $u(t) = -(I - e^{-t\mathcal{A}})\theta$ implying $u(T) + \theta = e^{-T\mathcal{A}}\theta$ on the other hand, it yields the necesssary conditions

$$\|\mathcal{B}u\|_{U_0} \leq \frac{1}{\underline{m}}\left(\|u\|_{U_0} + \|u(T)\|_{L^2}\right) \leq \frac{2}{\underline{m}}\|u\|_{U_0} \text{ for all } u \in U_0,$$

i.e., $\mathcal{B}: U_0 \to U_0$ bounded

and

$$\|\mathcal{B}(\underline{I}-e^{-\cdot\mathcal{A}})\theta\|_{U_0}+\|\mathcal{D}\theta\|_{H_0^1}\leq\frac{1}{\underline{m}}\|e^{-T\mathcal{A}}\theta\|_{L^2} \text{ for all } \theta\in X,$$

i.e., $\mathcal{D}e^{T\mathcal{A}}: L^2(\Omega)\to H_0^1(\Omega)$ bounded.

To obtain sufficient conditions for (1.53), with $f=(\partial_t+\mathcal{A})u+\mathcal{A}\theta$, $g=u(T)+\theta$, so that $\|\mathcal{G}(u,\theta)\|_{W'\times Y}=\|f\|_{L^2(H^{-1})}+\|g\|_{L^2}$, $u(t)=\int_0^t e^{-(t-s)\mathcal{A}}f(s)\,ds-(I-e^{-t\mathcal{A}})\theta$, hence we can express u and θ via f and g as

$$\begin{aligned} u(t) &= \int_0^t e^{-(t-s)\mathcal{A}}f(s)\,ds-(I-e^{-t\mathcal{A}})(e^{T\mathcal{A}}g-\int_0^T e^{s\mathcal{A}}f(s)\,ds),\\ \theta &= e^{T\mathcal{A}}g-\int_0^T e^{s\mathcal{A}}f(s)\,ds, \end{aligned}$$

and, therefore,

$$\begin{aligned} \|\psi(\mathcal{C}_0)(u,\theta)\|_{U\times X} &= \|\mathcal{B}u\|_{U_0}+\|\mathcal{D}\theta\|_{H_0^1}\\ &\leq \|\mathcal{B}\|_{L^\infty(L^2)\to U_0}\|\int_0^{\cdot} e^{-(\cdot-s)\mathcal{A}}f(s)\,ds\|_{L^\infty(L^2)}\\ &\quad+\left(\|\mathcal{B}e^{T\mathcal{A}}\|_{L^\infty(L^2)\to U_0}\|\underline{I}-e^{-\cdot\mathcal{A}}\|_{L^2\to L^\infty(L^2)}+\|\mathcal{D}e^{T\mathcal{A}}\|_{L^2\to H_0^1}\right)\\ &\qquad\cdot\left(\|g\|_{L^2}+\|\int_0^T e^{-(T-s)\mathcal{A}}f(s)\,ds\|_{L^2}\right), \end{aligned}$$

where $\|\underline{I}-e^{-\cdot\mathcal{A}}\|_{L^2\to L^\infty(L^2)}\leq 1$ and by self-adjoinedness of $\mathcal{A}$ as well as the Cauchy-Scharz inequality

$$\begin{aligned} &\|\int_0^{\cdot} e^{-(\cdot-s)\mathcal{A}}f(s)\,ds\|_{L^\infty(L^2)}\\ &= \sup_{t\in[0,T]\,v\in L^2\setminus\{0\}}\frac{1}{\|v\|_{L^2}}\int_0^t\int_\Omega e^{-(t-s)\mathcal{A}}\mathcal{A}^{1/2}v\,\mathcal{A}^{-1/2}f(s)\,dx\,ds\\ &\leq \sup_{t\in[0,T]\,v\in L^2\setminus\{0\}}\frac{1}{\|v\|_{L^2}}\left(\int_0^t\sum_{n=1}^\infty e^{-2(t-s)\frac{1}{\mu_n}}\frac{1}{\mu_n}\langle v,\phi_n\rangle_{L^2}^2\,ds\right)^{1/2}\|\mathcal{A}^{-1/2}f\|_{L^2(L^2)}\\ &\leq \frac{1}{2}\|f\|_{L^2(H^{-1})} \end{aligned}$$

with an eigensystem $(\mu_n,\phi_n)_{n\in\mathbb{N}}\subseteq\mathbb{R}\times L^2(\Omega)$ of $\mathcal{A}^{-1}$; likewise $\|\int_0^T e^{-(T-s)\mathcal{A}}f(s)\,ds\|_{L^2}\leq\frac{1}{2}\|f\|_{L^2(H^{-1})}$. Since these estimates are sharp when having to hold for arbitrary $f\in L^2(H^{-1})$, we can conclude that validity of (1.53) is equivalent to

$$\mathcal{B}e^{T\mathcal{A}}: L^\infty(L^2)\to U_0 \text{ and } \mathcal{D}e^{T\mathcal{A}}: L^2(\Omega)\to H_0^1(\Omega) \text{ bounded.} \tag{1.60}$$

Again the conditions for (1.53) and (1.54) are unfortunately contradictory. Still, for example the choice $\psi(\mathcal{C}_0) = \begin{pmatrix} \mathcal{A}^{1/2}e^{-T\mathcal{A}}\int_0^{\cdot} e^{-(\cdot-s)\mathcal{A}}\cdot(s)\,ds & 0 \\ 0 & \mathcal{A}^{-1/2}e^{-T\mathcal{A}} \end{pmatrix}$ satisfies (1.53) and therewith (1.49).

1.5.2 Heuristic Choice of $\mathcal{C}_0$ for the Backwards Heat Problem

To find out more about suitable operators fulfilling the link condition besides the trivial choice one attempt is made in the setting of the backwards heat problem. To do so, the norms are compared and so, the operator $\psi(\mathcal{C}_0)$ can be given by

$$\psi(\mathcal{C}_0) = \begin{pmatrix} I & \underline{I} - e^{-\mathcal{A}t} \\ \mathcal{A}^{-1}\delta_T + B & \mathcal{A}^{-1/2} \end{pmatrix},$$

where $\mathcal{A} := -\Delta$, $Bu := \int_0^T u(t)\ \mathrm{dt}$ and $(\underline{I}\theta)(t) = \theta$. This is a symmetric operator from $U_0 \times H_0^1(\Omega) \to U_0 \times H_0^1(\Omega)$ as

$$\begin{aligned}
((I-e^{-\mathcal{A}t})u, v)_{U_0} &= \int_0^T \int_\Omega \mathcal{A}^{-1/2}(\partial_t + \mathcal{A})(\underline{I} - e^{-\mathcal{A}t})u\mathcal{A}^{-1/2}(\partial_t + \mathcal{A})v\ \mathrm{dx\ dt} \\
&= \int_0^T \int_\Omega \mathcal{A}^{1/2}u\mathcal{A}^{-1/2}(\partial_t + \mathcal{A})v\ \mathrm{dx\ dt} \\
&= \int_0^T \int_\Omega \mathcal{A}^{1/2}u\mathcal{A}^{-1/2}\partial_t v\ \mathrm{dx\ dt} + \int_0^T \int_\Omega \mathcal{A}^{1/2}u\mathcal{A}^{1/2}v\ \mathrm{dx\ dt} \\
&= \int_\Omega \mathcal{A}^{1/2}u\mathcal{A}^{-1/2}v(T)\ \mathrm{dx} + \int_\Omega \mathcal{A}^{1/2}u\mathcal{A}^{1/2}\int_0^T v(t)\ \mathrm{dt\ dx},
\end{aligned}$$

$$\begin{aligned}
(u, (\mathcal{A}^{-1}\delta_T + B)v)_{H_0^1(\Omega)} &= \int_\Omega \mathcal{A}^{1/2}u\mathcal{A}^{1/2}(\mathcal{A}^{-1}\delta_T + B)v\ \mathrm{dx} \\
&= \int_\Omega \mathcal{A}^{1/2}u\mathcal{A}^{-1/2}v(T)\ \mathrm{dx} + \int_\Omega \mathcal{A}^{1/2}u\mathcal{A}^{1/2}\int_0^T v(t)\ \mathrm{dt}.
\end{aligned}$$

Now the norm of $\mathcal{G}$ and $\psi(\mathcal{C})$ are computed with the help of a rewriting of $\psi(\mathcal{C})$ as

$$\begin{aligned}
\psi(\mathcal{C}_0) &= \begin{pmatrix} I & \underline{I} - e^{-\mathcal{A}t} \\ \mathcal{A}^{-1}\delta_T + B & \mathcal{A}^{-1/2} \end{pmatrix} \qquad (1.61) \\
&= \underbrace{\begin{pmatrix} I & 0 \\ 0 & \mathcal{A}^{-1/2} \end{pmatrix}}_{=:\tilde{\mathcal{A}}} \underbrace{\begin{pmatrix} I & \underline{I} - e^{-\mathcal{A}t} \\ \mathcal{A}^{-1/2}\delta_T & \mathcal{A}^{-1/2} \end{pmatrix}}_{\tilde{\mathcal{C}}} + \underbrace{\begin{pmatrix} 0 & 0 \\ B & \mathcal{A}^{-1/2} - \mathcal{A}^{-1} \end{pmatrix}}_{=:\mathcal{R}}.
\end{aligned}$$

Instead of $\psi(\mathcal{C}_0)$ now we use $\tilde{\mathcal{C}}$ under the norm. The norms compute as follows for $x = (u, \theta) \in U_0 \times H_0^1$

$$\begin{aligned}
\|\mathcal{G}\mathbf{x}\|^2_{L^2(H^{-1})\times L^2} &= \|(\partial_t + \mathcal{A})u + \mathcal{A}\theta\|^2_{L^2(H^{-1})} + \|\delta_T u + I\theta\|^2_{L^2} \\
&= \|(\partial_t + \mathcal{A})u\|^2_{L^2(H^{-1})} + \|\mathcal{A}\theta\|^2_{L^2(H^{-1})} + 2((\partial_t + \mathcal{A})u, \mathcal{A}\theta)_{L^2(H^{-1})} \\
&\quad + \|\delta_T u\|^2_{L^2} + \|I\theta\|^2_{L^2} + 2(\delta_T u, I\theta)_{L^2} \\
&= \int_0^T \int_\Omega |\mathcal{A}^{-1/2}(\partial_t + \mathcal{A})u|^2 \text{ dx dt} + \int_0^T \int_\Omega |\mathcal{A}^{1/2}\theta|^2 \text{ dx dt} \\
&\quad + 2\int_0^T \int_\Omega \mathcal{A}^{-1/2}(\partial_t + \mathcal{A})u\mathcal{A}^{1/2}\theta \text{ dx dt} + \int_\Omega |u(T)|^2 \text{ dx} \\
&\quad + \int_\Omega |\theta|^2 \text{ dx} + 2\int_\Omega u(T)I\theta \text{ dx},
\end{aligned}$$

$$\begin{aligned}
\|\tilde{\mathcal{C}}\mathbf{x}\|^2_{U_0\times H_0^1} &= \|u + (\underline{I} - e^{-\mathcal{A}t}\theta)\|^2_{U_0} + \|\mathcal{A}^{-1/2}\delta_T u + \mathcal{A}^{-1/2}\theta\|^2_{H_0^1} \\
&= \|u\|^2_{U_0} + \|(I - e^{-\mathcal{A}t})\theta\|^2_{U_0} + 2(u, (\underline{I} - e^{-\mathcal{A}t})\theta)_{U_0} \\
&\quad + \|\mathcal{A}^{-1/2}\delta_T u\|^2_{H_0^1} + \|\mathcal{A}^{-1/2}\theta\|^2_{H_0^1} + 2(\mathcal{A}^{-1/2}\delta_T u, \mathcal{A}^{-1/2}\theta)_{H_0^1} \\
&= \int_0^T \int_\Omega |\mathcal{A}^{-1/2}(\partial_t + \mathcal{A})u|^2 \text{ dx dt} \\
&\quad + \int_0^T \int_\Omega |\mathcal{A}^{-1/2}(\partial_t + \mathcal{A})(I - e^{-\mathcal{A}t})\theta|^2 \text{ dx dt} \\
&\quad + 2\int_0^T \int_\Omega \mathcal{A}^{-1/2}(\partial_t + \mathcal{A})u\mathcal{A}^{-1/2}(\partial_t + \mathcal{A})(\underline{I} - e^{-\mathcal{A}t})\theta \text{ dx dt} \\
&\quad + \int_\Omega |\mathcal{A}^{1/2}\mathcal{A}^{-1/2}\delta_T u|^2 \text{ dx} \\
&\quad + \int_\Omega |\mathcal{A}^{1/2}\mathcal{A}^{-1/2}\theta|^2 \text{ dx} + 2\int_\Omega \mathcal{A}^{1/2}\mathcal{A}^{-1/2}\delta_T u\mathcal{A}^{1/2}\mathcal{A}^{-1/2}\theta \text{ dx} \\
&= \int_0^T \int_\Omega |\mathcal{A}^{-1/2}(\partial_t + \mathcal{A})u|^2 \text{ dx dt} + \int_0^T \int_\Omega |\mathcal{A}^{1/2}\theta|^2 \text{ dx dt} \\
&\quad + 2\int_0^T \int_\Omega \mathcal{A}^{-1/2}(\partial_t + \mathcal{A})u\mathcal{A}^{1/2}\theta \text{ dx dt} + \int_\Omega |u(T)|^2 \text{ dx} \\
&\quad + \int_\Omega |\theta|^2 \text{ dx} + 2\int_\Omega v(T)u \text{ dx}.
\end{aligned}$$

This shows that $\|\tilde{\mathcal{C}}\mathbf{x}\|^2 = \|\mathcal{G}\mathbf{x}\|^2$. Motivated by this, we use $\tilde{\mathcal{C}}$ in place of $\mathcal{C}$ as a prior covariance matrix. Note that estimating the remainder $\|\mathcal{R}\mathbf{x}\|$ by $\|\mathcal{G}\mathbf{x}\|$ unfortunately does not seem to be possible, since in $\mathcal{G}\mathbf{x}$ terms containing u and terms containing θ may possibly cancel. Nevertheless, since $\mathcal{R}$ contains negative order differential operators as compared to $\tilde{C}$, we can regard it as a perturbation of the latter and therefore skip it for computational purposes.

In Subsection 1.6.2.4 below we demonstrate numerically that block diagonal of $\tilde{C}$ as a prior yields reasonable results in the reconstruction.

1.5.3 Priors for the Inverse Source Problem

The choice of joint priors in this work relies on priors which are already well known in the literature and also implemented in hippylib, see, e.g., [9, 26]. We restrict ourselves to normal priors with the covariance operator given by

$$C_p = (-\gamma\Delta + \delta I)^{-n} \tag{1.62}$$

where n most often take the values 1 or 2. For joint priors for the parameter and the state, priors of the same type have shown to be useful in the numerical experiments in this study.

1.5.4 Prior for the State Variable of the Backwards Heat Problem

For the backwards heat problem we require a prior which is suitable for the initial condition, but in addition, we also need to find a prior for the state variable for every $t \in [0,T]$. To do so, the heat equation is analyzed. At first the solution to the heat equation is considered and the homogeneous case $f = 0$ is examined. In case of bounded Ω with, e.g., homogeneous Dirichlet boundary conditions and denoting by $\mathcal{A} = -\Delta$ the Laplace operator equipped with these boundary conditions, we can use semigroup theory to express u. To use the semigroup theory some preparatory work has to be done.

Definition 1.5.1 *(Section 7.4.1 in [11]) Let X be a real Banach space. A family of linear, bounded operators $\{S(t)\}_{t\geq 0}$, $S(t) : X \to X$ is called a semigroup iff*

$$S(0) = I \quad \text{and} \quad S(s+t) = S(s)S(t) \quad \forall t,s \geq 0.$$

As already assumed the solution of the heat equation with initial data θ can be written in terms of semigroups using the so called heat semigroup

$$S(t)\theta := u(t) \text{ where } \left\{ \begin{array}{rcl} u_t & = & \Delta u \text{ in } \Omega \times (0,\infty) \\ u & = & 0 \text{ on } \partial\Omega \times (0,\infty) \\ u & = & \theta \text{ on } \Omega \times \{0\} \end{array} \right. \tag{1.63}$$

with $X = L^2(\Omega)$. Clearly, $S(t)$ fulfills the conditions to be a semigroup. To investigate this equation the definition of the infinitesimal generator is needed.

Definition 1.5.2 *(Section 7.4.1 in [11]) Let $\{S(t)\}_{t\geq 0}$ be a semigroup on a Banach space X. Write*

$$D(A) := \left\{ u \in X : \lim_{t\to 0^+} \frac{S(t)u - u}{t} \text{ exists in } X \right\}$$

and

$$Au := \lim_{t\to 0+} \frac{S(t)u - u}{t} \qquad (u \in D(A)).$$

We call $A : D(A) \to X$ the infinitesimal generator of the semigroup $\{S(t)\}_{t\geq 0}$, $D(A)$ is the domain of A.

It can be shown, that the generator of the heat semigroup is defined by the Laplace operator with homogeneous Dirichet boundary conditions $\mathcal{A}$. Therewith, we can write u as

$$u(t,x) = (S(t)\theta)(x) = (e^{-t\mathcal{A}}\theta)(x). \tag{1.64}$$

In terms of finding a prior for the state $u(t,x)$ at any time t, this is a convenient setting as we can make use of the prior measure for $\theta(x)$. We denote the measure for the parameter θ by μ_0 and given by

$$\mu_0 = \mathcal{N}(m_0, C_p) \tag{1.65}$$

Using the properties of the normal distribution one can calculate the resulting prior for $u(t,x)$. In addition the fact that $e^{-t\mathcal{A}}$ is a self-adjoint operator is used. Then the prior for $u(t,x)$ is given by

$$\mu_s = \mathcal{N}(e^{-t\mathcal{A}}m_0, e^{-t\mathcal{A}}C_p e^{-t\mathcal{A}}). \tag{1.66}$$

In case $f \neq 0$, one can show that the solution to the heat equation changes to

$$u(t,x) = S(t)\theta(x) + \int_0^t S(t-s)f(s,x)\,\mathrm{ds} = e^{-t\mathcal{A}}\theta(x) + \int_0^t e^{-(t-s)\mathcal{A}}f(s,x)\,\mathrm{ds}. \tag{1.67}$$

In the corresponding prior measure only the expectation value has changed, as the covariance operator is invariant under translation. This leads to the new prior

$$\mu_s = \mathcal{N}(e^{-t\mathcal{A}}m_0 + \int_0^t e^{-(t-s)\mathcal{A}}f(s,x)\,\mathrm{ds}, e^{-t\mathcal{A}}C_p e^{-t\mathcal{A}}). \tag{1.68}$$

1.6 Numerical Experiments

In this section the prototypical inverse problems discussed in the previous section will be solved numerically. To do so, first the theoretical considerations for solving the problems are described, while later the implementation is discussed. In this work, we used the software FEniCS [7] with the extension of hIPPYlib

[26] which we extended further for the needs of our all-at-once formulations. In this work the method for discretizing and solving the inverse problem is based on the methods described in [25]. However, we change the computation of the Hessian including all the prior information we have in the all-at-once setting. The equation describing the relation between the data is given via

$$\mathbb{O}u = y + \eta, \tag{1.69}$$

where $\mathbb{O} : U \to Y$ is the operator which maps the state variable into the observation space Y and η is the random variable describing the noise in this equation. We assume that η is random white noise.

1.6.1 Lagrangian Method for Computing the Adjoint Based Hessian and Gradient

In this section we compute the adjoint based Hessian and gradient for a cost functional formulated in the all-at-once setting. This functional is then analyzed twice, first for the parameter and then also for the state variable.

For the computation of the Hessian with respect to the parameter we consider the following minimization problem

$$\min_{\theta} J_{\alpha}(\theta) = \|\mathbb{O}u - y\|_Y^2 + \frac{\alpha}{2}\mathcal{R}(u,\theta) \tag{1.70}$$

$$s.t. \;\; \mathbb{M}(u,\theta) = 0 \tag{1.71}$$

with the regularization given by the prior distribution and written as

$$\mathcal{R}(u,\theta) = \langle u, C_1 u\rangle_U + 2\langle u, C_2\theta\rangle_U + \langle \theta, C_3\theta\rangle_X, \tag{1.72}$$

with selfadjoint operators $C_1 : U \to U$, $C_3 : X \to X$. Together, this leads to the following Lagrange functional of $u \in U$, $\theta \in X$, $p \in W$,

$$\mathcal{L}_{\alpha}(u,\theta,p) := \frac{1}{2}\|\mathbb{O}u - y\|_Y^2 + \frac{\alpha}{2}\left(\langle u, C_1 u\rangle_U + 2\langle u, C_2\theta\rangle_U + \langle \theta, C_3\theta\rangle_X\right) \tag{1.73}$$

$$+\mathbb{M}(u,\theta)p, \tag{1.74}$$

which is used in order to derive adjoint based methods for gradient and Hessian computation. We start with computing the first derivatives and for this purpose use the Riesz isomorphisms $I_R^U : U \to U'$, $u \mapsto (v \mapsto \langle u, v\rangle_U)$, $I_R^X : X \to X'$

$$\frac{\partial \mathcal{L}_{\alpha}}{\partial p}(u,\theta,p) = \mathbb{M}(u,\theta) \in W' \tag{1.75}$$

$$\frac{\partial \mathcal{L}_{\alpha}}{\partial u}(u,\theta,p) = I_R^U\left(\mathbb{O}^*(\mathbb{O}u - y) + \alpha\,(C_1 u + C_2\theta)\right) + \frac{\partial \mathbb{M}}{\partial u}(u,\theta)^{\star} p \in U' \tag{1.76}$$

$$\frac{\partial \mathcal{L}_{\alpha}}{\partial \theta}(u,\theta,p) = \alpha I_R^X\,(C_2^* u + C_3\theta) + \frac{\partial \mathbb{M}}{\partial \theta}(u,\theta)^{\star} p \in X', \tag{1.77}$$

where the derivative with respect to p set to zero gives the forward problem. The following operators are now used as abbreviations of the derivatives of $\mathbb{M}(u,\theta)$

$$-\frac{\partial \mathbb{M}}{\partial u}(u,\theta) =: K : U \to W', \qquad \frac{\partial \mathbb{M}}{\partial \theta}(u,\theta) =: L : X \to W', \tag{1.78}$$

along with their Banach space adjoints $K^\star : W \to U'$, $L^\star : W \to X'$ and their liftings to U and X, respectively $K^* := (I_R^U)^{-1}K^\star : W \to U$, $L^* := (I_R^X)^{-1}L^\star : W \to X$. Since we deal with linear models here, K and L are in fact independent of u and θ and we can write $\mathbb{M}(u,\theta) = -Ku + L\theta + f$. Then, the derivative with respect to u when set to zero leads to the adjoint problem with the adjoint linearization of the model defining the differential operator and the residual plus some additional term from the prior define the right hand side

$$K^* p = \mathbb{O}^*(\mathbb{O}u - y) + \alpha(C_1 u + C_2\theta). \tag{1.79}$$

With $p = p(\theta)$ satisfying (1.79), and $u = u(\theta)$ (also inserted into (1.79)) satisfying the state equation (1.71), the derivative with respect to θ gives us the gradient of the reduced cost function $j_\alpha(\theta) = J_\alpha(u(\theta),\theta))$, which results in

$$\begin{aligned} j'_\alpha(\theta) &= \frac{d}{d\theta} J_\alpha(u(\theta),\theta) = \frac{d}{d\theta}\mathcal{L}_\alpha(u(\theta),\theta,p(\theta)) \\ &= \frac{\partial \mathcal{L}_\alpha}{\partial \theta}(u(\theta),\theta,p(\theta)) = \alpha I_R^X\,(C_2^* u + C_3\theta) + L^\star p(\theta). \end{aligned}$$

Now we can write down a new Lagrange functional for the computation of the Hessian matrix using the concept of second order adjoints. This new functional denoted by $\mathcal{L}^{\mathcal{H}}$ is given by

$$\begin{aligned} \mathcal{L}^{\mathcal{H}}(u,\theta,p;\hat{u},\hat{\theta},\hat{p}) &:= \frac{\partial \mathcal{L}_\alpha}{\partial p}(u,\theta,p)\hat{p} + \frac{\partial \mathcal{L}_\alpha}{\partial u}(u,\theta,p)\hat{u} + \frac{\partial \mathcal{L}_\alpha}{\partial \theta}(u,\theta,p)\hat{\theta} \\ &= \mathbb{M}(u,\theta)\hat{p} + \langle \mathbb{O}u - y, \mathbb{O}\hat{u}\rangle_Y + \alpha\langle C_1 u + C_2\theta, \hat{u}\rangle_U - \langle K\hat{u}, p\rangle_{W',W} \\ &\quad + \alpha\langle C_2^* u + C_3\theta, \hat{\theta}\rangle_X + \langle L\hat{\theta}, p\rangle_{W',W}. \end{aligned}$$

Again, the derivatives are computed and finally, the Hessian of the reduced cost functional can be given.

$$\begin{aligned} j''_\alpha(\theta)(\hat{\theta},h) &= \frac{d^2}{d\theta^2} J_\alpha(u(\theta),\theta)(\hat{\theta},h) = \frac{d}{d\theta}\mathcal{L}^H(u(\theta),\theta,p(\theta);\hat{u},\hat{\theta},\hat{p})h \\ &= \frac{\partial \mathcal{L}^H}{\partial u}(u(\theta),\theta,p(\theta);\hat{u},\hat{\theta},\hat{p})\frac{\partial u}{\partial \theta}(\theta)h + \frac{\partial \mathcal{L}^H}{\partial \theta}(u(\theta),\theta,p(\theta);\hat{u},\hat{\theta},\hat{p})h \\ &\quad + \frac{\partial \mathcal{L}^H}{\partial p}(u(\theta),\theta,p(\theta);\hat{u},\hat{\theta},\hat{p})\frac{\partial p}{\partial \theta}(\theta)h \end{aligned}$$

Choosing $\hat{u} = \hat{u}(\theta,\hat{\theta})$, $\hat{p} = \hat{p}(\theta,\hat{\theta})$ such that the first and the last term vanish for all h, i.e.,

$$\begin{aligned} 0 &= \frac{\partial \mathcal{L}^H}{\partial u}(u(\theta),\theta,p(\theta);\hat{u},\hat{\theta},\hat{p}) \\ &= I_R^U\left(-K^*\hat{p}(\theta,\hat{\theta}) + \mathbb{O}^*\mathbb{O}\hat{u}(\theta,\hat{\theta}) + \alpha(C_1^*\hat{u}(\theta,\hat{\theta}) + C_2\hat{\theta})\right), \\ 0 &= \frac{\partial \mathcal{L}^H}{\partial p}(u(\theta),\theta,p(\theta);\hat{u},\hat{\theta},\hat{p}) = -K\hat{u}(\theta,\hat{\theta}) + L\hat{\theta} = 0, \end{aligned}$$

where the lower equation is solved first and the resulting $\hat{u}(\theta)$ is inserted into the upper equation, which is the resolved for $\hat{p}(\theta)$. This together with

$$\frac{\partial \mathcal{L}^H}{\partial \theta}(u,\theta,p;\hat{u},\hat{\theta},\hat{p})h = \langle Lh,\hat{p}\rangle_{W',W} + \alpha\langle C_2 h,\hat{u}\rangle_U + \alpha\langle C_3 h,\hat{\theta}\rangle_U$$

yields, for any $h \in X$,

$$j''_\alpha(\theta)(\hat{\theta},h) = \langle L^*\hat{p}(\theta,\hat{\theta}) + \alpha\left(C_2^*\hat{u}(\theta,\hat{\theta}) + C_3\hat{\theta}\right), h\rangle_X,$$

thus, abbreviating $K^{-*} = (K^*)^{-1}$,

$$l j''_\alpha(\theta)(\hat{\theta},\check{\theta}) = \langle\left(L^*K^{-*}[\mathbb{O}^*\mathbb{O} + \alpha C_1]K^{-1}L + \alpha C_3 + \alpha L^*K^{-*}C_2 + \alpha C_2^*K^{-1}L\right)\hat{\theta},\check{\theta}\rangle_X.$$

Thus, altogether the gradient and Hessian of the reduced cost function j read as follows

$$\begin{aligned} j'_\alpha(\theta) &= \alpha I_R^X\left(C_2^*K^{-1}L + C_3\right)\theta + L^*K^{-*}\left[\mathbb{O}^*(\mathbb{O}K^{-1}L\theta - y) + \alpha(C_1K^{-1}L + C_2)\theta\right], \\ j''_\alpha(\theta) &= I_R^X H_\theta = I_R^X\left(L^*K^{-*}[\mathbb{O}^*\mathbb{O} + \alpha C_1]K^{-1}L + \alpha C_3 + \alpha L^*K^{-*}C_2 + \alpha C_2^*K^{-1}L\right). \end{aligned}$$

If L is invertible, then the role of u and θ in the above procedure can be exchanged and for the reduced cost function $\ell_\alpha(u) = J_\alpha(u,\theta(u))$ with $\theta(u) = L^{-1}(Ku - f)$ and $p(u) = -\alpha L^{-*}(C_2^*u + C_3\theta(u))$ we get

$$\begin{aligned} \ell'_\alpha(u) &= \frac{d}{du}J_\alpha(u,\theta(u)) = \frac{d}{du}\mathcal{L}_\alpha(u,\theta(u),p(u)) = \frac{\partial \mathcal{L}_\alpha}{\partial u}(u,\theta(u),p(u)) \\ &= I_R^U\left(\mathbb{O}^*(\mathbb{O}u - y) + \alpha\left(C_1u + C_2L^{-1}(Ku-f) + K^*L^{-*}(C_2^*u + C_3L^{-1}(Ku-f))\right)\right) \end{aligned}$$

and, with $\hat{\theta}(u,\hat{u}) = L^{-1}K\hat{u}$, $\hat{p}(u,\hat{u}) = -\alpha L^{-*}(C_2^* + C_3L^{-1}K)\hat{u}$,

$$\begin{aligned} \ell''_\alpha(u)(\hat{u},\check{u}) &= \frac{d}{du}\mathcal{L}^H(u,\theta(u),p(u);\hat{u},\hat{\theta}(u,\hat{u}),\hat{p}(u,\hat{u}))\check{u} \\ &= \frac{\partial \mathcal{L}^H}{\partial u}(u,\theta(u),p(u);\hat{u},\hat{\theta}(u,\hat{u}),\hat{p}(u,\hat{u}))\check{u} \\ &= \langle -K^*\hat{p}(u,\hat{u}) + \mathbb{O}^*\mathbb{O}\hat{u} + \alpha(C_1\hat{u} + C_2\hat{\theta}(u,\hat{u})),\check{u}\rangle_U \\ &= \langle\left[\mathbb{O}^*\mathbb{O} + \alpha(C_1 + C_2L^{-1}K + K^*L^{-*}C_2^* + K^*L^{-*}C_3L^{-1}K)\right]\hat{u},\check{u}\rangle_U \end{aligned}$$

that is, ℓ_α is the quadratic functional $\ell_\alpha(u) = \frac{1}{2}\langle Hu, u\rangle + \langle g, u\rangle$ with

$$H = (I_R^U)^{-1}\ell_\alpha''(u) = \mathbb{O}^*\mathbb{O} + \alpha(C_1 + C_2L^{-1}K + K^*L^{-*}C_2^* + K^*L^{-*}C_3L^{-1}K),$$
$$g = (I_R^U)^{-1}\ell_\alpha'(0) = -\mathbb{O}^*y - \alpha(C_2 + K^*L^{-*}C_3)L^{-1}f.$$

The computed Hessians can now be used to evaluate the MAP estimator for the posterior mean and the posterior covariance.

1.6.1.1 Inverse Source Problem

$U = H_0^1(\Omega)\cap H^2(\Omega)$, $X = Y = W = W' = L^2(\Omega)$, $\mathbb{M}(u,\theta) = -\mathcal{A}u + \theta$, $\mathbb{O}u = u$, $K = \mathcal{A} : H_0^1(\Omega)\cap H^2(\Omega) \to L^2(\Omega)$, $K^* = \mathcal{A}^{-1} : L^2(\Omega) \to H_0^1(\Omega)\cap H^2(\Omega)$, $L = \mathrm{id} : L^2(\Omega) \to L^2(\Omega)$, $L^* = \mathrm{id} : L^2(\Omega) \to L^2(\Omega)$, $\mathbb{O} : H_0^1(\Omega)\cap H^2(\Omega) \to L^2(\Omega)$, $\mathbb{O}^* = \mathcal{A}^{-2} : L^2(\Omega) \to H_0^1(\Omega)\cap H^2(\Omega)$, which results in

$$\begin{aligned} g_\theta(\theta) &:= (I_R^X)^{-1} j_\alpha'(\theta) \\ &= \alpha(C_2^*\mathcal{A}^{-1} + C_3)\theta + \mathcal{A}\big[\mathcal{A}^{-2}(\mathcal{A}^{-1}\theta - y) + \alpha(C_1\mathcal{A}^{-1} + C_2)\theta\big], \\ H_\theta &:= (I_R^X)^{-1} j_\alpha'' = \mathcal{A}(\mathcal{A}^{-2} + \alpha C_1)\mathcal{A}^{-1} + \alpha C_3 + \alpha \mathcal{A} C_2 + \alpha C_2^*\mathcal{A}^{-1}, \end{aligned}$$

for the parameter θ, where the computation of the adjoint is as described in Section 1.2. For the state u we have

$$\begin{aligned} g_u(u) &:= (I_R^U)^{-1}\ell_\alpha'(u) \\ &= \mathcal{A}^{-2}(u - y) + \alpha\Big(C_1u + C_2(\mathcal{A}u - f) + \mathcal{A}^{-1}(C_2^*u + C_3(\mathcal{A}u - f)\Big), \\ H_u &:= (I_R^U)^{-1}\ell_\alpha'' = \mathcal{A}^{-2} + \alpha(C_1 + C_2\mathcal{A} + \mathcal{A}^{-1}C_2^* + \mathcal{A}^{-1}C_3\mathcal{A})). \end{aligned}$$

1.6.1.2 Backwards Heat Problem

$U = U_0 = \{w \in L^2(H_0^1(\Omega)) \cap H^1(H^{-1}(\Omega)) : w(0,x) = 0\}$, $W = L^2(H_0^1(\Omega))$, $W' = L^2(H^{-1}(\Omega))$, $X = H_0^1(\Omega)$, $Y = L^2(\Omega)$, $\mathbb{M}(u,\theta) = (\partial_t + \mathcal{A})u + \underline{I}\mathcal{A}\theta$, $\mathbb{O} = \delta_T$, $K = (\partial_t + \mathcal{A}) : U_0 \to W'$, $K^{-1} = \int_0^\cdot e^{-\mathcal{A}(\cdot-s)}\cdot(s)\,ds : W' \to U_0$, $K^* = \int_0^\cdot e^{-\mathcal{A}(\cdot-s)}\cdot(s)\,ds : W' \to U_0$, $K^{-*} = K$, $L = \underline{I}\mathcal{A} : H_0^1(\Omega) \to W'$, $L^* = \mathcal{A}^{-1}\int_0^T \cdot(s)\,ds : W' \to H_0^1(\Omega)$, $K^{-1}L = \underline{I} - e^{\mathcal{A}\cdot} : H_0^1(\Omega) \to U_0$, $L^*K^{-*} = \mathcal{A}^{-1}\delta_T - \underline{I}^* : U_0 \to H_0^1(\Omega)$, $\mathbb{O} = \delta_T : U_0 \to L^2(\Omega)$, $\mathbb{O}^* = \frac{1}{2}(e^{-\mathcal{A}(T-.)} - e^{-\mathcal{A}(T+.)}) : L^2(\Omega) \to U_0$, resulting in the following instances

$$\begin{aligned} g_\theta(\theta) &:= (I_R^X)^{-1} j_\alpha'(\theta) = \alpha(C_2^*(\underline{I} - e^{\mathcal{A}\cdot}) + C_3)\theta + (\mathcal{A}^{-1}\delta_T - \underline{I}^*) \\ &\quad\cdot\Big[\tfrac{1}{2}(e^{-\mathcal{A}(T-.)} - e^{-\mathcal{A}(T+.)})(\delta_T[\underline{I} - e^{\mathcal{A}\cdot}]\theta - y) + \alpha(C_1[\underline{I} - e^{\mathcal{A}\cdot}] + C_2)\theta\Big], \\ H_\theta &:= (I_R^X)^{-1} j_\alpha'' = (\mathcal{A}^{-1}\delta_T - \underline{I}^*)\tfrac{1}{2}(e^{-\mathcal{A}(T-.)} - e^{-\mathcal{A}(T+.)})(\delta_T[\underline{I} - e^{\mathcal{A}\cdot}] \\ &\quad + \alpha\Big((\mathcal{A}^{-1}\delta_T - \underline{I}^*)C_1[\underline{I} - e^{\mathcal{A}\cdot}] + (\mathcal{A}^{-1}\delta_T - \underline{I}^*)C_2 + C_2^*(\underline{I} - e^{\mathcal{A}\cdot}) + C_3,\Big) \end{aligned}$$

for the parameter.

Since L is not invertible here, we substitute it by its right inverse $L^\sharp = \frac{1}{T}L^*$ to obtain, for the state,

$$\begin{aligned}
g_u(u) &:= (I_R^U)^{-1}\ell'_\alpha(u) = \tfrac{1}{2}(e^{-A(T-.)} - e^{-A(T+.)})(\delta_T u - y) \\
&+ \alpha\Big(C_1 u + C_2 A^{-1}\tfrac{1}{T}\textstyle\int_0^T((\partial_t + A)u - f)(s)\,\mathrm{d}s \\
&+ \tfrac{1}{T}(\mathrm{id} - e^{-At})\Big(C_2^* u + C_3\tfrac{1}{T}\textstyle\int_0^T((\partial_t + A)u - f)(s)\,\mathrm{d}s\Big)\Big), \\
H_u &:= (I_R^U)^{-1}\ell''_\alpha = \tfrac{1}{2}(e^{-A(T-.)} - e^{-A(T+.)})\delta_T \\
&+ \alpha\Big(C_1 + C_2 A^{-1}\tfrac{1}{T}\textstyle\int_0^T(\partial_t + A)\cdot(s)\,\mathrm{d}s \\
&+ \tfrac{1}{T}(\mathrm{id} - e^{-At})\Big(C_2^* + C_3\tfrac{1}{T}\textstyle\int_0^T(\partial_t + A)\cdot(s)\,\mathrm{d}s\Big).
\end{aligned}$$

1.6.2 Implementation

As already mentioned in the beginning of this section the analysis is done in python, with the help of Fenics and hippylib. With hippylib, the machinery of Bayesian inversion can be applied almost automatically to all stationary problems. However, concerning time-dependent problems a bit more work is necessary to get the results which are needed. In our case this means that the backwards heat problem had to be formulated in hippylib fashion to hand over to the algorithms for reconstruction. These algorithms were adapted to the all-at-once setting. In the following two sections the implementation of the problems as well as the results of the reconstruction are described in detail.

From now on, we fix the spatial domain Ω on which both inverse problems are considered to be the unit square and space discretization is done by means of Lagrange finite elements. For time discretization in the backwards heat problem we use zero order discontinuos Galerkin method as already described previously, which leads to a backward Euler time stepping scheme. The discretized versions of parameter and state will be denoted by u_h θ_h, the corresponding finite dimensional function spaces by U_h and X_h.

To generate the synthetic observations the forward model is solved with the true parameter. Here, the dimension of the spatial discretization space for the state and the parameter is both 1681. In order to avoid an inverse crime, this forward simulation is done on a finer grid as compared to the reconstruction, where the dimension is chosen to be 961. Discrete observation points are generated as 100 random points on the computational mesh, and the data at these points is perturbed with random noise. The measurement noise is assumed to follow a Gaussian distribution with zero mean and covariance $\Sigma = \delta^2 I$, where $\delta = 0.01$, and $I \in \mathbb{R}^{100\times 100}$. These synthetic observations are used (together with the prior) as input for the reconstructions.

1.6.2.1 Inverse Source Problem

The first test example considered for the implementation of the all-at-once version of Bayesian reconstruction is the inverse source problem. For this experiment the source is given by the function visualized in Figure 1.3(a). As described above, the Poisson equation with this source is solved and random discrete observations are constructed from the resulting state, see Figure 1.3(b) and 1.3(c). To reconstruct the source these observations are used together with the prior distribution. In this case the prior distribution is defined by

$$\mu_{\text{prior}} = \mathcal{N}(\mathbf{m}, \mathcal{C}_0), \text{ with } \mathbf{m} = \begin{pmatrix} m_u \\ m_\theta \end{pmatrix}, \mathcal{C}_0 = \begin{pmatrix} \kappa_s M + \gamma_s K & 0 \\ 0 & \kappa_p M + \gamma_p K \end{pmatrix}^{-1}, \tag{1.80}$$

with M and K denoting the mass and the stiffness matrix, respectively, cf. (1.27), (1.28), and chosen parameters $m_\theta = 0, \kappa_p = \kappa_s = 10^{-2}$ and $\gamma_p = \gamma_s = 35$. The prior matrix is chosen to be block diagonal, as operators on the off diagonal have not improved the reconstruction for this problem. The mean m_θ is chosen to be zero and the mean m_u is the output of the forward problem when the source is m_θ. The reconstruction using the synthetic observations and prior with the help of the CG-solver for the Hessian shown in the above computations leads to the results displayed in Figure 1.4(a) for the parameter and Figure 1.4(b) for the state. The posterior distribution is visualized with the help of samples for both the parameter in Figure 1.5 and the state in Figure 1.6. Let us comment on the choice of the parameters κ and γ in the prior covariance. The reconstruction of the parameter appears to be strongly influenced by the choice of κ_p, γ_p for the parameter prior, while the choice of κ_s, γ_s in the state prior do not really influence the reconstruction neither for the parameter nor for the state. Some comparison of different choices of parameters can be seen in Figure 1.7 for the parameter and Figure 1.8. Nonzero choices for the covariance operators C_2 or C_2^* other than zero have not improved the reconstructions for this example.

In Figures 1.4–1.8, the noise was set to 1% as described in the introduction of this section. However, the reconstructions are quite good up to a noise level of 3%, as it can be seen in Figure 1.9 and Figure 1.10.

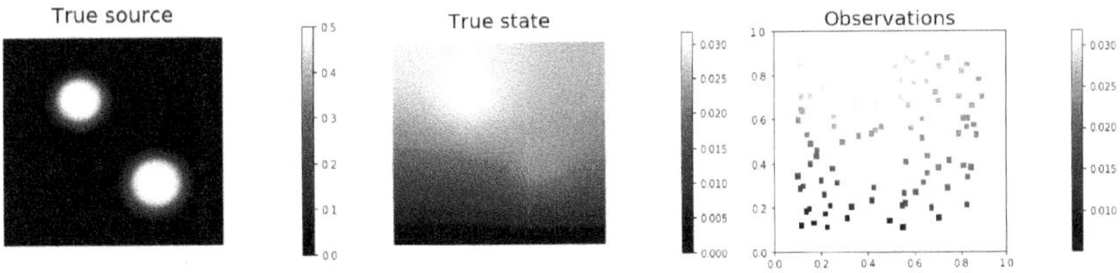

(a) True source. (b) True state. (c) Discrete observations.

Figure 1.3: Simulated observations for the inverse source problem.

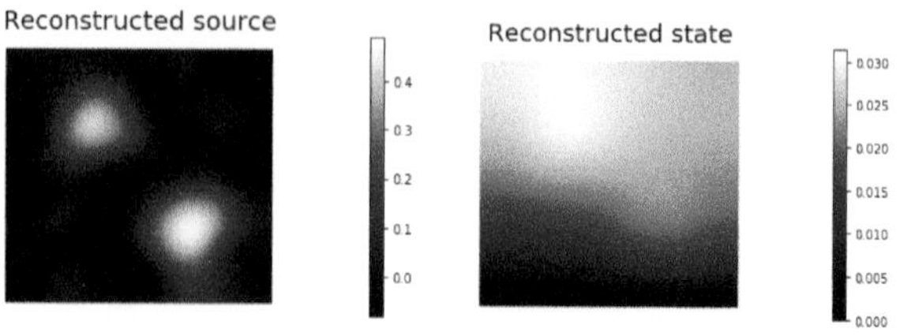

(a) Reconstructed source. (b) Reconstructed state.

Figure 1.4: Reconstructions for the inverse source problem.

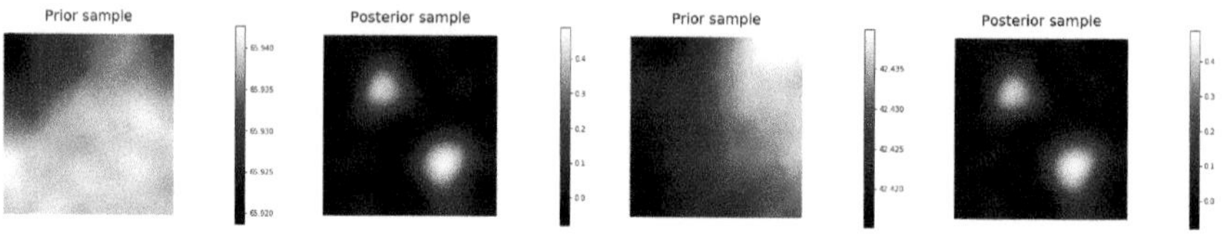

Figure 1.5: Samples from the posterior for the parameter variable of the inverse source problem.

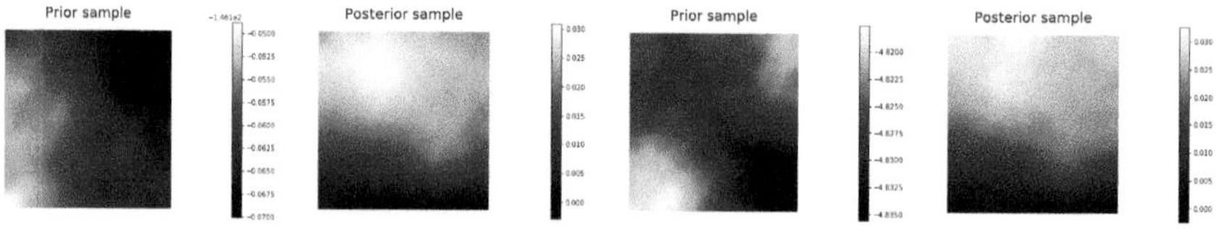

Figure 1.6: Samples from the posterior for the state variable of the inverse source problem.

1.6.2.2 Backwards Heat Equation, Sampled Initial Condition

For the backwards heat equation the prior as described in Section 1.5 is used, with the covariance operator for the initial condition chosen to be

$$C_p = (\kappa M + \gamma K)^{-1}, \tag{1.81}$$

where M and K are the mass and stiffness matrices resulting from the finite element discretization, with $\kappa = 1.5$ and $\gamma = 0.5$. The time variable is discretized in the same way as in Section 1.3 resulting in the covariance operator

$$C_s = \operatorname{diag}((e^{-t_i K} C_p e^{-t_i K})_{i=0}^{N}) \tag{1.82}$$

for the state variable, so that altogether we arrive at

$$\mathcal{C}_0 = \begin{pmatrix} C_s & 0 \\ 0 & C_p \end{pmatrix}.$$

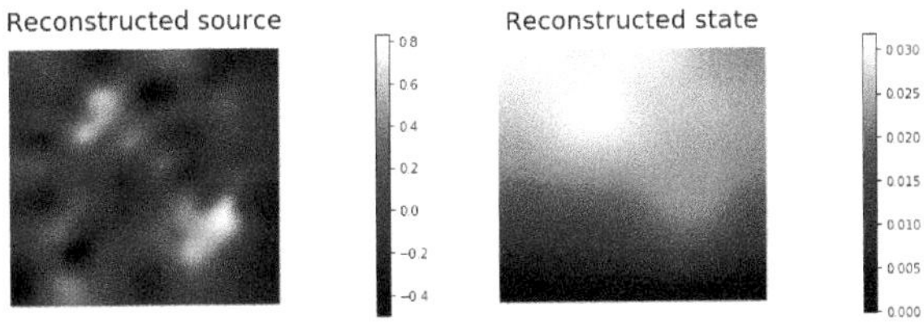

(a) Source: $\gamma_p = 1$ and $\kappa_p = 10^{-2}$. (b) State: $\gamma_p = 1$ and $\kappa_p = 10^{-2}$.

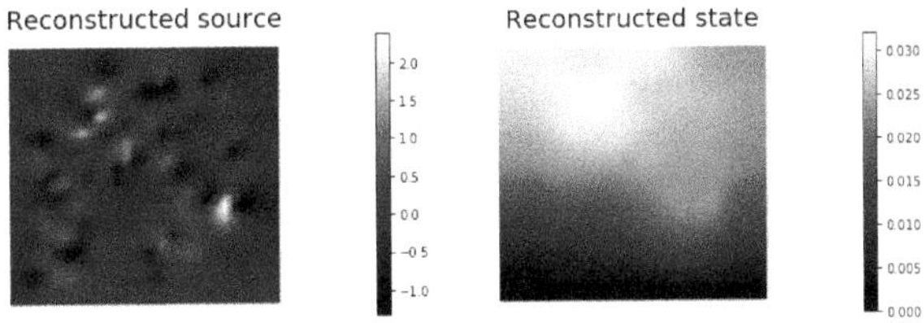

(c) Source: $\gamma_p = 10^{-2}$ and $\kappa_p = 70$. (d) State: $\gamma_p = 10^{-2}$ and $\kappa_p = 70$.

Figure 1.7: Reconstructions for the inverse source problem for different values for κ_p and γ_p and $\kappa_s = 10^{-2}$ and $\gamma_s = 35$.

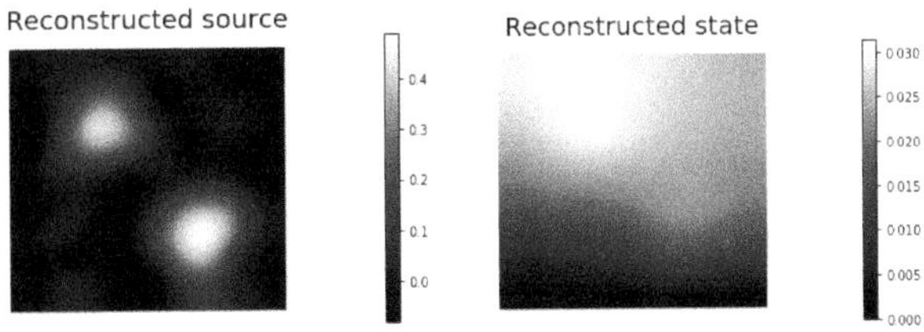

(a) Source: $\gamma_s = 10^{-2}$ and $\kappa_s = 70$. (b) State: $\gamma_s = 10^{-2}$ and $\kappa_s = 70$.

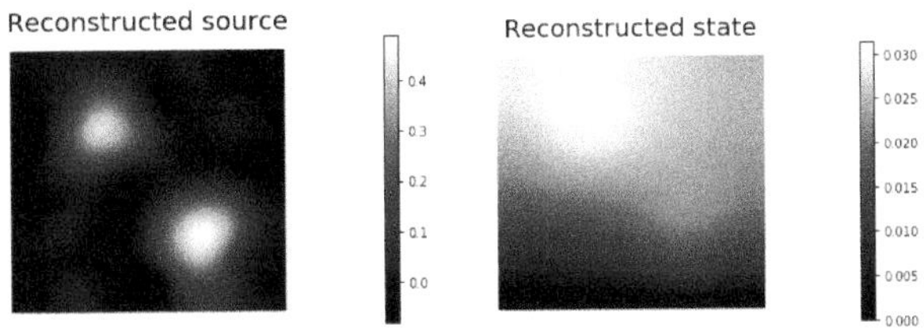

(c) Source: $\gamma_s = 10^{-5}$ and $\kappa_s = 100$. (d) State: $\gamma_s = 10^{-5}$ and $\kappa_s = 100$.

Figure 1.8: Reconstructions for the inverse source problem for different values for κ_s and γ_s and $\kappa_p = 10^{-2}$ and $\gamma_p = 35$.

Also here, nonzero covariance operators C_2 or C_2^* did not improve the reconstructions but would only complicate computation of powers of $\mathcal{C}_0$.

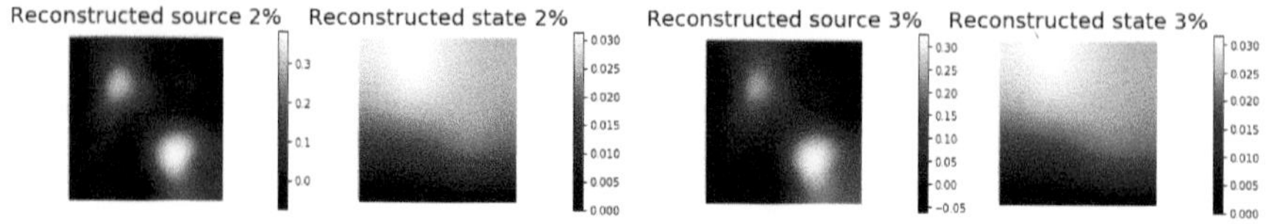

Figure 1.9: Reconstructions for the inverse source problem with different noise levels.

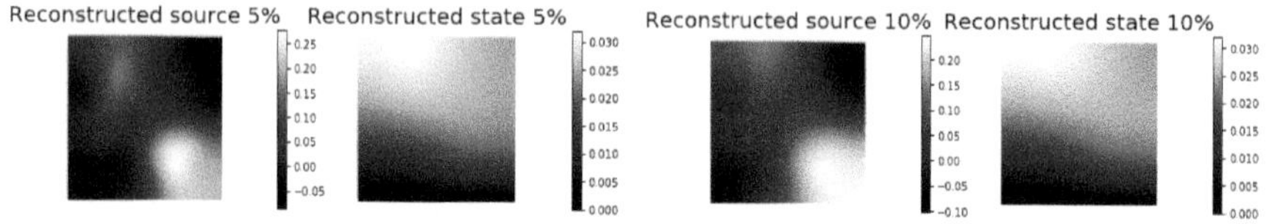

Figure 1.10: Reconstructions for the inverse source problem with different noise levels.

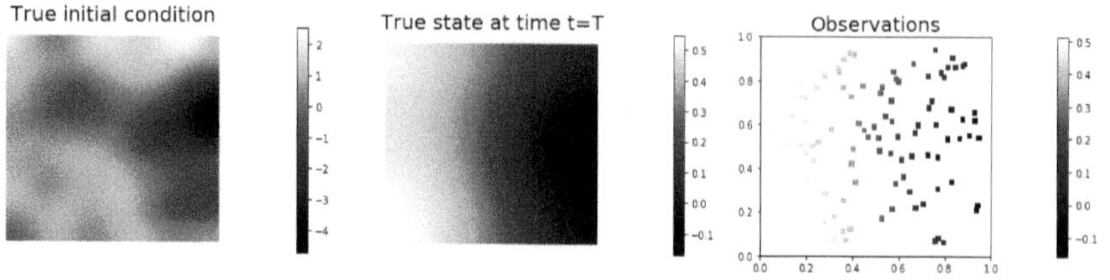

(a) True source. (b) True state. (c) Discrete observations.

Figure 1.11: Simulated observations for the backwards heat problem.

Here, we have the setting $T = 0.1, N = 4$ and $t_i = i\frac{T}{N}$. The prior mean for the initial condition is chosen to be zero, therefore, also the mean for the state is zero for each $t \in [0, T]$. Due to the diagonal structure of the operator matrix it is not necessary to save the whole matrix, instead for every time step only the application of the matrix vector product is needed. This overcomes the problem of block matrix usage in python. For the experiment, the initial condition is sampled from the prior distribution as seen in Figure 1.11(b). Then, the forward problem is solved (Figure 1.11(b) and discrete synthetic observations of the state at time $T = 0.1$ are constructed, see Figure 1.11(c). Finally, the MAP estimators can be computed as described in the beginning of this section for both the parameter and the state variable, see Figure 1.12. In this example the posterior samples are only shown for the parameter in Figure 1.13.

1.6.2.3 Backwards Heat Equation, Chosen Initial Condition

We now demonstrate performance of the method with a fixed initial condition as visualized in Figure 1.14(a). Again, discrete synthetic observations are made

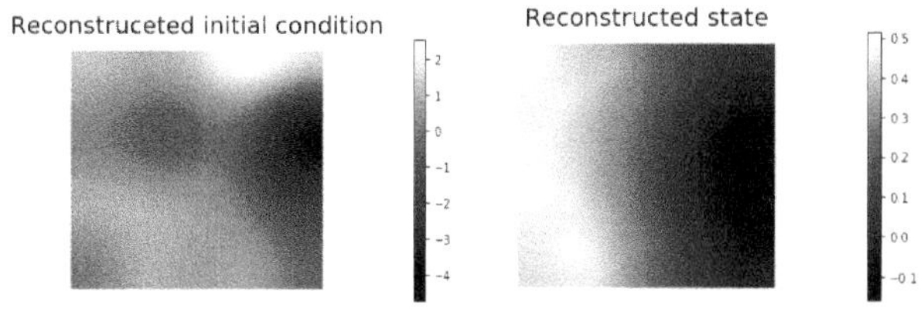

(a) Reconstructed source. (b) Reconstructed state.

Figure 1.12: Reconstructions for the backwards heat problem.

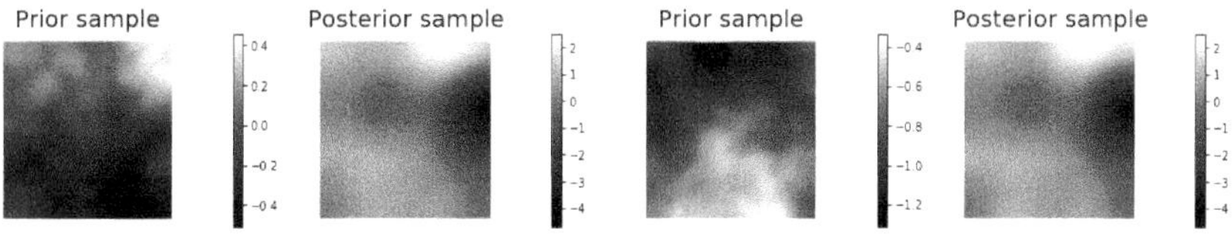

Figure 1.13: Samples from the posterior for the initial condition of the backwards heat problem.

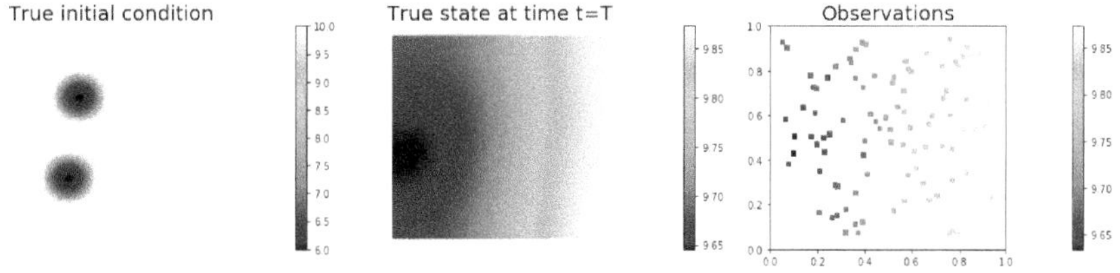

(a) True initial condition. (b) True state at time T. (c) Discrete observations.

Figure 1.14: Simulated observations for the backwards heat problem.

which are used for the reconstruction, see Figure 1.14(c). The prior is chosen as in Subsection 1.6.2.2. The reconstructions of the parameter and the state are shown in Figure 1.15. Samples are shown in Figure 1.16.

1.6.2.4 Backwards Heat Equation, Chosen Initial Condition, Prior Motivated by the Link Condition

Referring to Section 1.5.2 we do the same experiments as in the last section with the prior given by $\tilde{\mathcal{C}}$ as in (1.61) but skipping the off-diagonal blocks for ease of implementation

$$\mu_{\text{prior}} = \mathcal{N}(\mathbf{m}, \mathcal{C}_0), \text{ with } \mathbf{m} = \begin{pmatrix} m_u \\ m_\theta \end{pmatrix}, \quad \mathcal{C}_0 = \begin{pmatrix} \mathcal{M} & 0 \\ 0 & K^{1/2} \end{pmatrix}. \tag{1.83}$$

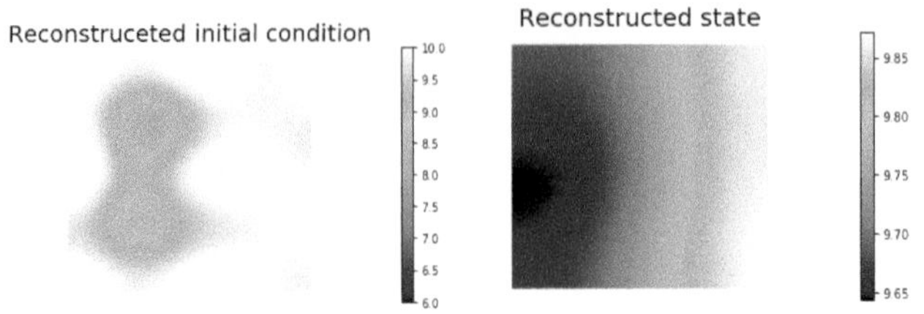

Figure 1.15: Reconstructions for the backwards heat problem.

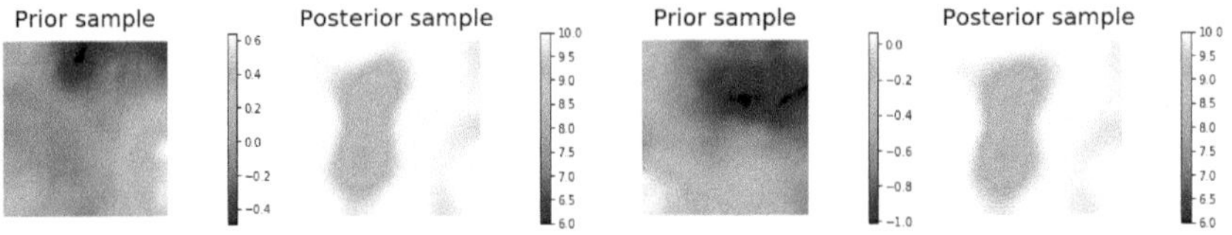

Figure 1.16: Samples from the posterior for the initial condition of the backwards heat problem.

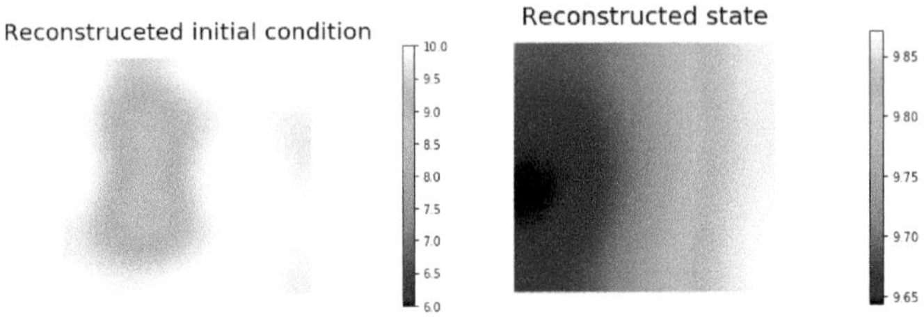

Figure 1.17: Reconstructions for the backwards heat problem with the heuristic prior.

The operator $\mathcal{M}$ denotes an operator consisting of the mass matrix M for every timestep $t \in [0, T]$. The setup of the numerical experiment is the same as in the last example concerning discretization, initial condition and observations. The reconstructions can be seen in Figure 1.17, which suggests quite a good fit also for this prior.

1.7 Conclusions and Remarks

In this chapter we have combined the Bayesian approach with an all-at-once formulation of the inverse problem. We have done so for linear problems, in particular focusing on two prototypical examples, namely the inverse source problem for the Poisson equation and the backwards heat equation.

Our next step will be to extend this approach to nonlinear problems such as the identification of coefficients in time dependent and stationary PDEs. Moreover we will further investigate the use of joint state and parameter priors, possibly also taking covariances between them into account.

Acknowledgment

This work was supported by the Austrian Science Fund FWF under the grants P30054 and DOC 78.

References

[1] Sergios Agapiou and Peter Mathé. Posterior contraction in bayesian inverse problems under gaussian priors. pp. 1–29. *In*: Bernd Hofmann, Antonio Leitão and Jorge P. Zubelli (eds.). *New Trends in Parameter Identification for Mathematical Models*. Springer International Publishing, Cham, 2018.

[2] Volkan Akcelik, George Biros, Andrei Draganescu, Omar Ghattas, Judith Hill and Bart G. van Bloemen Waanders. Inversion of airborne contaminants in a regional model. pp. 481–488. *In*: *Computational Science–ICCS 2006, 6th International Conference, Reading, UK, May 28–31, 2006, Proceedings, Part III*, 2006.

[3] Alen Alexanderian, Noemi Petra, Georg Stadler and Omar Ghattas. Optimal design of experiments for infinite-dimensional bayesian linear inverse problems with regularized l-sparsification. SIAM Journal on Scientific Computing, 36(5): A2122–A2148, 2014.

[4] A.W. van der Vaart, B.T. Knapik and J.H. van Zanten. Bayesian recovery of the initial condition for the heat equation. Communications in Statistics, Theory and Methods, 42, 2013.

[5] Martin Burger and Wolfram Mühlhuber. Iterative regularization of parameter identification problems by sequential quadratic programming methods. Inverse Problems, 18: 943–969, 2002.

[6] Martin Burger and Wolfram Mühlhuber. Numerical approximation of an sqp-type method for parameter identification. SIAM J. Numer. Anal., 40: 1775–1797, 2002.

[7] Christian Clason. Numerical partial differential equations. Lecture notes, University of Duisburg-Essen, 2017.

[8] Simon L. Cotter, Masoumeh Dashti and Andrew M. Stuart. Approximation of bayesian inverse problems for pdes. SIAM Journal on Numerical Analysis, 48(1): 322–345, 2010.

[9] Masoumeh Dashti and Andrew M. Stuart. The bayesian approach to inverse problems. pp. 311–428. *In*: Roger Ghanem, David Higdon and Houman Owhadi (eds.). *Handbook of Uncertainty Quantification*. Springer International Publishing, Cham, 2017.

[10] Klaus-Jochen Engel and Rainer Nagel. *One-Parameter Semigroups for Linear Evolution Equations*. Graduate Texts in Mathematics. Springer New York, 1999.

[11] Lawrence C. Evans. *Partial Differential Equations*, volume 19 of *Graduate Studies in Mathematics*. AMS, Providence, Rhode Island, 1998.

[12] Shota Gugushvili, A.W. van der Vaart and Dong Yan. Bayesian inverse problems with partial observations. ArXiv e-prints, Feb. 2018.

[13] Eldad Haber and Uri M. Ascher. Preconditioned all-at-once methods for large, sparse parameter estimation problems. Inverse Problems, 17(6): 1847–1864, Nov. 2001.

[14] H.P. Flath, Lucas C. Wilcox, Volkan Akcelik, Judith Hill, Bart Van Bloemen Waanders and Omar Ghattas. Fast algorithms for bayesian uncertainty quantification in large-scale linear inverse problems based on low-rank partial hessian approximations. SIAM J. Scientific Computing, 33, 2011.

[15] Barbara Kaltenbacher. All-at-once versus reduced iterative methods for time dependent inverse problems. Inverse Problems, 33(6): 064002, 2017.

[16] Barbara Kaltenbacher. Regularization based on all-at-once formulations for inverse problems. SIAM Journal on Optimization, 28: 620–645, 2018.

[17] Barbara Kaltenbacher, Manfred Kaltenbacher and Stefan Gombots. Inverse scheme for acoustic source localization using microphone measurements and finite element simulations. Acta Acustica united with Acustica, 647–656, 2018.

[18] Barbara Kaltenbacher, Alana Kirchner and Boris Vexler. Goal oriented adaptivity in the irgnm for parameter identification in pdes ii: all-at once formulations. Inverse Problems, 30: 045002, 2014.

[19] Richard Kowar and Otmar Scherzer. Attenuation models in photoacoustics. pp. 85–130. *In*: H. Ammari (ed.). *Mathematical Modeling in Biomedical Imaging II: Optical, Ultrasound, and Opto-Acoustic Tomographies*, volume 2035 of *Lecture Notes in Mathematics*. Springer Verlag, Berlin Heidelberg, 2012.

[20] James Martin, Lucas C. Wilcox, Carsten Burstedde and Omar Ghattas. A stochastic newton mcmc method for large-scale statistical inverse

problems with application to seismic inversion. SIAM Journal on Scientific Computing, 34(3): A1460–A1487, 2012.

[21] Peter Mathé. Bayesian inverse problems with non-commuting operators. Mathematics of Computation, 01 2018.

[22] Tram Thi Ngoc Nguyen. Landweber–kaczmarz for parameter identification in time-dependent inverse problems: all-at-once versus reduced version. Inverse Problems, 35(3): 035009, Feb. 2019.

[23] R.G. Douglas. On majorization, factorization, and range inclusion of operators on hilbert space. Proc. Amer. Math. Soc., 17: 413–415, 1966.

[24] Andreas Schuhmacher, Jorgen Hald, Karsten Bo Rasmussen and Per Christian Hansen. Sound source reconstruction using inverse boundary element calculations. J. Acoust. Soc. Am., 113: 114–127, 2003.

[25] James Martin Tan Bui-Thanh, Omar Ghattas and Georg Stadler. A computational framework for infinite-dimensional bayesian inverse problems Part I: The linearized case, with application to global seismic inversion. SIAM J. Scientific Computing, 35, 2013.

[26] Umberto Villa, Noemi Petra and Omar Ghattas. hIPPYlib: An extensible software framework for large-scale deterministic and bayesian inverse problems. Journal of Open Source Software, 3(30), 2018.

Chapter 2

On Iterated Tikhonov Kaczmarz Type Methods for Solving Systems of Linear Ill-posed Operator Equations

R Filippozzi, JC Rabelo and *A Leitão**

Mathematics Subject Classification (2000) 65J20, 47J06

2.1 Introduction

In this chapter we propose a nonstationary *iterated Tikhonov Kaczmarz* (iTK) type method for obtaining stable approximations to systems of linear ill-posed operator equations. The iTK methods are Kaczmarz type methods [13], where the steps are defined using the same heuristic as in the iterated Tikhonov (iT) method [3, Section 1.2].

The novelty of our approach consists in defining the Lagrange multipliers using a strategy inspired by [2]. That is the multipliers are chosen as to guarantee the residual of the next iterate to be in a *range* (use a different range as the one proposed in [2]).

Department of Mathematics, Federal University of St. Catarina, P.O. Box 476, 88040-900 Florianopolis SC, Brazil.
Emails: rafaela.filippozzi@gmail.com; joelrabelo@ufpi.edu.br
* Corresponding author: acgleitao@gmail.com

The inverse problems we are interested in consists of determining an unknown quantity $x \in X$ from the set of data $(y_0, \ldots, y_{N-1}) \in Y^N$, where X and Y are Hilbert spaces, and $N \geq 1$. In practical situations, one does not know the data exactly. Instead, only approximate measured data $y_i^\delta \in Y$ satisfying

$$\|y_i^\delta - y_i\| \leq \delta_i, \; i = 0, \ldots, N-1, \tag{2.1}$$

are available, where $\delta_i > 0$ are the (known) noise levels. The available data y_i^δ are obtained by indirect measurements of the parameter x, this process being described by the system of ill-posed operator equations

$$A_i x = y_i, \; i = 0, \ldots, N-1. \tag{2.2}$$

where $A_i : X \to Y$ are bounded linear operators, whose inverses $A_i^{-1} : R(A_i) \to X$ either do not exist, or are not continuous. Consequently, approximate solutions are extremely sensitive to noise in the data.

There is a vast literature on iterative methods for the stable solution of (2.2). We refer the reader to the text books [7, 12, 1, 16, 14, 5] and the references therein.

What concerns systems of linear ill-posed equations and Kaczmarz type methods, we refer the reader to [17]. In this article Nashed considered Kaczmarz (and Cimmino) methods for solving a problem related to the inverse Radon Transform, which is written in the form of abstract equations (see (1.1) to (1.4) in [17]). It is proven that the Kaczmarz method converges to a weighted least-squares solution of (2.2) [17, Section 2], which is defined by means of the *oblique generalized inverse* defined in [17, pg.167]. In this article Nashed also discusses the generalization of Kaczmarz (and Cimmino) method to operator equations in function spaces (this is the framework presented above in (2.2), (2.1)). The final paragraph in [17] reads:

> "It is hoped that the semicontinuous (or semidiscrete, depending on your viewpoint) analogues of the methods of Kaczmarz and Cimmino developed in this paper ... will be further adapted to the context of reconstruction problems."

It is our hope that the present manuscript is able to give a small step in the direction pointed by professor Nashed back in 1980.

Iterated Tikhonov Type Methods

Standard iterated Tikhonov (iT) type methods for solving the ill-posed problem (2.1), (2.2) are defined, after rewritting (2.2) as a single equation $\mathbf{A}x = \mathbf{y}$, where $\mathbf{A} = (A_0, \ldots, A_{N-1}) : X \to Y^N$ and $\mathbf{y}^\delta = (y_0^\delta, \ldots, y_{N-1}^\delta)$, by the iteration formula

$$x_{k+1}^\delta = \arg\min_{x \in X} \{\lambda_k \|\mathbf{A}x - \mathbf{y}^\delta\|^2 + \|x - x_k^\delta\|^2\} \tag{2.3}$$

or, equivalentely, by

$$\begin{aligned} x_{k+1}^{\delta} &= x_k^{\delta} - \lambda_k \big(I + \lambda_k \mathbf{A}^*\mathbf{A}\big)^{-1} \mathbf{A}^* \big(\mathbf{A}x_k^{\delta} - \mathbf{y}^{\delta}\big) \\ &= \big(\lambda_k^{-1} I + \mathbf{A}^*\mathbf{A}\big)^{-1} \big[\lambda_k^{-1} x_k^{\delta} + \mathbf{A}^*\mathbf{y}^{\delta}\big], \end{aligned} \tag{2.4}$$

where $\mathbf{A}^* : Y^N \to X$ is the adjoint operator to $\mathbf{A}$. The parameter $\lambda_k > 0$ can be viewed as the Lagrange multiplier of the problem of projecting x_k^{δ} onto a levelset of $\|\mathbf{A}x - \mathbf{y}^{\delta}\|^2$. If the sequence $\{\lambda_k = \lambda\}$ is constant, iteration (2.4) is called *stationary* iT [16, 7, 15], otherwise it is denominated *nonstationary* iT [6, 10, 3].

In the nonstationary iT methods, each λ_k is chosen either *a priori* (e.g., the geometrical choice $\lambda_k = q^k$, $q > 1$) or *a posteriori* [4, 2]. In this manuscript we focus on the *a posteriori* strategy investigated in [2], where the authors propose a choice for the Lagrange multipliers, which requires the residual at the next iterate to assume a prescribed value dependent on the current residual and also on the noise level. We extend the strategy used in [2], by defining a different range. This allow us to give convergence proof different to the one in [2], which boils down to a particular instance of [3, Theorem 1.4].

Iterated Tikhonov Kaczmarz Type Methods

The method proposed and analyzed in this manuscript for solving the the system of ill-posed problems (2.1), (2.2) is a Kaczmarz type method, where each step is defined as in the iT method (2.4) and the choice of Lagrange multipliers proposed in [2] is adopted. This iterative method is defined by

$$x_{k+1}^{\delta} = x_k^{\delta} + h_k, \tag{2.5}$$

where

$$h_k = \begin{cases} \lambda_k (I + \lambda_k A_{[k]}^* A_{[k]})^{-1} A_{[k]}^* \big(y_{[k]}^{\delta} - A_{[k]} x_k^{\delta}\big) & , \text{ if } \|A_{[k]}x_k^{\delta} - y_{[k]}^{\delta}\| > \tau\delta_{[k]} \\ 0 & , \text{ otherwise} \end{cases} \tag{2.6}$$

and

$$\lambda_k = \begin{cases} \text{chosen as in Algorithm 2.2.1} & , \text{ if } \|A_{[k]}x_k^{\delta} - y_{[k]}^{\delta}\| > \tau\delta_{[k]} \\ 0 & , \text{ otherwise.} \end{cases} \tag{2.7}$$

We use the notation $[k] = (k \bmod N) \in \{0, 1, \ldots, N-1\}$. Here $x_0^{\delta} \in X$ is an initial guess and $\tau > 1$ is a fixed constant.

Notice that, if $\|A_{[k]}x_k^{\delta} - y_{[k]}^{\delta}\| > \tau\delta_{[k]}$ for some k, then $h_k \in X$ is a tipical step of the iterated Tikhonov method for the $[k]$-th equation $A_{[k]}x = y_{[k]}$ of system (2.2). Otherwise, the computation of (λ_k, h_k) is avoided. We set $\lambda_k = 0$, $h_k = 0$ and $x_{k+1}^{\delta} = x_k^{\delta}$.

Following [2] we refer to this method as *range-relaxed iterated Tikhonov Kaczmarz* (rriTK) method. Essentialy, it consists in incorporating the Kaczmarz strategy into the iterated Tikhonov method investigated in [2]. This procedure is analog to the one introduced in [9, 8] regarding the Landweber Kaczmarz (LWK) iteration.

As usual in Kaczmarz type algorithms, a group of N subsequent steps (starting at some multiple of N) is called a cycle. In the noisy data case, the iTK iteration should be terminated when, for the first time, all x_k^δ are equal within a cycle. That is, the iteration is stopped at step $k_* = k_*\big(\{\delta_i\}_i, \{y_i^\delta\}_i\big)$ such that

$$k_* := \min\big\{lN : l \in N \text{ and } x_{lN}^\delta = x_{lN+1}^\delta = \cdots = x_{lN+N}^\delta\big\}. \tag{2.8}$$

In other words, $k_* \in \mathbb{N}$ is the smallest multiple of N such that $x_{k_*}^\delta = x_{k_*+1}^\delta = \cdots = x_{k_*+N}^\delta$ or, equivalently, such that $\lambda_{k_*} = \lambda_{k_*+1} = \cdots = \lambda_{k_*+N} = 0$.

Outline of the Manuscript

The article is organized as follows: In Section 2.2 we introduce the rriTK method, on which we focus on this manuscript. A detailed formulation of this method is given and some preliminary results are obtained, including an estimate for the "*gain*" (Proposition 2.2.4), as well as estimates for the Lagrange multipliers λ_k (Corollary 2.2.6) and for the stoping index k_* (Corollary 2.2.8). In Section 2.3 a convergence result for the rriTK method is presented. Section 2.4 is devoted to numerical experiments. A benchmark system of linear ill-posed equations (derived from the Hilbert matrix in $\mathbb{R}^{100,100}$) is considered. The performance of the rriTK method is compared against two other nonstationary iT type methods: the well established geometric iterated Tikhonov method (giT) with $\lambda_k = 2^k$ and the iT method in [2] (rriT). Section 2.5 is dedicated to final remarks and conclusions.

2.2 A Range-relaxed Iterated Tikhonov Kaczmarz Method

In the sequel we introduce the *range-relaxed iterated Tikhonov Kaczmarz* (rriTK) method for solving the ill-posed linear system (2.1), (2.2). Subsection 2.2.1 is devoted to main assumptions needed in the analysis. The new method is presented in Subsection 2.2.2 and a corresponding algorithm is discussed. In Subsection 2.2.3 we derive some basic properties of the proposed method, and prove preliminary results and estimates.

The implementable method proposed here happens to be a nonstationary iTK type method where, in each iteration, the set of feasible choices for the Lagrange multipliers is an interval, instead of a single real number. For this reason, this method is called a (nonstationary) range-relaxed iterated Tikhonov method.

2.2.1 Main Assumptions

For the remaining of this chapter we suppose that the following assumptions hold true:

(A1) There exists $x^\star \in X$ such that $A_i x^\star = y_i$, where $y_i \in R(A_i)$, $i = 0, \ldots, N-1$, are the exact data.

(A2) The operators $A_i : X \to Y$ is linear, bounded and ill-posed, i.e., even if the operator $A_i^{-1} : R(A_i) \to X$ (the left inverse of A_i) exists, it is not continuous.

From (A2) it follows the existence of $C > 0$ with $C := \max_i \|A_i\|$. Moreover, we write $\delta := \max_i \delta_i > 0$. Thus, $\delta = 0$ in the exact data case, and $\delta > 0$ in the noisy data case.

2.2.2 Description of the Method

As already discussed in the introduction, the iterative step of the rriTK method is analog to the one proposed in [2]. This step is discussed in the sequel.

For $i = 0, \ldots, N-1$ and $\mu > 0$ define the levelsets $\Omega_\mu^i := \{x \in X; \|A_i x - y_i^\delta\| \le \mu\}$ of the residual w.r.t. the ith-equation of system (2.2). Given $k \in \mathbb{N}$, set $i = [k]$. If x_k^δ does not belong to $\Omega_{\delta_i}^i$, the next iterate x_{k+1}^δ is computed by solving the *range-relaxed projection problem*

$$\begin{cases} \min_x \ \|x - x_k^\delta\|^2 \\ \text{s.t. } \|A_i x - y_i^\delta\|^2 \le \mu^2, \quad \bar{\Phi}(\|A_i x_k^\delta - y_i^\delta\|, \delta_i) \le \mu \le \bar{\bar{\Phi}}(\|A_i x_k^\delta - y_i^\delta\|, \delta_i) \end{cases} \tag{2.9}$$

for $(x, \mu) \in X \times \mathbb{R}$. Here

$$\bar{\Phi}(u,v) = (\bar{p}u + (1-\bar{p})v)^{\frac{1}{2}} \quad \text{and} \quad \bar{\bar{\Phi}}(u,v) = (\bar{\bar{p}}u + (1-\bar{\bar{p}})v), \quad \forall\, u, v \in \mathbb{R},$$

with $0 < \bar{p} < \bar{\bar{p}} < 1$.

If (x', μ') is a solution of (2.9), we define $x_{k+1}^\delta = x'$ and $\|A_i x_{k+1}^\delta - y_i^\delta\| = \mu'$ (see Lemma 2.2.1 below). As observed in [2], x_{k+1}^δ is generated from x_k^δ by projecting it onto any one of the range of convex sets $(\Omega_\mu^i)_{\bar{\Phi} \le \mu \le \bar{\bar{\Phi}}}$.

Since the solution of (2.9) is not unique, there are several possible choices for x_{k+1}^δ. The next lemma addresses this issue. For a proof we refer the reader to [2, Lemma 2.3].

Lemma 2.2.1 *Suppose $\|A_i x_k^\delta - y_i^\delta\| > \delta_i$. The following assertions are equivalent*

1. $x' = \Pi_{\Omega_\mu}(x_k^\delta)$ *and* $\bar{\Phi}(\|A_i x_k^\delta - y_i^\delta\|, \delta_i) \le \mu' \le \bar{\bar{\Phi}}(\|A_i x_k^\delta - y_i^\delta\|, \delta_i)$;

2. *$(x', \mu') \in X \times \mathbb{R}$ is a solution of the range-relaxed projection problem (2.9);*

3. *$x' = x_k^\delta - \lambda(I + \lambda A_i^* A_i)^{-1} A_i^*(A_i x_k^\delta - y_i^\delta)$, for some $\lambda > 0$,*

$$\bar{\Phi}(\|A_i x_k^\delta - y_i^\delta\|, \delta_i) \leq \|A_i x' - y_i^\delta\| \leq \bar{\bar{\Phi}}(\|A_i x_k^\delta - y_i^\delta\|, \delta_i),$$

and $\mu' = \|A_i x' - y_i^\delta\|$;

(here $\Pi_\Omega(x)$ represents the orthogonal projection of x onto the convex set Ω).

It follows from Lemma 2.2.1 that solving the range-relaxed projection problem in (2.9) sums up to solving the inequalities $\bar{\Phi}(\|A_i x_k^\delta - y_i^\delta|, \delta_i) \leq \|A_i x' - y_i^\delta\| \leq \bar{\bar{\Phi}}(\|A_i x_k^\delta - y_i^\delta\|, \delta_i)$, with $x' = x_k^\delta - \lambda(I + \lambda A_i^* A_i)^{-1} A_i^*(A_i x_k^\delta - y_i^\delta)$ and $\mu' = \|A_i x' - y_i^\delta\|$. This is the quintessential ingredient to define an implementable version of the range-relaxed iterated Tikhonov Kaczmarz (rriTK) method as follows:

Algorithm 2.2.1 Range-relaxed iterated Tikhonov Kaczmarz method (rriTK)

[1] *choose an initial guess $x_0 \in X$; set $k = 0$;*
[2] *choose $0 < \bar{p} < \bar{\bar{p}} < 1$ (with $\bar{p} > \delta \bar{\bar{p}}$) and $\tau > 1$;*
[3] **repeat**
  [3.1] $i = [k]$;
  [3.2] **if** $\left[\ \|A_i x_k^\delta - y_i^\delta\| > \tau \delta_i\ \right]$ **then**
    compute $(\lambda_k, h_k) \in \mathbb{R} \times X$ such that

$$\begin{cases} h_k = -\lambda_k \left(I + \lambda_k A_i^* A_i\right)^{-1} A_i^* \left(A_i x_k^\delta - y_i^\delta\right) \\ \bar{\Phi}(\|A_i x_k^\delta - y_i^\delta\|, \delta_i) \leq \|A_i(x_k^\delta + h_k) - y_i^\delta\| \leq \bar{\bar{\Phi}}(\|A_i x_k^\delta - y_i^\delta\|, \delta_i) \end{cases}$$

  else
    $\lambda_k = 0;\ h_k = 0;$
  [3.3] $x_{k+1}^\delta = x_k^\delta + h_k$;
  [3.4] $k = k + 1$;
  until $\left[\ ([k] = 0) \text{ and } (\lambda_{k-1} = \lambda_{k-2} = \cdots = \lambda_{k-N} = 0)\ \right]$;
[4] $k_* = k - N$;

An immediate consequence of Lemma 2.2.1 is the fact that Step [3.2] of Algorithm 2.2.1 is well defined, i.e., it is allways possible to solve the problem for (λ_k, h_k) in this step.

2.2.3 Preliminary Results

For simplicity of notation we write $b_k^\delta := y_i^\delta - A_i x_{k+1}^\delta = y_i^\delta - A_i x_k^\delta - A_i h_k$, with $i = [k]$, and $C > 0$ is defined as above. Moreover, for exact data $y = (y_0, \ldots, y_{N-1})$, the iterates in (2.5) are denoted by x_k, in contrast to x_k^δ in the noisy data case (analog notation for $b_k := y_i - A_i x_{k+1}$).

Our first result concerns basic properties of the iterative step of the rriTK method. The proofs of the assertions are straightforward and will be omitted.

Lemma 2.2.2 *Assume that (A1) and (A2) are satisfied and let x_k^δ, h_k, λ_k be defined by (2.5), (2.6) and (2.7) respectively. For all $0 \le k < k_*$ and $i = [k]$, the assertions*

a) $A_i x_{k+1}^\delta - y_i^\delta = (\lambda_k A_i A_i^* + I)^{-1} (A_i x_k^\delta - y_i^\delta)$;

b) $h_k = \lambda_k A_i^* \left(y_i^\delta - A_i x_{k+1}^\delta\right)$;

c) $\left(\bar{p} \, \|A_i x_k^\delta - y_i^\delta\|\right)^{\frac{1}{2}} \le \|A_i x_{k+1}^\delta - y_i^\delta\| \le \|A_i x_k^\delta - y_i^\delta\|$.

hold true whenever $\lambda_k > 0$.

Remark 2.2.3 *Let us consider the exact data case for a moment. From Step [3.2] of Algorithm 2.2.1 we learn that the residual w.r.t. the ith-equation (with $i = [k]$) reduces from iterate x_k to the next iterate x_{k+1}, namely*

$$\|A_i x_{k+1} - y_i\| \le \bar{\bar{p}} \, \|A_i x_k - y_i\| \,. \tag{2.10}$$

In other words, we have geometrical decay of this residual.

In what follows we estimate the "gain" $\|x_{k+1}^\delta - x^\star\|^2 - \|x_k^\delta - x^\star\|^2$. This is a central result for the analysis derived in this manuscript (all subsequent corollaries in this section derive from the next proposition).

Proposition 2.2.4 *Assume that (A1) and (A2) are satisfied and let x_k^δ, h_k, λ_k be defined by (2.5), (2.6) and (2.7) respectively. For $\delta = \max_i \delta_i$ sufficiently small, it holds*

$$\|x_{k+1}^\delta - x^\star\|^2 - \|x_k^\delta - x^\star\|^2 \le -2(\bar{p} - \delta \bar{\bar{p}}) \, \lambda_k \, \|A_i x_k^\delta - y_i^\delta\| - \|x_{k+1}^\delta - x_k^\delta\|^2, \tag{2.11}$$

for $k = 0, \ldots, k_* - 1$. In particular, in the exact data case ($y_i^\delta = y_i$) we have

$$\|x_{k+1} - x^\star\|^2 - \|x_k - x^\star\|^2 \le -2\bar{p} \, \lambda_k \, \|A_i x_k - y_i\| - \|x_{k+1} - x_k\|^2, \; k = 0, \ldots \tag{2.12}$$

Proof. Let $i = [k]$. If $\|A_i x_k^\delta - y_i^\delta\| \le \tau\delta_i$, then $\lambda_k = 0$ and $x_{k+1}^\delta = x_k^\delta$. Thus, (2.11) is trivial. Otherwise, it follows from Lemma 2.2.2 (b) that

$$\begin{aligned}
\|x_{k+1}^\delta - x^\star\|^2 - \|x_k^\delta - x^\star\|^2 & \\
&= 2\,\langle x_{k+1}^\delta - x_k^\delta,\, x_{k+1}^\delta - x^*\rangle - \|x_{k+1}^\delta - x_k^\delta\|^2 \\
&= 2\lambda_k\,\langle y_i^\delta - A_i x_{k+1}^\delta,\, A_i(x_{k+1}^\delta - x^\star)\rangle - \|x_{k+1}^\delta - x_k^\delta\|^2 \\
&= 2\lambda_k\,\langle y_i^\delta - A_i x_{k+1}^\delta,\, A_i x_{k+1}^\delta - y_i^\delta + y_i^\delta - A_i x^\star\rangle - \|x_{k+1}^\delta - x_k^\delta\|^2 \\
&\le 2\lambda_k\left[-\|b_k^\delta\|^2 + \|b_k^\delta\|\,\delta_i\right] - \|x_{k+1}^\delta - x_k^\delta\|^2 . \qquad (2.13)
\end{aligned}$$

If $\delta < 1$ then (2.11) follows from $\bar{p}\|A_i x_k^\delta - y_i^\delta\| + (1-\bar{p})\delta_i \le \|b_k^\delta\|^2$ and $\|b_k^\delta\| \le \bar{\bar{p}}\|A_i x_k^\delta - y_i^\delta\| + (1-\bar{\bar{p}})\delta_i$ (see Step [3.2] of Algorithm 2.2.1), together with $\bar{p} > \delta\bar{\bar{p}}$ (see Step [2]). To conclude the proof notice that, in the exact data case $\delta = 0$ and (2.12) follows directly from (2.11). □

Proposition 2.2.4 has several relevant consequences, namely: monotonicity of the iTK method (Corollary 2.2.5); a uniform estimate for the Lagrange multipliers (Corollary 2.2.6); the summability of important series (Corollary 2.2.7); finiteness of the stoping index k_* (Corollary 2.2.8).

Corollary 2.2.5 *Assume that (A1) and (A2) are satisfied and let x_k^δ, h_k, λ_k be defined by (2.5), (2.6) and (2.7) respectively. Then*

$$\|x_{k+1}^\delta - x^\star\|^2 \le \|x_k^\delta - x^\star\|^2 , \; k = 0,\ldots,k_* - 1 . \qquad (2.14)$$

Additionaly, in the exact data case we have $\|x_{k+1} - x^\star\|^2 \le \|x_k - x^\star\|^2$, *for* $k = 0, 1, \ldots$

Corollary 2.2.6 *Assume that (A1) and (A2) are satisfied and let x_k^δ, h_k, λ_k be defined by (2.5), (2.6) and (2.7) respectively. Moreover, let b_k^δ be defined as above. Then*

$$\lambda_k \ge \frac{\left(\|A_i x_k^\delta - y_i^\delta\| - \|b_k^\delta\|\right)\|A_i x_k^\delta - y_i^\delta\|}{\|A_i^*(A_i x_k^\delta - y_i^\delta)\|^2} , \; k = 0,\ldots,k_* - 1 . \qquad (2.15)$$

Moreover, if $\|A_i x_k^\delta - y_i^\delta\| > \tau\delta_i$ (for some $0 \le k < k_* - 1$) then $\lambda_k > C^{-2}(1-\bar{\bar{p}})(1-\frac{1}{\tau})$, with $C > 0$ defined as above.

Additionaly, in the exact data case we have $\lambda_k \ge C^{-2}(1-\bar{\bar{p}})$, for $k = 0, 1, \ldots$

Proof. Let $0 \le k < k_*$. If $\|A_i x_k^\delta - y_i^\delta\| \le \tau\delta_i$ then $\lambda_k = 0$ and $x_{k+1}^\delta = x_k^\delta$. Thus, (2.15) is trivial. On the other hand, if $\|A_i x_k^\delta - y_i^\delta\| > \tau\delta_i$, the proof of (2.15) follows the lines of [2, Corollary 2.5].

To prove the second assertion, notice that Step [3.2] of Algorithm 2.2.1 guarantees $\|b_k^\delta\| \le \bar{\bar{p}}\|A_i x_k^\delta - y_i^\delta\| + (1-\bar{\bar{p}})\delta_i$. Consequently, $\|A_i x_k^\delta - y_i^\delta\| - \|b_k^\delta\| \ge$

$(1-\bar{\bar{p}})(\|A_i x_k^\delta - y_i^\delta\| - \delta_i)$. Thus, we obtain from (2.15)

$$\lambda_k \ \geq \ \frac{\|A_i x_k^\delta - y_i^\delta\| - \|b_k^\delta\|}{C^2\|A_i x_k^\delta - y_i^\delta\|} \ \geq \ \frac{1}{C^2}(1-\bar{\bar{p}})\left(1-\delta_i/\|A_i x_k^\delta - y_i^\delta\|\right) \qquad (2.16)$$

and the second assertion follows from the aditional assumption $\|A_i x_k^\delta - y_i^\delta\| > \tau\delta_i$.

Finally, in the case of exact data, $\lambda_k \geq C^{-2}(1-\bar{\bar{p}})$ follows from the first inequality in (2.16) together with $\|b_k\| \leq \bar{\bar{p}}\|A_i x_k - y_i\|$. □

Corollary 2.2.7 *Assume that (A1) and (A2) are satisfied and let x_k, h_k, λ_k be defined by (2.5), (2.6) and (2.7) in the exact data case (i.e., $y_j^\delta = y_j$, $j = 0, \dots N-1$). Then the series*

$$\sum_{k=0}^{\infty} \|x_{k+1} - x_k\|^2, \ \sum_{k=0}^{\infty} \lambda_k \|A_{[k]} x_k - y_{[k]}\|, \ \sum_{k=0}^{\infty} \lambda_k \|b_k\|, \ \sum_{k=0}^{\infty} \lambda_k^2 \|b_k\|^2, \ \sum_{k=0}^{\infty} \|A_{[k]} x_k - y_{[k]}\|$$

are all summable.

Proof. The first two assertions follow from (2.12), using a telescopic series argument. The next two assertions follow from a comparison test and Lemma 2.2.2 (c). The last assertion follows from the second one and Corollary 2.2.6. □

Corollary 2.2.8 *Assume that (A1) and (A2) are satisfied and let x_k^δ, h_k, λ_k be defined by (2.5), (2.6) and (2.7). Then the stopping index k_* defined in (2.8) is finite and*

$$k_* \ \leq \ N\|x_0 - x^\star\|^2 \left[\frac{2(\bar{p} - \delta\bar{\bar{p}})(1-\bar{\bar{p}})(\tau-1)}{C^2}\,\delta_{\min}\right]^{-1}. \qquad (2.17)$$

Proof. Assume by contradiction that k_* is not finite, i.e., in each cycle $\{lN, \dots, lN+N-1\}$, $l \in \mathbb{N}$, of the rriTK method, there exists at least one index $j(l) \in \{0, \dots, N-1\}$ such that $\|A_{j(l)} x_{lN+j(l)} - y_{j(l)}^\delta\| \geq \tau\delta_{j(l)}$.
From Proposition 2.2.4 follows that (2.11) holds for $k \in \mathbb{N}$. Summing over k and using the fact that either $\|A_{[k]} x_k^\delta - y_{[k]}^\delta\| \geq \tau\delta_{[k]}$ or $\lambda_k = 0$, we obtain (with the notation $i = [k]$)

$$\begin{aligned}
\|x_0 - x^*\|^2 &\geq 2(\bar{p} - \delta\bar{\bar{p}}) \sum_{k=0}^{lN} \lambda_k \|A_i x_k^\delta - y_i^\delta\| \\
&\geq 2(\bar{p} - \delta\bar{\bar{p}}) \sum_{s=0}^{l} \lambda_{sN+j(s)} \|A_{j(s)} x_{sN+j(s)}^\delta - y_{j(s)}^\delta\| \\
&\geq 2(\bar{p} - \delta\bar{\bar{p}}) \sum_{s=0}^{l} \lambda_{sN+j(s)} \tau\delta_{j(s)} \ \geq \ l\,\tfrac{2(\bar{p}-\delta\bar{\bar{p}})(1-\bar{\bar{p}})(\tau-1)}{C^2}\,\delta_{\min}\,, \ l \in \mathbb{N}
\end{aligned} \qquad (2.18)$$

(the last inequality follows from Corollary 2.2.6). Since the right hand side of (2.18) becomes unbounded as $l \to \infty$ a contradiction is established, and the finiteness of k_* follows. Estimate (2.17) follows now substituting $k_* = lN$ in (2.18). □

2.3 A Convergence Result for Exact Data

Our main goal in this section is to prove convergence of the rriTK method in the case $\delta_i = 0$, $i = 0, \ldots, N-1$. Notice that, in this exact data case, $\lambda_k > 0$ and $h_k = x_{k+1} - x_k = 0$ if and only if $\|A_i x_k - y_i\| = 0$ (see Step [3.2] of Algorithm 2.2.1).

Theorem 2.3.1 ((Convergence for exact data)) *Assume that (A1) and (A2) are satisfied and let x_k, h_k, λ_k be defined by (2.5), (2.6) and (2.7) in the exact data case (i.e., $y_i^\delta = y_i$, $i = 0, \ldots N-1$). Then x_k converges to a solution of (2.2) as $k \to \infty$.*

Proof. We define $e_k := x^\star - x_k$. From Corolary 2.2.5 follows that $\|e_k\|$ is monotone non-increasing. Thus, $\|e_k\|$ converges to some $\varepsilon \geq 0$. In what follows we show that e_k is in fact a Cauchy sequence.

In order to prove that e_k is indeed a Cauchy sequence, it suffices to prove $|\langle e_n - e_k, e_n\rangle| \to 0$, $|\langle e_n - e_l, e_n\rangle| \to 0$ as $k, l \to \infty$ with $k \leq l$ for some $k \leq n \leq l$ [11, Theorem 2.3]. Let $k \leq l$ be arbitrary and write $k = k_0 N + k_1$, $l = l_0 N + l_1$, with $k_1, l_1 \in \{0, \ldots, N-1\}$. Now let $n_0 \in \{k_0, \ldots, l_0\}$ be such that

$$\sum_{s=0}^{N-1} \lambda_{n_0 N+s} \|A_s x_{n_0 N+s} - y_s\| \leq \sum_{s=0}^{N-1} \lambda_{i_0 N+s} \|A_s x_{i_0 N+s} - y_s\|, \text{ for all } i_0 \in \{k_0, \ldots, l_0\}, \tag{2.19}$$

and set $n = n_0 N + N - 1$. Therefore

$$\begin{aligned} |\langle e_n - e_k, e_n\rangle| &= \left|\textstyle\sum_{i=k}^{n-1} \langle (x_{i+1} - x_i), (x_n - x^\star)\rangle\right| \\ &= \left|\textstyle\sum_{i=k}^{n-1} \lambda_i \langle A_{[i]} x_{i+1} - y_{[i]}, A_{[i]} x_n - A_{[i]} x^\star\rangle\right| \\ &\leq \textstyle\sum_{i_0=k_0}^{n_0} \sum_{i_1=0}^{N-1} \lambda_i \|A_{i_1} x_{i+1} - y_{i_1}\| \, \|A_{i_1} x_n - y_{i_1}\| \\ &\leq \textstyle\sum_{i_0=k_0}^{n_0} \sum_{i_1=0}^{N-1} \lambda_i \|b_i\| \, \|A_{i_1} x_n - y_{i_1}\| \end{aligned} \tag{2.20}$$

(we use the notation $i = i_0 N + i_1$). The last term on the right hand side of (2.20) can be estimated by

$$\begin{aligned}
\|A_{i_1} x_n - y_{i_1}\| &= \|A_{i_1} x_{n_0 N+N-1} - y_{i_1}\| \\
&\leq \|A_{i_1} x_{n_0 N+i_1+1} - y_{i_1}\| + \sum_{s=i_1+1}^{N-2} \|A_{i_1} x_{n_0 N+s+1} - A_{i_1} x_{n_0 N+s}\| \\
&\leq \|A_{i_1} x_{n_0 N+i_1+1} - y_{i_1}\| + \sum_{s=i_1+1}^{N-2} C \|x_{n_0 N+s+1} - x_{n_0 N+s}\| \\
&= \|A_{i_1} x_{n_0 N+i_1+1} - y_{i_1}\| + \sum_{s=i_1+1}^{N-2} C \lambda_{n_0 N+s} \|A_s^*(A_s x_{n_0 N+s+1} - y_s)\| \\
&\leq \|A_{i_1} x_{n_0 N+i_1+1} - y_{i_1}\| + \sum_{s=0}^{N-1} C^2 \lambda_{n_0 N+s} \|A_s x_{n_0 N+s+1} - y_s\| \\
&\leq (\tfrac{1}{\lambda_{\min}} + C^2) \sum_{s=0}^{N-1} \lambda_{n_0 N+s} \|A_s x_{n_0 N+s+1} - y_s\|
\end{aligned}$$

(with $\lambda_{\min} = C^{-2}(1-\bar{p})$, cf. Corolary 2.2.6). Hence, by the minimality property (2.19) follows $\|A_{i_1} x_n - y_{i_1}\| \leq (\frac{1}{\lambda_{\min}} + C^2) \sum_{s=0}^{N-1} \lambda_{i_0 N+s} \|A_s x_{i_0 N+s+1} - y_s\|$, for $i_0 \in \{k_0, \dots, l_0\}$. Inserting this last inequality into (2.20) we obtain

$$\begin{aligned}
|\langle e_n - e_k, e_n \rangle| &\leq (\tfrac{2-\bar{\bar{p}}}{1-\bar{\bar{p}}}) C^2 \sum_{i_0=k_0}^{n_0} \sum_{i_1=0}^{N-1} \lambda_i \|b_i\| \left[\sum_{s=0}^{N-1} \lambda_{i_0 N+s} \|A_s x_{i_0 N+s+1} - y_s\| \right] \\
&= (\tfrac{2-\bar{\bar{p}}}{1-\bar{\bar{p}}}) C^2 \sum_{i_0=k_0}^{n_0} \left[\sum_{i_1=0}^{N-1} \lambda_i \|b_i\| \right]^2 \\
&\leq (\tfrac{2-\bar{\bar{p}}}{1-\bar{\bar{p}}}) C^2 N \sum_{i_0=k_0}^{n_0} \sum_{i_1=0}^{N-1} \lambda_i^2 \|b_i\|^2 \\
&= (\tfrac{2-\bar{\bar{p}}}{1-\bar{\bar{p}}}) C^2 N \sum_{i=k_0}^{n} \lambda_i^2 \|b_i\|^2 .
\end{aligned} \tag{2.21}$$

Hence by Corolary 2.2.7 the right hand side of (2.21) go to zero as $k,\, l \to \infty$. Analogously one shows that $|\langle e_n - e_l, e_n \rangle| \to 0$ as $k,\, l \to \infty$.

Thus, e_k is a Cauchy sequence and x_k converges to some $x^+ \in X$. Since the residuals $\|A_{[k]} x_k - y_{[k]}\|$ converge to zero as $k \to \infty$ (see Corolary 2.2.7), this x^+ is a solution of (2.2). □

2.4 Numerical Experiments

In this section the rriTK method (see Algorithm 2.2.1) is implemented for solving a benchmark problem, which happens to be a well known system of linear ill-posed equations.

The setup is inspired in [17, Introduction]. Let the operator $\mathbf{A} = \left[a_{i,j} = 1/(i+j-1)\right]_{i,j=1}^{24}$ be a Hilbert matrix. The Hilbert matrix is scaled such that each line a_i of $\mathbf{A}$ satisfy $\|a_i\| = 1$.

Set $N = 8$ and define $A_i \in \mathbb{R}^{3,24}$ to be the block of $\mathbf{A}$ formed by lines $a_{3i}, \dots, a_{3i+2}$, $i = 0, \dots, N-1$. In this setup we have $X = \mathbb{R}^{24}$ and $y_i \in Y = \mathbb{R}^3$.

The performance of the rriTK method is compared against three concurrent Kaczmarz type methods: (i) the Landweber Kaczmarz (LWK) method; (ii) the stationary iTK (siTK) method with constant $\lambda_k = 2$; (iii) the geometric iTK method (giTK) with $\lambda_k = 2^k$.

In our numerical experiments we set $x^\star = (1, \ldots, 1) \in X$ and compute the corresponding exact data $y_i = A_i x^\star$. The noise levels are $\delta_i = \delta = 0.1\%$; noisy data y_i^δ satisfying (2.1) is generated by adding to y_i randomly generated noise. The discrepancy principle constant is $\tau = 4.0$. Moreover, in Step [3.2] of Algorithm 2.2.1 we use the constants $\bar{p} = 0.1$ and $\bar{\bar{p}} = 0.8$

The first two plots in Figure 2.1 (TOP and CENTER) show the evolution of iteration error and residual (respectively) for the Kaczmarz type methods implemented in this section. The LWK (gray) reached the discrepancy principle after 3050 cycles; the siTK (black) after 1528 cycles, the giTK (blue) after 23 cycles, and the rriTK (red) after 10 cycles. In these plots the x-axis shows the number of computed cycles.

In the last plot of Figure 2.1 (BOTTOM) the values of $\|A_i x_{k+1}^\delta - y_i^\delta\|$, $i = [k]$, for the rriTK method are shown (black). Moreover, in order to verify the two inequalities in Step [3.2] of Algorithm 2.2.1, the upper bound $\bar{\bar{\Phi}}(\|A_i x_k^\delta - y_i^\delta\|, \delta_i)$ (green) and the lower bound $\bar{\Phi}(\|A_i x_k^\delta - y_i^\delta\|, \delta_i)$ (magenta) are shown. In this plot the x-axis shows the number of effectively computed iterates x_k^δ. Although 10 cycles were computed (i.e., a total of 80 steps), only 44 iterates x_k were actually computed. For the remaining 36 steps, the residual of the current equation $\|A_i x_k^\delta - y_i^\delta\|$ was below the discrepancy $\tau\delta_i$; consequently, $x_{k+1}^\delta = x_k^\delta$ in Step [3.2] avoiding the task of solving problem (2.9).

A careful reader will notice that the comparison of methods presented in Figure 2.1 is far from being fair. Indeed, in Kaczmarz type methods, the computation of an iterative step is avoided (i.e., $x_{k+1}^\delta = x_k^\delta$) whenever the residual satisfies $\|A_i x_k^\delta - y_i^\delta\| \le \tau\delta_i$. Consequently, the numerical burden of computing a cycle differs from method to method (as well as from cycle to cycle of the same method). Therefore, plotting iteration errors (or residuals) after each cycle does not give a proper comparison of the efficiency of these methods.

In Figure 2.2 the evolution of iteration error and residual (for the same Kaczmarz type methods as before) are plotted as functions of effectively computed iterates x_k. This allows a fair comparison between these methods, since the number of computed iterates is proportional to the total computational burden of a iTK type method.

It is worth noticing that, in Kaczmarz type methods we have monotonicity of the iteration error $\|x_k^\delta - x^\star\|$, see Corollary 2.2.5. However monotonicity of residual $\|\mathbf{A}x_k^\delta - \mathbf{y}^\delta\|$ cannot be guaranteed. In this regard, the best result available is Lemma 2.2.2 (c). These two facts can be observed in both Figures 2.1 and 2.2.

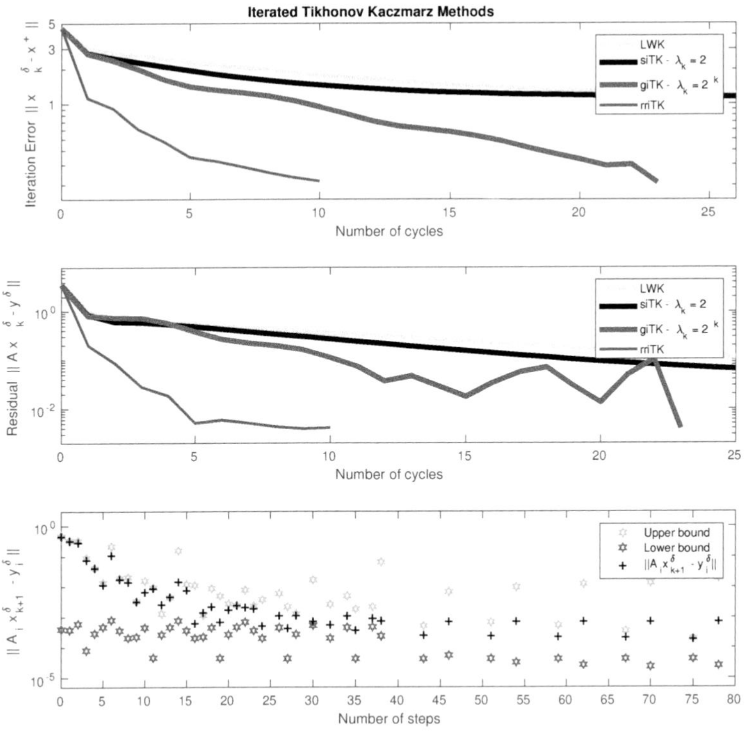

Figure 2.1: (TOP) Iteration error; (CENTER) Residual; (BOTTOM) Inequalities in Step [3.2].

2.5 Conclusions

We investigate nonstationary iTK type methods for computing stable approximate solutions to systems of linear ill-posed operator equations. The main contribution of this chapter is to extend the strategy for choosing the Lagrange multipliers in [2] (we propose a different range). This modification allow us to couple the iT method with the Kaczmarz strategy and also to give a convergence proof (Section 2.3) completely different from the one in [2].

This strategy is advantageous, since it allows each of these multipliers to belong to a non-degenerate interval. Consequently, the actual computation of Lagrange multipliers satisfying the theoretical requirements for the convergence analysis (Step [3.2]) is in much simplified.

We prove monotonicity of the proposed rriTK method (2.14) and verify geometrical decay of the residual (2.10). Moreover, we provide estimates to the "gain" $\|x^\star - x_k^\delta\|^2 - \|x^\star - x_{k+1}^\delta\|^2$ in (2.11) and (2.12), as well as a lower bound to the Lagrange multipliers (2.15), and an estimate to stopping index k_* (2.17). A convergence proof in the case of exact data is given (Theorem 2.3.1).

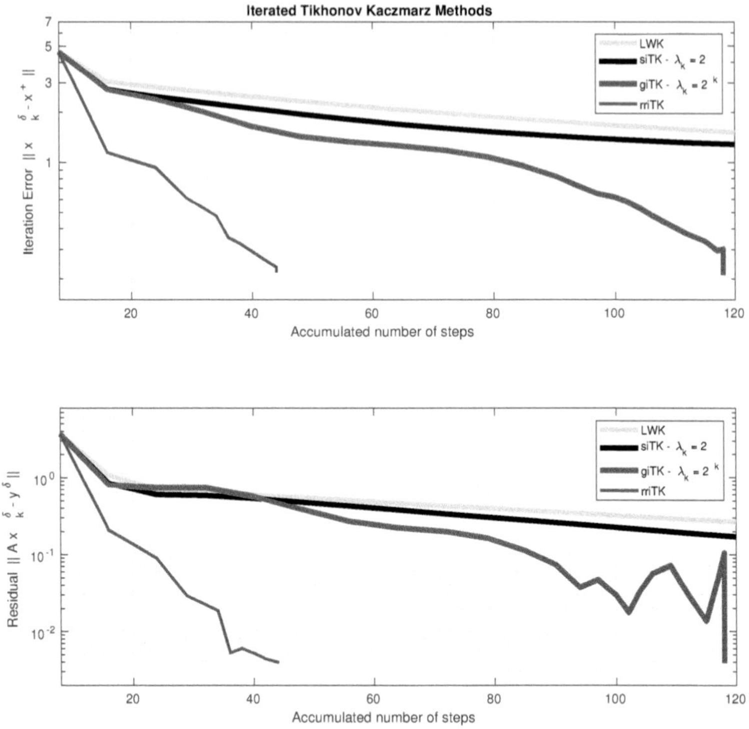

Figure 2.2: Iteration error and residual as functions of the accumulated number of steps.

An algorithmic implementation of the rriTK method is proposed (Algorithm 2.2.1). The resulting rriTK algorithm is competitive with giTK and also with other two well known Kaczmarz type methods (LWK and siTK).

The rriTK is tested for a well known benchmark problem modeled by a Hilbert matrix in the noisy data case. The obtained results validate the efficiency of our method.

Acknowledgments

J.C.R. is on leave from Department of Mathematics, Federal University of Piaui, 64049-550, Teresina PI, Brazil.

A.L. acknowledges support from the National Council for scientific and Technological Development—CNPq (grant 311087/2017-5), and from the AvH Foundation.

References

[1] Johann Baumeister. *Stable Solution of Inverse Problems*. Advanced Lectures in Mathematics, Friedr. Vieweg & Sohn, Braunschweig, 1987.

[2] R. Boiger, Antonio Leitão and Benar F. Svaiter. Range-relaxed criteria for choosing the Lagrange multipliers in nonstationary iterated Tikhonov method. IMA J. of Numerical Analysis, 40(1): 606–627, 2020.

[3] M. Brill and E. Schock. Iterative solution of ill-posed problems: A survey. pp. 13–38. *In*: A. Vogel (ed.). *Model Optimization in Exploration Geophysics*. Vieweg, Braunschweig, 1987.

[4] Marco Donatelli. On nondecreasing sequences of regularization parameters for nonstationary iterated Tikhonov. Numer. Algorithms, 60(4): 651–668, 2012.

[5] H.W. Engl, M. Hanke and A. Neubauer. *Regularization of Inverse Problems*. Kluwer Academic Publishers, Dordrecht, 1996.

[6] A.G. Fakeev. A class of iterative processes for solving degenerate systems of linear algebraic equations. U.S.S.R. Comput. Math. Math. Phys., 21(3): 15–22, 1981.

[7] C.W. Groetsch. *The Theory of Tikhonov Regularization for Fredholm Equations of the First Kind*. Research Notes in Mathematics, vol. 105, Pitman (Advanced Publishing Program), Boston, MA, 1984.

[8] M. Haltmeier, R. Kowar, A. Leitão and O. Scherzer. Kaczmarz methods for regularizing nonlinear ill-posed equations. II. Applications. Inverse Probl. Imaging, 1(3): 507–523, 2007.

[9] M. Haltmeier, A. Leitão and O. Scherzer. Kaczmarz methods for regularizing nonlinear ill-posed equations. I. Convergence Analysis. Inverse Probl. Imaging, 1(2): 289–298, 2007.

[10] M. Hanke and C.W. Groetsch. Nonstationary iterated Tikhonov regularization. J. Optim. Theory Appl., 98(1): 37–53, 1998.

[11] M. Hanke, A. Neubauer and O. Scherzer. A convergence analysis of Landweber iteration for nonlinear ill-posed problems. Numer. Math., 72: 21–37, 1995.

[12] B. Hofmann. *Regularization for Applied Inverse and Ill-Posed Problems.* Teubner-Texte zur Mathematik [Teubner Texts in Mathematics], vol. 85, BSB B. G. Teubner Verlagsgesellschaft, Leipzig, 1986, A numerical approach, With German, French and Russian summaries.

[13] S. Kaczmarz. Approximate solution of systems of linear equations. Internat. J. Control, 57(6): 1269–1271, 1993.

[14] A. Kirsch. *An Introduction to the Mathematical Theory of Inverse Problems.* Applied Mathematical Sciences, vol. 120, Springer-Verlag, New York, 1996.

[15] L.J. Lardy. *A series representation for the generalized inverse of a closed linear operator.* Atti della Accademia Nazionale dei Lincei, Rendiconti della Classe di Scienze Fisiche, Matematiche, e Naturali, Serie VIII, 58: 152–157, 1975.

[16] A. Louis. *Inverse und schlecht gestellte Probleme.* B.G. Teubner, Stuttgart, 1989.

[17] M.Z. Nashed. Continuous and semicontinuous analogues of iterative methods of Cimmino and Kaczmarz with applications to the inverse Radon transform. pp. 160–178. *In*: G.T. Herman and F. Natterer (eds.). *Mathematical Aspects of Computerized Tomography.* Springer, Berlin, 1981.

Chapter 3

On Numerical Approximation of Optimal Control for Stokes Hemivariational Inequalities

Xiaoliang Cheng[a], *Rongfang Gong*[b,*] and *Weimin Han*[c]

Mathematics Subject Classification. Primary: 65K10; Secondary: 35Q30, 49J24, 49J20

Dedicated to Professor Zuhair Nashed.

3.1 Introduction

In [10, 11], Fujita pioneered research on boundary value problems for viscous incompressible fluid flows with slip or leak boundary conditions of friction type. Theoretical results on solution existence, uniqueness and other properties for such Stokes problems can be found in [13, 12, 32]. In these references, the slip

[a] Department of Mathematics, Zhejiang University, Hangzhou, Zhejiang 310027, China.
[b] Department of Mathematics, Nanjing University of Aeronautics and Astronautics, Nanjing, Jiangsu 210016, China.
[c] Department of Mathematics, University of Iowa, Iowa City, IA 52242-1410, USA.
Emails: xiaoliangcheng@zju.edu.cn; weimin-han@uiowa.edu
* Corresponding author: grf_math@nuaa.edu.cn

or leak boundary conditions are of monotone type and the corresponding weak forms of the problems are variational inequalities. When the slip or leak boundary conditions are allowed to be non-monotone, the notion of hemivariational inequalities is needed. Hemivariational inequalities were first introduced by Panagiotopoulos in early 1980s ([29]) and it is closely related to the development of the concepts of the generalized directional derivative and subdifferential of a locally Lipschitz functional in the sense of Clarke ([4, 5]). Since then many publications have appeared on hemivariational inequalities, see for example the comprehensive references [30, 27, 26, 34]. In applications, numerical methods are needed to solve hemivariational inequalities, and the finite element method is a natural choice ([18]). Optimal order error estimates have been derived for the numerical solution of various hemivariational inequalities, starting with the paper [16]. Other numerical methods for solving hemivariational inequalities have also been studied, e.g., [9] on the use of the virtual element method. See [17] for a recent summarized account of numerical analysis of hemivariational inequalities.

Optimal control is an important research field closely tied to applications in a wide range of areas such as aviation and space technology, economics, electromagnetic waves, fluid flows, heat conduction, robotics, etc. In mathematical terms, an optimal control problem is often expressed in the form of optimization of a cost function with respect to one or more function variables. In the literature, many publications can be found on studies of optimal control problems governed by differential equations or variational inequalities, and here we only mention a few comprehensive references [22, 3, 28, 36]. Optimal control problems have been studied for variational-hemivariational inequalities in a number of papers, including [23, 19, 25, 24, 7, 25, 31, 33, 37] where existence of optimal pairs is proved, and applications in solid mechanics or fluid mechanics are illustrated. Since it is not realistic to expect closed form solution formulas, optimal control problems for variational-hemivariational inequalities need to be solved with numerical methods. Early references [23, 19] provide existence and approximation results for the optimal control of an elliptic hemivariational inequality posed over an entire function space, as well as convergence of numerical solutions. In a recent paper [15], convergence analysis is provided for numerical solutions of optimal control problems governed by general elliptic variational-hemivariational inequalities. In this chapter, we consider the numerical approximation of optimal control problems for Stokes hemivariational inequalities.

The rest of this paper is organized as follows. In Section 3.2, we introduce the notation and basic results needed later in the chapter. In Section 3.3, we present the Stokes hemivariational inequality and a corresponding optimal control problem. In Section 3.4, we study the numerical approximation of the optimal control problem and show the convergence of the numerical method in a rather general setting.

3.2 Notation and Preliminaries

We consider the flow problem in a Lipschitz domain Ω in $\mathbb{R}^d$ with the dimension $d \le 3$ for applications. The boundary $\Gamma = \partial\Omega$ is split into two parts: $\Gamma = \Gamma_0 \cup \Gamma_1$ such that $|\Gamma_0| > 0$, $|\Gamma_1| > 0$, and Γ_0 and Γ_1 have non-overlapping intersection. We will impose the homogeneous Dirichlet boundary condition on Γ_0 and a non-smooth slip boundary condition on Γ_1. Since Ω is a Lipschitz domain, the unit outward normal vector $n = (n_1, \cdots, n_d)^T$ exists a.e. on Γ. For a vector-valued function v defined on the boundary, we denote by $v_n = v \cdot n$ and $v_\tau = v - v_n n$ for its normal and tangential components. With the flow velocity field u and the pressure p, we define the strain tensor $\varepsilon(u) = \frac{1}{2}(\nabla u + (\nabla u)^T)$ and the stress tensor $\sigma = -pI + 2\nu\varepsilon(u)$, where I is the identity matrix and $\nu > 0$ is the viscosity coefficient. Let $\sigma_n = n \cdot \sigma n$ and $\sigma_\tau = \sigma n - \sigma_n n$ be the normal component and the tangential component of σ.

The canonical inner product and the corresponding norm on $\mathbb{R}^d$ are

$$u \cdot v = u_i v_i, \quad \|v\|_{\mathbb{R}^d} = (v \cdot v)^{1/2} \quad \forall u = (u_i),\, v = (v_i) \in \mathbb{R}^d.$$

The space $\mathbb{S}^d$ of second order symmetric tensors on $\mathbb{R}^d$ is endowed with the following inner product and norm:

$$\sigma : \tau = \sigma_{ij}\tau_{ij}, \quad \|\sigma\|_{\mathbb{S}^d} = (\sigma : \sigma)^{1/2} \quad \forall \sigma = (\sigma_{ij}),\, \tau = (\tau_{ij}) \in \mathbb{S}^d.$$

Throughout the chapter, the indices i and j run between 1 and d, and the summation convention over a repeated index is used.

We will use the generalized directional derivative and generalized gradient in the sense of Clarke to describe the slip boundary condition.

Definition 3.2.1 ([5]) *Let X be a Banach space, and let $\psi : X \to \mathbb{R}$ be a locally Lipschitz continuous function. The generalized directional derivative of ψ at $x \in X$ in the direction $z \in X$, denoted by $\psi^0(x;z)$, is defined by*

$$\psi^0(x;z) = \limsup_{y \to x,\, \lambda \to 0+} \frac{\psi(y + \lambda z) - \psi(y)}{\lambda}.$$

The generalized gradient or subdifferential of ψ at x, denoted by $\partial\psi(x)$, is a subset of the dual space X^* given by

$$\partial\psi(x) = \{\zeta \in X^* \mid f^0(x;z) \ge \langle \zeta, z \rangle_{X^* \times X}\ \forall z \in X\}. \tag{3.1}$$

We recall a few properties of the generalized directional derivative and the generalized gradient, in the context of Definition 3.2.1 ([26]).

For every $x \in X$, the function $X \ni z \mapsto \psi^0(x;z) \in \mathbb{R}$ is positively homogeneous and subadditive, i.e., $\psi^0(x;\lambda z) = \lambda \psi^0(x;z)$ for all $\lambda \ge 0$, $z \in X$ and $\psi^0(x;z_1 + z_2) \le \psi^0(x;z_1) + \psi^0(x;z_2)$ for all $z_1, z_2 \in X$, respectively.

The function $X \times X \ni (x,z) \mapsto \psi^0(x;z) \in \mathbb{R}$ is upper semicontinuous, i.e., for all $x \in X$, $z \in X$, $\{x_n\} \subset X$, $\{z_n\} \subset X$ such that $x_n \to x$ in X and $z_n \to z$ in X, we have $\limsup \psi^0(x_n;z_n) \le \psi^0(x;z)$.

For all $z \in X$, $\psi^0(x;z) = \max\{\langle \zeta, z \rangle_{X^* \times X} \mid \zeta \in \partial\psi(x)\}$.

3.3 Stokes Hemivariational Inequality and Optimal Control

The pointwise form of the boundary value problem of the Stokes equations is

$$-\nu\Delta u+\nabla p=f \quad \text{in } \Omega, \tag{3.2}$$

$$\operatorname{div} u=0 \quad \text{in } \Omega, \tag{3.3}$$

$$u=0 \quad \text{on } \Gamma_0, \tag{3.4}$$

$$u_n=0, \quad -\sigma_\tau\in\partial j(u_\tau) \quad \text{on } \Gamma_1. \tag{3.5}$$

Here, $j:\Gamma_1\times\mathbb{R}^d\to\mathbb{R}$ is assumed to be locally Lipschitz and ∂j is the subdifferential of $j(x,\cdot)$ in the sense of Clarke, $j(u_\tau)$ is a short-hand notation for $j(x,u_\tau)$, f is the density of external forces. In the literature, (3.5) is known as a slip boundary condition.

To study the problem (3.2)–(3.5), let us introduce some function spaces. Boldface symbols are used to denote vector-valued function spaces, e.g., $H^1(\Omega)=H^1(\Omega;\mathbb{R}^d)$. Let

$$V:=\{v\in H^1(\Omega)\mid v=0 \text{ on } \Gamma_0,\, v_n=0 \text{ on } \Gamma_1\},$$

$$Q:=L_0^2(\Omega)=\left\{q\in L^2(\Omega)\mid \int_\Omega q\,dx=0\right\}$$

be the spaces for the velocity variable and the pressure variable, respectively. We further let

$$V_0:=H_0^1(\Omega;\mathbb{R}^d),$$

$$H:=L^2(\Omega;\mathbb{R}^d)$$

and

$$\mathcal{H}:=\{\sigma=(\sigma_{ij})_{d\times d}\mid \sigma_{ij}=\sigma_{ji}\in L^2(\Omega),\,1\le i,j\le d\}.$$

Define the strain tensor $\varepsilon:H^1(\Omega)\to\mathcal{H}$ by

$$\varepsilon(u)=(\varepsilon_{ij}(u)),\ \varepsilon_{ij}(u)=\frac{1}{2}(u_{i,j}+u_{j,i}).$$

The following integration by parts formulas hold ([26, Chapter 2]):

$$\int_\Omega(u\operatorname{div}v+\nabla u\cdot v)\,dx=\int_{\partial\Omega}uv_n ds \quad \forall u\in H^1(\Omega),\, v\in H^1(\Omega), \tag{3.6}$$

$$\int_\Omega\sigma:\varepsilon(v)dx+\int_\Omega\operatorname{Div}\sigma\cdot v\,dx=\int_{\partial\Omega}\sigma n\cdot v\,ds \quad \forall v\in H^1(\Omega),\, \sigma\in H^1(\Omega;\mathbb{S}^d), \tag{3.7}$$

where $\operatorname{Div}\sigma=(\sigma_{ij,j})_d$.

Since $\text{meas}(\Gamma_0) > 0$, thanks to Korn's inequality (cf. [21, Lemma 6.2]), $\|\cdot\|_V = \|\varepsilon(\cdot)\|_{\mathcal{H}}$ defines a norm on V, and $(V, \|\cdot\|_V)$ is a Hilbert space. The space V_0 is a subspace of V. The space Q endowed with the $L^2(\Omega)$ inner product is a Hilbert space. In addition, H and $\mathcal{H}$ are Hilbert spaces equipped with the inner products

$$(u,v)_H = \int_\Omega u \cdot v\, dx, \quad (\sigma, \tau)_{\mathcal{H}} = \int_\Omega \sigma : \tau\, dx.$$

The duality pairing between V and V^* is denoted by $\langle \cdot, \cdot \rangle$. As usual, we identify H with its dual. Then we have an evolution triple $V \subset H \subset V^*$ with dense, continuous and compact embeddings. We denote by γ: $V \to L^2(\Gamma_1) := L^2(\Gamma_1; \mathbb{R}^d)$ the tangential component trace operator, defined by $\gamma v = v_\tau$ on Γ_1 for $v \in V$. By the Sobolev trace theorem, γ is a linear continuous operator from V to $L^2(\Gamma_1)$; we denote its operator norm by $\|\gamma\|$.

Introduce two bilinear forms:

$$a(u,v) = 2\nu\, (\varepsilon(u), \varepsilon(v))_{\mathcal{H}} \quad \forall u,v \in V, \tag{3.8}$$

$$b(v,q) = \int_\Omega q \,\text{div} v\, dx \quad \forall v \in V, q \in Q. \tag{3.9}$$

Obviously, $a(\cdot,\cdot)\colon V \times V \to \mathbb{R}$ and $b(\cdot,\cdot)\colon V \times Q \to \mathbb{R}$ are bounded. Moreover, $a(\cdot,\cdot)$ is coercive on V; indeed,

$$a(v,v) = 2\nu \|v\|_V^2, \quad \forall v \in V. \tag{3.10}$$

The following inf-sup condition holds ([35]): for a constant $\beta_1 > 0$,

$$\beta_1 \|q\|_{L^2(\Omega)} \le \sup_{v \in V_0} \frac{b(v,q)}{\|v\|_V} \quad \forall q \in Q. \tag{3.11}$$

On the superpotential j, we assume the following properties:

$H(j)$. $j : \Gamma_1 \times \mathbb{R}^d \to \mathbb{R}$ and

(i) $j(\cdot, \xi)$ is measurable on Γ_1 for all $\xi \in \mathbb{R}^d$, $j(\cdot, 0) \in L^1(\Gamma_1)$;

(ii) $j(x, \cdot)$ is locally Lipschitz on $\mathbb{R}^d$ for a.e. $x \in \Gamma_1$;

(iii) $\|\eta\|_{\mathbb{R}^d} \le c_0 + c_1 \|\xi\|_{\mathbb{R}^d}$ for all $\xi \in \mathbb{R}^d$, $\eta \in \partial j(x, \xi)$, a.e. $x \in \Gamma_1$ with constants $c_0, c_1 \ge 0$;

(iv) $(\eta_1 - \eta_2) \cdot (\xi_1 - \xi_2) \ge -m_\tau \|\xi_1 - \xi_2\|_{\mathbb{R}^d}^2$ for all $\xi_i \in \mathbb{R}^d$, $\eta_i \in \partial j(x, \xi_i)$, $i = 1, 2$, a.e. $x \in \Gamma_1$ with a constant $m_\tau \ge 0$.

The assumption $H(j)$ (iv) is equivalent to

$$j^0(x, \xi_1; \xi_2 - \xi_1) + j^0(x, \xi_2; \xi_1 - \xi_2) \le m_\tau \|\xi_1 - \xi_2\|_{\mathbb{R}^d}^2, \quad \forall \xi_1, \xi_2 \in \mathbb{R}^d, \text{a.e.}\, x \in \Gamma_1 \tag{3.12}$$

and it is known as a relaxed monotonicity condition.

Introduce the functional $J : L^2(\Gamma_1) \to \mathbb{R}$ defined by

$$J(v) = \int_{\Gamma_1} j(x, v)\, ds, \quad v \in L^2(\Gamma_1). \tag{3.13}$$

Following arguments similar to those in the proof of Theorem 3.47 in [26], we have the next result.

Lemma 3.3.1 *Assume $H(j)$. Then:*
(i) $J(\cdot)$ *is locally Lipschitz on* $L^2(\Gamma_1)$;
(ii) $\|z\|_{L^2(\Gamma_1)} \leq \sqrt{|\Gamma_1|}\, c_0 + c_1\|v\|_{L^2(\Gamma_1)}$ *for all* $v \in L^2(\Gamma_1)$, $z \in \partial J(v)$;
(iii) $\langle z_1 - z_2, v_1 - v_2\rangle_{L^2(\Gamma_1)^d} \geq -m_\tau\|v_1 - v_2\|^2_{L^2(\Gamma_1;\mathbb{R}^d)}$ *for all* $v_i \in L^2(\Gamma_1)$, $z_i \in \partial J(v_i)$, $i = 1,2$.

We assume $f \in H$. A weak formulations of the boundary value problem (3.2)–(3.5) is as follows ([6]):
Problem (P). Find $(u,p) \in V \times Q$ such that

$$a(u,v) - b(v,p) + \int_{\Gamma_1} j^0(u_\tau; v_\tau)\, ds \geq (f,v)_H \quad \forall v \in V, \tag{3.14}$$

$$b(u,q) = 0 \quad \forall q \in Q. \tag{3.15}$$

The following existence and uniqueness result for Problem (P) can be found in [6].

Theorem 3.3.2 *Assume $f \in H$, $H(j)$ and*

$$2\nu > m_\tau\|\gamma\|^2. \tag{3.16}$$

Then Problem (P) has a unique solution.

We now introduce an optimal control problem governed by the Stokes hemivariational inequality (P) with respect to the force density $f \in H$. Let $H_{ad} \subset H$ be a set of admissible controls. Consider a general objective functional $\mathcal{C} : H \to \mathbb{R}$ of the form

$$\mathcal{C}(f) = C(u(f), p(f), f),$$

where the cost function $C : V \times Q \times H \to \mathbb{R} \cup \{+\infty\}$, and for a given $f \in H$, $(u,p) = (u(f), p(f))$ is the solution of Problem (P).

For simplicity, we will denote the objective functional as

$$\mathcal{C}(f) = C(u,p,f), \tag{3.17}$$

with the understanding that $(u,p) \in V \times Q$ is the solution of the problem (3.14)–(3.15) corresponding to $f \in H$. Then the optimal control problem is

$$\inf\{\mathcal{C}(f) \mid f \in H_{ad}\}. \tag{3.18}$$

In the study of the problem (3.18), we introduce the following hypotheses:
$H(H_{ad})$: H_{ad} is a nonempty and weakly closed subset of H.

$H(C)$: $C : V \times Q \times H \to \mathbb{R} \cup \{+\infty\}$ is strongly-weakly lower semicontinuous, i.e., if $u_n \to u$ in V, $p_n \to p$ in Q and $f_n \rightharpoonup f$ in H, then

$$C(u,p,f) \le \liminf_{n\to\infty} C(u_n,p_n,f_n).$$

Moreover, if H_{ad} is unbounded, then for any $f \in H$,

$$\inf_{u\in V,\, p\in Q} C(u,p,f) \to \infty \quad \text{as } \|f\|_H \to \infty,\ f \in H_{ad}.$$

Note that if $H_{ad} \subset H$ is nonempty, closed and convex, then $H(H_{ad})$ is satisfied ([2, Section 3.3]).

As an example of a family of objective functionals, we mention

$$\mathcal{C}(f) = \frac{\theta_1}{2}\int_\Omega \|u(x)-u_d(x)\|^2_{\mathbb{R}^d}dx + \frac{\theta_2}{2}\int_\Omega |p(x)-p_d(x)|^2 dx + \frac{\theta_3}{2}\int_\Omega \|f(x)\|^2_{\mathbb{R}^d}dx, \tag{3.19}$$

where $f \in H$ is the control, (u,p) is the solution of Problem (P) with the force density function f, and u_d and p_d are the desired velocity field and the desired pressure function. The constants $\theta_1, \theta_2 \ge 0$ satisfy $\theta_1 + \theta_2 = 1$, and $\theta_3 > 0$. These constants provide relative weights of the three integral terms in $\mathcal{C}(f)$. If $\theta_1 = 0$, then the control is to match the desired pressure field only. If $\theta_2 = 0$, then the control is to match the desired velocity field only. The goal is to choose the control f in such a way that the corresponding velocity field u and the pressure field p are the best possible fit to the desired velocity field u_d and pressure field p_d. It is easy to see that $H(C)$ is satisfied. The model (3.19) on stationary flows of incompressible media is closely related to electrically conducting fluids that can be influenced by magnetic fields ([20, 36]).

As a corollary of [8, Theorem 3.3], under the conditions $H(j)$ and (3.16), if $f_n \rightharpoonup f$ in H, then the corresponding solutions of Problem (P) converge strongly:

$$u_n \to u \text{ in } V, \quad p_n \to p \text{ in } Q.$$

Then applying the standard argument in optimization theory in abstract function spaces (e.g., [2, Chapter 3]), it can be shown that under the conditions $H(j)$, $H(H_{ad})$, $H(C)$ and (3.16), the optimal control problem (3.18) has a solution $f \in H_{ad}$.

3.4 Numerical Approximation of the Optimal Control Problem

We turn to a study of numerical approximation of the optimal control problem (3.18). For this purpose, let $h > 0$ be a discretization parameter, and let $\{(V^h, Q^h, H^h_{ad})\}_h$ be a corresponding finite dimensional approximations of (V, Q, H_{ad}) as $h \to 0$. We make the following assumptions:

(H_V^h): $V^h \subset V$, and for any $v \in V$, there exists $v^h \in V^h$ with $\|v^h - v\|_V \to 0$ as $h \to 0$.

(H_Q^h): $Q^h \subset Q$, and for any $q \in Q$, there exists $q^h \in Q^h$ with $\|q^h - q\|_Q \to 0$ as $h \to 0$.

$(H_{H_{ad}}^h)$: $H_{ad}^h \subset H_{ad}$, and for any $f \in H_{ad}$, there exists $f^h \in H_{ad}^h$ with $\|f^h - f\|_H \to 0$ as $h \to 0$.

$(H_{V,Q}^h)$: There exists a constant $\beta > 0$ such that

$$\beta \, \|q^h\|_Q \leq \sup_{v^h \in V_0^h} \frac{b(v^h, q^h)}{\|v^h\|_V} \quad \forall q^h \in Q^h, \tag{3.20}$$

where $V_0^h = V^h \cap V_0$.

In the literature, $(H_{V,Q}^h)$ is known as the Babuška-Brezzi condition. We comment on the validity of these conditions for commonly used finite element spaces at the end of this section.

Then we introduce the following numerical approximation of (3.18).

$$\inf \left\{ C^h(f^h) \mid f^h \in H_{ad}^h \right\}, \tag{3.21}$$

where

$$C^h(f^h) = C(u^h, p^h, f^h) \tag{3.22}$$

and $(u^h, p^h) = (u^h(f^h), p^h(f^h))$ is the solution of the problem: $(u^h, p^h) \in V^h \times Q^h$ and

$$a(u^h, v^h) - b(v^h, p^h) + \int_{\Gamma_1} j^0(u_\tau^h; v_\tau^h)\, ds \geq (f^h, v^h)_H \quad \forall v^h \in V^h, \tag{3.23}$$

$$b(u^h, q^h) = 0 \quad \forall q^h \in Q^h. \tag{3.24}$$

Similar to the optimal control problem (3.18), under the assumptions $H(j)$, $H(H_{ad})$, $H(C)$, (3.16), and (H_V^h), (H_Q^h), $(H_{H_{ad}}^h)$, $(H_{V,Q}^h)$, the discrete problem (3.21) has a solution. As a preparation of the convergence analysis, we first prove a convergence result for the discrete solution (u^h, p^h) of (3.23)–(3.24) to the solution $(u, p) \in V \times Q$ of the problem (3.14)–(3.15) as $f^h \rightharpoonup f$ in H.

Theorem 3.4.1 *Assume $H(j)$, (3.16), and (H_V^h), (H_Q^h), $(H_{V,Q}^h)$. Let $(u, p) \in V \times Q$ and (u^h, p^h) be the solutions of the problem (3.14)–(3.15) and (3.23)–(3.24), respectively. Then as $f^h \rightharpoonup f$ in H, we have*

$$\|u^h - u\|_V + \|p^h - p\|_Q \to 0 \quad \text{as } h \to 0. \tag{3.25}$$

Proof. We split the proof into several steps. Since the embedding $H \subset V^*$ is compact, from $f^h \rightharpoonup f$ in H, we have a subsequence, still denoted by $\{f^h\}_h$ such that

$$f^h \to f \text{ in } V^*, \text{ as } h \to 0. \tag{3.26}$$

Step 1: We prove the uniform boundedness of the numerical solutions. We take $v^h = -u^h$ in (3.23) to get

$$a(u^h, u^h) \le \int_{\Gamma_1} j^0(u^h_\tau; -u^h_\tau)\, ds + (f^h, u^h)_H. \tag{3.27}$$

Apply the condition (3.12),

$$j^0(u^h_\tau; -u^h_\tau) \le m_\tau \|u^h_\tau\|^2_{\mathbb{R}^d} - j^0(0\ u^h_\tau).$$

By $H(j)$ (iii),

$$-j^0(0\ u^h_\tau) \le c_0 \|u^h_\tau\|_{\mathbb{R}^d}.$$

So from (3.27),

$$2\nu \|u^h\|^2_V \le m_\tau \|u^h_\tau\|^2_{L^2(\Gamma_1;\mathbb{R}^d)} + c_0 \|u^h_\tau\|_{L^2(\Gamma_1;\mathbb{R}^d)} + \|f^h\|_H \|u^h\|_H.$$

By the trace inequality

$$\|u^h_\tau\|_{L^2(\Gamma_1;\mathbb{R}^d)} \le \|\gamma\|\ \|u^h\|_V$$

and the modified Cauchy inequality

$$ab \le \varepsilon a^2 + c_\varepsilon b^2, \quad \varepsilon > 0,\ c_\varepsilon = \frac{1}{4\varepsilon},\ \forall a, b \in \mathbb{R},$$

we then find that for any small $\varepsilon > 0$, there is a constant c depending on ε such that

$$2\nu \|u^h\|^2_V \le \left(m_\tau \|\gamma\|^2 + \varepsilon\right) \|u^h\|^2_V + c\left(1 + \|f^h\|_H\right).$$

Due to the smallness assumption (3.16), we can choose $\varepsilon > 0$ sufficiently small in the above inequality to conclude the uniform boundedness of the sequence $\{\|u^h\|_V\}_h$.

By the Babuška-Brezzi condition (3.20),

$$\beta \|p^h\|_Q \le \sup_{v^h \in V^h_0} \frac{b(v^h, p^h)}{\|v^h\|_V}.$$

From (3.23),

$$a(u^h, v^h) - b(v^h, p^h) = (f^h, v^h)_H \quad \forall v^h \in V^h_0.$$

So

$$b(v^h, p^h) = a(u^h, v^h) - (f^h, v^h)_H \quad \forall v^h \in V^h_0.$$

Then

$$\beta \|p^h\|_Q \le \sup_{v^h \in V^h_0} \frac{a(u^h, v^h) - (f^h, v^h)_H}{\|v^h\|_V} \le c\left(\|u^h\|_V + \|f\|_H\right).$$

Therefore, since $\{\|u^h\|_V\}_h$ is bounded, so is $\{\|p^h\|_Q\}_h$.

Step 2: Since $\{\|u^h\|_V\}_h$ and $\{\|p^h\|_Q\}_h$ are bounded, there exist a subsequence, still denoted by $\{(u^h, p^h)\}_h$, and elements $\overline{u} \in V$, $\overline{p} \in Q$ such that

$$u^h \rightharpoonup \overline{u} \text{ in } V,\ u^h \to \overline{u} \text{ in } H,\ p^h \rightharpoonup \overline{p} \text{ in } Q, \quad \text{as } h \to 0. \tag{3.28}$$

Step 3: Let us prove that

$$b(\overline{u}, q) = 0 \quad \forall q \in Q. \tag{3.29}$$

For an arbitrarily fixed $q \in Q$, by (H_Q^h), there exists $q^h \in Q^h$ such that

$$q^h \to q \quad \text{in } Q. \tag{3.30}$$

By (3.24),

$$b(u^h, q^h) = 0. \tag{3.31}$$

Write

$$\begin{aligned} b(u^h, q^h) &= b(u^h - \overline{u}, q^h) + b(\overline{u}, q^h) \\ &= b(u^h - \overline{u}, q^h - q) + b(u^h - \overline{u}, q) + b(\overline{u}, q^h). \end{aligned}$$

Since $\|u^h - \overline{u}\|_V$ is bounded independent of h and $\|q^h - q\|_Q \to 0$ as $h \to 0$, we have

$$\left|b(u^h - \overline{u}, q^h - q)\right| \leq c\,\|u^h - \overline{u}\|_V \|q^h - q\|_Q \to 0 \quad \text{as } h \to 0.$$

Due to (3.28), as $h \to 0$,

$$b(u^h - \overline{u}, q) \to 0.$$

Thanks to (3.30), as $h \to 0$,

$$b(\overline{u}, q^h) \to b(\overline{u}, q).$$

Thus, taking the limit $h \to 0$ in (3.31), we obtain (3.29).

Step 4: We prove the strong convergence

$$u^h \to \overline{u} \text{ in } V, \quad \text{as } h \to 0. \tag{3.32}$$

By (H_V^h) and (H_Q^h), there exist $\overline{u}^h \in V^h$ and $\overline{p}^h \in Q^h$ such that

$$\overline{u}^h \to \overline{u} \text{ in } V,\ \overline{p}^h \to \overline{p} \text{ in } Q, \quad \text{as } h \to 0. \tag{3.33}$$

We start with

$$\begin{aligned} 2\nu\,\|\overline{u} - u^h\|_V^2 &\leq a(\overline{u} - u^h, \overline{u} - u^h) \\ &= a(\overline{u}, \overline{u} - u^h) - a(u^h, \overline{u} - \overline{u}^h) - a(u^h, \overline{u}^h - u^h). \end{aligned} \tag{3.34}$$

By (3.23) with $v^h = \overline{u}^h - u^h$,

$$-a(u^h,\overline{u}^h - u^h) \le -b(\overline{u}^h - u^h, p^h) + \int_{\Gamma_1} j^0(u^h_\tau;\overline{u}^h_\tau - u^h_\tau)\,ds - (f^h,\overline{u}^h - u^h)_H.$$

Then from (3.34),

$$\begin{aligned} 2\nu\,\|\overline{u} - u^h\|_V^2 \le{}& a(\overline{u},\overline{u} - u^h) - a(u^h,\overline{u} - \overline{u}^h) - b(\overline{u}^h - u^h, p^h) \\ &+ \int_{\Gamma_1} j^0(u^h_\tau;\overline{u}^h_\tau - u^h_\tau)\,ds - (f^h,\overline{u}^h - u^h)_H. \end{aligned} \tag{3.35}$$

Consider each term on the right side of (3.35). Since $u^h \rightharpoonup \overline{u}$ in V,

$$a(\overline{u},\overline{u} - u^h) \to 0.$$

Since $\|\overline{u} - \overline{u}^h\|_V \to 0$ and $\|u^h\|_V$ is bounded independent of h,

$$\left|a(u^h,\overline{u} - \overline{u}^h)\right| \le 2\nu\,\|u^h\|_V\,\|\overline{u} - \overline{u}^h\|_V \to 0.$$

Write

$$\begin{aligned} -b(\overline{u}^h - u^h, p^h) &= -b(\overline{u}^h, p^h) + b(u^h, p^h) \\ &= -b(\overline{u}^h, p^h) \\ &= -b(\overline{u}^h - \overline{u}, p^h) \\ &\le c\,\|p^h\|_Q\|\overline{u}^h - \overline{u}\|_V, \end{aligned}$$

where for the second equality, we used (3.24), and for the third equality, we used (3.29). Since $\|\overline{u} - \overline{u}^h\|_V \to 0$ and $\|p^h\|_Q$ is bounded independent of h, we obtain

$$-b(\overline{u}^h - u^h, p^h) \to 0.$$

Using $H(j)$ and for a subsequence, due to the compact embedding $H^1(\Omega) \subset L^2(\Gamma_1)$,

$$\|\overline{u}^h_\tau - u^h_\tau\|_{L^2(\Gamma_1;\mathbb{R}^d)} \le \|\overline{u}^h_\tau - \overline{u}_\tau\|_{L^2(\Gamma_1;\mathbb{R}^d)} + \|\overline{u}_\tau - u^h_\tau\|_{L^2(\Gamma_1;\mathbb{R}^d)} \to 0,$$

we have

$$\begin{aligned} \int_{\Gamma_1} j^0(u^h_\tau;\overline{u}^h_\tau - u^h_\tau)\,ds &\le \int_{\Gamma_1} \left(c_0 + c_1|u^h_\tau|\right)|\overline{u}^h_\tau - u^h_\tau|\,ds \\ &\le c\left(1 + \|u^h\|_V\right)\|\overline{u}^h_\tau - u^h_\tau\|_{L^2(\Gamma_1;\mathbb{R}^d)} \\ &\to 0. \end{aligned}$$

And,

$$\left|(f^h,\overline{u}^h - u^h)_H\right| \le \|f^h\|_H\|\overline{u}^h - u^h\|_H \to 0.$$

Hence, we obtain the strong convergence (3.32) from (3.35).

Step 5: We prove that the limit $(\overline{u},\overline{p})$ is the unique solution of the problem (3.14)–(3.15). For any $v \in V$ and $q \in Q$, by assumptions (H_V^h) and (H_Q^h), we have a sequence $\{(v^h,q^h)\} \subset V \times Q$ with $v^h \in V^h$, $q^h \in Q^h$ such that

$$v^h \to v \text{ in } V, \quad q^h \to q \text{ in } Q. \tag{3.36}$$

From (3.23),

$$a(u^h,v^h) - b(v^h,p^h) + \int_{\Gamma_1} j^0(u_\tau^h;v_\tau^h)\,ds \geq (f^h,v^h)_H. \tag{3.37}$$

Due to (3.36), (3.28) and $f^h \rightharpoonup f$ in H, we have, as $h \to 0$,

$$\begin{aligned} &a(u^h,v^h) \to a(\overline{u},v),\\ &b(v^h,p^h) \to b(v,\overline{p}),\\ &(f^h,v^h)_H \to (f,v)_H. \end{aligned}$$

Also, for subsequences, still denoted by $\{u_\tau^h\}_h$ and $\{v_\tau^h\}_h$, we have

$$u_\tau^h \to \overline{u}_\tau \text{ and } v_\tau^h \to v_\tau \quad \text{a.e. on } \Gamma_1,$$

and then

$$\limsup_{h\to 0} \int_{\Gamma_1} j^0(u_\tau^h;v_\tau^h)\,ds \leq \int_{\Gamma_1} \limsup_{h\to 0} j^0(u_\tau^h;v_\tau^h)\,ds \leq \int_{\Gamma_1} j^0(\overline{u}_\tau;v_\tau)\,ds.$$

Thus, we derive from (3.37) that

$$a(\overline{u},v) - b(v,\overline{p}) + \int_{\Gamma_1} j^0(\overline{u}_\tau;v_\tau)\,ds \geq (f,v)_H.$$

This relation and (3.29) show that $(\overline{u},\overline{p}) = (u,p)$ is the unique solution of the problem (3.14)–(3.15). Since the limit (u,p) is unique, the entire sequence converges: as $h \to 0$,

$$u^h \to u \text{ in } V, \quad q^h \to q \text{ in } Q.$$

Step 6: We prove the strong convergence:

$$p^h \to p \quad \text{in } Q. \tag{3.38}$$

By the Babuška-Brezzi condition (3.20),

$$\beta\,\|p^h - \overline{p}^h\|_Q \leq \sup_{v^h \in V_0^h} \frac{b(v^h,p^h-\overline{p}^h)}{\|v^h\|_V}.$$

Write

$$b(v^h,p^h-\overline{p}^h) = b(v^h,p^h-p) + b(v^h,p-\overline{p}^h).$$

From (3.23),

$$a(u^h,v^h)-b(v^h,p^h)=(f^h,v^h)_H \quad \forall v^h\in V_0^h.$$

From (3.14),

$$a(u,v^h)-b(v^h,p)=(f,v^h)_H \quad \forall v^h\in V_0^h.$$

Thus,

$$b(v^h,p^h-p)=a(u^h-u,v^h)-(f^h-f,v^h)_H.$$

Then,

$$\begin{aligned}\beta\,\|p^h-\overline{p}^h\|_Q &\le \sup_{v^h\in V_0^h}\frac{1}{\|v^h\|_V}\left[a(u^h-u,v^h)-(f^h-f,v^h)_H+b(v^h,p-\overline{p}^h)\right]\\ &\le c\left[\|u^h-u\|_V+\|f^h-f\|_{V^*}+\|p-\overline{p}^h\|_Q\right].\end{aligned}$$

By the triangle inequality

$$\|p^h-p\|_Q\le\|p^h-\overline{p}^h\|_Q+\|p-\overline{p}^h\|_Q,$$

we then obtain

$$\|p^h-p\|_Q\le c\left[\|u^h-u\|_V+\|f^h-f\|_{V^*}+\|p-\overline{p}^h\|_Q\right].$$

From this inequality and (3.32), (3.26), (3.33), noting that $\overline{u}=u$ and $\overline{p}=p$, we conclude that (3.38) holds.

Finally, we provide a convergence result on the numerical approximation defined by (3.21). For this purpose, we need a further assumption on the cost function C.

$H(C')$ If $u_n\to u$ in V, $p_n\to p$ in Q, and $f_n\to f$ in H, then

$$C(u,p,f)=\lim_{n\to\infty}C(u_n,p_n,f_n).$$

For a given $f^h\in H_{ad}^h$, we denote by $(u^h(f^h),p^h(f^h))\in V^h\times Q^h$ the solution of the problem (3.23)–(3.24).

Theorem 3.4.2 *Assume $H(j)$, $H(H_{ad})$, $H(C)$, (3.16), (H_V^h), (H_Q^h), $(H_{H_{ad}}^h)$, $(H_{V,Q}^h)$, and in addition $H(C')$. For each $h>0$, let f^h be a solution of the problem (3.21). Then there exist a subsequence, again denoted as $\{f^h\}$, and an element $f\in H_{ad}$ such that*

$$f^h\rightharpoonup f \text{ in } H,\; u^h(f^h)\to u(f) \text{ in } V,\; p^h(f^h)\to p(f) \text{ in } Q, \tag{3.39}$$

and $f\in H_{ad}$ is a solution of the optimal control problem (3.18).

Proof. Fix an arbitrary $f_0 \in H_{ad}$. Then by $(H^h_{H_{ad}})$, there exists $f^h_0 \in H^h_{ad}$ such that $f^h_0 \to f_0$ in H. Denote by $u^h_0 = u^h(f^h_0)$ and $p^h_0 = p^h(f^h_0)$ the solution of the problem (3.23)–(3.24) with f^h replaced by f^h_0, and by $u_0 = u(f_0)$ and $p_0 = p(f_0)$ the solution of the problem (3.14)–(3.15) with f replaced by f_0. By definition, $(u^h_0, p^h_0) \in V^h \times Q^h$ satisfies

$$a(u^h_0, v^h) - b(v^h, p^h_0) + \int_{\Gamma_1} j^0(u^h_{0\tau}; v^h_\tau)\, ds \geq (f^h_0, v^h)_H \quad \forall v^h \in V^h, \tag{3.40}$$

$$b(u^h_0, q^h) = 0 \quad \forall q^h \in Q^h, \tag{3.41}$$

and $(u_0, p_0) \in V \times Q$ satisfies

$$a(u_0, v) - b(v, p_0) + \int_{\Gamma_1} j^0(u_{0\tau}; v_\tau)\, ds \geq (f_0, v)_H \quad \forall v \in V, \tag{3.42}$$

$$b(u_0, q) = 0 \quad \forall q \in Q. \tag{3.43}$$

Applying Theorem 3.4.1, we have

$$u^h_0 \to u_0 \text{ in } V, \quad p^h_0 \to p_0 \text{ in } Q.$$

By $H(C')$,

$$\lim_{h\to 0} C^h(f^h_0) = C(f_0).$$

Since $C^h(f^h) \leq C^h(f^h_0)$, we deduce that the sequence $\{C^h(f^h)\}_h$ is bounded from above. By $H(C)$, $\{f^h\}_h$ is bounded in H. Thus, for a subsequence, still denoted by $\{f^h\}_h$, we have $f^h \rightharpoonup f$ in H for some element $f \in H$. Since H_{ad} is weakly closed and $f^h \in H^h_{ad} \subset H_{ad}$, we know that $f \in H_{ad}$. By Theorem 3.4.1, we have the convergence

$$u^h \to u \text{ in } V, \quad p^h \to p \text{ in } Q.$$

So by $H(C)$,

$$C(f) \leq \liminf_{h\to 0} C^h(f^h). \tag{3.44}$$

We need to show that f is a solution of (3.18). Let $\overline{f}$ be a solution of (3.18). By $(H^h_{H_{ad}})$, there exists $\overline{f}^h \in H^h_{ad}$ with

$$\overline{f}^h \to \overline{f} \quad \text{in } H.$$

Then by Theorem 3.4.1,

$$u^h(\overline{f}^h) \to u(\overline{f}) \text{ in } V, \quad p^h(\overline{f}^h) \to p(\overline{f}) \text{ in } Q.$$

By $H(C')$,

$$\lim_{h\to 0} C^h(\overline{f}^h) = C(\overline{f}). \tag{3.45}$$

From the definition of f^h,

$$\mathcal{C}^h(f^h) \le \mathcal{C}^h(\overline{f}^h).$$

Take the lower limit of both sides of the above inequality as $h \to 0$,

$$\liminf_{h\to 0} \mathcal{C}^h(f^h) \le \lim_{h\to 0} \mathcal{C}^h(\overline{f}^h).$$

This inequality, combined with (3.44) and (3.45), implies that

$$\mathcal{C}(f) \le \mathcal{C}(\overline{f}).$$

Thus, f is a solution of (3.18).

Finally, we comment that (H_V^h), (H_Q^h), $(H_{H_{ad}}^h)$, $(H_{V,Q}^h)$ are satisfied with stable finite element pairs (V^h, Q^h) and piecewise constant functions for H_{ad}^h. For simplicity, assume Ω is a polygonal domain ($d = 2$) or a polyhedral domain ($d = 3$). Let $\{\mathcal{T}^h\}_h$ be a regular family of finite element partitions of the domain $\overline{\Omega}$ into triangular/tetrahedral elements. Then we may choose $P_1 \oplus B(T)$-P_1 finite elements ([1])

$$V^h = \{v^h \in V \cap C^0(\overline{\Omega})^d : v^h|_T \in [P_1(T)]^d \oplus B(T) \ \forall T \in \mathcal{T}^h\},$$
$$Q^h = \{q^h \in Q \cap C^0(\overline{\Omega}) : q^h|_T \in P_1(T) \ \forall T \in \mathcal{T}^h\},$$

or P_2-P_1 finite elements ([14, Chapter II, Corollary 4.1])

$$V^h = \{v^h \in V \cap C^0(\overline{\Omega})^d : v^h|_T \in [P_2(T)]^d \ \forall T \in \mathcal{T}^h\}, \tag{3.46}$$
$$Q^h = \{q^h \in Q \cap C^0(\overline{\Omega}) : q^h|_T \in P_1(T) \ \forall T \in \mathcal{T}^h\}, \tag{3.47}$$

where for an integer $k \ge 0$, $P_k(T)$ is the space of polynomials of a total degree less than or equal to k in T, and $B(T)$ is the space of bubble functions on T. For these choices, the Babuška-Brezzi condition (3.20) is satisfied.

It is also possible to use a discontinuous pressure finite element space for Q^h in a pair (V^h, Q^h) such that the Babuška-Brezzi condition (3.20) is satisfied. For example, the P_2-P_0, $P_2 \oplus B(T)$-P_1 pairs (cf. [14]). If the optimal control problem in (3.19) requires to match the desired velocity only ($\theta_2 = 0$), then we can use a penalty or a stablization formulation by adding an $\varepsilon\,(p_h, q_h)$ term in (3.24) and can eliminate the pressure in the modified (3.23)–(3.24). In this way, we will need to solve a simpler optimal control problem with a hemivariational inequality as the constraint.

References

[1] D.N. Arnold, F. Brezzi and M. Fortin. A stable finite element for the Stokes equations. Calcolo, 21: 337–344, 1984.

[2] K. Atkinson and W. Han. *Theoretical Numerical Analysis: A Functional Analysis Framework*. Third edition, Springer, New York, 2009.

[3] V. Barbu. *Optimal Control of Variational Inequalities*. Pitman, London, 1983.

[4] F.H. Clarke. Generalized gradients and applications. Trans. Amer. Math. Soc., 205: 247–262, 1975.

[5] F.H. Clarke. *Optimization and Nonsmooth Analysis*. Wiley, Interscience, New York, 1983.

[6] C. Fang, K. Czuprynski, W. Han, X. Cheng and X. Dai. Finite element method for a stationary Stokes hemivariational inequality with slip boundary condition. IMA Journal of Numerical Analysis, 40: 2696–2716, 2020.

[7] C. Fang and W. Han. Well-posedness and optimal control of a hemivariational inequality for nonstationary Stokes fluid flow. Discrete Cont. Dyn.-A, 36: 5369–5386, 2016.

[8] C. Fang and W. Han. Stability analysis and optimal control of a stationary Stokes hemivariational inequality. Evolution Equations and Control Theory, 9: 995–1008, 2020.

[9] F. Feng, W. Han and J. Huang. Virtual element method for elliptic hemivariational inequalities. Journal of Scientific Computing, 81: 2388–2412, 2019.

[10] H. Fujita. *Flow Problems with Unilateral Boundary Conditions*. College de France, Lecons, 1993.

[11] H. Fujita. A mathematical analysis of motions of viscous incompressible fluid under leak or slip boundary conditions. RIMS Kôkyûroku, 888: 199–216, 1994.

[12] H. Fujita and H. Kawarada. Variational inequalities for the Stokes equation with boundary conditions of friction type. GAKUTO Int. Ser. Math. Sci. Appl., 11: 15–33, 1998.

[13] H. Fujita, H. Kawarada and A. Sasamoto. Analytical and numerical approaches to stationary flow problems with leak and slip boundary conditions. Lect. Notes Num. Appl. Anal., 14: 17–31, 1995.

[14] V. Girault and P.A. Raviart. *Finite Element Methods for Navier-Stokes Equations: Theory and Algorithms*. Springer-Verlag, Berlin, 1986.

[15] D. Han, W. Han, S. Migorski and J. Zhao. Convergence analysis of numerical solutions for optimal control of variational-hemivariational inequalities. Applied Mathematics Letters, 105: 106327, 2020.

[16] W. Han, S. Migórski and M. Sofonea. A class of variational-hemivariational inequalities with applications to frictional contact problems. SIAM J. Math. Anal., 46: 3891–3912, 2014.

[17] W. Han and M. Sofonea. Numerical analysis of hemivariational inequalities in contact mechanics. Acta Numerica, 28: 175–286, 2019.

[18] J. Haslinger, M. Miettinen and P.D. Panagiotopoulos. *Finite Element Method for Hemivariational Inequalities: Theory, Methods and Applications*. Kluwer Academic Publishers, Dordrecht, Boston, London, 1999.

[19] J. Haslinger and P.D. Panagiotopoulos. Optimal control of systems governed by hemivariational inequalities. Existence and approximation results. Nonlinear Analysis: Theory, Methods, and Applications, 24: 105–119, 1995.

[20] L.S. Hou and S.S. Ravindran. Computations of boundary optimal control problems for an electrically conducting fluid. Journal of Computational Physics, 128: 319–330, 1996.

[21] N. Kikuchi and J.T. Oden. *Contact Problems in Elasticity*. SIAM, Philadelphia, 1988.

[22] J.-L. Lions. *Optimal Control of Systems Governed by Partial Differential Equations*. Springer, Heidelberg, Berlin, 1971.

[23] M. Miettinen and J. Haslinger. Approximation of optimal control problems of hemivariational inequalities. Numer. Funct. Anal. Optim., 13: 43–68, 1992.

[24] S. Migórski. A note on optimal control problem for a hemivariational inequality modeling fluid flow. Discrete and Continuous Dynam. Systems—Supplement, 545–554, 2013.

[25] S. Migórski and A. Ochal. Optimal control of parabolic hemivariational inequalities. J. Global Optim., 17: 285–300, 2000.

[26] S. Migórski, A. Ochal and M. Sofonea. *Nonlinear Inclusions and Hemivariational Inequalities. Models and Analysis of Contact Problems*. Advances in Mechanics and Mathematics 26, Springer, New York, 2013.

[27] Z. Naniewicz and P.D. Panagiotopoulos. *Mathematical Theory of Hemivariational Inequalities and Applications*. Dekker, New York, 1995.

[28] P. Neittaanmaki, J. Sprekels and D. Tiba. *Optimization of Elliptic Systems: Theory and Applications*. Springer, New York, 2006.

[29] P.D. Panagiotopoulos. Nonconvex energy functions, hemivariational inequalities and substationary principles. Acta Mech., 42: 160–183, 1983.

[30] P.D. Panagiotopoulos. *Hemivariational Inequalities: Applications in Mechanics and Engineering*. Springer Verlag, Berlin, 1993.

[31] Z. Peng and K. Kunisch. Optimal control of elliptic variational-hemivariational inequalities. J. Optim. Theory Appl., 178: 1–25, 2018.

[32] F. Saidi. Non-Newtonian Stokes flow with frictional boundary conditions. Math. Model. Anal., 12: 483–495, 2007.

[33] M. Sofonea. Convergence results and optimal control for a class of hemivariational inequalities. SIAM J. Math. Anal., 50: 4066–4086, 2018.

[34] M. Sofonea and S. Migórski. *Variational-Hemivariational Inequalities with Applications*. Chapman & Hall/CRC Press, Boca Raton-London, 2018.

[35] R. Temam. *Navier-Stokes Equations: Theory and Numerical Analysis*. North-Holland, Amsterdam, 1979.

[36] F. Tröltzsch. *Optimal Control of Partial Differential Equations*. American Mathematical Society, Providence, Rhode Island, 2010.

[37] Y. Xiao and M. Sofonea. On the optimal control of variational-hemivariational inequalities. J. Math. Anal. Appl., 475: 364–384, 2019.

Chapter 4

Nonlinear Tikhonov Regularization in Hilbert Scales with Oversmoothing Penalty: Inspecting Balancing Principles

Bernd Hofmann[a,*], *Christopher Hofmann*[a], *Peter Mathé*[b] and *Robert Plato*[c]

2010 Mathematics Subject Classification. 65J20, 47J06, 47A52

Dedicated to Zuhair Nashed, our esteemed colleague and outstanding Professor, doyen of operator theory and regularization theory for inverse and ill-posed problems.

4.1 Introduction

In the past years, a new facet has found interest in the theory of inverse problems. When considering variational (Tikhonov-type) regularization for the stable

[a] Faculty of Mathematics, Chemnitz University of Technology, 09107 Chemnitz, Germany.
[b] Weierstraß Institute for Applied Analysis and Stochastics, Mohrenstraße 39, 10117 Berlin, Germany.
[c] Department Mathematik, Emmy-Noether-Campus, Universität Siegen, Walter-Flex-Str. 3, 57068 Siegen, Germany.
Emails: christopher.hofmann@mathematik.tu-chemnitz.de; mathe@wias-berlin.de;
plato@mathematik.uni-siegen.de
* Corresponding author: bernd.hofmann@mathematik.tu-chemnitz.de

approximate solution of *ill-posed* operator equations

$$F(x) = y \tag{4.1}$$

in Hilbert spaces the treatment of *oversmoothing penalties* gained attention. The current state of the art concerning that facet shows gaps. The present chapter aims at closing some of them. Specifically, we analyze variants of the balancing principle as parameter choice for the regularization parameter. Moreover, we would like to illustrate the theory by numerical case studies.

The forward operator $F : \mathcal{D}(F) \subseteq X \to Y$, which is preferably assumed to be *nonlinear*, maps between the separable infinite dimensional Hilbert spaces X and Y and possesses the convex and closed subset $\mathcal{D}(F)$ of X as domain of definition. In the sequel, let $x^\dagger \in \mathcal{D}(F)$ be a solution to equation (4.1) for given exact right-hand side $y = F(x^\dagger) \in Y$. We throughout assume that $x^\dagger \in \operatorname{int}(\mathcal{D}(F))$, which means that the solution belongs to the interior of the domain $\mathcal{D}(F)$ of the operator F. Given the noise level $\delta \geq 0$, we consider the deterministic noise model

$$\|y - y^\delta\|_Y \leq \delta,$$

which means that instead of y, only perturbed data $y^\delta = y + \delta\xi \in Y$ with $\|\xi\|_Y \leq 1$ are available.

The equation (4.1) is ill-posed at least locally at $x^\dagger$, and finding stable solutions requires some regularization. We apply Tikhonov regularization with quadratic misfit and penalty functionals in a *Hilbert scale* setting.

4.1.1 Hilbert Scales with Respect to an Unbounded Operator

The Hilbert scale is generated by some densely defined, unbounded and self-adjoint linear operator $B\colon \mathcal{D}(B) \subset X \to X$ with domain $\mathcal{D}(B)$. This operator B is assumed to be strictly positive such that we have for some $\underline{m} > 0$

$$\|Bx\|_X \geq \underline{m}\|x\|_X \quad \text{for all} \quad x \in \mathcal{D}(B).$$

The Hilbert scale $\{X_\tau\}_{\tau\in\mathbb{R}}$, generated by B, is characterized by the formulas $X_\tau = \mathcal{D}(B^\tau)$ for $\tau > 0$, $X_\tau = X$ for $\tau \leq 0$ and $\|x\|_\tau := \|B^\tau x\|_X$ for $\tau \in \mathbb{R}$. We do not need in our setting the topological completion of the spaces $X_\tau = X$, for $\tau < 0$, with respect to the norm $\|\cdot\|_\tau$.

4.1.2 Tikhonov Regularization with Smoothness Promoting Penalty

The operator B is used for Tikhonov regularization in the corresponding functional

$$T_\alpha^\delta(x) := \|F(x) - y^\delta\|_Y^2 + \alpha\,\|B(x-\overline{x})\|_X^2, \quad x \in \mathcal{D} := \mathcal{D}(F) \cap \mathcal{D}(B), \tag{4.2}$$

where $\|F(x)-y^\delta\|^2$ characterizes the misfit or fidelity term, and $\bar{x} \in X$ is an initial guess occurring in the penalty functional $\|B(x-\bar{x})\|_X^2$. Throughout this chapter we suppose that $\bar{x} \in \mathcal{D}$. Given a regularization parameter $\alpha > 0$ the corresponding regularized solutions x_α^δ to $x^\dagger$ are obtained as the minimizers of the Tikhonov functional T_α^δ on the set $\mathcal{D}$. By definition of the Hilbert scale we have that $\|B(x-\bar{x})\|_X^2 = \|x-\bar{x}\|_1^2$ and consequently $x_\alpha^\delta \in \mathcal{D}(B) = X_1$ for all data $y^\delta \in Y$ and $\alpha > 0$. In order to ensure *existence* and *stability* of the regularized solutions x_α^δ for all $\alpha > 0$ (cf. [8, § 3], [25, Section 3.2] and [26, Section 4.1.1]), we additionally suppose that the forward operator F is weakly sequentially continuous.

Our focus will be on oversmoothing penalties, when $x^\dagger \notin \mathcal{D}(B)$ and hence $T_\alpha^\delta(x^\dagger) = \infty$. In this case, the regularizing property $T_\alpha^\delta(x_\alpha^\delta) \le T_\alpha^\delta(x^\dagger)$, which often is a basic tool for obtaining error estimates does not yield consequences.

4.1.3 State of the Art

The seminal study for Tikhonov regularization, including the case of oversmoothing penalty, and for linear ill-posed operator equations, was published by Natterer in 1984, cf. [20]. For linear bounded operator $F = A : X \to Y$, Natterer used for this study a two-sided inequality chain

$$c_a\|x\|_{-a} \le \|Ax\|_Y \le C_a\|x\|_{-a} \quad \text{for all} \quad x \in X,$$

with constants $0 < c_a \le C_a < \infty$ and a *degree of ill-posedness* $a > 0$. Here, we adapt this to the nonlinear mapping $F : \mathcal{D}(F) \subset X \to Y$ as

$$c_a\,\|x-x^\dagger\|_{-a} \le \|F(x)-F(x^\dagger)\|_Y \le C_a\|x-x^\dagger\|_{-a} \qquad \text{for all } x \in \mathcal{D}, \tag{4.3}$$

and rely upon (4.3) as an intrinsic *nonlinearity condition* for the mapping F under consideration.

This specific nonlinearity condition was first used within the present context in [9]. It was shown that a discrepancy principle yields optimal order convergence under the power type smoothness assumption that $x^\dagger \in X_p,\ 0 < p < 1$. One major tool was to use certain *auxiliary elements* $\hat{x}_\alpha$ of proximal type, which are minimizers of the functional

$$\widehat{T}_\alpha(x) := \|x-x^\dagger\|_{-a}^2 + \alpha\|x-\bar{x}\|_1^2, \quad x \in X, \tag{4.4}$$

and hence belong to $X_1 = \mathcal{D}(B)$. This study was complemented in [2] within the proceedings *Inverse Problems and Related Topics: Shanghai, China, October 12–14, 2018*, Springer, 2020, by case studies showing intrinsic problems when using oversmoothing penalties. The same issue contains results on *a priori* parameter choice $\alpha_* \sim \delta^{(2a+2)/(a+p)}$, i.e., when the smoothness p is assumed to be known, see [10].

However, the first decomposition of the error into a smoothness dependent increasing term (as a function of α tending to zero as $\alpha \to +0$), and a smoothness independent decreasing term proportional to $\delta/\alpha^{a/(2a+2)}$ was developed in [13]. As a consequence, there is something special about this study that norm convergence of regularized solutions to the exact solution can be shown for a wide region of a priori parameter choices and for a specific discrepancy principle without to make any specific smoothness assumption on $x^\dagger$. It is highlighted there that such error decomposition also allows for low order convergence rates under low order smoothness assumptions on $x^\dagger$. But it was observed in [7] that the error decomposition from [13] extends to power type smoothness $x^\dagger \in X_p$, $0 < p < 1$, and hence yields optimal rates of convergence under the a priori parameter choice.

4.1.4 Goal of the Present Study

The present chapter complements the series of articles mentioned before.

On the one hand, it extends the error decomposition from [13, 7] to more general smoothness assumptions. On the other hand, we present new results for the *balancing principle* for choosing the regularization parameter in Tikhonov regularization for nonlinear problems with oversmoothing penalties in a Hilbert scale setting. This work was essentially motivated by the recent paper [23]. Pricop-Jeckstadt has also analyzed the balancing principle for nonlinear problems in Hilbert scales, but only for non-oversmoothing penalties. In this sense, we try to close a gap in the theory.

The material is organized as follows. In Section 4.2 we highlight the decomposition of the error under smoothness in terms of source conditions. This provides us with the required structure in order to found the balancing principles in Section 4.3. We give a brief account of the history of such principles, and formulate several specifications for the setup under consideration. The results presented in this part are general and may be of independent interest. Finally, in Section 4.4 we discuss the exponential growth model, both theoretically, and as subject for a numerical case study.

4.2 General Error Estimate for Tikhonov Regularization in Hilbert Scales with Oversmoothing Penalty

The basis for an analytical treatment of the balancing principle is formed by general error estimates for Tikhonov regularization in Hilbert scales with oversmoothing penalty. Under the inequality chain (4.3) and for $x^\dagger \in \mathrm{int}(\mathcal{D}(F))$ such estimates have been developed recently in [9], [13], and [7] by using *auxiliary elements* as minimizers of (4.4). Introducing the injective linear operator $G := B^{-(2a+2)}$, the corresponding minimizers $\hat{x}_\alpha$ can be expressed explicitly as

$$\hat{x}_\alpha = \overline{x} + G(G+\alpha \mathrm{I})^{-1}(x^\dagger - \overline{x}) = x^\dagger - \alpha(G+\alpha \mathrm{I})^{-1}(x^\dagger - \overline{x}).$$

4.2.1 Smoothness in Terms of Source Conditions

General error estimates were obtained under general source conditions, given in terms of index functions ψ.

Definition 4.2.1 *A continuous and non-decreasing function $\varphi : (0,\infty) \to (0,\infty)$ with $\lim_{t\to+0} \varphi(t) = 0$ is called* index function. *We call this index function sub-linear if there is some $t_0 > 0$ such that the quotient $t/\varphi(t)$ is non-decreasing for $0 < t \le t_0$.*

In these terms, for an index function ψ, a general source condition for the unknown solution $x^\dagger$ is given in the form of

$$x^\dagger - \bar{x} = \psi(G)\,w, \quad w \in X. \tag{4.5}$$

Here the linear operator $\psi(G)$ is obtained from the operator G by spectral calculus.

4.2.2 Error Decomposition

The balancing principle relies on an error bound in a specific form, and the corresponding fundamental error bound is given next.

Theorem 4.2.2 *Let $x^\dagger \in \operatorname{int}(\mathcal{D}(F))$ and let hold the inequality chain (4.3), by which the degree of ill-posedness $a > 0$ is given. Moreover, let ψ be an index function such that ψ^{2a+2} is sub-linear. If $x^\dagger$ satisfies a source condition (4.5) for that ψ, then we have for some constant $c_1 > 0$ depending on w the general error estimate*

$$\| x_\alpha^\delta - x^\dagger \|_X \le c_1 \psi(\alpha) + \frac{\delta}{\lambda(\alpha)}, \tag{4.6}$$

where $\lambda(\alpha) = \frac{1}{K_2}\alpha^{a/(2a+2)}$, and $K_2 = \max\{1, \frac{2}{c_a}\}$.

The proof follows the arguments of Proposition 3.4 in [13], and we briefly sketch these.

Proof. A substantial ingredient of the proof is the fact that due to [19] sub-linear index functions are qualifications for the classical Tikhonov regularization approach with norm square penalty, and the verification of formula (25) in [7], which in turn is based on the bounds (21)–(23) ibid. As can be seen from there it is enough to show that under the above assumptions, and for $0 \le \theta \le \frac{2a+1}{2a+2}$, we have that

$$\alpha^{1-\theta} \| G^\theta (G + \alpha I)^{-1} (x^\dagger - \bar{x}) \|_X \le C\psi(\alpha), \quad \alpha > 0. \tag{4.7}$$

To this end we start from the observation that under the source condition (4.5) we have

$$\| G^\theta (G + \alpha I)^{-1} (x^\dagger - \bar{x}) \|_X \le \| w \|_X \| G^\theta (G + \alpha I)^{-1} \psi(G) \|_{X \to X}.$$

By introducing the residual function for (classical) Tikhonov regularization $r_\alpha(t) := \alpha/(t+\alpha)$, for $t, \alpha > 0$, it suffices to bound

$$\frac{1}{\alpha} \| r_\alpha(G) G^\theta \psi(G) \|_{X \to X}.$$

The function $t \mapsto t^\theta \psi(t)$ plainly constitutes an index function. We shall establish that it is sub-linear. To this end we write

$$\left[\frac{t}{t^\theta \psi(t)}\right]^{2a+2} = \frac{t^{(1-\theta)(2a+2)}}{\psi^{2a+2}(t)} = t^{(1-\theta)(2a+2)-1} \frac{t}{\psi^{2a+2}(t)}, \quad 0 < t \leq t_0.$$

Under the made sub-linearity assumption we find that $t \mapsto t^\theta \psi(t)$ is sub-linear provided that $(1-\theta)(2a+2) - 1 \geq 0$, which corresponds to $\theta \leq \frac{2a+1}{2a+2}$. Thus in this range the function $t^\theta \psi(t)$ is a qualification for Tikhonov regularization, and we conclude that

$$\frac{1}{\alpha} \| r_\alpha(G) G^\theta \psi(G) \|_{X \to X} \leq C \frac{1}{\alpha} \alpha^\theta \psi(\alpha) = C \alpha^{\theta - 1} \psi(\alpha), \quad \alpha > 0,$$

which yields (4.7). □

We note that the error estimate (4.6) does not correspond to the natural estimate $\| x_\alpha^\delta - x^\dagger \|_X \leq \| x_\alpha - x^\dagger \|_X + \| x_\alpha^\delta - x_\alpha \|_X$.

We highlight the above result for the prototypical examples, as studied previously.

Example 4.2.3 (power-type smoothness) Theorem 4.2.2 applies for *Hölder-type source conditions* of the form

$$x^\dagger - \bar{x} = B^{-p} w = G^{p/(2a+2)} \quad \text{for} \quad 0 < p \leq 1, \tag{4.8}$$

which characterize for this type the case of oversmoothing penalties. Indeed, the corresponding function ψ is $\psi(t) = t^{\frac{p}{2a+2}}$, such that $\psi^{2a+2}(t) = t^p$ is sub-linear whenever $0 < p \leq 1$. Then the a priori parameter choice $\alpha_* := \delta^{\frac{2a+2}{a+p}}$ yields under the source condition (4.8) a Hölder-type convergence rate of the form

$$\|x_{\alpha_*}^\delta - x^\dagger\|_X = \mathcal{O}(\delta^{\frac{p}{a+p}}) \quad \text{as} \quad \delta \to 0. \tag{4.9}$$

Such power-type rates correspond to *moderately ill-posed problems*.

We note that the same convergence rate (4.9) can also be obtained for α_*, determined by the discrepancy principle in the sense of formula (4.51) below, cf. [9].

Example 4.2.4 (low order smoothness) Theorem 4.2.2 also applies for *low order source conditions* with ψ, for which ψ^{2a+2} is always sub-linear. Most prominently, we assume that there is some exponent $\mu > 0$, such that $\psi(t) =$

$K(\log^{-\mu}(1/t))$ for $0 < t \le t_0 = e^{-1}$, and continuously extended as constant for $t_0 < t \le \|G\|_{X \to X}$. Moreover, the a priori parameter choice resulting in $\alpha_* := \delta$ yields the rate of convergence

$$\|x_{\alpha_*}^{\delta} - x^{\dagger}\|_X = \mathcal{O}(\log^{-\mu}(1/\delta)) \quad \text{as} \quad \delta \to 0. \tag{4.10}$$

Such logarithmic rates correspond to *severely ill-posed problems* (cf. [14]).

Example 4.2.5 (no explicit smoothness) Theorem 4.2.2 provides us with an upper bound of the error, once a smoothness condition of the form (4.5) is available such that ψ^{2a+2} is sub-linear. Now we argue as follows. For the operator B^{-1} there is an index function φ such that $x^{\dagger} - \bar{x} = \varphi(G)v$, $v \in X$, see [18] for compact B^{-1}, and [11] for the general case. In the compact case it is shown in [18, Cor. 2] that this index function may be chosen concave, and hence sub-linear. Then letting $\psi := \varphi^{1/(2a+2)}$ we can apply Theorem 4.2.2 for this index function ψ. In particular we conclude the following. If $\alpha_* := \alpha_*(y^{\delta}, \delta)$ is any parameter choice such that $\alpha_* \to 0$, and also $\delta/\alpha_*^{a/(2a+2)} \to 0$ as $\delta \to 0$, then $\| x_{\alpha_*}^{\delta} - x^{\dagger} \|_X \to 0$. For the general case of B, which includes B^{-1} non-compact, the latter result may be found in [13, Thm. 4.1] by an alternative proof based on the Banach–Steinhaus theorem.

4.3 Balancing Principles

Vast majority of regularization theory for ill-posed equations is concerned with asymptotic properties of regularization, as this is convergence, and if so, rates of convergence. For given operator $F : \mathcal{D}(F) \subseteq X \to Y$ between Hilbert spaces X and Y, let $Y \ni y^{\delta} \mapsto x_{\alpha}^{\delta} := R_{\alpha}(y^{\delta}) \in X$ be any regularization scheme for the stable approximate determination of $x^{\dagger} \in \mathcal{D}(F)$ from data $y^{\delta} \in Y$ such that $\| F(x^{\dagger}) - y^{\delta} \|_Y \le \delta$. Its error at $x^{\dagger}$ is then considered uniformly for admissible data as

$$e(x^{\dagger}, R_{\alpha}, \delta) := \sup_{y^{\delta} :\, \| F(x^{\dagger}) - y^{\delta} \|_Y \le \delta} \| x_{\alpha}^{\delta} - x^{\dagger} \|_X .$$

We call a parameter choice $\alpha = \alpha(y^{\delta}, \delta)$ *convergent* if $e(x^{\dagger}, R_{\alpha(y^{\delta},\delta)}, \delta) \to 0$ whenever $\delta \to 0$. In most cases, convergence of regularization parameter choices is analyzed *uniformly on some class* $\mathcal{M} \subset X$, i.e., it is studied when we have $\sup_{x^{\dagger} \in \mathcal{M}} e(x^{\dagger}, R_{\alpha(y^{\delta},\delta)}, \delta) \to 0$.

In contrast, there are studies which highlight a different paradigm: What is the quality of a particular regularization and parameter choice at any given data y^{δ}? This is relevant, since in practice we are given just one instance of data y^{δ}. Then convergence is not an issue, rather the aim is to do the best possible for any such instance. Balancing principles may be used for this purpose.

Lepskiĭ's balancing principle is most prominent for the latter paradigm. It arose in a series of papers, starting from [16], and it gained special attention in statistics within the subject of 'oracle inequalities' for the purpose of model selection since then.

Within classical regularization theory it was first studied in [19]; fundamental discussions are given in [21, 17]. A variation of this statistically motivated approach was followed starting from [24], where the above mentioned paradigm was called quasi-optimality. The original presentation of this idea dates back to [15], called point-wise pseudo-optimal. It is shown ibid. Theorem 7, and for Tikhonov regularization, that the choice α_*, obtained as solutions of the extremal problem

$$\| \alpha \frac{dx_\alpha^\delta}{d\alpha} \|_X + \frac{\delta}{\sqrt{\alpha}} \longrightarrow \min$$

is point-wise pseudo-optimal. Here we follow the approach from [24, 5] by using the concept of *quasi-optimality*.

4.3.1 Quasi-optimality

In what follows, we assume that for some fixed searched-for element $x^\dagger \in X$ and $x_\alpha^\delta = R_\alpha(y^\delta) \in X$ $(\alpha > 0,\ 0 < \delta \le \delta_0)$ obtained from some noisy data $y^\delta \in Y$ and by using some regularization scheme R_α not further specified, the estimate

$$\| x_\alpha^\delta - x^\dagger \|_X \le \varphi(\alpha) + \frac{\delta}{\lambda(\alpha)} \qquad (\alpha > 0) \tag{4.11}$$

holds, where $\varphi,\ \lambda : (0,\infty) \to (0,\infty)$ are both index functions. The function $\alpha \mapsto \lambda(\alpha)$ is assumed to be known. This approach is generic and we shall not make use of any specific properties of the operator F, nor of any specific conditions on the noisy data y^δ.

Definition 4.3.1 *Suppose that the error bound (4.11) holds true. A parameter choice strategy $\alpha_* = \alpha_*(y^\delta, \delta)$ $(0 < \delta \le \delta_0)$ is called* quasi-optimal, *if there is a constant $c_2 > 0$ such that for $0 < \delta \le \delta_0$ an estimate of the following kind is satisfied:*

$$\| x_{\alpha_*}^\delta - x^\dagger \|_X \le c_2 \inf_{\alpha > 0} \left(\varphi(\alpha) + \frac{\delta}{\lambda(\alpha)} \right). \tag{4.12}$$

Note that the constant c_2 in Definition 4.3.1, called the *error constant* below, may depend on the function φ. In addition, note that Definition 4.3.1 also includes a posteriori parameter choices since in applications, x_α^δ rely on data $y^\delta \in Y$.

We highlight a general feature of quasi-optimal parameter choice.

Proposition 4.3.2 *Suppose that the error bound (4.11) holds true.*

1. *If for some parameter choice rule $\alpha_+ = \alpha_+(y^\delta, \delta)$ we can guarantee a rate*

$$\varphi(\alpha_+) + \frac{\delta}{\lambda(\alpha_+)} = \mathcal{O}(\rho(\delta)), \quad as \quad \delta \to 0,$$

for some index function ρ*, then any quasi-optimal parameter choice* $\alpha_* = \alpha_*(y^\delta, \delta)$ *yields the convergence rate*

$$\|x^\delta_{\alpha_*} - x^\dagger\|_X = \mathcal{O}(\rho(\delta)) \quad as \quad \delta \to 0.$$

2. *Any quasi-optimal parameter choice* $\alpha_* = \alpha_*(y^\delta, \delta)$ *yields convergence* $\|x^\delta_{\alpha_*} - x^\dagger\|_X \to 0$ *as* $\delta \to 0$.

Proof. The first part is obvious. For the second part, one may consider the right-hand side of (4.12) with any parameter choice $\alpha_+ = \alpha_+(y^\delta, \delta)$ such that both $\alpha_+ \to 0$ and $\delta/\lambda(\alpha_+) \to 0$ as $\delta \to 0$. □

We stress once again, the focus of quasi-optimality of a parameter choice strategy is not convergence, rather it emphasizes an *oracle property*: If (by some oracle) we are given a parameter choice rule $\alpha_+ := \alpha_+(y^\delta, \delta)$ which realizes

$$\varphi(\alpha_+) + \frac{\delta}{\lambda(\alpha_+)} \le C \inf_{\alpha>0} \left(\varphi(\alpha) + \frac{\delta}{\lambda(\alpha)}\right), \tag{4.13}$$

then the quasi-optimal rule is (up to the constant c_2) as good as the oracle choice.

In the sub-sequent sections, we shall describe variants of the balancing principle and we shall show that these are quasi-optimal.

4.3.2 The Balancing Principles: Setup and Formulation

We constrain to the following setup. First, we shall assume that the noise amplification term is of the form

$$\lambda(\alpha) = \frac{\alpha^\varkappa}{K_2}, \tag{4.14}$$

where $K_2 > 0$ and $\varkappa > 0$. For standard regularization schemes for selfadjoint and non-selfadjoint linear problems in Hilbert spaces, we have $\varkappa = 1$ and $\varkappa = \frac{1}{2}$, respectively. In the situation of Section 4.2, representation (4.14) holds for $\varkappa = \frac{a}{2a+2}$ and $K_2 = \max\{1, \frac{2}{c_a}\}$.

The following result will be utilized at several occasions.

Lemma 4.3.3 *Let* $\alpha_+ = \alpha_+(y^\delta, \delta) > 0$ *be any parameter choice satisfying*

$$\varphi(\alpha_+) \le c_3 \frac{\delta}{\lambda(\alpha_+)}, \qquad \frac{\delta}{\lambda(\rho\alpha_+)} \le c_4 \varphi(\rho\alpha_+), \tag{4.15}$$

where c_3, $c_4 > 0$ *and* $\rho \ge 1$ *denote some finite constants chosen independently of* δ*. Then* α_+ *satisfies the oracle estimate (4.13), with a constant that may by chosen as* $C = \rho^\varkappa(1 + \max\{c_3, c_4\})$.

Proof. Consider the case $0 < \alpha \leq \rho\alpha_+$, first. From $\varphi(\alpha_+) \leq c_3 \frac{\delta}{\lambda(\alpha_+)}$ we then obtain

$$\varphi(\alpha_+) + \frac{\delta}{\lambda(\alpha_+)} \leq (c_3+1)\frac{\delta}{\lambda(\alpha_+)} \leq \rho^{\varkappa}(c_3+1)\frac{\delta}{\lambda(\alpha)}$$
$$\leq \rho^{\varkappa}(c_3+1)\Big(\varphi(\alpha) + \frac{\delta}{\lambda(\alpha)}\Big).$$

Next we consider the case $\alpha \geq \rho\alpha_+$. Then the estimate $\frac{\delta}{\lambda(\alpha_+)} \leq c_4\rho^{\varkappa}\varphi(\rho\alpha_+)$ yields

$$\varphi(\alpha_+) + \frac{\delta}{\lambda(\alpha_+)} \leq (1+c_4\rho^{\varkappa})\varphi(\rho\alpha_+) \leq (1+c_4\rho^{\varkappa})\Big(\varphi(\alpha) + \frac{\delta}{\lambda(\alpha)}\Big).$$

This completes the proof of the lemma. □

For the numerical realization of the balancing principle considered below, we utilize the following finite set of regularization parameters:

$$\Delta_\delta = \{\, \alpha_0 < \alpha_1 < \cdots < \alpha_N \,\}, \tag{4.16}$$

where each element of Δ_δ as well as $N \geq 0$ may depend on the noise level δ. We further assume that the elements of Δ_δ form a finite geometric sequence, i.e.,

$$\alpha_j = q^j\alpha_0, \quad j = 0, 1, \ldots, N, \quad \text{with } q > 1, \tag{4.17}$$

where the spacing parameter q is assumed to be independent of δ. We confine the search for the regularization parameter to the set Δ_δ. Given a tuning parameter $0 < \sigma \leq 1$, we consider the set

$$M_\delta := \Big\{ \alpha \in \Delta_\delta : \varphi(\alpha) \leq \sigma \frac{\delta}{\lambda(\alpha)} \Big\}. \tag{4.18}$$

The case $\sigma > 1$ does not provide any improvement and thus is excluded from the considerations below. For α_0 chosen sufficiently small and α_N sufficiently large in a way such that the set M_δ is not empty and in addition satisfies $M_\delta \neq \Delta_\delta$, then the maximum value $\alpha_+ = \max M_\delta$ enjoys quasi-optimality. This immediately follows from Lemma 4.3.3, applied with $\rho = q$, $c_3 = \sigma$, and $c_4 = \frac{1}{\sigma}$. However, such a parameter choice strategy is not implementable since the function φ is not available, in general. Thus we look for feasible sets which contain M_δ and are as close as possible to M_δ.

For $c_5, c_6, c_7 > 0$ fixed, below we assume that

$$0 < \alpha_0 \leq c_5\delta^{1/\varkappa}, \qquad c_6 \leq \alpha_N \leq c_7, \tag{4.19}$$

which guarantees that a sufficiently large interval is covered by the set Δ_δ introduced in (4.16).

Below we discuss several such balancing principles. These differ, e.g., in the number of comparisons executed at each step, and it is seen from the discussion in Section 4.3.3 that by increasing the number of comparisons we can decrease the error constant c_2.

In each of the subsequent versions, the balancing is controlled by a parameter $\tau_{\mathrm{L}} > 0$, therefore called *balancing constant*, and it is assumed to satisfy

$$\tau_{\mathrm{L}} > 1 + q^{-\varkappa}, \tag{4.20}$$

where $q > 1$ is the spacing parameter from (4.17).

First version

Here we consider

$$H_\delta := \left\{ \alpha_k \in \Delta_\delta : \| x_{\alpha_j}^\delta - x_{\alpha_{j-1}}^\delta \|_X \le \tau_{\mathrm{L}} \frac{\delta}{\lambda(\alpha_{j-1})} \text{ for any } 1 \le j \le k \right\}. \tag{4.21}$$

In order to find the maximum value $\alpha_* = \max H_\delta$, we shall start from $k = 0$, and increase k until $\| x_{\alpha_{k+1}}^\delta - x_{\alpha_k}^\delta \|_X > \tau_{\mathrm{L}} \frac{\delta}{\lambda(\alpha_k)}$ is satisfied for the first time, and take $\alpha_* = \alpha_k$ then. In the exceptional case that there is no such $k \le N-1$, it terminates with $k = N$. There is no need to compute the candidate approximations $x_{\alpha_{k+1}}^\delta, x_{\alpha_{k+2}}^\delta, \ldots, x_{\alpha_N}^\delta$ for this version. In the present chapter, our focus will be on this version.

Standard version

The standard version of the balancing principle is related to the set

$$\widetilde{H}_\delta := \left\{ \alpha_k \in \Delta_\delta : \| x_{\alpha_k}^\delta - x_{\alpha_j}^\delta \|_X \le \tau_{\mathrm{L}} \frac{\delta}{\lambda(\alpha_j)} \text{ for any } 0 \le j < k \right\}, \tag{4.22}$$

and it uses the maximum value $\alpha_* = \max \widetilde{H}_\delta$ as regularizing parameter, cf., e.g., [17, 21, 23]. In order to find the maximum value $\alpha_* = \max H_\delta$, one may start from $k = N$, and decrease k until the condition considered in (4.22) is satisfied for the first time.

This version of the balancing principle requires more comparisons than the first version introduced above, but on the other hand it allows to reduce the error constant. More details on the latter issue are given in Section 4.3.3.

A third version

Finally we consider a variant of the standard version given through

$$\widehat{H}_\delta := \left\{ \alpha_k \in \Delta_\delta : \| x_{\alpha_i}^\delta - x_{\alpha_j}^\delta \|_X \le \tau_{\mathrm{L}} \frac{\delta}{\lambda(\alpha_i)} \text{ for any } 0 \le i < j \le k \right\}, \tag{4.23}$$

and consider the maximum value $\alpha_* = \max \widehat{H}_\delta$ as regularizing parameter. This variant is considered in [22] in a special framework. In order to find the maximum value $\alpha_* = \max \widehat{H}_\delta$, we shall start from $k = 0$, and increase k until, for the first time, the condition $\| x^\delta_{\alpha_{k+1}} - x^\delta_{\alpha_j} \|_X > \tau_L \frac{\delta}{\lambda(\alpha_j)}$ is satisfied for some index $0 < j \leq k$, and take $\alpha_* = \alpha_k$ then. In the exceptional case that there is no such index $k \leq N-1$, the algorithm terminates with $k = N$. Only the candidate approximations $x^\delta_{\alpha_0}, x^\delta_{\alpha_1}, \ldots, x^\delta_{\alpha_k}$ have to be computed in the course of this procedure.

Typically one expects $\widetilde{H}_\delta = \widehat{H}_\delta$, and one can show that this identity in fact holds, e.g., for Lavrentiev's method for solving linear, symmetric, positive semidefinite ill-problems. However, in general $\widehat{H}_\delta \subset \widetilde{H}_\delta$ can be guaranteed only, and the set $\widetilde{H}_\delta$ man have gaps in Δ_δ. Under such general circumstances, the standard version of the balancing procedure requires the computation of all elements $x^\delta_{\alpha_0}, x^\delta_{\alpha_1}, \ldots, x^\delta_{\alpha_N}$ and consequently has a larger cost than the third version.

Remark 4.3.4 *In its original form, as introduced by Lepskiĭ, the principle is based on $\sigma = 1$ for the set M_δ from (4.18). In this case the standard technique only allows choices $\tau_L \geq 4$. Numerical experiments show that sometimes smaller balancing constants τ_L produce better results. We note that in the present chapter, we verify quasi-optimality of the balancing principle for a range of balancing constants τ_L which is bounded from below by the number given in (4.20). Note that condition (4.20) even permits τ_L close to 1 provided that q is chosen large. The latter case, however, corresponds to a maybe undesirable coarse grid Δ_δ. In addition, it leads to a large error constant, as is shown below, cf. Proposition 4.3.10 and the discussion following that proposition.*

Finally we mention that within the present context, the analog of Leonov's proposal would read as

$$\| x^\delta_{\alpha_i} - x^\delta_{\alpha_{i-1}} \|_X + \frac{\delta}{\lambda(\alpha_{i-1})} \longrightarrow \min.$$

We shall establish the quasi-optimality for the first variant with some details. The corresponding proofs for the other variants are similar, and hence omitted. The quasi-optimality of Leonov's approach is not clear for the present context of nonlinear ill-posed problems.

We start with the following observation.

Lemma 4.3.5 *Suppose that the error bound (4.11) holds true, where $\lambda(\alpha)$ is of the form (4.14). In addition, let (4.16), (4.17) and (4.20) be satisfied. Let the tuning parameter $0 < \sigma \leq 1$ used in the definition of the set M_δ, cf. (4.18), be chosen sufficiently small such that $(\sigma + 1)(1 + q^{-\varkappa}) \leq \tau_L$ holds. Then we have $M_\delta \subset H_\delta$.*

Proof. Let $\alpha = \alpha_k \in M_\delta$ and $1 \le j \le k$. Then $\alpha_j, \alpha_{j-1} \in M_\delta$, and thus

$$\begin{aligned}
\| x^\delta_{\alpha_j} - x^\delta_{\alpha_{j-1}} \|_X &\le \| x^\delta_{\alpha_j} - x^\dagger \|_X + \| x^\delta_{\alpha_{j-1}} - x^\dagger \|_X \\
&\le \varphi(\alpha_j) + \frac{\delta}{\lambda(\alpha_j)} + \varphi(\alpha_{j-1}) + \frac{\delta}{\lambda(\alpha_{j-1})} \\
&\le (\sigma+1)\Big(\frac{1}{\lambda(\alpha_j)} + \frac{1}{\lambda(\alpha_{j-1})}\Big)\delta = (\sigma+1)(1+q^{-\varkappa})\frac{\delta}{\lambda(\alpha_{j-1})} \\
&\le \tau_{\mathrm{L}} \frac{\delta}{\lambda(\alpha_{j-1})}.
\end{aligned}$$

Thus, each $\alpha \in M_\delta$ obeys the estimate in (4.21), and the proof is complete. □

Lemma 4.3.5 and the considerations at the end of Section 4.3.1 give rise to the following a posteriori choice of the parameter $\alpha = \alpha_*$:

$$\alpha_* = \max H_\delta. \tag{4.24}$$

Theorem 4.3.6 *Suppose that the error bound (4.11) holds true, where $\lambda(\alpha)$ is of the form (4.14). Let (4.16), (4.17), (4.19) and (4.20) be satisfied. Then the balancing principle (4.24) is quasi-optimal.*

Proof. The proof will distinguish three cases, and as a preparation we first prove the following assertion. For any $\alpha \in \Delta_\delta$ with $\alpha \le \alpha_*$, we have

$$\| x^\delta_{\alpha_*} - x^\dagger \|_X \le \varphi(\alpha) + c_8 \frac{\delta}{\lambda(\alpha)}, \tag{4.25}$$

where $c_8 = 1 + \frac{\tau_{\mathrm{L}}}{1-q^{-\varkappa}}$. In fact, there are indices $0 \le k \le N$ and $0 \le m \le N-k$, such that $\alpha = \alpha_k$ and $\alpha_* = \alpha_{k+m}$. We can bound

$$\begin{aligned}
\| x^\delta_{\alpha_*} - x^\dagger \|_X &\le \| x^\delta_{\alpha} - x^\dagger \|_X + \sum_{j=0}^{m-1} \| x^\delta_{\alpha_{k+j+1}} - x^\delta_{\alpha_{k+j}} \|_X \\
&\le \varphi(\alpha) + \frac{\delta}{\lambda(\alpha)} + \tau_{\mathrm{L}}\delta \sum_{j=0}^{m-1} \frac{1}{\lambda(\alpha_{k+j})} \\
&= \varphi(\alpha) + \frac{\delta}{\lambda(\alpha)} + \frac{\tau_{\mathrm{L}}\delta}{\lambda(\alpha)} \sum_{j=0}^{m-1} q^{-j\varkappa} \le \varphi(\alpha) + \Big(1 + \frac{\tau_{\mathrm{L}}}{1-q^{-\varkappa}}\Big)\frac{\delta}{\lambda(\alpha)}.
\end{aligned}$$

This proves (4.25) with constant c_8 as given.

We turn to the main part of the proof. Assume that $\sigma > 0$ is chosen as in Lemma 4.3.5. Clearly, $M_\delta \subset \Delta_\delta$.

Case (i) ($M_\delta \neq \varnothing$ and $M_\delta \neq \Delta_\delta$)

The property $M_\delta \neq \varnothing$ allows to consider

$$\alpha_+ := \max M_\delta. \tag{4.26}$$

From the definition of M_δ and the assumption $M_\delta \neq \Delta_\delta$, we obtain $(\varphi\lambda)(\alpha_+) \leq \sigma\delta \leq (\varphi\lambda)(q\alpha_+)$. Thus, by Lemma 4.3.3, the parameter α_+ satisfies an oracle inequality of the form (4.13). In addition, by Lemma 4.3.5 we have that $M_\delta \subset H_\delta$, such that the inequality $\alpha_+ \leq \alpha_*$ holds. Quasi-optimality of α_* under the current situation now immediately follows from the error estimate (4.25) applied with $\alpha = \alpha_+$.

Case (ii) ($M_\delta = \Delta_\delta$)

For α_+ given by (4.26), this in fact means $\alpha_+ = \alpha_* = \alpha_N$ and thus

$$(\varphi\lambda)(\alpha_*) \leq \sigma\delta. \tag{4.27}$$

For the lower bound of $(\varphi\lambda)(\alpha_*)$, we make use of $\alpha_* \geq c_6$ which implies that $\varphi(\alpha_*) \geq \varphi(c_6)$ as well as $\lambda(\alpha_*) \geq \lambda(c_6) = c_6^\varkappa / K_2$. We therefore arrive at

$$\delta \leq c_4(\varphi\lambda)(\alpha_*) \quad \text{with } c_4 = \frac{\delta_0 K_2}{\varphi(c_6)c_6^\varkappa}. \tag{4.28}$$

This implies that α_* satisfies an estimate of the form (4.15) and thus is quasi-optimal. This completes the considerations of the case (ii).

Case (iii) ($M_\delta = \varnothing$)

In this case we may consider $\alpha_+ := \alpha_0$. This by (4.19) means $\alpha_+ = \alpha_0 \leq c_5\delta^{1/\varkappa}$, and thus $\lambda(\alpha_+) \leq (c_5^\varkappa / K_2)\delta$ and $\varphi(\alpha_+) \leq \varphi(c_5\delta_0^{1/\varkappa})$. Then, by the definition of M_δ, we have

$$\sigma\delta \leq (\varphi\lambda)(\alpha_+) \leq \frac{c_5^\varkappa \varphi(c_5\delta_0^{1/\varkappa})}{K_2}\delta. \tag{4.29}$$

This implies that α_+ satisfies an estimate of the form (4.15) and thus also the oracle inequality (4.13). As in case (i), employing estimate (4.25), we deduce an estimate of the form (4.12) for α_* for this particular case.

The proof of the theorem is thus completed. □

Remark 4.3.7 *We stress that the case (i) considered in the above proof is prototypical. For, if the maximum noise level δ_0 is sufficiently small, the cases (ii) and (iii) cannot occur. This follows from the estimates (4.27) and (4.29), which lead to contradictions then, respectively. However, larger levels δ_0 give rise for the cases (ii) and (iii), respectively.*

Remark 4.3.8 *Lemma 4.3.5 and Theorem 4.3.6 also hold for the other two balancing principles given by the sets $\widetilde{H}_\delta$ and $\widehat{H}_\delta$, respectively. More precisely, the same range of balancing constants τ_L, cf. (4.20), and tuning parameters σ may be used. In the wording of Lemma 4.3.5, only H_δ has to be replaced by $\widehat{H}_\delta$ and $\widetilde{H}_\delta$, respectively. In (4.25) in the proof of Theorem 4.3.6, the constant c_8 may be reduced to $c_8 = 1 + \tau_L$, which in fact has an impact on the corresponding error constant c_2, cf. the discussion in Section 4.3.3 below.*

4.3.3 Discussion

We shall discuss several aspects concerning the balancing principles.

Comparison of the three considered variants of the balancing principle

We continue with a comparison of the considered variants of the balancing principle. Since we have

$$M_\delta \subset \widehat{H}_\delta \subset H_\delta, \qquad M_\delta \subset \widehat{H}_\delta \subset \widetilde{H}_\delta,$$

the latter balancing principle, which is related to the set $\widehat{H}_\delta$, seems to be superior to the other versions. In fact, the set $\widehat{H}_\delta$ it closer to the oracle set M_δ than the other two sets H_δ and $\widetilde{H}_\delta$. In addition, the latter version related to the set $\widehat{H}_\delta$ requires less computational complexity, since the number of x_α^δ to be computed does not exceed the related number for the other versions. Note that for the classical balancing principle related to the set $\widetilde{H}_\delta$, one always has to compute x_α^δ for each $\alpha \in \Delta_\delta$.

Oracle property of the parameter choices

It may be of interest to consider quasi-optimality-type estimates without assuming (4.19), in particular, the minimum value α_0, and the maximal α_N are misspecified. The following result is obtained as a corollary of Theorem 4.3.1 and its proof.

Corollary 4.3.9 *For any of the three considered variants of the balancing principle, we have*

$$\|x_{\alpha_*}^\delta - x^\dagger\|_X \le c_2 \inf_{\alpha_0 \le \alpha \le \alpha_N} \left(\varphi(\alpha) + \frac{\delta}{\lambda(\alpha)} \right),$$

where $c_2 > 0$ denotes some finite constant.

Proof. We consider the first balancing principle only. The proofs for the other two balancing principles are quite similar, and are left to the reader. Below, for different situations, we verify estimates of the form

$$\|x_{\alpha_*}^\delta - x^\dagger\|_X \le c_2 \inf_{\alpha \in \mathcal{I}} \left(\varphi(\alpha) + \frac{\delta}{\lambda(\alpha)} \right), \tag{4.30}$$

with appropriate intervals $\mathcal{I}$ and constants c_2, respectively. This in fact follows by a careful inspection of the proofs of Lemma 4.3.3 and Theorem 4.3.6. In the following considerations, σ denotes a constant satisfying the conditions of Lemma 4.3.5, and for the meaning of the constant c_8, we refer to (4.25).

For case (i) considered in Theorem 4.3.6, i.e., $M_\delta \neq \varnothing$ and $M_\delta \neq \Delta_\delta$, we have (4.30) with $\mathcal{I} = (0, \infty)$ and $c_2 = q^{\varkappa} \frac{\sigma + c_8}{\sigma}$.

For case (ii) in that theorem, i.e., $M_\delta = \Delta_\delta$, we have $\alpha_* = \alpha_+ = \alpha_N$ and $\varphi(\alpha_*) \leq \sigma \frac{\delta}{\lambda(\alpha_*)}$. The first part of the proof of Lemma 4.3.3, applied with $\rho = 1$, then gives (4.30) with $\mathcal{I} = (0, \alpha_N]$ and $c_2 = \sigma + c_8$.

Finally, for case (iii) considered in the theorem, i.e., $M_\delta = \varnothing$, we have $\alpha_+ = \alpha_0$ and $\varphi(\alpha_+) \geq \sigma \frac{\delta}{\lambda(\alpha_+)}$. The second part of the proof of Lemma 4.3.3 then gives (4.30) with $\mathcal{I} = [\alpha_0, \infty)$ and $c_2 = \frac{1}{\sigma}(\sigma + c_8)$. A combination of those three cases finally gives the statement of the corollary. □

The assertion of Corollary 4.3.9 may be considered as *oracle type*: If the range of parameters $[\alpha_0, \alpha_N]$ is not specified correctly, then the chosen parameter α_* is, up to the constant c_2, at least as good as the best value within the specified range.

Controlling the error constant

The following proposition specifies the error constant c_2 for each of the considered balancing principles.

Proposition 4.3.10 *Let the maximum noise level δ_0 be sufficiently small, and in addition, let (4.17), (4.19) and (4.20) be satisfied. Then the error constant may be chosen as*

$$c_2 = q^{\varkappa} \frac{\sigma + c_8}{\sigma}, \tag{4.31}$$

where $\sigma \leq \min\{\frac{\tau_L}{1+q^{-\varkappa}} - 1, 1\}$. In addition, $c_8 := 1 + \frac{\tau_L}{1-q^{-\varkappa}}$ for the balancing principle (4.21), and $c_8 := 1 + \tau_L$ for the versions from (4.22) and (4.23), respectively.

Proof. Under the given assumptions on δ_0, case (i) in the proof of Theorem 4.3.6 applies, i.e., we have $M_\delta \neq \varnothing$ and $M_\delta \neq \Delta_\delta$ there. For α_+ as in (4.26), an application of the estimate in (4.25) for $\alpha = \alpha_+$, and a careful inspection of the proof of Lemma 4.3.3 gives

$$\begin{aligned} \| x_{\alpha_*}^\delta - x^\dagger \|_X &\leq \max \Big\{ \Big(1 + \frac{q^{\varkappa} c_8}{\sigma} \Big) \varphi(\alpha),\, q^{\varkappa} (\sigma + c_8) \frac{\delta}{\lambda(\alpha)} \Big\} \\ &\leq q^{\varkappa} \frac{\sigma + c_8}{\sigma} \Big(\varphi(\alpha) + \frac{\delta}{\lambda(\alpha)} \Big) \qquad (\alpha > 0). \end{aligned} \tag{4.32}$$

For the balancing principle (4.21) this was shown to hold for $c_8 = 1 + \frac{\tau_L}{1-q^{-\varkappa}}$. For the balancing principles from (4.22) and (4.23) the reasoning in Theorem 4.3.6

simplifies, and the bound (4.25) holds with $c_8 := 1 + \tau_L$. This completes the sketch of this proof.

We note that the special form of σ considered in Proposition 4.3.10 is caused by the requirement made in Lemma 4.3.5.

We next discuss the optimal choice of the parameters used in the balancing principle (4.24) to minimize the error constant c_2. First, we consider the spacing parameter $q > 1$ to be fixed. Thus, in order to minimize c_2 we need to consider $\frac{\sigma + c_8}{\sigma}$ only. The constant c_8, as a function of τ_L is monotone, such that the smallest possible value of τ_L minimizes c_8, and, taking into account the requirements in Lemma 4.3.5, we let $\tau_L(q^{\varkappa}) := (\sigma + 1)(1 + q^{-\varkappa})$. Now we need to distinguish the values for c_8 as indicated in Proposition 4.3.10. For the first balancing principle, based on (4.21), we find that

$$c_2 = q^{\varkappa}\frac{\sigma + c_8}{\sigma} = \frac{\sigma + 1}{\sigma}\frac{2q^{\varkappa}}{1 - q^{-\varkappa}} \geq \frac{4q^{\varkappa}}{1 - q^{-\varkappa}},$$

the latter being achieved for $\sigma = 1$. This can further be optimized with respect to the spacing parameter q, and it is minimized for $q^{\varkappa} = q_{\text{opt}}^{\varkappa} := 2$. With these specifications we find that

$$\tau_{L,\text{opt}} = 3, \quad \text{and} \quad c_{2,\text{opt}} = 16.$$

We next consider the size of the error constants of the other two balancing principles related with the sets given by (4.22) and (4.23), respectively. In either case, the error constant c_2 is again of the form (4.31), with $c_8 = 1 + \tau_L$.

Thus, for $\tau_L = (\sigma + 1)(1 + q^{-\varkappa})$ we have that

$$c_2 = q^{\varkappa}\frac{\sigma + c_8}{\sigma} = q^{\varkappa}\frac{\sigma + 1}{\sigma}(2 + q^{-\varkappa}).$$

Again, this is minimized for $\sigma := 1$, and it gives

$$c_{2,\text{opt}} = 2\,(2q^{\varkappa} + 1) \tag{4.33}$$

with corresponding $\tau_{L,\text{opt}} = 2(1 + q^{-\varkappa}) < 4$. This means that the error constant becomes smaller as the grid Δ_δ becomes finer, with $c_2 \to 6$ as $q \to 1$. For the best grid independent choice of the parameter τ_L, we find that $\tau_L = 4$, and hence we recover the original Lepskiĭ principle with constant $c_2 = 6q^{\varkappa}$.

Remark 4.3.11 *The quasi-optimality results for all three methods considered in the present work can also be written in the frequently used form*

$$\|x_{\alpha_*}^{\delta} - x^{\dagger}\|_X \leq c_2\varphi(\alpha_+), \tag{4.34}$$

where the parameter $\alpha_+ > 0$ satisfies $\varphi(\alpha_+) = \frac{\delta}{\lambda(\alpha_+)}$, and the error constant c_2 is given by (4.31). This can be seen by considering estimate (4.32) in the proof of

Proposition 4.3.10. Note that we have $\varphi(\alpha_+) \le \inf_{\alpha>0}(\varphi(\alpha) + \frac{\delta}{\lambda(\alpha)}) \le 2\varphi(\alpha_+)$, *so quasi-optimality is in fact equivalent to (4.34) for some constant* c_2.

For the standard balancing principle (4.22), utilized with the traditional balancing constant $\tau_L = 4$, *the error constant in estimate (4.34) takes the form* $c_2 = 6q^{\varkappa}$,*which is a well-known result, cf., e.g., [17, 21]. The above discussion shows that the error constant* c_2 *in (4.34) can be reduced to the form (4.33) by choosing* τ_L *somewhat smaller.*

4.3.4 Specific Impact on Oversmoothing Penalties

After the presentation of various facets of the general theory for balancing principles in the preceding paragraphs of this section, we return to the specific situation of oversmoothing penalties as outlined in Sections 4.1 and 4.2. To characterize the impact of the general theory on that situation, we recall the error estimate (4.6) with the specific index function $\lambda(\alpha) = \frac{1}{K_2}\alpha^{a/(2a+2)}$ and with the specific constant $K_2 = \max\{1, \frac{2}{c_a}\}$.

In Examples 4.2.3 and 4.2.4 we have explicitly described a priori parameter choice rules as well as the discrepancy principle as an a posteriori choice rule. For the nonlinear inverse problem (4.1) at hand, the corresponding convergence rates are given in (4.9) for the Hölder case, and (4.10) for the logarithmic case. Here, we complement those rate results by analog assertions for the balancing principles. The results are based on the quasi-optimality of the balancing principles under consideration, in connection with the first part of Proposition 4.3.2.

In case that no explicit smoothness for the solution of the nonlinear inverse problem (4.1) is available, we note that any quasi-optimal rule for Tikhonov regularization with oversmoothing penalty yields convergence. For B^{-1} compact, this can be seen by consulting Example 4.2.5 and the second part of Proposition 4.3.2.

We briefly summarize the impact of the theory of the first balancing principle (4.24), when applied to nonlinear Tikhonov regularization with oversmoothing penalty, by the following corollary. Note that the assertions of the corollary can be formulated in an analog manner for the other two balancing principles, and we refer to Remark 4.3.8 above.

Corollary 4.3.12 *Consider nonlinear Tikhonov regularization with oversmoothing penalty as introduced in Sections 4.1 and 4.2, with the regularization parameter* α_* *determined by the balancing principle (4.24) under the required conditions (4.19) and (4.20). For Hölder-type smoothness (4.8) as considered in Example 4.2.3, with* $0 < p \le 1$, *one has*

$$\|x^\delta_{\alpha_*} - x^\dagger\|_X = \mathcal{O}(\delta^{\frac{p}{a+p}}) \quad \text{as } \delta \to 0.$$

Similarly, for logarithmic source conditions as considered in Example 4.2.4, we obtain logarithmic rates

$$\|x^{\delta}_{\alpha_*} - x^{\dagger}\|_X = \mathcal{O}(\log^{-\mu}(1/\delta)) \quad as \;\; \delta \to 0.$$

Proof. This is an immediate consequence of quasi-optimality of the balancing principle (4.24), and of the convergence rate results in Examples 4.2.3 and 4.2.4 in connection with the first part of Proposition 4.3.2. □

We explicitly highlight the following fact, intrinsic in the proof: If the parameter $\alpha_*(\delta)$, obtained by the a priori choice, cf. Examples 4.2.3–4.2.5, is in the interval $[\alpha_0(\delta), \alpha_N(\delta)]$, then the corresponding convergence rates for the parameter choice according to the balancing principle are valid. Otherwise Corollary 4.3.9 applies.

As already noticed, the study [23] by Pricop-Jeckstadt is close to our approach on balancing principles. However, it does not include the case of oversmoothing penalties, a gap which is closed here. Despite the fact that the nonlinearity requirements of [23] are slightly different, the main difference lies in the following fact: The proofs (for the non-oversmoothing case) in ibid. are based on an error decomposition into a noise amplification error, and a bias that occurs when the data are noise-free. This technique fails in the oversmoothing case, where instead a certain auxiliary element is used.

4.4 Exponential Growth Model: Properties and Numerical Case Study

For a case study we shall collect the theoretical properties of the exponential growth model, first presented in [4, Section 3.1]. More details about properties of the nonlinear forward map F as in (4.36), below, can be found in [6]. Then we highlight different behavior for the reconstruction in the oversmoothing and non-oversmoothing cases, respectively.

4.4.1 *Properties*

For analytical and numerical studies we are going to exploit the exponential growth model

$$y'(t) = x(t)\,y(t) \quad (0 \le t \le 1), \qquad y(0) = 1, \tag{4.35}$$

considered in the Hilbert space $L^2(0,1)$. The inverse problem consists in the identification of the square-integrable time-dependent function $x(t)$ $(0 \le t \le 1)$ in (4.35) from noisy data $y^{\delta} \in L^2(0,1)$ of the solution $y(t)$ $(0 \le t \le 1)$ to the corresponding initial value O.D.E. problem. In this context, we suppose a deterministic noise model $\|y^{\delta} - y\|_{L^2(0,1)} \le \delta$ with noise level $\delta > 0$. This identification problem can be written in form of an operator equation (4.1) with the nonlinear forward operator

$$[F(x)](t) = \exp\left(\int_0^t x(\tau)d\tau\right) \qquad (0 \le t \le 1) \tag{4.36}$$

mapping in $L^2(0,1)$ with full domain $\mathcal{D}(F) = L^2(0,1)$.

Evidently, F is globally *injective*. One can also show on the one hand that F is *weakly sequentially continuous* and on the other hand that F is *Fréchet differentiable* everywhere. It possesses for all $x \in L^2(0,1)$ the Fréchet derivative $F'(x)$, explicitly given as

$$[F'(x)h](t) = [F(x)](t) \int_0^t h(\tau)d\tau \quad (0 \le t \le 1,\ h \in L^2(0,1)). \tag{4.37}$$

This Fréchet derivative is a compact linear operator mapping in $L^2(0,1)$, because it is a composition $F'(x) = M \circ J$ of the bounded linear multiplication operator M mapping in $L^2(0,1)$ defined as $[Mg](t) = [F(x)](t)\, g(t)$ $(0 \le t \le 1)$ and the compact linear integration operator J mapping in $L^2(0,1)$ defined as

$$[Jh](t) = \int_0^t h(\tau)d\tau \quad (0 \le t \le 1). \tag{4.38}$$

We mention that the continuous multiplier function $F(x)$ in M is bounded below and above by finite positive values due to

$$\exp(-\|x\|_{L^2(0,1)}) \le [F(x)](t) \le \exp(\|x\|_{L^2(0,1)}) \quad (0 \le t \le 1,\ x \in L^2(0,1)), \tag{4.39}$$

and hence $F(x) \in L^\infty(0,1)$.

Let us denote by

$$\mathcal{B}_r(x^\dagger) = \{z \in L^2(0,1) : \|z - x^\dagger\|_{L^2(0,1)} \le r\},$$

the closed ball with radius $r > 0$ and center $x^\dagger$.

The following lemma highlights, that F satisfies a nonlinearity condition of tangential cone-type.

Lemma 4.4.1 *For the nonlinear operator F from (4.36), the inequality*

$$\|F(x) - F(x^\dagger) - F'(x^\dagger)(x - x^\dagger)\|_{L^2(0,1)} \le \|x - x^\dagger\|_{L^2(0,1)}\, \|F(x) - F(x^\dagger)\|_{L^2(0,1)} \tag{4.40}$$

is valid for all $x, x^\dagger \in L^2(0,1)$. Consequently, we have for arbitrary but fixed $r > 0$ and $x^\dagger \in L^2(0,1)$ the inequality

$$\frac{1}{1+r}\|F'(x^\dagger)(x - x^\dagger)\|_{L^2(0,1)} \le \|F(x) - F(x^\dagger)\|_{L^2(0,1)} \tag{4.41}$$

for all $x \in \mathcal{B}_r(x^\dagger)$. *Moreover, whenever* $0 < r < 1$ *we have that*

$$\|F(x) - F(x^\dagger)\|_{L^2(0,1)} \le \frac{1}{1-r} \|F'(x^\dagger)(x - x^\dagger)\|_{L^2(0,1)} \tag{4.42}$$

for all $x \in \mathcal{B}_r(x^\dagger)$.

Proof. By setting $\theta(t) := [J(x - x^\dagger)](t)$ $(0 \le t \le 1)$ we have

$$[F(x) - F(x^\dagger)](t) = [F(x^\dagger)](t)\,(\exp(\theta(t)) - 1)$$

and

$$[F(x) - F(x^\dagger) - F'(x^\dagger)(x - x^\dagger)](t) = [F(x^\dagger)](t)\,(\exp(\theta(t)) - 1 - \theta(t)).$$

Then the general estimate

$$|\exp(\theta) - 1 - \theta| \le |\theta|\,|\exp(\theta) - 1|,$$

which is valid for all $-\infty < \theta < +\infty$, leads to

$$|[F(x) - F(x^\dagger) - F'(x^\dagger)(x - x^\dagger)](t)| \le |\theta(t)|\,|[F(x) - F(x^\dagger)](t)| \quad (0 \le t \le 1).$$

By using the Cauchy–Schwarz inequality this implies

$$|[F(x) - F(x^\dagger) - F'(x^\dagger)(x - x^\dagger)](t)| \le \|x - x^\dagger\|_{L^2(0,1)}\,|[F(x) - F(x^\dagger)](t)| \quad (0 \le t \le 1).$$

This yields the inequality (4.40). Both inequalities (4.41) and (4.42) are immediate consequences by applying the triangle inequality. The proof of the lemma is complete. □

We are going to establish that the forward operator F from (4.36) obeys the nonlinearity condition (4.3). To this end we use the Hilbert scale model as introduced in Section 4.1.1. Here, the Hilbert scale $\{X_\tau\}_{\tau \in \mathbb{R}}$ with $X_0 = X = L^2(0,1)$, $X_\tau = \mathcal{D}(B^\tau)$ for $\tau > 0$ and $X_\tau = X$ for $\tau < 0$, is generated by the unbounded, self-adjoint, and positive definite linear operator

$$B := (J^* J)^{-1/2} \tag{4.43}$$

induced by the integration operator J from (4.38). The domain $\mathcal{D}(B)$ of B is dense in $L^2(0,1)$ and its range $\mathcal{R}(B)$ coincides with $L^2(0,1)$. For each $\tau \in \mathbb{R}$ one can define the norm

$$\|x\|_\tau := \|B^\tau x\|_{L^2(0,1)} \quad \text{defined for all} \quad x \in X_\tau.$$

The powers of B are linked to the powers of J. By analyzing the Riemann–Liouville fractional integral operator J^p for levels p from the interval $(0,1]$ we have that

$$X_p = \mathcal{D}(B^p) = \mathcal{R}((J^* J)^{p/2}) \quad \text{for} \quad 0 < p \le 1.$$

Due to [3, Lemma 8] this gives the explicit representation

$$X_p = \begin{cases} H^p(0,1) & \text{for} \quad 0 < p < \frac{1}{2} \\ \{x \in H^{\frac{1}{2}}(0,1) : \int\limits_0^1 \frac{|x(t)|^2}{1-t} dt < \infty\} & \text{for} \quad p = \frac{1}{2} \\ \{x \in H^p(0,1) : x(1) = 0\} & \text{for} \quad \frac{1}{2} < p \leq 1 \end{cases}, \tag{4.44}$$

where $H^p(0,1)$ denotes the corresponding fractional hilbertian Sobolev space. Note that for $0 < p < \frac{1}{2}$ the spaces X_p and the hilbertian Sobolev spaces $H^p(0,1)$ coincide, whereas for $p > \frac{1}{2}$ an additional homogeneous boundary condition occurs at the right end of the interval.

Using the Hilbert scale introduced above we have collected now all ingredients for verifying an inequality chain of type (4.3) with a degree $a = 1$ of ill-posedness.

We start with

$$\|Jh\|_{L^2(0,1)} = \|(J^*J)^{1/2}h\|_{L^2(0,1)} = \|B^{-1}h\|_{L^2(0,1)} = \|h\|_{-1} \quad \text{for all} \quad h \in L^2(0,1)$$

and aim at applying Lemma 4.4.1. In this context, we set on the one hand $k_0 := \exp(-\|x^\dagger\|_{L^2(0,1)})$, $K_0 := \exp(\|x^\dagger\|_{L^2(0,1)})$ and on the other hand $c_1 := \frac{k_0}{1+r}$ and $C_1 := \frac{K_0}{1-r}$. Then we have $0 < k_0 \leq [F(x^\dagger)](t) \leq K_0 < \infty$ from (4.39). By using formula (4.37) we obtain, for all $r > 0$ and arbitrary $x^\dagger \in L^2(0,1)$, the left-side estimate

$$c_1\|x - x^\dagger\|_{-1} = \frac{k_0}{1+r}\|J(x - x^\dagger)\|_{L^2(0,1)} \leq \frac{1}{1+r}\|F'(x^\dagger)(x - x^\dagger)\|_{L^2(0,1)} \tag{4.45}$$

whenever $x \in \mathcal{B}_r(x^\dagger)$. In the same manner one deduces that, for all $0 < r < 1$ and arbitrary $x^\dagger \in L^2(0,1)$, the right-side estimate

$$\frac{1}{1-r}\|F'(x^\dagger)(x - x^\dagger)\|_{L^2(0,1)} \leq \frac{K_0}{1-r}\|J(x - x^\dagger)\|_{L^2(0,1)} = C_1\|x - x^\dagger\|_{-1}$$

holds true whenever $x \in \mathcal{B}_r(x^\dagger)$. By Lemma 4.4.1 this yields the inequality chain

$$c_1\|x - x^\dagger\|_{-1} \leq \|F(x) - F(x^\dagger)\|_{L^2(0,1)} \leq C_1\|x - x^\dagger\|_{-1} \text{ for } x \in \mathcal{B}_r(x^\dagger)\ (0 < r < 1),$$

which proves the assertion of the following proposition.

Proposition 4.4.2 *For $X = Y = L^2(0,1)$ we consider the nonlinear operator F from (4.36). Its domain $\mathcal{D}(F)$ is restricted to a closed ball $\mathcal{B}_r(x^\dagger)$ around some element $x^\dagger \in X$, and with radius $r < 1$.*

Within the Hilbert scale generated by the operator B from (4.43), induced by the integration operator J from (4.38), the operator F obeys the nonlinearity condition (4.3) with $a = 1$. The positive constants c_1 and C_1 depend on $x^\dagger$ and r.

Next we discuss assertions on missing stability and well-posedness for the operator equation (4.1).

Proposition 4.4.3 *For arbitrary solution $x^\dagger \in L^2(0,1)$ the operator equation (4.1) with $F : \mathcal{D}(F) = X = L^2(0,1) \to Y = L^2(0,1)$ from (4.36) is locally ill-posed (cf. [12, Definition 3]). It is not stably solvable at y (cf. [12, Definition 1]) for arbitrary right-hand element $y \in \mathcal{R}(F) := \{z \in L^2(0,1) : z = F(\xi),\ \xi \in L^2(0,1)\}$ from the range of F.*

Proof. One can easily show that, as a consequence of the compactness of J in $L^2(0,1)$, the operator $F : \mathcal{D}(F) = X = L^2(0,1) \to Y = L^2(0,1)$ from (4.36) is *strongly continuous* in the sense of Definition 26.1 (c) from [28]. Thus weakly convergent sequences $x_n \rightharpoonup x_0$ in $L^2(0,1)$ imply norm convergent image sequences such that $\lim_{n\to\infty} \|F(x_n) - F(x_0)\|_{L^2(0,1)} = 0$. For any orthonormal system $\{e_n\}_{n=1}^\infty$ in $L^2(0,1)$ and any radius $r > 0$ we then have $x_n = x^\dagger + re_n \rightharpoonup x^\dagger$, $x_n \in \mathcal{B}_r(x^\dagger)$, and $\lim_{n\to\infty} \|F(x_n) - F(x_0)\|_{L^2(0,1)} = 0$. On the one hand this proves the local ill-posedness at $x^\dagger$. On the other hand, since F is injective with the inverse operator $F^{-1} : \mathcal{R}(F) \subset L^2(0,1) \to L^2(0,1)$, the mapping F^{-1} cannot be continuous at $y = F(x^\dagger)$, which contradicts the stable solvability of the operator equation at y. The proof is complete. □

Note that for injective forward operators stable solvability and continuity of the inverse operator coincide. Moreover note that in the Hilbert space $L^2(0,1)$ the strong continuity of F implies that F is compact (cf. [28, Proposition 26.2]).

Remark 4.4.4 *Due to the local ill-posedness of F defined by formula (4.36) and mapping from $X_0 = X = L^2(0,1)$ to $Y = L^2(0,1)$ with the associated norm topologies, we have that for arbitrarily small $r > 0$ there is no constant $c_0 > 0$ such that*

$$c_0 \|x - x^\dagger\|_{L^2(0,1)} \le \|F(x) - F(x^\dagger)\|_{L^2(0,1)} \text{ for all } x \in \mathcal{B}_r(x^\dagger).$$

However, if the weaker X_{-1}-norm $\|\cdot\|_{-1} = \|B^{-1}\cdot\|_{L^2(0,1)} = \|J\cdot\|_{L^2(0,1)}$ applies for the pre-image space of F, one can see from the estimates (4.41) and (4.45) that for all $r > 0$ there exists a constant $c_1 > 0$ depending on $x^\dagger$ and r such that

$$c_1 \|x - x^\dagger\|_{-1} \le \|F(x) - F(x^\dagger)\|_{L^2(0,1)} \text{ for all } x \in \mathcal{B}_r(x^\dagger),$$

which proves that (4.1) is locally well-posed everywhere for that norm pairing. For the convergence theory of Tikhonov regularization in Hilbert scales in case of oversmoothing penalties, however, this requires an a priori restriction of the domain $\mathcal{D}(F)$ to bounded sets (balls), because (4.3) is originally needed in [13] with respect to that example with the full domain $\mathcal{D}(F) = L^2(0,1)$.

On the other hand, there exists no global constant $c_1 > 0$ depending only on $x^\dagger$ such that $c_1 \|x - x^\dagger\|_{-1} \le \|F(x) - F(x^\dagger)\|_{L^2(0,1)}$ for each $x \in L^2(0,1)$. This follows, for any $x^\dagger$, by considering, e.g., the functions

$$x(t) = x_n(t) \equiv -n \text{ for } n = 1, 2, \ldots .$$

In fact, we then have $[Jx_n](t) = -nt$ *and* $[F(x_n)](t) = \exp(-nt)$, *and thus*

$$\|Fx_n\|^2_{L^2(0,1)} = \frac{1}{2n}(1-e^{-2n}) \to 0, \quad \text{but } \|x_n\|_{-1} = \|Jx_n\|_{L^2(0,1)} = \frac{n}{\sqrt{3}} \to \infty,$$

as $n \to \infty$.

The restriction to a small ball with radius $r < 1$ *for the right-hand inequality of (4.3), as caused by the condition (4.42), is not problematic for the theory (cf. [9, 13]). This part is only used by auxiliary elements that are close to* $x^\dagger$ *for sufficiently small regularization parameters* $\alpha > 0$ *whenever* $x^\dagger$ *is supposed to be an interior point of* $\mathcal{D}(F)$, *which is trivial for* $\mathcal{D}(F) = X$.

The character of ill-posedness of the operator equation (4.1) with F from (4.36) can be illustrated at the exact solution

$$x^\dagger(t) \equiv 1 \quad (0 \le t \le 1), \tag{4.46}$$

which will be used in the numerical study below. In this case we have $[F(x^\dagger)](t) = \exp(t)$ $(0 \le t \le 1)$. If we perturb this exact right-hand side by a continuously differentiable noise function $\eta(t)$ $(0 \le t \le 1)$ with $\eta(0) = 0$, then the pre-image of $F(x^\dagger) + \eta$ attains the explicit form

$$x_\eta(t) = \frac{\exp(t) + \eta'(t)}{\exp(t) + \eta(t)} \quad (0 \le t \le 1).$$

In particular, for $\eta(t) = \delta \sin(nt)$ $(0 \le t \le 1)$ with multiplier $\delta > 0$ and $\|\eta\|_{L^2(0,1)} \le \delta$ we have $x_\eta = x_n$ defined as

$$x_n(t) = \frac{\exp(t) + n\,\delta\,\cos(nt)}{\exp(t) + \delta\,\sin(nt)} \quad (0 \le t \le 1), \tag{4.47}$$

as well as $\|F(x_n) - F(x^\dagger)\|_{L^2(0,1)} \le \delta$ for all $n \in \mathbb{N}$ and $\delta > 0$. The next proposition emphasizes for F from (4.36) that in spite of very small image deviations $\|F(x) - F(x^\dagger)\|_{L^2(0,1)}$ the corresponding error norm $\|x - x^\dagger\|_{L^2(0,1)}$ can be arbitrarily large.

Proposition 4.4.5 *For arbitrarily small* $\delta > 0$ *the pre-image set* $F^{-1}(\mathcal{B}_\delta(F(x^\dagger)))$ *for* $x^\dagger$ *from (4.46) is not bounded in* $L^2(0,1)$, *i.e., there exist sequences* $\{x_n\}_{n=1}^\infty \subset F^{-1}(\mathcal{B}_\delta(F(x^\dagger)))$ *with* $\lim_{n\to\infty} \|x_n\|_{L^2(0,1)} = +\infty$.

Proof. To this end we shall use the explicit sequence $\{x_n\}_{n=1}^\infty$ from (4.47), for which the estimate

$$\|x_n\|^2_{L^2(0,1)} = \int_0^1 \frac{(\exp(t) + n\,\delta\,\cos(nt))^2}{(\exp(t) + \delta\,\sin(nt))^2}\,dt = \int_0^1 \frac{(1 + n\,\delta\,\frac{\cos(nt)}{\exp(t)})^2}{(1 + \delta\,\frac{\sin(nt)}{\exp(t)})^2}\,dt$$

$$\geq \frac{n^2\delta^2 \int_0^1 (\cos(nt))^2 dt}{e^2(1+\delta)^2} = \frac{n^2\delta^2}{e^2(1+\delta)^2}\left(\frac{1}{2} + \frac{\sin(n)\cos(n)}{2n}\right)$$

holds true. Consequently, we have $\|x_n\|_{L^2(0,1)} \geq \frac{n\delta}{2e(1+\delta)}$ for sufficiently large $n \in \mathbb{N}$, such that $\lim_{n\to\infty} \|x_n\|_{L^2(0,1)} = +\infty$. □

4.4.2 Numerical Case Study

The following numerical case study operates in the setting of Section 4.4.1 and complements the theoretical results. Therefore we minimize the Tikhonov functional of type (4.2) with $\bar{x} = 0$ and forward operator (4.36) derived from the exponential growth model. Recall that the inequality chain (4.3) holds with degree of ill-posedness $a = 1$. Further, set $X = Y = L^2(0,1)$. To obtain the X_1-norm in the penalty, use $\|\cdot\|_1 = \|\cdot\|_{H^1(0,1)}$ and additionally enforce the boundary condition $x(1) = 0$ in accordance with the construction of the Hilbert scale (4.44). In all experiments we use the exact solution $x^\dagger(t) = 1$ $(0 < t \leq 1)$. As this particular exact solution is smooth, but violates the boundary condition $x^\dagger(1) = 0$, we have $x^\dagger \in X_p$ for all $0 < p < \frac{1}{2}$. This means, a Hölder-type source condition as outlined in Example 4.2.3 holds. A discretization level of $N = 1000$ in the time domain is used. The noise is then constructed by sampling one realization of a vector $\xi = (\xi_1, \dots, \xi_{1000})$ of 1000 i.i.d. standard Gaussian random variables. This is then normalized to have $\|\xi\|_{L^2(0,1)} = 1$, and $\delta\xi$ added to the exact data y. For noise level δ this yields $\|y - y^\delta\|_Y = \delta$. The minimization problem itself is solved using the MATLAB®-routine `fmincon`. Integrals are discretized using the trapezoid rule.

Further, a modification of the first variant (4.21) of the balancing principle is implemented. Precisely, we modify H_δ introduced in formula (4.21) as

$$H_\delta^{mod} := \left\{ \alpha_k \in \Delta_\delta : \|x_{\alpha_j}^\delta - x_{\alpha_{j-1}}^\delta\|_X \leq C_{BP} \frac{\delta}{\alpha_{j-1}^{a/(2a+2)}} \text{ for any } 1 \leq j \leq k \right\}. \tag{4.48}$$

This is necessary, because the constant K_2, which is required to be known in (4.14), is not available. So, we use the constant C_{BP} as a replacement for $\tau_L K_2$, instead. Then we set $\alpha_* = \alpha_{BP} := \max H_\delta^{mod}$.

Since $x^\dagger$ is known we can compute the regularization errors $\|x_\alpha^\delta - x^\dagger\|_X$. This can be interpreted as a function of δ and justifies a regression for the model function

$$\|x_\alpha^\delta - x^\dagger\|_X \leq c_x \delta^{\kappa_x}. \tag{4.49}$$

Similarly we estimate the asymptotic behavior of the selected regularization parameter through the ansatz

$$\alpha \sim c_\alpha \delta^{\kappa_\alpha}. \tag{4.50}$$

Both exponents κ_x and κ_α as well as the corresponding multipliers c_x and c_α are obtained using a least squares regression based on samples for varying δ.

In a first case study we consider several constants C_{BP} used in the balancing principle, the results of which are displayed in Table 4.1. Recall the results of Theorem 4.2.2 as well as Example 4.2.3: if a Hölder-type source condition holds, we expect $\kappa_x = \frac{p}{a+p}$. As $a = 1$ and $p \approx \frac{1}{2}$, this corresponds very well with the numerical observations in the third column of Table 4.1. Further recall the a priori parameter choice $\alpha_* = \delta^{\frac{2a+2}{a+p}}$, which here reads as $\alpha_* = \delta^{\frac{8}{3}}$. The fifth column of Table 4.1 shows the resulting $\alpha-$rates for the balancing principle. We therefore conclude that the resulting rates coincide with this particular a priori choice.

Table 4.1: Exponential growth model with $x^\dagger(t) \equiv 1$; $(0 < t \leq 1)$. Numerically computed results for the balancing principle (4.21) yielding multipliers and exponents of regularization error (4.49) and α-rates (4.50) for various C_{BP}.

C_{BP}	c_x	κ_x	c_α	κ_α
0.02	0.5275	0.3373	3.3750	3.0000
0.05	0.5241	0.3337	2.2241	2.8613
0.1	0.7188	0.3426	5.8352	2.5925

Figure 4.1 shows the realized regularization parameters α_{BP} (left) obtained by the balancing principle and the corresponding regularization errors (right) as well as their respective approximations. We observe an excellent fit which confirms our confidence in this approach, and in the implementation.

Next we fix the noise level δ and compare various parameter choice rules. Besides the balancing principle, we consider a discrepancy principle, where the

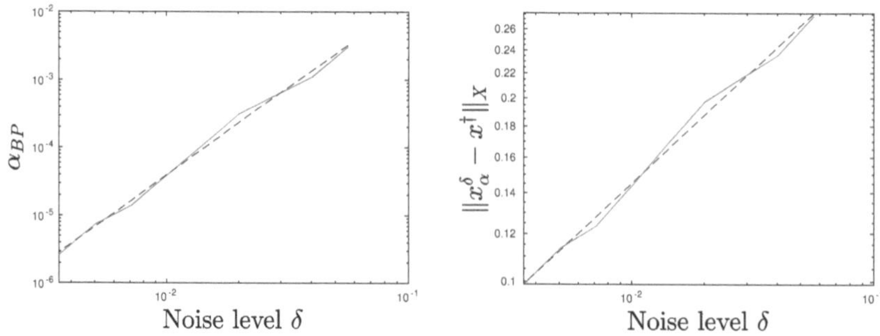

Figure 4.1: Exponential growth model with $x^\dagger(t) \equiv 1$; $(0 < t \leq 1)$ and parameter choice using the balancing principle (4.21) with $C_{BP} = 0.1$. α_{BP} in red for various δ and best approximating regression line in blue/dashed on a log-log scale (left) and approximation error $\|x_\alpha^\delta - x^\dagger\|_X$ in red and approximate rate in blue/dashed (right).

parameter is chosen a posteriori such that

$$\|F(x_\alpha^\delta) - y^\delta\|_Y = C_{DP}\,\delta \tag{4.51}$$

for given noise level δ and suitable constant $C_{DP} > 0$. Recall, that this parameter choice rule also yields the order optimal convergence rate. Additionally we study the heuristic parameter choice originally developed by Tikhonov, Glasko and Leonov* [15, 27] violating the Bakushinskij veto established in [1]. Hence we consider a sequence of regularization parameters

$$\alpha_k = \alpha_0 q^k : \; k = 0, 1, \ldots, M \tag{4.52}$$

for $q > 0$, some suitable α_0 and appropriate M. Here, $x_{\alpha_k}^\delta$ denotes the regularized solutions to the functional (4.2) with regularization parameter α_k. Using the series of parameters (4.52) the suitable regularization parameter according to this parameter choice rule is then chosen by minimizing

$$\|x_{\alpha_{k+1}}^\delta - x_{\alpha_k}^\delta\|_X \to \min \quad 1 \le k \le M-1$$

with respect to α_k. Moreover consider α_{opt} which minimizes the error $\|x_\alpha^\delta - x^\dagger\|_X$, i.e.,

$$\alpha_{\text{opt}} := \min_{\alpha} \|x_\alpha^\delta - x^\dagger\|_X \tag{4.53}$$

assuming the exact solution is known.

All of the above parameter choices are visualized in Figure 4.2 for $\delta = 0.0179$. Regularization error $\|x_\alpha^\delta - x^\dagger\|_X$ and the term $\|x_{\alpha_i}^\delta - x_{\alpha_{i-1}}^\delta\|_X$ are plotted for various regularization parameters on a log-log scale. Their respective minima are marked as parameter choices α_{opt} and α_{QO}. The colored graphs correspond to the right hand term of the balancing principle (4.48) for different choices of C_{BP}. The parameter choice rule can then be interpreted in the following way: the balancing principle chooses the largest regularization parameter from the admissible set, such that the left hand term in (4.48) is less or equal to the right hand side. Visually speaking this means choosing the regularization parameter at the intersect or just below the intersect of the blue and colored lines, again depending on C_{BP}. Larger C_{BP} leads to larger regularization parameters and vice versa. The resulting parameters for parameter choice using the discrepancy principle and the respective regularization error are also marked for various C_{DP}.

In this situation, with fixed noise level, we observe that the heuristic parameter choice α_{QO} performs surprisingly well. Parameter choice using the discrepancy principle follows our intuition: for smaller constants C_{DP} the regularization error decreases and vice versa. The success of the balancing principle highly

*The authors in the respective publications call this parameter choice quasioptimality. In order to avoid ambiguity with respect to Definition 4.3.1 we avoid this terminology here, but denote the resulting regularization parameter as α_{QO}.

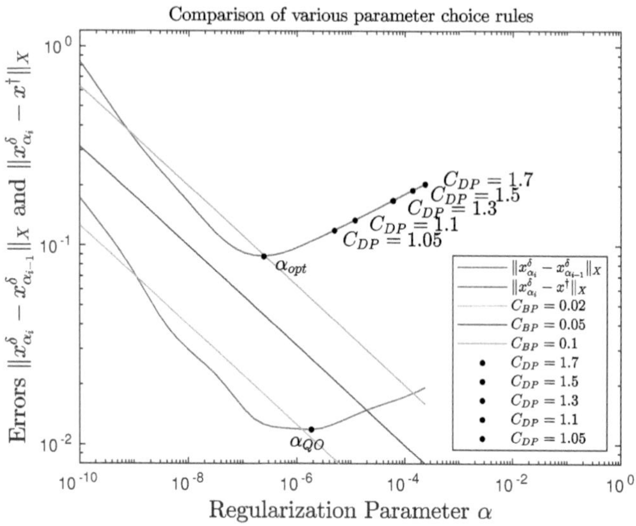

Figure 4.2: Exponential growth model with $x^\dagger(t) \equiv 1$; $(0 < t \leq 1)$ and $\delta = 0.0179$. Visualization of $\|x^\delta_{\alpha_{k+1}} - x^\delta_{\alpha_k}\|_X$ and $\|x^\delta_\alpha - x^\dagger\|_X$ as well as parameter choice using the balancing principle, discrepancy principle, quasi-optimality and α_{opt} for various C_{BP} and C_{DP}.

depends on the choice C_{BP}. Although theoretical results on the choice of this constant exist it is difficult to choose this accordingly in practice.

Finally, we highlight the differences between oversmoothing to non-oversmoothing penalties. We therefore remain in the same setting and consider regularized solutions $x^\dagger(t) \equiv 1$ $(0 < t \leq 1)$ with $x^\dagger \in X_p$ $(0 < p < \frac{1}{2})$ (oversmoothing case) and $\hat{x}^\dagger(t) = -(t - \frac{1}{2})^2 + \frac{1}{4}$ $(0 < t \leq 1)$ with $\hat{x}^\dagger \in X_1$ (non-oversmoothing case). We again minimize the Tikhonov functional (4.2) for various parameter choice rules. Understand that $\hat{x}^\dagger \in X_p$ for some $p > 1$ and therefore the penalty is not oversmoothing. The exact and regularized solution for various parameter choice are visualized in Figure 4.3. The left column considers $x^\dagger$, the right column $\hat{x}^\dagger$. Parameter choice $\alpha \approx 9.52e{-}09$ is chosen a priori and too small in both instances. Regularized solutions are displayed in the first row. We therefore see highly oscillating regularized solutions and an insufficient noise suppression. In the second row, $\alpha \approx 2.44e{-}07$ is the optimal parameter choice in the sense of (4.53) for the oversmoothing situation. Similarly, $\alpha \approx 2.12e{-}05$ (third row) is the optimal parameter choice for the non oversmoothing situation. We see that the first parameter choice leads to highly oscillating regularized solutions in the non oversmoothing case. Further, we obverse a phenomenon inherent to regularization with oversmoothing regularization (left): when comparing the parameter choices $\alpha \approx 2.44e{-}07$ and $\alpha \approx 2.12e{-}05$ it becomes evident that the regularized solution for the first parameter choice oscillates mildly, while the latter appears much smoother. This occurs, as regularized solution have to adhere to

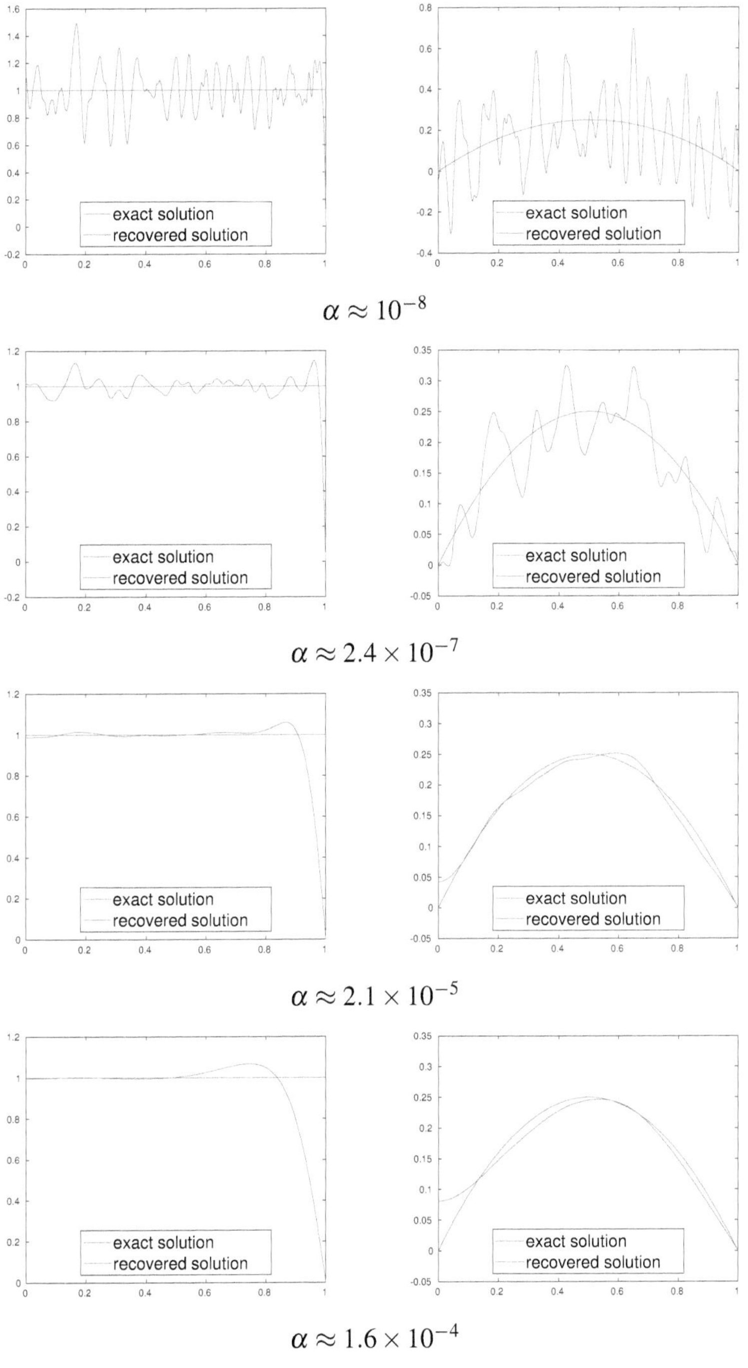

Figure 4.3: Exponential growth model with $x^\dagger(t) \equiv 1$; $(0 < t \leq 1)$ (left) and $\hat{x}^\dagger(t) = -(t - \frac{1}{2})^2 + \frac{1}{4}$; $(0 < t \leq 1)$, $\delta = 0.0179$. Regularized and exact solutions for various regularization parameters.

the boundary condition $x^\dagger(1) = 0$. Therefore a trade off between noise suppression and boundary condition occurs. This is in agreement with results in [9, 13]. The fourth column shows the regularized solutions for too large regularization parameters $\alpha \approx 1.60e{-}04$. Noise is effectively suppressed, but in both instances the regularized solutions are too smooth.

Acknowledgments

The research of Bernd Hofmann, Christopher Hofmann and Robert Plato was supported by the German Research Foundation (DFG grants HO 1454/12-1, HO 1454/13-1 and PL 182/8-1).

References

[1] A.B. Bakushinskij. Remarks on choosing a regularization parameter using the quasi-optimality and ratio criterion. U.S.S.R. Comput. Math. Math. Phys., 24(4): 181–182, 1984. Translation from Zh. Vychisl. Mat Mat. Fiz., 24(8): 1258–1259, 1984 (Russian).

[2] D. Gerth, B. Hofmann and C. Hofmann. Case studies and a pitfall for nonlinear variational regularization under conditional stability. pp. 177–203. Chapter 9. *In*: J. Cheng, S. Lu and M. Yamamoto (eds.). *Inverse Problems and Related Topics: Shanghai, China, October 12–14, 2018*, Springer Proceedings in Mathematics & Statistics, Vol. 310. Springer Nature, Singapore, 2020.

[3] R. Gorenflo and M. Yamamoto. Operator-theoretic treatment of linear Abel integral equations of first kind. Japan J. Indust. Appl. Math., 16(1): 137–161, 1999.

[4] C.W. Groetsch. *Inverse Problems in the Mathematical Sciences*. Vieweg Mathematics for Scientists and Engineers. Friedr. Vieweg & Sohn, Braunschweig, 1993.

[5] U. Hämarik and T. Raus. About the balancing principle for choice of the regularization parameter. Numer. Funct. Anal. Opt., 30(9-10): 951–970, 2009.

[6] B. Hofmann. A local stability analysis of nonlinear inverse problems. pp. 313–320. *In*: D. Delaunay et al. (eds.). *Inverse Problems in Engineering-Theory and Practice*. The American Society of Mechanical Engineers, New York, 1998.

[7] B. Hofmann and C. Hofmann. The impact of the discrepancy principle on the Tikhonov-regularized solutions with oversmoothing penalties. Mathematics-www.mdpi.com/journal/mathematics, 8(3): 331 (16pp), 2020.

[8] B. Hofmann, B. Kaltenbacher, C. Pöschl and O. Scherzer. A convergence rates result for Tikhonov regularization in Banach spaces with non-smooth operators. Inverse Problems, 23(3): 987–1010, 2007.

[9] B. Hofmann and P. Mathé. Tikhonov regularization with oversmoothing penalty for non-linear ill-posed problems in Hilbert scales. Inverse Problems, 34(1): 015007 (14pp), 2018.

[10] B. Hofmann and P. Mathé. A priori parameter choice in Tikhonov regularization with oversmoothing penalty for non-linear ill-posed problems. pp. 169–176. Chapter 8. *In*: J. Cheng, S. Lu and M. Yamamoto (eds.). *Inverse Problems and Related Topics: Shanghai, China, October 12–14, 2018*, Springer Proceedings in Mathematics & Statistics, Vol. 310. Springer Nature, Singapore, 2020.

[11] B. Hofmann, P. Mathé and H. von Weizsäcker. Regularization in Hilbert space under unbounded operators and general source conditions. Inverse Problems, 25(11): 115013 (15pp), 2009.

[12] B. Hofmann and R. Plato. On ill-posedness concepts, stable solvability and saturation. J. Inverse Ill-Posed Probl., 26(2): 287–297, 2018.

[13] B. Hofmann and R. Plato. Convergence results and low order rates for nonlinear Tikhonov regularization with oversmoothing penalty term. Electronic Transactions on Numerical Analysis, 53: 313–328, 2020.

[14] T. Hohage. Regularization of exponentially ill-posed problems. Numer. Funct. Anal. Optim., 21(3-4): 439–464, 2000.

[15] A.S. Leonov. On the accuracy of Tikhonov regularizing algorithms and the quasi-optimal choice of regularization parameter. Dokl. Akad. Nauk SSSR, 321(3): 460–465, 1991.

[16] O.V. Lepskiĭ. A problem of adaptive estimation in Gaussian white noise. Teor. Veroyatnost. i Primenen., 35(3): 459–470, 1990.

[17] P. Mathé. The Lepskiĭ principle revisited. Inverse Problems, 22(3): L11–L15, 2006.

[18] P. Mathé and B. Hofmann. How general are general source conditions? Inverse Problems, 24(1): 015009 (5pp), 2008.

[19] P. Mathé and S.V. Pereverzev. Geometry of linear ill-posed problems in variable Hilbert scales. Inverse Problems, 19(3): 789–803, 2003.

[20] F. Natterer. Error bounds for Tikhonov regularization in Hilbert scales. Appl. Anal., 18(1-2): 29–37, 1984.

[21] S. Pereverzev and E. Schock. On the adaptive selection of the parameter in regularization of ill-posed problems. SIAM J. Numer. Anal., 43(5): 2060–2076, 2005.

[22] R. Plato. The regularizing properties of multistep methods for first kind Volterra integral equations with smooth kernels. Comput. Methods Appl. Math., 17(1): 139–159, 2017.

[23] M. Pricop-Jeckstadt. Nonlinear Tikhonov regularization in Hilbert scales with balancing principle tuning parameter in statistical inverse problems. Inverse Probl. Sci. Eng., 27(2): 205–236, 2019.

[24] T. Raus and U. Hämarik. On the quasioptimal regularization parameter choices for solving ill-posed problems. J. Inv. Ill-Posed Problems, 15: 419–439, 2007.

[25] O. Scherzer, M. Grasmair, H. Grossauer, M. Haltmeier and F. Lenzen. *Variational Methods in Imaging*, volume 167 of *Applied Mathematical Sciences*. Springer, New York, 2009.

[26] T. Schuster, B. Kaltenbacher, B. Hofmann and K.S. Kazimierski. *Regularization Methods in Banach Spaces*. Walter de Gruyter, Berlin/Boston, 2012.

[27] A.N. Tikhonov and V.B. Glasko. The approximate solution of Fredholm integral equations of the first kind. U.S.S.R. Comput. Math. Math. Phys., 4(3): 236–247, 1964. Translation from Zh. Vychisl. Mat Mat. Fiz., 4(3): 564–571, 1964 (Russian).

[28] E. Zeidler. *Nonlinear Functional Analysis and Its Applications–Nonlinear Monotone Operators*, volume II/B. Springer-Verlag, New York, 1990. Translated from the German.

Chapter 5

An Optimization Approach to Parameter Identification in Variational Inequalities of Second Kind-II

Joachim Gwinner

2010 Mathematics Subject Classification. 49J40, 49N45, 90C26

The chapter is dedicated to Professor Zuhair Nashed for his great contribution on variational inequalities and inverse problems.

5.1 Introduction

This chapter continues the work of [16] and is concerned with the inverse problem of parameter identification in variational inequalities of the second kind following the terminology of [12]. A prominent example of this class is the following *direct* problem: Find the function u in the standard Sobolev space $H^1(\Omega) = \{v \in L^2(\Omega) : \nabla v \in (L^2(\Omega))^d\}$ on a bounded Lipschitz domain $\Omega \subset \mathbb{R}^d$ $(d = 2,3)$ such that for any $v \in H^1(\Omega)$ there holds

Institute of Mathematics, Department of Aerospace Engineering, Universität der Bundeswehr München, Werner-Heisenberg-Weg 39, 85577 Neubiberg/Munich, Germany.
Email: joachim.gwinner@unibw.de

$$\int_\Omega e(x)\, [\nabla u \cdot \nabla(v-u) + u(v-u)]\, dx + \int_{\partial\Omega} f(s)\, (|v| - |u|)\, ds$$
$$\geq \int_\Omega g(x)\, (v-u)\, dx. \tag{5.1}$$

This variational inequality (VI) is related to the Helmholtz partial differential equation $-\Delta u + u = g$ rendering the coercive bilinear form $\nabla u \cdot \nabla v + u\, v$. (5.1) provides a simplified scalar model of the Tresca frictional contact problem in linear elasticity, as detailed later in the text. By the classic theory of variational inequalities [23] there is a unique solution u of (5.1) if the datum g that enters the right-hand side is given in $L^2(\Omega)$ and moreover, the "ellipticity" parameter $e > 0$ in $L^\infty(\Omega)$ and the "friction" parameter $f > 0$ in $L^\infty(\partial\Omega)$ are known. Here we study the *inverse* problem that asks for the distributed parameters e and f, when the state u or, what is more realistic, some approximation $\tilde{u}$ from measurement is known.

We loosely follow the optimization approach of [16] to this inverse problem. This approach uses an output-least squares formulation that involves the variational inequality of the second kind as constraint. As already shown in [16], the parameter-to-solution map is Lipschitz, however not differentiable in general.

The main objective of this contribution is the derivation of optimality conditions of first order. To this purpose we adopt a regularization approach that is similar to the regularization approach to optimal control of elliptic variational inequalities that goes back to the work of V. Barbu [6, 7]. Here we apply well-known technics in the study of numerical methods for the solution of finite-dimensional variational inequalities, see [10], and use smoothing functions to the plus function and to the related modulus function. Thus we can regularize the nonsmooth part in the variational inequality and obtain an optimization problem for which the constraint variational inequality is replaced by the regularized variational equation. For this case, the smoothness of the parameter-to-solution map is studied and convergence analysis and optimality conditions are given.

For a review of literature on inverse problems in VI up to 2017 we refer to [16]. More recent works are [22, 24].

So in contrast to the work cited above, this contribution on the inverse problem of parameter identification in variational inequalities does not only treat the parameter e linked to a bilinear form, but importantly also the parameter f linked to a nonlinear nonsmooth function, like the modulus function above.

This chapter is organized as follows. The next Section 2 collects some more variational inequalities of the second kind which model frictional contact and are drawn from other non-smooth problems in continuum mechanics. Here we also give an abstract framework for parameter identification of the ellipticity parameter linked to the bilinear form and of an friction parameter linked to a non-smooth function. Then in Section 3 we present an regularization procedure smoothing the modulus function. By this approach we arrive at a regularized VI equivalent to a variational equation for which we can prove the differentiability of the parameter-to-solution map. Moreover we provide an estimate of the error between the solution of the original VI and the solution of the regularized VI. Section 4 develops the least squares optimization approach to the parameter identification problems where the original VI, respectively the regularized VI appear as constraint. Beyond existence results for these optimization problems we establish an approximation result for the optimal solutions associated to the regularized VI to an optimal solution associated to the original VI when the regularization parameter goes to zero. Finally we present optimality conditions of first order for the regularized optimization problem with the regularized VI as constraint. The chapter ends with a short outlook to related parameter identification problems and their solution.

5.2 Some Variational Inequalities and an Abstract Framework for Parameter Identification

Let Ω be a bounded domain $\subset \mathbb{R}^d$ $(d = 2,3)$ with Lipschitz boundary Γ and nonempty boundary part $\Gamma_C \subset\subset \Gamma$. Further, let $0 < e \in L^\infty(\Omega)$, $0 < f \in L^\infty(\Gamma_C)$, $g \in L^2(\Omega)$, $V = \{v \in H^1(\Omega) : v|\Gamma\backslash\Gamma_C = 0\}$. Then one may consider the VI: Find $u \in V$ such that for all $v \in V$,

$$\int_\Omega e\, \nabla u \cdot \nabla(v-u) + \int_{\Gamma_C} f(|v| - |u|) \geq \int_\Omega g(v-u). \tag{5.2}$$

This scalar VI is more related than (5.1) to the Tresca frictional contact problem which reads as follows: Find $u \in V := \{v \in H^1(\Omega, \mathbb{R}^d) : v|\Gamma\backslash\Gamma_C = 0\}$ $(d = 2,3)$ such that for all $v \in V$,

$$\int_\Omega [E\, \sigma(u) : \sigma(v-u) + \int_{\Gamma_C} f\,(|v\cdot n| - |u\cdot n|) \geq \int_\Omega g\cdot(v-u), \tag{5.3}$$

where now $E \in L^\infty(\Omega, \mathbb{R}^{d\times d}_{\text{symm}})$, $E > 0$ (that is, E is positive definite) is the anisotropic elasticity tensor, $\sigma = \sigma(u), \sigma = 1/2\,(\nabla u + (\nabla u)^T)$ denotes the strain field associated to the displacement field u, n stands for the outward unit normal, and now $g \in L^2(\Omega, \mathbb{R}^d)$.

A vectorial VI of second kind similar to (5.3) appears in Stokes flow with leaky boundary condition or with Tresca friction boundary condition; see [11, 4, 3].

When replacing the functional $\int_{\Gamma_C} f\,|w|$ by $\int_\Omega f\,|\nabla w|$ in (5.1) or in (5.2) one obtains a VI of second kind that models laminar flow of a Bingham fluid, see, e.g., [12]. More general than Bingham fluid is the vectorial viscoplastic fluid flow problem studied in [13].

All these VIs can be covered by the abstract framework of [16] as follows. Let (as above) V be a real Hilbert space, where in virtue of the Riesz isomorphism we identify the dual space V^* with V. Moreover let E, F real Banach spaces with convex closed cones $E_+ \subset E$ and $F_+ \subset F$. Let as with [14], $t : E \times V \times V \to \mathbb{R}, (e,u,v) \mapsto t(e,u,v)$ a trilinear form and $l : V \to \mathbb{R}, v \mapsto l(v)$ a linear form. Assume that t is continuous such that $t(e,\cdot,\cdot)$ is $V-$elliptic for any fixed $e \in \operatorname{int} E_+$. Now in addition we have a "semisublinear form" $s : F \times V \to \mathbb{R}, (f,u) \mapsto s(f,u)$, that is, for any $u \in V$, $s(f,u)$ is linear in its first argument f on F and for any $f \in F_+$, $s(f,\cdot)$ is sublinear, continuous, and nonnegative on V. Moreover assume that $s(f, 0_V) = 0$ for any $f \in F$.

Then the forward problem is the following VI: Given $e \in \operatorname{int} E_+$ and $f \in F_+$, find $u \in V$ such that

$$t(e;u,v-u) + s(f;v) - s(f;u) \geq l(v-u)\,, \forall v \in V\,. \tag{5.4}$$

Now with given convex closed subsets $E^{\mathrm{ad}} \subset \operatorname{int} E_+$ and $F^{\mathrm{ad}} \subset F_+$ we seek to identify two parameters, namely the "ellipticity" parameter e in E^{ad} and the "friction" parameter f in F^{ad}.

In the model problem we have some convex closed cone $E_+ \subseteq \{e \in L^\infty(\Omega) : e \geq 0 \text{ a.e. on } \Omega\}$ containing the convex closed "feasible" set $E^{\mathrm{ad}} = \{e \in E_+ : \underline{e} \leq e \leq \overline{e} \text{ a.e. on } \Omega\}$, where the bounds $\underline{e} < \overline{e}$ are given in $\mathbb{R}_{++} = \{r \in \mathbb{R} : r > 0\}$. Likewise we have some convex closed cone $F_+ \subseteq \{f \in L^\infty(\Gamma_C) : f \geq 0 \text{ a.e. on } \Gamma_C\}$ containing the convex closed "feasible" set $F^{\mathrm{ad}} = \{f \in F_+ : \underline{f} \leq f \leq \overline{f} \text{ a.e. on } \Gamma_C\}$, where the bounds $0 \leq \underline{f} < \overline{f}$ are given.

As with M. S. Gockenbach and A. A. Khan in [14] we can assume that $t(e;\cdot,\cdot)$ is symmetric and

$$t(e;u,v) \leq \bar{t}\, ||e||_E\, ||u||_V\, ||v||_V, \forall e \in E,\ u \in V,\ v \in V \tag{5.5}$$

$$t(e;u,u) \geq \underline{t}\, ||u||_V^2, \forall e \in E^{\mathrm{ad}} \subset E,\ u \in V\,. \tag{5.6}$$

In fact, $\bar{t} < \infty$ directly follows from the assumed continuity of t, where in the model problem $\bar{t} = 1$, and $\underline{t} > 0$ comes from Poincaré inequality; respectively in the elastic friction contact problem from Korn's inequality.

In the following we specify the abstract approach of [16] and give the sublinear functional s a more concrete form. Let D be some finite dimensional bounded open domain. We fix $F := L^\infty(D)$ and $F_+ := L^\infty_+(D)$. Introduce the L^2 scalar product $(\cdot,\cdot)$ on D and let $\gamma : V \to L^2(D)$ a linear continuous map. Then use the modulus function $|\cdot|$ and define

$$s(f;v) := (f, |\gamma(v)|) = \int_D f\, |\gamma(v)|\, ds,\ \forall f \in L^\infty(D), v \in V\,. \tag{5.7}$$

In the model problem we have the trace map $\gamma : V = H^1(\Omega) \to L^2(D)$ with $D = \partial\Omega$, whereas in the elastic friction contact problem we have the trace map γ: $V = \{v \in H^1(\Omega, \mathbb{R}^d) : v|\Gamma\backslash\Gamma_C = 0\} \to L^2(D)$ with $D = \Gamma_c$ defined by $v \to v \cdot n$.

In the Bingham flow problem or (simplified) plasticity problem, simply $D = \Omega$, $\gamma : v \in V \mapsto \nabla v \in L^2(\Omega)$, and the modulus function changes to the modulus of a vector in an obvious way.

5.3 The Regularization Procedure

In this section we show how the VI (5.4) of the second kind that appears as constraint in the parameter identification problem regularizes in a variational equation. This regularization procedure is based on an appropriate smoothing of the modulus function.

5.3.1 Smoothing the Modulus Function

The modulus function $m, m(t) = |t|$ is related to the plus function $p, p(t) = t_+ = \max(t, 0)$, $(t \in \mathbb{R})$ by

$$m(t) = p(t) + p(-t),$$
$$p(t) = 1/2(t + m(t)).$$

Therefore smoothing functions for the plus function easily translate to those for the modulus function.

The general methods for constructing smoothing functions go back to the works of Sobolev, see [1], and are based on convolution. Let $\rho : \mathbb{R} \to \mathbb{R}_+ := \{s \in \mathbb{R} : s \geq 0\}$ be the density of a probability distribution on $\mathbb{R}$, that is,

- ρ is Lebesgue integrable
- $\int_{\mathbb{R}} \rho(s) ds = 1$.

Let $\mathbb{R}_{++} := \{\varepsilon \in \mathbb{R} : \varepsilon > 0\}$. Then define the smoothing function $P : \mathbb{R}_{++} \times \mathbb{R} \to \mathbb{R}$ via convolution for the plus function p by

$$P(\varepsilon, t) = \int_{\mathbb{R}} p(t - \varepsilon s) \rho \, ds = \int_{-\infty}^{\frac{t}{\varepsilon}} (t - \varepsilon s) \rho(s) \, ds. \tag{5.8}$$

Further, we focus $\rho : \mathbb{R} \to \mathbb{R}_+$ to be a density function of finite absolute mean, that is,

$$k := \int_{\mathbb{R}} |s| \rho(s) \, ds < \infty. \tag{5.9}$$

Referring to [10, Proposition 11.8.10] we have the following approximation result.

Proposition 5.3.1 *Let the density function $\rho : \mathbb{R} \to \mathbb{R}_+$ satisfy (5.9). Then for any $\varepsilon > 0, t \in \mathbb{R}$*

$$|P(\varepsilon, t) - p(t)| \leq k \, \varepsilon \, . \tag{5.10}$$

Further for any $\varepsilon > 0$, $P(\varepsilon,\cdot)$ *is convex and twice continuously differentiable on* $\mathbb{R}$ *with*

$$P_t(\varepsilon,t) = \int_{-\infty}^{\frac{t}{\varepsilon}} \rho(s)\,ds,\; P_{tt}(\varepsilon,t) = \frac{1}{\varepsilon}\rho(\frac{t}{\varepsilon}),$$

and $0 \le P_t(\varepsilon,t) \le 1$ *for all* $t \in \mathbb{R}$.

By the above relation between the plus function and the modulus function, we define the smoothing function $M : \mathbb{R}_{++} \times \mathbb{R} \to \mathbb{R}$ for the modulus function m by

$$M(\varepsilon,t) = P(\varepsilon,t) + P(\varepsilon,-t) \tag{5.11}$$

and obtain from Proposition 5.3.1 the direct consequence:

Corollary 5.3.2 *Let the density function* $\rho : \mathbb{R} \to \mathbb{R}_+$ *satisfy (5.9). Then for any* $\varepsilon > 0, t \in \mathbb{R}$

$$|M(\varepsilon,t) - m(t)| \le 2k\varepsilon. \tag{5.12}$$

Further for any $\varepsilon > 0$, $M(\varepsilon,\cdot)$ *is convex and twice continuously differentiable on* $\mathbb{R}$ *with*

$$M_t(\varepsilon,t) = \int_{-\frac{t}{\varepsilon}}^{\frac{t}{\varepsilon}} \rho(s)ds,\; M_{tt}(\varepsilon,t) = \frac{1}{\varepsilon}[\rho(\frac{t}{\varepsilon}) + \rho(\frac{-t}{\varepsilon}],\tag{5.13}$$

and $0 \le M_t(\varepsilon,t) \le 2$ *for all* $t \in \mathbb{R}$.

Since the smoothing function for the modulus function is based on the smoothing function for the plus function, some examples from [10] and the references therein are in order.

Example 5.3.3

$$P_1(\varepsilon,t) = \int_{-\infty}^{\frac{t}{\varepsilon}} (t-\varepsilon s)\,\rho_1(s)\,ds = t + \varepsilon\, ln(1+e^{-\frac{t}{\varepsilon}}) = \varepsilon\, ln(1+e^{\frac{t}{\varepsilon}}),$$

where $\rho_1(s) = \frac{e^{-s}}{(1+e^{-s})^2}$.

Example 5.3.4

$$P_2(\varepsilon,t) = \int_{-\infty}^{\frac{t}{\varepsilon}} (t-\varepsilon s)\,\rho_2(s)\,ds = \frac{\sqrt{t^2+4\varepsilon^2}+t}{2},$$

where $\rho_2(s) = \frac{2}{(s^2+4)^{3/2}}$.

Example 5.3.5

$$P_3(\varepsilon,t) = \int_{-\infty}^{\frac{t}{\varepsilon}} (t-\varepsilon s)\,\rho_3(s)\,ds = \begin{cases} 0, & \text{if } t < -\frac{\varepsilon}{2}, \\ \frac{1}{2\varepsilon}(t+\frac{\varepsilon}{2})^2, & \text{if } -\frac{\varepsilon}{2} \le t \le \frac{\varepsilon}{2}, \\ t, & \text{if } t > \frac{\varepsilon}{2}, \end{cases}$$

where $\rho_3(s) = \begin{cases} 1, & \text{if } -\frac{1}{2} \le s \le \frac{1}{2}, \\ 0, & \text{otherwise.} \end{cases}$

Example 5.3.6

$$P_4(\varepsilon,t) = \int_{-\infty}^{\frac{t}{\varepsilon}} (t-\varepsilon s)\,\rho_4(s)\,ds = \begin{cases} 0, & \text{if } t<0, \\ \frac{t^2}{2\varepsilon}, & \text{if } 0 \le t \le \varepsilon, \\ t-\frac{\varepsilon}{2}, & \text{if } t>\varepsilon, \end{cases}$$

where $\rho_4(s) = \begin{cases} 1, & \text{if } 0 \le s \le 1, \\ 0, & \text{otherwise.} \end{cases}$

Remark 5.3.7 *The regularization used in the analysis of state constrained semilinear elliptic VIs in [29, Section 5.2] is similar, but different. Indeed, here we regularize the special convex nonsmooth modulus function which has the maximal monotone graph*

$$\beta(t) := \partial m(t) = \begin{cases} -1 & : \; t<0 \\ [-1,1] & : \; t=0 \\ 1 & : \; t>0. \end{cases}$$

So β *is single-valued a.e. and [29, p. 113] regularizes* β *to*

$$\begin{aligned} \beta_\varepsilon(t) &= \int_{-\infty}^{\infty} \beta(t+\varepsilon\, s)\rho(s)\,ds \\ &= -\int_{-\infty}^{-\frac{t}{\varepsilon}} \rho(s)\,ds + \int_{-\frac{t}{\varepsilon}}^{\infty} \rho(s)\,ds, \end{aligned}$$

what differs from the corresponding $M_t(\varepsilon,t)$ *in (5.13) - apart from the regularizing kernel in [29] assumed to be* C^∞ *with support in* $[0,1]$, *whereas we require that the density function* ρ *has finite absolute mean.*

5.3.2 Regularizing the VI of Second Kind

Using the smoothing function $M_\varepsilon := M(\varepsilon,\cdot)$ to the modulus function $m = |\cdot|$, we define the smoothing approximation to s by

$$S_\varepsilon(f,v) := \int_D f\, M_\varepsilon(\gamma(v))\; ds, \;\; \forall f \in L^\infty(D), v \in V, \varepsilon \in \mathbb{R}_{++}. \qquad (5.14)$$

Thus with $\varepsilon \in \mathbb{R}_{++}$ fixed, we can now regularize the above VI of second kind (5.4) by the following VI: Given $e \in \operatorname{int} E_+$ and $f \in F_+$, find $u_\varepsilon \in V$ such that

$$t(e;u_\varepsilon, v-u_\varepsilon) + S_\varepsilon(f,v) - S_\varepsilon(f;u_\varepsilon) \ge l(v-u_\varepsilon), \forall v \in V. \qquad (5.15)$$

Since M'_ε is bounded, we obtain in virtue of the Lebesgue theorem of majorized convergence

$$\begin{aligned}\frac{d}{dt}S_\varepsilon(f,u+tw)|_{t=0} &= \int_D f\,M'_\varepsilon(\gamma u)\gamma(w)\,ds\\ &= (f\,M'_\varepsilon(\gamma u),\gamma(w))\\ &= \langle\gamma^*(f\,M'_\varepsilon(\gamma u)),w\rangle_{V\times V},\end{aligned}$$

hence the partial derivative of S_ε with respect to v:

$$D_v S_\varepsilon(f,u)=\gamma^*(f\,M'_\varepsilon(\gamma u))\in V\,. \tag{5.16}$$

Further $S_\varepsilon(f,\cdot)$ is convex. Therefore the VI (5.15) is indeed equivalent to the *variational equation*: Find $u_\varepsilon\in V$ such that

$$T(e)u_\varepsilon\,+\,D_v S_\varepsilon(f,u_\varepsilon)=l\,, \tag{5.17}$$

where the parameter dependent linear operator $T(e)$ is defined by

$$\langle T(e)v,w\rangle = t(e;v,w)\,.$$

By the classic theory of variational inequalities [23] there is a unique solution u of (5.4) and a unique solution u_ε of (5.15) for given "ellipticity" parameter e in E^{ad} and "friction" parameter f in F^{ad}. This leads to uniquely defined solution maps $(e,f)\in E^{\mathrm{ad}}\times F^{\mathrm{ad}}\mapsto u=\mathcal{S}(e,f)$, $(e,f)\in E^{\mathrm{ad}}\times F^{\mathrm{ad}}\mapsto u_\varepsilon=\mathcal{S}_\varepsilon(e,f)$, respectively. In [16] we have shown that the solution map $\mathcal{S}$ is Lipschitz both in ellipticity and in friction parameter. However, the parameter-to-solution map $\mathcal{S}$ is not smooth in general.

An advantage of replacing the variational inequality by the regularized equation is that for the latter the parameter-to-solution map $\mathcal{S}_\varepsilon$ is *smooth* as shown below.

Theorem 5.3.8 *Let* $\varepsilon>0$.

1. *Fix* $f\in F^{ad}$. *Then the map* $e\mapsto v_\varepsilon(e):=\mathcal{S}_\varepsilon(e,f)$ *is differentiable at any point* e *in the interior of* E^{ad}. *For any direction* $\delta e\in\hat{E}$, *the derivative* $\delta v_\varepsilon = Dv_\varepsilon(e)(\delta e)$ *is the unique solution of the following equation:*

$$T(e)\delta v_\varepsilon+\gamma^*(fM''_\varepsilon(\gamma v_\varepsilon)(\gamma\delta v_\varepsilon)) = -T(\delta e)v_\varepsilon \tag{5.18}$$

2. *Fix* $e\in E^{ad}$. *Then the map* $f\mapsto w_\varepsilon(f):=\mathcal{S}_\varepsilon(e,f)$ *is differentiable at any point* f *in the interior of* F^{ad}. *For any direction* $\delta f\in\hat{F}$, *the derivative* $\delta w_\varepsilon = Dw_\varepsilon(f)(\delta f)$ *is the unique solution of the following equation:*

$$T(e)\delta w_\varepsilon+\gamma^*(fM''_\varepsilon(\gamma w_\varepsilon)(\gamma\delta w_\varepsilon)) = -\gamma^*(\delta f M'_\varepsilon(\gamma w_\varepsilon)) \tag{5.19}$$

3. *The map* $(e,f) \in E^{ad} \times F^{ad} \mapsto u_\varepsilon = \mathcal{S}_\varepsilon(e,f)$ *is differentiable at any point* (e,f) *in the interior of* $E^{ad} \times F^{ad}$. *From (5.18),(5.19) one obtains the derivative* $\delta u_\varepsilon = Du_\varepsilon(e,f)(\delta e, \delta f) = (\delta v_\varepsilon, \delta w_\varepsilon)$ *for any direction* $(\delta e, \delta f) \in \hat{E} \times \hat{F}$.

Proof.

1. The differentiability of the map $e \mapsto v_\varepsilon(e) = \mathcal{S}_\varepsilon(e,f)$ follows by applying the implicit function theorem to the map $G : \hat{E} \times V \to V$ mapping $(e,v) \mapsto T(e)v + \gamma^*(fM_\varepsilon'(\gamma v))$. The derivative $D_v G(e,v) : V \to V$ is given by $D_v G(e,v)(\delta v) = T(e)\delta v + \gamma^*(fM_\varepsilon''(\gamma v)(\gamma \delta v))$. For every $l \in V$, the variational equation

$$t(e; \delta v, w) + (fM_\varepsilon''(\gamma v)(\gamma \delta v), \gamma w)_{L^2(D)\times L^2(D)} = \langle l, w \rangle_{V \times V}, \forall w \in V$$

possesses a unique solution δv, since t is uniformly coercive by (5.6) and $M_\varepsilon''(\gamma v) \geq 0$ by (5.13) and $\rho \geq 0$. Therefore $D_v G(e, \cdot)(v) : V \to V$ is surjective and the differentiability follows from the implicit function theorem. From (5.17) we have

$$T(\delta e)v_\varepsilon + T(e)\delta v_\varepsilon + \gamma^*(fM_\varepsilon''(\gamma v_\varepsilon)(\gamma \delta v_\varepsilon)) = 0,$$

and (5.18) follows.

2. Similarly the differentiability of the map $f \mapsto w_\varepsilon(f) = \mathcal{S}_\varepsilon(e,f)$ follows by applying the implicit function theorem to the map $H : \hat{F} \times V \to V$ mapping $(f,w) \mapsto T(e)w + \gamma^*(fM_\varepsilon'(\gamma w))$. The derivative $D_w H(f,w) : V \to V$ is given by $D_w H(f,w)(\delta w) = T(e)\delta w + \gamma^*(fM_\varepsilon''(\gamma w)(\gamma \delta w))$. Similarly as above $D_w H(f, \cdot)(w) : V \to V$ is seen to be surjective and the differentiability follows from the implicit function theorem. Again from (5.17) we have

$$T(e)\delta w_\varepsilon + \gamma^*(\delta f M_\varepsilon'(\gamma w_\varepsilon)) + \gamma^*(fM_\varepsilon''(\gamma w_\varepsilon)(\gamma \delta w_\varepsilon)) = 0,$$

and (5.19) follows.

3. Clear from above.

The proof is complete. □

Remark 5.3.9 *The assumption on interior points in Theorem 5.3.8 does not pose a restriction of generality. Indeed, some feasible* $f \in F^{ad} = \{f \in L_+^{infty}(D) : \underline{f} \leq f \leq \overline{f}$ *a.e. on* $D\} =: F_{\underline{f}}^{\overline{f}}$ *is an interior point of* $F_{\underline{f}/2}^{2\overline{f}}$ *and so apply the above result in the latter larger set, simlarly for* $e \in E^{ad}$.

5.3.3 An Estimate of the Regularization Error

To conclude this section we give an estimate of the error between the solution $u = \mathcal{S}(e,f)$ of the original VI (5.4) and the solution $u_\varepsilon = \mathcal{S}_\varepsilon(e,f)$ of the regularized VI (5.15).

Theorem 5.3.10 *Let the density function $\rho : \mathbb{R} \to \mathbb{R}_+$ satisfy (5.9). Let $e \in E^{ad}$ and $f \in F^{ad}$. Then for the solution $u = \mathcal{S}(e,f)$ of the original VI (5.4) and the solution $u_\varepsilon = \mathcal{S}_\varepsilon(e,f)$ of the regularized VI (5.15) there holds the error estimate*

$$\|S_\varepsilon(e,f) - S(e,f)\|_V = \mathcal{O}(\varepsilon^{\frac{1}{2}}). \tag{5.20}$$

Proof. Inserting $v = u_\varepsilon$ in the original VI (5.4) and $v = u$ in the regularized VI (5.15), gives

$$t(e;u,u_\varepsilon - u) + \int_D f\,[m(\gamma(u_\varepsilon)) - m(\gamma(u))]\,ds \geq l(u_\varepsilon - u),$$

$$t(e;u_\varepsilon,u - u_\varepsilon) + \int_D f\,[M_\varepsilon(\gamma(u)) - M_\varepsilon(\gamma(u_\varepsilon))]\,ds \geq l(u - u_\varepsilon).$$

A rearrangement of the above yields, where we use (5.6) and Corollary 5.3.2, (5.12),

$$\begin{aligned}
&\underline{t}\|u_\varepsilon - u\|_V^2 \leq t(e;u_\varepsilon - u, u_\varepsilon - u)\\
&\leq \int_D f\,[m(\gamma(u_\varepsilon)) - M_\varepsilon(\gamma(u_\varepsilon)) + M_\varepsilon(\gamma(u)) - m(\gamma(u))]\,ds\\
&\leq 4c\;\varepsilon\;|D|\|f\|_{L^\infty(D)},
\end{aligned}$$

where $|D|$ is the Lebesgue measure of D. This proves the claimed error estimate. □

5.4 The Optimization Approach

Let an observation $\hat{v} \in V$ be given. Then the parameter identification problem studied in this paper reads: Find parameters $e \in E^{ad}, f \in F^{ad}$ such that $u = \mathcal{S}(e,f)$ "fits best" $\hat{v}$, where $u \in V$ satisfies the VI (5.4), namely

$$t(e;u,v-u) + s(f;v) - s(f;u) \;\geq\; l(v-u), \forall v \in V.$$

Similar to [21, 15, 14] and similar to parameter estimation in linear elliptic equations [5] we follow an optimization approach and introduce the "misfit function"

$$J(e,f) := \frac{1}{2}\;\|\mathcal{S}(e,f) - \hat{v}\|^2$$

to be minimized.

Here we assume similar to [21] that the sought ellipticity and friction parameters are smooth enough to satisfy with compact imbeddings

$$E^{\mathrm{ad}} \subset \hat{E} \subset\subset E; F^{\mathrm{ad}} \subset \hat{F} \subset\subset F = L^{\infty}(D) \subset L^{2}(D).$$

Some examples are in order. By the Rellich-Kondrachev Theorem [1, Theorem 6.3], $H^1(\Omega) \subset\subset C^0_B(\Omega)$, the space of bounded, continuous functions on Ω, provided Ω satisfies the cone condition; clearly $C^0_B(\Omega) \subset L^\infty(\Omega)$. Thus $\hat{E} = H^1(\Omega) \subset\subset L^\infty(\Omega)$. More general Sobolev spaces of fractional order can also be used, see, e.g., [2] treating the identification of the ellipticity parameter in linear elliptic Dirichlet problems.

For simplicity let $\hat{E}, \hat{F}$ be Hilbert spaces (or more generally reflexive Banach spaces). Thus with given weights $\alpha > 0, \beta > 0$ we pose the stabilized optimization problem

$$(OP) \qquad \text{minimize } J(e,f) + \frac{\alpha}{2}\, \|e\|^2_{\hat{E}} + \frac{\beta}{2} \|f\|^2_{\hat{F}}$$

$$\text{subject to } e \in E^{\mathrm{ad}},\ f \in F^{\mathrm{ad}}$$

Under these assumptions we have the following solvability theorem.

Theorem 5.4.1 *Suppose the above compact imbeddings. Suppose that the trilinear form t satisfies (5.5) and (5.6) and that the semisublinear form s is given by (5.7). Then (OP) admits an optimal (not necessarily unique!) solution $(e^*, f^*, u) \in E^{ad} \times F^{ad} \times V$, where $u = \mathcal{S}(e^*, f^*)$. i.e., $u \in V$ solves the VI (5.4) for the optimal parameter (e^*, f^*).*

Proof. For details see the proof of [16, Theorem 4.1]. □

We now consider an analogue of (OP) where the underlying variational inequality has been replaced by a regularized variational inequality that is equivalent to a variational equation:

$$(OP)_\varepsilon \qquad \text{minimize } J_\varepsilon(e,f) + \frac{\alpha}{2}\, \|e\|^2_{\hat{E}} + \frac{\beta}{2} \|f\|^2_{\hat{F}}$$

$$\text{subject to } e \in E^{\mathrm{ad}},\ f \in F^{\mathrm{ad}},$$

where

$$J_\varepsilon(e,f) := \frac{1}{2}\, \|\mathcal{S}_\varepsilon(e,f) - \hat{v}\|^2 .$$

We give the following existence and convergence result:

Theorem 5.4.2 *Suppose the above compact imbeddings. Suppose that the trilinear form t satisfies (5.5) and (5.6) and that the semisublinear form s is given by (5.7). Moreover, let the density function $\rho : \mathbb{R} \to \mathbb{R}_+$ in the definition (5.14) of* *the regularizing function S_ε satisfy (5.9). Then for any $\varepsilon > 0$, $(OP)_\varepsilon$ has an optimal solution $(\bar{e}_\varepsilon, \bar{f}_\varepsilon)$. Moreover for any sequence $\{\varepsilon_k\}_{k\in\mathbb{N}} \subset \mathbb{R}_{++}$ with $\varepsilon_k \to 0$ for $k \to \infty$, there is a subsequence $\{(\bar{e}_n, \bar{f}_n, \bar{u}_n)\}_{n\in N}$, where $\bar{u}_n = \mathcal{S}_{\varepsilon_n}(\bar{e}_n, \bar{f}_n)$ for $n \in N \subset \mathbb{N}$, such that for $n \to \infty$ we have $(\bar{e}_n, \bar{f}_n) \to (\tilde{e}, \tilde{f})$ in $E \times F$, $\bar{u}_n \to \tilde{u}$ in V where $(\tilde{e}, \tilde{f})$ is a solution of (OP) and $\tilde{u} = \mathcal{S}(\tilde{e}, \tilde{f})$.*

Proof. For a fixed $\varepsilon > 0$, the existence of a solution $(\bar{e}_\varepsilon, \bar{f}_\varepsilon)$ follows by arguments similar to those used in the proof of Theorem 5.4.1. The proof of the convergence result is split into the following three steps.

Step 1: An a priori estimate and convergence of some subsequence $\{\bar{e}_n, \bar{f}_n\}$ to some $(\tilde{e}, \tilde{f})$

We observe that for any optimal solution $(e_k, f_k) := (\bar{e}_{\varepsilon_k}, \bar{f}_{\varepsilon_k})$ of $(OP)_{\varepsilon_k}$ and for any optimal solution (e^*, f^*). of (OP),

$$\begin{aligned}
&J_{\varepsilon_k}(e_k, f_k) + \frac{\alpha}{2}\,\|e_k\|_{\hat{E}}^2 + \frac{\beta}{2}\|f_k\|_{\hat{F}}^2 \\
&= \frac{1}{2}\,\|\mathcal{S}_{\varepsilon_k}(e_k, f_k) - \hat{v}\|^2 + \frac{\alpha}{2}\,\|e_k\|_{\hat{E}}^2 + \frac{\beta}{2}\|f_k\|_{\hat{F}}^2 \\
&\le \frac{1}{2}\,\|\mathcal{S}_{\varepsilon_k}(e^*, f^*) - \hat{v}\|^2 + \frac{\alpha}{2}\,\|e^*\|_{\hat{E}}^2 + \frac{\beta}{2}\|f^*\|_{\hat{F}}^2 .
\end{aligned}$$

Moreover, by the error estimate (5.20),

$$\|\mathcal{S}_{\varepsilon_k}(e^*, f^*) - \hat{v}\| \le \|\mathcal{S}(e^*, f^*) - \hat{v}\| + \mathcal{O}(\varepsilon_k^{\frac{1}{2}}) .$$

Hence, the boundedness of $\|e_k\|_{\hat{E}} + \|f_k\|_{\hat{F}}$ follows. Therefore there exists a subsequence $\{(e_n, f_n)\}_{n\in N}$ with $N \subset \mathbb{N}$ that converges weakly to some $(\tilde{e}, \tilde{f}) \in E^{\text{ad}} \times F^{\text{ad}}$ in the reflexive space $\hat{E} \times \hat{F}$. In view of the assumed compact imbeddings there is a further subsequence again denoted by $\{(e_n, f_n)\}_{n\in N}$, such that for $n \to \infty$, $(e_n, f_n) \to (\tilde{e}, \tilde{f})$ in $E \times F$ strongly.

Step 2: Convergence $\mathcal{S}_{\varepsilon_n}(e_n, f_n) \to \mathcal{S}(\tilde{e}, \tilde{f})$

Let $u_n := \mathcal{S}_{\varepsilon_n}(e_n, f_n), \tilde{u} := \mathcal{S}(\tilde{e}, \tilde{f})$. Then inserting $v = u_n$ in the original VI (5.4) with parameter $(\tilde{e}, \tilde{f})$ and $v = \tilde{u}$ in the regularized VI (5.15) with parameter (e_n, f_n), gives

$$t(\tilde{e}; \tilde{u}, u_n - \tilde{u}) + \int_D f\,[M(\gamma(u_n)) - M(\gamma(u))]\,ds \ge l(u_n - \tilde{u}),$$

$$t(e_n; u_n, \tilde{u} - u_n) + \int_D f_n\,[M_{\varepsilon_n}(\gamma(\tilde{u})) - M_{\varepsilon_n}(\gamma(u_n))]\,ds \ge l(\tilde{u} - u_n) .$$

A rearrangement of the above yields by (5.6) and (5.5)

$$\begin{aligned}
&\underline{t}\|u_n - \tilde{u}\|_V^2 \le t(e_n; u_n - \tilde{u}, u_n - \tilde{u}) \\
&\le t(\tilde{e} - e_n; \tilde{u}, u_n - \tilde{u}) + R_n \\
&\le \bar{t}\;\|e_n - \tilde{e}\|_E\;\|\tilde{u}\|_V\;\|u_n - \tilde{u}\|_V + R_n ,
\end{aligned}$$

where using Corollary 5.3.2, (5.12),

$$\begin{aligned} R_n &= s(\tilde{f},u_n) - S_{\varepsilon_n}(f_n,u_n) + S\varepsilon_n(f_n,\tilde{u}) - s(\tilde{f},\tilde{u}) \\ &= \int_D (\tilde{f} - f_n)\ [M(\gamma u_n) + f_n[M(\gamma u_n) - M_{\varepsilon_n}(\gamma u_n)] \\ &\quad + (f_n - \tilde{f})M(\gamma\tilde{u}) + f_n[M(\gamma\tilde{u}) - M_{\varepsilon_n}(\gamma\tilde{u})]\ ds \\ &\leq \|\tilde{f} - f_n\|_{L^\infty(D)}\|\gamma\|_{V\to L^1(D)}\|u_n\|_V + 4c_0\ \varepsilon_n\ |D|\|f_n\|_{L^\infty(D)} \\ &\quad + \|\tilde{f} - f_n\|_{L^\infty(D)}\|\gamma\|_{V\to L^1(D)}\|\tilde{u}\|_V + 4c_0\ \varepsilon_n\ |D|\|f_n\|_{L^\infty(D)}\,. \end{aligned}$$

These estimates show that

$$\underline{t}\|u_n - \tilde{u}\|_V^2 \leq c_1\|u_n - \tilde{u}\|_V + c_2$$

holds for some constants $c_1 > 0, c_2 > 0$. Hence $\{u_n\}$ is bounded, say $\max(\|u_n\|_V, \|u_n - \tilde{u}\|_V) \leq \tilde{c} < \infty$. Thus the above estimates give

$$\underline{t}\|u_n - \tilde{u}\|_V^2 \leq \bar{t}\ \tilde{c}\ \|\tilde{u}\|_V\ \|e_n - \tilde{e}\|_E + R_n\,,$$

where

$$R_n \leq 2\tilde{c}\ \|\gamma\|_{V\to L^1(D)}\ \|\tilde{f} - f_n\|_{L^\infty(D)} + 8c_0\ \varepsilon_n\ |D|\|f_n\|_{L^\infty(D)}$$

and so $R_n \to 0$ for $n \to \infty$. The convergence $u_n \to \tilde{u}$ follows.

Step 3: $(\tilde{e},\tilde{f})$ is a solution of (OP)

Take $(e_0,f_0) \in E^{ad} \times F^{ad}$ arbitrarily. Let $u_0 := S(e_0,f_0), \bar{u}_n := S_{\varepsilon_n}(e_0,f_0)$. Then firstly by Theorem 5.3.10, $\bar{u}_n \to u_0$ in V for $n \in N \to \infty$, secondly (e_0,f_0) is feasible for the regularized optimization problem $(OP)_{\varepsilon_n}$. Hence

$$\begin{aligned} &J(\tilde{e},\tilde{f}) + \frac{\alpha}{2}\ \|\tilde{e}\|_{\hat{E}}^2 + \frac{\beta}{2}\|\tilde{f}\|_{\hat{F}}^2 \\ &= \frac{1}{2}\ \|\tilde{u} - \hat{v}\|^2 + \frac{\alpha}{2}\ \|\tilde{e}\|_{\hat{E}}^2 + \frac{\beta}{2}\|\tilde{f}\|_{\hat{F}}^2 \\ &\leq \liminf_{n\to\infty}\frac{1}{2}\ \|u_n - \hat{v}\|^2 + \liminf_{n\to\infty}\ [\frac{\alpha}{2}\ \|e_n\|_{\hat{E}}^2 + \frac{\beta}{2}\|f_n\|_{\hat{F}}^2] \\ &\leq \liminf_{n\to\infty}[\frac{1}{2}\ \|u_n - \hat{v}\|^2 + \frac{\alpha}{2}\ \|e_n\|_{\hat{E}}^2 + \frac{\beta}{2}\|f_n\|_{\hat{F}}^2] \\ &= \liminf_{n\to\infty}[J_{\varepsilon_n}(e_n,f_n) + \frac{\alpha}{2}\ \|e_n\|_{\hat{E}}^2 + \frac{\beta}{2}\|f_n\|_{\hat{F}}^2] \\ &\leq \liminf_{n\to\infty}[J_{\varepsilon_n}(e_0,f_0) + \frac{\alpha}{2}\ \|e_0\|_{\hat{E}}^2 + \frac{\beta}{2}\|f_0\|_{\hat{F}}^2] \\ &= \liminf_{n\to\infty}[\frac{1}{2}\ \|\bar{u}_n - \hat{v}\|^2 + \frac{\alpha}{2}\ \|e_0\|_{\hat{E}}^2 + \frac{\beta}{2}\|f_0\|_{\hat{F}}^2] \\ &= \frac{1}{2}\ \|u_0 - \hat{v}\|^2 + \frac{\alpha}{2}\ \|e_0\|_{\hat{E}}^2 + \frac{\beta}{2}\|f_0\|_{\hat{F}}^2 \\ &= J(e_0,f_0) + \frac{\alpha}{2}\ \|e_0\|_{\hat{E}}^2 + \frac{\beta}{2}\|f_0\|_{\hat{F}}^2\,, \end{aligned}$$

what shows the optimality of $(\tilde{e}, \tilde{f})$.

The proof is complete.

□

Remark 5.4.3 *Note that the optimization problems (OP) and $(OP)_\varepsilon$ typically have multiple solutions. To overcome the ill-posedness, we could use the well-known method of Browder-Tykhonov regularization, see, e.g., [25]. More specifically, if we have some a priori information of a solution of these problems, then this could be incorporated in the regularized problem $(OP)_\varepsilon$ in a similar way as it was done in the work [17] that was focused to the identification of the ellipticity parameter e.*

Now we apply the general theory of optimality conditions in optimal control in the differentiable case presented in [26] and derive from [26, Theorem 3.1.7] the following optimality condition (of first order) for the regularized problem $(OP)_\varepsilon$.

Theorem 5.4.4 *Suppose the above compact imbeddings. Suppose that the trilinear form t satisfies (5.5) and (5.6) and that the semisublinear form s is given by (5.7). Moreover, let the density function $\rho : \mathbb{R} \to \mathbb{R}_+$ in the definition (5.14) of the regularizing function S_ε satisfy (5.9). Then for any $\varepsilon > 0$, for any optimal solution $(\bar{e}_\varepsilon, \bar{f}_\varepsilon)$ of $(OP)_\varepsilon$, there exists $\bar{p}_\varepsilon \in V$, uniformly bounded in V, such that*

$$T(\bar{e}_\varepsilon\ \bar{p}_\varepsilon + \gamma^*(fM_\varepsilon^{''}(\gamma\bar{u}_\varepsilon)\gamma\bar{p}_\varepsilon) = \grave{v} - \bar{u}_\varepsilon\,, \tag{5.21}$$

$$\alpha\langle e-\bar{e}_\varepsilon, \bar{e}_\varepsilon\rangle_{\hat{E}\times\hat{E}} + t(e-\bar{e}_\varepsilon, \bar{u}_\varepsilon, \bar{p}_\varepsilon) \geq 0, \quad \forall e \in E^{ad}\,, \tag{5.22}$$

$$\beta\langle f-\bar{f}_\varepsilon, \bar{f}_\varepsilon\rangle_{\hat{F}\times\hat{F}} + (M_\varepsilon^{'}(\gamma\bar{u}_\varepsilon)\ \gamma\bar{p}_\varepsilon), f-\bar{f}_\varepsilon) \geq 0, \quad \forall f \in F^{ad}\,. \tag{5.23}$$

Proof. Let $\varepsilon > 0$ be fixed. Here we minimize

$$L(u_\varepsilon, e, f) = 1/2\ \|u_\varepsilon - \hat{v}\|^2 + 1/2\ \alpha\|e\|_{\hat{E}}^2 + 1/2\ \beta\|f\|_{\hat{F}}^2$$

and we have the constraint equation

$$A(u,e,f) = T(e)u + \gamma^*(fM_\varepsilon^{'}(\gamma u)) - l = 0\,.$$

The partial derivative $D_u A(u,e,f)$ is given by

$$\partial u \mapsto T(e)\delta u + \gamma^*(fM_\varepsilon^{''}(\gamma u)\delta u)\,.$$

We compute the adjoints via

$$\langle T(e)\delta u, w\rangle_{V\times V} = \langle T(e)w, \delta u\rangle_{V\times V}$$

by the symmetry of $t(e;\cdot,\cdot)$ and since $f \in L^\infty(D)$,

$$\langle \gamma^*(fM_\varepsilon^{''}(\gamma u)\ \gamma\,\delta u), w\rangle_{V\times V} = (fM_\varepsilon^{''}(\gamma u)\ \gamma\,\delta u, \gamma w)_{L^2(D)\times L^2(D)}$$
$$= (\gamma\,\delta u, fM_\varepsilon^{''}(\gamma u)\gamma w)_{L^2(D)\times L^2(D)} = \langle \delta u, \gamma^*(fM_\varepsilon^{''}(\gamma u)\gamma w)\rangle_{V\times V}\,.$$

Hence with the partial derivative $D_u L$ we obtain for the optimal solution

$$T(\bar{e}_\varepsilon \, \bar{p}_\varepsilon) + \gamma^*(f M''_\varepsilon(\gamma \bar{u}_\varepsilon) \gamma \bar{p}_\varepsilon) + \bar{u}_\varepsilon - \hat{v} = 0_V \, ,$$

what is (5.21). By coercivity - see the arguments in the proof of Theorem 5.3.8 - this equation uniquely determines the adjoint variable $\bar{p}_\varepsilon$.

The partial derivative $D_e A(u,e,f)$ is given by $\partial e \mapsto T(\delta e)u$. Then with the partial derivative $D_e L$ and similar to the proof of [17, Theorem 3.6] we obtain using the symmetry of $t(e,\cdot,\cdot)$ (5.22).

Finally the partial derivative $D_f A(u,e,f)$ is given by

$$\partial f \mapsto \gamma^*(\delta f M'_\varepsilon(\gamma u)) \in V \, .$$

Since $P'_\varepsilon(t) \in [0,1]$ and hence $M'_\varepsilon(\gamma v) \in L^\infty(D)$ for any $v \in V$, we can compute the adjoint:

$$\begin{aligned} &\langle \gamma^*(\delta f M'_\varepsilon(\gamma u)), w \rangle_{V \times V} \\ &= (\delta f M'_\varepsilon(\gamma u), \gamma w)_{L^2(D) \times L^2(D)} \\ &= (\delta f, M'_\varepsilon(\gamma u) \gamma w)_{L^2(D) \times L^2(D)} \, . \end{aligned}$$

Hence with the partial derivative $D_f L$, (5.23) follows.

We still need to show that $\{\bar{p}_\varepsilon\}$ is uniformly bounded. For this, we take $v = \bar{p}_\varepsilon$ in the variational equation to the adjoint equation (5.21) and by using ellipticity of t and $M''_\varepsilon \geq 0$, we obtain

$$\underline{t} \, \|\bar{p}_\varepsilon\|_V^2 \leq t(\bar{a}_\varepsilon; \bar{p}_\varepsilon, \bar{p}_\varepsilon) + \langle \gamma^*(f M''_\varepsilon(\gamma \bar{u}_\varepsilon) \gamma \bar{p}_\varepsilon), \bar{p}_\varepsilon \rangle \leq C_1 \, \|\bar{p}_\varepsilon\|_V \, ,$$

where we also used the fact that $\{\bar{u}_\varepsilon\}$ is also bounded. The proof is complete. □

5.5 Concluding Remarks—An Outlook

The field of Inverse Problems and Parameter Identification is very vast. There are many books on this subject, see also the interesting surveys [8, 28].

In this paper we have studied a parameter identification problem for nonlinear non-smooth problems in the setting of variational inequalities of the second kind. Thus our results are confined to the class of inverse problem where the associated direct problem is a convex variational problem.

On the other hand, there are interesting nonconvex variational problems resulting from nonmonotone boundary conditions in contact mechanics that describe adhesion and delamination phenomena; see, e.g., [18] for the forward problem. Here the identification of the nonmonotone contact laws is a challenging task. Also in fluid mechanics nonmonotone boundary conditions are encountered, see, e.g., [9]. Here also interesting parameter identification problems arise. When the nonmonotone boundary conditions are of max or min or min-max type, advanced regularization techniques, see [27, 19] for the forward problem, are applicable.

With linear partial differential equations with constant coefficients, as with linear elasticity and Stokes flow, boundary integral methods are available. Then boundary element methods [20] could be developed for the efficient and reliable solution of the friction parameter identification problem.

References

[1] R.A. Adams and J.J.F. Fournier. *Sobolev Spaces*, volume 140 of *Pure and Applied Mathematics (Amsterdam)*. Elsevier/Academic Press, Amsterdam, second edition, 2003.

[2] U. Aßmann and A. Rösch. Identification of an unknown parameter function in the main part of an elliptic partial differential equation. Z. Anal. Anwend., 32(2): 163–178, 2013.

[3] M. Ayadi, L. Baffico, M.K. Gdoura and T. Sassi. Error estimates for Stokes problem with Tresca friction conditions. ESAIM Math. Model. Numer. Anal., 48: 1413–1429, 2014.

[4] L. Baffico and T. Sassi. Existence result for a fluid structure interaction problem with friction type slip boundary condition. ZAMM Z. Angew. Math. Mech., 95: 831–844, 2015.

[5] H.T. Banks and K. Kunisch. *Estimation Techniques for Distributed Parameter Systems*. Birkhäuser Boston, Inc., Boston, MA, 1989.

[6] V. Barbu. Necessary conditions for nonconvex distributed control problems governed by elliptic variational inequalities. J. Math. Anal. Appl., 80(2): 566–597, 1981.

[7] V. Barbu. *Optimal Control of Variational Inequalities*, volume 100 of *Research Notes in Mathematics*. Pitman (Advanced Publishing Program), Boston, MA, 1984.

[8] M. Bonnet and A. Constantinescu. Inverse problems in elasticity. Inverse Problems, 21(2): R1–R50, 2005.

[9] S. Dudek, P. Kalita and S. Migórski. Stationary flow of non-Newtonian fluid with nonmonotone frictional boundary conditions. Z. Angew. Math. Phys., 66(5): 2625–2646, 2015.

[10] F. Facchinei and J.S. Pang. *Finite-dimensional Variational Inequalities and Complementarity Problems*, volume II. Springer, New York, 2003.

[11] H. Fujita. A mathematical analysis of motions of viscous incompressible fluid under leak or slip boundary conditions. RIMS Kokyuroku, 888: 199–216, 1994.

[12] R. Glowinski. *Numerical Methods for Nonlinear Variational Problems*. Springer-Verlag, Berlin, 2008. Reprint of the 1984 original.

[13] R. Glowinski and A. Wachs. On the numerical simulation of viscoplastic fluid flow. pp. 483–717. *In*: *Handbook of numerical analysis. Vol XVI. Special Volume: Numerical methods for non-Newtonian fluids*. Amsterdam: Elsevier/North Holland, 2011.

[14] M.S. Gockenbach and A.A. Khan. An abstract framework for elliptic inverse problems. I. An output least-squares approach. Math. Mech. Solids, 12(3): 259–276, 2007.

[15] G.A. González. Theoretical framework of an identification problem for an elliptic variational inequality with bilateral restrictions. J. Comput. Appl. Math., 197: 245–252, 2006.

[16] J. Gwinner. An optimization approach to parameter identification in variational inequalities of second kind. Optim. Lett., 12: 1141–1154, 2018.

[17] J. Gwinner, B. Jadamba, A.A. Khan and M. Sama. Identification in variational and quasi-variational inequalities. J. Convex Anal., 25: 545–569, 2018.

[18] J. Gwinner and N. Ovcharova. From solvability and approximation of variational inequalities to solution of nondifferentiable optimization problems in contact mechanics. Optimization, 64: 1683–1702, 2015.

[19] J. Gwinner and N. Ovcharova. A Garding inequality based unified approach to various classes of semi-coercive variational inequalities applied to non-monotone contact problems with a nested max-min superpotential. Minimax Theory Appl., 5(1): 103–128, 2020.

[20] J. Gwinner and E.P. Stephan. *Advanced Boundary Element Methods—Treatment of Boundary Value, Transmission and Contact Problems*, volume 52 of *Springer Series in Computational Mathematics*. Springer, Cham, 2018.

[21] M. Hintermüller. Inverse coefficient problems for variational inequalities: optimality conditions and numerical realization. M2AN Math. Model. Numer. Anal., 35: 129–152, 2001.

[22] A.A. Khan, S. Migórski and M. Sama. Inverse problems for multi-valued quasi variational inequalities and noncoercive variational inequalities with noisy data. Optimization, 68(10): 1897–1931, 2019.

[23] D. Kinderlehrer and G. Stampacchia. *An Introduction to Variational Inequalities and their Applications*. Society for Industrial and Applied Mathematics (SIAM), Philadelphia, PA, 2000. Reprint of the 1980 original.

[24] S. Migórski, A.A. Khan and S. Zeng. Inverse problems for nonlinear quasivariational inequalities with an application to implicit obstacle problems of p-Laplacian type. Inverse Problems, 35(3): 035004, 14, 2019.

[25] M.Z. Nashed and F. Liu. On nonlinear ill-posed problems. II. Monotone operator equations and monotone variational inequalities. pp. 223–240. *In*: *Theory and Applications of Nonlinear Operators of Accretive and Monotone Type*, volume 178 of *Lecture Notes in Pure and Appl. Math.* Dekker, New York, 1996.

[26] P. Neittaanmaki, J. Sprekels and D. Tiba. *Optimization of Elliptic Systems*. Springer Monographs in Mathematics. Springer, New York, 2006. Theory and applications.

[27] N. Ovcharova and J. Gwinner. A study of regularization techniques of nondifferentiable optimization in view of application to hemivariational inequalities. J. Optim. Theory Appl., 162: 754–778, 2014.

[28] K. Shirota and K. Onishi. Adjoint method for numerical solution of inverse boundary value and coefficient identification problems. Surv. Math. Ind., 11(1-4): 43–93, 2005.

[29] D. Tiba. *Optimal Control of Nonsmooth Distributed Parameter Systems*, volume 1459 of *Lecture Notes in Mathematics*. Springer-Verlag, Berlin, 1990.

Chapter 6

Generalized Variational-hemivariational Inequalities in Fuzzy Environment

Shengda Zeng[a,*], *Jinxia Cen*[b], *Stanisław Migórski*[c] and *Van Thien Nguyen*[d]

2010 Mathematics Subject Classification. 35Jxx, 47J20, 49Jxx, 58Exx, 80M30.

The chapter is dedicated to Professor Zuhair Nashed for his great contribution on variational inequalities and inverse problems.

6.1 Introduction

The theory of variational inequalities can be efficiently employed to describe the principles of virtual work and power which was initially proposed by Fourier

[a] Guangxi Colleges and Universities Key Laboratory of Complex System Optimization and Big Data Processing, Yulin Normal University, Yulin 537000, Guangxi, P.R. China, and Jagiellonian University in Krakow, Faculty of Mathematics and Computer Science, ul. Lojasiewicza 6, 30348 Krakow, Poland.

[b] School of Science, Institute for artificial intelligence, Southwest Petroleum University, Chengdu, Sichuan 610500, P. R. China.

[c] Jagiellonian University in Krakow, Faculty of Mathematics and Computer Science, ul. Lojasiewicza 6, 30348 Krakow, Poland.

[d] Department of Mathematics, FPT University, Education zone, Hoa Lac high tech park, Km29 Thang Long highway, Thach That ward, Hanoi, Vietnam.

Emails: jinxiacen@163.com; stanislaw.migorski@uj.edu.pl; Thiennv15@fe.edu.vn

* Corresponding author: zengshengda@163.com

in 1823. The prototypes, which lead to a class of variational inequalities, are the problems of Signorini-Fichera and of frictional contact in elasticity. The first complete proof of unique solvability to the Signorini problem was provided by Signorini's student Fichera in 1964. The solution of the Signorini problem coincides with the birth of the field of variational inequalities. For more on the initial developments of elasticity theory and variational inequalities, cf., e.g., [1]. With the gradual improvement of the theory of variational inequalities, there are numerous monographs dedicated to solving various complex phenomena in contact mechanics with different bodies and foundations, see, for instance [10, 11, 13, 23] and others. As the generalization of variational inequalities, the theory of hemivariational inequalities was first introduced and studied by P.D. Panagiotopoulos in [22]. The mathematical theory of hemivariational inequalities has been of great interest recently, which is due to the intensive development of applications of hemivariational inequalities in contact mechanics, control theory, games and so forth. Some comprehensive references are [18, 19, 20].

On the other side, the concept of a fuzzy set was first introduced and studied by Zadeh [26] in 1965. Since then, the fuzzy set theory gained a substantial amount of attention, because it can be used as a powerful tool to model some uncertain problems. After that, in 1972, Chang-Zadeh [8] proposed the notion of a fuzzy mapping and considered a simple fuzzy variational inequality. A large amount of problems, such as image processing, contact mechanics problems and dynamic traffic networks, eventually can be formulated by fuzzy variational inequalities. So, variational inequalities in fuzzy environment have attracted a wide range of attention of researchers, for instance, Chang-Lee-Lee [4, 5] introduced and investigated a vector quasi-variational inequality driven by fuzzy mappings, Chang-Salahuddin [6] proved the existence of solution to a fuzzy vector quasi-variational-like inequalities, under suitable monotonicity and coercivity conditions Huang-Li-O'Regan [15] investigated a class of f-complementary problems through applying KKM theorem, and Tang-Zhao-Wan-He [25] explored an existence result for a perturbed variational inequality with a fuzzy mapping in a finite dimensional space. For more details on these topics the reader is welcome to consult [2, 7, 14, 15, 16] and the references therein.

To the best of our knowledge, up to now, there has not been any study on fuzzy variational-hemivariational inequalities. Based on this motivation, our goal is to fill in this gap and provide new results in this area. Let E and X be two real reflexive Banach spaces, E^* be the topological dual of E, K be a nonempty, closed and convex subset of E, and $\varphi\colon E \to \overline{\mathbb{R}} := \mathbb{R} \cup \{+\infty\}$ be a convex, proper (i.e., finite at least in one point) and lower semicontinuous function. Given a fuzzy mapping $H\colon K \to \mathcal{F}(E^*)$ (in what follows, we denote by $H(x,y) = H_x(y)$ for all $x \in K$ and all $y \in E^*$), a locally Lipschitz function $J\colon X \to \mathbb{R}$, an operator $\gamma\colon E \to X$, an element $q \in E^*$, and a function $\alpha\colon K \to (0,1]$, in this paper, we are concerned with the study of existence of solution for the following generalized fuzzy variational-hemivariational inequality (FVHVI, for short).

Problem 6.1.1 *Find $u \in K$ such that*

$$\begin{cases} \langle w+q, v-u\rangle + \varphi(v) - \varphi(u) + J^0(\gamma u; \gamma(v-u)) \geq 0 \quad \text{for all } v \in K, \\ H(u,w) \geq \alpha(u). \end{cases} \tag{6.1}$$

The goal of the current work is twofold. In the first part of the chapter, we use a monotonicity argument and a fixed principle for set-valued operators to explore the nonemptiness, boundedness and weak closedness of the solution set for fuzzy variational-hemivariational inequality in Problem 6.1.1. Moreover, the second part of the chapter is devoted to an optimal control problem described by a fuzzy variational-hemivariational inequality. Under mild assumptions, an existence result for the optimal control problem is delivered by applying a Weierstrass type theorem.

The rest of the chapter is organized as follows. In Section 6.2 we survey preliminary material needed in the sequel. In Section 6.3, we apply the monotonicity argument and a fixed point theorem for set-valued operators to prove a result that the set of solutions of Problem 6.1.1 is nonempty, bounded and weakly closed. Finally, in Section 6.4, we introduce an optimal control problem driven by a fuzzy variational-hemivariational inequality, and establish an existence result for the optimal control problem under consideration.

6.2 Mathematical Prerequisites

In this section we recall notation and collect basic results needed later. For more details, we refer to [9, 17, 21, 7, 4, 12, 27].

Let X and Y be two topological vector spaces, and D be a subset of X. We denote by 2^X the set of all subsets of X. We say that

(i) a function $A\colon X \to [0,1]$ is called a fuzzy set on X, and denote by $\mathcal{F}(X)$ the collection of all fuzzy sets on X,

(ii) a function F from D into $\mathcal{F}(Y)$, i.e., $F\colon D \to \mathcal{F}(Y)$, is called fuzzy mapping on D.

Remark 6.2.1 *If $F\colon D \to \mathcal{F}(Y)$ is a fuzzy mapping, then for all $x \in D$, $F(x) \in \mathcal{F}(Y)$ is a fuzzy set on Y, namely, $F(x)$ is a function from Y to $[0,1]$. In what follows, we write $F_x(y) = F(x,y)$ for all $x \in D$ and $y \in Y$. For any $y \in Y$, $F_x(y)$ is usually called the degree of membership of y in the fuzzy set F_x.*

Definition 6.2.2 *Let $F\colon D \subset X \to \mathcal{F}(Y)$ be a fuzzy mapping, and A be a fuzzy set on Y.*

(i) *We say that F is convex, if for any $x \in D$, the fuzzy set F_x satisfies the inequality*

$$F_x(ty + (1-t)z) \geq \min\{F_x(y), F_x(z)\} \quad \text{for all } t \in [0,1] \text{ and } y, z \in Y.$$

(ii) *We say that F is closed, if the binary function $(x,y) \mapsto F_x(y)$ is upper semicontinuous on $D \times Y$, i.e.,*

$$\limsup_{n\to\infty} F_{x_n}(y_n) \le F_x(y)$$

for any $\{x_n\} \subset D$ and $\{y_n\} \subset Y$ with $x_n \to x$ in D and $y_n \to y$ in Y.

(iii) *If $Y = X^*$, F is said to be monotone on D if for any x, $y \in D$ and any u, $w \in X^*$ with $F_x(u) > 0$ and $F_y(w) > 0$, the inequality $\langle w-u, y-x\rangle \ge 0$ holds.*

(iv) *Given $\alpha \in [0,1]$, the α-cut set and the strong α-cut set of A are defined by*

$$(A)_\alpha := \{y \in Y \mid A(y) \ge \alpha\} \ \text{ and } \ [A]_\alpha := \{y \in Y \mid A(y) > \alpha\},$$

respectively.

For more details on fuzzy mappings the reader is refered to [3, 14] and the references therein.

A function $J\colon X \to \mathbb{R}$, defined on a Banach space X, is called locally Lipschitz at $u \in X$ if there exist a neighborhood $N(u)$ of u in X and a constant $L_u > 0$ such that

$$|J(w) - J(v)| \le L_u \|w-v\|_X \ \text{ for all } \ w, v \in N(u).$$

Definition 6.2.3 *Given a locally Lipschitz function $J\colon X \to \mathbb{R}$, we denote by $J^0(u;v)$ the generalized directional derivative of J at the point $u \in X$ in the direction $v \in X$ defined by*

$$J^0(u;v) = \limsup_{\lambda\to 0^+,\, w\to u} \frac{J(w+\lambda v) - J(w)}{\lambda}.$$

The generalized gradient of $J\colon X \to \mathbb{R}$ at $u \in X$ is given by

$$\partial J(u) = \{\, \xi \in X^* \mid J^0(u;v) \ge \langle \xi, v\rangle \ \text{ for all } \ v \in X \,\}.$$

Basic properties are collected in the statement below, see, e.g., [21, Proposition 3.23].

Proposition 6.2.4 *Assume that the function $J\colon X \to \mathbb{R}$ is locally Lipschitz. Then, we have*

(i) *for every $x \in X$, the function $X \ni v \mapsto J^0(x;v) \in \mathbb{R}$ is positively homogeneous and subadditive, i.e., $J^0(x;\lambda v) = \lambda J^0(x;v)$ for all $\lambda \ge 0$, $v \in X$ and $J^0(x; v_1+v_2) \le J^0(x;v_1) + J^0(x;v_2)$ for all v_1, $v_2 \in X$,*

(ii) *for every $v \in X$, it holds $J^0(x;v) = \max\{\, \langle \xi, v\rangle \mid \xi \in \partial J(x) \,\}$,*

(iii) *the function $X \times X \ni (u,v) \mapsto J^0(u;v) \in \mathbb{R}$ is upper semicontinuous.*

We conclude this section with the following fixed point principle for set-valued mappings which will play a significant role in the proof of existence of solutions to the inequality problems in Section 6.3. Its proof can be found in [24].

Theorem 6.2.5 *Let K be a nonempty and convex subset of a Hausdorff topological vector space E. Let $F\colon K \to 2^K$ be a set-valued map such that*

(i) *for each $u \in K$, the set $F(u)$ is a nonempty convex subset of K,*

(ii) *for each $v \in K$, $F^{-1}(v) = \{u \in K \mid v \in F(u)\}$ contains a relatively open subset O_v (O_v may be empty for some v),*

(iii) $\bigcup_{v\in K} O_v = K$,

(iv) *there exists a nonempty set K_0 contained in a compact convex subset K_1 of K such that $D = \bigcap_{v\in K_0} O_v^c$ is either empty or compact, where O_v^c denotes the complement of O_v.*

Then, there exists $u_0 \in K$ such that $u_0 \in F(u_0)$.

6.3 Fuzzy Variational-hemivariational Inequalities

In this section we study existence of solution to Problem 6.1.1. First, we define the set–valued mapping $\mathcal{H}\colon K \to 2^{E^*}$ by

$$\mathcal{H}(u) := \{w \in E^* \mid H(u,w) \geq \alpha(u)\} \text{ for all } u \in K. \tag{6.2}$$

We impose the following hypotheses on the data of Problem 6.1.1.

(A_1) $H\colon K \to \mathcal{F}(E^*)$ is a convex and monotone fuzzy mapping which is closed with respect to the strong topology of E and the weak topology of E^* (see Definition 6.2.2), and $\alpha\colon K \to (0,1]$ is a lower semicontinuous function such that $\mathcal{H}$ is a bounded mapping, namely, for each bounded set $B \subset K$, there exists a constant $M_B > 0$ satisfying

$$\|\mathcal{H}(B)\|_{E^*} := \sup_{u\in B} \{\|w\|_{E^*} \mid w \in \mathcal{H}(u)\} \leq M_B. \tag{6.3}$$

(A_2) $J\colon X \to \mathbb{R}$ is a locally Lipschitz function, $\gamma\colon E \to X$ is a linear and compact operator, and $\varphi\colon E \to \overline{\mathbb{R}}$ is a proper, convex and lower semicontinuous function.

Lemma 6.3.1 *If (A_1) and (A_2) hold, then the map $\mathcal{H}\colon K \to 2^{E^*}$ defined by (6.2) is strongly–weakly closed, strongly–weakly upper semicontinuous, and for all $u \in K$ the set $\mathcal{H}(u)$ is weakly closed and convex in E^*.*

Proof. Let $u \in K$ be arbitrary. We demonstrate the convexity of $\mathcal{H}(u)$. For all w_1, $w_2 \in \mathcal{H}(u)$ and $\lambda \in (0,1)$, we have

$$H(u,w_i) \geq \alpha(u) \text{ for } i = 1,2.$$

The convexity of H implies

$$H(u,w_\lambda) \geq \min\{H(u,w_1), H(u,w_2)\} \geq \alpha(u),$$

where $w_\lambda := \lambda w_1 + (1-\lambda)w_2$. This means that $w_\lambda \in \mathcal{H}(u)$, so, $\mathcal{H}(u)$ is convex for all $u \in K$. Next, let $\{w_n\} \subset \mathcal{H}(u)$ be a sequence such that $w_n \rightharpoonup w$ in E^* as $n \to \infty$ for some $w \in E^*$. The closedness of H leads to

$$H(u,w) \geq \limsup_{n\to\infty} H(u,w_n) \geq \alpha(u).$$

Hence, we conclude that $w \in \mathcal{H}(u)$, which implies that $\mathcal{H}(u)$ is weakly closed in E^*.

We will show that $\mathcal{H}$ is closed from E endowed with the norm topology to the subsets of E^* endowed with the weak topology. To this end, let $\{u_n\} \subset K$ and $\{w_n\} \subset E^*$ be such that $u_n \to u$ in E and $w_n \rightharpoonup w$ in E^* as $n \to \infty$ with $w_n \in \mathcal{H}(u_n)$ for all $n \in \mathbb{N}$. Then, for each $n \in \mathbb{N}$, we have

$$H(u_n,w_n) \geq \alpha(u_n). \tag{6.4}$$

Using the closedness of H and lower semicontinuity of α reveals

$$H(u,w) \geq \limsup_{n\to\infty} H(u_n,w_n) \geq \limsup_{n\to\infty} \alpha(u_n) \geq \liminf_{n\to\infty} \alpha(u_n) \geq \alpha(u). \tag{6.5}$$

We conclude that $w \in \mathcal{H}(u)$, and therefore, $\mathcal{H}$ is strongly–weakly closed.

Finally, we shall verify that $\mathcal{H}$ is upper semicontinuous from E endowed with the norm topology to the subsets of E^* endowed with the weak topology. Invoking [21, Proposition 3.8], it is enough to prove that for each weakly closed subset D in E^*, the set $\mathcal{H}^{-1}(D)$ is closed in K, where $\mathcal{H}^{-1}(D)$ is defined by

$$\mathcal{H}^{-1}(D) := \{u \in K \mid \mathcal{H}(u) \cap D \neq \emptyset\}.$$

Let $\{u_n\} \subset \mathcal{H}^{-1}(D)$ be a sequence such that $u_n \to u$ in K as $n \to \infty$ for some $u \in K$. So, we can find $w_n \in \mathcal{H}(u_n) \cap D$ for each $n \in \mathbb{N}$. Hence

$$H(u_n,w_n) \geq \alpha(u_n). \tag{6.6}$$

Moreover, condition (A_1) ensures that $\{w_n\}$ is a bounded sequence in E^* due to $u_n \to u$ as $n \to \infty$. Passing to a subsequence, we may assume that $w_n \rightharpoonup w$ in E^* as $n \to \infty$ for some $w \in D$. This together with the convergence $u_n \to u$ and the strong–weak closedness of $\mathcal{H}$ implies $w \in \mathcal{H}(u) \cap D$. Consequently, we have $u \in \mathcal{H}^{-1}(D)$, thus, $\mathcal{H}$ is strongly–weakly upper semicontinuous. □

The Minty type inequality corresponding to Problem 6.1.1 is formulated as follows.

Problem 6.3.2 *Find $u \in K$ such that*

$$\langle w+q, v-u\rangle + \varphi(v) - \varphi(u) + J^0(\gamma u; \gamma(v-u)) \geq 0 \text{ for all } w \in \mathcal{H}(v) \text{ and all } v \in K. \tag{6.7}$$

Employing Lemma 6.3.1, we deduce the following result.

Theorem 6.3.3 *Assume that* (A_1) *and* (A_2) *hold. Then* $u \in K$ *is a solution of Problem 6.1.1 if and only if it solves Problem 6.3.2.*

Proof. "$\Longrightarrow$" Let $u \in K$ be an arbitrary solution to Problem 6.1.1. Then, there exists $w \in E^*$ such that the second inequality in (6.1) is satisfied. From the monotonicity of H and the fact $\alpha(v) > 0$ for each $v \in K$, it follows that for each $v \in K$ and $\widehat{w} \in E^*$ with $H(v, \widehat{w}) \geq \alpha(v) > 0$, we have

$$\langle \widehat{w} - w, v - u \rangle \geq 0.$$

Combining the latter with the first inequality of (6.1), one finds

$$\begin{aligned} &\langle \widehat{w} + q, v - u \rangle + \varphi(v) - \varphi(u) + J^0(\gamma u; \gamma(v - u)) \\ &\geq \langle w + q, v - u \rangle + \varphi(v) - \varphi(u) + J^0(\gamma u; \gamma(v - u)) \geq 0 \end{aligned}$$

for all $\widehat{w} \in \mathcal{H}(v)$ and all $v \in K$. Hence, u is also a solution to Problem 6.3.2.
"$\Longleftarrow$" Assume that $u \in K$ solves Problem 6.3.2. Then

$$\langle \widehat{w} + q, v - u \rangle + \varphi(v) - \varphi(u) + J^0(\gamma u; \gamma(v - u)) \geq 0 \text{ for all } \widehat{w} \in \mathcal{H}(v) \text{ and all } v \in K.$$

Let $v \in K$ and $\lambda \in (0, 1)$ be arbitrary. We insert $v = v_\lambda := \lambda v + (1 - \lambda)u \in K$ into the above inequality to get

$$\begin{aligned} 0 &\leq \langle \widehat{w}_\lambda + q, v_\lambda - u \rangle + \varphi(v_\lambda) - \varphi(u) + J^0(\gamma u; \gamma(v_\lambda - u)) \\ &\leq \lambda \left[\langle \widehat{w}_\lambda + q, v - u \rangle + \varphi(v) - \varphi(u) + J^0(\gamma u; \gamma(v - u)) \right] \end{aligned}$$

for all $\widehat{w}_\lambda \in \mathcal{H}(v_\lambda)$. Here, we have used the convexity of φ and the fact that $v \mapsto J^0(u; v)$ is positively homogeneous (see Proposition 6.2.4(i)). Hence

$$\langle \widehat{w}_\lambda + q, v - u \rangle + \varphi(v) - \varphi(u) + J^0(\gamma u; \gamma(v - u)) \geq 0 \text{ for all } \widehat{w}_\lambda \in \mathcal{H}(v_\lambda).$$

Using the convergence $v_\lambda \to u$ as $\lambda \to 0^+$ and the hypothesis that $\mathcal{H}$ is a bounded mapping, we infer that the sequence $\{\widehat{w}_\lambda\}$ is bounded in E^*. Therefore, by passing to a subsequence if necessary, we suppose such that $\widehat{w}_\lambda \to w$ weakly in E^* as $\lambda \to 0^+$ for some $w \in E^*$. Recall that the fuzzy function H is closed with respect to the strong topology of E and the weak topology of E^*. It gives

$$H(u, w) \geq \limsup_{\lambda \to 0^+} H(v_\lambda, \widehat{w}_\lambda) \geq \limsup_{\lambda \to 0^+} \alpha(v_\lambda) \geq \liminf_{\lambda \to 0^+} \alpha(v_\lambda) \geq \alpha(u),$$

and proves that $w \in \mathcal{H}(u)$. Finally, the latter together with the following estimate

$$\begin{aligned} &\langle w + q, v - u \rangle + \varphi(v) - \varphi(u) + J^0(\gamma u; \gamma(v - u)) \\ &= \lim_{\lambda \to 0^+} \left[\langle \widehat{w}_\lambda + q, v - u \rangle + \varphi(v) - \varphi(u) + J^0(\gamma u; \gamma(v - u)) \right] \geq 0 \end{aligned}$$

for all $v \in K$, implies that u is a solution to Problem 6.1.1. This completes the proof. □

Let $D(\varphi) := \{u \in E \mid \varphi(u) < +\infty\}$ be the domain of φ and $\gamma^* : X^* \to E^*$ be the adjoint operator to γ.

In what follows, we need the following coercivity condition.

(A_3) There exists an element $v^* \in K \cap D(\varphi)$ such that

$$\lim_{u \in K,\, \|u\|_E \to +\infty} \frac{\inf_{w \in \mathcal{H}(u), \xi \in \partial J(\gamma u)} \langle w + \gamma^* \xi, u - v^* \rangle}{\|u\|_E} = +\infty. \tag{6.8}$$

Remark 6.3.4 *It is easy to observe that hypothesis (6.8) allows one to find a function $r\colon [0,+\infty) \to \mathbb{R}$ with $r(k) \to \infty$ as $k \to \infty$ such that*

$$\inf_{w \in \mathcal{H}(u), \xi \in \partial J(\gamma u)} \langle w + \gamma^* \xi, u - v^* \rangle + \varphi(u) - \varphi(v^*) \ge r(\|u\|_E)\, \|u\|_E$$

for all $u \in K$.

Subsequently, we denote by $SOL(K, H+q, \varphi, J)$ the solution set to Problem 6.1.1. The existence result for Problem 6.1.1 reads as follows.

Theorem 6.3.5 *Under hypotheses (A_1) and (A_2), if, in addition, the set K is bounded or (A_3) holds, then for each $q \in E^*$ fixed, the set $SOL(K, H+q, \varphi, J)$ is nonempty, bounded and weakly closed.*

Proof. We first prove the existence of solution to Problem 6.1.1. We distinguish the following two cases:

(a) K is bounded in E;

(b) K is unbounded in E.

Suppose that (a) holds. Arguing by contradiction, we assume that Problem 6.1.1 has no solution, so, for each $u \in K$, we are able to find $v \in K$ such that

$$\langle w + q, v - u \rangle + J^0(\gamma u; \gamma(v-u)) + \varphi(v) - \varphi(u) < 0$$

for all $w \in E^*$ with $H(u,w) \ge \alpha(u)$. Consider the mapping $\Lambda\colon K \to 2^K$ defined by

$$\Lambda(u) := \left\{ u \in K \mid \sup_{\widehat{w} \in \mathcal{H}(u)} \langle \widehat{w} + q, v - u \rangle + J^0(\gamma u; \gamma(v-u)) + \varphi(v) - \varphi(u) < 0 \right\}$$

for all $u \in K$. Moreover, the assumption that Problem 6.1.1 has no solution shows that

(i) $\Lambda(u) \neq \emptyset$ for all $u \in K$,

(ii) Λ has no fixed point in K.

In order to show the existence of solution to Problem 6.1.1, we shall trigger the contradiction that the set–valued mapping Λ has at least one fixed point in K. We have the following claims.

Claim 1. *For all $u \in K$, the set $\Lambda(u)$ is convex in K.*

Let $u \in K$, $v_1, v_2 \in \Lambda(u)$, and $t \in (0,1)$ be arbitrary. Set $v_t := tv_1 + (1-t)v_2$. For $i = 1, 2$, one has

$$\sup_{\widehat{w}\in\mathcal{H}(u)} \langle \widehat{w}+q, v_i - u\rangle + J^0(\gamma u; \gamma(v_i - u)) + \varphi(v_i) - \varphi(u) < 0.$$

Hence, we have

$$\begin{aligned}&\sup_{\widehat{w}\in\mathcal{H}(u)} \langle \widehat{w}+q, v_t - u\rangle + J^0(\gamma u; \gamma(v_t - u)) + \varphi(v_t) - \varphi(u)\\ &\quad\le t\Big[\sup_{\widehat{w}\in\mathcal{H}(u)} \langle \widehat{w}+q, v_1 - u\rangle + J^0(\gamma u; \gamma(v_1 - u)) + \varphi(v_1) - \varphi(u)\Big]\\ &\qquad+(1-t)\Big[\sup_{\widehat{w}\in\mathcal{H}(u)} \langle \widehat{w}+q, v_2 - u\rangle + J^0(\gamma u; \gamma(v_2 - u)) + \varphi(v_2) - \varphi(u)\Big] < 0,\end{aligned}$$

where we have used the convexity of φ and the positive homogeneity and subadditivity of $v \mapsto J(u;v)$. Therefore, we deduce that $\Lambda(u)$ is convex in K.

In addition, for every $v \in K$ fixed, let us define the set O_v by

$$O_v := \big\{u \in K \mid \inf_{w\in\mathcal{H}(v)} \langle w+q, v-u\rangle + J^0(\gamma u; \gamma(v-u)) + \varphi(v) - \varphi(u) < 0\big\}.$$

Claim 2. *For all $v \in K$, the set O_v is weakly open, and $\Lambda^{-1}(v)$ contains O_v, where*

$$\Lambda^{-1}(v) := \big\{u \in K \mid v \in \Lambda(u)\big\} \text{ for all } v \in K.$$

It is not difficult to see that this claim is equivalent to the assertion that the set $O_v^{\complement}$ is weakly closed and

$$\big[\Lambda^{-1}(v)\big]^{\complement} \subset O_v^{\complement} \tag{6.9}$$

for each $v \in K$. For any $u \in \big[\Lambda^{-1}(v)\big]^{\complement}$, we have

$$\sup_{\widehat{w}\in\mathcal{H}(u)} \langle \widehat{w}+q, v-u\rangle + J^0(\gamma u; \gamma(v-u)) + \varphi(v) - \varphi(u) \ge 0.$$

Note that $\mathcal{H}$ has bounded, closed and convex values, so, there exists an element $w \in E^*$ with $H(u,w) \ge \alpha(u)$ such that

$$\langle w+q, v-u\rangle + J^0(\gamma u; \gamma(v-u)) + \varphi(v) - \varphi(u) \ge 0.$$

The latter combined with the monotonicity of H entails

$$\langle \widetilde{w}+q, v-u\rangle + J^0(\gamma u; \gamma(v-u)) + \varphi(v) - \varphi(u) \ge 0$$

for all $\widetilde{w} \in \mathcal{H}(v)$. This means that

$$\inf_{\widetilde{w}\in\mathcal{H}(v)} \langle \widetilde{w}+q, v-u\rangle + J^0(\gamma u;\gamma(v-u)) + \varphi(v) - \varphi(u) \geq 0.$$

So, we have $u \in O_v^{\complement}$, i.e., (6.9) is proved.

We now show that the set $O_v^{\complement}$ is weakly closed. Let $\{u_n\} \subset O_v^{\complement}$ be a sequence such that $u_n \to u$ weakly in E, as $n \to \infty$, for some $u \in K$. Then, one has

$$\langle \widetilde{w}+q, v-u_n\rangle + J^0(\gamma u_n;\gamma(v-u_n)) + \varphi(v) - \varphi(u_n) \geq 0$$

for all $\widetilde{w} \in E^*$ with $H(v,\widetilde{w}) \geq \alpha(v)$. Passing to the upper limit as $n \to \infty$ in the above inequality, we could apply the compactness of γ, the weak lower semicontinuity of φ, and Proposition 6.2.4(iii) to obtain

$$\begin{aligned}
&\langle \widetilde{w}+q, v-u\rangle + J^0(\gamma u;\gamma(v-u)) + \varphi(v) - \varphi(u) \\
&\quad \geq \lim_{n\to\infty} \langle \widetilde{w}+q, v-u_n\rangle + \limsup_{n\to\infty} J^0(\gamma u_n;\gamma(v-u_n)) + \varphi(v) - \liminf_{n\to\infty} \varphi(u_n) \\
&\quad \geq \limsup_{n\to\infty} \left[\langle \widetilde{w}+q, v-u_n\rangle + J^0(\gamma u_n;\gamma(v-u_n)) + \varphi(v) - \varphi(u_n)\right] \geq 0
\end{aligned}$$

for all $\widetilde{w} \in E^*$ with $H(v,\widetilde{w}) \geq \alpha(v)$. Hence

$$\inf_{\widetilde{w}\in\mathcal{H}(v)} \langle \widetilde{w}+q, v-u\rangle + J^0(\gamma u;\gamma(v-u)) + \varphi(v) - \varphi(u) \geq 0.$$

This means that $u \in O_v^{\complement}$ which implies that $O_v^{\complement}$ is weakly closed in V. Therefore, we conclude that O_v is weakly open for each $v \in K$.

Claim 3. *We have* $\cup_{v\in K} O_v = K$.

It is obvious that $\cup_{v\in K} O_v \subset K$, so, we shall only show that the inclusion $K \subset \cup_{v\in K} O_v$ is valid. Let $u \in K$ be arbitrary. Recall that Problem 6.1.1 has no solution, so we use Theorem 6.3.3 to find elements $v \in K$ and $\widetilde{w} \in E^*$ with $H(v,\widetilde{w}) \geq \alpha(v)$ such that

$$\langle \widetilde{w}+q, v-u\rangle + J^0(\gamma u;\gamma(v-u)) + \varphi(v) - \varphi(u) < 0.$$

Hence,

$$\inf_{\widetilde{w}\in\mathcal{H}(v)} \langle \widetilde{w}+q, v-u\rangle + J^0(\gamma u;\gamma(v-u)) + \varphi(v) - \varphi(u) < 0.$$

This guarantees that $u \in O_v$, which shows that $K \subset \cup_{v\in K} O_v$.

Claim 4. *The set* $\cap_{v\in K} O_v^{\complement}$ *is weakly compact, if it is nonempty.*

Suppose that $\cap_{v\in K} O_v^{\complement}$ is nonempty. Claim 2 indicates that $\cap_{v\in K} O_v^{\complement}$ is weakly closed, due to the weak closedness of $O_v^{\complement}$. On the other hand, the boundedness, convexity and closedness of K together with the reflexivity of E imply that K

is weakly compact. This implies that the set $\cap_{v\in K} O_v^{\complement}$ is weakly compact, and therefore the claim is valid.

Combining Claims 1–4 and the fixed point principle of Theorem 6.2.5, we infer that Λ has at least one fixed point in K. This gives a contradiction, so, we conclude that Problem 6.1.1 admits a solution in K.

Further, we consider the case (b) when K is unbounded in E. For every $n \in \mathbb{N}$, consider the set $K_n := \{u \in K \mid \|u - v^*\|_E \leq n\}$, where the element $v^* \in K$ is given in hypothesis (A_3). Analogously to the preceding proof, for each $n \in \mathbb{N}$, we may find $u_n \in K_n$ such that

$$\begin{cases} \langle w_n + q, v - u_n\rangle + J^0(\gamma u_n; \gamma(v - u_n)) + \varphi(v) - \varphi(u_n) \geq 0 \quad \text{for all } v \in K_n, \\ H(u_n, w_n) \geq \alpha(u_n). \end{cases}$$

We are going to show that there exists $n \in \mathbb{N}$ large enough such that for all $u_n \in SOL(K_n, H + q, \varphi, J)$, we have

$$\|u_n - v^*\|_E < n. \tag{6.10}$$

If the above inequality is not true, then for each $n \in \mathbb{N}$, we have

$$\begin{cases} \langle w_n + q, v - u_n\rangle + J^0(\gamma u_n; \gamma(v - u_n)) + \varphi(v) - \varphi(u_n) \geq 0 \quad \text{for all } v \in K_n, \\ w_n \in E^* \text{ with } H(u_n, w_n) \geq \alpha(u_n), \\ \|u_n - v^*\|_E = n. \end{cases}$$

Invoking the coercivity hypothesis (A_3), we deduce that there exist a constant $N_0 > 0$ and a function $r\colon = [0, +\infty) \to \mathbb{R}$ with $r(k) \to \infty$, as $k \to \infty$, such that

$$\inf_{w\in\mathcal{H}(u_n),\, \xi_n \in \partial J(\gamma u_n)} \langle w + \gamma^* \xi_n, u_n - v^*\rangle + \varphi(u_n) - \varphi(v^*) \geq r(\|u_n\|_E)\, \|u_n\|_E$$

for each $\|u_n\|_E > N_0$. Taking $n > \max\{N_0, \|v^*\|_E\}$ large enough such that

$$r(n - \|v^*\|_E) > \|q\|_{E^*} + \frac{\|q\|_{E^*}\|v^*\|_E}{n - \|v^*\|_E},$$

we obtain

$$\begin{aligned} 0 &\geq \langle w_n + \gamma^* \xi_n + q, u_n - v^*\rangle + \varphi(u_n) - \varphi(v^*) \geq \langle q, u_n - v^*\rangle + r(\|u_n\|_E)\, \|u_n\|_E \\ &\geq -\|q\|_{E^*}\|u_n - v^*\|_E + (\|u_n - v^*\|_E - \|v^*\|_E) r(\|u_n - v^*\|_E - \|v^*\|_E) \\ &\geq (n - \|v^*\|_E)(-\|q\|_{E^*} + r(n - \|v^*\|_E)) - \|q\|_{E^*}\|v^*\|_E > 0 \end{aligned}$$

with $w_n \in \mathcal{H}(u_n)$ and $\xi_n \in \partial J(\gamma u_n)$. This leads a contradiction. Hence, (6.10) is valid.

Now, we assume that $u_n \in SOL(K_n, H + q, \varphi, J)$ is such that (6.10) holds. Indeed, we will show that u_n is also a solution to Problem 6.1.1. For any $v \in K$, we can find $\lambda \in (0,1)$ small enough such that $v_\lambda := \lambda v + (1-\lambda)u_n \in K_n$. Then, using the convexity of φ and the positive homogeneity and subadditivity of $v \mapsto J(u;v)$, we obtain

$$\begin{aligned} 0 &\le \langle w_n + q, v_\lambda - u_n\rangle + J^0(\gamma u_n; \gamma(v_\lambda - u_n)) + \varphi(v_\lambda) - \varphi(u_n) \\ &\le \lambda\left[\langle w_n + q, v - u_n\rangle + J^0(\gamma u_n; \gamma(v - u_n)) + \varphi(v) - \varphi(u_n)\right]. \end{aligned}$$

This implies

$$\begin{cases} \langle w_n + q, v - u_n\rangle + J^0(\gamma u_n; \gamma(v - u_n)) + \varphi(v) - \varphi(u_n) \ge 0 \quad \text{for all } v \in K, \\ H(u_n, w_n) \ge \alpha(u_n). \end{cases}$$

Therefore, $u_n \in SOL(K, H+q, \varphi, J) \neq \emptyset$.

It remains to prove that the set $SOL(K, H+q, \varphi, J)$ is bounded and weakly closed.

Claim 5. *The set $SOL(K, H+q, \varphi, J)$ is bounded and weakly closed.*

Suppose that $SOL(K, H+q, \varphi, J)$ is unbounded. So, there exists a sequence $\{u_n\} \subset SOL(K, H+q, \varphi, J)$ such that

$$\|u_n\|_E \to \infty, \quad \text{as } n \to \infty.$$

Further, a simple computation gives

$$\begin{aligned} 0 &\ge \langle w_n + \gamma^*\xi_n + q, u_n - v^*\rangle + \varphi(u_n) - \varphi(v^*) \\ &\ge -\|q\|_{E^*}\|u_n - v^*\|_E + (\|u_n - v^*\|_E - \|v^*\|_E)\, r(\|u_n - v^*\|_E - \|v^*\|_E) \end{aligned}$$

for all $n \in \mathbb{N}$, where $r\colon [0,+\infty) \to \mathbb{R}$ is such that $r(k) \to \infty$, as $k \to \infty$. Letting $n \to \infty$ in the above inequality, this leads to a contradiction. Thus, $SOL(K, H+q, \varphi, J)$ is a bounded set.

Finally, we prove the weak closedness of $SOL(K, H+q, \varphi, J)$. Let $\{u_n\} \subset SOL(K, H+q, \varphi)$ be such that $u_n \to u$ weakly in E as $n \to \infty$ for some $u \in K$. Then, Theorem 6.3.3 entails

$$\langle \widehat{w} + q, v - u_n\rangle + J^0(\gamma u_n; \gamma(v - u_n)) + \varphi(v) - \varphi(u_n) \ge 0$$

for all $\widehat{w} \in \mathcal{H}(v)$, all $v \in K$ and $n \in \mathbb{N}$. Recall that φ is weakly lower semicontinuous and γ is compact, which gives

$$\begin{aligned} &\langle \widehat{w} + q, v - u\rangle + J^0(\gamma u; \gamma(v - u)) + \varphi(v) - \varphi(u) \\ &\quad \ge \limsup_{n\to\infty} \langle \widehat{w} + q, v - u_n\rangle + \limsup_{n\to\infty} J^0(\gamma u_n; \gamma(v - u_n)) + \varphi(v) - \liminf_{n\to\infty} \varphi(u_n) \\ &\quad \ge \limsup_{n\to\infty} \left[\langle \widehat{w} + q, v - u_n\rangle + J^0(\gamma u_n; \gamma(v - u_n)) + \varphi(v) - \varphi(u_n)\right] \ge 0 \end{aligned}$$

for all $\widehat{w} \in \mathcal{H}(v)$ and all $v \in K$. Therefore, from Theorem 6.3.3, we conclude that $SOL(K, H+q, \varphi, J)$ is a weakly closed set. This completes the proof. □

As a byproduct of Theorem 6.3.5, we have the following result.

Lemma 6.3.6 *Assume hypotheses* (A_1)–(A_3). *Then, for each positive integer* $n \in \mathbb{N}$, *there exists a constant* $M_n > 0$ *such that*

$$\|u\|_E \le M_n \text{ for all } u \in \{u \in SOL(K,H+q,\varphi,J) \mid q \in E^* \text{ with } \|q\|_{E^*} \le n\}. \tag{6.11}$$

Proof. We argue by contradiction. Assume that there exist $N_1 > 0$ and sequences $\{q_k\} \subset E^*$, $\{u_k\} \subset K$ with $u_k \in SOL(K, H+q_k, \varphi, J)$, $\|q_k\|_{E^*} \le N_1$ and $\|u_k\|_E > k$ for each $k \in \mathbb{N}$. From Remark 6.3.4, it follows that there exist a constant $N_0 > 0$ large enough and a function $r\colon \mathbb{R}_+ \to \mathbb{R}$ with $r(k) \to \infty$ as $k \to \infty$ such that

$$\inf_{w \in \mathcal{H}(u)} \langle w, u - v^* \rangle - J^0(\gamma u; \gamma(v^* - u)) + \varphi(u) - \varphi(v^*) \ge \|u\|_E r(\|u\|_E)$$

for each $\|u\|_E > N_0$. So, we can take k large enough such that

$$r(k) > \|q\|_{E^*} + \frac{\|q\|_{E^*}\|v^*\|_E}{k}.$$

This implies

$$\begin{aligned} 0 &\le \langle w_k + q, v^* - u_k \rangle + \varphi(v^*) - \varphi(u_k) + J^0(\gamma u_k; \gamma(v^* - u_k)) \\ &\le \langle q, v^* - u_k \rangle - \|u_k\|_E r(\|u_k\|_E) \\ &\le \|q\|_{E^*}\|v^*\|_E + \|u_k\|_E(\|q\|_{E^*} - r(\|u_k\|_E)) < 0. \end{aligned}$$

This leads to a contradiction. Consequently, (6.11) holds, which completes the proof. □

6.4 Optimal Control Problem

In this section, we are interested in the study of the following optimal control problem driven by the fuzzy variational-hemivariational inequality in Problem 6.4.1. Let $V \subset E^*$ be a reflexive Banach space such that the embedding from V to E^* is compact.

Problem 6.4.1 *Find* $q \in U$ *such that*

$$G(q) := \inf_{u \in S(q)} L(u) + R(q) = \inf_{p \in U} \Big(\inf_{u \in S(p)} L(u) + R(p) \Big), \tag{6.12}$$

where $S(q) = SOL(K, H+q, \varphi, J)$, *the set* U *is a weakly closed subset of* V, *and* $L\colon K \to \mathbb{R}$ *and* $R\colon U \to \mathbb{R}$ *are two given functions.*

We need the following hypothesis.

(A_4) $L\colon K \to \mathbb{R}_+$ is a weakly lower semicontinuous function bounded from below, $R\colon U \to \mathbb{R}$ is a weakly lower semicontinuous function such that

$$R(p) \geq \|p\|_V + c_R \text{ for all } p \in U \tag{6.13}$$

with some $c_R \in \mathbb{R}$.

The main result in the section is provided as follows.

Theorem 6.4.2 *Assume that* (A_1)–(A_4) *hold. Then, Problem 6.4.1 has at least one solution in* U.

Proof. It is based on the Weierstrass type theorem and uses the lower semicontinuity argument. First, we remark that the function $G\colon U \to \mathbb{R}$ defined by $G(q) = \inf_{u\in S(q)} L(u) + R(q)$ for $q \in U$, is well-defined. For any $q \in U$, Theorem 6.3.5 shows that the set $S(q)$ is bounded and weakly closed. Since the function L is bounded from below, then there exists a minimizing sequence $\{u_n\} \subset S(q)$ for L, i.e.,

$$\lim_{n\to\infty} L(u_n) = \inf_{u\in S(q)} L(u).$$

Moreover, the boundedness and weak closedness of $S(q)$ guarantee that there exist a subsequence of $\{u_n\}$, still denoted in the same way, and an element $u^* \in S(q)$ such that

$$u_n \to u^* \text{ weakly in } E, \text{ as } n \to \infty.$$

This convergence combined with the weak lower semicontinuity of L gives

$$L(u^*) \leq \liminf_{n\to\infty} L(u_n) = \lim_{n\to\infty} L(u_n) = \inf_{u\in S(q)} L(u) \leq L(u^*),$$

that is, $\inf_{u\in S(q)} L(u) = L(u^*)$. So, we conclude that G is well-defined.

Next, by the definition of G and hypothesis (A_4), we have

$$G(q) = \inf_{u\in S(q)} L(u) + R(q) \geq c_L + \|q\|_V + c_R \geq c_L + c_R,$$

where $c_L \in \mathbb{R}$ is such that $L(u) \geq c_L$ for all $u \in K$. This means that G is bounded from below. So, let $\{q_n\} \subset U$ be a minimizing sequence for G, i.e.,

$$\lim_{n\to\infty} G(q_n) = \inf_{p\in U} G(p). \tag{6.14}$$

From the following estimate

$$G(q_n) \geq c_L + \|q_n\|_V + c_R,$$

we infer that the sequence $\{q_n\}$ is bounded in V. Therefore, without any loss of generality, we may suppose that $q_n \to q^*$ weakly in V as $n \to \infty$ for some $q^* \in U$, due to the weak closedness of U. The latter combined with the compactness of the embedding of V to E^* ensures

$$q_n \to q^* \text{ in } E^* \text{ as } n \to \infty. \tag{6.15}$$

Let $\{u_n\} \subset K$ be such that

$$L(u_n) = \inf_{u \in S(q_n)} L(u). \tag{6.16}$$

Further, Lemma 6.3.6 implies that the sequence $\{u_n\}$ is bounded. By passing to a subsequence, we may assume that $u_n \to u$ weakly in E as $n \to \infty$ for some $u \in K$. We assert that $u \in S(q^*)$. For each $n \in \mathbb{N}$, we have

$$\langle \widetilde{w} + q_n, v - u_n \rangle + J^0(\gamma u_n; \gamma(v - u_n)) + \varphi(v) - \varphi(u_n) \geq 0$$

for all $\widetilde{w} \in E^*$ with $H(v, \widetilde{w}) \geq \alpha(v)$ and all $v \in K$. Passing to the upper limit as $n \to \infty$ and taking into account the compactness of γ, weak lower semicontinuity of φ and Proposition 6.2.4(iii), one obtains

$$\begin{aligned}
&\langle \widetilde{w} + q^*, v - u \rangle + J^0(\gamma u; \gamma(v - u)) + \varphi(v) - \varphi(u) \\
&\geq \lim_{n\to\infty} \langle \widetilde{w} + q_n, v - u_n \rangle + \limsup_{n\to\infty} J^0(\gamma u_n; \gamma(v - u_n)) + \varphi(v) - \liminf_{n\to\infty} \varphi(u_n) \\
&\geq \limsup_{n\to\infty} \left[\langle \widetilde{w} + q_n, v - u_n \rangle + J^0(\gamma u_n; \gamma(v - u_n)) + \varphi(v) - \varphi(u_n) \right] \geq 0
\end{aligned}$$

for all $\widetilde{w} \in E^*$ with $H(v, \widetilde{w}) \geq \alpha(v)$ and all $v \in K$, where we have applied the convergence (6.15). Hence, using Theorem 6.3.3, we conclude that $u \in S(q^*)$. On the other hand, the weak lower semicontinuity of R and the convergence $q_n \to q^*$ weakly in V, as $n \to \infty$, imply

$$\liminf_{n\to\infty} R(q_n) \geq R(q^*), \tag{6.17}$$

and similarly, it holds

$$\liminf_{n\to\infty} L(u_n) \geq L(u). \tag{6.18}$$

Therefore, from (6.17) and (6.18), we have

$$\begin{aligned}
G(q^*) &= \inf_{u \in S(q^*)} L(u) + R(q^*) \\
&\geq \inf_{p \in U} G(p) = \lim_{n\to\infty} G(q_n) \\
&= \liminf_{n\to\infty} G(q_n) = \liminf_{n\to\infty} \Big(\inf_{u \in S(q_n)} L(u) + R(q_n) \Big) \\
&\geq \liminf_{n\to\infty} L(u_n) + \liminf_{n\to\infty} R(q_n) \\
&\geq L(u) + R(q^*) \geq \inf_{u \in S(q^*)} L(u) + R(q^*) = G(q^*).
\end{aligned}$$

Finally, we conclude that $q^* \in U$ is a solution to Problem 6.4.1. This completes the proof of the theorem. □

Acknowledgement

Project supported by NNSF of China Grants Nos. 12001478 and 12026256, the European Unions Horizon 2020 Research and Innovation Programme under the Marie Skłodowska-Curie grant agreement No. 823731 CONMECH, the National Science Center of Poland under Preludium Project No. 2017/25 /N/ST1/00611, the NSF of Guangxi (Grant No: 2018GXNSFAA281353), the Ministry of Science and Higher Education of Republic of Poland under Grants Nos. 4004/GG-PJII/H2020/2018/0 and 440328/PnH2/2019, the Startup Project of Doctor Scientific Research of Yulin Normal University No. G2020ZK07, and the Beibu Gulf University under Project No. 2018KYQD06.

References

[1] S.S. Antman. The influence of elasticity on analysis: Modern developments. B. Am. Math. Soc., 9: 267–291, 1983.

[2] Y.R. Bai, S. Migórski and S.D. Zeng. Generalized vector complementarity problem in fuzzy environment. Fuzzy Sets Syst., 347: 142–151, 2018.

[3] M.S. Chang and H.K. Chen. A fuzzy user-optimal route choice problem using a link-based fuzzy variational inequality formulation. Fuzzy Sets Syst., 114: 339–345, 2000.

[4] S.S. Chang, G.M. Lee and B.S. Lee. Vector quasivariational inequalities for fuzzy mappings (I). Fuzzy Sets Syst., 87: 307–315, 1997.

[5] S.S. Chang, G.M. Lee and B.S. Lee. Vector quasivariational inequalities for fuzzy mappings (II). Fuzzy Sets Syst., 102: 333–344, 1999.

[6] S.S. Chang and Salahuddin. Existence theorems for vector quasivariational-like inequalities for fuzzy mappings. Fuzzy Sets Syst., 233: 89–95, 2013.

[7] S.S. Chang and Y.G. Zhu. On variational inequalities for fuzzy mappings. Fuzzy Sets Syst., 32: 359–367, 1989.

[8] S.S. Chang and L.A. Zadeh. On fuzzy mappings and control. IEEE Trans. Syst. Man Cybern., 2: 30–34, 1972.

[9] F.H. Clarke. *Optimization and Nonsmooth Analysis*. Wiley, Interscience, New York, 1983.

[10] G. Duvant and J.L. Lions. *Inequalities in Mechanics and Physics*, vol. 219. Springer Science & Business Media, 2012.

[11] G. Eck, J. Jarušek and M. Krbec. *Unilateral Contact Problems: Variational Methods and Existence Theorems*. Chapman Hall/CRC Press, 2005.

[12] A. Granas and J. Dugundji. *Fixed Point Theory*. Springer-Verlag, New York, 2003.

[13] I. Hlavacek, J. Haslinger, J. Necas and J. Lovisek. *Solution of Variational Inequalities in Mechanics*, vol. 66. Springer Science & Business Media, 2012.

[14] N.J. Huang and H.Y. Lan. A couple of nonlinear equations with fuzzy mappings in fuzzy normed spaces. Fuzzy Sets Syst., 152: 209–222, 2005.

[15] N.J. Huang, J. Li and D. O'Regan. Generalized F-complementary problems in Banach spaces. Nonlinear Anal., 68: 3828–3840, 2008.

[16] N.V. Hung, V.M. Tam, T. Nguyen and D. O'Regan. Regularized gap functions and error bounds for generalized mixed weak vector quasivariational inequality problems in fuzzy environments. Fuzzy Sets and Syst., 400: 162–176, 2020.

[17] M. Kamenskii, V. Obukhovskii and P. Zecca. *Condensing Multivalued Maps and Semilinear Differential Inclusions in Banach Space*. Walter de Gruyter, Berlin, 2001.

[18] Z.H. Liu. Anti-periodic solutions to nonlinear evolution equations. J. Funct. Anal., 258: 2026–2033, 2010.

[19] Z.H. Liu, S. Migórski and S.D. Zeng. Partial differential variational inequalities involving nonlocal boundary conditions in Banach spaces. J. Differential Equations, 263: 3989–4006, 2017.

[20] Z.H. Liu, S.D. Zeng and D. Motreanu. Evolutionary problems driven by variational inequalities. J. Differential Equations, 260: 6787–6799, 2016.

[21] S. Migórski, A. Ochal and M. Sofonea. *Nonlinear Inclusions and Hemivariational Inequalities. Models and Analysis of Contact Problems*. Advances in Mechanics and Mathematics 26, Springer, New York, 2013.

[22] P.D. Panagiotopoulos. Nonconvex energy functions. hemivariational inequalities and substationarity principles. Acta Mech., 48: 111–130, 1983.

[23] M. Shillor, M. Sofonea and J.J. Telega. *Models and Analysis of Quasistatic Contact: Variational Methods*. Springer Science & Business Media, 2004.

[24] E. Tarafdar. A fixed point theorem equivalent to the Fan-Knaster-Kuratowski-Mazurkiewicz theorem. J. Math. Anal. Appl., 128: 475–479, 1987.

[25] G.J. Tang, T. Zhao, Z.P. Wan and D.X. He. Existence results of a perturbed variational inequality with a fuzzy mapping. Fuzzy Sets Syst., 331: 68–77, 2018.

[26] L.A. Zadeh. Fuzzy sets. Inf. Control, 8: 338–353, 1965.

[27] E. Zeidler. *Nonlinear Functional Analysis and its Applications II/B. Nonlinear Monotone Operators*. Springer-Verlag, New York, 1990.

Chapter 7

Boundary Stabilization of the Linear MGT Equation with Feedback Neumann Control

Marcelo Bongarti[a] and *Irena Lasiecka*[b,*]

Mathematics Subject Classification. 93B, 93C, 93D15, 35, 37L30, 37L05, 35B, 35B40.

7.1 Introduction

Let $\Omega \subset \mathbb{R}^3$ bounded with C^2–boundary denoted by Γ. With $T > 0$ (could also be $T = \infty$), the third-order (in time) quasilinear JMGT–equation is given by

$$\tau u_{ttt} + (\alpha - 2ku)u_{tt} - c^2\Delta u - b\Delta u_t = 2ku_t^2 \text{ in } (0,T)\times\Omega \qquad (7.1)$$

where $k > 0$ is a nonlinearity parameter, $c > 0$ denotes the speed of sound, $\tau > 0$ denotes thermal relaxation parameter, $b := \delta + \tau c^2 > 0$ where δ denotes the sound diffusivity and α refers to viscoelastic friction. The parameter $\tau > 0$ – introduced when the Fourier's law of heat conduction is replaced my the Maxwell–Catanneo's (MC) law – plays an important role: it removes the paradox of infinite speed of propagation in heat waves.

[a] Department of Mathematical Sciences, University of Memphis, Memphis, TN 38152 USA.

[b] Department of Mathematical Sciences, University of Memphis, Memphis, TN 38152 USA, IBS, Polish Academy of Sciences, Warsaw.

* Corresponding author: lasiecka@memphis.edu

A multitude of applications ranging from acoustics, image processing, thermodynamics, etc. have brought a considerable attention to the dynamics behind the hyperbolic (third–order in time) acoustic wave models. As a consequence, a rich literature on the topic has been developed during the last decade [1, 2, 3, 4, 5, 7, 10, 11, 13, 16, 17, 18, 26, 30, 31, 32, 33, 36, 37, 39, 40, 41]. The interest behind the propagation of waves through viscous fluids and other heterogeneous media, has been already pointed out – almost two centuries ago – by Professor Stokes in his prominent article [43] in 1851. Stokes' work was rooted on the idea that heat propagation – in particular within acoustic media – was hyperbolic. Later experimental studies indicated the presence of heat *waves* in such materials thereby dictating the presence of the (nowadays known as) thermal relaxation parameter $\tau > 0$.

There is a strong connection between the Stokes–model and the JMGT model, both revealing the basic principles of acoustic waves propagation in the presence of the heat waves. This also led to a creation of other models accounting for a more detailed information about the material and the medium [21, 12, 44]. In these models, standard time derivative may be replaced by material derivative, which depends on the medium. Dependence of the heat flux upon the media, its surroundings and other thermal–material dependent quantities: thermal inertia, specific heat, velocity field, etc. are taken into account in the respective modeling processes. For a broader understanding of hyperbolic heat and modern nonlinear acoustics, we refer to the works [8, 9, 20, 21, 27, 44] and references therein. Recent review of pertinent modeling aspects of acoustic waves can also be found in [20, 26, 34]. In order to focus our work on boundary stabilization and the related technical details, in the present work we consider $\tau > 0$ and fixed. However, other generalizations may be possible and, indeed, welcome.

Typical boundary conditions associated with the model (7.1) and its linearization are homogenous Dirichlet $u = 0$ imposed on Γ. Questions such as wellposedness of solutions and their stability were extensively studied [22, 23, 24, 35]. With $k = 0$ equation (7.1) is linear and reads

$$\tau u_{ttt} + \alpha u_{tt} - c^2 \Delta u - b \Delta u_t = 0 \text{ in } (0,T) \times \Omega \tag{7.2}$$

(here we allow $\alpha \in \mathbb{R}$). The structurally damped case ($b > 0$) corresponds to a group generator defined on the phase space $H_0^1(\Omega) \times H_0^1(\Omega) \times L^2(\Omega)$. In the absence of structural damping ($b = 0$), however, semigroup generation fails and the problem is ill-posed, a property dating back to Fattorini [19] in 1969. Nonlinear semigroups corresponding to (7.1) were shown to exist in the following phase spaces $H^2(\Omega) \cap H_0^1(\Omega) \times H_0^1(\Omega) \times L^2(\Omega)$, $[H^2(\Omega) \cap H_0^1(\Omega)]^2 \times H_0^1(\Omega)$. First with the data assumed to be small at the level of the underlying phase space [24] and later with smallness required only in the lower topology, namely $H_0^1(\Omega) \times H_0^1(\Omega) \times L^2(\Omega)$ [2].

The parameter $\gamma := \alpha - \frac{\tau c^2}{b}$ is critical for stability of solutions: both linear and nonlinear semigroups are exponentially stable provided that $\gamma > 0$. When $\gamma = 0$ the linear dynamics is conservative and therefore there is no decay of solutions. This brings us to the goal of the present chapter, namely the *linear* stabilization: how to stabilize the model with critical γ-i.e γ can be degenerate? It is known by now that specifically constructed memory terms may have stabilizing effects on the critical dynamics [16, 18, 31]. In this work we are interested how to achieve stabilization in the critical case via a boundary feedback only.It is known, that boundary of the region is accessible to external manipulations, hence a good place for placing actuators and sensors. Within this spirit, we shall show that a suitable boundary feedback implemented on the boundary Γ will lead to exponential stability of the resulting semigroup. This result is important not only on its own rights, but also within the context of the quasilinear equations where questions of stability are strongly linked to decay properties of linearized solutions [24].

7.1.1 The Linearized PDE Model with Space-dependent Viscoelasticity

Let the domain $\Omega \subset \mathbb{R}^n (n = 2, 3)$ with the boundary $\Gamma = \partial\Omega$ be of class C^2. Let Γ be divided into two disjoint parts, Γ_0 and Γ_1, both non-empty, with Γ_1 relatively open in Γ. We consider the linear version of (7.1) but with a space–dependent coeficient $\alpha \in C(\overline{\Omega})$

$$\tau u_{ttt} + \alpha(x)u_{tt} - c^2\Delta u - b\Delta u_t = 0 \text{ in } (0,T)\times\Omega \tag{7.3}$$

and subject to the Robin-*type* (on Γ_0) and Dirichlet (on Γ_1) boundary conditions

$$\frac{\partial u}{\partial \nu} + \eta u_t = 0 \text{ on } (0,T)\times\Gamma_0 \text{ and } u = 0 \text{ on } (0,T)\times\Gamma_1 \tag{7.4}$$

where $\eta > 0$, and the initial conditions are given by

$$u(0) = u_0, u_t(0) = u_1, u_{tt}(0) = u_2. \tag{7.5}$$

In addition to continuity, we assume that the damping coefficient $\alpha(x) > 0$ is such that stability parameter $\gamma \in C(\overline{\Omega})$ satisfies

$$\gamma(x) := \alpha(x) - \frac{\tau c^2}{b} \geqslant 0. \tag{7.6}$$

Remark 7.1.1 *The above assumption will be used only for the stability estimates. The generation of a semigroup is valid without assuming (7.6).*

Since the damping typically depends on local properties of the material, assuming variability of the damping $\alpha(x)$ is physically relevant and, in most cases, necessary. We shall show that under suitable geometric conditions imposed on Ω the linear system is exponentially stable in the topology of the natural phase space.

Notation: Throughout this chapter, $L^2(\Omega)$ denotes the space of Lebesgue measurable functions whose squares are integrable and $H^s(\Omega)$ denotes the $L^2(\Omega)$-based Sobolev space of order s. Moreover, we use the notation $H^1_\Gamma(\Omega)$ to represent the space

$$H^1_\Gamma(\Omega) := \{u \in H^1(\Omega); u|_\Gamma = 0\} \tag{7.7}$$

instead of the standard $H^1_0(\Omega)$ in order to emphasize the portion of the boundary on what the trace is vanishing . We also denote by $H^2_\Gamma(\Omega)$ the space $H^2(\Omega) \cap H^1_\Gamma(\Omega)$. We denote the inner product in $L^2(\Omega)$ and $L^2(\Gamma)$ respectively by

$$(u,v) = \int_\Omega uv d\Omega \text{ and } (u,v)_\Gamma = \int_\Gamma uv d\Gamma$$

and the respective induced norms in $L^2(\Omega)$ and $L^2(\Gamma)$ are denoted by $\|\cdot\|_2$ and $\|\cdot\|_\Gamma$ respectively.

7.1.2 Main Results and Discussion

We begin with the abstract version of equation (7.3). To this end, let $A : \mathcal{D}(A) \subset L^2(\Omega) \to L^2(\Omega)$ be the operator defined as

$$A\xi = -\Delta\xi, \ \mathcal{D}(A) = \left\{ \xi \in H^2(\Omega);\ \xi \Big|_{\Gamma_1} = \frac{\partial \xi}{\partial \nu}\Big|_{\Gamma_0} \equiv 0 \right\}. \tag{7.8}$$

It is well known that A is a positive ($\Gamma_1 \neq 0$), self-adjoint operator with compact resolvent and that $\mathcal{D}\left(A^{1/2}\right) = H^1_{\Gamma_1}(\Omega)$ (equivalent norms). In addition, up to a bit of abuse of notation we denote (also) by $A : L^2(\Omega) \to [\mathcal{D}(A)]'$ the extension (by duality) of the operator $A : \mathcal{D}(A) \subset L^2(\Omega) \to L^2(\Omega)$ defined in (7.8).

Next, for $\varphi \in L^2(\Gamma_0)$, let $\psi = N(\varphi)$ be the unique solution of the elliptic problem

$$\begin{cases} \Delta\psi = 0 & \text{in } \Omega \\ \dfrac{\partial \psi}{\partial \nu} = \varphi & \text{on } \Gamma_0 \\ \psi = 0 & \text{on } \Gamma_1. \end{cases}$$

It follows from elliptic theory that $N \in \mathcal{L}(H^s(\Gamma_0), H^{s+3/2}(\Omega))^*$ ($s \in \mathbb{R}^*_+$) and

$$N^* A\xi = \begin{cases} \xi \text{ on } & \Gamma_0 \\ 0 \text{ on } & \Gamma_1 \end{cases} \tag{7.9}$$

$^*\mathcal{L}(X,Y)$ denote the space of linear bounded operators from X to Y.

for all $\xi \in \mathcal{D}(A)$, where N^* represents the adjoint of N when the latter is considered as an operator from $L_2(\Gamma_0)$ to $L_2(\Omega)$.

The introduction of A and N will allow us to write equation (7.3) abstractly as

$$\tau u_{ttt} + \alpha(x)u_{tt} + c^2 A(u + \eta NN^* Au_t) + bA(u_t + \eta\eta NN^* Au_{tt}) = f. \tag{7.10}$$

The abstract version of our model gives rise to the natural phase space we are going to consider. We define $\mathbb{H}$ as

$$\mathbb{H} := H^1_{\Gamma_1}(\Omega) \times H^1_{\Gamma_1}(\Omega) \times L^2(\Omega) \tag{7.11}$$

The computations leading to (7.10) show formally that u is a solution of (7.3) with boundary condition given by (7.4) if and only if $\Phi = (u, u_t, u_{tt})^\top$ is a solution for the first other system

$$\begin{cases} \Phi_t = \mathscr{A}\Phi + F \\ \Phi(0) = \Phi_0 = (u_0, u_1, u_2)^\top, \end{cases} \tag{7.12}$$

with $\mathscr{A} : \mathcal{D}(\mathscr{A}) \subset \mathbb{H} \to \mathbb{H}$ given by

$$\begin{aligned} \mathscr{A}(\xi_1, \xi_2, \xi_3)^\top := (\xi_2, \xi_3, -\alpha\tau^{-1}\xi_3 - c^2\tau^{-1}A(\xi_1 + \eta NN^* A\xi_2) \\ - b\tau^{-1}A(\xi_2 + \eta NN^* A\xi_3)) \end{aligned} \tag{7.13}$$

where

$$\begin{aligned} \mathcal{D}(\mathscr{A}) &= \left\{(\xi_1, \xi_2, \xi_3)^\top \in \mathbb{H};\ \xi_3 \in \mathcal{D}\left(A^{1/2}\right),\ \xi_1 + \eta NN^* A\xi_2 \in \mathcal{D}(A),\ \xi_2 + \eta NN^* A\xi_3 \in \mathcal{D}(A)\right\} \\ &= \left\{(\xi_1, \xi_2, \xi_3)^\top \in \left[H^2_{\Gamma_1}(\Omega)\right]^2 \times \mathcal{D}\left(A^{1/2}\right);\ \left[\frac{\partial \xi_1}{\partial \nu} + \eta\xi_2\right]\Big|_{\Gamma_0} = \left[\frac{\partial \xi_2}{\partial \nu} + \eta\xi_3\right]\Big|_{\Gamma_0} = 0\right\} \end{aligned} \tag{7.14}$$

and $F^\top = (0, 0, f)$.

We now recall that, topologically, the space $\mathbb{H}$ is equivalent to

$$\mathcal{D}\left(A^{1/2}\right) \times \mathcal{D}\left(A^{1/2}\right) \times L^2(\Omega) \tag{7.15}$$

with the topology induced by the inner product

$$\begin{aligned} ((\xi_1, \xi_2, \xi_3)^\top, (\varphi_1, \varphi_2, \varphi_3))_{\mathbb{H}} = (A^{1/2}\xi_1, A^{1/2}\varphi_1) + b(A^{1/2}\xi_2, A^{1/2}\varphi_2) \\ + (\xi_3, \varphi_3), \end{aligned} \tag{7.16}$$

for all $(\xi_1, \xi_2, \xi_3)^\top, (\varphi_1, \varphi_2, \varphi_3)^\top \in \mathbb{H}$. Because of this equivalence we will be using the same $\mathbb{H}$ to denote both spaces.

We are then in position to state our wellposedness of the phase space solutions.

Theorem 7.1.2 *Assume $f \in L^1((0,T),L^2(\Omega))$, and $\eta \geq 0$, $\alpha \in C(\Omega)$. For every initial data $\Phi_0 := (u_0,u_1,u_2)$ in $\mathbb{H}$, there exists a unique semigroup solution $\Phi = (u,u_t,u_{tt})$ such that $\Phi \in C([0,T],\mathbb{H})$ for every $T > 0$. Moreover, if the initial datum belongs to $\mathcal{D}(\mathscr{A})$ and $f \in C^1([0,T],L^2(\Omega))$ the corresponding solution is in $C((0,T];D(\mathscr{A})) \cap C^1([0,T],\mathbb{H})$.*

Our main results is exponential stability of the solutions refereed to in Theorem 7.1.2. In order to formulate the result we need to impose geometric condition:

Assumption 7.1.3 *Choose a point $x_0 \in \mathbb{R}^n$* outside *of $\overline{\Omega}$. and we define the vector field $h : \mathbb{R}^n \to \mathbb{R}^n$ given by $h(x) = x - x_0$. With $\nu(x)$ denoting the outwards normal unit vector at x we define $\Gamma_0, \Gamma_1 \subseteq \Gamma$ by*

$$\Gamma_0 = \{x \in \Gamma;\ \nu(x) \cdot h(x) > 0\}, \quad \Gamma_1 = \{x \in \Gamma;\ \nu(x) \cdot h(x) \leqslant 0\}.$$

Remark 7.1.4 *The geometric condition imposed above can be substantially relaxed. For instance, if the feedback control is active on the full Γ, there is no need for any geometric coonditions. However, this would require some microlocal analysis and becomes rather technical [28, 29, 45]. For this reason we opted for a more restrictive geometry, as to make the exposition fully independent.*

Theorem 7.1.5 *Let Assumption 7.1.3 and condition (7.6) be satisfied. Then, there exist $\omega > 0$ and $M > 0$ such that*

$$||\Phi(t)||_{\mathbb{H}} \leqslant Me^{-\omega t}||\Phi_0||_{\mathbb{H}} \tag{7.17}$$

for all $t \geqslant 0$.

As mentioned earlier, the *wellposedness* of the MGT equation with homogenous boundary conditions is well known by now [23, 24, 35]. However, in the case of non-homogeneous boundary conditions, the situation is much more complicated due to the fact that "wave" operator with Neumann boundary data does not satisfy the Lopatinski condition [42, 45], unless Ω is one dimensional. This leads to a *loss* of $1/3$ derivative when looking at the map from the boundary with L_2 data into the $H^1 \times L^2$ solutions. This has been known for some time in the case of wave equation, but only recently studied for MGT equation [5, 7, 46]. In fact, an open loop control problem for MGT equation with L^2–Neumann controls leads to only distributional solutions [6]. However, for both the wave and MGT equations, a *boundary feedback via Neumann boundary conditions does recover this lo* leading to the recuperation of the full energy. This is due to the boundary dissipativity with $\eta \geq 0$. The main mathematical issue in dealing with the nonhomogenous Neumann boundary data is to deal with *unbounded and uncloseable* perturbations within the context of the third order hyperbolic dynamics. In fact, this is the first result on wellposedness of feedback generator for MGT dynamics. Also, notice that applying feedback $\frac{\partial u}{\partial \nu} + \eta u_t = 0$, with $\eta < 0$

leads to the ill-posed dynamics. This corresponds to anti–damping which shifts the spectrum to a "wrong" complex half–plane-thus denying wellposedness of a semigroup. While the analog of stability result in Theorem 7.1.5 is known for the case of wave equation, this result is new for the MGT ($\tau > 0$) with critical stability parameter γ. The difficulties encountered in the proof of wellposedness in Theorem 7.1.2 are compounded, when proving Theorem 7.1.5, by geometric considerations necessary when studying dissipation with restricted geometric support (such as portion of the boundary).Geometric condition assumed in Assumption (7.1.3) can be, however, substantially relaxed. For instance, when the dissipation is active on the full boundary there is no need for any geometric constraints [28, 29]. However, this brings forward microlocal analysis arguments which are known by now, however tedious. In order to ease readability and focus of the analysis, we have opted for a more restrictive version of geometric assumption.

It should be noted that the result of Theorem 7.1.5 is critical when studying optimal boundary feedback control problem for MGT equation. While the feedback synthesis for this model has been carried out in [6] for a finite horizon problem, analysis of *infinite horizon* problem requires stabilizability condition, which is provided by Theorem 7.1.5.

7.2 Wellposedness: Proof of Theorem 7.1.2

The thermal relaxation parameter $\tau > 0$ plays no significant role in the study of the wellposedness of (7.3), therefore for the sake of readability we are assuming $\tau = 1$ in this section.

The main goal of this section is to prove that the operator $\mathscr{A} : \mathcal{D}(\mathscr{A}) \subset \mathbb{H} \to \mathbb{H}$ generates a strongly continuous semigroup. It is convenient to introduce the following change of variables $bz = bu_t + c^2 u$ (see [35]) which reduces the problem to a PDE- abstract ODE coupled system.

Let $M \in \mathcal{L}(\mathbb{H})$ defined by

$$M(\xi_1, \xi_2, \xi_3)^\top = \left(\xi_1, \xi_2 + \frac{c^2}{b}\xi_1, \xi_3 + \frac{c^2}{b}\xi_2\right)$$

which has inverse $M^{-1} \in \mathcal{L}(\mathbb{H})$ given by

$$M^{-1}(\xi_1, \xi_2, \xi_3)^\top = \left(\xi_1, \xi_2 - \frac{c^2}{b}\xi_1, \xi_3 - \frac{c^2}{b}\xi_2 + \frac{c^4}{b^2}\xi_1\right)$$

and therefore is an isomorphism of $\mathbb{H}$. The next lemma makes precise the translation of (7.3) to the system involving z.

Lemma 7.2.1 *Assume that the compatibility condition*

$$\frac{\partial}{\partial \nu} u_0 + \eta u_1 = 0 \text{ on } \Gamma_0 \tag{7.18}$$

holds. Then $\Phi \in C^1(0,T;\mathbb{H}) \cap C(0,T;\mathcal{D}(\mathscr{A}))$ *is a strong solution for (7.12) if, and only if,* $\Psi = M\Phi \in C^1(0,T;\mathbb{H}) \cap C(0,T;\mathcal{D}(\mathbb{A}))$ *is a strong solution for*

$$\begin{cases} \Psi_t = \mathbb{A}\Psi + G \\ \Psi(0) = \Psi_0 = M\Phi_0 = \left(u_0, u_1 + \dfrac{c^2}{b}u_0, u_2 + \dfrac{c^2}{b}u_1\right)^\top, \end{cases} \tag{7.19}$$

where $G = MF$ *and* $\mathbb{A} = M\mathscr{A}M^{-1}$ *with*

$$\mathcal{D}(\mathbb{A}) = \left\{ (\xi_1,\xi_2,\xi_3)^\top \in \left[H^2_{\Gamma_1}(\Omega)\right]^2 \times \mathcal{D}\left(A^{1/2}\right); \left[\frac{\partial \xi_2}{\partial \nu} + \eta\xi_3\right]\Bigg|_{\Gamma_0} = 0 \right\} \tag{7.20}$$

Proof. It is simple to check that if $\Phi \in C^1(0,T;\mathbb{H}) \cap C(0,T;\mathcal{D}(\mathscr{A}))$ is a strong solution for (7.12) then $\Psi = M\Phi$ belongs to $C^1(0,T;\mathbb{H}) \cap C(0,T;\mathcal{D}(\mathbb{A}))$ and satisfy (7.19).

For the reverse implication, the only non-trivial step is to prove that boundary conditions match. To this end, assume that $\Psi = (u,z,z_t) \in C^1(0,T;\mathbb{H}) \cap C(0,T;\mathcal{D}(\mathbb{A}))$ is a strong solution for (7.19). Let

$$\Upsilon(t) := \left(\frac{\partial u(t)}{\partial \nu} + \eta u_t(t)\right)\Bigg|_{\Gamma_0}, \; t \geqslant 0$$

and notice that $b\Upsilon_t + c^2\Upsilon = 0$ for all t. This along with the compatibility condition ($\Upsilon(0) = 0$) implies that $\Upsilon \equiv 0$ hence $(u,u_t,u_{tt}) \in \mathcal{D}(\mathscr{A})$ for all t. The proof is then complete. □

For $(\xi_1,\xi_2,\xi_3)^\top \in \mathcal{D}(\mathbb{A})$ a basic algebraic computation yields the explicit formula for $\mathbb{A}$.

$$\mathbb{A}(\xi_1,\xi_2,\xi_3)^\top = \left(\xi_2 - \frac{c^2}{b}\xi_1, \xi_3, -\gamma\left(\xi_3 - \frac{c^2}{b}\xi_2 + \frac{c^4}{b^2}\xi_1\right) - bA\xi_2 - b\eta ANN^*A\xi_3\right). \tag{7.21}$$

We are ready for our generation result.

Theorem 7.2.2 *The operator* $\mathscr{A}$ *generates a strongly continuous semigroup on* $\mathbb{H}$.

Proof. Equivalently, we show that $\mathbb{A}$ generates a strongly continuous semigroup on $\mathbb{H}$. If $\{S(t)\}_{t\geqslant 0}$ is the said semigroup then $\{T(t)\}_{t\geqslant 0}$ $(T(t) := M^{-1}S(t)M, t \geqslant 0)$ will be the semigroup generated by $\mathscr{A}$.

Write $\mathbb{A} = \mathbb{A}_d + P$ where

$$P(\xi_1,\xi_2,\xi_3) = \left(\xi_2, 0, \frac{\gamma c^2}{b}\left(\xi_2 - \frac{c^2}{b}\xi_1\right) + (1-\gamma)\xi_3\right), \quad (\xi_1,\xi_2,\xi_3)^\top \in \mathbb{H}$$

is bounded in $\mathbb{H}$ and

$$\mathbb{A}_d(\xi_1,\xi_2,\xi_3) = \left(-\frac{c^2}{b}\xi_1,\xi_3,-\xi_3 - bA\xi_2 - b\eta ANN^*A\xi_3\right), \ (\xi_1,\xi_2,\xi_3)^\top \in \mathcal{D}(\mathbb{A}_d), \tag{7.22}$$

where $\mathcal{D}(\mathbb{A}_d) := \mathcal{D}(\mathbb{A})$. It then suffices to prove generation of $\mathbb{A}_d$ on $\mathbb{H}$.

We start by showing dissipativity: for $(\xi_1,\xi_2,\xi_3)^\top \in \mathcal{D}(\mathbb{A})$ we have

$$\begin{aligned}(\mathbb{A}_d(\xi_1,\xi_2,\xi_3),(\xi_1,\xi_2,\xi_3))_{\mathbb{H}} &= -\frac{c^2}{b}\|A^{1/2}\xi_1\|_2^2 + b\left(A^{1/2}\xi_3, A^{1/2}\xi_2\right)\\ &\quad - \|\xi_3\|_2^2 - b(A^{1/2}\xi_2,A^{1/2}\xi_3) - b\eta\|\xi_3\|_{\Gamma_0}^2\\ &= -\frac{c^2}{b}\|A^{1/2}\xi_1\|_2^2 - \|\xi_3\|_2^2 - b\eta\|\xi_3\|_{\Gamma_0}^2 \leqslant 0,\end{aligned}$$

hence, $\mathbb{A}_d$ is dissipative in $\mathbb{H}$.

For maximality in $\mathbb{H}$, given any $L = (f,g,h) \in \mathbb{H}$ we need to show that there exists $\Psi = (\xi_1,\xi_2,\xi_3)^\top \in \mathcal{D}(\mathbb{A})$ such that $(\lambda - \mathbb{A}_d)\Psi = L$, for some $\lambda > 0$. This leads to the system of equations:

$$\begin{cases}\lambda\xi_1 + \dfrac{c^2}{b}\xi_1 = f,\\ \lambda\xi_2 - \xi_3 = g,\\ \lambda\xi_3 + \xi_3 + bA[\xi_2 + \eta NN^*A\xi_3] = h,\end{cases} \tag{7.23}$$

which implies $\xi_1 = \left(\lambda + \dfrac{c^2}{b}\right)^{-1} f \in \mathcal{D}(A^{1/2})$. Moreover, since $A^{-1} \in \mathcal{L}(L^2(\Omega))$ the third equation above yields

$$\left[(\lambda^2+\lambda)A^{-1} + b + b\lambda\eta NN^*A\right]\xi_3 = \lambda A^{-1}h - bg$$

and then by the strictly positivity (in $\mathcal{D}(A^{1/2})$) of the operator K_λ defined as

$$K_\lambda := (\lambda^2+\lambda)A^{-1} + b + b\lambda\eta NN^*A$$

(in fact recall $(NN^*A\xi,\xi)_{\mathcal{D}(A^{1/2})} = \|N^*A\xi\|_{\Gamma_0}^2$ for all $\xi \in \mathcal{D}(A^{1/2})$ therefore $K_\lambda^{-1} \in \mathcal{L}(\mathcal{D}(A^{1/2})))$ we can write $\xi_3 = K_\lambda^{-1}(\lambda A^{-1}h - bg) \in \mathcal{D}(A^{1/2})$. Finally, $\xi_2 = \lambda^{-1}(\xi_3 + g) = \lambda^{-1}(K_\lambda^{-1}(\lambda A^{-1}h - bg) + g) \in \mathcal{D}(A^{1/2})$.

The final step for concluding membership of (ξ_1,ξ_2,ξ_3) in $\mathcal{D}(\mathbb{A})$ follows from

$$b\lambda(\xi_2 + \eta NN^*A\xi_3) = -(\lambda^2+\lambda)A^{-1}\xi_3 + \lambda A^{-1}h \in \mathcal{D}(A).$$

Generation is then achieved. □

Applying standard semigroup arguments [38] to the result of Theorem 7.2.2, we obtain the following corollary, which in turn completed the proof of Theorem 7.1.2.

Corollary 7.2.3 (Wellposedness and Regularity) *Assume $f \in L^1(\mathbb{R}_+, L^2(\Omega))$ and that condition (7.18) is at force. Denote by $\{T(t)\}_{t\geqslant 0}$ the semigroup given by Theorem 7.2.2.*

(i) *If $\Phi_0 \in \mathbb{H}$, then the function $\Phi \in C([0,T];\mathbb{H})$ defined as*

$$\Phi(t) \equiv T(t)\Phi_0 + \int_0^t T(t-\sigma)F(\sigma)d\sigma, \ t \in [0,T]$$

is the unique mild solution for (7.12) in $\mathbb{H}$.

(ii) *If $\Phi_0 \in \mathcal{D}(\mathscr{A})$ and, in addition, $f \in C^1(\mathbb{R}_+, L^2(\Omega)$ then the function $\Phi \in C^1([0,T];\mathbb{H}) \cap C((0,T);\mathcal{D}(\mathscr{A}))$ defined as*

$$\Phi(t) \equiv T(t)\Phi_0 + \int_0^t T(t-\sigma)F(\sigma)d\sigma \ t \in [0,T]$$

is the unique classical solution for (7.12) in $\mathbb{H}$.

Remark 7.2.4 *We notice here that condition (7.18) is not essential for well-posedness of weak solutions. However, it is critical for the regularity of solutions which allows to interpret mild (semigroup) solution in a strong form of equation (7.3).*

7.2.1 Stabilization in $\mathbb{H}$: Proof of Theorem 7.1.5

In order to allow future tracking stability rates with respect to the parameter τ we now resume considering $\tau > 0$. Moreover, we will use the notation $a \lesssim b$ to say that $a \leqslant Cb$ where C is a constant possibly depending on the physical parameters of the model ($\tau, c, b > 0$) but independent of space, time and $\gamma \in C(\overline{\Omega})$.

We will introduce several energy functionals which will be used to describe long time behavior of mild solutions to (7.3). For a classical solution (u, u_t, u_{tt}) of (7.12) in $\mathbb{H}$, we define the corresponding energy by $E(t) = E_0(t) + E_1(t)$ where $E_i : [0,T] \to \mathbb{R}_+$ $(i = 0,1)$ are defined by

$$\begin{aligned} E_1(t) &:= \frac{b}{2}\left\|A^{1/2}\left(u_t + \frac{\tau c^2}{b}u\right)\right\|_2^2 + \frac{\tau}{2}\left\|u_{tt} + \frac{c^2}{b}u_t\right\|_2^2 + \frac{c^2}{2b}\|\gamma^{1/2}u_t\|_2^2 \\ &= \frac{b}{2}\|A^{1/2}z\|_2^2 + \frac{\tau}{2}\|z_t\|_2^2 + \frac{c^2}{2b}\|\gamma^{1/2}u_t\|_2^2 \end{aligned} \tag{7.24}$$

(where we have omitted the variable x in $\gamma(x)$) and

$$E_0(t) := \frac{1}{2}\|\alpha^{1/2}u_t\|_2^2 + \frac{c^2}{2}\|A^{1/2}u\|_2^2 \tag{7.25}$$

where we have omitted x in $\alpha(x)$.

The next lemma guarantees that stability of solutions in $\mathbb{H}$ is equivalent to uniform exponential decay of the function $t \mapsto E(t)$.

Lemma 7.2.5 *Let $\Phi = (u, u_t, u_{tt})$ be a weak solution for (7.12) in $\mathbb{H}$ and assume condition (7.18) holds. Then the following statements are equivalent:*

a) $t \mapsto \|\Phi(t)\|_{\mathbb{H}}^2$ *decays exponentially.*

b) $t \mapsto \|M\Phi(t)\|_{\mathbb{H}}^2 = \|(u, z, z_t)\|_{\mathbb{H}}^2$ *decays exponentially.*

c) $t \mapsto E(t)$ *decays exponentially.*

Proof. Observe that $\Sigma : \mathbb{H} \to \mathbb{R}_+$ defined as

$$\Sigma((\xi_1, \xi_2, \xi_3)^\top) = \frac{c^2}{2}\|A^{1/2}\xi_1\|_2^2 + \frac{1}{2}\left\|\alpha^{1/2}\left(\xi_2 - \frac{c^2}{b}\xi_1\right)\right\|_2^2 + \frac{c^2}{2b}\left\|\gamma^{1/2}\left(\xi_2 - \frac{c^2}{b}\xi_1\right)\right\|_2^2 + \frac{b}{2}\|A^{1/2}\xi_2\|_2^2 + \frac{\tau}{2}\|\xi_3\|_2^2$$

is such that $\|\cdot\|_{\mathbb{H}}^2 \sim \Sigma(\cdot)$. The proof follows by noticing that $E(t) = \Sigma(M\Phi(t))$.
□

Remark 7.2.6 *The equivalence in Lemma 7.2.5 is uniform with respect to $\gamma \in C(\overline{\Omega})$.*

The next proposition provides the set of main identities for the linear stabilization in $\mathbb{H}$.

Proposition 7.2.7 *If (u, z, z_t) is a classical solution of (7.19) then for all $0 \leqslant s < t \leqslant T$ the following identities hold*

$$E_1(t) + b\eta\int_s^t \|z_t\|_{\Gamma_0}^2 d\sigma + \int_s^t \|\gamma^{1/2}u_{tt}\|_2^2 d\sigma = E_1(s) + \frac{c^2}{b}\int_s^t (f, \gamma u_{tt}) d\sigma \quad (7.26)$$

$$\int_s^t \left[b\|A^{1/2}z\|_2^2 - \|z_t\|_2^2\right] d\sigma = -\int_s^t (\gamma u_{tt}, z) d\sigma - \left[(z_t, z) + \frac{b\eta}{2}\|z\|_{\Gamma_0}^2\right]\Big|_s^t + \int_s^t (f, z) d\sigma \quad (7.27)$$

$$\int_s^t \left[\frac{n}{2}\|z_t\|_2^2 - \frac{b(n-2)}{2}\|A^{1/2}z\|_2^2\right] d\sigma = (b+1)\int_s^t \int_{\Gamma_0} |z_t|^2 h\nu \, d\Gamma_0 d\sigma - \int_s^t (\gamma u_{tt}, h\nabla z) d\sigma - (z_t, h\nabla z)\Big|_s^t + \int_s^t (f, h\nabla z) d\sigma \quad (7.28)$$

where h is the vector field defined as $h(x) = x - x_0$, see Assumption 7.1.3.

Proof.

1. **Proof of (7.26):** Let, on $\mathbb{H}$, the bilinear form $\langle\cdot,\cdot\rangle$ be given by

$$\langle(\xi_1,\xi_2,\xi_3)^\top,(\varphi_1,\varphi_2,\varphi_3)\rangle = b\left(A^{1/2}\left(\xi_2+\frac{c^2}{b}\xi_1\right),A^{1/2}\left(\varphi_2+\frac{c^2}{b}\varphi_1\right)\right) + \left(\xi_3+\frac{c^2}{b}\xi_2,\varphi_3+\frac{c^2}{b}\varphi_2\right)+\frac{c^2}{b}(\xi_2,\gamma\varphi_2), \tag{7.29}$$

which is clearly continuous. Moreover, recalling that $\Phi(t)=(u(t),u_t(t),u_{tt}(t))$ it follows that $2E_1(t)=\langle\Phi(t),\Phi(t)\rangle$ (see (7.24)) therefore – mostly omitting the parameters $t\in[0,T]$ and x in $\gamma(x)$ we obtain

$$\begin{aligned}\frac{dE_1(t)}{dt} &= \left\langle\frac{d\Phi(t)}{dt},\Phi(t)\right\rangle = \langle\mathscr{A}\Phi(t)+F,\Phi(t)\rangle\\ &= \langle(u_t,u_{tt},-\alpha u_{tt}-c^2A(u-\eta NN^*Au_t)-bA(u_t-\eta NN^*Au_{tt}))^\top,(u,u_t,u_{tt})\rangle\\ &+\frac{c^2}{b}(f,\gamma u_{tt})\\ &\overset{(*)}{=} b\left(A^{1/2}z_t,A^{1/2}z\right)+\left(-\gamma u_{tt}-c^2A(u+NN^*Au_t)-bA(u_t+NN^*Au_{tt}),z_t\right)\\ &+\frac{c^2}{b}(\gamma u_{tt},u_t)+\frac{c^2}{b}(f,\gamma u_{tt})\\ &= -\|\gamma^{1/2}u_{tt}\|_2^2-b\eta\|z_t\|_{\Gamma_0}^2+\frac{c^2}{b}(f,\gamma u_{tt}),\end{aligned} \tag{7.30}$$

where, in $(*)$ above we have used the definition of $\langle\cdot,\cdot\rangle$ along with $bz(t)=u_t(t)+c^2u(t)$ from what it follows that $-\alpha u_{tt}(t)+\frac{c^2}{b}u_{tt}(t)=-\gamma u_{tt}(t)$ and we directly computed

$$\begin{aligned}(bA(z+\eta NN^*Az_t),z_t) &= b(A^{1/2}(z+\eta NN^*Az_t),A^{1/2}z_t)\\ &= b(A^{1/2}z,A^{1/2}z_t)+b\eta\|N^*Az_t\|_{L^2(\Gamma)}^2\\ &= b(A^{1/2}z,A^{1/2}z_t)+b\eta\|z_t\|_{L^2(\Gamma)}^2\end{aligned} \tag{7.31}$$

by using self-adjointness of A and the characterization (7.9). The identity (7.26) then follows by integration on (s,t) for $0\leqslant s<t\leqslant T$.

2. **Proof of (7.27):** Observe that taking the L^2–inner product of

$$z_{tt}+bA(z+\eta ANN^*Az_t)=-\gamma u_{tt}+f$$

with z we have, for the left hand side:

$$(z_{tt}+bA(z+\eta ANN^*Az_t),z)=\frac{d}{dt}(z_t,z)-\|z_t\|_2^2+b\|A^{1/2}z\|_2^2+\frac{b\eta}{2}\frac{d}{dt}\|z_t\|_{\Gamma_0}^2,$$

while for the right hand side we have

$$(-\gamma u_{tt}+f,z)=(-\gamma u_{tt},z)+(f,z).$$

Then, putting right and left hand sides together and integrating on (s,t) for $0\leqslant s<t\leqslant T$ yields (7.27).

3. **Proof of (7.28):** From divergence theorem, recall that for a vector field h and a function $\varphi : \mathbb{R}^n \to \mathbb{R}$ we have that

$$\int_\Omega h\nabla\varphi d\Omega = \int_\Gamma \varphi h\cdot v d\Gamma - \int_\Omega \varphi \text{div}(h) d\Omega. \tag{7.32}$$

Considering $h(x) = x - x_0$, $x \in \overline{\Omega}$ we go back to the original (non-abstract) z–equation

$$z_{tt} - b\Delta z = -\gamma u_{tt} + f \tag{7.33}$$

– with boundary conditions $\dfrac{\partial z}{\partial v} + \eta z_t = 0$ on Γ_0 and $z = 0$ on Γ_1 – and multiply it by $h\nabla z$. We next analyze each of the involved terms in the resulting expression, omitting the variable t in most steps. For the first term we obtain

$$(z_{tt}, h\nabla z) = \frac{d}{dt}(z_t, h\nabla z) - (z_t, h\nabla z_t)$$

which, by chain rule $\nabla(\theta^2) = 2\theta\nabla\theta$ can be rewritten as

$$(z_{tt}, h\nabla z) = \frac{d}{dt}(z_t, h\nabla z) - \frac{1}{2}\int_\Omega h\nabla(z_t^2(t))d\Omega \tag{7.34}$$

and then we can apply the Divergence Theorem (with $\varphi = z_t^2$). For this we notice that since $h = x - x_0 = (x_1 - x_{01}, \cdots, x_n - x_{0n})$, we have

$$\text{div}(h) = \sum_{k=0}^{n} \frac{\partial(x_i - x_{0i})}{\partial x_i} = n.$$

Hence recalling that $z_t(t) = 0$ on Γ_1 for all t, we can further rewrite (7.34) as

$$(z_{tt}, h\nabla z) = \frac{d}{dt}(z_t, h\nabla z) - \frac{1}{2}\int_{\Gamma_0} z_t^2 hv d\Gamma_0 + \frac{n}{2}\|z_t\|_2^2. \tag{7.35}$$

Moving to the next term, we first apply Green's first Theorem to get

$$(\Delta z, h\nabla z) = -(\nabla z, \nabla(h\nabla z)) + \left(h\nabla z, \frac{\partial z}{\partial v}\right)_{\Gamma_0} \tag{7.36}$$

and then recalling the product rule for gradients along with the fact that the Jacobian Matrix of h is the identity we have

$$\begin{aligned}\nabla z\nabla(h\nabla z) &= \nabla z(h\nabla(\nabla z) + Jh\nabla z) \\ &= h\nabla z\nabla(\nabla z) + Jh|\nabla z|^2 = \frac{h}{2}\nabla(|\nabla z|^2) + |\nabla z|^2\end{aligned}$$

which then allows us to rewrite (7.36) as

$$(\Delta z, h\nabla z) = -\frac{1}{2}\int_\Omega h\nabla(|\nabla z|^2)d\Omega - \|\nabla z\|_2^2 + \left(h\nabla z, \frac{\partial z}{\partial v}\right)_{\Gamma_0}, \tag{7.37}$$

and then again application of divergence theorem (with $\varphi = |\nabla z|^2$) gives

$$(\Delta z, h\nabla z) = -\frac{1}{2}\int_{\Gamma_0} |\nabla z|^2 h\nu d\Gamma_0 + \left(\frac{n}{2}-1\right)\|\nabla z\|_2^2 + \left(h\nabla z, \frac{\partial z}{\partial \nu}\right)_{\Gamma_0}, \quad (7.38)$$

and finally recalling the definition of normal derivative $\left(\frac{\partial z}{\partial \nu} = \nabla z \cdot \nu\right)$ we get

$$(\Delta z, h\nabla z) = \frac{1}{2}\int_{\Gamma_0} |\nabla z|^2 h\nu d\Gamma_0 + \left(\frac{n}{2}-1\right)\|\nabla z\|_2^2,. \quad (7.39)$$

The identity (7.28) then follows by putting together equations (7.39) (multiplied by $-b$) and (7.35) along with the right hand side of (7.33) multiplied by $h\nabla z$.

□

Remark 7.2.8 *Take $f=0$. Observe that if $\gamma \equiv 0$ and one has no other source of dissipation – zero boundary data and no interior damping – then it follows from identity (7.26) that the $E_1(t) \equiv E_1(0)$, for all $t \geqslant 0$. With the presence of the boundary dissipation, however, E_1 is decreasing even for $\gamma \equiv 0$.*

Theorem 7.2.9 *Let $\Psi = (u, z, z_t)$ be a classical solution of (7.19) in $\mathbb{H}$. Then for all $0 \leqslant s < t \leqslant T$, if $f=0$, the following estimate holds*

$$E(t) + \int_s^t E(\sigma)d\sigma \lesssim E(s). \quad (7.40)$$

Proof.

Step 1. Take $f=0$ and let $\varepsilon > 0$ to be given. Hölder's Inequality[†] along with Trace Theorem[‡] and identity (7.26) allow the left hand side of identity (7.27) to be estimated as

$$\int_s^t \left[b\|A^{1/2}z\|_2^2 - \|z_t\|_2^2\right] d\sigma \lesssim E_1(s) + \varepsilon\overline{\gamma}\int_s^t \|A^{1/2}z\|_2^2 d\sigma, \quad (7.41)$$

where $\overline{\gamma} = \sup_{x\in\overline{\Omega}} \gamma(x)$. In fact, we estimate the terms on the right side of (7.27) as follows:

[†]Hölder's Inequality: $\|fg\|_1 \leqslant \|f\|_p\|g\|_q$ for $p, q \in [1,\infty)$ such that $p+q = pq$. Here we used for $p=q=2$.

[‡]Trace Theorem: $\|f\|_\Gamma^2 \lesssim \|A^{1/2}f\|_2^2$.

$$-\int_s^t (\gamma u_{tt}, z)d\sigma - \left[(z_t, z) + \frac{b}{2}\|z\|^2_{\Gamma_0}\right]\Big|_s^t \lesssim C_\varepsilon \int_s^t \|\gamma^{1/2} u_{tt}\|_2^2 + \varepsilon\overline{\gamma}\int_s^t \|A^{1/2}z\|_2^2$$
$$+E_1(t) + E_1(s) \tag{7.42}$$

and then, under (7.26) with $f = 0$, (7.41) follows.

Step 2. Next, recalling that $\max_{x\in\overline{\Omega}} |h(x)| < \infty$ and using again identity (7.26) we also estimate the left hand side of (7.28) as

$$\int_s^t \left[\frac{n}{2}\|z_t\|_2^2 - \frac{b(n-2)}{2}\|A^{1/2}z\|_2^2\right] d\sigma \lesssim E_1(s) + \varepsilon\overline{\gamma}\int_s^t \|A^{1/2}z\|_2^2 d\sigma, \tag{7.43}$$

for which we have used the fact that, for $f = 0$, identity (7.26) allows us to control the time integrals $\int_s^t \|z_t\|^2_{\Gamma_0} d\sigma$ and $\int_s^t \|\gamma^{1/2}u_{tt}\|_2^2 d\sigma$ along with

$$(\gamma u_{tt}, h\nabla z) \lesssim \varepsilon\overline{\gamma}\|\nabla z\|^2 + C_\varepsilon\|\gamma^{1/2}u_{tt}\|^2$$

Step 3. Now notice that adding (7.43) with $(n-1)/2$ – times (7.41) gives

$$\int_s^t \left[\frac{b}{2}\|A^{1/2}z\|_2^2 + \frac{1}{2}\|z_t\|_2^2\right] d\sigma \lesssim E_1(s) + \varepsilon\overline{\gamma}\int_s^t \|A^{1/2}z\|_2^2 d\sigma,$$

from where it follows, by taking ε small, that

$$\int_s^t \left[\|A^{1/2}z\|_2^2 + \|z_t\|_2^2\right] d\sigma \lesssim E_1(s). \tag{7.44}$$

Remark 7.2.10 *Notice that none of the arguments for Steps 1–3 depend on the requirement that $\gamma > 0$. Therefore it is valid for $\gamma \geqslant 0$.*

Step 4. Finally, from $bz = bu_t + c^2u$ we get, from (7.44)

$$\|A^{1/2}u\|_2^2 + \int_s^t \|A^{1/2}u\|_2^2 d\sigma \lesssim \int_s^t \|A^{1/2}z\|_2^2 d\sigma \lesssim E_1(s), \tag{7.45}$$

and then (7.40) follows by adding (7.45), (7.44) and (7.26).

This proves the inequality in Theorem 7.2.9 valid for classical solutions. The extension to mild solutions follows from the density of the domain of the generator in $\mathbb{H}$ and from weak lower-semi-continuity of the energy functions. □

The proof of the final result in Theorem 7.1.5 follows from Datko's Theorem [38].

Acknowledgment

Research partially supported by NSF-DMS Grant Nr 1713506.

References

[1] M.O. Alves, A.H. Caixeta, M.A. Jorge Silva and J.H. Rodrigues. Moore–Gibson–Thompson equation with memory in a history framework: A semigroup approach. Z. Angew. Math. Phys., 69(4): 106, Aug. 2018.

[2] Marcelo Bongarti, Sutthirut Charoenphon and Irena Lasiecka. Singular thermal relaxation limit for the Moore-Gibson-Thompson equation arising in propagation of acoustic waves. pp. 147–182. *In*: *Semigroups of Operators—Theory and Applications*, volume 325. Springer, 2020.

[3] Marcelo Bongarti, Sutthirut Charoenphon and Irena Lasiecka. Vanishing relaxation time dynamics of the Jordan Moore-Gibson-Thompson equation arising in nonlinear acoustics. arXiv: 2011.11141, Nov. 2020.

[4] Salah Boulaaras, Abderrahmane Zaraï and Alaeddin Draifia. Galerkin method for nonlocal mixed boundary value problem for the Moore-Gibson-Thompson equation with integral condition. Math Meth. Appl. Sci., 42(8): 2664–2679, May 2019.

[5] Francesca Bucci and Matthias Eller. The Cauchy-Dirichlet problem for the Moore-Gibson-Thompson equation. arXiv: 2004.11167, Apr. 2020.

[6] Francesca Bucci and Irena Lasiecka. Feedback control of the acoustic pressure in ultrasonic wave propagation. Optimization, 68(10): 1811–1854, Oct. 2019.

[7] Francesca Bucci and Luciano Pandolfi. On the regularity of solutions to the Moore–Gibson–Thompson equation: A perspective via wave equations with memory. J. Evol. Equ., 20(3): 837–867, Sep. 2020.

[8] C. Cattaneo. A form of heat-conduction equations which eliminates the paradox of instantaneous propagation. Comptes Rendus, 247: 431, 1958.

[9] C. Cattaneo. Sulla Conduzione Del Calore. pp. 485–485. *In*: A. Pignedoli (ed.). *Some Aspects of Diffusion Theory*. Springer Berlin Heidelberg, Berlin, Heidelberg, 2011.

[10] Valéria Neves Domingos Cavalcanti, Irena Lasiecka and Arthur Henrique Caixeta. On long time behavior of Moore-Gibson-Thompson equation with molecular relaxation. EECT, 5(4): 661–676, Oct. 2016.

[11] Wenhui Chen and Alessandro Palmieri. Nonexistence of global solutions for the semilinear Moore-Gibson-Thompson equation in the conservative case. Discrete & Continuous Dynamical Systems-A, 40(9): 5513–5540, 2020.

[12] C.I. Christov and P.M. Jordan. Heat conduction paradox involving second-sound propagation in moving media. Phys. Rev. Lett., 94(15): 154301, April 2005.

[13] J. Alberto Conejero, Carlos Lizama and Francisco Rodenas. Chaotic behaviour of the solutions of the Moore-Gibson-Thompson equation. Applied Mathematics & Information Sciences, 9(5): 2233–2238, 2015.

[14] F. Coulouvrat. On the equations of non linear acoustics. Journal d'acoustique (Les Ulis), 5(4): 321–359, 1992.

[15] D.G. Crighton. Model equations of nonlinear acoustics. Annu. Rev. Fluid Mech., 11(1): 11–33, Jan. 1979.

[16] Filippo Dell'Oro, Irena Lasiecka and Vittorino Pata. The Moore–Gibson–Thompson equation with memory in the critical case. Journal of Differential Equations, 261(7): 4188–4222, Oct. 2016.

[17] Filippo Dell'Oro, Irena Lasiecka and Vittorino Pata. A note on the Moore–Gibson–Thompson equation with memory of type II. J. Evol. Equ., Dec. 2019.

[18] Filippo Dell'Oro and Vittorino Pata. On the Moore–Gibson–Thompson equation and its relation to linear viscoelasticity. Appl. Math. Optim., 76(3): 641–655, Dec. 2017.

[19] H.O. Fattorini. Ordinary differential equations in linear topological spaces, I. Journal of Differential Equations, 5(1): 72–105, Jan. 1969.

[20] Pedro Jordan. Nonlinear acoustic phenomena in viscous thermally relaxing fluids: Shock bifurcation and the emergence of diffusive solitons. The Journal of the Acoustical Society of America, 124(4): 2491–2491, Oct. 2008.

[21] Pedro M. Jordan. Second-sound phenomena in inviscid, thermally relaxing gases. Discrete & Continuous Dynamical Systems-B, 19(7): 2189, 2014.

[22] Barbara Kaltenbacher and Irena Lasiecka. Exponential decay for low and higher energies in the third order linear Moore-Gibson-Thompson equation with variable viscosity. Palestine Journal of Mathematics 1(1): 1–10, 2012.

[23] Barbara Kaltenbacher, Irena Lasiecka and Richard Marchand. Wellposedness and exponential decay rates for the Moore-Gibson-Thompson equation arising in high intensity ultrasound. Control and Cybernetics, 40: 971–988, 2011.

[24] Barbara Kaltenbacher, Irena Lasiecka and Maria K. Pospieszalska. Wellposedness and exponential decay of the energy of the energy in the nonlinear Jordan-Moore-Gibson-Thompson equation arising in high intensity ultrasound. Math. Models Methods Appl. Sci., 22(11): 1250035, Nov. 2012.

[25] Barbara Kaltenbacher and Vanja Nikolić. On the Jordan-Moore-Gibson-Thompson equation: Well-posedness with quadratic gradient nonlinearity and singular limit for vanishing relaxation time. arXiv: 1901.02795, Oct. 2019.

[26] Barbara, Alpen-Adria-Universität Klagenfurt, Universitätsstraße 65–67, 9020 Klagenfurt Kaltenbacher. Mathematics of nonlinear acoustics. Evolution Equations & Control Theory, 4(4): 447–491, 2015.

[27] W. Michael Lai, David Rubin and Erhard Krempl. *Introduction to Continuum Mechanics*. Butterworth-Heinemann/Elsevier, Amsterdam; Boston, 4th edition, 2010.

[28] I. Lasiecka and D. Tataru. Uniform boundary stabilization of semilinear wave equations with nonlinear boundary damping. Differential Integral Equations, 6(3): 507–533, 1993.

[29] I. Lasiecka and R. Triggiani. Uniform stabilization of the wave equation with Dirichlet or Neumann feedback control without geometrical conditions. Appl Math Optim, 25(2): 189–224, Mar. 1992.

[30] Irena Lasiecka and Xiaojun Wang. Moore–Gibson–Thompson equation with memory, Part II: General decay of energy. Journal of Differential Equations, 259(12): 7610–7635, Dec. 2015.

[31] Irena Lasiecka and Xiaojun Wang. Moore–Gibson–Thompson equation with memory, Part I: Exponential decay of energy. Z. Angew. Math. Phys., 67(2): 17, Apr. 2016.

[32] Shitao Liu and Roberto Triggiani. Inverse problem for a linearized Jordan–Moore–Gibson–Thompson equation. pp. 305–351. *In*: *New Prospects in*

Direct, Inverse and Control Problems for Evolution Equations, volume 10. Springer, 2014.

[33] Wenjun Liu and Zhijing Chen. General decay rate for a Moore–Gibson–Thompson equation with infinite history. Z. Angew. Math. Phys., 71(2): 43, Apr. 2020.

[34] Pedro M. Jordan, Barbara Kaltenbacher. U.S. Naval Research Laboratory, USA, and Alpen-Adria-Universität Klagenfurt, Austria. Introduction to the special issue Nonlinear wave phenomena in continuum physics: Some recent findings. Evolution Equations & Control Theory, 8(1): 1–3, 2019.

[35] R. Marchand, T. McDevitt and R. Triggiani. An abstract semigroup approach to the third-order Moore-Gibson-Thompson partial differential equation arising in high-intensity ultrasound: structural decomposition, spectral analysis, exponential stability. Math. Meth. Appl. Sci., 35(15): 1896–1929, Oct. 2012.

[36] Vanja Nikolić and Belkacem Said-Houari. Mathematical analysis of memory effects and thermal relaxation in nonlinear sound waves on unbounded domains. arXiv: 2003.11840, Oct. 2020.

[37] Vanja Nikolić and Belkacem Said-Houari. On the Jordan-Moore-Gibson-Thompson wave equation in hereditary fluids with quadratic gradient nonlinearity. arXiv: 2005.07245, May 2020.

[38] Amnon Pazy. *Semigroups of linear operators and applications to partial differential equations*. Number 44 in Applied mathematical sciences. Springer, New York, NY, corr. 2. print edition, 1992.

[39] Marta Pellicer and Belkacem Said-Houari. On the Cauchy problem for the standard linear solid model with heat conduction: Fourier versus Cattaneo. arXiv: 1903.10181, Mar. 2019.

[40] Marta Pellicer and Joan Solà-Morales. Optimal scalar products in the Moore-Gibson-Thompson equation. Evolution Equations & Control Theory, 8(1): 203–220, 2019.

[41] Reinhard Racke and Belkacem Said-Houari. Global well-posedness of the Cauchy problem for the 3D Jordan–Moore–Gibson–Thompson equation. Communications in Contemporary Mathematics, 2050069, 2020.

[42] Reiko Sakamoto. *Hyperbolic Boundary Value Problems*. Cambridge University Press, Cambridge [Cambridgeshire]; New York, 1st english edition, 1982.

[43] Stokes. An examination of the possible effect of the radiation of heat on the propagation of sound. The London, Edinburgh, and Dublin Philosophical Magazine and Journal of Science, 1(4): 305–317, Apr. 1851.

[44] Brian Straughan. *Heat Waves*. Springer-Verlag New York, 2014.

[45] Daniel Tataru. On the regularity of boundary traces for the wave equation. Annali della Scuola Normale Superiore di Pisa-Classe di Scienze, 26(1): 185–206, 1998.

[46] Roberto Triggiani. Sharp interior and boundary regularity of the SMGTJ equation with dirichlet or neumann boundary control. pp. 379–426. *In*: *Semigroups of Operators–Theory and Applications*, volume 325. Springer, 2020.

Chapter 8

Sweeping Process Arguments in the Analysis and Control of a Contact Problem

Mircea Sofonea[a,*] and *Yi-bin Xiao*[b]

Mathematics Subject Classification (2000) 74M15, 74M10, 47J22, 49J40, 49J21, 34G25.

8.1 Introduction

Contact phenomena between deformable bodies arise in industry and everyday life. They are modeled by strongly nonlinear boundary value problems in which, besides the balance equation and the classical displacement-traction boundary condition, the main ingredients are the constitutive law and the interface law. The constitutive law describes the specific material's behavior which could be the elastic, plastic, viscous, with or without hardening, with or without damage, etc. The interface law describes the contact with a rigid or deformable foundation, which could be frictional or frictionless, with or without adhesion, and with or without wear. The diversity of real materials and interface laws lead to a large variety of boundary value problems which, usually, do not have classi-

[a] Laboratoire de Mathématiques et Physique, University of Perpignan Via Domitia, 52 Avenue Paul Alduy, 66860 Perpignan, France.

[b] School of Mathematical Sciences, University of Electronic Science and Technology of China, Chengdu, Sichuan, 611731, PR China.

* Corresponding author: sofonea@univ-perp.fr

cal solutions. Therefore, their study is made by using a variational approach, that consists to replace the strong formulation of the problem by a weak or variational formulation, which is more convenient for mathematical analysis and numerical simulations.

The weak formulation of contact problems vary from problem to problem, from author to author and even from paper to paper. For most of them, the variational formulation is given in a form of an elliptic or evolutionary variational inequality in which the unknown is the displacement field. References in the field include [8, 10, 11, 12, 13, 28, 31]. On occasion, when the problem has a nonconvex structure, its weak formulation is provided by a hemivariational inequality or by a so-called variational-hemivariational inequality. References in the field are [19, 27, 29] and, more recently, [32]. Currently, there is an interest in variational formulation of contact models in the form of a sweeping process. Sweeping processes represent a special class of differential inclusions associated to the normal cone of a nonempty set and have been introduced in the pioneering works of Moreau [20, 21, 22]. References in the field are [9, 14, 18, 23, 26], for instance. Sweeping process formulation for contact problems in which the unknown is the displacement field have been considered in [1, 2]. Sweeping process formulation for contact problems in which the unknown is the strain field have been studied in our recent works [24, 25].

In most of the references above, besides the weak formulation of the contact models, existence and uniqueness results for the weak solution have been obtained. To this end, various functional arguments have been used, including arguments of monotonicity, convexity, nonsmooth analysis, multivalued analysis and fixed point. The dependence of the solution with respect the data and parameters was also studied and various convergence results have been obtained. Nevertheless, the literature concerning optimal control problems in the study of mathematical models of contact is quite limited. The reason is the strong nonlinearities which arise in the boundary conditions involved in such models. Results on optimal control for various contact problems with elastic materials can be found in [3, 7, 8, 15, 16, 17, 30] and the references therein.

The aim of this current chapter is to study the optimal control of a new model of contact. To the best of our knowledge, our work has three traits of novelty. The first one concerns the model we consider, which is new and nonstandard. It describes the frictional contact of a viscoelastic body with a foundation made by a deformable material covered by a layer of a viscous material, say a viscous fluid. The second novelty consists in the variational formulation of the model, which is given in the form of a sweeping process for the strain tensor. We use this formulation in order to deduce the existence of a unique weak solution to the contact problem. Finally, the third novelty consists in the optimal control problem we consider, associated to the contact model. It is quite general and allows to provide various relevant examples, in which the choice of the control can be either the initial density of tractions, or the friction bound, or the initial displacement field, for instance. The existence of the optimal pairs for the optimal control we consider is based on a continuous dependence result which has some interest in its own.

The chapter is organized as follows. In Section 8.2 we present some notation and preliminary material which are needed in the rest of the chapter. It concerns the properties of the function spaces we use, background on convex analysis, and an abstract result for a class of sweeping processes. In Section 8.3 we describe the mechanical assumptions we consider and the resulting mathematical model of contact. Then we list the hypotheses on the data. In Section 8.4 we derive a variational formulation of the problem and prove an existence and uniqueness result. This allows us to define the concept of a weak solution to the contact model. Section 8.5 is devoted to the study of the dependence of the weak solution with respect to the data. In Section 8.6 we consider an associated optimal control problem for which we prove a general existence result. We also provide three examples which differ by the choice of the control and cost function, together with the corresponding mechanical interpretation. Finally, we end this chapter with Section 8.7 in which we present some concluding remarks.

8.2 Notation and Preliminaries

The preliminary material we present in this section concerns basic notation, an existence and uniqueness result for a class of sweeping processes and some properties of the function spaces in Contact Mechanics. Everywhere in this section X represents a real Hilbert space endowed with an inner product $(\cdot,\cdot)_X$ and its associated norm $\|\cdot\|_X$, and 2^X denotes the set of parts of X.

Basic notation. We use the notation N_K for the outward normal cone of a nonempty closed convex subset $K \subset X$. It is well known that $N_K : X \to 2^X$ and, for any $u, f \in X$, we have

$$f \in N_K(u) \iff u \in K, \quad (f, v-u)_X \leq 0 \quad \text{for all } v \in K. \tag{8.1}$$

We also recall that a function $\varphi : X \to \mathbb{R}$ is said to be subdifferentiable (in the sense of the convex analysis) if for any $u \in X$ there exists an element $\xi \in X$ such that

$$\varphi(v) - \varphi(u) \geq (\xi, v-u)_X \quad \text{for all } \ v \in X. \tag{8.2}$$

Consider now an interval of time $I \subset \mathbb{R}$ which could be either of the form $I = [0,T]$ with $T > 0$ or the unbounded interval $\mathbb{R}_+ = [0,+\infty)$. We denote by $C(I;X)$ and $C^1(I;X)$ the space of continuous and continuously differentiable functions defined on I with values in X, respectively. For $v \in C^1(I;X)$ we use $\dot{v}$ for the derivative of v with respect to the time variable $t \in I$ and we recall that the following equality holds:

$$v(t) = \int_0^t \dot{v}(s)\,ds + v(0) \quad \text{for all } \ t \in I. \tag{8.3}$$

For an operator $\mathcal{S}\colon C(I;X) \to C(I;X)$ and a function $u \in C(I;X)$ we use the shorthand notation $\mathcal{S}u(t)$ to represent the value of the function $\mathcal{S}u$ at the point $t \in I$, that is, $\mathcal{S}u(t) := (\mathcal{S}u)(t)$. Moreover, if $A : X \to X$, then $A + \mathcal{S}$ will represent a shorthand notation for the operator which maps any function $u \in C(I;X)$ to the function $t \mapsto Au(t) + \mathcal{S}u(t) \in C(I;X)$.

Sweeping process. Consider a set-valued mapping $K : I \to 2^X$, the operators $A : X \to X$, $B : X \to X$, $\mathcal{S} : C(I;X) \to C(I;X)$, and an element u_0 which satisfy the following conditions.

($\mathcal{K}$) $K : I \to 2^X$ and there exist a nonempty closed convex $K_0 \subset X$ and a function $f \in C(I;X)$ such that

$$K(t) = K_0 + f(t) \quad \text{for all } t \in I.$$

($\mathcal{A}$) $A : X \to X$ is a strongly monotone and Lipschitz continuous operator with constants m_A and $L_A > 0$, i.e.,

$$(Au - Av, u - v)_X \geq m_A \|u - v\|_X^2 \quad \text{for all } u, v \in X.$$

$$\|Au - Av\|_X \leq L_A \|u - v\|_X \quad \text{for all } u, v \in X.$$

($\mathcal{B}$) $B : X \to X$ is a Lipschitz continuous operator with Lipschitz constant $L_B > 0$, i.e.,

$$\|Bu - Bv\|_X \leq L_B \|u - v\|_X \quad \text{for all } u, v \in X.$$

($\mathcal{S}$) $\mathcal{S} : C(I;X) \to C(I;X)$ is a history-dependent operator, i.e., if for any nonempty compact set $J \subset I$, there exists $L_J > 0$ such that

$$\|\mathcal{S}u_1(t) - \mathcal{S}u_2(t)\|_X \leq L_J \int_0^t \|u_1(s) - u_2(s)\|_X \, ds$$

for all $u_1, u_2 \in C(I;X)$ and $t \in J$.

($\mathcal{U}$) $u_0 \in X$.

Under these assumptions we consider the sweeping process problem of finding a function $u : I \to X$ such that

$$\begin{cases} -\dot{u}(t) \in N_{K(t)}(A\dot{u}(t) + Bu(t) + \mathcal{S}\dot{u}(t)) & \text{for all } t \in I, \\ u(0) = u_0. \end{cases} \tag{8.4}$$

We have the following existence and uniqueness result.

Theorem 8.2.1 *Assume that* ($\mathcal{K}$), ($\mathcal{A}$), ($\mathcal{B}$), ($\mathcal{S}$) *and* ($\mathcal{U}$) *hold. Then, the sweeping process* (8.4) *has a unique solution* $u \in C^1(I;X)$.

Theorem 8.2.1 represents a direct consequence of Theorem 4.1 and Corollary 5.4 in [24]. Its proof is based on arguments of convex analysis, monotone operators and a fixed point result for history-dependent operators.

Function spaces. For the contact problem we introduce some specific notation we need in the following sections. First, $\mathbb{S}^d$ stands for the space of second order symmetric tensors on $\mathbb{R}^d$ with $d \in \{2,3\}$. Moreover, "$\cdot$" and $\|\cdot\|$ represent the inner product and the Euclidean norm on the spaces $\mathbb{R}^d$ and $\mathbb{S}^d$, respectively. In addition, $\Omega \subset \mathbb{R}^d$ is a bounded domain with a Lipschitz continuous boundary Γ. The outward unit normal at Γ will be denoted by ν and Γ_1 is a measurable part of Γ with positive measure.

We use the standard notation for the Lebesgue and Sobolev spaces associated to Ω and Γ. Typical examples are the spaces $L^2(\Omega)^d$, $L^2(\Gamma)^d$ and $H^1(\Omega)^d$ equipped with their canonical Hilbertian structure. For an element $v \in H^1(\Omega)^d$ we still write v for the trace $\gamma v \in L^2(\Gamma)^d$ and v_ν, v_τ for the normal and tangential traces on the boundary, i.e., $v_\nu = v \cdot \nu$ and $v_\tau = v - v_\nu \nu$. Moreover, $\varepsilon(v)$ will denote the symmetric part of the gradient of v, i.e.,

$$\varepsilon(v) = \frac{1}{2}(\nabla v + \nabla^T v).$$

In addition, for the displacement field we need the space V and for the stress and strain fields we need the space Q, defined as follows:

$$V = \{v \in H^1(\Omega)^d : \ v = 0 \ \text{ on } \ \Gamma_1\}, \tag{8.5}$$
$$Q = \{\sigma = (\sigma_{ij}) : \ \sigma_{ij} = \sigma_{ji} \in L^2(\Omega) \ \ \forall i, j = \overline{1,d}\}. \tag{8.6}$$

The spaces V and Q are real Hilbert spaces endowed with the inner products

$$(u,v)_V = \int_\Omega \varepsilon(u) \cdot \varepsilon(v)\, dx, \qquad (\sigma,\tau)_Q = \int_\Omega \sigma \cdot \tau\, dx. \tag{8.7}$$

The associated norms on these spaces will be denoted by $\|\cdot\|_V$ and $\|\cdot\|_Q$, respectively. Recall that the completeness of the space $(V, \|\cdot\|_V)$ follows from the assumption $meas\,(\Gamma_1) > 0$, which allows the use of Korn's inequality. Note also that, by the definition of the inner product in the spaces V and Q, we have

$$\|v\|_V = \|\varepsilon(v)\|_Q \quad \text{for all } \ v \in V \tag{8.8}$$

and, using the Sobolev theorem, we deduce that

$$\|v\|_{L^2(\Gamma)^d} \le c_{tr}\, \|v\|_V \quad \text{for all } \ v \in V. \tag{8.9}$$

Here c_{tr} is a positive constant which depends on Ω and Γ_1.

We also use "$\to$" and "$\rightharpoonup$" for the strong and weak convergence in various spaces which will be specified, except in the case when these convergence hold in $\mathbb{R}$. Moreover, all the limits, lower limits and upper limits will be considered as $n \to \infty$, even if we do not mention it explicitly.

We end this section with the following result we shall use in the rest of the chapter .

Lemma 8.2.2 *There exists a linear continuous operator $G : Q \to V$ such that for any $\omega \in Q$ and $u \in V$ the following implication holds:*

$$\omega = \varepsilon(u) \quad \Longrightarrow \quad u = G\omega. \tag{8.10}$$

Proof. First, we recall that the range of the deformation operator $\varepsilon : V \to Q$, denoted $\varepsilon(V)$, is a closed subspace of Q. A proof of this result can be found in [32, p.212]. Denote by $P: Q \to \varepsilon(V)$ the orthogonal projection operator on $\varepsilon(V) \subset Q$ and note that equality (8.8) shows that $\varepsilon : V \to \varepsilon(V)$ is a linear invertible operator. In what follows, we denote by $\varepsilon^{-1} : \varepsilon(V) \to V$ the inverse of ε. The ingredients above allow us to define the operators $G : Q \to V$ by equality

$$G\omega = (\varepsilon^{-1}P\omega) \quad \text{for all } \omega \in Q. \tag{8.11}$$

It is obvious to see that G is a linear continuous operator and, moreover, the implication (8.10) holds. □

8.3 The Contact Model

We now turn to describe the mathematical model of contact we consider in this chapter. The physical setting is the following: a viscoelastic body occupies, in its reference configuration, a bounded domain $\Omega \subset \mathbb{R}^d$ ($d \in \{2,3\}$), with boundary $\partial\Omega = \Gamma$. The body is fixed on a part of its boundary, is acted upon by body forces and surface tractions and is in contact with an obstacle, the co-called foundation. As a result, its mechanical state evolves. To describe its evolution we denote by I the time interval of interest and we assume that I is either of the form $I = [0,T]$ with $T > 0$ or $I = \mathbb{R}_+$. Moreover, as usual, we use the dot above to represent the derivative with respect to the time variable $t \in I$. In addition, x will represent a typical point in $\Omega \cup \Gamma$ and, for simplicity, we sometimes skip the dependence of various functions on the spatial variable x. We denote by $\sigma : \Omega \times I \to \mathbb{S}^d$ the stress field and by $u : \Omega \times I \to \mathbb{R}^d$ the displacement field. We consider the framework of linearized theory and, therefore, $\varepsilon(u) : \Omega \times I \to \mathbb{S}^d$ will represent the strain tensor.

We model the material's behavior with a viscoelastic constitutive law of the form

$$\sigma(t) = \mathcal{A}\varepsilon(\dot{u}(t)) + \mathcal{B}\varepsilon(u(t)) + \int_0^t \mathcal{C}(t-s)\varepsilon(\dot{u}(s))\,ds \quad \text{in } \Omega \tag{8.12}$$

where $\mathcal{A}$ is the viscosity operator, $\mathcal{B}$ is the elasticity operator, $\mathcal{C}$ is the relaxation tensor and, here and below, $t \in I$. Such kind of laws have been considered in

[4, 5, 6, 32] in order to model the properties of various materials like metals, rubbers, polymers and so on. Note that, when $\mathcal{C}$ vanishes, equation (8.12) reduces to the well-known Kelvin-Voigt constitutive law.

We assume that the process is quasistatic and, therefore, the stress field satisfies the equilibrium equation, i.e.,

$$\operatorname{Div}\sigma(t) + f_0(t) = 0 \quad \text{in } \Omega. \tag{8.13}$$

Here "Div" denotes the divergence operator and $f_0 : \Omega \times I \to \mathbb{R}^d$ denotes the density of applied body forces like gravity forces, for instance.

Next, we assume that the boundary Γ is divided in three measurable disjoint parts Γ_1, Γ_2 and Γ_3 such that $meas(\Gamma_1) > 0$. The set Γ_1 represents the part of the boundary where the viscoelastic body is fixed and, therefore, we use the displacement boundary condition

$$u(t) = 0 \quad \text{on } \Gamma_1. \tag{8.14}$$

The set Γ_2 represents the part of the boundary where the body is acted by surface tractions and, therefore,

$$\sigma(t)\nu = f_2(t) \quad \text{on } \Gamma_2. \tag{8.15}$$

Here $f_2 : \Gamma_2 \times I \to \mathbb{R}^d$ denotes the density of applied traction.

Finally, Γ_3 is the part of the boundary where the contact arises. To describe the interface law on this boundary we use σ_ν and σ_τ for the normal and tangential components of the stress vector $\sigma\nu$ on Γ, i.e., $\sigma_\nu = \sigma\nu \cdot \nu$ and $\sigma_\tau = \sigma\nu - \sigma_\nu \nu$. We assume that the foundation is made by a deformable obstacle covered by a layer of viscous material, say a fluid, which completely fills the gap between the body and the foundation, at any time moment t. Then, the normal stress has an additive decomposition of the form

$$\sigma_\nu(t) = \sigma_\nu^1(t) + \sigma_\nu^2(t) \tag{8.16}$$

where $\sigma_\nu^1(t)$ represents the reaction of the fluid towards the body and $\sigma_\nu^2(t)$ is the reaction of the deformable obstacle. Assume that

$$-\sigma_\nu^1(t) = \xi_\nu(t), \quad \xi_\nu(t) \in [F_1, F_2], \quad \xi_\nu(t) = \begin{cases} F_1 & \text{if } \dot{u}_\nu(t) < 0, \\ F_2 & \text{if } \dot{u}_\nu(t) > 0, \end{cases} \tag{8.17}$$

where $F_2 \geq F_1 \geq 0$. This condition shows that the pressure exerted by the fluid on the viscoelastic body is F_1 in extension, and F_2 in compression. The reaction of the deformable obstacle is described by a normal compliance condition in the form with a gap function, i.e.,

$$-\sigma_\nu^2(t) = p(u_\nu(t) - g), \tag{8.18}$$

where g represents the initial depth of the viscous fluid and p is a given function which will be described below. We now gather conditions (8.16)–(8.18) to see that

$$\left.\begin{array}{l} -\sigma_\nu(t) = \xi_\nu(t) + p(u_\nu(t) - g), \\[2ex] \xi_\nu(t) \in [F_1, F_2], \quad \xi_\nu(t) = \begin{cases} F_1 & \text{if} \quad \dot{u}_\nu(t) < 0, \\ F_2 & \text{if} \quad \dot{u}_\nu(t) > 0, \end{cases} \end{array}\right\} \text{ on } \Gamma_3. \qquad (8.19)$$

Note that in the particular case when $F_1 = F_2$ and p vanishes, the boundary condition (8.19) represents an example of the so-called of normal damped response condition. In the case when $F_1 = F_2 = 0$ the boundary condition (8.19) becomes the classical normal compliance contact condition. It models the contact of the viscoelastic body with a deformable obstacle situated at the distance g from the body, measured along the outward normal. For more details on these classical contact conditions see [12, 31, 32], for instance.

We complete the contact condition (8.19) with the Tresca friction law

$$\|\sigma_\tau(t)\| \le F_b, \quad -\sigma_\tau(t) = F_b \frac{\dot{u}_\tau(t)}{\|\dot{u}_\tau(t)\|} \quad \text{if} \quad \dot{u}_\tau(t) \neq 0 \quad \text{on } \Gamma_3, \qquad (8.20)$$

in which $F_b \ge 0$ is a given friction bound. In particular, when F_b vanishes the contact is frictionless. This represents an idealization since, even lubricated, the real surfaces generate reaction on sliding.

Finally, since the problem is evolutionary, we impose the initial condition

$$u(0) = u_0 \qquad \text{in } \Omega, \qquad (8.21)$$

where u_0 represents a given initial displacement.

We now gather the above equations and conditions to obtain the following formulation of our contact model.

Problem $\mathcal{P}$. *Find a displacement field $u\colon \Omega \times I \to \mathbb{R}^d$ and a stress field $\sigma\colon \Omega \times I \to \mathbb{S}^d$ such that* (8.12)–(8.15), (8.19), (8.20) *hold, for all $t \in I$ and, moreover,* (8.21) *holds, too.*

In the study of Problem $\mathcal{P}$ we assume that the viscosity and the elasticity operators satisfy the following conditions.

$$\left\{\begin{array}{l}\text{(a) } \mathcal{A}\colon \Omega\times\mathbb{S}^d\to\mathbb{S}^d.\\ \text{(b) There exists } L_{\mathcal{A}}>0 \text{ such that}\\ \qquad \|\mathcal{A}(x,\varepsilon_1)-\mathcal{A}(x,\varepsilon_2)\|\le L_{\mathcal{A}}\|\varepsilon_1-\varepsilon_2\|\\ \qquad\quad \text{for all } \ \varepsilon_1,\varepsilon_2\in\mathbb{S}^d, \text{ a.e. } x\in\Omega.\\ \text{(c) There exists } m_{\mathcal{A}}>0 \text{ such that}\\ \qquad (\mathcal{A}(x,\varepsilon_1)-\mathcal{A}(x,\varepsilon_2))\cdot(\varepsilon_1-\varepsilon_2)\ge m_{\mathcal{A}}\,\|\varepsilon_1-\varepsilon_2\|^2\\ \qquad\quad \text{for all } \ \varepsilon_1,\varepsilon_2\in\mathbb{S}^d, \text{ a.e. } \boldsymbol{x}\in\Omega.\\ \text{(d) The mapping } \ x\mapsto\mathcal{A}(x,\varepsilon) \text{ is measurable on } \Omega,\\ \qquad \text{for all } \varepsilon\in\mathbb{S}^d.\\ \text{(e) The mapping } x\mapsto\mathcal{A}(x,0) \text{ belongs to } Q.\end{array}\right. \tag{8.22}$$

$$\left\{\begin{array}{l}\text{(a) } \mathcal{B}\colon \Omega\times\mathbb{S}^d\to\mathbb{S}^d.\\ \text{(b) There exists } L_{\mathcal{B}}>0 \text{ such that}\\ \qquad \|\mathcal{B}(x,\varepsilon_1)-\mathcal{A}(x,\varepsilon_2)\|\le L_{\mathcal{A}}\|\varepsilon_1-\varepsilon_2\|\\ \qquad\quad \text{for all } \ \varepsilon_1,\varepsilon_2\in\mathbb{S}^d, \text{ a.e. } x\in\Omega.\\ \text{(c) The mapping } \ x\mapsto\mathcal{B}(x,\varepsilon) \text{ is measurable on } \Omega,\\ \qquad \text{for all } \varepsilon\in\mathbb{S}^d.\\ \text{(d) The mapping } x\mapsto\mathcal{B}(x,0) \text{ belongs to } Q.\end{array}\right. \tag{8.23}$$

Moreover, the relaxation tensor is such that

$$\mathcal{C}\in C(I;\mathbf{Q}_\infty), \tag{8.24}$$

where, here and below, $\mathbf{Q}_\infty$ is the space of fourth order tensor fields defined by

$$\mathbf{Q}_\infty=\{\mathcal{C}=(c_{ijkl})\ :\ c_{ijkl}=c_{jikl}=c_{klij}\in L^\infty(\Omega)\},$$

equipped with the norm

$$\|\mathcal{C}\|_{\mathbf{Q}_\infty}=\max_{0\le i,j,k,l\le d}\|c_{ijkl}\|_{L^\infty(\Omega)}.$$

In addition, the normal compliance function p satisfies the following condition.

$$\left\{\begin{array}{l}\text{(a) } p\colon \Gamma_3\times\mathbb{R}\to\mathbb{R}.\\ \text{(b) There exists } L_p>0 \text{ such that}\\ \qquad |p(x,r_1)-p(x,r_2)|\le L_p|r_1-r_2|\\ \qquad\quad \text{for all } \ r_1,r_2\in\mathbb{R}, \text{ a.e. } x\in\Gamma_3.\\ \text{(c) The mapping } x\mapsto p(x,r) \text{ is measurable on } \Gamma_3\\ \qquad\quad \text{for all } r\in\mathbb{R}.\\ \text{(c) } p(x,r)=0 \ \text{ for all } r\le 0,\ p(x,r)\ge 0\\ \qquad\quad \text{for all } r>0, \text{ a.e. } x\in\Gamma_3.\end{array}\right. \tag{8.25}$$

The density of applied forces, the depth function and the initial displacement have the regularity

$$f_0 \in C(I; L^2(\Omega)^d). \tag{8.26}$$

$$f_2 \in C(I; L^2(\Gamma_2)^d). \tag{8.27}$$

$$g \in L^2(\Gamma_3), \quad g(x) \geq 0 \quad \text{a.e. on } \Gamma_3. \tag{8.28}$$

$$u_0 \in V. \tag{8.29}$$

Finally, recall that

$$F_2 \geq F_1 \geq 0, \qquad F_b \geq 0. \tag{8.30}$$

We shall keep assumptions (8.22)–(8.30) in the next two sections, even if we do not mention it explicitly. Our main aim there is to provide the variational analysis of Problem $\mathcal{P}$, including existence, uniqueness and convergence results.

8.4 An Existence and Uniqueness Result

We now turn to the variational formulation of Problem $\mathcal{P}$ and, to this end, we introduce the operators $A : V \to V$, $B : V \to V$ and $\mathcal{S} : C(I;Q) \to C(I;Q)$ defined by equalities:

$$(A\omega, \tau)_Q = \int_\Omega \mathcal{A}\omega \cdot \tau \, dx \quad \text{for all } \omega,\, \tau \in Q, \tag{8.31}$$

$$(B\omega, \tau) = \int_\Omega \mathcal{B}\omega \cdot \tau \, dx + \int_{\Gamma_3} p((G\omega)_\nu - g)(G\tau)_\nu \, da \quad \text{for all } \omega, \tau \in Q, \tag{8.32}$$

$$(\mathcal{S}\omega(t), \tau)_Q = (\int_0^t \mathcal{C}(t-s)\omega(s)) \, ds, \tau)_Q \quad \text{for all } \omega \in C(I;Q),\, \tau \in Q. \tag{8.33}$$

Recall that, here and below, G is the operator defined in Lemma 8.2.2. On the other hand, we consider the functions $j : V \to \mathbb{R}$, $f : I \to V$, the set-valued mapping $\Sigma : I \to 2^Q$ and the element ω_0 defined by

$$j(v) = \int_{\Gamma_3} (F_2 v_\nu^+ - F_1 v_\nu^-) \, da + \int_{\Gamma_3} F_b \|v_\tau\| \, da \quad \text{for all } v \in V, \tag{8.34}$$

$$(f(t), v)_V = \int_\Omega f_0(t) \cdot v \, dx + \int_{\Gamma_2} f_2(t) \cdot v \, da \quad \text{for all } v \in V,\, t \in I, \tag{8.35}$$

$$\Sigma(t) = \{\tau \in Q : (\tau, \varepsilon(v))_Q + j(v) \geq (f(t), v)_V \;\; \forall \tau \in Q\} \text{ for all } t \in I, \tag{8.36}$$

$$\omega_0 = \varepsilon(u_0). \tag{8.37}$$

Note that in (8.34) as well as in the rest of the chapter notations r^+ and r^- represent the positive and negative part of r, that is $r^+ = max\{r, 0\}$ and $r^- = max\{-r, 0\}$.

Assume now that (u,σ) represents a regular solution of Problem $\mathcal{P}$ and let $v \in V$, $t \in I$ be arbitrary fixed. Then, using integration by parts and equalities (8.13)–(8.15) we find that

$$\begin{aligned}
&\int_{\Omega} \sigma(t)\cdot(\varepsilon(v)-\varepsilon(\dot{u}(t)))\,dx \qquad (8.38)\\
&\quad = \int_{\Omega} f_0(t)\cdot(v-\dot{u}(t))\,dx + \int_{\Gamma_2} f_2(t)\cdot(v-\dot{u}(t))\,da\\
&\quad + \int_{\Gamma_3} \sigma_\nu(t)(v_\nu-\dot{u}_\nu(t))\,da + \int_{\Gamma_3} \sigma_\tau\cdot(v_\tau-\dot{u}_\tau(t))\,da.
\end{aligned}$$

On the other hand, the boundary conditions (8.19) and (8.20) yield

$$\begin{aligned}
&\sigma_\nu(t)(v_\nu-\dot{u}_\nu(t)) \ge F_2((\dot{u}_\nu(t))^+ - v_\nu^+) - F_1((\dot{u}_\nu(t))^- - v_\nu^-)\\
&\qquad -p(u_\nu(t)-g)(v_\nu-\dot{u}_\nu(t)),\\
&\sigma_\tau(t)\cdot(v_\tau-\dot{u}_\tau(t)) \ge F_b(\|\dot{u}_\tau(t)\| - \|v_\tau\|)
\end{aligned}$$

on Γ_3 and, therefore, (8.38) implies that

$$\begin{aligned}
&\int_{\Omega} \sigma(t)\cdot(\varepsilon(v)-\varepsilon(\dot{u}(t)))\,dx + \int_{\Gamma_3} p(u_\nu(t)-g)(v_\nu-\dot{u}_\nu(t))\,da \qquad (8.39)\\
&\quad + \int_{\Gamma_3} (F_2 v_\nu^+ - F_1 v_\nu^-)\,da - \int_{\Gamma_3} (F_2(\dot{u}_\nu(t))^+ - F_1(\dot{u}_\nu(t))^-)\,da\\
&\quad + \int_{\Gamma_3} F_b(\|v_\tau\| - \|\dot{u}_\tau(t)\|)\,da\\
&\quad \ge \int_{\Omega} f_0(t)\cdot(v-\dot{u}(t))\,dx + \int_{\Gamma_2} f_2(t)\cdot(v-\dot{u}(t))\,da.
\end{aligned}$$

Denote by $\widetilde{\sigma}(t)$ the element of Q given by

$$\widetilde{\sigma}(t) = A\varepsilon(\dot{u}(t)) + B\varepsilon(u(t)) + \mathcal{S}\varepsilon(\dot{u})(t). \qquad (8.40)$$

Then, using inequality (8.39), the constitutive law (8.12) and notations (8.31)–(8.35), (8.40) we see that

$$(\widetilde{\sigma}(t), \varepsilon(v)-\varepsilon(\dot{u}(t)))_Q + j(v) - j(\dot{u}(t)) \ge (f(t), v-\dot{u}(t))_V. \qquad (8.41)$$

We now take $v = 2\dot{u}(t)$ and $v = 0_V$ in (8.41) to obtain that

$$(\widetilde{\sigma}(t), \varepsilon(\dot{u}(t)))_Q + j(\dot{u})(t) = (f(t), \dot{u}(t))_V. \qquad (8.42)$$

Then, using (8.41), (8.42) and (8.36) it follows that

$$\widetilde{\sigma}(t) \in \Sigma(t), \quad (\tau - \widetilde{\sigma}(t), \varepsilon(\dot{u}(t)))_Q \ge 0 \quad \text{for all } \tau \in \Sigma(t). \qquad (8.43)$$

Next, we use (8.1) to write inequality (8.43) in the equivalent form

$$-\varepsilon(\dot{u}(t)) \in N_{\Sigma(t)}(\widetilde{\sigma}(t)). \tag{8.44}$$

Finally, we introduce the notation $\varepsilon(u) = \omega$ and use the inclusion (8.44) together with equalities (8.40) and (8.37) to obtain the following variational formulation of Problem $\mathcal{P}$.

Problem $\mathcal{P}_V$. *Find a strain field $\omega : I \to V$ such that*

$$-\dot{\omega}(t) \in N_{\Sigma(t)}\big(\mathcal{A}\dot{\omega}(t) + \mathcal{B}\omega(t) + \mathcal{S}\dot{\omega}(t)\big) \quad \text{for all } t \in I,$$

$$\omega(0) = \omega_0.$$

Note that Problem $\mathcal{P}_V$ represents a sweeping process in which the unknown is the strain field. To the best of our knowledge, this problem is new and nonstandard since, usually, the variational formulation of quasistatic viscoelastic contact problems are in a form of a history-dependent variational inequality for the displacement field, as shown in [31] and the references therein.

We now state and prove the following existence and uniqueness result.

Theorem 8.4.1 *Assume that* (8.22)–(8.30) *hold. Then Problem $\mathcal{P}_V$ has a unique solution $\omega \in C^1(I;Q)$.*

Proof. We use Theorem 8.2.1 with $X = Q$ and $K(t) = \Sigma(t)$ for all $t \in I$ and, to this end, we check in what follows the validity of the assumptions $(\mathcal{K})$, $(\mathcal{A})$, $(\mathcal{B})$, $(\mathcal{S})$ and $(\mathcal{U})$.

We start with assumption $(\mathcal{K})$. First, we define the set

$$\Sigma_0 = \{\, \tau \in Q \,:\, (\tau, \varepsilon(v))_Q + j(v) \geq 0 \quad \forall\, v \in V \,\}.$$

It follows from (8.30) that the function $v \mapsto j(v) : V \to \mathbb{R}$ is convex and lower semicontinuous and, therefore, it is subdifferentiable. Moreover, since $j(0_V) = 0$, we deduce from (8.2) that there exists an element $w \in V$ such that $j(v) \geq (w, v)_V$ for all $v \in V$. In addition, equality $(w, v)_V = (\varepsilon(w), \varepsilon(v)_V$, valid for all $v \in V$, implies that $-\varepsilon(w) \in \Sigma_0$ and, therefore, Σ_0 is not empty. Next, it is easy to see that Σ_0 is a closed convex subset of Q. On the other hand, assumptions (8.26) and (8.27) imply that the element f given by (8.35) has the regularity $f \in C(I;V)$ and, hence, $\varepsilon(f) \in C(I;Q)$. Finally, since $(f(t), v)_V = (\varepsilon(f(t)), \varepsilon(v)_Q$ we deduce that

$$\Sigma(t) = \Sigma_0 + \varepsilon(f(t) \qquad \text{for all } t \in I.$$

It follows from above that condition $(\mathcal{K})$ is satisfied.

Next, note that assumptions (8.22), (8.23), (8.25) and (8.28) imply that the operators (8.31) and (8.32) satisfy conditions $(\mathcal{A})$ and $(\mathcal{B})$, respectively. The proof is standard and, therefore, we skip it. Assume now that $J \subset I$ is an nonempty compact set, $t \in J$ and let $\omega_1, \omega_2 \in C(I;Q)$. Also, let

$$b(J) = \max\{\, r : r \in J \,\}. \tag{8.45}$$

Then, using assumption (8.24) and inequality

$$\|\mathcal{C}(r)\tau\|_Q \leq d\,\|\mathcal{C}(r)\|_{\mathbf{Q}_\infty}\|\tau\|_Q, \tag{8.46}$$

valid for all $\tau \in Q$ and $r \in I$, it is easy to see that

$$\|\mathcal{S}\omega_1(t) - \mathcal{S}\omega_2(t)\|_Q \leq d \max_{r\in[0,b(J)]} \|\mathcal{C}(r)\|_{\mathbf{Q}_\infty} \int_0^t \|\omega_1(s) - \omega_2(s)\|_Q\, ds.$$

This inequality proves that the operator $\mathcal{S}$ satisfies condition $(\mathcal{S})$.

Finally, assumption (8.29) guarantees that $\omega_0 = \varepsilon(u_0) \in Q$ and, therefore, condition $(\mathcal{U})$ is satisfied. It follows from above that we are in a position to apply Theorem 8.2.1 to conclude the proof. □

We complete Theorem 8.4.1 with the following existence and uniqueness result.

Corollary 8.4.2 *Assume that* (8.22)–(8.30) *hold. Then, there exists a unique couple of functions $u \in C^1(I;V)$, $\widetilde{\sigma} \in C(I;Q)$ such that*

$$\widetilde{\sigma}(t) = A\varepsilon(\dot{u}(t) + B\varepsilon(u(t) + \mathcal{S}\varepsilon(\dot{u})(t), \tag{8.47}$$

$$\widetilde{\sigma}(t) \in \Sigma(t), \qquad (\tau - \widetilde{\sigma}(t), \varepsilon(\dot{u}(t)))_Q \geq 0 \quad \text{for all } t \in I, \tag{8.48}$$

$$u(0) = u_0. \tag{8.49}$$

Proof. Let $\omega \in C^1(I;Q)$ be the solution of Problem $\mathcal{P}_V$ obtained in Theorem 8.4.1 and denote by $\widetilde{\sigma}$ the function given by by

$$\widetilde{\sigma}(t) = A\dot{\omega}(t) + B\omega(t) + \mathcal{S}\dot{\omega}(t) \quad \text{for all } t \in I. \tag{8.50}$$

Then, $\widetilde{\sigma} \in C(I,Q)$ and

$$-\dot{\omega}(t) \in N_{\Sigma(t)}(\widetilde{\sigma}(t)) \quad \text{for all } t \in I, \tag{8.51}$$

$$\omega(0) = \omega_0. \tag{8.52}$$

Moreover, (8.1) yields

$$\widetilde{\sigma}(t) \in \Sigma(t), \qquad (\tau - \widetilde{\sigma}(t), \dot{\omega}(t))_Q \geq 0 \qquad \text{for all } t \in I. \tag{8.53}$$

Let $t \in I$ and let $z \in Q$ be such that

$$(z, \varepsilon(v))_Q = 0 \qquad \text{for all } v \in V. \tag{8.54}$$

Then, it is easy to see that $\tau = \widetilde{\sigma}(t) \pm z \in \Sigma(t)$ and, testing with these elements in (8.53) implies that

$$(z, \dot{\omega}(t))_Q = 0. \tag{8.55}$$

Equalities (8.54) and (8.55) show that $\dot{\omega}(t) \in \varepsilon(V)^{\perp\perp} = \varepsilon(V)$ where $M^\perp$ represents the orthogonal of M in Q and $M^{\perp\perp} = (M^\perp)^\perp$. Therefore, since $\varepsilon : V \to$

$\varepsilon(V)$ is a linear invertible operator, it follows that $\varepsilon^{-1}\dot{\omega} \in C(I;V)$. Consider now the function $u : I \to V$ given by

$$u(t) = \int_0^t \varepsilon^{-1}\dot{\omega}(s)\,ds + u_0 \qquad \text{for all } t \in I \tag{8.56}$$

and note that, obviously, $u \in C^1(I;V)$. Moreover, using notation (8.37) we deduce that $\varepsilon(u) = \omega$ and, therefore, (8.50) and (8.53) imply that (8.47) and (8.48) hold. In addition, equality (8.49) is a direct consequence of the equalities $\varepsilon(u) = \omega$, $\varepsilon(u_0) = \omega_0$ and $\omega(0) = \omega_0$. This proves the existence part in Corollary 8.4.2.

To prove the uniqueness part, consider two couples of functions $(u_i, \widetilde{\sigma}_i)$ with regularity $u_i \in C^1(I;V)$, $\widetilde{\sigma}_i \in C(I;Q)$ such that (8.47) –(8.49) hold, with $i = 1,2$. Let $\omega_i = \varepsilon(u_i)$. Then, it is easy to see that ω_i is a solution of Problem $\mathcal{P}_V$, with regularity $\omega_i \in C^1(I;Q)$. We now use the uniqueness part in Theorem 8.4.1 to see that $\omega_1 = \omega_2$ which, in turn, implies that $u_1 = u_2$ and $\widetilde{\sigma}_1 = \widetilde{\sigma}_1$. □

Denote by $(u, \widetilde{\sigma})$ the solution of problem (8.47)–(8.49) obtained in Corollary 8.4.2 and let $\sigma : I \to Q$ be the function defined by (8.12). Then, we refer to the couple (u, σ) as a weak solution to the viscoelastic contact problem $\mathcal{P}$. We conclude from above that, under assumptions, (8.22)–(8.30), Problem $\mathcal{P}$ has a unique weak solution, with regularity $u \in C^1(I;V)$, $\sigma \in C(I;Q)$. Moreover, the weak solution satisfies

$$\omega(t) = \varepsilon(u(t)), \tag{8.57}$$

$$\sigma(t) = \mathcal{A}\dot{\omega}(t) + \mathcal{B}\omega(t) + \int_0^t \mathcal{C}(t-s)\dot{\omega}(s)\,ds \tag{8.58}$$

for all $t \in I$ where, recall, ω is the solution of Problem $\mathcal{P}_V$.

8.5 A Continuous Dependence Result

In this section we study the dependence of the weak solution of Problem $\mathcal{P}$ with respect to the data. To this end we assume in what follows that (8.22)–(8.30) hold and we denote by ω the solution of Problem $\mathcal{P}_V$ obtained in Theorem 8.4.1. Moreover, for each $n \in \mathbb{N}$ we assume that f_{0n}, f_{2n}, F_{1n}, F_{2n}, F_{bn} and u_{0n} represent a perturbation of f_0, f_2, F_1, F_2, F_b, and u_0, respectively, such that

$$f_{0n} \in C(I;L^2(\Omega)^d). \tag{8.59}$$

$$f_{2n} \in C(I;L^2(\Gamma_2)^d). \tag{8.60}$$

$$F_{2n} \geq F_{1n} \geq 0, \qquad F_{bn} \geq 0. \tag{8.61}$$

$$u_{0n} \in V. \tag{8.62}$$

Next, we consider the functions $j_n : V \to \mathbb{R}$, $f_n : I \to V$, the set-valued mapping $\Sigma_n : I \to 2^Q$ and the element ω_{0n} defined by

$$j_n(v) = \int_{\Gamma_3} (F_{2n}v_\nu^+ - F_{1n}v_\nu^-)\,da + \int_{\Gamma_3} F_{bn}\|v_\tau\|\,da \quad \text{for all } v \in V, \tag{8.63}$$

$$(f_n(t), v)_V = \int_\Omega f_{0n}(t)\cdot v\,dx + \int_{\Gamma_2} f_{2n}(t)\cdot v\,da \quad \text{for all } v \in V,\ t \in I, \tag{8.64}$$

$$\Sigma_n(t) = \{\tau \in Q : (\tau, \varepsilon(v))_Q + j_n(v) \geq (f_n(t), v)_V \ \forall \tau \in Q\} \text{ for all } t \in I, \tag{8.65}$$

$$\omega_{0n} = \varepsilon(u_{0n}). \tag{8.66}$$

Then, using Theorem 8.4.1 we deduce the existence of a unique function $\omega_n \in C^1(I; Q)$ such that

$$-\dot{\omega}_n(t) \in N_{\Sigma_n(t)}\big(\mathcal{A}\dot{\omega}_n(t) + \mathcal{B}\omega_n(t) + \mathcal{S}\dot{\omega}_n(t)\big) \quad \text{for all } t \in I, \tag{8.67}$$

$$\omega_n(0) = \omega_{0n}. \tag{8.68}$$

Consider now the following assumptions.

$$\left\{\begin{array}{l} \text{(a) } f_{0n}(t) \rightharpoonup f_0(t) \ \text{ in } L^2(\Omega)^d \ \text{ as } n \to \infty, \ \text{ for all } t \in I. \\ \text{(b) For any nonemty compact set } J \subset I \text{ there exists } w_{0J} > 0 \\ \qquad \text{such that } \|f_{0n}(t)\|_{L^2(\Omega)^d} \leq w_{0J} \ \text{ for all } n \in \mathbb{N},\ t \in J. \end{array}\right. \tag{8.69}$$

$$\left\{\begin{array}{l} \text{(a) } \boldsymbol{f}_{2n}(t) \rightharpoonup \boldsymbol{f}_2(t) \ \text{ in } L^2(\Gamma_3)^d \ \text{ as } n \to \infty, \ \text{ for all } t \in I. \\ \text{(b) For any nonempty compact set } J \subset I \text{ there exists } w_{2J} > 0 \\ \qquad \text{such that } \|f_{2n}(t)\|_{L^2(\Omega)^d} \leq w_{2J} \ \text{ for all } n \in \mathbb{N},\ t \in J. \end{array}\right. \tag{8.70}$$

$$F_{1n} \to F_1, \quad F_{2n} \to F_2, \quad F_{bn} \to F_b \quad \text{as} \quad n \to \infty. \tag{8.71}$$

$$u_{0n} \to u_0 \quad \text{in} \quad V \quad \text{as} \quad n \to \infty. \tag{8.72}$$

Our main result in this section is the following.

Theorem 8.5.1 *Assume that* (8.22)–(8.30), (8.59)–(8.62) *and* (8.69)–(8.72) *hold. Then, for any $t \in I$ the following convergences hold:*

$$\dot{\omega}_n(t) \to \dot{\omega}(t) \quad \text{in } Q, \quad \omega_n(t) \to \omega(t) \quad \text{in } Q, \quad \text{as} \quad n \to \infty. \tag{8.73}$$

Proof. Denote by u, $\widetilde{\sigma}$ the functions obtained in Corollary 8.4.2. Then, it follows that (8.47)–(8.49) hold and, moreover, (8.53) and (8.57) hold, too.

Let $t \in I$, $n \in \mathbb{N}$ and let J be a nonempty compact subset of I such that $t \in J$. Using the subdifferentiability of the function j at $\dot{u}(t)$ we know that there exists an element $w(t) \in V$ such that

$$j(v) - j(\dot{u}(t)) \geq (w(t), v - \dot{u}(t))_V = (\varepsilon(w(t)), \varepsilon(v) - \varepsilon(\dot{u}(t)))_Q$$

and, taking $\tau_0(t) := \varepsilon(f(t)) - \varepsilon(w(t))$ we deduce that

$$(\tau_0(t), \varepsilon(v) - \varepsilon(\dot{u}(t)))_Q + j(v) - j(\dot{u}(t)) \geq (f(t), v - \dot{u}(t))_V \quad \text{for all } v \in V. \tag{8.74}$$

We now test with $v = 2\dot{u}(t)$ and $v = 0_V$ in this inequality to deduce that

$$(\tau_0(t), \varepsilon(\dot{u}(t)))_Q + j(\dot{u}(t)) = (f(t), \dot{u}(t))_V. \tag{8.75}$$

Therefore, combining (8.74) and (8.75) we find that

$$(\tau_0(t), \varepsilon(v))_Q + j(v) \geq (f(t), \dot{u}(t))_V \quad \text{for all } v \in V,$$

which shows that $\tau_0(t) \in \Sigma(t)$. This regularity, (8.53) and (8.57) imply that

$$(\tau_0(t), \varepsilon(\dot{u}(t)))_Q \geq (\widetilde{\sigma}(t), \varepsilon(\dot{u}(t)))_Q$$

and, using (8.75), yields

$$(\widetilde{\sigma}(t), \varepsilon(\dot{u}(t)))_Q + j(\dot{u}(t)) \leq (f(t), \dot{u}(t))_V. \tag{8.76}$$

On the other hand, since $\widetilde{\sigma}(t) \in \Sigma(t)$ and $\dot{u}(t) \in V$ the converse inequality holds, i.e.,

$$(\widetilde{\sigma}(t), \varepsilon(\dot{u}(t)))_Q + j(u(t)) \geq (f(t), \dot{u}(t))_V. \tag{8.77}$$

It follows now from (8.76) and (8.77) that

$$(\widetilde{\sigma}(t), \varepsilon(\dot{u}(t)))_Q + j(u(t)) = (f(t), \dot{u}(t))_V. \tag{8.78}$$

We now combine the regularity $\widetilde{\sigma}(t) \in \Sigma(t)$ in (8.53) with (8.78) to see that

$$\begin{aligned}(\widetilde{\sigma}(t), \varepsilon(v) - \varepsilon(\dot{u}(t))) + j(v) - j(\dot{u}(t))& \\ \geq (f(t), v - \dot{u}(t))_V \quad \text{for all } v \in V.&\end{aligned} \tag{8.79}$$

Similar arguments show that

$$\begin{aligned}(\widetilde{\sigma}_n(t), \varepsilon(v) - \varepsilon(\dot{u}_n(t))) + j_n(v) - j_n(\dot{u}_n(t))& \\ \geq (f_n(t), v - \dot{u}_n(t))_V \quad \text{for all } v \in V,&\end{aligned} \tag{8.80}$$

where u_n, $\widetilde{\sigma}_n$ are the functions obtained in Corollary 8.4.2 for the perturbed data. Recall also that the following equalities hold:

$$\widetilde{\sigma}_n(t) = A\dot{\omega}_n(t) + B\omega_n(t) + \mathcal{S}\dot{\omega}_n(t), \tag{8.81}$$

$$\varepsilon(u_n(t)) = \omega_n(t). \tag{8.82}$$

We now take $v = \dot{u}_n(t)$ in (8.79), $v = \dot{u}(t)$ in (8.80) and add the resulting inequalities to obtain that

$$\begin{aligned}&(\widetilde{\sigma}_n(t) - \widetilde{\sigma}(t), \varepsilon(\dot{u}_n(t)) - \varepsilon(\dot{u}(t)))_Q \\ &\quad \leq j(\dot{u}_n(t)) - j(\dot{u}(t)) + j_n(\dot{u}(t)) - j_n(\dot{u}_n(t)) + (f_n(t) - f(t), \dot{u}_n(t) - \dot{u}(t))_V.\end{aligned}$$

Then, using equalities (8.81), (8.47), (8.82) and (8.57) we find that

$$(\widetilde{\sigma}_n(t)-\widetilde{\sigma}_n(t),\varepsilon(\dot{u}_n(t))-\varepsilon(\dot{u}(t)))_Q=(A\dot{\omega}_n(t)-A\dot{\omega}(t),\dot{\omega}_n(t)-\dot{\omega}(t))_Q \qquad (8.83)$$
$$+(B\omega_n(t)-B\omega(t),\dot{\omega}_n(t)-\dot{\omega}(t))_Q+(\mathcal{S}\dot{\omega}_n(t)-\mathcal{S}\dot{\omega}(t),\dot{\omega}_n(t)-\dot{\omega}(t))_Q.$$

On the other hand, a standard calculation based on the definitions (8.34), (8.63) and the trace inequality (8.9) shows that there exists a positive constant $c>0$ such that

$$j(\dot{u}_n(t))-j(\dot{u}(t))+j_n(\dot{u}(t))-j_n(\dot{u}_n(t)) \qquad (8.84)$$
$$\le c\big(|F_{1n}-F_1|+|F_{2n}-F_2|+|F_{bn}-F_b|\big)\|\dot{u}_n(t)-\dot{u}(t)\|_V$$

and, obviously,

$$(f_n(t)-f(t),\dot{u}_n(t)-\dot{u}(t))_V\le\|f_n(t)-f(t)\|_V\|\dot{u}_n(t)-\dot{u}(t)\|_V. \qquad (8.85)$$

Here and below c and $\widetilde{c}$ represent positive constants which may depend on J but do not depend on n and t and whose value may change from line to line.

We now combine relations (8.83)–(8.85) and use the properties $(\mathcal{A})$, $(\mathcal{B})$ and $(\mathcal{S})$ of the operators A, B and $\mathcal{S}$, respectively, to obtain that

$$\|\dot{\omega}_n(t)-\dot{\omega}(t)\|_Q \qquad (8.86)$$
$$\le c\big(|F_{1n}-F_1|+|F_{2n}-F_2|+|F_{bn}-F_b|+\|f_n(t)-f(t)\|_V\big)$$
$$+\widetilde{c}\int_0^t\|\dot{\omega}_n(s)-\dot{\omega}(s)\|_Q\,ds.$$

Denote by $h_n:I\to\mathbb{R}$ the function given by

$$h_n(s)=c\big(|F_{1n}-F_1|+|F_{2n}-F_2|+|F_{bn}-F_b|+\|f_n(s)-f(s)\|_V\big) \qquad (8.87)$$

for all $s\in I$. Then, (8.86) and (8.87) yield

$$\|\dot{\omega}_n(t)-\dot{\omega}(t)\|_Q\le h_n(t)+\widetilde{c}\int_0^t\|\dot{\omega}_n(s)-\dot{\omega}(s)\|_Q\,ds$$

and, using the Gronwall argument, it follows that

$$\|\dot{\omega}_n(t)-\dot{\omega}(t)\|_Q\le h_n(t)+\widetilde{c}\int_0^t e^{\widetilde{c}(t-s)}h_n(s)\,ds. \qquad (8.88)$$

We now use assumptions (8.69)(b), (8.70)(b) and definition (8.64) to see that $\|f_n(s)\|_V\le c$ for each $s\in J$ and, combining this inequality with (8.71) and (8.87) we find that

$$|h_n(s)|\le c \qquad \text{for all } s\in J. \qquad (8.89)$$

Next, assumptions (8.69)(a), (8.70)(a) and definition (8.64) guarantee that

$$(\boldsymbol{f}_n(s), \boldsymbol{v})_V \to (\boldsymbol{f}(s), \boldsymbol{v})_V$$

for each $\boldsymbol{v} \in V$ and $s \in J$. This means that

$$\boldsymbol{f}_n(s) \rightharpoonup \boldsymbol{f}(s) \quad \text{in } V, \qquad \text{for all } s \in J$$

and, using a standard compactness argument it follows that

$$\boldsymbol{f}_n(s) \to \boldsymbol{f}(s) \text{ in } L^2(\Omega)^d, \quad \boldsymbol{f}_n(s) \to \boldsymbol{f}(s) \text{ in } L^2(\Gamma)^d, \quad \text{as} \quad n \to \infty, \tag{8.90}$$

for all $s \in J$. Therefore, since

$$\|\boldsymbol{f}_n(s) - \boldsymbol{f}(s)\|_V^2 = (\boldsymbol{f}_n(s) - \boldsymbol{f}(s), \boldsymbol{f}_n(s) - \boldsymbol{f}(s))_V$$

$$= \int_\Omega (\boldsymbol{f}_{0n}(s) - \boldsymbol{f}_0(s))(\boldsymbol{f}_n(s) - \boldsymbol{f}(s))\,dx + \int_{\Gamma_2} (\boldsymbol{f}_{2n}(s) - \boldsymbol{f}_2(s))(\boldsymbol{f}_n(s) - \boldsymbol{f}(s))\,da,$$

using the convergences (8.69)(a), (8.70)(a) and (8.90) we deduce that

$$\|\boldsymbol{f}_n(s) - \boldsymbol{f}(s)\|_V \to 0 \qquad \text{for all } s \in J. \tag{8.91}$$

We now use (8.87), (8.71) and (8.91) to find that

$$h_n(s) \to 0 \qquad \text{for all } s \in J. \tag{8.92}$$

The properties (8.89) and (8.92) allow us to apply the Lebesque theorem in (8.88) in order to find that

$$\dot{\boldsymbol{\omega}}_n(t) \to \dot{\boldsymbol{\omega}}(t) \quad \text{in } Q \quad \text{as} \quad n \to \infty. \tag{8.93}$$

This implies that for any $s \in J$, the following convergence hold:

$$\dot{\boldsymbol{\omega}}_n(s) \to \dot{\boldsymbol{\omega}}(s) \quad \text{in } Q \quad \text{as} \quad n \to \infty. \tag{8.94}$$

On the other hand, (8.88) and (8.89) show that

$$\|\dot{\boldsymbol{\omega}}_n(s) - \dot{\boldsymbol{\omega}}(s)\|_Q \le c \qquad \text{for all } s \in J. \tag{8.95}$$

It follows from (8.94), (8.95) and the Lebesgue theorem that

$$\int_0^t \|\dot{\boldsymbol{\omega}}_n(s) - \dot{\boldsymbol{\omega}}(s)\|_Q\,ds \to 0. \tag{8.96}$$

Moreover, since $\boldsymbol{\omega}_n(0) = \boldsymbol{\omega}_{0n} = \boldsymbol{\varepsilon}(\boldsymbol{u}_{0n})$ and $\boldsymbol{\omega}(0) = \boldsymbol{\omega}_0 = \boldsymbol{\varepsilon}(\boldsymbol{u}_0)$, we have

$$\boldsymbol{\omega}_n(t) - \boldsymbol{\omega}(t) = \int_0^t \|\dot{\boldsymbol{\omega}}_n(s) - \dot{\boldsymbol{\omega}}(s)\|_Q\,ds + \boldsymbol{\varepsilon}(\boldsymbol{u}_{0n}) - \boldsymbol{\varepsilon}(\boldsymbol{u}_0). \tag{8.97}$$

We now use (8.96), (8.97) and (8.72) to find that

$$\omega_n(t) \to \omega(t) \quad \text{in } Q \quad \text{as} \quad n \to \infty. \tag{8.98}$$

The convergence (8.73) follows now from (8.93) and (8.98). □

We denote in what follows by (u, σ) the weak solution of Problem $\mathcal{P}$ with the data f_0, f_2, F_1, F_2, F_b, and u_0 and, for each $n \in \mathbb{N}$, let (u_n, σ_n) be the weak solution of the same problem with the data f_{0n}, f_{2n}, F_{1n}, F_{2n}, F_{bn} and u_{0n}. We have the following consequence of Theorem 8.5.1.

Corollary 8.5.2 *Assume that* (8.22)–(8.30), (8.59)–(8.62) *and* (8.69)–(8.72) *hold. Then, for any $t \in I$ the following convergences hold:*

$$\dot{u}_n(t) \to \dot{u}(t), \quad u_n(t) \to u(t) \quad \text{in} \quad V \quad \text{as} \quad n \to \infty \tag{8.99}$$

$$\sigma_n(t) \to \sigma(t) \quad \text{in} \quad Q \quad \text{as} \quad \to \infty. \tag{8.100}$$

Proof. The convergences (8.99) represent a direct consequence of (8.82), (8.57) and (8.73). To prove the convergence (8.100) we recall (8.58) and we note that, for each $n \in \mathbb{N}$, we have

$$\sigma_n(t) = \mathcal{A}\dot{\omega}_n(t) + \mathcal{B}\omega_n(t) + \int_0^t \mathcal{C}(t-s)\dot{\omega}_n(s)\, ds \quad \text{for all } t \in I. \tag{8.101}$$

We combine (8.58) and (8.101) then use standard arguments based on the properties of the operators $\mathcal{A}$, $\mathcal{B}$ and $\mathcal{S}$ to see that for any $t \in I$ we have

$$\begin{aligned} \|\sigma_n(t) - \sigma(t)\|_Q \ \leq\ & L_A\|\dot{\omega}_n(t) - \dot{\omega}(t)\|_Q + L_B\|\omega_n(t) - \omega(t)\|_Q \\ & + d \max_{s\in[0,b(J)]} \|\mathcal{C}(s)\|_{\mathbf{Q}_\infty} \int_0^t \|\dot{\omega}_n(s) - \dot{\omega}(s)\|_Q\, ds, \end{aligned}$$

where, recall, $b(J)$ is given by (8.45). Therefore, using the convergences (8.73) and (8.96) we deduce that (8.100) holds, which concludes the proof. □

In addition to the mathematical interest in the convergences (8.99) and (8.100), they are important from mechanical point of view sine they show that the weak solution of the frictional contact problem $\mathcal{P}$ depends continuously on the bounds F_1, F_2 and F_b, the density of the applied forces f_0 and f_2, and the initial displacement u_0, as well.

8.6 An Optimal Control Problem

Throughout this section we assume that (8.22)–(8.25), (8.28) and (8.29) hold. We consider the product space $W = L^2(\Omega)^d \times L^2(\Gamma_2)^d \times \mathbb{R}^3$ together with its canonical Hilbertian structure. A typical point of W will be denoted by $q =$

$(\widetilde{f}_0, \widetilde{f}_2, F_1, F_2, F_b)$. Let U be a nonempty subset of W with the following property

$$q = (\widetilde{f}_0, \widetilde{f}_2, F_1, F_2, F_b, u_0) \in U \implies \text{(8.30) holds.} \tag{8.102}$$

Assume now that θ_0 and θ_2 are real valued functions which satisfy the conditions

$$\theta_0 \in C(I;\mathbb{R}), \qquad \theta_0(0) = 1. \tag{8.103}$$

$$\theta_2 \in C(I;\mathbb{R}), \qquad \theta_2(0) = 1 \tag{8.104}$$

and, for each $q \in U$, define the functions f_0, f_2 by equalities

$$f_0(t) = \theta_0(t)\widetilde{f}_0 \quad \text{for all } t \in I. \tag{8.105}$$

$$f_2(t) = \theta_2(t)\widetilde{f}_2 \quad \text{for all } t \in I. \tag{8.106}$$

Then, the functions f_0 and f_2 satisfy conditions (8.26) and (8.27), respectively. Therefore, the results in Section 8.4 show that for each $q = (\widetilde{f}_0, \widetilde{f}_2, F_1, F_2, F_b) \in U$ there exists a unique weak solution to Problem $\mathcal{P}$ with the data f_0, f_2, F_1, F_2, F_b, u_0. This solution depends on q and, for this reason, we denote it in what follows by (u_q, σ_q). Its regularity is $u_q \in C^1(I;V)$ and $\sigma_q \in C(I;Q)$. Moreover, note that (8.103)–(8.106) imply that the function $\widetilde{f}_0$ and $\widetilde{f}_2$ represent the initial density of body forces and surface tractions, respectively.

Consider now a cost function $\mathcal{L} : V \times V \times Q \times U \to \mathbb{R}$. Then, the optimal control problem we study in this section is the following.

Problem $\mathcal{Q}$. *Given $t \in I$, find $q^* \in U$ such that*

$$\mathcal{L}(u_{q^*}(t), \dot{u}_{q^*}(t), \sigma_{q^*}(t), q^*) = \min_{q \in U} \mathcal{L}(u_q(t), \dot{u}_q(t), \sigma_q(t), q). \tag{8.107}$$

In the study of this problem we consider the following assumptions.

U is a nonempty weakly closed bounded subset of W such that (8.102) holds. (8.108)

$$\left\{ \begin{array}{l} \text{For all sequences } \{u_n\} \subset V,\ \{v_n\} \subset V,\ \{\sigma_n\} \subset Q,\ \{q_n\} \subset U \text{ such that} \\ u_n \to u \text{ in } V,\ v_n \to v \text{ in } V,\ \sigma_n \to \sigma \text{ in } Q,\ q_n \rightharpoonup q \text{ in } W, \text{ we have} \\ \liminf\limits_{n\to\infty} \mathcal{L}(u_n, v_n, \sigma_n, q_n) \geq \mathcal{L}(u, v, \sigma, q). \end{array} \right. \tag{8.109}$$

Our main result of this section is the following.

Theorem 8.6.1 *Under the previous assumptions, for each $t \in I$, the optimal control problem $\mathcal{Q}$ has at least one solution q^*.*

Proof. Let $t \in I$ be fixed and consider the function $J_t : U \to \mathbb{R}$ defined by

$$J_t(q) = \mathcal{L}(u_q(t), \dot{u}_q(t), \sigma_q(t), q) \quad \text{for all } q \in U. \tag{8.110}$$

We associate to Problem $\mathcal{Q}$ the problem of finding $q^* \in U$ such that

$$J_t(q^*) = \min_{q \in U} J_t(q). \tag{8.111}$$

Consider now a sequence $\{q_n\} \subset U$ and an element $q \in U$ such that

$$q_n \rightharpoonup q \quad \text{in} \quad W. \tag{8.112}$$

Assume that $q_n = (\widetilde{f}_{0n}, \widetilde{f}_{2n}, F_{1n}, F_{2n}, F_{bn})$ for each $n \in \mathbb{N}$ and, moreover, assume that $q = (\widetilde{f}_0, \widetilde{f}_2, F_1, F_2, F_b)$. In addition, recall (8.105), (8.106) and, for each $n \in \mathbb{N}$, define the functions

$$f_{0n}(s) = \theta_0(s)\widetilde{f}_{0n} \quad \text{for all } s \in I, \tag{8.113}$$

$$f_{2n}(s) = \theta_2(s)\widetilde{f}_{2n} \quad \text{for all } s \in I. \tag{8.114}$$

Then, it is easy to see that (8.112) implies that the convergences (8.69)–(8.72) hold, the last one with $u_{0n} = u_0$, for each $n \in \mathbb{N}$. We now apply Corollary 8.5.2 to see that the convergences (8.99) and (8.100) hold, too. Using these convergence, (8.112) and the property (8.109) of the cost functional $\mathcal{L}$ we find that

$$\liminf_{n\to\infty} \mathcal{L}(u_{q_n}(t), \dot{u}_{q_n}(t), \sigma_{q_n}(t), q_n) \geq \mathcal{L}(u_q(t), \dot{u}_q(t), \sigma_q(t), q).$$

Therefore, using the definition (8.110) yields

$$\liminf_{n\to\infty} J_t(q_n) \geq J_t(q), \tag{8.115}$$

which shows that J_t is a weakly lower semicontinuous function. Recall that W is a reflexive Banach space and U is a weakly closed subset of W. Then the existence of at least one solution to problem (8.111) is a direct consequence of a well-known Weierstrass theorem. This means that there exists a minimizer $q^* \in U$ for J_t which, in turn, guarantees that Problem $\mathcal{Q}$ has at least one solution. □

We now provide some relevant examples of optimal control problems of the form $\mathcal{Q}$. For all the examples below we precise the cost functional $\mathcal{L}$ and the set U, then we check the validity of conditions (8.108) and (8.109). This guarantee that Theorem 8.6.1 holds for all the examples we present below.

Example 8.6.2 *In the first example the control is the initial density of the surface tractions on Γ_2 and the cost function is related to the normal displacement. This represents a particular case of the general optimal control problem $\mathcal{Q}$ that will be described as follows.*

Fix $\widetilde{f}_0 \in L^2(\Omega)^d$ and F_1, F_2, F_b, such that (8.30) *holds. Moreover, consider the set $U \subset W$ defined by*

$$U = \{q = (\widetilde{f}_0, \widetilde{f}_2, F_1, F_2, F_b) \in W \ : \ \|\widetilde{f}_2\|_{L^2(\Gamma_2)^d} \leq \widetilde{M}_2\}, \tag{8.116}$$

where $\widetilde{M}_2$ is given positive constant. Let $\mathcal{L} : V \times V \times Q \times U \to \mathbb{R}$ be the cost function given by

$$\mathcal{L}(u, v, \sigma, q) = \int_{\Gamma_3} (u_\nu - \phi)^2 \, da \quad \text{for all } (u, v, \sigma, q) \in V \times V \times Q \times U, \tag{8.117}$$

where $\phi \in L^2(\Gamma_3)$ is given. Then, it is easy to see that the set (8.116) *satisfies condition* (8.108) *and the function* (8.117) *satisfies condition* (8.109). *Therefore, Theorem* 8.6.1 *works in this case.*

The mechanical interpretation of the corresponding optimal control problem $\mathcal{Q}$ is the following: given a contact process of the form (8.12)–(8.15), (8.19)–(8.21), *a time moment $t \in I$ and a constant $\widetilde{M}_2 > 0$, we are looking for an initial density of surface tractions $\widetilde{f}_2 \in L^2(\Gamma_2)^d$ with $\|\widetilde{f}_2\|_{L^2(\Gamma_2)^d} \leq \widetilde{M}_2$ such that the corresponding penetration of the body at t is as close as possible to the "desired penetration" ϕ. Theorem* 8.6.1 *guarantees the existence of such an optimal choice.*

Example 8.6.3 *In the second example the control is the friction bound and the cost function is related to the stress field. This represents a particular case of the general optimal control problem $\mathcal{Q}$ that will be described as follows.*

Fix $\widetilde{f}_0 \in L^2(\Omega)^d$, $\widetilde{f}_2 \in L^2(\Gamma_2)^d$ and F_1, $F_2 \in \mathbb{R}$ such that $F_2 \geq F_1 \geq 0$. Moreover, consider the set $U \subset W$ defined by

$$U = \{q = (\widetilde{f}_0, \widetilde{f}_2, F_1, F_2, F_b) \in W \ : \ 0 \leq F_b \leq M_b\}, \tag{8.118}$$

where M_b is given positive constant. Let $\mathcal{L} : V \times V \times Q \times U \to \mathbb{R}$ be the cost function given by

$$\mathcal{L}(u, v, \sigma, q) = \int_{\Omega} \|\sigma\|^2 \, dx \quad \text{for all } (u, v, \sigma, q) \in V \times V \times Q \times U. \tag{8.119}$$

Then, it is easy to see that the set (8.118) *satisfies condition* (8.108) *and the function* (8.119) *satisfies condition* (8.109). *Therefore, Theorem* 8.6.1 *works in this case.*

The mechanical interpretation of the corresponding optimal control problem $\mathcal{Q}$ is the following: given a contact process of the form (8.12)–(8.15), (8.19)–(8.21), *a time moment $t \in I$ and a constant $M_b > 0$, we are looking for a friction bound $F_b \in [0, M_b]$ such that the corresponding stress in the body at t is as small as possible. Theorem* 8.6.1 *guarantees the existence of such an optimal choice.*

Example 8.6.4 *In the third example the control is the pressure of the fluid in compression and the cost function is related to the slip-rate. This represents a particular case of the general optimal control problem* $\mathcal{Q}$ *that will be described as follows.*

Fix $\widetilde{f}_0 \in L^2(\Omega)^d$, $\widetilde{f}_0 \in L^2(\Omega)^d$ *and* $F_1, F_b \in \mathbb{R}$ *such that* $F_1 \geq 0,\ F_b \geq 0$. *Moreover, consider the set* $U \subset W$ *defined by*

$$U = \{q = (\widetilde{f}_0, \widetilde{f}_2, F_1, F_2, F_b) \in W \ : \ F_1 \leq F_2 \leq M_2\}, \tag{8.120}$$

where M_2 *is given positive constant. Let* $\mathcal{L} : V \times V \times Q \times U \to \mathbb{R}$ *be the cost function given by*

$$\mathcal{L}(u, v, \sigma, q) = \int_{\Gamma_3} \|v_\tau\|^2 da \quad \text{for all } (u, v, \sigma, q) \in V \times V \times Q \times U. \tag{8.121}$$

Then, it is easy to see that the set (8.120) *satisfies condition* (8.108) *and the function* (8.121) *satisfies condition* (8.109). *Therefore, Theorem* 8.6.1 *can be applied in this case.*

The mechanical interpretation of the corresponding optimal control problem $\mathcal{Q}$ *is the following: given a contact process of the form* (8.12)–(8.15), (8.19)–(8.21), *a time moment* $t \in I$ *and a constant* $M_2 > 0$, *we are looking for a pressure* $F_2 \in [F_1, M_2]$ *such that the corresponding slip-rate on the contact surface at* t *is as small as possible. Theorem* 8.6.1 *guarantees the existence of such an optimal choice.*

8.7 Conclusion

In this chapter we considered a boundary value problem which describes the frictional contact of a viscoelastic body with a foundation. We associated to this contact model a sweeping process problem in which the unknown is the strain field. For the sweeping process we provided an existence and uniqueness result and its continuous dependence with respect to the data. Then, using the constitutive operators we recovered the corresponding results for the weak solution of the contact problem, in terms of displacement and stress fields. We also considered an associated optimal control problem for which we proved the existence of optimal pairs. The question of deriving necessary optimality conditions was left open.

The present work shows that, besides the classical tools provided by the theory of variational and hemivariational inequalities, the sweeping process theory, initiated by the pioneering works of Moreau in early seventies, can be used in the study of contact problems. Nevertheless, using sweeping process arguments in the study of our contact model and, more general, in the Mathematical Theory of Contact Mechanics, gives rise to several open problems that we describe in what follows. Any progress in these directions will complete our work and will open the way for new advances and ideas.

First, it would be interesting to study the dynamic version of the contact model presented in this chapter , by using arguments of sweeping process. Another question is to study the weak solvability of Problem $\mathcal{P}$ in the case when the viscosity operator vanishes. To the best of our knowledge this is an open problem which requires a new existence and uniqueness result in the study of sweeping process of the form (8.4) with $A \equiv 0$.

More general, recall that the mathematical modelling of the large variety of mechanical processes, with different constitutive laws, interface boundary conditions and specific geometry, leads to a large variety of boundary value problems. Therefore, it is expected that these problems would give rise to various classes of sweeping process in which the unknown is either the displacement field or the strain field. So, there is a need to complete the existence and uniqueness result in the literature with new abstract existence and uniqueness results for sweeping precesses which could be used in the corresponding contact models. Another problem would be to obtain results on the control problems associated to the corresponding classes of sweeping processes. An interesting continuation of the results presented in this chapter would be the study of contact models with nonconvex boundary conditions. This would give rise to sweeping processes with nonconvex sets.

We end this section by recalling that the control of mathematical models of contact, as well as their optimal shape design, deserves to make the object of important studies in the future. These topics are of considerable theoretical and applied interest. Any result in this direction will illustrate the cross fertilization between models and applications, in one hand, and the nonlinear functional analysis, on the other hand. The question whether the sweeping process arguments could be used to obtain such kind of results represents an open problem which, clearly, deserves to be investigated in the future.

Acknowledgements

This work has received funding from the European Union's Horizon 2020 Research and Innovation Programme under the Marie Sklodowska-Curie Grant Agreement No 823731 CONMECH. It has also been partially supported by the National Natural Science Foundation of China (11771067), the Applied Basic Project of Sichuan Province (2019YJ0204) and the Fundamental Research Funds for the Central Universities (ZYGX2019J095).

References

[1] S. Adly and T. Haddad. An implicit sweeping process approach to quasistatic evolution variational inequalities. SIAM J. Math. Anal., 50: 761–778, 2018.

[2] S. Adly and M. Sofonea. Time-dependent inclusions and sweeping processes in contact mechanics. J. Appl. Math. Phys. (ZAMP), 70, 2019 Art. 39, 19 pp. https://doi.org/10.1007/s00033-019-1084-4.

[3] A. Amassad, D. Chenais and C. Fabre. Optimal control of an elastic contact problem involving Tresca friction law. Nonlinear Anal., 48: 1107–1135, 2002.

[4] H.T. Banks, S. Hu and Z.R. Kenz. A brief review of elasticity and viscoelasticity for solids. Adv. Appl. Math. Mech., 3: 1–51, 2011.

[5] H.T. Banks, G.A. Pinter, L.K. Potter, J.M. Gaitens and L.C. Yanyo. Modeling of quasistatic and dynamic load responses of filled viscoelastic materials. pp. 229–252. Chapter 11 *In*: E. Cumberbatch and A. Fitt (eds.). *Mathematical Modeling: Case Studies from Industry*. Cambridge University Press, 2011.

[6] H.T. Banks, G.A. Pinter, L.K. Potter, B.C. Munoz and L.C. Yanyo. Estimation and control related issues in smart material structure and fluids. pp. 19–34. *In*: L. Caccetta et al. (eds.). *Optimization Techniques and Applications*. Curtain University Press, 1998.

[7] A. Capatina. Optimal control of Signorini problem. Numer. Funct. Anal. Optim., 21: 817–828, 2000.

[8] A. Capatina. *Variational Inequalities and Frictional Contact Problems*. Advances in Mechanics and Mathematics 31, Springer, Heidelberg, 2014.

[9] G. Colombo and V.V. Goncharov. The sweeping processes without convexity. Set-Valued Anal., 7: 357–374, 1999.

[10] G. Duvaut and J.-L. Lions. *Inequalities in Mechanics and Physics*. Springer-Verlag, Berlin, 1976.

[11] C. Eck, J. Jarušek and M. Krbeč. *Unilateral Contact Problems: Variational Methods and Existence Theorems*. Pure and Applied Mathematics 270, Chapman/CRC Press, New York, 2005.

[12] W. Han and M. Sofonea. *Quasistatic Contact Problems in Viscoelasticity and Viscoplasticity*. Studies in Advanced Mathematics 30, Americal Mathematical Society, Providence, RI–International Press, Somerville, MA, 2002.

[13] N. Kikuchi and J.T. Oden. *Contact Problems in Elasticity: A Study of Variational Inequalities and Finite Element Methods*. SIAM, Philadelphia, 1988.

[14] M. Kunze and M.D.P. Monteiro Marques. On parabolic quasi-variational inequalities and state-dependent sweeping processes. Topol. Methods Nonlinear Anal., 12: 179–191, 1998.

[15] A. Matei and S. Micu. Boundary optimal control for nonlinear antiplane problems. Nonlinear Anal.: TMA, 74: 1641–1652, 2011.

[16] A. Matei and S. Micu. Boundary optimal control for a frictional contact problem with normal compliance. Appl. Math. Optim., 78: 379–401, 2018.

[17] A. Matei, S. Micu and C. Niţă. Optimal control for antiplane frictional contact problems involving nonlinearly elastic materials of Hencky type. Math. Mech. Solids, 23: 308–328, 2018.

[18] M.D.P. Monteiro Marques. *Differential inclusions in nonsmooth mechanical problems. Shocks and dry friction*. Progress in Nonlinear Differential Equations and their Applications 9, Birkhäuser Verlag, Basel, 1993.

[19] S. Migórski, A. Ochal and M. Sofonea. *Nonlinear Inclusions and Hemivariational Inequalities. Models and Analysis of Contact Problems*. Advances in Mechanics and Mathematics 26, Springer, New York, 2013.

[20] J.J. Moreau. Sur l'évolution d'un système élastoplastique. C. R. Acad. Sci. Paris, Sér A-Bn, 273, A118–A121, 1971.

[21] J.J. Moreau. On unilateral constraints, friction and plasticity. pp. 173–322. *In*: G. Capriz and G. Stampacchia (eds.). *New Variational Techniques in Mathemaical Physics*. C.I.M.E. II, Ciclo 1973, Edizione Cremonese, Roma, 1974.

[22] J.J. Moreau. Evolution problem associated with a moving convex in a Hilbert space. J. Diff. Eqs., 26: 347–374, 1977.

[23] F. Nacry. Truncated nonconvex state-dependent sweeping process: implicit and semi-implicit adapted Moreau's catching-up algorithms. J. Fixed Point Theory Appl., 20: Art 121, 32 pp, 2018.

[24] F. Nacry and M. Sofonea. A class of nonlinear inclusions and sweeping processes in solid mechanics. Acta Applicandae Mathematicae, in press.

[25] F. Nacry and M. Sofonea. A history-dependent sweeping processes in contact mechanics, *preprint*.

[26] F. Nacry and L. Thibault. Regularization of sweeping process: old and new. Pure Appl. Funct. Anal., 4: 59–117, 2019.

[27] Z. Naniewicz and P.D. Panagiotopoulos. *Mathematical Theory of Hemivariational Inequalities and Applications*. Marcel Dekker, Inc., New York, Basel, Hong Kong, 1995.

[28] P.D. Panagiotopoulos. *Inequality Problems in Mechanics and Applications*. Birkhäuser, Boston, 1985.

[29] P.D. Panagiotopoulos. *Hemivariational Inequalities, Applications in Mechanics and Engineering*. Springer-Verlag, Berlin, 1993.

[30] M. Sofonea. Optimal control of variational-hemivariational inequalities. Appl. Math. Optim., 79: 621–646, 2019.

[31] M. Sofonea and A. Matei. *Mathematical Models in Contact Mechanics*. London Mathematical Society Lecture Note Series 398, Cambridge University Press, 2012.

[32] M. Sofonea and S. Migórski. *Variational-Hemivariational Inequalities with Applications*. Pure and Applied Mathematics, Chapman & Hall/CRC Press, Boca Raton-London, 2018.

Chapter 9

Anderson Acceleration for Degenerate and Nondegenerate Problems

Sara Pollock

Mathematics Subject Classification. 65N22, 65B05.

9.1 Introduction

Solving systems of nonlinear equations is a problem of fundamental importance in numerical analysis, and across many areas of science, engineering, finance, mathematics and data science. In general, solving nonlinear problems is an iterative process, accomplished by generating a sequence of approximations to the solution; often, using an iteration of fixed-point type. Fixed-point iterations include widely used processes such as Newton and Picard iterations. A fixed-point iteration to find a zero x of a function f can be defined by $x_{k+1} = g(x_k)$, where $g(x) = x + f(x)$. Similarly, setting $g(x) = x - f'(x)^{-1}f(x)$, with $f'(x)$ the Jacobian of f at x, defines a Newton iteration in fixed-point form. In this chapter, we discuss recent developments in the theory and implementation of Anderson acceleration (AA), an extrapolation technique used to accelerate sequences of fixed-point iterations.

AA was introduced by D. Anderson in 1965 in [3], in the context of integral equations. Given an algorithmic depth m, at each step of the algorithm a linear combination of the $m+1$ most recent iterates and fixed-point update steps is used to define the next iterate. The combination is determined by the solution to

Department of Mathematics, University of Florida, Gainesville, FL 32611, USA.
Email: s.pollock@ufl.edu

a (least-squares) optimization problem. The method has been of continuing interest as it provides a low-cost improvement on linearly-converging fixed-point iterations. Often it is used in cases where higher-order methods are too computationally intensive or unstable. A few applications where it has been found beneficial include nonlinear flow problems [5, 11, 14, 16], multiphysics [2, 23, 24], electronic structure computations [7], and optimization [13].

In [6, 7], AA was shown to be in the class of generalized multisecant or Broyden methods. For linear problems, a certain implementation was further shown in [26] to be "essentially equivalent" to the method of generalized minimal residual (GMRES). The performance of AA on solving the systems of equations resulting from the discretization of several nonlinear partial differential equations (PDE) is also presented in [26], accompanied by a discussion of efficient and stable implementation practices. Local convergence theory for contractive operators was first presented in [25], refined in [10], and extended to settings with inexact function evaluations in [23]. The first theory to show AA improves convergence of linearly-converging iterations was developed by the present author and collaborators in [5, 14], and extended in [15]. These contributions will be further discussed in the next section.

The remainder of the chapter is organized as follows. Subsection 9.1.1 states the AA algorithm, and the basic assumptions used in the theory, including the degeneracy and nondegeneracy conditions. Section 9.2 reviews recent results by the author on convergence and acceleration of AA under the nondegeneracy condition, illustrated by a numerical example. Section 9.3 reviews recent numerical results in the degenerate setting, and provides an analysis of AA applied to Newton's method in the simple case of one variable.

9.1.1 Mathematical Setting and Algorithm

Suppose X is a normed vector space, and let $g : X \to X$. Suppose we are seeking a fixed-point of $g(x)$, or equivalently a zero of $f(x) = g(x) - x$. Define the difference between consecutive iterates and nonlinear residual (update step) by

$$e_k := x_k - x_{k-1}, \quad w_{k+1} := g(x_k) - x_k. \tag{9.1}$$

Anderson acceleration with algorithmic depth m is defined as follows.

Algorithm 9.1.1 (AA with depth m) *Set depth $m \geq 0$ and choose x_0.*
Compute $w_1 = g(x_0) - x_0$. Set $x_1 = x_0 + w_1$.
For $k = 1, 2, \ldots$, set $m_k = \min\{k, m\}$
 Compute $w_{k+1} = g(x_k) - x_k$
 Set $F_k = \big((w_{k+1} - w_k) \ \ \cdots \ \ (w_{k-m+2} - w_{k-m+1})\big)$, and $E_k = \big(e_k \ \ \cdots \ \ e_{k-m+1}\big)$
 Compute $\gamma_k = \operatorname{argmin}_{\gamma \in \mathbb{R}^m} \|w_{k+1} - F_k \gamma\|$
 For damping factor $0 < \beta_k \leq 1$, set $x_{k+1} = x_k + \beta_k w_{k+1} - (E_k + \beta_k F_k)\gamma_k$

In the remainder, we will restrict ourselves to a Hilbert space setting, where the optimization problem reduces to a least-squares problem which can be solved efficiently using a QR factorization. More precisely, we consider finding a fixed-point of $g : X \to X$, or equivalently finding a zero of $f(x) = g(x) - x$, under the following assumptions.

Assumption 9.1.2 *Let $g : X \to X$ be a Fréchet differentiable operator for Hilbert space $X \subseteq \mathbb{R}^n$ equipped with inner product $(\cdot, \cdot)$ and induced norm $\| \cdot \|$, under the following conditions. Assume $g \in C^1(X)$ has a fixed point x^* in X, and there are positive constants κ_g and $\hat{\kappa}_g$ with*

1. $\|g'(x)z\| \leq \kappa_g \|z\|$ *for all* $x, z \in X$.
2. $\|g'(x)z - g'(y)z\| \leq \hat{\kappa}_g \|x - y\| \|z\|$ *for all* $x, y, z \in X$.

In Section 9.2 we will review recent results from [15] which describe how AA accelerates the fixed-point iteration defined by an operator g that satisfies the following nondegeneracy condition.

Assumption 9.1.3 *There is a constant $\sigma > 0$ for which the stage-j iterates and residuals satisfy*

$$\|w_{j+1} - w_j\| \geq \sigma \|e_j\|. \tag{9.2}$$

In Section 9.3, we will consider the specific case of Anderson accelerated Newton iterations (AA-Newton) under the following contrasting assumption, posed in terms of the zero-finding problem for $f(x) = g(x) - x$.

Assumption 9.1.4 *Suppose $f : X \to X$ has a zero x^* for which $f'(x^*)$, the Jacobian of f at x^*, is singular.*

Assumption 9.1.4 could also be stated as: 1 is an eigenvalue of $g'(x^*)$. We next describe how Assumption 9.1.4 contrasts with 9.1.3, and further explain why we refer to 9.1.3 as a nondegeneracy condition.

9.1.2 The Nondegeneracy Condition

As discussed in [15], two important instances in which Assumption 9.1.3 holds are if either g is contractive, or if the smallest singular value of f' is bounded away from zero. First, if g is contractive, the Lipschitz constant κ_g from Assumption 9.1.2 satisfies $\kappa_g < 1$. In that case

$$\|w_{j+1} - w_j\| = \|g(x_j) - x_j - (g(x_{j-1}) - x_{j-1})\| \geq (1 - \kappa_g) \|x_j - x_{j-1}\|,$$

so (9.2) holds with $\sigma = (1 - \kappa_g)$. This case covers an iteration for nonlinear operators ϕ that satisfy the strong monotonicity condition $(\phi(x) - \phi(y), x - y) \geq \nu \|x - y\|^2$, and Lipschitz continuity with constant κ_ϕ. As discussed in [4, 8], it then holds that $\kappa_\phi \geq \nu$, and defining the fixed-point operator $g(x) = x - (\nu/\kappa_\phi^2)\phi(x)$, g is then Lipschitz continuous with constant $\kappa_g = \sqrt{1 - \nu^2/\kappa_\phi^2} < 1$. Other contractive operators g include the fixed-point operator associated with the Picard iteration for the steady Navier-Stokes or Boussinesq equations, under a small-data condition [5, 14, 16]. The assumption that g is contractive was also made in the original convergence proofs for AA [10, 25]. Here we see it as one instance of the more general condition of Assumption 9.1.3.

Considering the results of [7] which cast AA as a quasi-Newton method, it should be expected that local convergence results also hold under more Newton-like conditions. Let x^* be a zero of f. Then similarly to how one considers convergence of Newton methods, we have

$$w_{j+1} - w_j = f(x_j) - f(x_{j-1}) = f'(x_j)e_j + \int_0^1 (f'(x_{j-1} + te_j) - f'(x_j))e_j \, \mathrm{d}t.$$

Suppose in addition to Assumption 9.1.2 it holds that the smallest singular value of $f'(y)$, the Jacobian of f at y, is bounded away from zero by constant σ_f in the ball $B(x^*, \delta)$ centered at x^*, with radius $\delta = \sigma_f/(2\kappa_g)$. Then for $x_j, x_{j-1} \in B(x^*, \delta)$ it holds that

$$\|w_{j+1} - w_j\| \geq \sigma_f \|e_j\| - \frac{\kappa_g}{2}\|e_j\|^2 \geq \frac{\sigma_f}{2}\|e_j\|, for \|e_j\| \leq \frac{\sigma_f}{\kappa_g}.$$

This is why Assumption 9.1.3 is called a nondegeneracy condition, and it extends the analysis of AA from strictly contractive operators, as in [5, 10, 14, 25], to those which satisfy Newton-like nondegeneracy properties.

9.2 Nondegenerate Problems

The acceleration property of AA has so far been primarily understood in nondegenerate settings, as developed in [5, 14, 15, 16]; and, for the specific case of Newton iterations in [17]. We next review the main results developed in the most recent analysis of [15], noting where it diverges from the analysis of [5]. The remaining two papers mentioned above are application specific. The first analysis showing that AA improves the convergence rate of fixed-point iterations was developed specifically for Picard iterations for stable finite element discretizations of the steady Navier-Stokes equations in [14]. Those results were generalized to cover more general contractive fixed-point operators in [5]. The results of [15] improve the approximation of the higher-order terms in the residual expansion shown in [5], and relax the condition that g must be contractive to the more general Assumption 9.1.3. This framework was applied to develop acceleration theory for Picard iterations for the Boussinesq system in [16]. The updated analysis in [15] also points to a filtering scheme that has been demonstrated to improve convergence.

The analysis in both [5] and [15] starts with an expansion of the residual, under the conditions of Assumption 9.1.2. We first introduce some notation for the optimization problem and update step of Algorithm 9.1.1. The optimization problem for a step with algorithmic depth m specifies

$$\gamma_k = \mathrm{argmin}_{\gamma \in \mathbb{R}^m} \left\| w_{k+1} - F_k \gamma \right\|. \tag{9.3}$$

Now define

$$w_{k+1}^{\alpha} = \min_{\gamma \in \mathbb{R}^m} \left\| w_{k+1} - F_k \gamma \right\| = w_{k+1} - F_k \gamma_k, \text{ and } \theta_{k+1} = \frac{\left\| w_{k+1}^{\alpha} \right\|}{\left\| w_{k+1} \right\|}, \tag{9.4}$$

where γ_k will be referred to as the *optimization coefficient*, and θ_k as the *optimization gain*. These two quantities and the relation between them are critical for understanding how AA improves convergence in fixed-point iterations. The update step of Algorithm 9.1.1 can now be written as

$$x_{k+1} = x_k + \beta_k w_{k+1} - (E_k + \beta F_k)\gamma_k = x_k^{\alpha} + \beta_k w_{k+1}^{\alpha}, \tag{9.5}$$

where $x_k^{\alpha} = x_k - E_k \gamma_k$. From Algorithm 9.1.1, the matrices F_k and E_k whose respective columns are the $m+1$ most recent differences between residuals and iterates are given by

$$F_k = \left((w_{k+1} - w_k) \quad \dots \quad (w_{k-m+2} - w_{k-m+1}) \right), \quad E_k = \left(e_k \quad \dots \quad e_{k-m+1} \right).$$

We will return to relating the quantities defined by (9.3)–(9.5) in a Hilbert space setting, after distilling the residual w_{k+1} into its higher- and lower- order terms.

The details of this residual expansion can be found in [5, Section 3.1] and [15, Section 3], and involve several steps of reindexing sums and applying Taylor's theorem, resulting in

$$\begin{aligned} w_{k+1} = & \int_{t=0}^{1} (1 - \beta_{k-1}) w_k^{\alpha} + \beta_{k-1} g'(z_k(t)) w_k^{\alpha} \, dt \\ & + \sum_{j=k-m_{k-1}}^{k-1} \sum_{n=j}^{k-1} \int_{t=0}^{1} \left(g'(z_n(t)) - g'(z_{n+1}(t)) \right) e_j \gamma_k(j) \, dt, \end{aligned}$$

where $\gamma_k(j)$ is the jth entry in γ_k, and $z_n(t) = x_{n-1} + t e_n$. Applying triangle inequalities and the definition of the optimization gain in (9.4) leads to the normed estimate

$$\begin{aligned} \left\| w_{k+1} \right\| = & \ \theta_k \left((1 - \beta_{k-1}) + \kappa_g \beta_{k-1} \right) \left\| w_k \right\| + \\ & \frac{\hat{\kappa}_g}{2} \sum_{n=k-m_{k-1}}^{k-1} \left(\left\| e_{n+1} \right\| + \left\| e_n \right\| \right) \sum_{j=n}^{k-1} \left\| e_j \gamma_k(j) \right\|. \end{aligned} \tag{9.6}$$

Three important observations to make about (9.6) are:

- Without acceleration ($m = 0$), the standard fixed-point residual (using the same damping factor) satisfies $\|w_{k+1}\| \leq ((1-\beta_{k-1}) + \kappa_g \beta_{k-1}) \|w_k\|$, whereby (9.6) improves the first-order term by a factor of the optimization gain θ_k, which satisfies $0 \leq \theta_k \leq 1$.
- The cost of the acceleration is the accumulated higher-order terms that multiply $\hat{\kappa}$, the Lipschitz constant of g' in (9.6).
- The higher-order terms in the residual bound are written in terms of the differences between consecutive iterates, $e_j = x_j - x_{j-1}$, rather than the previous residuals $w_j = g(x_{j-1}) - x_{j-1}$.

The analysis proceeds by bounding the differences between consecutive iterates by the residuals. At this juncture, the updated analysis of [15] diverges from that in [5].

9.2.1 Relating Residuals to Differences Between Consecutive Iterates

We now make use of the Hilbert space setting from Assumption 9.1.2. From Algorithm 9.1.1 on iteration k, the m_k columns of matrix F_k are the differences of consecutive residuals, starting on the left with $w_{k+1} - w_k$. The most recent residual or update step w_{k+1} has a unique decomposition into the columnspace of F_k and the nullspace of F_k^T

$$w_{k+1} = F_k\gamma_k + (w_{k+1} - F_k\gamma_k) = F_k\gamma_k + w_{k+1}^{\alpha}.$$

Now consider a reduced (economy) QR decomposition [9] of $F_k = Q_k R_k$. Then γ_k, the least squares solution to (9.3) is $\gamma_k = R_k^{-1} Q_k^T w_{k+1}$, and we have expressions

$$w_{k+1}^{\alpha} = (I - Q_k Q_k^T) w_{k+1}, \qquad \|(I - Q_k Q_k^T) w_{k+1}\| = \theta_k \|w_{k+1}\|$$

$$F_k\gamma_k = Q_k Q_k^T w_{k+1}, \qquad \|Q_k Q_k^T w_{k+1}\| = \sqrt{1-\theta_k^2}\, \|w_{k+1}\|.$$

From the above expressions and the defined update (9.5), $e_{j+1} = x_{j+1} - x_j$ has the expansion

$$x_{j+1} - x_j = E_j\gamma_j + \beta_j(w_{j+1} - F_j\gamma_j) = E_j R_j^{-1} Q_j^T w_{j+1} + \beta_j (I - QQ^T) w_{j+1},$$

hence

$$\|e_{j+1}\| \leq \sqrt{1-\theta_j^2}\, \|E_j R_j^{-1}\| \, \|w_{j+1}\| + \beta_j \theta_j \|w_{j+1}\|.$$

It is shown in some technical estimates of [15, Lemma 5.4] that there is a constant $C(\sigma, c_s)$ for which

$$\|E_j R_j^{-1}\| \leq C(\sigma, c_s),$$

where c_s is a lower bound on the direction sines between each column of F_j and the subspace spanned by the columns to its left. The diagonal values of R_j, denoted r_{ii}, are nothing but $r_{ii} = \|f_i\| \, |\sin(f_i, \text{span}\{f_1, \dots, f_{i-1}\})|$, with f_i denoting column i of F_k. Hence it is possible to control the constant c_s by filtering out columns of F_k where $r_{ii}/\|f_i\|$ are less than a desired value. This strategy is demonstrated in [15, Section 6]. The second dependence of $C(\sigma, c_s)$ is the constant σ from the nondegeneracy condition, Assumption 9.1.3.

The other quantity from (9.6) that is desirable to bound is $\|e_j\gamma_k(j)\|$, the jth component of vector $E_k\gamma_k$. By similar technical estimates, it is also shown in [15, Lemma 5.4], that $\|e_j\gamma_k(j)\| \le \beta_{k-1}C(\sigma, c_s)\sqrt{1-\theta_k^2}\,\|w_k\|$.

9.2.2 Full Residual Bound

Putting together the bounds on each term $\|e_j\|$ and $\|e_j\gamma_k(j)\|$ that appears in (9.6) leads to Theorem 5.5, the main result of [15]. This theorem, in somewhat simplified form, is given below.

Theorem 9.2.1 ([15, Theorem 5.5]) *Suppose Assumptions 9.1.2 and 9.1.3 hold. Let $Q_jR_j = F_j$ be the economy QR decomposition of F_j for each $j \le k$, and suppose each $|R_j(i,i)|/\|F_j(:,i)\| \ge c_s$, where $R_j(i,i)$ are the diagonal elements of R_j and $F_j(:,i)$ are the corresponding columns of F_j. Then the residual $w_{k+1} = g(x_k) - x_k$ from depth m acceleration satisfies the following bound*

$$\|w_{k+1}\| \le \|w_k\| \left(\theta_k((1-\beta_{k-1}) + \kappa\beta_{k-1}) + \frac{C(\sigma, c_s)\hat{\kappa}\sqrt{1-\theta_k^2}}{2} \left(\|w_k\|\,h(\theta_k) \right.\right.$$
$$\left.\left. +2 \sum_{n=k-m_{k-1}+1}^{k-1} (k-n)\,\|w_n\|\,h(\theta_n) + m_{k-1}\left\|w_{k-m_{k-1}}\right\| h(\theta_{k-m_{k-1}}) \right)\right) \tag{9.7}$$

where each $h(\theta_j) \le C\sqrt{1-\theta_j^2} + \beta_{j-1}\theta_j$, and C depends on c_s (sufficient linear independence of columns of each F_j)

Three important observations to make about (9.7) are

- As mentioned above after the first residual bound (9.6), this improves the first order term in the residual expansion by a factor of the optimization gain θ_k, as compared with the fixed-point algorithm with the same damping factor where no acceleration is applied.
- A successful optimization yields θ_k small, reducing the influence of the first order term, but increases the influence of the higher-order terms by a factor of $\sqrt{1-\theta_k^2}$. Likewise, if w_{k+1} is poorly represented in the columns

of F_k, then θ_k will be close to one, but $\sqrt{1-\theta_k^2}$, will be close to zero, and the lowest order term carries more weight.

- The constant $C(\sigma, c_s)$ that multiplies the higher-order terms can be controlled by filtering out columns of each F_k for which $|R_j(i,i)|/\|F_j(:,i)\| \leq c_T$ for some user-defined $0 < c_T \leq 1$.

We finish this section with a numerical demonstration.

9.2.3 Numerical Examples (Nondegenerate)

Extensive numerical results are shown for the 2D and 3D steady Navier-Stokes equations in [5, 14, 15], for the p-Laplacian in [5, 15], a nonlinear Helmholtz equation in [15], and the Boussinesq equations in [16]. In [15], examples include using a filtering strategy for the p-Laplacian which removes each column i from each F_k for which $|R_k(i,i)|/\|F_k(:,i)\| < 0.25$. For that problem, this safeguarding strategy is seen to be as effective as starting the iteration with a small values of algorithmic depth m (zero or one), and increasing the depth as the residual decreases.

The reasoning behind the last *dynamic depth* strategy is that from (9.7), an increased number of higher-order residual terms, and their increased scaling for θ_k smaller, is dominated by the first-order term, once $\|w_k\|$ is small enough. Along similar lines, a depth-switching strategy is demonstrated in [5, 15] for the steady Navier-Stokes, Boussinesq, and a nonlinear Helmoltz equation, in which the depth is switched from a smaller value (like $m=2$) to a larger value (like $m=10$) once the residual decreases past a given threshold, such at $\|w_k\| < 10^{-2}$. These practical strategies are discussed in more depth in [15, Section 5.1]. An example of dynamically chosen damping factors β_k for the p-Laplacian can be found in [5]. Developing efficient and robust dynamic parameter selection strategies is a current area of research for the author and collaborators.

Here we look at P_1 finite element discretization of a strongly monotone quasilinear PDE

$$-\text{div}\,(\mu(|\nabla u|)\nabla u) = f, \quad \mu(|\nabla u|) = 1 + \arctan(|\nabla u|), \quad f = \pi,$$

on the domain $(0,2)\times(0,2)$, with homogeneous Dirichlet boundary conditions. The iteration is defined by solving the sequence of linear sytems: Find $w_{k+1} \in V_h$ such that

$$(\nabla(w_{k+1}), \nabla v) = (f, v) - (\mu(|\nabla u_k|)\nabla u_k, \nabla v), \text{ for all } v \in V_h.$$

For these simulations, V_h is the P_1 finite element space on a uniform triangulation of the domain with 128 subdivisions in each of the x and y directions and 66049 degrees of freedom. The examples were run using the FEniCS finite element library [1]. In accordance with the discussion in Subsection

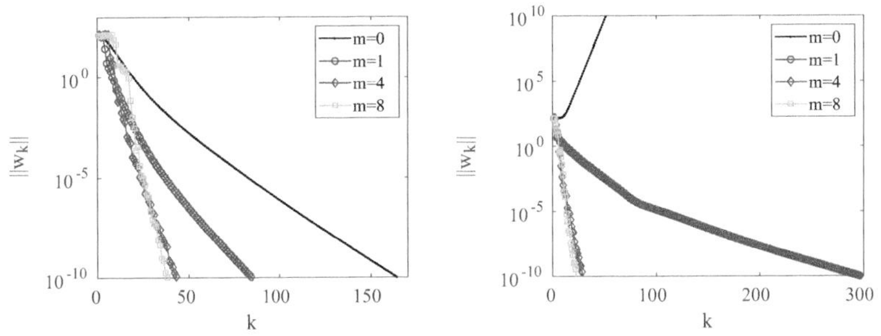

Figure 9.1: Residual $\|w_k\|$ with depths $m = \{0,1,4,8\}$, for $-\text{div}\,(\mu(|\nabla u|\nabla u) = f$, with $\mu(|\nabla u|) = 1 + \arctan(|\nabla u|)$. Left: contractive iteration with $\beta = (1+\sqrt{3}/2+\pi/3)^{-2}$. Right: noncontractive iteration with $\beta = 1$.

9.1.2, and [4, Example 1], the iteration $u_{k+1} = u_k + \beta w_{k+1}$ is contractive for $0 < \beta \leq (1+\sqrt{3}/2+\pi/3)^{-2}$. Each of iterations are started with $u_0 = 0$ and run to a residual tolerance of $\|w_k\| \leq 10^{-10}$.

Figure 9.1 shows the fixed-point iteration without acceleration ($m = 0$) together with the Anderson accelerated iterations using depths $m = \{1,4,8\}$. On the left, the damping factor $\beta_k = \beta = (1+\sqrt{3}/2+\pi/3)^{-2}$ ensures the fixed-point iteration with $m = 0$ is contractive. Consistent with the theory, AA with depths $m = 1,4,8$ each improve convergence of the iteration. Depths $m = 4$ and $m = 8$ solve to residual tolerance in a similar number of iterations, with $m = 8$ finding a better asymptotic rate. This is consistent with the theory, as once the residual is small enough so that the increase in the higher-order terms does not interfere with convergence, it is preferable to use a greater depth to enable a smaller optimization gain θ_k. The figure on the right shows the iteration with $\beta = 1$, which is not contractive, and for which the initial fixed-point iteration diverges. Each of the accelerated iterations converges, with $m = 4$ and $m = 8$ yielding similar performance. The computational cost for implementing AA is low, as m is much less than the number of degrees of freedom n, and the cost for the QR decomposition is of order n. An useful property of AA illustrated by Figure 9.1, is that the accelerated iterates are often less sensitive to the damping factor than those without acceleration.

9.3 Degenerate Problems

We now consider convergence of AA-Newton under Assumptions 9.1.2 and 9.1.4. As demonstrated in [17], AA-Newton can provide superlinear convergence to solutions of degenerate problems, $f : \mathbb{R}^n \to \mathbb{R}^n$, whose Jacobians are singular at a solution. In [17, Section 2.2], this superlinear convergence of AA-Newton with algorithmic depth $m = 1$ is demonstrated on both classical polynomial examples from [20], and the degenerate Chandrashekhar H-equation as discretized in [10]. In this degenerate situation, Newton's method converges only linearly [20, 21]. It has also been observed numerically that AA-Newton can enlarge the domain of convergence in the nondegenate setting of Assumptions 9.1.2 and 9.1.3 [5, 16]. The precise reason for this has yet to be thoroughly investigated, although superlinear convergence of AA-Newton in the nondegenerate setting is shown analytically in [17]. While the full analysis in the degenerate setting has also yet to be thoroughly investigated, an elementary proof provided here shows superlinear convergence for higher-order roots of smooth functions $f : \mathbb{R} \to \mathbb{R}$, together with accurate detection of the multiplicity of the root. The numerical examples of Subsection 9.3.4 demonstrate the behavior predicted by the theory. Several examples benchmarking the behavior of AA-Newton in both the nondegenerate and degenerate systems settings can be found in [17].

9.3.1 Scalar AA-Newton

In the scalar case, $f : \mathbb{R} \to \mathbb{R}$, the optimization problem in Algorithm 9.1.1 reduces to a linear equation for a single scalar coefficient, $w_{k+1} - \gamma_k(w_{k+1} - w_k) = 0$, solved by $\gamma_k = w_{k+1}/(w_{k+1} - w_k)$. Then the accelerated iterate x_{k+1}, for $k \geq 1$ is given by

$$x_{k+1} = x_k + w_{k+1} - \frac{w_{k+1}}{w_{k+1} - w_k}((x_k + w_{k+1} - (x_{k-1} + w_k)) = x_k - \frac{x_k - x_{k-1}}{w_{k+1} - w_k} w_{k+1}. \tag{9.8}$$

If the fixed-point scheme $x_{k+1} = x_k + f(x_k)$ is used, then $w_{k+1} = f(x_k)$, which results in the secant method. If the Newton iteration

$$x_{k+1} = x_k - f(x_k)/f'(x_k), \tag{9.9}$$

is accelerated, then plugging in $w_{k+1} = -f(x_k)/f'(x_k)$ yields the update step for AA-Newton, summarized in the algorithm below.

Algorithm 9.3.1 (AA-Newton rootfinding method)
Choose x_0. *Compute* $w_1 = -f(x_0)/f'(x_0)$. *Set* $x_1 = x_0 + w_1$
For $k = 1, 2, \ldots$

$$\begin{aligned} &\textit{Compute} \quad w_{k+1} &&= -f(x_k)/f'(x_k) \\ &\textit{Set} \quad x_{k+1} &&= x_k - \frac{x_k - x_{k-1}}{w_{k+1} - w_k} w_{k+1} \end{aligned}$$

As recalled above, AA applied to $w_{k+1} = f(x_k)$ results in a generalized multisecant method for $f : \mathbb{R}^n \to \mathbb{R}^n$ [6, 7], and the standard secant method in the scalar case. In this view, scalar AA-Newton is the secant method applied to $-f/f'$. This technique is mentioned (but not analyzed) as a rootfinding method for higher multiplicity roots in the classical text [19, Chapter 8.6], where it is mentioned that the method is subject to poles from the zeros of f' which are not common to f. Here we will see that in the absence of such poles, AA-Newton converges superlinearly and accurately detects the multiplicity of the root.

9.3.2 Methods for Higher-order Roots

In this subsection we review some of the standard methods for converging to higher-order roots. One of the most common methods of obtaining a solution to the nonlinear equation $f(x) = 0$ is Newton's method, (9.9). Newton's method is well-known for its quadratic convergence to simple zeros, supposing the iteration is started close enough to some root of a function f. Here we consider non-simple (higher multiplicity) roots, by which Assumption 9.1.4 is satisfied. For a root c of multiplicity $p > 1$, Newton's method converges only linearly, and $\lim_{k\to\infty} |x_{k+1} - c|/|x_k - c| = 1 - 1/p$, [18, Section 6.3]. A modified Newton method

$$x_{k+1} = x_k - p\frac{f(x_k)}{f'(x_k)}, \tag{9.10}$$

can be seen to restore quadratic convergence. However, this requires knowledge of the multiplicity p of the root which is generally *a priori* unknown.

Even if p is unknown, it may be approximated in the course of the iterative process. A method that performs this approximation based on Aitken's acceleration process is provided in [18, Section 6.6.2]. This approximate or adaptive modified Newton method is given by the iteration $x_{k+1} = x_k - p_k f(x_k)/f'(x_k)$ with $p_0 = 1$ and for $k \geq 1$,

$$p_k = \frac{x_{k-1} - x_{k-2}}{2x_{k-1} - x_k - x_{k-2}},$$

where p_k is recomputed on each iteration where the convergence rate is sufficiently stable (see [18, Program 56]). Algorithm (9.3.1) will be seen to produce a different approximation to p_k, shown to compare favorably to the adaptive method of [18] in the numerical tests of Subsection 9.3.4.

Finally it is remarked that another approach to quadratic convergence for non-simple roots discussed in for instance [12] is a modified Newton-Raphson method

$$x_{k+1} = x_k - \frac{f(x_k)f'(x_k)}{(f'(x_k))^2 - f(x_k)f''(x_k)},$$

which bears close resemblence to Halley's method [22]. However, the computation of the second derivative may be considered unnecessarily laborious as it will be seen in Subsection 9.3.4 that the superlinear convergence of Algorithm 9.3.1 is nearly as fast as that of the modified Newton method (9.10) but without the *a priori* knowledge of the multiplicity of the zero.

9.3.3 Analysis of the AA-Newton Rootfinding Method

An alternative approach to the following analysis is to exploit the interpretation of Algorithm 9.3.1 as a secant method used to find the (simple) zero of $-f(x)/f'(x)$, yielding the usual order of convergence for the secant method, $(1+\sqrt{5})/2$. The results that follow, however, give a direct proof that the method has an order of convergence of at least $(1+\sqrt{5})/2$; and, show that it gives an accurate approximation to the multiplicity of the root (also demonstrated numerically in Subsection 9.3.4), which is very useful if deflation is used to find additional roots.

To fix some notation for the remainder of this section, let $e(x) = c - x$, Suppose c is a non-simple root of a function $f(x)$ expressed in the form $f(x) = (x-c)^p g(x)$, $p > 1$, for some function g which is assumed not to have a zero (or pole) in some neighborhood of c. The following lemma shows the AA-Newton rootfinding method approximates the modified Newton method (9.10); and, it makes a precise statement regarding how $(x_{k+1}-x_k)/w_{k+1} = (x_k - x_{k-1})/(w_{k+1}-w_k)$, provides an approximation to the multiplicity of the zero of f at $x = c$. The theorem that follows provides a local convergence analysis of Algorithm 9.3.1.

Lemma 9.3.2 *Let $f(x) = (x-c)^p g(x)$ for $p > 1$ where $g : \mathbb{R} \to \mathbb{R}$ is a C^2 function for which both $g'(x)/g(x)$ and $g''(x)/g(x)$ are bounded in an open interval $\mathcal{N}$ containing c.*

Define the constants

$$M_0 = \max_{x\in\mathcal{N}} \frac{1}{p}\left|\left(\frac{g'(x)}{g(x)}\right)^2 - \frac{g''(x)}{g(x)}\right|, \quad \text{and } M_1 = \max_{x\in\mathcal{N}} \frac{1}{p}\left|\frac{g'(x)}{g(x)}\right|. \tag{9.11}$$

Then, if $x_{k-1}, x_k \in \mathcal{N}_0 := \{x \in \mathcal{N} : e(x)^2 < M_0^{-1} \text{ and } |e(x)| < M_1^{-1}\}$, the iterate x_{k+1} given by Algorithm 9.3.1 satisfies $x_{k+1} = x_k + p_k w_{k+1}$ with

$$p_k = \left(p - 2e(\eta_k)\frac{g'(\eta_k)}{g(\eta_k)} + \mathcal{O}(e(\eta_k)^2)\right), \quad \text{for some } \eta_k \in \mathcal{I}_k. \tag{9.12}$$

The hypotheses on g maintain that g is reasonably smooth and does not have a zero in the vicinity of c.

Proof. The Newton update step is $w_k = -f(x_{k-1})/f'(x_{k-1})$ so writing $w_k = w(x_{k-1})$, the update step from Algorithm 9.3.1 reads as

$$x_{k+1} = x_k - \left(\frac{x_k - x_{k-1}}{w(x_k) - w(x_{k-1})}\right) w_{k+1} = x_k + p_k w_{k+1}, \tag{9.13}$$

with $p_k = -(x_k - x_{k-1})/(w(x_k) - w(x_{k-1}))$. The aim is now to show $p_k \to p$ as $e(x_k) \to 0$.

For $f(x)$ given by $f(x) = (x-c)^p g(x)$, the first two derivatives are given by

$$\begin{aligned} f'(x) &= (x-c)^{p-1}\big(pg(x) + (x-c)g'(x)\big) \\ f''(x) &= (x-c)^{p-2}\big(p(p-1)g(x) + 2p(x-c)g'(x) + (x-c)^2 g''(x)\big). \end{aligned} \tag{9.14}$$

Writing $w(x_k)$ in terms of $f(x_k) = (x-c)^p g(x_k)$, and $f'(x_k)$ given by (9.14), gives $w(x_k) = e(x_k)g(x_k)/(pg(x_k) - e(x_k)g'(x_k))$, whose denominator is bounded away from zero for $x_k \in \mathcal{N}_0$. By the mean value theorem, there is an $\eta_k \in I_k$ for which $w(x_k) - w(x_{k-1}) = w'(\eta_k)(x_k - x_{k-1})$, by which (9.13) reduces to $x_{k+1} = x_k - w_{k+1}/w'(\eta_k)$. Temporarily dropping the subscript on η_k for clarity of notation, taking the derivative of $w(\eta) = -f(\eta)/f'(\eta)$ yields

$$p_k = \frac{-1}{w'(\eta)} = \frac{f'(\eta)^2}{(f'(\eta))^2 - f(\eta)f''(\eta)}.$$

Applying the expansions of f' and f'' from (9.14), cancelling common factors of $e(x)^{p-2}$ and simplifying allows the expansion of $-1/w'(\eta)$ as

$$\begin{aligned} &\frac{\big(pg(\eta) - e(\eta)g'(\eta)\big)^2}{\big(pg(\eta) - e(\eta)g'(\eta)\big)^2 - g(\eta)\big(p(p-1)g(\eta) - 2pe(\eta)g'(\eta) + e(\eta)^2 g''(\eta)\big)} \\ &= \frac{p - 2e(\eta)\frac{g'(\eta)}{g(\eta)} + \frac{1}{p}e(\eta)^2\left(\frac{g'(\eta)}{g(\eta)}\right)^2}{1 + \frac{1}{p}e(\eta)^2\left(\left(\frac{g'(\eta)}{g(\eta)}\right)^2 - \frac{g''(\eta)}{g(\eta)}\right)}. \end{aligned} \tag{9.15}$$

By hypothesis, x_k and x_{k-1} are in $\mathcal{N}_0$ which implies $\eta_k \in \mathcal{I}_k \subset \mathcal{N}_0$, so the denominator of the right hand side of (9.15) is of the form $1 + \alpha$ with $|\alpha| < 1$. Expanding the denominator in a geometric series shows that

$$-\frac{1}{w'(\eta_k)} = p - 2e(\eta_k)\frac{g'(\eta_k)}{g(\eta_k)} + \mathcal{O}(e(\eta_k)^2). \tag{9.16}$$

This shows there is an $\eta_k \in \mathcal{I}_k$ for which the update (9.13) of Algorithm 9.3.1 satisfies (9.12). □

Remark 9.3.3 *Both the adaptive method of [18, (6.39)–(6.40)] and the AA-Newton update given by (9.8), can be written in the form* $x_{k+1} = x_k + p_k w_{k+1}$*, so it makes sense to compare the two expressions for* p_k*. Letting* $\{y_k\}$ *represent the sequence generated by [18, (6.39)-(6.40)], and setting* $w_k = -f(y_{k-1})/f'(y_{k-1})$*, the resulting iteration may be written*

$$y_{k+1} = y_k + \frac{y_{k-1} - y_{k-2}}{(y_k - y_{k-1}) - (y_{k-1} - y_{k-2})} w_{k+1} = y_k + \frac{y_{k-1} - y_{k-2}}{p_{k-1}w_k - p_{k-2}w_{k-1}} w_{k+1},$$

which differs from update (9.13) of Algorithm 9.3.1 both in terms of the set of iterates used in the numerator of p_k*:* $\{y_{k-1}, y_{k-2}\}$ *compared to* $\{x_k, x_{k-1}\}$*; and, in the form of the denominator* $p_{k-1}w_k - p_{k-2}w_{k-1}$ *as opposed to* $w_{k+1} - w_k$*. As such,* p_k *of the adaptive scheme appears more complicated to analyze as an approximation to* p*, and the two methods will only be compared numerically, in Subsection 9.3.4.*

The previous Lemma 9.3.2 shows the update step of Algorithm 9.3.1 is of the form $x_{k+1} = x_k + p_k w_k$ where $p_k \to p$ so long as $x_k \to c$. The next theorem shows that $x_k \to c$, and that the order of convergence is greater than one (and, in fact, no worse than $(1+\sqrt{5})/2$).

Theorem 9.3.4 *Let* $f(x) = (x-c)^p g(x)$*, for* $p > 1$ *where* $g : \mathbb{R} \to \mathbb{R}$ *is a* C^2 *function for which both* $g'(x)/g(x)$ *and* $g''(x)/g(x)$ *are bounded in an open interval* $\mathcal{N}$ *containing* c*. Define the interval* $\mathcal{N}_1 = \{x \in \mathcal{N}_0 : |e(x)| < 1/(2M_1)\}$*, where* $\mathcal{N}_0$ *and* M_1 *are given in the statement of Lemma 9.3.2. Then there exists an interval* $\mathcal{N}_* \subseteq \mathcal{N}_1$ *such that if* $x_{k-1}, x_k \in \mathcal{N}_*$*, all subsequent iterates remain in* $\mathcal{N}_*$ *and the iterates defined by Algorithm 9.3.1 converge superlinearly to the root* c*.*

Proof. Suppose $x_k, x_{k-1} \in \mathcal{N}_1$. Let $p_k = -(x_k - x_{k-1})/(w_{k+1} - w_k)$. Then the error in iterate x_{k+1} satisfies

$$e(x_{k+1}) = c - (x_k + p_k w_{k+1}) = e(x_k) - p_k w_{k+1}. \tag{9.17}$$

Similarly to the computations of the previous lemma

$$w_{k+1} = -\frac{f(x_k)}{f'(x_k)} = \frac{e(x_k)g(x_k)}{pg(x_k) - e(x_k)g'(x_k)},$$

which together with (9.17) shows

$$e(x_{k+1}) = e(x_k)\left(1 - \frac{p_k g(x_k)}{pg(x_k) - e(x_k)g'(x_k)}\right) = e(x_k)\left(1 - \frac{p_k/p}{1 - \frac{1}{p}e(x_k)\frac{g'(x_k)}{g(x_k)}}\right). \tag{9.18}$$

For $x_k \in \mathcal{N}_0$ the denominator of (9.18) can be expanded as a geometric series to obtain

$$e(x_{k+1}) = e(x_k)\left(1 - \frac{p_k}{p}\sum_{j=0}^{\infty}\left(\frac{1}{p}e(x_k)\frac{g'(x_k)}{g(x_k)}\right)^j\right). \tag{9.19}$$

For x_k and x_{k-1} in $\mathcal{N}_1 \subset \mathcal{N}_0$, the results of Lemma 9.3.2 hold, and applying the resulting expansion of p_k to (9.19) shows

$$
\begin{aligned}
e(x_{k+1}) &= e(x_k)\left\{1-\left(1-\frac{2}{p}e(\eta_k)\frac{g'(\eta_k)}{g(\eta_k)}+\mathcal{O}(e(\eta_k)^2)\right)\sum_{j=0}^{\infty}\left(\frac{1}{p}e(x_k)\frac{g'(x_k)}{g(x_k)}\right)^j\right\}\\
&= e(x_k)\left\{1-\left(1-\frac{2}{p}e(\eta_k)\frac{g'(\eta_k)}{g(\eta_k)}+\mathcal{O}(e(\eta_k)^2)\right)\times\right.\\
&\left.\left(1+\frac{1}{p}e(x_k)\frac{g'(x_k)}{g(x_k)}+\left(\frac{1}{p}e(x_k)\frac{g'(x_k)}{g(x_k)}\right)^2\sum_{j=0}^{\infty}\left(\frac{1}{p}e(x_k)\frac{g'(x_k)}{g(x_k)}\right)^j\right)\right\}\\
&= e(x_k)\left\{1-\left(1-\frac{2}{p}e(\eta_k)\frac{g'(\eta_k)}{g(\eta_k)}+\mathcal{O}(e(\eta_k)^2)\right)\times\right.\\
&\left.\left(1+\frac{1}{p}e(x_k)\frac{g'(x_k)}{g(x_k)}+\mathcal{O}(e(x_k)^2)\right)\right\},
\end{aligned}
\tag{9.20}
$$

for some $\eta_k \in \mathcal{I}_k$. Multiplying out terms in (9.20) shows the error satisfies

$$
e(x_{k+1}) = e(x_k)e(\eta_k)\frac{2}{p}\frac{g'(\eta_k)}{g(\eta_k)} - e(x_k)^2\frac{1}{p}\frac{g'(x_k)}{g(x_k)} + \mathcal{O}(e(x_k)e(\eta_k)^2), \tag{9.21}
$$

which, for x_k, x_{k-1} in an interval $\mathcal{N}_* \subseteq \mathcal{N}_1$, shows the iterates stay in $\mathcal{N}_*$, and converge superlinearly to c. □

The standard secant method, when used to approximate a simple root, has an order of convergence of $(1+\sqrt{5})/2$, and the lowest order term in its error expansion is multiple of $e(x_k)e(x_{k-1})$. From (9.21), the lowest order term in the error expansion of AA-Newton, when approaching a higher-multiplicity root, is a multiple of $e(x_k)e(\eta_k)$, where η_k (from a mean value theorem) is between x_k and x_{k-1}. This implies the order of convergence for the method is at least $(1+\sqrt{5})/2$, and generally less than 2 unless $g'/g \to 0$.

9.3.4 Numerical Examples (Degenerate)

In this section, numerical examples are provided to illustrate the efficiency of AA-Newton for rootfinding. In these examples, Algorithm 9.3.1 is compared with the Newton method (9.9), the modified Newton method (9.10) (assuming *a priori* knowledge of the multiplicity p of the zero), and the adaptive method of [18, Section 6.6.2], implemented as described therein. Additionally, results are shown for the secant method (using x_0 as stated, and $x_{-1} = x_0 - 10^{-3}$). The secant method is included because, as shown in (9.8), scalar AA-Newton can be interpreted as a secant method applied to the Newton update step, or a secant method to find the zero of $w(x) = -f(x)/f'(x)$.

9.3.4.1 Example 1

The first example is taken from [18, Example 6.11]. The problem tested is finding the zero of $f(x) = (x^2 - 1)^q \log x$, which has a zero of multiplicity $p = q + 1$ at $x = 1$. The condition to exit the iterations are those from [18, Example 6.11], namely $|x_{k+1} - x_k| < 10^{-10}$. The iteration counts starting from $x_0 = 0.8$ (for standard, adaptive and modifed Newton methods) agree with those stated in [18]. Tables 9.1–9.2 show the respective iteration counts for $q = \{2, 6\}$ for each method starting from initial iterates $x_0 = \{0.8, 2, 10\}$. The final value of p_k is shown in parentheses after the iteration count for the AA-Newton and adaptive Newton methods.

Consistent with the analysis from Lemma 9.3.2 and Theorem 9.3.4, the performance of AA-Newton is linked to its accurate approximation of the root's multiplicity. For the result below in Tables 9.1–9.2, the final value of p_k in AA-Newton was accurate to $\mathcal{O}(10^{-8})$, except for the last experiment in Table 9.1, where it was $\mathcal{O}(10^{-7})$.

Table 9.1: Iterations to $|x_{k+1} - x_k| < 10^{-10}$ for $f(x) = (x^2 - 1)^2 \log x$.

x_0	modified N.	AA-Newton	adaptive N.	Newton	secant
0.8	4	6 (3.0000)	13 (2.9860)	51	72
2.0	5	7 (3.0000)	17 (3.0178)	56	79
10.0	7	8 (3.0000)	30 (4.1984)	63	89

Table 9.2: Iterations to $|x_{k+1} - x_k| < 10^{-10}$ for $f(x) = (x^2 - 1)^6 \log x$.

x_0	modified N.	AA-Newton	adaptive N.	Newton	secant
0.8	5	7 (7.0000)	18 (6.7792)	127	179
2.0	6	8 (7.0000)	29 (7.3274)	140	198
10.0	8	10 (7.0000)	80 (12.1095)	162	229

9.3.4.2 Example 2

The second example is a nonsmooth version of the first: $f(x) = \text{sign}(x-1)(x^2 - 1)^q$, for $q = \{2, 6\}$, which has a zero of multiplicity q at $x = 1$. This function features a discontinuity in the qth derivative at $x = 1$. The iterations were started from an initial iterate $x_0 = 4$, and run until $|x_{k+1} - x_k| < 10^{-10}$.

As seen in Figure 9.2, AA-Newton behaves similarly to modified Newton in both cases, but without preknowledge of the multiplicity of the root. The remaining methods display a lower order of convergence, although the adaptive Newton method is seen to be advantageous in comparison with Newton for $q = 2$ (on the left). For $q = 2$, Newton eventually converges after 37 iterations, adaptive Newton after 19, and secant after 52. For $q = 6$, Newton converges to tolerance after

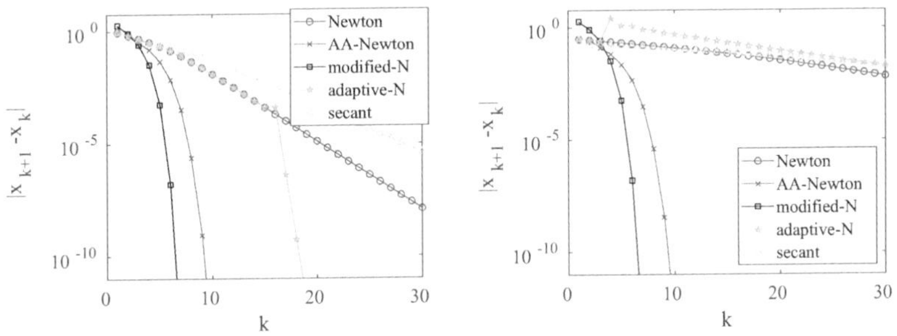

Figure 9.2: $|x_{k+1} - x_k|$ for $f(x) = \text{sign}(x-1)(x^2-1)^q$ starting with $x_0 = 4$, for the first 30 iterations. Left: $q = 2$; right: $q = 6$.

130 iterations, adaptive Newton after 150, and secant after 183. All methods converge to the root at $x = 1$.

9.4 Conclusion

The purpose of this discussion is to review recent results on the acceleration of fixed-point iterations using AA. We focus on two mathematical settings. In the first, the fixed-point operator is assumed nondegenerate, which includes contractive fixed-point iterations, and iterations to find the zero of a function f, where the smallest singular value of the Jacobian of f at a solution is bounded away from zero. This theory has been substantially developed by the author and collaborators, and current efforts focus on using the theory to develop robust and efficient methods by dynamically updating the algorithm parameters. In the second part of the chapter, we discuss the specific case of accelerating Newton iterations for degenerate problems. In this setting, AA-Newton with depth $m = 1$ has been shown numerically to provide superlinear convergence. Here we also give a proof of the superlinear convergence for the simple case of higher-multiplicity rootfinding in 1D. We show AA-Newton converges superlinearly, and also provides an accurate estimate of the order of the root.

Acknowledgements

The author was partially supported by NSF DMS 1852876.

References

[1] M.S. Alnæs, J. Blechta, J. Hake, A. Johansson, B. Kehlet, A. Logg, C. Richardson, J. Ring, M.E. Rognes and G.N.Wells. The FEniCS project version 1.5. Archive of Numerical Software, 3(100), 2015.

[2] H. An, X. Jia and H.F. Walker. Anderson acceleration and application to the three-temperature energy equations. Journal of Computational Physics, 347: 1–19, 2017.

[3] D.G. Anderson. Iterative procedures for nonlinear integral equations. J. Assoc. Comput. Mach., 12(4): 547–560, 1965.

[4] S. Congreve and T.P. Wihler. Iterative Galerkin discretizations for strongly monotone problems. Journal of Computational and Applied Mathematics, 311: 457–472, 2017.

[5] C. Evans, S. Pollock, L. Rebholz and M. Xiao. A proof that Anderson acceleration increases the convergence rate in linearly converging fixed point methods (but not in those converging quadratically). SIAM J. Numer. Anal., 58(1): 788–810, 2020.

[6] V. Eyert. A comparative study on methods for convergence acceleration of iterative vector sequences. J. Comput. Phys., 124(2): 271–285, 1996.

[7] H. Fang and Y. Saad. Two classes of multisecant methods for nonlinear acceleration. Numer. Linear Algebra Appl., 16(3): 197–221, 2009.

[8] G. Gantner, A. Haberl, D. Praetorius and B. Stiftner. Rate optimal adaptive FEM with inexact solver for nonlinear operators. IMA Journal of Numerical Analysis, 38(4): 1797–1831, 2017.

[9] G.H. Golub and C.F. Van Loan. *Matrix Computations (3rd Ed.)*. Johns Hopkins University Press, Baltimore, MD, USA, 1996.

[10] C.T. Kelley. Numerical methods for nonlinear equations. Acta Numerica, 27: 207–287, 2018.

[11] P.A. Lott, H.F. Walker, C.S. Woodward and U.M. Yang. An accelerated Picard method for nonlinear systems related to variably saturated flow. Adv. Water Resour., 38: 92–101, 2012.

[12] J.H. Mathews. An improved Newton's method. The AMATYC Review, 10(2): 9–14, 1989.

[13] Y. Peng, B. Deng, J. Zhang, F. Geng, W. Qin and L. Liu. Anderson acceleration for geometry optimization and physics simulation. ACM Trans. Graph., 37(4), 2018.

[14] S. Pollock, L. Rebholz and M. Xiao. Anderson-accelerated convergence of Picard iterations for incompressible Navier-Stokes equations. SIAM J. Numer. Anal., 57(2): 615–637, 2019.

[15] S. Pollock and L.G. Rebholz. Anderson acceleration for contractive and noncontractive operators. IMA J. Numer. Anal., 2020. Accepted.

[16] S. Pollock, L.G. Rebholz and M. Xiao. Acceleration of nonlinear solvers for natural convection problems. Journal of Numerical Mathematics, 2020.

[17] S. Pollock and H. Schwartz. Benchmarking results for the newton–anderson method. Results in Applied Mathematics, 8, 2020.

[18] A. Quarteroni, R. Sacco and F. Saleri. *Numerical Mathematics (Texts in Applied Mathematics)*. Springer-Verlag, Berlin, Heidelberg, 2006.

[19] A. Ralston and P. Rabinowitz. *A First Course in Numerical Analysis*. International series in pure and applied mathematics. McGraw-Hill, 1978.

[20] G. Reddien. Newton's method and high order singularities. Computers & Mathematics with Applications, 5(2): 79–86, 1979.

[21] G.W. Reddien. On Newton's method for singular problems. SIAM J. Numer. Anal., 15(5): 993–996, 1978.

[22] T.R. Scavo and J.B. Thoo. On the geometry of Halley's method. The American Mathematical Monthly, 102(5): 417–426, 1995.

[23] A. Toth, J.A. Ellis, T. Evans, S. Hamilton, C.T. Kelley, R. Pawlowski and S. Slattery. Local improvement results for anderson acceleration with inaccurate function evaluations. SIAM Journal on Scientific Computing, 39(5): S47–S65, 2017.

[24] A. Toth, C. Kelley, S. Slattery, S. Hamilton, K. Clarno and R. Pawlowski. Analysis of Anderson acceleration on a simplified neutronics/thermal hydraulics system. *Proceedings of the ANS MC2015 Joint International Conference on Mathematics and Computation (M&C), Supercomputing in Nuclear Applications (SNA) and the Monte Carlo (MC) Method*, ANS MC2015 CD: 1–12, 2015.

[25] A. Toth and C.T. Kelley. Convergence analysis for Anderson acceleration. SIAM J. Numer. Anal., 53(2): 805–819, 2015.

[26] H.F. Walker and P. Ni. Anderson acceleration for fixed-point iterations. SIAM J. Numer. Anal., 49(4): 1715–1735, 2011.

Chapter 10

Approximate Coincidence Points for Single-valued Maps and Aubin Continuous Set-valued Maps

Mohamed Ait Mansour[a,*], *Mohamed Amin Bahraoui*[b] and *Adham El Bekkali*[c]

2010 Mathematics Subject Classification. 37C25, 47H09, 47H10.

10.1 Introduction

Let X be a metric space whose metric is denoted by ρ. For a given set-valued map $\Phi : X \rightrightarrows X$, a point $x \in X$ is said to be a *fixed point* if $x \in \Phi(x)$. In the sequel, $\mathrm{Fix}(\Phi)$ denotes the set of fixed points Φ. If X is complete and Φ is a contraction, then as known Nadler's result [22, Theorem 5] (see also [13, Theorem 5E.3]) ensures the existence of a fixed point for Φ. Many efforts have been devoted in the recent literature to fixed point Theory in the context of metric

[a] Département de Physiques, LPFAS, Faculté Poly-disciplinaire, Safi, Université Cadi Ayyad, Morocco.
[b] Département de Mathématiques, FST, Tanger, Université Abdelmalek Essaadi, Morocco.
[c] Département de Mathématiques, Faculté des Sciences et techniques, Université Abdelmalek Essaadi, Morocco.
* Corresponding author: ait.mansour.mohamed@gmail.com

regularity and/or its equivalent conditions that is openness at a linear rate and Aubin continuity, without being exhaustive we quote here [5, 6, 9, 13, 11, 14].

Outside complete metric structures, for contractions, approximate fixed points have been recently proved in the sense that for every $\varepsilon \geq 0$, there exists $x \in X$ such that

$$d\big(x, \Phi(x)\big) \leq \varepsilon,$$

see [4, 1, 2]. Such approximate points, whose set will be denoted by ε-Fix(Φ), are infinitely multiple though the contracting property of the underlying map.

In [1] we present a global approximate contraction mapping principle that estimates the distance from a point to the set of the approximate fixed points of a set-valued map by the use of completion techniques and extension of globally Lipschitz maps from a dense subset to the whole space. This of course extends the recent results by A.L. Dontchev and R.T Rockafellar in [13, Theorem 5I.3, pp. 339] and by A. Arutyunov [5, Theorem 2] to the non-complete metric framework. Precisely, in [1, Theorem 2.1.] we state and prove the following.

Theorem 10.1.1 *Let X be a metric space and $\Phi : X \rightrightarrows X$ be a contraction with a constant $\kappa \in (0,1)$. Then, for every $\varepsilon > 0$, the set of ε-fixed points of Φ is nonempty, i.e., ε-Fix$(\Phi) \neq \emptyset$ and moreover the following estimate is satisfied:*

$$d(x, \varepsilon\text{-Fix}(\Phi)) \leq \frac{1}{1-\kappa} d(x, \Phi(x)) \quad \textit{for all } x \in X. \tag{10.1}$$

Here, for $x \in X$ and a subset $A \subset X$, $d(x,A)$ stands for the distance from x to A.

In [2, Theorem 4] we give another proof of the result in Theorem 10.1.1 with other independent arguments based on direct numerical procedures. The paper [2] emphasizes that the Painlevé-Kuratowski convergence of $(\varepsilon\text{-Fix}(\Phi))_\varepsilon$ to the set of exact fixed points Fix(Φ) and we show that this is not of course enough to pass to the limit in (10.1) over $\varepsilon \to 0$. This has been proved to necessitate rather the Wijsman convergence of $(\varepsilon\text{-Fix}(\Phi))_\varepsilon$ that is the pointwise convergence of $d\left(x, \varepsilon\text{-Fix}(\Phi)\right)$ to $d\left(x, \text{Fix}(\Phi)\right)$, but this may not succeed in general in noncomplete metric spaces, see our counter-example in [2, Example 3]. One may observe that the Pompeiu-Hausdorff convergence, whenever it is satisfied for the underlying sets of approximate points to the set of exact ones, do the same job as the Wijsman mode.

In this chapter, our primary goal is to provide a quite different proof of Theorem 10.1.1 for the case of single-valued maps by considering approximate coincidence points. Examples and applications are then given with respect to abstract elliptic equations and general parametric systems of equations formulated in metric spaces. Our contribution in this part is also situated within the close recent results such as those of [1, 2, 5]. Secondary, extensions of Theorem 10.1.1 to the local case with the Aubin property in the same general metric setting are envisaged. In this way, we first put the contraction mapping principle in a local approximate expression by involving approximate fixed points for Aubin continuous set-valued maps, which we discuss with the results by A. L Dontchev and H. Frankowska [11]. Then, we present a general unified result from which we easily derive many assertions such as those of Theorems of existence of fixed and/or ε-fixed points. Consequently, we obtain new conclusions concerning several extensions of classic Theorems such as Lyusternik-Graves Theorem, wherein we confirm that Hausdorff upper continuity could be an alternative of the closedness assumption as done in the global case in [2]. Consequent sharp regularity estimates are then obtained for approximate fixed points of Aubin continuous multi-maps and stability of local metric regularity under the sum considering single-valued locally Lipschitz perturbations, the case of set-valued perturbation can not be covered as shows [13, Example 5I.1, p. 338].

The plan of the chapter is organized as follows. Section 2 is devoted to preliminaries and notation. Section 3 deals with approximate and exact coincidence points of single-valued maps. In Section 4 our attention is in focus of an application of the results of Section 3. In Section 5 we consider an approximate version of the well-known contraction mapping principle for ε-fixed points of Aubin continuous multi-maps. In Section 6, we give an extended Lyusternik-Graves Theorem, which permits to get further extensions of other classic results such as up-dated Graves and Milyutin Theorems.

10.2 Notation

Throughout this chapter, X and Y are metric spaces unless otherwise is specified. Any metric is denoted by $\rho(.,.)$. If one of the spaces has in addition a linear structure then its metric ρ will be said shift-invariant if for all x,y,z, $\rho(x+z,y+z)=\rho(x,y)$. We denote by $B_r(\omega)$ the closed ball centred at ω with radius r indifferently in X or Y for any ω in X or Y. For any nonempty subset A of X and any point $x\in X$, $d(x,A)=\inf\{\rho(x,y)\ :\ y\in A\}$ will stand for the distance from x to A whereas $d(x,\emptyset)=\infty$. If B is another nonempty subset of X, $e(A,B)$ denotes the *excess* of A on B given by $e(A,B)=\sup\{d(a,B)\ :\ a\in A\}$. We adopt the convention $e(\emptyset,A)=0$ for any subset $\emptyset\neq A\subset X$ and $e(A,\emptyset)=+\infty$. The *extended Hausdorff distance* between two subsets A and B of X is given by

$$h(A,B)=\max\{e(A,B),e(B,A)\}.$$

Notice that the word "extended" refers to the possibility of the distance to be ∞. The minimal distance between two nonempty subsets A,B of X is denoted and given by

$$d(A,B)=\inf\{\rho(x,y)\ :\ (x,y)\in A\times B\}.$$

When one of the sets A and B is empty we set $d(A,B)=h(A,B)=+\infty$. By a *set-valued map* from X to Y we mean a correspondence F which assigns to each point $x\in X$ a subset $F(x)\subset Y$. We will denote a set-valued map by $F:X\rightrightarrows Y$ and its *graph* by $\mathrm{gph}(F)$ which is given by $\mathrm{gph}(F) = \{(x,y)) \in X \times Y \ : \ y \in F(x)\}$. The *domain* of F denoted by $\mathrm{dom}(F)$ is given by $\mathrm{dom}(F) = \{x \in X \ : \ F(x) \neq \emptyset\}$ and its range is given by $\mathrm{rge}(F) = \{y \in Y \ : \ \exists x \in X \text{ such that } y \in F(x)\}$.

The *inverse* of a set-valued map $F : X \rightrightarrows Y$ is the set-valued map $F^{-1} : Y \rightrightarrows X$ defined for every $y \in Y$ by $F^{-1}(y) = \{x \in X \ : \ y \in F(x)\}$. Observe that $(F^{-1})^{-1} = F$. Given another metric space Z and another set-valued map $G : Y \rightrightarrows Z$ we mean by $G \circ F$ the *set-valued map composition* of G with F defined from X to Z which whose graph is the set consisting of all pairs $(x,z) \in X \times Z$ such that there exists $y \in Y$ with $(x,y) \in \mathrm{gph}(F)$ and $(y,z) \in \mathrm{gph}(G)$. If Y is a vector space and $F, G : X \rightrightarrows Y$ are two set-valued maps, we define the set-valued map $F + G : X \rightrightarrows Y$ given for every $x \in X$ by

$$(F+G)(x) = F(x) + G(x) := \{y + z \ : \ y \in F(x) \text{ and } z \in G(x)\}.$$

A map $F : X \rightrightarrows Y$ is said to be *Lipschitz continuous* relatively to a subset D of X if there exists $\kappa \geq 0$ such that

$$h(F(x), F(x')) \leq \kappa \rho(x,x') \qquad \text{for all } x, x' \in D. \tag{10.2}$$

When the constant κ in the last definition is such that $\kappa \in (0,1)$ then F is said to be a *contraction* with constant κ. If $D = X$ and (10.2) is satified then F is said to be globally Lipschitz continuous with constant κ.

A map $F : X \rightrightarrows Y$ is said to be *locally complete* at $(\bar{x}, \bar{y})$ if $(\bar{x}, \bar{y}) \in \mathrm{gph} F$ and there exists neighborhoods U of $\bar{x}$ and V of $\bar{y}$ such that $\mathrm{gph}(F) \cap (U \times V)$ is complete.

A set-valued map $\Gamma : X \rightrightarrows Y$ is said to be *Hausdorff upper continuous* or *Hausdorff upper semicontinuous* (resp. *Hausdorff lower semicontinuous*), H-u.c (resp. H-l.c) in short, at a point $x_0 \in X$ if, and only if $\lim_{x \to x_0} e(\Gamma(x), \Gamma(x_0)) = 0$. If Γ is H-u.c (resp. H-l.c) at any point $x \in X$ then Γ is said to be H-u.c (resp. H-u.c). Obviously, every Lipschitz set-valued map is H-u.c and H-l.c.

A map $F : X \rightrightarrows Y$ is said to be *upper semicontinuous* (following [17, (a) Definition 2.5.1, pp 51], see also [8]) at a point $x_0 \in X$ if for every open $V \subset X$, $F(x_0) \subset V$, there exists a neighborhood U of x_0 such that for all $x \in U : F(x) \subset V$, i.e.,

$$\limsup_{x \to x_0} F(x) \subseteq F(x_0).$$

A set-valued map $F : X \rightrightarrows Y$ with closed values is said to be *lower semicontinuous* ([7]) at $x_0 \in \mathit{dom} F$ if

$$F(x_0) \subseteq \liminf_{x \to x_0} F(x).$$

We recall now the concepts of Aubin property, metric regularity and linear openness at a linear rate of a set-valued map around a reference point. Notice that linear open mapping are also recognized in the literature under covering maps, see [5, 6].

Definition 10.2.1 *Let X,Y be metric spaces, $F : X \rightrightarrows Y$ be a set-valued mapping and $(\bar{x},\bar{y}) \in \text{gph}(F)$.*

1. *F is said to be Aubin continuous at $\bar{x}$ for $\bar{y}$ if there exists $\kappa > 0$ with neighborhoods U of $\bar{x}$ and V of $\bar{y}$ such that F is Aubin continuous on $U \times V$ with constant κ, i.e.,*

$$e(F(x) \cap V, F(x')) \leq \kappa\rho(x,x') \quad \text{for all } x,x' \in U. \tag{10.3}$$

The infimum of κ over all combinations κ, U and V for which (10.3) holds is called the Lipschitz modulus *of F at $\bar{x}$ for $\bar{y}$ and denoted by* $\text{lip}(F;\bar{x} \mid \bar{y})$.

2. *F is said to be metrically regular at $\bar{x}$ for $\bar{y}$ if there exists $\kappa > 0$ with neighborhoods U of $\bar{x}$ and V of $\bar{y}$ such that F is metrically regular on $U \times V$ with constant κ, i.e.,*

$$d(x, F^{-1}(y)) \leq \kappa d(y, F(x)) \quad \text{for all } (x,y) \in U \times V. \tag{10.4}$$

The infimum of κ over all combinations κ, U and V for which (10.4) holds is called the regularity modulus *or* regularity moduli *of F at $\bar{x}$ for $\bar{y}$ and denoted by* $\text{reg}(F;\bar{x} \mid \bar{y})$.

3. *F is said to be linearly open at $\bar{x}$ for $\bar{y}$ if there exists $\kappa > 0$ with neighborhoods U of $\bar{x}$ and V of $\bar{y}$ such that F is linearly open on $U \times V$ with constant κ, i.e.,*

$$B_{\kappa r}(y) \cap V \subset F(B_r(x)) \quad \text{for all } r > 0 \text{and all} (x,y) \in \text{gph}(F) \cap (U \times V). \tag{10.5}$$

The supremum of κ over all combinations κ, U and V for which (10.5) holds is called the Linear openness modulus of F at $\bar{x}$ for $\bar{y}$ and denoted by $\text{lop}(F;\bar{x} \mid \bar{y})$.

For the equivalence between these three notions, see, e.g., [23, Theorem 9.43], [21, Theorem 1.52] or [14, Theorem 2.2]. It is worth equally to recall the definitions of these concepts on fixed sets which are more general than their counterparts at a reference point.

Definition 10.2.2 *Let X,Y be metric spaces, U, V be nonempty subsets of X and Y respectively, and $F : X \rightrightarrows Y$ be a set-valued mapping.*

1. *F is said to be Aubin continuous on $U \times V$ with constant κ if for all $x,x' \in U$,*

$$e(F(x) \cap V, F(x')) \leq \kappa\rho(x,x'). \tag{10.6}$$

2. *F is said to be metrically regular on $U \times V$ with constant κ if for all $(x,y) \in U \times V$,*

$$d(x, F^{-1}(y)) \leq \kappa d(y, F(x) \cap V). \tag{10.7}$$

3. *F is said to be linearly open on $U \times V$ with constant κ if for all $r > 0$ and all $(x,y) \in \mathrm{gph}(F) \cap (U \times V)$,*

$$B_{\kappa r}(y) \cap V \subset F(B_r(x)). \tag{10.8}$$

If F is metrically regular at a point $(\bar{x},\bar{y}) \in \mathrm{gph}(F)$ with constant κ and neighborhoods U and V of $\bar{x}$ and $\bar{y}$ respectively, then F is metrically regular on $U \times V$ with the same constant κ. Note also that in this case the Aubin continuity on $U \times V$ reduces to the classical Aubin continuity around $(\bar{x},\bar{y})$. The same observation holds for linear openness, see [13, Chapter 5, 5.8] and [15]. For other discussions of these notions, we refer to [5, 12]. In our contribution, we adopt these concepts defined on sets for our main result, and when we extend Lyusternik-Graves Theorem we rather employ the local definition to simply the comparison of our results with the corresponding ones in the literature.

10.3 Coincidence and Approximate Coincidence Points of Single-valued Maps

Let $f,g : X \longrightarrow Y$ be two single-valued maps. We denote by $\mathrm{Coin}(f,g)$ the set of coincidence points given by

$$\mathrm{Coin}(f,g) = \{x \in X \,|\, f(x) = g(x)\}.$$

Then we have

$$\mathrm{Coin}(f,g) = \mathrm{Fix}(f^{-1} \circ g). \tag{10.9}$$

If f is injective then $f^{-1} \circ g$ is a single-valued map. For every $\varepsilon > 0$, we define the set of ε-coincidence points of f and g by

$$\varepsilon\text{-}\mathrm{Coin}(f,g) = \varepsilon\text{-}\mathrm{Fix}(f^{-1} \circ g).$$

Let us state of first result of this section wherein we get a similar conclusion to [1, Theorem 2.1] and [2, Theorem 4] (stated in Theorem 10.1.1 above) for the case of single-valued maps by considering coincidence points but with a more simple proof.

Theorem 10.3.1 *Let X and Y be metric spaces. Let κ and μ be positive constants such that $\kappa\mu < 1$. Consider two single-valued mappings $f,g : X \longrightarrow Y$ such that f is injective. Assume moreover that $g : X \longrightarrow Y$ is Lipschitz continuous with constant μ and f is metrically regular with constant κ, i.e., for all $x \in X$ and all $y \in Y$,*

$$\rho(x, f^{-1}(y)) \leq \kappa\rho(y, f(x)).$$

Then for every $\varepsilon > 0$, ε*-Coin*(f,g) *is nonempty and the following estimate holds:*

$$d\Big(x, \varepsilon\text{-Coin}(f,g)\Big) \leq \frac{\varepsilon}{1-\kappa\mu} + \frac{\kappa}{1-\kappa\mu}\rho\left(f(x), g(x)\right), \textit{ for all } x \in X. \quad (10.10)$$

Proof. Let $\varepsilon > 0$. By definition, we have $\varepsilon\text{-Coin}(f,g) = \varepsilon\text{-Fix}\left(f^{-1} \circ g\right)$. Then, from [4, Thorem 2.1] it follows that ε-Coin(f,g) is nonempty*. Let us prove the estimate (10.10). Observe first that f^{-1} is a single-valued map since f is injective. Let $x \in X$. Take $v = f^{-1}(y)$, $y = g(x)$ and $u \in \varepsilon\text{-Coin}(f,g)$. Then,

$$\rho\left(u, f^{-1} \circ g(u)\right) \leq \varepsilon.$$

With the triangle inequality we write

$$\begin{aligned} d(x, \varepsilon\text{-Coin}(f,g)) &\leq \rho(x,u) \\ &\leq \rho(x, f^{-1}(y)) + \rho(f^{-1}(y), f^{-1} \circ g(u)) + \rho(f^{-1} \circ g(u), u). \end{aligned}$$

Thus,

$$d(x, \varepsilon\text{-Coin}(f,g)) \leq \rho(x, f^{-1}(y)) + \rho(f^{-1}(y), f^{-1} \circ g(u)) + \varepsilon. \quad (10.11)$$

Put $w = g(u)$ and see that (10.11) becomes

$$d(x, \varepsilon\text{-Coin}(f,g)) \leq \rho\left(x, f^{-1}(y)\right) + \rho\left(f^{-1}(y), f^{-1}(w)\right) + \varepsilon. \quad (10.12)$$

But, with the metric regularity of f with constant κ, we obtain that f^{-1} is Lipschitz continuous with constant κ. Hence,

$$d(x, \varepsilon\text{-Coin}(f,g)) \leq \rho\left(x, f^{-1}(y)\right) + \kappa\rho(y,w) + \varepsilon. \quad (10.13)$$

Now, with $w = g(u)$ and $y = g(x)$, (10.13) gives us

$$d(x, \varepsilon\text{-Coin}(f,g)) \leq \rho\left(x, f^{-1}(y)\right) + \kappa\rho\left(g(x), g(u)\right) + \varepsilon. \quad (10.14)$$

Next, we involve the Lipschitz continuity of g (with constant μ) in (10.14) and see that

$$d(x, \varepsilon\text{-Coin}(f,g)) \leq \rho\left(x, f^{-1}(y)\right) + \kappa\mu\rho(x,u) + \varepsilon. \quad (10.15)$$

Accordingly, if we pass to the infimum in (10.15) over $u \in \varepsilon\text{-Coin}(f,g)$ we infer

$$d(x, \text{Coin}(f,g)) \leq \rho\left(x, f^{-1}(y)\right) + \kappa\mu d(x, \varepsilon\text{-Coin}(f,g)) + \varepsilon. \quad (10.16)$$

*In the proof of [2, Theorem 4] we construct an infinite sequence of approximate fixed points.

This implies that

$$d\big(x, \varepsilon\text{-Coin}(f,g)\big) \leq \frac{1}{1-\kappa\mu}\Big(\rho\big(x, f^{-1}(y)\big) + \varepsilon\Big).$$

Finally, involve once more the metric regularity of f in the last estimate and conclude that

$$d\big(x, \varepsilon\text{-Coin}(f,g)\big) \leq \frac{\varepsilon}{1-\kappa\mu} + \frac{\kappa}{1-\kappa\mu}\rho\big(f(x), g(x)\big).$$

The proof is then complete. □

Example 10.3.2 *Let us provide a general problem formulated as an abstract elliptic equation that arises in partial differential equations (see for instance [10, 16, 20]). Let U,V be Banach spaces with compact and dense embeddings $U \hookrightarrow V \hookrightarrow U^*$, U^* is the dual space of U. The duality pairing between U and U^* is simply denoted by $\langle .,. \rangle$. $\|.\|_X$ will stand for the norm for any normed space X. Let $A : U \longrightarrow U^*$ be a linear operator, which is supposed to be elliptic, i.e., there exists $\alpha > 0$ such that*

$$\langle Au, u\rangle \geq \alpha \|u\|_U^2, \ \forall u \in U \quad (\textit{Ellipticity condition}). \tag{10.17}$$

Of course, elliptic operators are necessarily injective.

Let $B : V \longrightarrow U^*$ be a nonlinear operator. For a given $\xi \in U^*$, the aim is to find $u \in U$ such that

$$Au + Bu = \xi. \tag{10.18}$$

The restriction of B to U is denoted again by B, i.e., $B_{|_U} = B$. Clearly, solutions to (10.18) are exactly coincidence points of A and $\xi - B(.)$, i.e., $\text{Coin}\,(A, \xi - B(.))$ expresses the set of solutions to (10.18).

Let κ be the norm of A, i.e.,

$$\kappa = \|A\| := \sup_{\|u\|_U \leq 1} \|Au\|_{U^*}.$$

Suppose that B is Lipschitz continuous with constant μ such that $\kappa\mu < 1$, i.e., $\|A\| < \frac{1}{\mu}$, and see that all of the required conditions of Theorem 10.3.1 are satisfied. Then, for every $\varepsilon > 0$, we have the following estimate for approximate solutions to the elliptic problem (10.18) as follows: for all $u \in U$,

$$d\Big(u, \varepsilon\text{-Coin}\,\big(A, \xi - B(.)\big)\Big) \leq \frac{\varepsilon}{1-\kappa\mu} + \frac{\kappa}{1-\kappa\mu}\big\|A(u) + B(u) - \xi\big\|_{U^*}.$$

One possibility to obtain a regularity estimate for exact coincidence points is to find conditions trough which we are able to pass to the limit in (10.10) of Theorem 10.3.1 when ε goes to 0. This is the object of the following result.

Corollary 10.3.3 *Assume that conditions of Theorem 10.3.1 hold with the same data and suppose moreover that one of the following assumptions is satisfied:*

i) X is complete;

ii) There exists a compact $K \subset X$ such that ε-$\mathrm{Fix}(f^{-1} \circ g) \subset K$ for every $\varepsilon > 0$.

Then, $\mathrm{Coin}(f,g)$ *reduces to a singleton and moreover the following is satisfied*

$$\rho(x,x_0) \leq \frac{\kappa}{1-\kappa\mu}\rho\big(f(x),g(x)\big), \text{ for all } x \in X. \tag{10.19}$$

Proof. From [2, Theorem 6], by using one of the assumptions under the choice i) or ii), we are able to pass to the limit in (10.10) over $\varepsilon \to 0$, which ensures the required assertion in (10.19). □

Let us highlight that it is possible to improve Corollary 10.3.3 by removing assumptions i) or ii) provided that $\mathrm{Coin}(f,g)$ is nonempty. Precisely, with a slight adjustment of the proof of Theorem 10.3.1 we state the following.

Theorem 10.3.4 *Let X and Y be metric spaces. Let κ and μ be positive constants such that $\kappa\mu < 1$. Consider two single-valued mappings $f,g : X \longrightarrow Y$ such that f is injective. Assume moreover that $g : X \longrightarrow Y$ is Lipschitz continuous with constant μ and f is metrically regular with constant κ, i.e., for all $x \in X$ and all $y \in Y$,*

$$\rho(x,f^{-1}(y)) \leq \kappa\rho(y,f(x)).$$

If $\mathrm{Coin}(f,g)$ *is nonempty then it is reduced to a singleton $\{x_0\}$ and the following estimate holds:*

$$\rho(x,x_0) \leq \frac{\kappa}{1-\kappa\mu}\rho\big(f(x),g(x)\big), \text{ for all } x \in X. \tag{10.20}$$

Remark 10.3.5 *Observe that*

1. *A sufficient condition for* $\mathrm{Coin}(f,g)$ *to be nonempty is to suppose that Y is complete. In this case, since* $\mathrm{Coin}(f,g)$ *is exactly* $\mathrm{Fix}(f^{-1} \circ g)$, *f and g admit a unique coincidence point in view of Banach's contracting principle applied to the composition $f^{-1} \circ g$, which is of course a contraction with the constant $\kappa\mu$.*

2. *In the result by A. Arutyunov [5, Theorem 1] the same conclusion of our Theorem 10.3.4 has been obtained but with the following differences:*

   - *The main assumption in [5, Theorem 1] is that Y is complete while in our case it is any metric space. Instead, the alternative of our case is that one of the single-valued maps should be injective while this condition is not needed in [5].*

- *The set of coincidence points of the underlying maps contains at most one point in our Theorem 10.3.4 (thanks to the injectivity assumption on f) while the uniqueness in [5, Theorem 1] is not fulfilled in general.*
- *The paper [5] adopts the concept of α-covering mapping, $\alpha > 0$, which is equivalent to metric regularity of the corresponding inverse map with constant $\frac{1}{\alpha}$.*
- *The proof of [5, Theorem 1] uses iterative methods based on closedness and completeness conditions while here we devise computations of regularity bounds directly.*
- *In A. Arutyunov et al. [6, Theorem 1], the authors extend [5, Theorem 1] by considering covering and Lipschitz continuous maps with respect to fixed sets. Our local treatment in the following section shall also meet the local counterpart of these previous results with the fundamental novelty of introducing approximate coincidence and/or fixed points in our contribution.*

Proof of Theorem 10.3.4. Let $x \in X$. Take $v = f^{-1}(y)$ and $y = g(x)$. Let us denote by w the common value of $f(x_0)$ and $g(x_0)$. Of course we have

$$\rho(x,x_0) \leq \rho(x,x_0) \leq \rho(x,f^{-1}(y)) + \rho(f^{-1}(y),x_0). \tag{10.21}$$

Since f is injective then $x_0 = f^{-1}(w)$. Then (10.21) becomes

$$\rho(x,x_0) \leq \rho\left(x,f^{-1}(y)\right) + \rho\left(f^{-1}(y),f^{-1}(w)\right). \tag{10.22}$$

As already seen, f^{-1} is Lipschitz continuous with constant κ, then we arrive at

$$\rho(x,x_0) \leq \rho(x,f^{-1}(y)) + \kappa\rho(y,w). \tag{10.23}$$

Therefore, with $w = g(x_0)$, $y = g(x)$ and the Lipschitz property of g we see that

$$\begin{aligned} \rho(x,x_0) &\leq \rho\left(x,f^{-1}(y)\right) + \kappa\rho\left(g(x),g(x_0)\right) \\ &\leq \rho\left(x,f^{-1}(y)\right) + \kappa\mu\rho(x,x_0). \end{aligned}$$

This implies that

$$\rho(x,x_0) \leq \frac{1}{1-\kappa\mu}\rho\left(x,f^{-1}(y)\right).$$

Finally, involve the metric regularity of f in the last estimate and conclude that

$$\rho(x,x_0) \leq \frac{\kappa}{1-\kappa\mu}\rho\left(f(x),g(x)\right).$$

This completes the proof. □

Remark 10.3.6 *If X is complete then in Theorem 10.3.4 the existence and uniqueness of the coincidence point of f and g comes from Banach's contraction principle.*

As a straight consequence of Theorem 10.3.4, we obtain the following.

Corollary 10.3.7 *Let X be a metric space. Let κ be a positive constants such that $\kappa < 1$. Consider a mapping $g : X \longrightarrow X$ which is contraction with constant κ. If $\mathrm{Fix}(g)$ is nonempty then it is reduced to a singleton $\{x_0\}$ and the following inequality is satisfied:*

$$\rho(x, x_0) \leq \frac{1}{1-\kappa} \rho\left(x, g(x)\right), \textit{ for all } x \in X. \tag{10.24}$$

Proof. It suffices to take, in Theorem 10.3.4, the identity mapping for f, i.e., $f = I_X$.

□

Remark 10.3.8 *If $\tilde{g} : X \longrightarrow X$ is another contracting map such that $\mathrm{Fix}(\tilde{g})$ is nonempty then $\mathrm{Fix}(\tilde{g})$ is reduced to a singleton $\{\tilde{x}_0\}$ and moreover the following single-valued version of Lim's Lemma [19, Lemma 1] is satisfied:*

$$\rho(\tilde{x}_0, x_0) \leq \frac{1}{1-\kappa} \sup_{x \in X} \rho\left(\tilde{g}(x), g(x)\right). \tag{10.25}$$

A statement of a parametric form of (10.25) by considering rather approximate coincidence points is of a particular relevance from the applications viewpoint as shown below. This is the aim of our Theorem 10.3.9 below. So, let P another metric space (space of parameters) whose distance is denoted by $\mathbf{d}_P$. Let us present the following.

Theorem 10.3.9 *Let $g : P \times X \longrightarrow Y$ be a map. Assume that*

a) g is a contraction in x uniformly in p with constant $\gamma \in (0,1)$;

b) g is Lipschitz or Hölder continuous in p uniformly in x, i.e., for all $p, p' \in P$,

$$\sup_{x \in X} \rho\left(g(p,x), g(p',x)\right) \leq \nu\, \mathbf{d}_P^{\alpha}(p, p'), \tag{10.26}$$

where $\nu \in (0,1)$ and $\alpha \in (0,1]$.

Then, for every $\varepsilon > 0$, for all $p \in P$, ε-$\mathrm{Fix}(g(p,.)$ is nonempty and, for any other $p' \in P$, the following quantitative stability holds

$$h\big(\varepsilon\text{-}\mathrm{Fix}(g(p,.), \varepsilon\text{-}\mathrm{Fix}(g(p',.))\big) \leq \frac{\varepsilon}{1-\gamma} + \frac{\nu}{1-\gamma} \mathbf{d}_P^{\alpha}(p, p'). \tag{10.27}$$

Proof. Let $\varepsilon > 0$ and $p \in P$. Take $f = Id_X$ and $g = g(p,.)$ and derive from Theorem 10.3.1 that ε-Coin(f,g) is nonempty. At the meantime, observe that ε-Fix$(g(p,.) = \varepsilon$-Coin(f,g). Now, by using the assumption a), from [2, Theorem 15], it follows that

$$h(\varepsilon\text{-Fix}(g(p,.), \varepsilon\text{-Fix}(g(p',.))) \leq \frac{\varepsilon}{1-\gamma} + \frac{1}{1-\gamma} \sup_{x \in X} h(g(p,x), g(p',x)).$$

Therefore, (10.26) combined with the previous inequality gives us the required estimate (10.27). □

Remark 10.3.10 *Let us emphasize that*

- *[2, Theorem 15] is an approximate version of Lim's Lemma [19] and extends also the result in [15, Corollary 4.1].*
- *In Theorem 10.3.1 if in addition X is complete then for all $p \in P$,* Fix$(g(p,.)$ *is reduced to a singleton $\{x_p\}$ and, for any other $p' \in P$, the following estimate holds*

$$\rho(x_p, x_{p'}) \leq \frac{\nu}{1-\kappa} \mathbf{d}_P^\alpha(p,p'). \tag{10.28}$$

10.4 An Application: Parametric Abstract Systems of Equations

In this section we present an abstract example of application to illustrate our main results above. The first one concerns a general system of equations. Let $(X_i, |\,.\,|_i)$, $i = 1, ..., n$ be normed spaces whose the zero vector is indifferently denoted by 0, $n \in \mathbb{N}$ and let $X = X_1 \times X_2 \times ... \times X_n$ be the product normed space equipped with the supremum nom $\|\,.\,\|_\infty$ defined for any $x = (x_1, ..., x_n) \in X$ by

$$\|x\|_\infty = \max_{i=1,...,n} |x|_i.$$

We consider a further parametric metric space denoted by $(P, \mathbf{d}_P)$ as in Theorem 10.3.9 above. Let $(g_i)_{i=1,...n}$ be a finite sequence of functions given as $g_i : P \times X \longrightarrow X_i$ such that for every $p \in P$ and every $i \in \{1, ..., n\}$, $g_i(p,.) : X \longrightarrow X_i$ converges uniformly in x to a function $g_i^0 : X \longrightarrow X_i$. Put $g_0 : X \longrightarrow X$ defined for every $x = (x_1, ..., x_n) \in X$ by $g_0(x) = \left(g_1^0(x), ..., g_n^0(x)\right)$. With these objects we define an initial system of equations by:

$$(\mathbf{S}_0) \quad g_i^0(x_1, ..., x_n) = 0, \; i = 1, ..., n. \tag{10.29}$$

Then the parametric format of $(\mathbf{S}_0)$ is naturally given, for every $p \in P$, by

$$(\mathbf{S}_p) \quad g_i(p, x_1, ..., x_n) = 0, \; i = 1, ..., n. \tag{10.30}$$

Notation:

- $\mathbb{S}_0$ will stand for the set of solutions to the system (10.29);
- $\mathbb{S}_p$ designs the set of solutions to (10.30), every $p \in P$;
- $\mathbb{S}_0^{\varepsilon}$ will be recognized as the set of ε-approximate solutions to the system (10.29), for every $\varepsilon > 0$;
- $\mathbb{S}_p^{\varepsilon}$ will mean the set of ε-approximate solutions to (10.30), for every $p \in P$;
- π_i, for every $i \in \{1,...,n\}$, expresses the projection map $\pi_i : X \longrightarrow X_i$, which to every $x = (x_1,...,x_n)$ assigns x_i.

Theorem 10.4.1 *Assume that the following conditions are satisfied: for every $i \in \{1,...,n\}$,*

a) $g_i + \pi_i$ is a contraction in x uniformly in p with constant $\gamma_i \in (0,1)$;

b) g_i is Lipschitz or Hölder continuous in p uniformly in x, i.e., for all $p, p' \in P$,

$$\sup_{x \in X} \rho\left(g_i(p,x), g_i(p',x)\right) \leq \nu_i \mathbf{d}_P^{\alpha}(p,p'), \tag{10.31}$$

where $\nu_i \in (0,1)$ and $\alpha \in (0,1]$.

Then, for every $\varepsilon > 0$ and all $p \in P$, $\mathbb{S}_p^{\varepsilon}$ is nonempty and moreover for any other $p' \in P$, we have

$$h\left(\mathbb{S}_p^{\varepsilon}, \mathbb{S}_{p'}^{\varepsilon}\right) \leq \frac{\varepsilon}{1-\gamma} + \frac{\nu}{1-\gamma}\mathbf{d}_P^{\alpha}(p,p'), \tag{10.32}$$

where $\nu = \max\left\{\nu_i|, i \in \{1,...,n\}\right\}$ and $\gamma = \max\left\{\gamma_i|, i \in \{1,...,n\}\right\}$.

Remark 10.4.2 *If, besides assumptions of Theorem 10.4.1, X is complete then the exact solutions's set $\mathbb{S}_p$ reduces to a unique solution x_p for any $p \in P$ (thanks to the Banach's contraction principle). In this case, (10.32) tuns out to be*

$$\rho(x_p, x_{p'}) \leq \frac{\nu}{1-\kappa}\mathbf{d}_P^{\alpha}(p,p'). \tag{10.33}$$

Proof of Theorem 10.4.1. Let us define, for each $i \in \{1,...,n\}$, the function $f_i = P \times X \longrightarrow X_i$ given for all $p \in P$ and $x = (x_1,...,x_n) \in X$ by $f_i(x) = x_i + g_i(x)$. We shall also set $f(x) = f(x_1,...,x_n) = (f_1(x),..., f_n(x))$ and $f_0 : X \longrightarrow X$ defined by $f_0(x) = \left(f_1^0(x),..., f_n^0(x)\right)$, where $f_i^0(x) = x_i + g_i^0(x)$ for each $i \in \{1,...,n\}$. With these notation remark that for every $p \in P$, it is a straight matter to check that a vector $x = (x_1,...,x_n)$ is solution to $(\mathbf{S}_p)$ $\big($resp. $(\mathbf{S}_0)\big)$ if and only if x is a fixed point of f (resp. f_0).

Now, observe that condition assumption a) implies that f is a contraction in x uniformly in p with constant $\gamma = \max\left\{\gamma_i|, i \in \{1,...,n\}\right\}$, which is of course in $(0,1)$, while the condition b) ensures that f is Lipschitz or Hölder continuous in p uniformly in x with constant $\nu = \max\left\{\nu_i|, i \in \{1,...,n\}\right\}$. Then, the estimate in question in (10.32) is a consequence of Theorem 10.3.9. □

In the initial system (10.29), the maps g_i^0, $i \in \{1,...,n\}$, correspond indeed to an initial value p_0 of the parameter p. In this way, Theorem 10.4.1 reads a stability result of approximate solutions to the input (initial) system $(\mathbf{S}_0)$ with respect to the parametric perturbation p that generates stable approximations of solutions to the output (exit) system. Formally, we claim the following:

Theorem 10.4.3 *Suppose that conditions of Theorem 10.4.1 hold and, moreover, the map g_i^0 verifies the assumptions a) and b) of this Theorem for every $i \in \{1,...,n\}$. Then, for every $\varepsilon > 0$ and all $p \in P$, $\mathbb{S}_p^\varepsilon$ is nonempty and the following estimate holds*

$$h\left(\mathbb{S}_p^\varepsilon, \mathbb{S}_0^\varepsilon\right) \leq \frac{\varepsilon}{1-\gamma} + \frac{\nu}{1-\gamma}\mathbf{d}_P^\alpha(p, p_0), \tag{10.34}$$

where ν and γ are as given above.

Remark 10.4.4 *In the conditions of Theorem 10.4.3, for any sequence of parameters $(p_k)_k$ converging to p_0 with respect to the metric $\mathbf{d}_P$, $(\mathbb{S}_{p_k}^\varepsilon)$ converges in the sense of Hausdorff to $\mathbb{S}_0^\varepsilon$. In particular, we infer the following qualitative stability properties:*

$$\mathbb{S}_0^\varepsilon \subseteq \liminf_{k\to\infty} \mathbb{S}_{p_k}^\varepsilon \tag{10.35}$$

and

$$\limsup_{k\to\infty} \mathbb{S}_{p_k}^\varepsilon \subseteq \mathbb{S}_0^\varepsilon. \tag{10.36}$$

Then, we conclude that the approximate solution map of the considered system is at the meantime lower and upper semicontinuous with respect to the parametric perturbation. In fact, (10.35) means that every ε-solution to the initial system (10.29) can be approached by a sequence of ε-solutions to the parametric system (10.30) while, following (10.36), the limit of any sequence of approximate solutions to (10.30) is necessarily an approximate solution to (10.29). Note that the hypotheses done on the functions g_i are strong but the conclusions are also strong assertions. This convergence analysis can be stated similarly as in Remark 10.4.2 for the case of a unique exact solution.

10.5 Approximate Local Contraction Mapping Principle and ε-Fixed Points

Let us recall now the well-known contraction mapping principle for set valued mapping, which is a more general result than Nadler's Theorem and ensures the existence of fixed point for Aubin continuous set-valued mapping under completeness and closeness assumptions.

Theorem 10.5.1 ([13, Theorem 5E.2]) *Let X be a complet metric space, and consider a mapping $\Phi : X \rightrightarrows X$ and a point $\bar{x} \in X$. Suppose that there exist scalars $c > 0$ and $\lambda \in (0,1)$ such that the set* $\operatorname{gph}(\Phi) \cap (B_c(\bar{x}) \times B_c(\bar{x}))$ *is closed and*

(a) $d(\bar{x}, \Phi(\bar{x})) < c(1-\lambda)$,

(b) Φ *is Aubin continuous on* $B_c(\bar{x}) \times B_c(\bar{x})$*, i.e.,*

$$e(\Phi(x) \cap B_c(\bar{x}), \Phi(x')) \leq \lambda \rho(x, x') \quad \textit{for all } x, x' \in B_c(\bar{x}).$$

Then, Φ has a fixed point in $B_c(\bar{x})$, that is, there exists $x \in B_c(\bar{x})$ such that $x \in \Phi(x)$.

Remark 10.5.2 *In the recent literature there are well improved and advances results of this principle as proved by Ioffe [18, Theorem 4] under an approximate calmness property in complete metric spaces.*

In the following step we obtain an approximative format of Theorem 10.5.1 for ε-fixed points of set-valued mapping satisfying the Aubin property without recourse to completeness and closeness assumptions. The main assertion of this result could be considered implicit in [13, Theorem 5E.2] and also in [11, Theorem 2] but approximate fixed points have not however been declared in [11, 13].

Theorem 10.5.3 *Let X be a metric space and consider a mapping $\Phi : X \rightrightarrows X$ and a point $\bar{x} \in X$. Suppose that there exists scalars $c > 0$ and $\lambda \in (0,1)$ such that*

(a) $d(\bar{x}, \Phi(\bar{x})) < c(1-\lambda)$;

(b) Φ *is Aubin continuous on* $B_c(\bar{x}) \times B_c(\bar{x})$*, i.e.,*

$$e(\Phi(x) \cap B_c(\bar{x}), \Phi(x')) \leq \lambda \rho(x, x') \quad \textit{for all } x, x' \in B_c(\bar{x}).$$

Then, for every $\varepsilon > 0$, Φ has a ε-fixed point in $B_c(\bar{x})$, that is, there exists $x \in B_c(\bar{x})$ such that $d(x, \Phi(x)) \leq \varepsilon$.

Proof. Let $\varepsilon > 0$. We intend to construct a sequence (x_n) satisfying

$$x_{n+1} \in \Phi(x_n) \cap B_c(\bar{x}) \quad \text{and} \quad \rho(x_n, x_{n+1}) < c(1-\lambda)\lambda^n, \ \forall n \in \mathbb{N}. \tag{10.37}$$

Define $x_0 := \bar{x}$. By assumption (a), there exists $x_1 \in \Phi(x_0)$ such that

$$\rho(x_0, x_1) < c(1-\lambda). \tag{10.38}$$

Hence, $x_1 \in \Phi(x_0) \cap B_c(\bar{x})$.
Now, suppose we have already found $x_0, x_1, \ldots, x_m$ satisfying (10.37) for $n = 0, 1, \ldots, m-1$, for some $m \in \mathbb{N}^*$.
By assumption of induction, $x_m \in \Phi(x_{m-1}) \cap B_c(\bar{x})$ and $x_{m-1} \in B_c(\bar{x})$. Then, by using the assumption (b) with $x = x_{m-1}$ and $x' = x_m$ we obtain

$$d(x_m, \Phi(x_m)) \leq e(\Phi(x_{m-1}) \cap B_c(\bar{x}), \Phi(x_m)) \leq \lambda \rho(x_{m-1}, x_m) < c(1-\lambda)\lambda^m. \tag{10.39}$$

This implies that there exists $x_{m+1} \in \Phi(x_m)$ such that

$$\rho(x_m, x_{m+1}) < c(1-\lambda)\lambda^m. \tag{10.40}$$

Accordingly, the triangle inequality together with the assumption of induction imply

$$\rho(x_{m+1}, \bar{x}) = \leq \sum_{n=0}^{m} \rho(x_n, x_{n+1}) < c(1-\lambda) \sum_{n=0}^{m} \lambda^n = c(1-\lambda^{m+1}) < c. \tag{10.41}$$

Thus, $x_{m+1} \in \Phi(x_m) \cap B_c(\bar{x})$. Thus, the induction step is complete and (10.37) holds for all $n \in \mathbb{N}$.
Moreover, thanks to (10.37), for all $n \in \mathbb{N}$,

$$d(x_n, \Phi(x_n)) \leq \rho(x_n, x_{n+1}) \leq c(1-\lambda)\lambda^n \xrightarrow[n \to +\infty]{} 0. \tag{10.42}$$

Then there exists $n_0 \in \mathbb{N}$ such that, for all $n \geq n_0$,

$$d(x_n, \Phi(x_n)) \leq \varepsilon. \tag{10.43}$$

This means that Φ has ε-fixed points in $B_c(\bar{x})$, completing the proof. □

As a consequence of Theorem 10.5.3, we immediately derive the assertion a) of [2, Proposition 4].

Corollary 10.5.4 *Let X be a metric space and consider a contraction mapping $\Phi : X \rightrightarrows X$ with a constant $\mu \in (0,1)$. Then, Φ has ε-fixed points for every $\varepsilon > 0$.*

Proof. Let $\bar{x} \in X$ and take a real $a > \dfrac{d(\bar{x}, \Phi(\bar{x})}{(1-\lambda)}$ so that

$$d(\bar{x}, \Phi(\bar{x})) < a(1-\lambda). \tag{10.44}$$

For every $x, x' \in B_a(\bar{x})$ observe that

$$e(\Phi(x) \cap B_c(\bar{x}), \Phi(x')) \leq e(\Phi(x), \Phi(x')) \leq h(\Phi(x), \Phi(x')) \leq \lambda \rho(x, x'). \tag{10.45}$$

Consequently, the existence of ε-fixed points for the mapping Φ follows immediately from Theorem 10.5.3. □

10.6 Lyusternik-Graves Theorem and ε-Fixed Points for Aubin Continuous Set-valued Maps

We formulate now a further result on the Aubin property and ε-fixed points which can be deduced directly from the proof of [11, Theorem 5]. Our statement is however new and of a particular importance from the application stand point, see [3] in this regard, wherein the approximation purpose generates new concepts of solutions to quasi-optimization and programming problems via appropriate implicit solutions maps. Furthermore, in the present context, we infer an extension to the local case of our previous result in Theorem 10.1.1 above.

Theorem 10.6.1 *Let X be a metric space and α, μ be positive constants such that $\mu < 1$. Consider a mapping $\Phi : X \rightrightarrows X$ and $(\bar{x}, \bar{y}) \in X^2$. Assume that Φ is Aubin continuous on $B_\alpha(\bar{x}) \times B_\alpha(\bar{y})$ with constant μ, i.e.,*

$$e(\Phi(x) \cap B_\alpha(\bar{y}), \Phi(x')) \leq \mu\rho(x, x') \quad \text{for all } x, x' \in B_\alpha(\bar{x}). \tag{10.46}$$

Let a and b any positive reals such that

$$\frac{a+b}{1-\mu} + a < \alpha \quad \text{and} \quad \frac{a+b}{1-\mu} + b < \alpha. \tag{10.47}$$

Then, for every $\varepsilon > 0$ and any $x \in B_a(\bar{x})$,

$$d\big(x, \varepsilon\text{-Fix}(\Phi)\big) \leq \frac{1}{1-\mu} d\big(x, \Phi(x) \cap B_b(\bar{x}) \cap B_b(\bar{y})\big). \tag{10.48}$$

If $\alpha = +\infty$ in the assumption of Φ , then one can take $a = b = +\infty$ in (10.48).

Remark 10.6.2 *Let us emphasize that:*

1. *Taking into account the domain of Aubin continuity property of Φ, the estimate (10.48) can also be adjusted into*

$$d\big(x, \varepsilon\text{-Fix}(\Phi) \cap B_\alpha(\bar{x})\big) \leq \frac{1}{1-\mu} d\big(x, \Phi(x) \cap B_b(\bar{x}) \cap B_b(\bar{y})\big). \tag{10.49}$$

2. *In Theorem 10.6.1 with $\alpha = +\infty$, we find again the result concerning globally metrically regular and Lipschitz maps in Theorem 10.1.1, which in turn implies Nadler's theorem for the case when X is complete and Φ is closed-valued. At the mean time, we cover the particular case of composition $\Phi = F^{-1} \circ G$ of [13, Theorem 51.3, pp 339] established under the completeness condition on X and Y.*

3. *As proved in the global case in [2], the estimate in (10.48) with $\alpha = +\infty$ implies the global exact formulation of Lyusternik-Graves Theorem presented in [13, Theorem 51.2] but in the local case corresponding rather to $\alpha < 1$, this interesting implication can not be a direct consequence of (10.48). Nevertheless, we are able in our subsequent result in Theorem 10.6.7 to cover the local Lyusternik-Graves Theorem with the help of an appropriate sequence (x_n) under suitable adjustments (see Proposition 12.64 below).*

4. *In the proof of Theorem 10.6.1, the condition $\frac{a+b}{1-\mu} + a < \alpha$ was involved to prove that $x_n \in B_\alpha(\bar{x})$, for all $n \in \mathbb{N}^*$, while the condition $\frac{a+b}{1-\mu} + b < \alpha$ was used to ensure that $x_n \in B_\alpha(\bar{y})$, for all $n \in \mathbb{N}^*$.*

Remark that in the case when $\bar{y} = \bar{x}$, in Theorem 10.6.1 the condition $\frac{a+b}{1-\mu} + b < \alpha$ can be removed. Precisely, we state the following:

Theorem 10.6.3 *Let X be a metric space and α, μ be positive constants such that $\mu < 1$. Consider a mapping $\Phi : X \rightrightarrows X$ and a point $\bar{x} \in X$. Assume that Φ is Aubin continuous on $B_\alpha(\bar{x}) \times B_\alpha(\bar{x})$ with constant μ, i.e.,*

$$e(\Phi(x) \cap B_\alpha(\bar{x}), \Phi(x')) \leq \mu\rho(x, x') \quad \text{for all } x, x' \in B_\alpha(\bar{x}). \tag{10.50}$$

Let a and b any positive reals such that

$$\frac{a+b}{1-\mu} + a < \alpha. \tag{10.51}$$

Then, for any $x \in B_a(\bar{x})$,

$$d\big(x, \varepsilon\text{-Fix}(\Phi)\big) \leq \frac{1}{1-\mu} d\big(x, \Phi(x) \cap B_b(\bar{x})\big) \quad \text{for every } \varepsilon > 0. \tag{10.52}$$

Remark 10.6.4 *Using (10.49) of Remark 10.6.2, in Theorem 10.6.3 the estimate (10.52) can be replaced with the following*

$$d\big(x, \varepsilon\text{-Fix}(\Phi) \cap B_\alpha(\bar{x})\big) \leq \frac{1}{1-\mu} d\big(x, \Phi(x) \cap B_b(\bar{x})\big) \quad \text{for every } \varepsilon > 0. \tag{10.53}$$

We are now ready to derive both of the approximate contraction principle in non-complete metric spaces (Theorem 10.5.3) and the classic contraction principle in complete spaces (Theorem 10.5.1).

Proof of Theorem 10.5.3. Let $\varepsilon > 0$. The idea is to apply Theorem 10.6.3 with $\alpha = c$ and $\mu = \lambda$. Let b and a be real numbers such that $d(\bar{x}, \Phi(\bar{x})) < b < c(1-\lambda)$ and

$$\frac{a+b}{1-\mu} + a < \alpha. \tag{10.54}$$

Hence, apply (i) of Theorem 10.6.3 with $x = \bar{x}$ and obtain

$$d(\bar{x}, \varepsilon\text{-Fix}(\Phi)) \leq \frac{1}{1-\mu} d(\bar{x}, \Phi(\bar{x}) \cap B_b(\bar{x})). \tag{10.55}$$

By the choice of b, there exists $y \in \Phi(\bar{x})$ such that $\rho(y, \bar{x}) < b$. Hence $y \in \Phi(\bar{x}) \cap B_a(\bar{x})$. Combine this with (10.55) and deduce that '

$$d(\bar{x}, \varepsilon\text{-Fix}(\Phi)) \leq \frac{1}{1-\mu} d(\bar{x}, \Phi(\bar{x}) \cap B_b(\bar{x})) \leq \frac{1}{1-\mu} \rho(y, \bar{x}) < \frac{b}{1-\mu} < c. \tag{10.56}$$

Therefore, Φ has ε-fixed points in $B_c(\bar{x})$. □

Proof of Theorem 10.5.1. Consider the same real numbers a and b as suggested above in the proof of Theorem 10.5.3. Apply (ii) of Theorem 10.6.3 with $x = \bar{x}$ and obtain

$$d(\bar{x}, \text{Fix}(\Phi)) \leq \frac{1}{1-\mu} d(\bar{x}, \Phi(\bar{x}) \cap B_b(\bar{x})). \tag{10.57}$$

By the choice of b, there exists $y \in \Phi(\bar{x})$ such that $\rho(y, \bar{x}) < b$. Hence $y \in \Phi(\bar{x}) \cap B_a(\bar{x})$. Therefore, from (10.57) we deduce that

$$d(\bar{x}, \text{Fix}(\Phi)) \leq \frac{b}{1-\mu} < c. \tag{10.58}$$

Therefore, Φ has a fixed point in $B_c(\bar{x})$. □

Now, we present a proposition which is useful for local Lyusternik-Graves's type assertion. Precisely, we obtain more information on regularity estimates as follows.

Proposition 10.6.5 *Let X be a metric space and α, μ be positive constants such that $\mu < 1$. Consider a mapping $\Phi : X \rightrightarrows X$ and $(\bar{x}, \bar{y}) \in X^2$. Assume that Φ is Aubin continuous on $B_\alpha(\bar{x}) \times B_\alpha(\bar{y})$ with constant μ, i.e.,*

$$e(\Phi(x) \cap B_\alpha(\bar{y}), \Phi(x')) \leq \mu \rho(x, x') \quad \textit{for all } x, x' \in B_\alpha(\bar{x}). \tag{10.59}$$

Let a and b any positive real numbers such that

$$\frac{a+b}{1-\mu} + a < \alpha \quad \textit{and} \quad \frac{a+b}{1-\mu} + b < \alpha. \tag{10.60}$$

Then, for any $\varepsilon > 0$ and $x \in B_a(\bar{x})$ such that $\Phi(x) \cap B_b(\bar{x}) \cap B_b(\bar{y}) \neq \emptyset$, there exists a sequence (x_n) of elements of X such that for all $n \in \mathbb{N}$,

$$x_{n+1} \in \Phi(x_n), \quad \rho(x_{n+1}, x_n) \xrightarrow[n \to +\infty]{} 0 \tag{10.61}$$

and

$$\rho(x, x_{n+1}) \leq \frac{1}{1-\mu} \left(d(x, \Phi(x) \cap B_b(\bar{x}) \cap B_b(\bar{y})) + \varepsilon \right). \tag{10.62}$$

Proof. Let $\varepsilon > 0$ and $x \in B_a(\bar{x})$ such that $\Phi(x) \cap B_b(\bar{x}) \cap B_b(\bar{y}) \neq \emptyset$. Thus, there exists $y \in \Phi(x) \cap B_b(\bar{x}) \cap B_b(\bar{y})$ such that

$$\rho(x,y) < d(x, \Phi(x) \cap B_b(\bar{x}) \cap B_b(\bar{y})) + \varepsilon. \tag{10.63}$$

If $y = x$, then it is clear that the constant sequence equal to x satisfies (10.61) and (10.62). Next, assume that $y \neq x$ and choose $\gamma \in (\mu, 1)$ satisfying

$$\frac{1}{1-\gamma}\rho(x,y) \leq \frac{1}{1-\mu}\left(d(x, \Phi(x) \cap B_b(\bar{x}) \cap B_b(\bar{y})) + \varepsilon\right). \tag{10.64}$$

and

$$\frac{a+b}{1-\gamma} + a \leq \alpha \quad \text{and} \quad \frac{a+b}{1-\gamma} + b \leq \alpha.$$

According to Theorem 10.6.1, there exists a sequence (x_n) of elements of X satisfying:

$$x_{n+1} \in \Phi(x_n) \cap B_\alpha(\bar{x}), \rho(x_{n+1}, x_n) \leq \gamma^n \rho(x,y) \text{ and } d(x, x_{n+1}) \leq \frac{1}{1-\mu}\rho(x,y). \tag{10.65}$$

Since $\gamma \in (0,1)$, from (10.65) we obtain (10.61) and by combining (10.63)–(10.65), we deduce that the sequence (x_n) satisfies (10.62). This ends the proof. □

From Proposition 12.64 we get the following.

Corollary 10.6.6 *Let X be a metric space and α, μ be positive constants such that $\mu < 1$. Consider a mapping $\Phi : X \rightrightarrows X$ and $\bar{x} \in X$. Assume that Φ is Aubin continuous on $B_\alpha(\bar{x}) \times B_\alpha(\bar{x})$ with constant μ, i.e.,*

$$e(\Phi(x) \cap B_\alpha(\bar{x}), \Phi(x')) \leq \mu\rho(x,x') \quad \textit{for all } x, x' \in B_\alpha(\bar{x}). \tag{10.66}$$

Let a and b any positive real numbers such that

$$\frac{a+b}{1-\mu} + a < \alpha. \tag{10.67}$$

Then, for any $\varepsilon > 0$ and $x \in B_a(\bar{x})$ such that $\Phi(x) \cap B_b(\bar{x}) \cap B \neq \emptyset$, there exists a sequence (x_n) of elements of X such that, for all $n \in \mathbb{N}$,

$$x_{n+1} \in \Phi(x_n), \quad \rho(x_{n+1}, x_n) \xrightarrow[n \to +\infty]{} 0 \tag{10.68}$$

and

$$\rho(x, x_{n+1}) \leq \frac{1}{1-\mu}\left(d(x, \Phi(x) \cap B_b(\bar{x})) + \varepsilon\right). \tag{10.69}$$

We are by now in a position to state an extension to the local case of [2, Theorem 13], which also improves the conclusions of the Theorems by Lyusternik-Graves and Milyutin ([13, Theorem 5E.7]) without supposing that gph$F$ is locally complete at $(\bar{x}, \bar{y})$. Instead we require the Hausdorff upper continuity on the inverse mapping of $F + g$:

Theorem 10.6.7 *Let X be a metric space, Y be a linear metric space with shift-variant metric. Consider a mapping $F : X \rightrightarrows Y$, a point $(\bar{x}, \bar{y})$ of graph of F and a function $f : X \to Y$. Assume that F is metrically regular at $\bar{x}$ for $\bar{y}$, that g is Lipschitz continuous in neighborhood of $\bar{x}$, and that there exists constants κ and μ such that*

$$\kappa\mu < 1, \quad \operatorname{reg}(F;\bar{x} \mid \bar{y}) < \kappa \quad \textit{and} \quad \operatorname{lip}(g;\bar{x}) \leq \mu.$$

Then $F + g$ is approximatively metrically regular at $\bar{x}$ for $\bar{y} + g(\bar{x})$ with constant $\frac{\kappa}{1-\kappa\mu}$ in the sense that for $\varepsilon > 0$, there exist a neighborhood $\overline{U}$ of $\bar{x}$ and a neighborhood $\overline{V}$ of $\bar{y} + g(\bar{x})$ such that for every $(x,y) \in \overline{U} \times \overline{V}$ there exists a sequence (y_n) of Y converging to y satisfying

$$d\big(x,(F+g)^{-1}(y_n)\big) \leq \frac{\kappa}{1-\kappa\mu}\big(d(y,F(x)+g(x))+\varepsilon\big) \quad \textit{for all } n \in \mathbb{N}. \tag{10.70}$$

If in addition, $(F+g)^{-1}$ is Hausdorff upper continuous then every $(x,y) \in \overline{U} \times \overline{V}$,

$$d\big(x,(F+g)^{-1}(y)\big) \leq \frac{\kappa}{1-\kappa\mu}\big(d(y,F(x)+g(x))\big).$$

Proof. The idea is similar to [2, Theorem 13] by adapting the same technical arguments of [11, Theorem 3].

□

At this stage, we involve Theorem 10.6.7 to extend the updated Graves Theorem ([13, Theorem 5D.3]) to the setting of linear normed spaces.

Theorem 10.6.8 *Let X and Y be linear normed spaces whose norms are denoted $\|.\|$. Let $A \in \mathcal{L}(X,Y)$ surjective and satisfy $reg(A) \leq \kappa$ for some $\kappa \geq 0$. Consider a function $f : X \to Y$ and a point $\bar{x} \in X$ such that $lip(f - A)(\bar{x}) \leq \mu$ for some μ with $\kappa\mu < 1$. Then, for every $\varepsilon > 0$ there exist neighborhoods U and V of $\bar{x}$ and $f(\bar{x})$ respectively such that for all $(x,y) \in U \times V$, there exists a sequence (y_n) converging to y such that for all $n \in \mathbb{N}$,*

$$d\big(x,f^{-1}(y_n)\big) \leq \frac{\kappa}{1-\kappa\mu}\Big(\|y - f(x)\| + \varepsilon\Big).$$

If in addition, f^{-1} is Hausdorff upper continuous, then for all $(x,y) \in U \times V$,

$$d\big(x,f^{-1}(y)\big) \leq \frac{\kappa}{1-\kappa\mu}\|y - f(x)\|.$$

The result in Theorem 10.6.8 implies in turn an extension of Graves Theorem ([13, Theorem 5D.2]) from Banach spaces to linear normed spaces as follows.

Theorem 10.6.9 *Let X and Y be linear normed spaces whose norms are denoted $\|.\|_X$ and $\|.\|_X$ respectively. Let $\overline{x} \in X$. Let $A \in \mathcal{L}(X,Y)$ surjective and satisfy $reg(A) \leq \kappa$ for some $\kappa \geq 0$. Consider a function $f : X \to Y$ continuous in a neighborhood of $\overline{x}$ such that such that f^{-1} is Hausdorff upper continuous, $lip(f-A)(\overline{x}) \leq \mu$ for some μ with $\kappa\mu < 1$. Then, for any y close to $\overline{y}$, the equation $y = f(x)$ has a solution close to $\overline{x}$.*

Proof. Let $\varepsilon > 0$. Let also $\overline{U}$ and $\overline{V}$ be as in the proof of Theorem 10.6.8. So by this theorem, for every $x \in \overline{U}$ and $y \in \overline{V}$,

$$d\left(x, f^{-1}(y)\right) \leq \frac{\kappa}{1-\kappa\mu}(\|y - f(x)\| + \varepsilon). \tag{10.71}$$

Let x and y in $\overline{U}$ and $\overline{V}$ respectively. Wlog we can assume that $y \neq f(x)$. Following the correction function of Graves Theorem [13, 5D.4], consider a nonnegative constant μ' such that $\mu < \mu'$. Clearly, $\frac{\kappa}{1-\kappa\mu} < \frac{\kappa}{1-\kappa\mu'}$ and then

$$d\left(x, f^{-1}(y)\right) < \frac{\kappa}{1-\kappa\mu'}(\|y - f(x)\| + \varepsilon). \tag{10.72}$$

Therefore, there exists $\eta \in f^{-1}(y)$ such that $\|x - \eta\| \leq \frac{\kappa}{1-\kappa\mu'}(\|y - f(x)\| + \varepsilon)$ otherwise

$$\|x - \eta\| > \frac{\kappa}{1-\kappa\mu'}(\|y - f(x)\| + \varepsilon), \ \forall \eta \in f^{-1}(y).$$

Whence $d\left(x, f^{-1}(y)\right) \geq \frac{\kappa}{1-\kappa\mu'}(\|y - f(x)\| + \varepsilon)$, a contradiction with (10.72). Then it follows that $f(\eta) = y$ where η is in a neighborhood of $\overline{x}$ (since $y \in \overline{V}$ and f is continuous).

□

References

[1] M. Ait Mansour, M.A. Bahraoui and A. El Bekkali. A global approximate contraction mapping principle in non-complete metric spaces. J. Nonlinear Var. Anal., 4(1): 153–157, 2020.

[2] M. Ait Mansour, M.A. Bahraoui and A. El Bekkali. Metric regularity and lyusternik-graves theorem via approximate fixed points of set-valued maps in noncomplete metric spaces. Set Valued Var. Anal. Published online: http://dx.doi.org/10.1007/s11228-020-00553-1.

[3] M. Ait Mansour, M.A. Bahraoui and A. El Bekkali. Sharp estimates for approximate and exact solutions to quasi-optimization problems. Optimization. Published online: https://doi.org/10.1080/023319340.2021.1873986, 2021.

[4] M. Ait Mansour, M.A. Bahraoui and A. El Bekkali. Metric regularity and lyusternik-graves theorem via approximate fixed points of set-valued maps in noncomplete metric spaces. Le Matematiche, LXXIV: 411–415, 2019.

[5] A.V. Arutyunov. Covering mappings in metric spaces and fixed points. pp. 665–668. *In*: *Doklady Mathematics*, volume 76. Springer, 2007.

[6] A.V. Arutyunov, E. Avakov, B. Gel'man, A. Dmitruk and V. Obukhovskii. Locally covering maps in metric spaces and coincidence points. Journal of Fixed Point Theory and Applications, 5(1): 105–127, 2009.

[7] J.-P. Aubin. Lipschitz behavior of solutions to convex minimization problems. Mathematics of Operations Research, 9(1): 87–111, 1984.

[8] J.-P. Aubin and H. Frankowska. *Set-valued Analysis*. Springer Science & Business Media, 2009.

[9] M. Bianchi, G. Kassay and R. Pini. Linear openness of the composition of set-valued maps and applications to variational systems. Set-Valued and Variational Analysis, 24(4): 581–595, 2016.

[10] H. Brezis, P.G. Ciarlet and J.L. Lions. *Analyse Fonctionnelle: Théorie et Applications*, volume 91. Dunod Paris, 1999.

[11] A.L. Dontchev and H. Frankowska. Lyusternik-graves theorem and fixed points. Proceedings of the American Mathematical Society, 139(2): 521–534, 2011.

[12] A.L. Dontchev and H. Frankowska. Lyusternik-graves theorem and fixed points II. J. Convex Analysis, 19: 955–973, 2012.

[13] A.L. Dontchev and R.T. Rockafellar. Implicit functions and solution mappings. *Springer Monographs in Mathematics*. Springer, 208, 2009.

[14] M. Durea and R. Strugariu. Chain rules for linear openness in general banach spaces. SIAM Journal on Optimization, 22(3): 899–913, 2012.

[15] M. Durea and R. Strugariu. Metric subregularity of composition set-valued mappings with applications to fixed point theory. Set-Valued and Variational Analysis, 24(2): 231–251, 2016.

[16] L.C. Evans. Partial differential equations. graduate studies in mathematics. American Mathematical Society, 2: 1998, 1998.

[17] A. Göpfert, H. Riahi, C. Tammer and C. Zalinescu. *Variational Methods in Partially Ordered Spaces*. Springer Science & Business Media, 2006.

[18] A.D. Ioffe. Towards variational analysis in metric spaces: metric regularity and fixed points. Mathematical Programming, 123(1): 241, 2010.

[19] T.-C. Lim. On fixed point stability for set-valued contractive mappings with applications to generalized differential equations. Journal of Mathematical Analysis and Applications, 110(2): 436–441, 1985.

[20] J.-L. Lions. Sur quelques problèmes aux limites relatifs à des opérateurs différentiels elliptiques. Bulletin de la société mathématique de France, 83: 225–250, 1955.

[21] B.S. Mordukhovich. *Variational Analysis and Generalized Differentiation I: Basic Theory*, volume 330. Springer Science & Business Media, 2006.

[22] S. Nadler. Multi-valued contraction mappings. Pacific Journal of Mathematics, 30(2): 475–488, 1969.

[23] R.T. Rockafellar and R.J.-B. Wets. *Variational Analysis*, volume 317. Springer Science & Business Media, 2009.

Chapter 11

Stochastic Variational Approach for Random Cournot-Nash Principle

Annamaria Barbagallo[a,*], *Massimiliano Ferrara*[b] and *Paolo Mauro*[c]

2000 Mathematics Subject Classification. 49J40; 58E35; 91A15; 49N15; 49N45.

11.1 Introduction

In recent years a lot of attention has been devoted to the study of stochastic variational inequalities arising from problems with conditions of randomness where the data are affected by a certain degree of uncertainty. Such problems are called random equilibrium problems (see for instance [18, 19, 21, 22, 23, 20]). In [21] the authors present a class of linear stochastic variational inequalities on random sets in a Hilbert space setting and the measurability, the existence and the uniqueness of the solution are studied. Moreover, in the same paper, they provide an approximation procedure for a particular case. In [23], such a theory is applied for the treatment of nonlinear random traffic equilibrium problem. A

[a] Department of Mathematics and Applications "R. Caccioppoli", University of Naples Federico II, via Cintia - 80126 Naples, Italy.

[b] Department of Law, Economics and Human Sciences, University Mediterranea of Reggio Calabria, via dell'Università 25 - 89124 Reggio Calabria, Italy.

[c] Department of Mathematics and Computer Science, University of Catania, Viale A. Doria, 6 - 95125 Catania - Italy.

Emails: massimiliano.ferrara@unirc.it; mauro@dmi.unict.it

* Corresponding author: annamaria.barbagallo@unina.it

more complete detailed analysis is carried out in [13, 16] where the authors show the importance of constraints through the associated Lagrange multipliers.

The aim of this chapter is to introduce and analyze the oligopolistic market equilibrium problem under conditions of uncertainty. The need to consider the random problem arises because the constraints or the data are often variable over time in a non-regular and unpredictable manner. It is sufficient to think about unpredictable events and sudden accidents. So we propose a model which is able to handle random constraints. Let us highlight that we choose a Hilbert space setting because this functional space is very general and allows to obtain overall existence and regularity results. In the last part of the chapter we study a model in which control policies may be imposed to regulate the amounts of exportation in random way. More precisely, control policies are implemented by imposing higher taxes or subsidies in order to restrict or encourage the exportation. Such a model is a policymaker optimization problem. We prove that the system that controls the commodity exportations in random way is expressed by a stochastic inverse variational inequality. Thanks to such an inequality, the existence of control with uncertainty is obtained.

The oligopolistic market equilibrium problem has its origin with Cournot [10], who introduces the so-called duopoly problem. Later, Nash [30, 31] extends Cournot's duopoly problem to n agents, each acting according to his own self-interest, the so-called noncooperative game. A more complete and efficient study is done by Nagurney in [11, 27, 29, 28] but the problem is still faced in a static case through a finite-dimensional variational approach. Finally, in [2] the time dependence is considered in the model. Such a dynamic formulation is very useful to explore the adjustment of behavior of equilibrium states modelled over a time interval of interest. Furthermore, in [3] the authors describe the behavior of the market by using the Lagrange multipliers of the infinite-dimensional duality theory developed in [14, 12, 15, 17]. Lately, in [4] and [5], the model presented in [2] has been improved with the addition of production excesses and both production and demand excesses, respectively, and a numerical scheme is presented in [1]. In [6], the authors abandon the study of the problem from a producer's point of view whose purpose is to maximize its own profit. Moreover, they focus their attention to the policy-maker's perspective whose aim is to control the commodity exportations by means of the imposition of taxes or incentives. Hence, they formulate the resulting optimization problem as an inverse variational inequality. Finally, in [7, 8], the authors consider the model in which the constraint set depends on the expected equilibrium solution. In fact, the perception of the expected equilibrium solution influences the choice of the firms and the demand markets. For this reason, in this case, the problem is called elastic or with adaptive constraint set. As a consequence, the capacity constraint set is defined by means of a multivalued function and the equilibrium conditions are expressed by an evolutionary quasi-variational inequality.

The chapter is organized as follows. In Section 11.2, the random oligopolistic market equilibrium problem is presented. Furthermore the equivalence between the random Cournot-Nash equilibrium condition and an appropriate stochastic variational inequality is proved. In Section 11.3, an existence result is shown. In Section 11.4 the Lagrange theory is recalled and in Section 11.5 it is applied to the random problem. Section 11.6 is devoted to present the random optimal equilibrium control problem. Finally, in Section 11.7 a numerical example is provided.

11.2 The Random Model

The random oligopolistic market equilibrium problem is the problem of finding a trade equilibrium in a supply-demand market between a finite number of spatially separated firms which produce a homogeneous commodity and ship the commodity to some demand markets and where the data are affected by a certain degree of uncertainty.

For the reader's convenience we introduce in detail the random model. Let (Ω, A, P) be a probability space. Let us denote by $L^2(\Omega, \mathbb{R}^k, P)$ the Hilbert space of random vectors V from Ω to $\mathbb{R}^k$ such that the expectation

$$E\|V\|^2 = \int_\Omega \|V(\omega)\|^2 dP_\omega < \infty.$$

Moreover, we define in $L^2(\Omega, \mathbb{R}^k, P)$ the following bilinear form on $L^2(\Omega, \mathbb{R}^k, P)^* \times L^2(\Omega, \mathbb{R}^k, P)$, through the expectation, by

$$\langle\langle \phi, \mathrm{w} \rangle\rangle_E = \int_\Omega \langle \phi(\omega), \mathrm{w}(\omega) \rangle \, dP_\omega,$$

where $\phi \in (L^2(\Omega, \mathbb{R}^k, P))^* = L^2(\Omega, \mathbb{R}^k, P)$, $w \in L^2(\Omega, \mathbb{R}^k, P)$ and

$$\langle \phi(\omega), w(\omega) \rangle = \sum_{l=1}^{k} \phi_l(\omega) w_l(\omega).$$

Let us consider m firms P_i, $i = 1, \ldots, m$, which produce a homogeneous commodity and n demand markets Q_j, $j = 1, \ldots, n$, which are generally spatially separated. Assume that the homogeneous commodity, produced by the m firms and consumed by the n markets, is considered depending on/upon random variables. Let p_i, $i = 1, \ldots, m$, denote the random variable expressing the nonnegative commodity output produced by firm P_i and suppose that $p_i = p_i(\omega)$, $\omega \in \Omega$. Let q_j, $j = 1, \ldots, n$, denote the random variable expressing the nonnegative demand for the commodity of demand market Q_j, namely $q_j = q_j(\omega)$, $\omega \in \Omega$. Let x_{ij}, $i = 1, \ldots, m$, $j = 1, \ldots, n$, denote the random variable expressing the nonnegative commodity shipment between the supply producer P_i and the demand market Q_j, namely $x_{ij} = x_{ij}(\omega)$, $\omega \in \Omega$. In particular, let us set the vector

$x_i(\omega) = (x_{i1}(\omega), \dots, x_{in}(\omega))$, $i = 1, \dots, m$, $\omega \in \Omega$, as the strategy vector for the firm P_i.

Let us assume that the following feasibility conditions hold:

$$p_i(\omega) = \sum_{j=1}^{n} x_{ij}(\omega), \quad i = 1, \dots, m, \text{ P} - \text{a.s.}, \tag{11.1}$$

$$q_j(\omega) = \sum_{i=1}^{m} x_{ij}(\omega), \quad j = 1, \dots, n, \text{ P} - \text{a.s.} \tag{11.2}$$

Hence, the random quantity produced by each firm P_i must be equal to the random commodity shipments from that firm to all the demand markets. Moreover, the random quantity demanded by each demand market Q_j must be equal to the random commodity shipments from all the firms to that demand market.

Furthermore, we assume that the nonnegative random commodity shipment between the producer P_i and the demand market Q_j has to satisfy two capacity constraints, namely there exist two nonnegative random variables $\underline{x}, \overline{x} : \Omega \longrightarrow \mathbb{R}^{mn}_{+}$ such that

$$0 \le \underline{x}_{ij}(\omega) \le x_{ij}(\omega) \le \overline{x}_{ij}(\omega), \quad \forall i = 1, \dots, m, \ \forall j = 1, \dots, n, \text{ P} - \text{a.s.} \tag{11.3}$$

In order to guarantee general existence results under minimal assumptions we set our problem in the framework of suitable Hilbert spaces, precisely,

$$x \in L^2(\Omega, \mathbb{R}^{mn}_{+}, P), \quad \underline{x} \in L^2(\Omega, \mathbb{R}^{mn}_{+}, P), \quad \overline{x} \in L^2(\Omega, \mathbb{R}^{mn}_{+}, P).$$

As a consequence, we have $p \in L^2(\Omega, \mathbb{R}^{m}_{+}, P)$, $q \in L^2(\Omega, \mathbb{R}^{n}_{+}, P)$. Then, the set of feasible vectors $x \in L^2(\Omega, \mathbb{R}^{mn}_{+}, P)$ is

$$\mathbb{K} = \Big\{ x \in L^2(\Omega, \mathbb{R}^{mn}_{+}, P) : \underline{x}_{ij}(\omega) \le x_{ij}(\omega) \le \overline{x}_{ij}(\omega),$$
$$\forall i = 1, \dots, m, \ \forall j = 1, \dots, n, \ P - \text{a.s.} \Big\}. \tag{11.4}$$

This set is convex, closed and bounded in the Hilbert space $L^2(\Omega, \mathbb{R}^{mn}_{+}, P)$.

Furthermore, let us associate a random variable denoting the production cost f_i, with each firm P_i, $i = 1, \dots, m$, and assume that the production cost of a firm P_i may depend upon the entire production pattern, namely $f_i = f_i(x(\omega))$. Similarly, let us associate a random variable denoting the demand price for unity of the commodity d_j, with each demand market Q_j, and assume that the demand price of a demand market Q_j may depend upon the entire consumption pattern, $j = 1, \dots, n$, namely $d_j = d_j(x(\omega))$. Finally, let c_{ij} denote the random variable expressing the transaction cost, which includes the transportation cost associated with trading the commodity between firm P_i and demand market Q_j, $i = 1,\dots,m$, $j = 1,\dots,n$. Here we allow that the transaction cost depends on the entire shipment pattern, namely $c_{ij} = c_{ij}(x(\omega))$. Let η_{ij} be the random variable expressing the supply or resource tax imposed on the supply market P_i for the transaction with the demand market Q_j, $i = 1,\dots,m$, $j = 1,\dots,n$. Let λ_{ij} be the random variable expressing the incentive pay imposed on the supply market P_i for the transaction with the demand market Q_j, $i = 1,\dots,m$, $j = 1,\dots,n$. Moreover, let h_{ij} be the random variable expressing the difference between the supply tax and the incentive pay imposed on the supply market P_i for the transaction with the demand market Q_j, namely, $h_{ij}(\omega) = \eta_{ij}(\omega) - \lambda_{ij}(\omega)$. As above, we suppose that $\eta,\lambda \in L^2(\Omega,\mathbb{R}^{mn}_+,P)$, and, hence, $h \in L^2(\Omega,\mathbb{R}^{mn}_+,P)$.

The profit $v_i(x(\omega))$ of the firm P_i, $i = 1,\dots,m$, is, then,

$$\begin{aligned} v_i(x(\omega)) = &\sum_{j=1}^{n} d_j(x(\omega))x_{ij}(\omega) - f_i(x(\omega)) - \sum_{j=1}^{n} c_{ij}(x(\omega))x_{ij}(\omega) \\ &- \sum_{j=1}^{n} h_{ij}(\omega)x_{ij}(\omega), \end{aligned}$$

namely, it is equal to the price which the demand markets are disposed to pay minus the production costs, the transportation costs and the taxes.

Let us denote by $\nabla_D v = \left(\dfrac{\partial v_i}{\partial x_{ij}}\right)_{\substack{i=1,\dots,m\\ j=1,\dots,n}}$ and $x_i = \left(x_{ij}\right)_{j=1,\dots,n} \in L^2(\Omega,\mathbb{R}^n_+,P)$, $i = 1,\dots,m$. Let us assume the following assumptions:

(i) $v_i(\cdot)$ is continuously differentiable for each $i = 1,\dots,m$,

(ii) $\nabla_D v(\cdot)$ is a Carathéodory function such that there exists $\tau \in L^2(\Omega,P)$:

$$\|\nabla_D v(x(\omega))\|_{mn} \le \tau(\omega)\,\|x(\omega)\|_{mn}, \quad \forall x \in L^2(\Omega,\mathbb{R}^{mn}_+,P),\ P-\text{a.s.}, \tag{11.5}$$

(iii) $v_i(\cdot)$ is pseudoconcave with respect to the variables x_i, $i = 1,\dots,m$.

For the reader's convenience, we recall that a function $v_i(\cdot)$, continuously differentiable, is called *pseudoconcave* with respect to x_i, $i = 1,\dots,m$, (see [24]) if the following condition holds:

$$\begin{aligned} &\left\langle \frac{\partial v_i}{\partial x_i}(x_1,\dots,x_i,\dots,x_m), x_i - y_i \right\rangle \ge 0 \\ &\qquad \Rightarrow\ v_i(x_1,\dots,x_i,\dots,x_m) \ge v_i(x_1,\dots,y_i,\dots,x_m). \end{aligned}$$

Now let us consider the random oligopolistic market, in which the m firms supply the commodity in a noncooperative fashion, each one trying to maximize its own profit function considered the optimal distribution pattern for the other firms. We seek to determine a nonnegative commodity distribution for which the m firms and the n demand markets will be in a state of equilibrium as defined below by the random Cournot-Nash principle.

Definition 11.2.1 *$x^* \in \mathbb{K}$ is a random oligopolistic market equilibrium distribution if and only if for each $i = 1,\ldots,m$ and P-a.s. we have*

$$v_i(x^*(\omega)) \geq v_i(x_i(\omega), \hat{x}_i^*(\omega)), \tag{11.6}$$

where

$$\hat{x}_i^*(\omega) = (x_1^*(\omega),\ldots,x_{i-1}^*(\omega), x_{i+1}^*(\omega),\ldots,x_m^*(\omega)).$$

It is possible to prove that under assumptions (i), (ii), (iii), Definition 11.2.1 can be expressed by a stochastic variational inequality, as the following result establishes.

Theorem 11.2.2 *Let us suppose that assumptions* (i), (ii), (iii) *are satisfied. Then, $x^* \in \mathbb{K}$ is a random oligopolistic market equilibrium distribution if and only if it is a solution to the stochastic variational inequality*

$$\ll -\nabla_D v(x^*(\omega)), x(\omega) - x^*(\omega)) \gg_E \geq 0, \quad \forall x \in \mathbb{K}. \tag{11.7}$$

Proof. Firstly let us prove that the stochastic variational inequality (11.7)

$$\begin{aligned}
&\langle\langle -\nabla_D v(x^*), x - x^*\rangle\rangle_E \\
&= \int_\Omega \langle -\nabla_D v(x^*(\omega)), x(\omega) - x^*(\omega)\rangle \, dP_\omega \\
&= \int_\Omega \sum_{i=1}^m \sum_{j=1}^n -\frac{\partial v_i(x^*(\omega))}{\partial x_{ij}}(x_{ij}(\omega) - x_{ij}^*(\omega)) dP_\omega \geq 0, \quad \forall x \in \mathbb{K},
\end{aligned}$$

is equivalent to the following point-to-point stochastic variational inequality:

$$\begin{aligned}
&\langle -\nabla_D v(x^*(\omega)), x(\omega) - x^*(\omega)\rangle \\
&= \sum_{i=1}^m \sum_{j=1}^n -\frac{\partial v_i(x^*(\omega))}{\partial x_{ij}}(x_{ij}(\omega) - x_{ij}^*(\omega)) \geq 0, \quad \forall x(\omega) \in \mathbb{K}(\omega),
\end{aligned} \tag{11.8}$$

where

$$\mathbb{K}(\omega) = \left\{ x(\omega) \in \mathbb{R}^{mn} : \underline{x}_{ij}(\omega) \leq x_{ij}(\omega) \leq \overline{x}_{ij}(\omega), \ \forall i = 1,\ldots,m, \ \forall j = 1,\ldots,n \right\}.$$

In fact, we suppose by absurdum that (11.8) does not hold, namely there exists some $\overline{\Omega} \subseteq \Omega$ with $P(\overline{\Omega}) > 0$ such that for each $\omega \in \overline{\Omega}$, there is some $x(\omega) \in \mathbb{K}(\omega)$ such that

$$\langle -\nabla_D v(x^*(\omega)), x(\omega) - x^*(\omega)\rangle < 0, \quad P-\text{a.s. in } \overline{\Omega}.$$

We can choose

$$x(\omega) = \begin{cases} x^*(\omega), & P-\text{a.s. in } \Omega \setminus \overline{\Omega}, \\ \bar{x}(\omega), & P-\text{a.s. in } \overline{\Omega}. \end{cases}$$

Then, by integrating over Ω, we obtain:

$$\begin{aligned} \langle\langle -\nabla_D v(x^*), x - x^* \rangle\rangle_E = & \int_{\Omega\setminus\overline{\Omega}} \langle -\nabla_D v(x^*(\omega)), x(\omega) - x^*(\omega) \rangle \, dP_\omega \\ & + \int_{\overline{\Omega}} \langle -\nabla_D v(x^*(\omega)), \bar{x}(\omega) - x^*(\omega) \rangle \, dP_\omega < 0. \end{aligned}$$

This is an absurdum. The vice versa is immediate. Hence, the equivalence between the stochastic variational inequalities (11.7) and (11.8) is shown.

Let us prove, now, the equivalence between the random Cournot-Nash principle and the stochastic variational inequality (11.7). Let us suppose that $x^*(\omega) \in \mathbb{K}(\omega)$ is an equilibrium distribution according to Definition 11.2.1, namely:

$$v_i(x^*(\omega)) \geq v_i(x(\omega), \hat{x}^*(\omega)), \quad \forall x(\omega) \in \mathbb{K}(\omega),\ \forall i = 1, \ldots, m,\ \text{P}-\text{a.s.} \quad (11.9)$$

For well known theorems of Optimization, we have that for every $i = 1, \ldots, m$, for every $x(\omega) \in \mathbb{K}(\omega)$, P-a.s.

$$\begin{aligned} & \langle -\nabla_D v_i(x^*(\omega)), x_i(\omega) - x_i^*(\omega) \rangle \\ & = \sum_{j=1}^{n} -\frac{\partial v_i(x^*(\omega))}{\partial x_{ij}} (x_{ij}(\omega) - x_{ij}^*(\omega)) \geq 0. \end{aligned} \quad (11.10)$$

By assumptions on $\nabla_D v_i$ and since $x, x^* \in L^2(\Omega, \mathbb{R}^{mn}, P)$, we have that

$$\omega \mapsto \langle -\nabla_D v_i(x^*(\omega)), x_i(\omega) - x_i^*(\omega) \rangle \in L^2(\Omega, \mathbb{R}, P).$$

Hence, by integrating over Ω, we get

$$\langle\langle -\nabla_D v_i(x^*), x_i - x_i^* \rangle\rangle_E \geq 0, \quad \forall x \in \mathbb{K},$$

from which, by summing for each firm P_i, for $i = 1, \ldots, m$, we obtain

$$\sum_{i=1}^{m} \langle\langle -\nabla_D v_i(x^*), x_i - x_i^* \rangle\rangle_E = \langle\langle -\nabla_D v(x^*), x - x^* \rangle\rangle_E \geq 0, \quad \forall x \in \mathbb{K}.$$

Vice versa, let us suppose that $x^* \in \mathbb{K}$ is a solution to the stochastic variational inequality (11.7), but not an equilibrium solution according to random Cournot-Nash principle, namely there exists some $I \subseteq \Omega$ with $P(I) > 0$, such that for each $\omega \in I$, there is some $\bar{i} \in \{1, \ldots, m\}$ and $\widetilde{x}_{\bar{i}}(\omega)$ such that

$$v_{\bar{i}}(x^*(\omega)) < v_{\bar{i}}(\widetilde{x}_i, \hat{x}^*(\omega)).$$

Since the profit function $v_{\bar{i}}(x(\omega))$ is pseudoconcave with respect to $x_{\bar{i}}$, we have

$$\langle -\nabla_D v_{\bar{i}}(x^*(\omega)), \widetilde{x}_{\bar{i}}(\omega) - x^*_{\bar{i}}(\omega)\rangle < 0, \quad \mathrm{P-a.s.\ in}\ I. \tag{11.11}$$

Analogously to what done above, we can choose $x \in \mathbb{K}$ such that

$$x_i(\omega) = \begin{cases} x_i^*(\omega), & \text{in } \Omega \setminus \mathrm{I},\ \forall \mathrm{i} = 1,\ldots,\mathrm{m}, \\ x_i^*(\omega), & \text{in I, if } \mathrm{i} \neq \bar{\mathrm{i}}, \\ \widetilde{x}_i, & \text{in I, if } \mathrm{i} = \bar{\mathrm{i}}. \end{cases}$$

As a consequence, it results

$$\begin{aligned} &\int_\Omega \langle -\nabla_D v(x^*(\omega)), x(\omega) - x^*(\omega)\rangle \, dP_\omega \\ &\quad = \int_I \langle -\nabla_D v_{\bar{i}}(x^*(\omega)), \widetilde{x}_{\bar{i}}(\omega) - x^*_{\bar{i}}(\omega)\rangle \, dP_\omega < 0. \end{aligned}$$

Hence, we obtain the contradiction. □

11.3 Existence Results

This section is devoted to show some existence results for equilibrium distributions to the random oligopolistic market equilibrium problem. There are two standard approaches to the existence: with and without monotonicity assumptions (see [26]). We shall employ some definitions.

Let X be a reflexive Banach space over the reals, let K be a nonempty, closed and convex subset of X and let X^* be the dual space of X equipped with the weak* topology.

Definition 11.3.1 *Let $A : K \longrightarrow X^*$ be a mapping.*

- *The mapping is called pseudomonotone in the sense of Brezis (B-pseudomonotone) iff*

  1. *for each sequence $\{x_n\}_n$ weakly converging to x (in short $x_n \rightharpoonup x$) in K and such that $\limsup_n \langle A(x_n), x_n - x\rangle \le 0$, it results*

  $$\liminf_n \langle A(x_n), x_n - y\rangle \ge \langle A(x), x - y\rangle, \quad \forall y \in K;$$

  2. *for each $y \in \mathbb{K}$ the function $x \mapsto \langle A(x), x - y\rangle$ is lower bounded on the bounded subset of $\mathbb{K}$.*

- *The mapping is hemicontinuous in the sense of Fan (F-hemicontinuous) iff for every $y \in K$ the function $x \mapsto \langle A(x), x - y\rangle$ is weakly lower semicontinuous on K.*

Now, we set

$$A : L^2(\Omega, \mathbb{R}^{mn}, P) \longrightarrow L^2(\Omega, \mathbb{R}^{mn}, P),$$

$$A(x) = \left(-\frac{\partial v_i(x)}{\partial x_{ij}}\right)_{\substack{i=1,\dots,m \\ j=1,\dots,n}}, \quad \forall x \in L^2(\Omega, \mathbb{R}^{mn}, P).$$

The following existence result holds.

Theorem 11.3.2 *If A is B-pseudomonotone or F-hemicontinuous, then the stochastic variational inequality*

$$\ll A(x^*), x - x^* \gg_E \geq 0, \quad \forall x \in K, \tag{11.12}$$

admits a solution.

Proof. Let us note that K is clearly a nonempty, closed, convex and bounded subset of $L^2(\Omega, \mathbb{R}^{mn}, P)$ and, consequently, it is a weakly compact subset of $L^2(\Omega, \mathbb{R}^{mn}, P)$, being $L^2(\Omega, \mathbb{R}^{mn}, P)$ a reflexive Banach space. Then, the claim is achieved by applying Theorems 2.6 and 2.7 in [26]. □

In order to examine the monotone approach, we recall the following definitions.

Definition 11.3.3 *Let $A : K \longrightarrow X^*$ be a mapping.*

- *The mapping is called pseudomonotone in the sense of Karamardian (K-pseudomonotone) iff for every $x, y \in \mathbb{K}$*

$$\langle A(y), x - y \rangle \geq 0 \Rightarrow \langle A(x), x - y \rangle \geq 0.$$

- *The mapping is lower hemicontinuous along line segments, iff the function $\xi \mapsto \langle A(\xi), x - y \rangle$ is lower semicontinuous for every $x, y \in K$ on the line segments $[x, y]$.*

The following result holds.

Theorem 11.3.4 *If A is K-pseudomonotone and lower hemicontinuous along line segments, then the variational inequality* (11.12) *admits a solution.*

Proof. Since $\mathbb{K}$ is a weakly compact subset of $L^2(\Omega, \mathbb{R}^{mn}, P)$ and taking into account Corollary 3.7 in [26], we obtain the existence of an equilibrium distribution. □

Let us remark that if we assume that the profit function v is continuously differentiable and verifies the condition

$$\exists c > 0 : \ \|\nabla_D v(x(\omega))\| \leq c \|x(\omega)\|, \quad \forall x \in L^2(\Omega, \mathbb{R}^{mn}_+, P), \ \mathrm{P-a.s.},$$

then $\nabla_D v$ belongs to the class of Nemytskii operators and is lower hemicontinuous along line segments.

11.4 The Infinite-dimensional Duality Theory

We recall some results on the infinite-dimensional duality theory (see, for instance, [12, 15, 14, 17]).

Let X denote a real normed space, let X^* be its topological dual space and let C be a subset of X. Given an element $x \in \text{Cl}(C)$, the set:

$$T_C(x) = \left\{ h \in X : \; h = \lim_{n\to\infty} \lambda_n(x_n - x), \; \lambda_n > 0, \; x_n \in C, \; \forall n \in \mathbb{N}, \; \lim_{n\to\infty} x_n = x \right\}$$

is called the tangent cone to C at x.

Let X be a real linear topological space and let S be a nonempty convex subset of X and let $(Y, \|\cdot\|_Y)$ be a real normed space partially ordered by a convex cone C. Let $f : S \to \mathbb{R}$ and $g : S \to Y$ be two convex functions.

Let us consider the problem

$$\min_{x\in K} f(x), \tag{11.13}$$

where $K = \{x \in S : \; g(x) \in -C\}$, and the dual problem

$$\max_{\substack{u\in C^* \\ v\in Z^*}} \inf_{x\in S} \{f(x) + \langle u, g(x)\rangle\}, \tag{11.14}$$

where $C^* = \{u \in Y^* : \; \langle u, y\rangle \geq 0, \quad \forall y \in C\}$ is the dual cone of C.

We say that *Assumption S* is fulfilled at a point $x_0 \in K$ if and only if it results

$$T_{\widetilde{M}}(0, \theta_Y) \cap \left( ]-\infty, 0[\times \{\theta_Y\} \right) = \emptyset, \tag{11.15}$$

where $\widetilde{M} = \{(f(x) - f(x_0) + \alpha, g(x) + y) : \; x \in S \setminus K, \; \alpha \geq 0, \; y \in C\}$.

The following theorem holds (see [12]).

Theorem 11.4.1 *Under the above assumptions, if problem* (11.13) *is solvable and* Assumption S *is fulfilled at the extremal solution* $x_0 \in K$*, then also problem* (11.14) *is solvable, the extreme values of both problems are equal and if* $(x_0, \overline{u}) \in K \times C^*$ *is the optimal point of problem* (11.14)*, it results*

$$\langle \overline{u}, g(x_0)\rangle = 0.$$

It is worth to emphasize that *Assumption S*, besides being a sufficient condition, is also a necessary condition to guarantee the strong duality in every setting (see [9]).

Making use of Theorem 11.4.1, we are able to show the usual relationship between a saddle point of the so-called Lagrange functional

$$\mathcal{L}(x, u, v) = f(x) + \langle u, g(x)\rangle, \quad \forall x \in S, \; \forall u \in C^*, \tag{11.16}$$

and the solution of the constraint optimization problem (11.13) (see [12]).

Theorem 11.4.2 *Let us assume that the assumptions of Theorem* 11.4.1 *are satisfied. Then* $x_0 \in K$ *is a minimal solution to problem* (11.13) *if and only if there exists* $\overline{u} \in C^*$ *such that* $(x_0, \overline{u})$ *is a saddle point of the Lagrange functional* (11.16), *namely*

$$\mathcal{L}(x_0, u) \leq \mathcal{L}(x_0, \overline{u}) \leq \mathcal{L}(x, \overline{u}), \quad \forall x \in S, \ \forall u \in C^*,$$

and, moreover, it results

$$\langle \overline{u}, g(x_0) \rangle = 0. \tag{11.17}$$

11.5 The Lagrange Formulation of the Random Model

This section deals with the application of the infinite-dimensional duality theory [12, 14, 17] which has a reasonable role in the economical field in order to characterize the random oligopolistic market equilibrium conditions in terms of Lagrange multipliers. To this aim, we prove a preliminary lemma.

Lemma 11.5.1 *Let* $x^* \in \mathbb{K}$ *be a solution to the stochastic variational inequality* (11.7) *and let us set*

$$E_{ij}^- = \left\{ \omega \in \Omega : x_{ij}^*(\omega) = \underline{x}_{ij}(\omega) \right\}, \quad \forall i = 1, \ldots, m, \ \forall j = 1, \ldots, n,$$
$$E_{ij}^0 = \left\{ \omega \in \Omega : \underline{x}_{ij}(\omega) < x_{ij}^*(\omega) < \overline{x}_{ij}(\omega) \right\}, \quad \forall i = 1, \ldots, m, \ \forall j = 1, \ldots, n,$$
$$E_{ij}^+ = \left\{ \omega \in \Omega : x_{ij}^*(\omega) = \overline{x}_{ij}(\omega) \right\}, \quad \forall i = 1, \ldots, m, \ \forall j = 1, \ldots, n.$$

Then, we have

$$\frac{\partial v_i(\underline{x}(\omega))}{\partial x_{ij}} \leq 0, \quad P\text{-a.s. in } E_{ij}^-,$$
$$\frac{\partial v_i(x^*(\omega))}{\partial x_{ij}} = 0, \quad P\text{-a.s. in } E_{ij}^0,$$
$$\frac{\partial v_i(\overline{x}(\omega))}{\partial x_{ij}} \geq 0, \quad P\text{-a.s. in } E_{ij}^+.$$

Proof. It results

$$
\begin{aligned}
&\int_{\Omega} -\sum_{i=1}^{m}\sum_{j=1}^{n} \frac{\partial v_i(x^*(\omega))}{\partial x_{ij}}(x_{ij}(\omega)-x^*_{ij}(\omega))dP_\omega \\
&= \int_{E^-_{ij}} -\sum_{i=1}^{m}\sum_{j=1}^{n} \frac{\partial v_i(x^*(\omega))}{\partial x_{ij}}(x_{ij}(\omega)-\underline{x}_{ij}(\omega))dP_\omega \\
&+ \int_{E^0_{ij}} -\sum_{i=1}^{m}\sum_{j=1}^{n} \frac{\partial v_i(x^*(\omega))}{\partial x_{ij}}(x_{ij}(\omega)-x^*_{ij}(\omega))dP_\omega \\
&+ \int_{E^+_{ij}} -\sum_{i=1}^{m}\sum_{j=1}^{n} \frac{\partial v_i(x^*(\omega))}{\partial x_{ij}}(x_{ij}(\omega)-\overline{x}_{ij}(\omega))dP_\omega \geq 0, \quad \forall x \in \mathbb{K}.
\end{aligned}
$$

If we choose $x \in \mathbb{K}$ such that $x_{lr}(\omega) = x^*_{lr}(\omega)$ for $l \neq i$ and $r \neq j$, we have for every $\underline{x}_{ij}(\omega) \leq x_{ij}(\omega) \leq \overline{x}_{ij}(\omega), \quad \forall i = 1,\ldots,m, \ \forall j = 1,\ldots,n,$

$$
\begin{aligned}
&\int_{\Omega} -\frac{\partial v_i(x^*(\omega))}{\partial x_{ij}}(x_{ij}(\omega)-x^*_{ij}(\omega))dP_\omega \\
&= \int_{E^-_{ij}} -\frac{\partial v_i(x^*(\omega))}{\partial x_{ij}}(x_{ij}(\omega)-\underline{x}_{ij}(\omega))dP_\omega \\
&+ \int_{E^0_{ij}} -\frac{\partial v_i(x^*(\omega))}{\partial x_{ij}}(x_{ij}(\omega)-x^*_{ij}(\omega))dP_\omega \\
&+ \int_{E^+_{ij}} -\frac{\partial v_i(x^*(\omega))}{\partial x_{ij}}(x_{ij}(\omega)-\overline{x}_{ij}(\omega))dP_\omega \geq 0. \qquad (11.18)
\end{aligned}
$$

If we choose $x \in \mathbb{K}$ such that

$$
x_{ij}(\omega) \begin{cases} > \underline{x}_{ij}(\omega), & \text{in } E^-_{ij}, \\ = x^*_{ij}(\omega), & \text{in } E^0_{ij}, \\ = x^*_{ij}(\omega), & \text{in } E^+_{ij}, \end{cases}
$$

then, (11.18) becomes

$$
\begin{aligned}
&\int_{\Omega} -\frac{\partial v_i(x^*(\omega))}{\partial x_{ij}}(x_{ij}(\omega)-x^*_{ij}(\omega))dP_\omega \\
&= \int_{E^-_{ij}} -\frac{\partial v_i(x^*(\omega))}{\partial x_{ij}}(x_{ij}(\omega)-\underline{x}_{ij}(\omega))dP_\omega \geq 0. \qquad (11.19)
\end{aligned}
$$

Since $x_{ij}(\omega) > \underline{x}_{ij}(\omega)$, we obtain that $\frac{\partial v_i(x^*(\omega))}{\partial x_{ij}} \leq 0$. In fact if there exists a subset F of $E_{ij}^- \in \mathcal{A}$ with $P(F) > 0$ such that $\frac{\partial v_i(x^*(\omega))}{\partial x_{ij}} > 0$ in F, choosing

$$x_{ij}(\omega) \begin{cases} = \underline{x}_{ij}(\omega), & \text{in } E_{ij}^- \setminus F, \\ > \underline{x}_{ij}(\omega), & \text{in } F, \end{cases}$$

it follows

$$\int_\Omega -\frac{\partial v_i(x^*(\omega))}{\partial x_{ij}}(x_{ij}(\omega) - x_{ij}^*(\omega))dP_\omega = \int_F -\frac{\partial v_i(x^*(\omega))}{\partial x_{ij}}(x_{ij}(\omega) - \underline{x}_{ij}(\omega))dP_\omega < 0$$

which is in contradiction with (11.19).

Hence,

$$\frac{\partial v_i(\underline{x}(\omega))}{\partial x_{ij}} \leq 0, \quad \text{P-a.s. in } E_{ij}^-.$$

If we choose $x \in \mathbb{K}$ such that

$$x_{ij}(\omega) \begin{cases} = x_{ij}^*(\omega)), & \text{in } E_{ij}^-, \\ = x_{ij}^*(\omega), & \text{in } E_{ij}^0, \\ < \overline{x}_{ij}(\omega), & \text{in } E_{ij}^+, \end{cases}$$

then we can rewrite (11.18) as

$$\begin{aligned} &\int_\Omega -\frac{\partial v_i(x^*(\omega))}{\partial x_{ij}}(x_{ij}(\omega) - x_{ij}^*(\omega))dP_\omega \\ &\quad = \int_{E_{ij}^+} -\frac{\partial v_i(x^*(\omega))}{\partial x_{ij}}(x_{ij}(\omega) - \overline{x}_{ij}(\omega))dP_\omega \geq 0. \end{aligned} \tag{11.20}$$

Since $x_{ij}(\omega) < \overline{x}_{ij}(\omega)$, it results that $\frac{\partial v_i(x^*(\omega))}{\partial x_{ij}} \geq 0$. In fact if there exists a subset F of $E_{ij}^- \in \mathcal{A}$ with $P(F) > 0$ such that $\frac{\partial v_i(x^*(\omega))}{\partial x_{ij}} < 0$ in F, choosing

$$x_{ij}(\omega) \begin{cases} = \overline{x}_{ij}(\omega), & \text{in } E_{ij}^- \setminus F, \\ < \overline{x}_{ij}(\omega), & \text{in } F, \end{cases}$$

we have

$$\int_\Omega -\frac{\partial v_i(x^*(\omega))}{\partial x_{ij}}(x_{ij}(\omega) - x_{ij}^*(\omega))dP_\omega = \int_F -\frac{\partial v_i(x^*(\omega))}{\partial x_{ij}}(x_{ij}(\omega) - \overline{x}_{ij}(\omega))dP_\omega < 0$$

in contradiction with (11.20).

Hence,

$$\frac{\partial v_i(\underline{x}(\omega))}{\partial x_{ij}} \geq 0, \quad \text{P-a.s. in } E_{ij}^+.$$

In E_{ij}^0, proceeding in analogous manner of the previous cases, it can be easily proved that $\frac{\partial v_i(\underline{x}(\omega))}{\partial x_{ij}}$ cannot be either negative or positive on any set with positive probability. As a consequence,

$$\frac{\partial v_i(\underline{x}(\omega))}{\partial x_{ij}} = 0, \quad \text{P-a.s. in } E_{ij}^0.$$

□

Now, we are able to prove the following result.

Theorem 11.5.2 *$x^* \in \mathbb{K}$ is a random oligopolistic market equilibrium distribution if and only if for each $i = 1, \ldots, m$ and P-a.s. in Ω there exist $\alpha_{ij}^* \in L^2(\Omega)$, $\beta_{ij}^* \in L^2(\Omega)$ such that*

$$-\frac{\partial v_i(x^*(\omega))}{\partial x_{ij}} + \beta_{ij}^*(\omega) = \alpha_{ij}^*(\omega), \tag{11.21}$$

$$\alpha_{ij}^*(\omega)(\underline{x}_{ij}(\omega) - x_{ij}^*(\omega)) = 0, \qquad \alpha_{ij}^*(\omega) \geq 0, \tag{11.22}$$

$$\beta_{ij}^*(\omega)(x_{ij}^*(\omega) - \overline{x}_{ij}(\omega)) = 0, \qquad \beta_{ij}^*(\omega) \geq 0. \tag{11.23}$$

Proof. Let us assume that (11.21)–(11.23) hold. Then, taking into account that $\alpha_{ij}^*(\omega)(\underline{x}_{ij}(\omega) - x_{ij}^*(\omega)) = 0$ and $\beta_{ij}^*(\omega)(x_{ij}^*(\omega) - \overline{x}_{ij}(\omega)) = 0$, P-a.s., we have for every $x \in \mathbb{K}$, P-a.s.,

$$\begin{aligned}
&-\frac{\partial v_i(x^*(\omega))}{\partial x_{ij}}(x_{ij}(\omega) - x_{ij}^*(\omega)) \\
&= -\beta_{ij}^*(\omega)(x_{ij}(\omega) - x_{ij}^*(\omega)) + \alpha_{ij}^*(\omega)(x_{ij}(\omega) - x_{ij}^*(\omega)) \\
&= -\beta_{ij}^*(\omega)(x_{ij}(\omega) - \overline{x}_{ij}(\omega)) + \alpha_{ij}^*(\omega)(x_{ij}(\omega) - \underline{x}_{ij}(\omega)) \geq 0,
\end{aligned}$$

and, as a consequence, summing over $i = 1, \ldots, m$ and $j = 1, \ldots, n$, and integrating on Ω, it results

$$\int_\Omega \sum_{i=1}^m \sum_{j=1}^n -\frac{\partial v_i(x^*(\omega))}{\partial x_{ij}}(x_{ij}(\omega) - x_{ij}^*(\omega))dP_\omega \geq 0, \quad \forall x \in \mathbb{K}.$$

Hence, we obtain (11.7).

Vice versa, let $x^* \in \mathbb{K}$ be a solution to (11.7) and let us apply the infinite dimensional duality theory. First of all, let us prove that the Assumption S is fulfilled. To this aim, let us set, for $x \in L^2(\Omega, \mathbb{R}^{mn}, P)$,

$$\Psi(x) = \int_\Omega \sum_{i=1}^m \sum_{j=1}^n -\frac{\partial v_i(x^*(\omega))}{\partial x_{ij}}(x_{ij}(\omega) - x_{ij}^*(\omega))dP_\omega$$

and

$$\widetilde{M} = \Bigg\{ (\Psi(x)+\alpha, -x+\underline{x}+y, x-\overline{x}+u) : x \in L^2(\Omega,\mathbb{R}^{mn}_+,P)\setminus\mathbb{K},\ \alpha \geq 0,$$
$$y,u \in L^2(\Omega,\mathbb{R}^{mn}_+,P) \Bigg\}.$$

We must show that if $(l, \theta_{L^2(\Omega,\mathbb{R}^{mn}_+,P)}, \theta_{L^2(\Omega,\mathbb{R}^{mn}_+,P)})$ belongs to $T_{\widetilde{M}}(0, \theta_{L^2(\Omega,\mathbb{R}^{mn}_+,P)}, \theta_{L^2(\Omega,\mathbb{R}^{mn}_+,P)})$, namely

$$\lim_{n\to+\infty} \lambda_n(\Psi(x^n)+\alpha_n) = l,$$
$$\lim_{n\to+\infty} \lambda_n(-x^n+\underline{x}+y^n) = \theta_{L^2(\Omega,\mathbb{R}^{mn}_+,P)},$$
$$\lim_{n\to+\infty} \lambda_n(x^n-\overline{x}+u^n) = \theta_{L^2(\Omega,\mathbb{R}^{mn}_+,P)},$$

with $\lambda_n \geq 0$, $x^n \in L^2(\Omega,\mathbb{R}^{mn}_+,P)\setminus\mathbb{K}$, $\alpha_n \geq 0$, $y^n, u^n \in L^2(\Omega,\mathbb{R}^{mn}_+,P)$, $\forall n \in \mathbb{N}$, and

$$\lim_{n\to+\infty} (\Psi(x^n)+\alpha_n) = 0,$$
$$\lim_{n\to+\infty} (-x^n+\underline{x}+y^n) = \theta_{L^2(\Omega,\mathbb{R}^{mn}_+,P)},$$
$$\lim_{n\to+\infty} (x^n+\overline{x}+u^n) = \theta_{L^2(\Omega,\mathbb{R}^{mn}_+,P)},$$

then l is nonnegative.

As a consequence, it follows

$$\begin{aligned}
l &= \lim_{n\to+\infty} \lambda_n(\Psi(x^n)+\alpha_n) \\
&= \lim_{n\to+\infty} \lambda_n \left(\int_\Omega \sum_{i=1}^m \sum_{j=1}^n -\frac{\partial v_i(x^*(\omega))}{\partial x_{ij}} (x^n_{ij}(\omega)-x^*_{ij}(\omega))dP_\omega + \alpha_n \right) \\
&\geq \lim_{n\to+\infty} \lambda_n \Bigg(\int_{E^-_{ij}} \sum_{i=1}^m \sum_{j=1}^n -\frac{\partial v_i(x^*(\omega))}{\partial x_{ij}} (x^n_{ij}(\omega)-\underline{x}_{ij}(\omega))dP_\omega \\
&\quad + \int_{E^0_{ij}} \sum_{i=1}^m \sum_{j=1}^n -\frac{\partial v_i(x^*(\omega))}{\partial x_{ij}} (x^n_{ij}(\omega)-x^*_{ij}(\omega))dP_\omega \\
&\quad + \int_{E^+_{ij}} \sum_{i=1}^m \sum_{j=1}^n -\frac{\partial v_i(x^*(\omega))}{\partial x_{ij}} (x^n_{ij}(\omega)-\overline{x}_{ij}(\omega))dP_\omega \Bigg).
\end{aligned}$$

We can note that

$$\lim_{n\to+\infty} \lambda_n \int_{E^0_{ij}} \sum_{i=1}^m \sum_{j=1}^n -\frac{\partial v_i(x^*(\omega))}{\partial x_{ij}} (x^n_{ij}(\omega)-x^*_{ij}(\omega))dP_\omega = 0, \tag{11.24}$$

being $-\dfrac{\partial v_i(x^*(\omega))}{\partial x_{ij}} = 0$, P-a.s. in E_{ij}^0, $\forall i = 1, \dots, m$, $\forall j = 1, \dots, n$.

We will prove that

$$\lim_{n\to+\infty} \lambda_n \int_{E_{ij}^-} \sum_{i=1}^{m}\sum_{j=1}^{n} -\frac{\partial v_i(\underline{x}(\omega)))}{\partial x_{ij}}(x_{ij}^n(\omega) - \underline{x}_{ij}(\omega))dP_\omega \geq 0, \tag{11.25}$$

$$\lim_{n\to+\infty} \lambda_n \int_{E_{ij}^+} \sum_{i=1}^{m}\sum_{j=1}^{n} -\frac{\partial v_i(\overline{x}(\omega))}{\partial x_{ij}}(x_{ij}^n(\omega) - \overline{x}_{ij}(\omega))dP_\omega \geq 0. \tag{11.26}$$

In fact, it results

$$\begin{aligned}
&\lim_{n\to+\infty} \lambda_n \int_{E_{ij}^-} \sum_{i=1}^{m}\sum_{j=1}^{n} -\frac{\partial v_i(\underline{x}(\omega))}{\partial x_{ij}}(x_{ij}^n(\omega) - \underline{x}_{ij}(\omega))dP_\omega \\
&= \lim_{n\to+\infty} \lambda_n \int_{E_{ij}^-} \sum_{i=1}^{m}\sum_{j=1}^{n} \Bigg(-\frac{\partial v_i(\underline{x}(\omega))}{\partial x_{ij}}(x_{ij}^n(\omega) - \underline{x}_{ij}(\omega) - y_{ij}^n(\omega)) \\
&\quad - \frac{\partial v_i(\underline{x}(\omega))}{\partial x_{ij}}(y_{ij}^n(\omega)) \Bigg) dP_\omega
\end{aligned}$$

By virtue of the previous remarks and Lemma 11.5.1, by using the properties of the tangent cone, we obtain the inequality (11.25) and, with analogous considerations, we have the inequality (11.26).

Therefore, thanks to (11.24), (11.25) and (11.26), it follows that

$$\begin{aligned}
l &= \lim_{n\to+\infty} \lambda_n(\Psi(x^n) + \alpha_n) \\
&= \lim_{n\to+\infty} \lambda_n \left(\int_\Omega \sum_{i=1}^{m}\sum_{j=1}^{n} -\frac{\partial v_i(x^*(\omega))}{\partial x_{ij}}(x_{ij}^n(\omega) - x_{ij}^*(\omega))dP_\omega + \alpha_n \right)
\end{aligned}$$

is nonnegative.

Taking into account Theorems 11.4.1 and 11.4.2, if we consider the Lagrange function

$$\begin{aligned}
\mathcal{L}(x,\alpha,\beta) =& \Psi(x) + \sum_{i=1}^{m}\sum_{j=1}^{n} \int_\Omega \alpha_{ij}(\omega)(\underline{x}_{ij}(\omega) - x_{ij}(\omega))dP_\omega \\
&+ \sum_{i=1}^{m}\sum_{j=1}^{n} \int_\Omega \beta_{ij}(\omega)(x_{ij}(\omega) - \overline{x}_{ij}(\omega))dP_\omega,
\end{aligned}$$

for every $x \in L^2(\Omega, \mathbb{R}_+^{mn}, P)$, $\alpha, \beta \in L^2(\Omega, \mathbb{R}_+^{mn}, P)$, we have that there exist $\alpha^*, \beta^* \in L^2(\Omega, \mathbb{R}_+^{mn}, P)$ such that

$$\mathcal{L}(x^*, \alpha, \beta) \leq \mathcal{L}(x^*, \alpha^*, \beta^*) \leq \mathcal{L}(x, \alpha^*, \beta^*), \tag{11.27}$$

for every $x \in L^2(\Omega,\mathbb{R}^{mn}_+,P)$, $\alpha,\beta \in L^2(\Omega,\mathbb{R}^{mn}_+,P)$, and

$$\langle\langle \alpha^*, \underline{x}-x^* \rangle\rangle = \int_\Omega \sum_{i=1}^m \sum_{j=1}^n \alpha^*_{ij}(\omega)(\underline{x}_{ij}(\omega)-x^*_{ij}(\omega))dP_\omega = 0,$$

$$\langle\langle \beta^*, x^*-\overline{x} \rangle\rangle = \int_\Omega \sum_{i=1}^m \sum_{j=1}^n \beta^*_{ij}(\omega)(x^*_{ij}(\omega)-\overline{x}_{ij}(\omega))dP_\omega = 0.$$

Hence, we have

$$\alpha^*_{ij}(\omega)(\underline{x}_{ij}(\omega)-x^*_{ij}(\omega)) = 0, \quad \forall i=1,\dots,m, \ \forall j=1,\dots,n, \tag{11.28}$$

$$\beta^*_{ij}(\omega)(x^*_{ij}(\omega)-\overline{x}_{ij}(\omega)) = 0, \quad \forall i=1,\dots,m, \ \forall j=1,\dots,n. \tag{11.29}$$

Then, for conditions (11.28), (11.29), $\mathcal{L}(x^*,\alpha^*,\beta^*)=0$, by virtue of the right-hand side of (11.27) and the equalities (11.28), (11.29), we obtain

$$\begin{aligned}\mathcal{L}(x,\alpha^*,\beta^*) =& \sum_{i=1}^m \sum_{j=1}^n \int_\Omega -\frac{\partial v_i(x^*(\omega))}{\partial x_{ij}}(x_{ij}(\omega)-x^*_{ij}(\omega))dP_\omega \\ & -\sum_{i=1}^m \sum_{j=1}^n \int_\Omega \alpha^*_{ij}(\omega)(x_{ij}(\omega)-x^*_{ij}(\omega))dP_\omega \\ & +\sum_{i=1}^m \sum_{j=1}^n \int_\Omega \beta^*_{ij}(\omega)(x_{ij}(\omega)-x^*_{ij}(\omega))dP_\omega \\ \geq & \mathcal{L}(x^*,\alpha^*,\beta^*) = 0, \qquad \forall x \in L^2(\Omega,\mathbb{R}^{mn}_+,P).\end{aligned}$$

Then, $\mathcal{L}(x,\alpha^*,\beta^*)$ has a minimal point in x^*.

Let $x^1 = x^*+\varepsilon$ and $x^2 = x^*-\varepsilon$, for every $\varepsilon \in L^2(\Omega,\mathbb{R}^{mn}_+,P)$. We observe that

$$\mathcal{L}(x^1,\alpha^*,\beta^*) = \sum_{i=1}^m \sum_{j=1}^n \int_\Omega \left(-\frac{\partial v_i(x^*(\omega))}{\partial x_{ij}} - \alpha^*_{ij}(\omega)+\beta^*_{ij}(\omega)\right)\varepsilon_{ij}(\omega)dP_\omega \geq 0,$$
$$\forall \varepsilon \in L^2(\Omega,\mathbb{R}^{mn}_+,P),$$

and

$$\mathcal{L}(x^2,\alpha^*,\beta^*) = -\left\{\sum_{i=1}^m \sum_{j=1}^n \int_\Omega \left(-\frac{\partial v_i(x^*(\omega))}{\partial x_{ij}} - \alpha^*_{ij}(\omega)+\beta^*_{ij}(\omega)\right)\varepsilon_{ij}(\omega)dP_\omega\right\} \geq 0,$$
$$\forall \varepsilon \in L^2(\Omega,\mathbb{R}^{mn}_+,P),$$

from which it results

$$\sum_{i=1}^m \sum_{j=1}^n \int_\Omega \left(-\frac{\partial v_i(x^*(\omega))}{\partial x_{ij}} - \alpha^*_{ij}(\omega)+\beta^*_{ij}(\omega)\right)\varepsilon_{ij}(\omega)dP_\omega = 0, \ \forall \varepsilon \in L^2(\Omega,\mathbb{R}^{mn}_+,P).$$

For the arbitrariness of $\varepsilon \in L^2(\Omega, \mathbb{R}^{mn}_+, P)$, it follows

$$-\frac{\partial v_i(x^*(\omega))}{\partial x_{ij}} - \alpha^*_{ij}(\omega) + \beta^*_{ij}(\omega) = 0, \quad \forall i = 1,\ldots,m,\ \forall j = 1,\ldots,n,\ P-\text{a.s.}$$

□

Conditions (11.21)–(11.23) give the optimal distribution pattern for the firm P_i. The terms $\alpha^*_{ij}(\omega)$ and $\beta^*_{ij}(\omega)$ are the Lagrange multipliers associated to the constraints $x^*_{ij}(\omega) \geq \underline{x}_{ij}(\omega)$, $x^*_{ij}(\omega) \leq \overline{x}_{ij}(\omega)$, respectively. They, as it is well known, have a topical importance on the understanding and the management of the market. In fact, for a fixed outcome $\omega \in \Omega$, it results:

(a) if $\alpha^*_{ij}(\omega) > 0$ then, using (11.22), we have $x^*_{ij}(\omega) = \underline{x}_{ij}(\omega)$, namely the commodity shipment between the firm P_i and the demand market Q_j is minimum;

(b) if $x^*_{ij}(\omega) > \underline{x}_{ij}(\omega)$ then, taking into account (11.22), $\alpha^*_{ij}(\omega) = 0$ and, making use of (11.21), it results $\beta^*_{ij}(\omega) = \dfrac{\partial v_i(x^*(\omega))}{\partial x_{ij}}$, namely $\beta^*_{ij}(\omega)$ is equal to the marginal utility function;

(c) if $\beta^*_{ij}(\omega) > 0$ then, using (11.23), we have $x^*_{ij}(\omega) = \overline{x}_{ij}(\omega)$, namely the commodity shipment between the firm P_i and the demand market Q_j is maximum;

(d) if $x^*_{ij}(\omega) < \overline{x}_{ij}(\omega)$ then, making use of (11.23), $\beta^*_{ij}(\omega) = 0$ and, taking into account (11.21), we obtain $\alpha^*_{ij}(\omega) = -\dfrac{\partial v_i(x^*(\omega))}{\partial x_{ij}}$, namely $\alpha^*_{ij}(\omega)$ is equal to the opposite of the marginal utility function.

11.6 The Inverse Problem

In this section, we analyze the policymaker's point of view of the random oligopolistic market equilibrium problem and present a stochastic optimal control equilibrium problem. In particular, we exchange the point of view in the analysis of the problem by introducing an optimal control problem in which the random variable h represents the difference between the random supply tax η and the random incentive pay λ for the transactions. Consequently, the term h which is a fixed parameter in Section 11.2, is here a variable. Now, it is possible to control the random resource exportations $x(\omega, h(\omega))$ at firms by adjusting taxes $h(\omega)$. In this perspective, the random tax adjustment is an efficient means of regulating exportation. In particular, if the policymaker wants to restrict the exportation and, hence, the production of a certain commodity, then the government will impose higher taxes, otherwise if the policymaker wants to encourage the exportation of a certain commodity, the government will give subsidies.

Let $x(h) = x(\omega, h(\omega))$ be the random function of regulatory taxes, with $h(\omega) \in \mathbb{R}^{mn}$, P-a.s. We suppose that $x(\omega, h(\omega))$ is a Carathéodory function and there exists $\gamma(\omega) \in L^2(\Omega, P)$ such that

$$\|x(\omega, h(\omega))\|_{mn} \leq \gamma(\omega) + \|h(\omega)\|_{mn}, \quad \forall h \in L^2(\Omega, \mathbb{R}^{mn}_+, P),\ P-\text{a.s.} \tag{11.30}$$

The set of feasible states is given by

$$W = \left\{ w \in L^2([0,T], \mathbb{R}^{mn}, P) : \underline{x}_{ij}(t) \leq w_{ij}(t) \leq \overline{x}_{ij}(t), \right.$$
$$\left. \forall i = 1, \ldots, m,\ \forall j = 1, \ldots, n,\ P-\text{a.s.} \right\},$$

and the random optimal regulatory tax as follows.

Definition 11.6.1 *A random regulatory tax $h^* \in L^2(\Omega, \mathbb{R}^{mn}_+, P)$ is an optimal regulatory tax if $x(h^*) \in \Omega$ and for $i = 1, \ldots, m$, $j = 1, \ldots, n$ and P-a.s. the following conditions hold:*

$$x_{ij}(\omega, h^*(\omega)) = \underline{x}_{ij}(\omega) \quad \Rightarrow \quad h^*_{ij}(\omega) \leq 0, \tag{11.31}$$
$$\underline{x}_{ij}(\omega) < x_{ij}(\omega, h^*(\omega)) < \overline{x}_{ij}(\omega) \quad \Rightarrow \quad h^*_{ij}(\omega) = 0, \tag{11.32}$$
$$x_{ij}(\omega, h^*(\omega)) = \overline{x}_{ij}(\omega) \quad \Rightarrow \quad h^*_{ij}(\omega) \geq 0. \tag{11.33}$$

Definition 11.6.1 must be interpreted as follows: the random optimal regulatory tax h^* is such that the corresponding state $x(\omega, h^*(\omega))$ has to satisfy capacity constraints, namely $x(\omega, h^*(\omega)) \in \Omega$. Moreover, if $x_{ij}(\omega, h^*(\omega)) = \underline{x}_{ij}(\omega)$, then it means to encourage the random exportations, namely the random optimal choice is that taxes must be less than or equal to the random incentive pays. If $x_{ij}(\omega, h^*(\omega)) = \overline{x}_{ij}(\omega)$, then the random exportations must be reduced, hence random taxes must be greater than or equal to the random incentive pays. Finally, if $\underline{x}_{ij}(\omega) < x_{ij}(t, h^*(\omega)) < \overline{x}_{ij}(\omega)$ is satisfied, random taxes equal random incentive pays.

Next, we establish the stochastic inverse variational inequality formulation of the random optimal equilibrium control problem.

Theorem 11.6.2 *A random regulatory tax $h^* \in L^2(\Omega, \mathbb{R}^{mn}_+, P)$ is a random optimal regulatory tax if and only if it solves the stochastic inverse variational inequality*

$$\int_\Omega \sum_{i=1}^{m} \sum_{j=1}^{n} \left(w_{ij}(\omega) - x_{ij}(\omega, h^*(\omega)) \right) h^*_{ij}(\omega) dP_\omega \leq 0, \quad \forall w \in W. \tag{11.34}$$

Proof. We consider a random optimal regulatory tax h^* and $w \in W$. For $i \in \{1, \ldots, m\}$ and $j \in \{1, \ldots, n\}$ fixed, we have that $\underline{x}_{ij}(\omega) \leq w_{ij}(\omega) \leq \overline{x}_{ij}(\omega)$, P-a.s. The following cases can occur:

1. if $x_{ij}(\omega,h^*(\omega)) = \underline{x}_{ij}(\omega)$, P-a.s., making use of (11.31) it results that $h^*_{ij}(\omega) \leq 0$, P-a.s., and, then, $\left(w_{ij}(\omega) - x_{ij}(\omega,h^*(\omega))\right) h^*_{ij}(\omega) \leq 0$, P-a.s.;
2. if $\underline{x}_{ij}(\omega) < x_{ij}(\omega,h^*(\omega)) < \overline{x}_{ij}(\omega)$, P-a.s., by (11.31) we obtain $h^*_{ij}(\omega) = 0$, P-a.s., and, hence, $\left(w_{ij}(\omega) - x_{ij}(t,h^*(\omega))\right) h^*_{ij}(\omega) = 0$, P-a.s.;
3. if $x_{ij}(\omega,h^*(\omega)) = \overline{x}_{ij}(\omega)$, P-a.s., taking into account (11.31) it follows that $h^*_{ij}(\omega) \geq 0$, P-a.s., and, consequently, $\left(w_{ij}(\omega) - x_{ij}(\omega,h^*(\omega))\right) h^*_{ij}(\omega) \leq 0$, P-a.s.

In any case, for every $i \in \{1,\ldots,m\}$, for every $j \in \{1,\ldots,n\}$ and for every $w \in W$, we deduce

$$\left(w_{ij}(\omega) - x_{ij}(\omega,h^*(\omega))\right) h^*_{ij}(\omega) \leq 0, \quad P-\text{a.s.}$$

By summing over $i \in \{1,\ldots,m\}, j \in \{1,\ldots,n\}$ and integrating on Ω, we have the stochastic inverse variational inequality (11.34).

Vice versa, we suppose that h^* satisfies the stochastic inverse variational inequality (11.34). Fixing $i \in \{1,\ldots,m\}$, $j \in \{1,\ldots,n\}$, setting $w_{hk}(\omega) = x_{ij}(\omega,h^*(\omega))$, P-a.s., for every $h \neq i$, $k \neq j$ and using (11.34), we obtain

$$\int_\Omega \left(w_{ij}(\omega) - x_{ij}(\omega,h^*(\omega))\right) h^*_{ij}(\omega) dP_\omega \leq 0, \qquad \forall w_{ij}(\omega) \in L^2(\Omega,P): \quad (11.35)$$
$$\underline{x}_{ij}(\omega) \leq w_{ij}(\omega) \leq \overline{x}_{ij}(\omega).$$

We show that if $x_{ij}(\omega,h^*(\omega)) = \underline{x}_{ij}(\omega)$, P-a.s., then, $h^*_{ij}(\omega) \leq 0$, P-a.s. By contradiction, we assume that there exists a set $\Xi \subseteq \Omega$, with $P(\Xi) > 0$, such that $h^*_{ij}(\omega) > 0$, P-a.s. in Ξ. Choosing

$$w_{ij}(\omega) = \begin{cases} \overline{x}_{ij}(\omega), & P-\text{a.s. in } \Xi, \\ x_{ij}(\omega,h^*(\omega)), & P-\text{a.s. in } \Omega \setminus \Xi, \end{cases}$$

it results

$$\int_\Omega \left(w_{ij}(\omega) - x_{ij}(\omega,h^*(\omega))\right) h^*_{ij}(\omega) dP_\omega = \int_\Xi (\overline{x}_{ij}(\omega) - \underline{x}_{ij}(\omega)) h^*_{ij}(\omega) dP_\omega > 0,$$

which contradicts (11.35).

Moreover we prove that if $x_{ij}(\omega,h^*(\omega)) = \overline{x}_{ij}(\omega)$, P-a.s., then $h^*_{ij}(\omega) \geq 0$, P-a.s. By contradiction, we assume that there exists a set $\Sigma \subseteq \Omega$, with $P(\Sigma) > 0$, such that $h^*_{ij}(\omega) < 0$, P-a.s. in Σ. Choosing

$$\omega_{ij}(\omega) = \begin{cases} \underline{x}_{ij}(\omega), & \omega \in \Sigma, \\ x_{ij}(\omega,h^*(\omega)), & P-\text{a.s. in } \Omega \setminus \Sigma, \end{cases}$$

it follows

$$\int_\Omega \left(w_{ij}(\omega) - x_{ij}(\omega,h^*(\omega))\right) h^*_{ij}(\omega) dP_\omega = \int_\Sigma (\underline{x}_{ij}(\omega) - \overline{x}_{ij}(\omega)) h^*_{ij}(\omega) dP_\omega > 0,$$

which contradicts (11.35).

Finally, if $\underline{x}_{ij}(\omega) < x_{ij}(\omega, h^*(\omega)) < \overline{x}_{ij}(\omega)$, P-a.s., making use of the same procedures as in the previous cases, it can be easily shown that $h^*(\omega) = 0$, P-a.s. □

We present a classical stochastic variational inequality formulation of the random optimal equilibrium control problem. Thanks to such a formulation, we are able to use all the theoretical and numerical results of the theory of stochastic variational inequalities to deal fully with the problem. Let us set

$$Z = L^2(\Omega, \mathbb{R}^{mn}_+, P) \times \Omega, \qquad F : \Omega \times Z \to L^2(\Omega, \mathbb{R}^{2mn}_+, P),$$

$$z(\omega) = \begin{pmatrix} h(\omega) \\ w(\omega) \end{pmatrix}, \qquad F(\omega, z(\omega)) = \begin{pmatrix} w(\omega) - x(\omega, h(\omega)) \\ -h(\omega) \end{pmatrix}.$$

We remark that Z is a closed, convex and not bounded subset of $L^2(\Omega, \mathbb{R}^{2mn}_+, P)$. It is possible to prove that the stochastic inverse variational inequality (11.34) is equivalent to a stochastic variational inequality, as the following result states.

Theorem 11.6.3 *The stochastic inverse variational inequality* (11.34) *is equivalent to the stochastic variational inequality*

$$\int_\Omega \sum_{l=1}^{2m} \sum_{j=1}^{n} F_{lj}(\omega, z^*(\omega)) \left(z_{lj}(\omega) - z^*_{lj}(\omega)\right) dP_\omega \geq 0, \quad \forall z \in Z. \tag{11.36}$$

Proof. Let us assume that (11.36) holds true. As a consequence, we have $z^* = (h^*, w^*)^T \in Z$, and

$$\int_\Omega \left(\sum_{i=1}^{m} \sum_{j=1}^{n} (w^*_{ij}(t) - x_{ij}(\omega, h^*(\omega)))(h_{ij}(\omega) - h^*_{ij}(\omega)) \right) dP_\omega$$
$$- \int_\Omega \left(\sum_{i=1}^{m} \sum_{j=1}^{n} h^*_{ij}(\omega)(w_{ij}(\omega) - w^*_{ij}(\omega)) \right) dP_\omega \geq 0, \ \forall z = (h, w)^T \in Z. \tag{11.37}$$

Let us set $h(\omega) = h^*(\omega) - w^*(\omega) + x(\omega, h^*(\omega))$ and $w(\omega) = w^*(\omega)$ in (11.37). Hence, we obtain

$$- \int_\Omega \sum_{i=1}^{m} \sum_{j=1}^{n} (w^*_{ij}(\omega) - x_{ij}(\omega, h^*(\omega)))^2 dP_\omega \geq 0,$$

then $x(\omega, h^*(\omega)) = w^*(\omega)$, P-a.s. Consequently $x(\omega, h^*(\omega)) \in W$ and, by (11.37), (11.34) follows.

Vice versa, if $h^* \in L^2(\Omega, \mathbb{R}^{mn}_+, P)$ is a solution of (11.34), then $z^* = (h^*(\omega), x(\omega, h^*))^T \in Z$ is a solution to (11.36). In fact

$$\underbrace{\int_\Omega \sum_{i=1}^m \sum_{j=1}^n (x_{ij}(\omega, h^*(\omega)) - x_{ij}(\omega, h^*(\omega)))(h_{ij}(\omega) - h^*_{ij}(\omega))dP_\omega}_{=0}$$

$$\underbrace{-\int_\Omega \sum_{i=1}^m \sum_{j=1}^n h^*_{ij}(\omega)(w_{ij}(\omega) - x_{ij}(\omega, h^*(\omega)))dP_\omega}_{\geq 0} \geq 0.$$

□

Thanks to the equivalence established above, we can rewrite analogous existence results as in Section 11.3 for the random optimal equilibrium control problem.

11.7 A Numerical Example

An example of random oligopolistic market equilibrium problem which emphasizes the central role in the study of the model of the uncertainty is provided. To this aim, let us analyze an economic network made up of two firms and two demand markets, as in Figure 11.1.

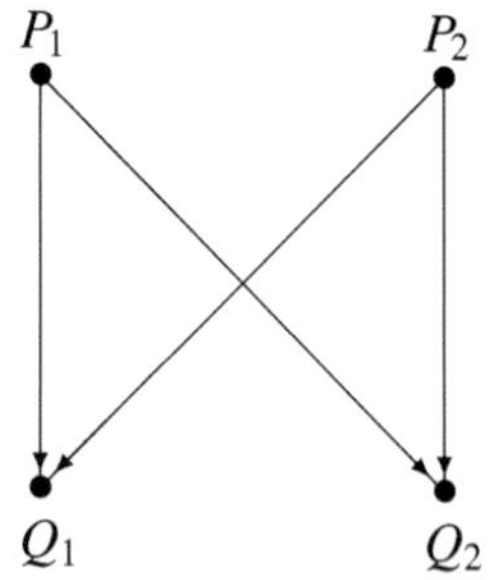

Figure 11.1: Network structure of the numerical random spatial oligopoly problem.

Let us introduce the set of feasible vectors $x \in L^2(\Omega, \mathbb{R}^4_+, P)$ as

$$\mathbb{K} = \left\{ x \in L^2(\Omega, \mathbb{R}^4_+, P) : \ x_{ij}(\omega) \geq 0, \ \ \forall i = 1,2, \ \forall j = 1,2, \ \mathrm{P-a.s.} \right\}.$$

Let us consider the profit function $v \in L^2(L^2(\Omega, \mathbb{R}^4, P), \mathbb{R}^2)$ given by

$$\begin{aligned} v_1(x(\omega)) =& \frac{3}{2}x_{11}^2(\omega) + x_{12}^2(\omega) + x_{11}(\omega)x_{12}(\omega) + x_{12}(\omega)x_{21}(\omega) - \alpha_1 x_{11}(\omega) \\ &- \rho_1 x_{12}(\omega), \\ v_2(x(\omega)) =& \frac{3}{2}x_{21}^2(\omega) + \frac{1}{2}x_{22}^2(\omega) + x_{12}(\omega)x_{21}(\omega) + x_{11}(\omega)x_{22}(\omega) + x_{12}(\omega)x_{22}(\omega) \\ &- \alpha_2 x_{21}(\omega) - \rho_2 x_{22}(\omega), \end{aligned}$$

where α_1 and α_2 are random variables uniformly distributed in the intervals $[95, 100]$ and $[0, 5]$, respectively, and ρ_1 and ρ_2 are two constants such that $35 \leq \rho_1 \leq 190$ and $2\rho_1 - 5\rho_2 \leq -100$. We assume that α_1 and α_2 are independent of random variables. Their densities are

$$f_{\alpha_1}(x) = \begin{cases} \frac{1}{5}, & 95 \leq x \leq 100, \\ 0, & \text{elsewhere}, \end{cases} \tag{11.38}$$

and

$$f_{\alpha_2}(x) = \begin{cases} \frac{1}{5}, & 0 \leq x \leq 5, \\ 0, & \text{elsewhere}, \end{cases} \tag{11.39}$$

respectively. As a consequence, the operator $-\nabla_D v \in L^2([0,1] \times L^2([0,1], \mathbb{R}^4), \mathbb{R}^4)$ is given by

$$-\nabla_D v(x(\omega)) = \begin{bmatrix} -3x_{11}(\omega) - x_{12}(\omega) + \alpha_1 & -x_{11}(\omega) - 2x_{12}(\omega) - x_{21}(\omega) + \rho_1 \\ -x_{12}(\omega) - 3x_{21}(\omega) + \alpha_2, & -x_{11}(\omega) - x_{12}(\omega) - x_{22}(\omega) + \rho_2 \end{bmatrix}.$$

The governing stochastic variational inequality is the following problem:

$$\ll -\nabla_D v(x^*), x - x^* \gg_E \geq 0, \quad \forall x \in \mathbb{K}. \tag{11.40}$$

Applying the direct method (see [25]), we have to solve the following system

$$\begin{cases} -3x_{11}^*(\omega) - x_{12}^*(\omega) + \alpha_1 = 0, \\ -x_{11}^*(\omega) - 2x_{12}^*(\omega) - x_{21}^*(\omega) + \rho_1 = 0, \\ -x_{12}^*(\omega) - 3x_{21}^*(\omega) + \alpha_2 = 0, \\ -x_{11}^*(\omega) - x_{12}^*(\omega) - x_{22}^*(\omega) + \rho_2 = 0. \end{cases} \tag{11.41}$$

Then we obtain that the solution to (11.41) is

$$\begin{cases} x_{11}^*(\omega) = \frac{1}{12}(5\alpha_1 + \alpha_2 - 3\rho_1), \\ x_{12}^*(\omega) = \frac{1}{4}(-\alpha_1 - \alpha_2 + 3\rho_1), \\ x_{21}^*(\omega) = \frac{1}{12}(\alpha_1 + 5\alpha_2 - 3\rho_1), \\ x_{22}^*(\omega) = \frac{1}{6}(-\alpha_1 + \alpha_2 - 3\rho_1 - 6\rho_2). \end{cases} \tag{11.42}$$

Since $x^*_{ij}(\omega) \geq 0$, for $i = 1,2,\ j = 1,2$, it results

$$\begin{cases} 5\alpha_1 + \alpha_2 \geq 3\rho_1, \\ \alpha_1 + \alpha_2 \leq 3\rho_1, \\ \alpha_1 + 5\alpha_2 \geq 3\rho_1, \\ \alpha_1 - \alpha_2 \leq -3\rho_1 - 6\rho_2. \end{cases} \tag{11.43}$$

Moreover, the densities of the random variables $5\alpha_1+\alpha_2, \alpha_1+\alpha_2, \alpha_1+5\alpha_2, \alpha_1-\alpha_2$ are:

$$f_{5\alpha_1+\alpha_2}(x) = \begin{cases} \dfrac{x-475}{125}, & 475 \leq x \leq 480, \\ \dfrac{1}{25}, & 480 < x \leq 500, \\ \dfrac{505-x}{125}, & 500 < x \leq 505, \\ 0, & \text{elsewhere}, \end{cases}$$

$$f_{\alpha_1+\alpha_2}(x) = \begin{cases} \dfrac{x-95}{25}, & 95 \leq x \leq 100, \\ \dfrac{105-x}{25}, & 100 < x \leq 105, \\ 0, & \text{elsewhere}, \end{cases}$$

$$f_{\alpha_1+5\alpha_2}(x) = \begin{cases} \dfrac{x-95}{125}, & 95 \leq x \leq 100, \\ \dfrac{1}{25}, & 100 < x \leq 120, \\ \dfrac{125-x}{125}, & 120 < x \leq 125, \\ 0, & \text{elsewhere}, \end{cases}$$

$$f_{\alpha_1-\alpha_2}(x) = \begin{cases} \dfrac{x-90}{25}, & 90 \leq x \leq 95, \\ \dfrac{100-x}{25}, & 95 < x \leq 100, \\ 0, & \text{elsewhere}, \end{cases}$$

respectively. It is clear that (11.42) is not a solution because the event $x^*_{21}(\omega) \geq 0$ is not P-a.s. true for $35 \leq \rho_1 \leq 190$. As a consequence, let us consider the new set of feasible vectors $x \in L^2(\Omega, \mathbb{R}^4_+, P)$ given by

$$\tilde{\mathbb{K}} = \Big\{ x \in L^2(\Omega, \mathbb{R}^4_+, P) : x_{ij}(\omega) \geq 0,\ \forall i = 1,2,\ \forall j = 1,2,\ (i,j) \neq (2,1),\ \mathrm{P-a.s.} \\ x_{21}(t) = 0,\ P-\text{a.s.} \Big\}. \tag{11.44}$$

Now, we solve the following system:

$$\begin{cases} -3x^*_{11}(\omega) - x^*_{12}(\omega) + \alpha_1 = 0, \\ -x^*_{11}(\omega) - 2x^*_{12}(\omega) + \rho_1 = 0, \\ x^*_{21}(\omega) = 0, \\ -x^*_{11}(\omega) - x^*_{12}(\omega) - x^*_{22}(\omega) + \rho_2 = 0. \end{cases} \tag{11.45}$$

We obtain that the solution to (11.45) is

$$\begin{cases} x^*_{11}(\omega) = \frac{1}{5}(2\alpha_1 - \rho_1), \\ x^*_{12}(\omega) = \frac{1}{5}(-\alpha_1 + 3\rho_1), \\ x^*_{21}(\omega) = 0, \\ x^*_{22}(\omega) = \frac{1}{5}(-\alpha_1 - 2\rho_1 + 5\rho_2), \end{cases}$$

under the following conditions:

$$\begin{cases} \alpha_1 \geq \frac{1}{2}\rho_1, \\ \alpha_1 \leq 3\rho_1, \\ \alpha_1 \leq -2\rho_1 + 5\rho_2, \\ \alpha_1 + 5\alpha_2 \leq 8\rho_1. \end{cases} \tag{11.46}$$

Let us remark that the last condition in (11.46) is assumed to characterize the solutions in a face of the convex set $\mathbb{K}$. Here, it results

$$P\left(\alpha_1 \geq \frac{1}{2}\rho_1\right) = P(\alpha_1 \leq 3\rho_1) = P(\alpha_1 \leq -2\rho_1 + 5\rho_2) = P(\alpha_1 + 5\alpha_2 \leq 8\rho_1) = 1,$$

namely the solution belongs to the new constraints set $\tilde{\mathbb{K}}$. As a consequence, the random equilibrium solution is

$$x^*(\omega) = \begin{pmatrix} \frac{1}{5}(2\alpha_1 - \rho_1) & \frac{1}{5}(-\alpha_1 + 3\rho_1) \\ 0 & \frac{1}{5}(-\alpha_1 - 2\rho_1 + 5\rho_2) \end{pmatrix}.$$

Moreover, the expected value of the solution is

$$E(x^*) = \begin{pmatrix} \frac{1}{5}(195 - \rho_1) & \frac{1}{10}(-195 + 6\rho_1) \\ 0 & \frac{1}{10}(-195 - 4\rho_1 + 10\rho_2) \end{pmatrix},$$

and the variance of the solution is

$$\operatorname{var}(x^*) = \begin{pmatrix} \frac{1}{3} & \frac{1}{12} \\ 0 & \frac{1}{12} \end{pmatrix}.$$

11.8 Concluding Remarks

In this chapter we consider Cournot-Nash equilibrium principle in Lebesgue spaces with probability measure and derive its equivalent variational formulation. More precisely, we propose a model of oligopolistic market with uncertain data and derive the stochastic variational inequality formulation. Thanks to this we are able to obtain some existence results. Moreover, the use of the qualification condition, the so-called *Assumption S*, allows us to prove the existence of the Lagrange multipliers. It worth to emphasize the important role of the Lagrange variables in order to understand the features of the random market. Then we introduce random control policies for the regulation of exportations, we change the perspective of the situation that leads us to a policymaker optimization problem. In particular, we present the optimal control equilibrium conditions and express them by a stochastic inverse variational inequality. Finally we rewrite it with a classical stochastic variational inequality.

Acknowledgements

The first author was partially supported by PRIN 2017 "Nonlinear Differential Problems via Variational, Topological and Set-valued Methods" (Grant 2017AYM8XW).

References

[1] A. Barbagallo. Advanced results on variational inequality formulation in oligopolistic market equilibrium problem. Filomat, 5: 935–947, 2012.

[2] A. Barbagallo and M.-G. Cojocaru. Dynamic equilibrium formulation of oligopolistic market problem. Math. Comput. Model., 49: 966–976, 2009.

[3] A. Barbagallo and A. Maugeri. Duality theory for the dynamic oligopolistic market equilibrium problem. Optim., 60: 29–52, 2011.

[4] A. Barbagallo and P. Mauro. Evolutionary variational formulation for oligopolistic market equilibrium problems with production excesses. J. Optim. Theory Appl., 155: 1–27, 2012.

[5] A. Barbagallo and P. Mauro. Time-dependent variational inequality for oligopolistic market equilibrium problem with production and demand excesses., Abstr. Appl. Anal., 2012: 651975, 2012.

[6] A. Barbagallo and P. Mauro. Inverse variational inequality approach and applications. Numer. Funct. Anal. Optim., 35: 851–867, 2014.

[7] A. Barbagallo and P. Mauro. A quasi variational approach for the dynamic oligopolistic market equilibrium problem. Abstr. Appl. Anal., 2013: 952915, 2013.

[8] A. Barbagallo and P. Mauro. A general quasi-variational problem of Cournot-Nash type and its inverse formulation. J. Optim. Theory Appl., 170: 476–492, 2016.

[9] R.I. Boţ, E.R. Csetnek and A. Moldovan. Revisiting some dual theorems via the quasirelative interior in convex optimization. J. Optim. Theory Appl., 139: 67–84, 2000.

[10] A. Cournot. *Researches into the Mathematical Principles of the Theory of Wealth.* MacMillan, London, 1897.

[11] S. Dafermos and A. Nagurney. Oligopolistic and competitive behavior of spatially separated markets. Regional Science and Urban Economics, 17: 245–254, 1987.

[12] P. Daniele and S. Giuffrè. General infinite dimensional duality and applications to evolutionary network equilibrium problems. Optim. Lett., 1: 227–243, 2007.

[13] P. Daniele and S. Giuffrè. Random variational inequalities and the random traffic equilibrium problem. J. Optim. Theory Appl., 167: 363–381, 2015.

[14] P. Daniele, S. Giuffrè, G. Idone and A. Maugeri. Infinite dimensional duality and applications. Math. Ann., 339: 221–239, 2007.

[15] P. Daniele, S. Giuffrè and A. Maugeri. Remarks on general infinite dimensional duality with cone and equality constraints. Communications in Applied Analysis, 13: 567–578, 2009.

[16] P. Daniele, S. Giuffrè and A. Maugeri. General traffic equilibrium problem with uncertainty and random variational inequalities. pp. 89–96. *In*: T.M. Russias, C.A. Floudas and S. Butenko (eds.). *Optimization in Science and Engineering*. Springer, New York, 2014.

[17] M.B. Donato. The infinite dimensional Lagrange multiplier rule for convex optimization problems. J. Funct. Anal., 261: 2083–2093, 2011.

[18] I.V. Evstigneev and M.I. Taksar. Equilibrium states of random economies with locally interacting agents and solutions to stochastic variational inequalities in $\langle L_1, L_\infty \rangle$. Ann. Oper. Res., 114: 145–165, 2002.

[19] A. Ganguly and K. Wadhwa. On random variational inequalities. J. Math. Anal. Appl., 206: 315–321, 1997.

[20] G. Gürkan, A.Y. Özge and S.M. Robinson. Sample-path solution of stochastic variational inequalities. Math. Program., 84: 313–333, 1999.

[21] J. Gwinner and F. Raciti. On a class of random variational inequalities on random sets. Numer. Funct. Anal. Optim., 27: 619–636, 2006.

[22] J. Gwinner and F. Raciti. Random equilibrium problems on networks. Math. Computer Model., 43: 880–891, 2006.

[23] J. Gwinner and F. Raciti. Some equilibrium problems under uncertainty and random variational inequalities. Numer. Funct. Anal. Optim., 200: 299–319, 2012.

[24] O. Mangasarian. Pseudoconvex functions. Journal of the Society for Industrial and Applied Mathematics, Series A Control, 3: 281–290, 1965.

[25] A. Maugeri. Convex programming, variational inequalities and applications to the traffic equilibrium problem. Appl. Math. Optim., 16: 169–185, 1987.

[26] A. Maugeri and F. Raciti. On existence theorems for monotone and non-monotone variational inequalities. J. Convex Anal., 16: 899–911, 2009.

[27] A. Nagurney. Algorithms for oligopolistic market equilibrium problems. Regional Science and Urban Economics, 18: 425–445, 1988.

[28] A. Nagurney. *Network Economics: A Variational Inequality Approach.* Kluwer Academic Publishers, Boston, 1998.

[29] A. Nagurney, P. Dupuis and D. Zhang. A dynamical systems approach for network oligopolies and variational inequalities. The Annals of Regional Science, 28: 263–283, 1994.

[30] J.F. Nash. Equilibrium points in n-person games. Proc. Natl. Acad. Sci. USA, 36: 48–49, 1950.

[31] J.F. Nash. Non-cooperative games. Ann. Math., 54: 286–295, 1951.

[32] R.T. Rockafellar and R.J.B. Wets. *Variational Analysis.* Springer, Berlin, 1998.

Chapter 12

Augmented Lagrangian Methods For Optimal Control Problems Governed by Mixed Variational-Hemivariational Inequalities Involving a Set-valued Mapping

O Chadli[a] and *RN Mohapatra*[b,*]

2000 Mathematics Subject Classification. 47J20, 49J20, 49N15

12.1 Introduction

The optimal control problems considered in this chapter is an optimization problem in infinite-dimensional Banach spaces where the objective function is non-

[a] Department of Economics, Faculty of Economics and Social Sciences, Ibn Zohr University, B.P. 8658 Poste Dakhla, Agadir, Morocco.

[b] Department of Mathematics, University of Central Florida, USA.

Email: o.chadli@uiz.ac.ma

* Corresponding author: ram.mohapatra@ucf.edu

convex and nonsmooth, and whose state is a solution to a mixed variational-hemivariational problem depending on the control itself involving set-valued mapping and a pseudomonotone bifunction in the sense of Brézis. Variational-hemivariational inequalities represent a special class of inequalities, in which both convex and nonconvex functions are involved. This come from the fact that the theory of variational inequalities was built on arguments of monotonicity and convexity, including properties of the subdifferential of a convex function, while, on the other hand, the theory of hemivariational inequalities is based on properties of the Clarke subdifferential, defined for locally Lipschitz functions which may be nonconvex. Since their apparitions, respectively in early sixties and eighties, variational inequalities and hemivariational inequalities have gone through substantial developments and provided us with a convenient mathematical apparatus for studying a wide range of problems arising in diverse fields such as engineering sciences, physics, contact mechanics, economics and others; see [2, 6, 7, 14, 29, 27, 23, 28, 16].

The optimal control problem studied here contains precisely the optimal control of variational inequalities and hemivariational inequalities. For some studies related to optimal control of variational and hemivariational inequalities, we refer an interested reader to the papers [31, 19, 34, 3, 40, 35, 22, 42, 4, 17, 18, 15, 13] and the references therein.

The method developed in this chapter is based on the most well-known methods for reducing a constrained optimization problem to unconstrained optimization. We construct, similarly as in the paper by Rubinov et al. [33], via a Lagrangian function, a dual problem to the optimal control problem studied. Note that in optimization theory and more precisely in duality theory, methods incorporating Lagrangian type functions are successful when the optimal value of the dual problem is equal to that of the original (primal) problem. This leads to a condition known as the *zero duality gap property*.

At the out set, we use some general coercivity assumptions and monotonicity-type conditions, to obtain the existence of solutions for the optimal control problem governed by mixed variational-hemivariational inequality. Then, we establish the zero duality gap property between the optimal control problem and its nonlinear Lagrangian dual problem. More precisely, the optimal control problem is explored through a general result on the existence of optimal control of systems governed by mixed variational-hemivariational inequality associated with a pseudomonotone bifunction in the topological sense of Brézis [6]. Regarding the notion of pseudomonotonicity for bifunctions in topological sense, it is worth mentioning that it has been considered by Gwinner [10, 11] as a logical extension of pseudomonotone operators following Brézis [6]. A recent paper by Steck [37] has shown the importance of this notion and showed how it is strictly weaker that the notion called the *Ky Fan hemicontinuity* (see [37, Definition 2.1]) which has been used in [18] and many other references in literature related to the problem studied in this paper; see for instance [17, 41]. To obtain the zero duality gap between the primal and dual problems, we proceed similarly as in the paper by Rubinov et al. [33] by introducing a perturbation function associated to the primal problem and we show that the lower semicontinuity at zero of this perturbation function is an equivalent condition for the zero duality gap property. Under some monotonicity-type conditions and some coercivity conditions, we establish several sufficient conditions that guaranty the lower semicontinuity of the perturbation function at zero and therefore the zero duality gap property is obtained. It important to mention that Zhou et al. [43] investigated the zero duality property for an optimal control problem governed by a variational inequality, Wang et al. [39] studied the zero duality property for an optimal control problem governed by a mixed quasi-variational inequality, and very recently Long and Zeng [20, 21] gave several sufficient conditions for the zero duality gap property between the optimal control problem governed by multivalued hemivariational inequalities.

The approach developed in this chapter leads us to obtain new results and improve considerably some recent results in the literature, mainly in [39] and [20, 21] where some ambiguities have been pointed out, this is discussed in the last section of the chapter.

As applications, we consider the optimal control of a frictional contact problem from the theory of elasticity with subdifferential boundary conditions.

Following this introduction, the rest of the chapter is structured as follows. In Section 2, we introduce some definitions and preliminaries needed in the sequel. In Section 3, we provide some results on the existence of optimal control and we give several sufficient conditions for the zero duality gap property between the optimal control problem and its nonlinear dual problem. In Section 4, we give an application to the optimal control of a unilateral contact problem for elastic materials in which the frictional contact conditions are in a subdifferential form. We end the chapter with some comments and comparisons with recent results in literature.

12.2 Problem Statement and Preliminaries

Let X be a reflexive Banach space and X^* its topological dual. By $\langle \cdot, \cdot \rangle$ we denote the duality pairing between X^* and X. The norms of X and X^* are denoted by $\| \cdot \|$. For each subset M of X, we denote by $\text{conv}(M)$ the convex hull of M, by $\text{cl}(M)$ the closure of M in X and by M^c the complementary set of M. We shall use $\mathcal{F}(M)$ to denote the family of all finite subsets of M. For a multivalued mapping $T : X \rightrightarrows X^*$, $\mathcal{D}(T) := \{x \in X : T(x) \neq \emptyset\}$ is the domain of T, and $\mathcal{G}(T) := \{(x,x^*) \in X \times X^* : x \in \mathcal{D}(T) \text{ and } x^* \in T(x)\}$ is the graph of T. We denote by " $\rightarrow$ " the strong convergence and by " $\rightharpoonup$ " the weak convergence.

Let E and W be reflexive Banach spaces, $U_{ad} \subset W$ be the set of admissible controls and $K : U_{ad} \to 2^X$ be a set-valued mapping with nonempty values. We suppose throughout this paper that U_{ad} is a nonempty, closed and convex subset of W. Let $T : K(U_{ad}) \to 2^{X^*}$, $\mathcal{J} : U_{ad} \times X \to \mathbb{R}$, $B : U_{ad} \to X^*$ and $\gamma : X \to E$ be given mappings, and $f : X \times X \to \mathbb{R}$ be a bifunction such that $f(u,u) = 0$ for every $u \in X$. Let $J : E \to \mathbb{R}$ be a locally Lipschitz function, we denote by $J^0(u; v)$ the generalized directional derivative of J at the point $u \in E$ in the direction $v \in E$.

Given a control $w \in U_{ad}$, we consider the optimal control of the following set-valued variational-hemivariational inequality:

$$\begin{cases} \text{Find } u \in K(w) \text{ such that for all } u^* \in T(u) \\ \langle u^* + B(w), v - u \rangle + f(u,v) + J^0(\gamma(u); \gamma(v) - \gamma(u)) \geq 0 \quad \text{for all } v \in K(w). \end{cases} \tag{12.1}$$

We shall denote by $\mathbb{S}(w)$ the solution set of the state control system (12.1).

We consider the following optimal control problem:

$$\begin{array}{c} \min \mathcal{J}(w,u) \\ w \in U_{ad},\ u \in \mathbb{S}(w) \end{array} \tag{12.2}$$

Particular forms of this problem have been considered in [39, 4, 31, 42, 18, 32].

For $u \in K(w)$, we define the following function:

$$h_w(u) = \inf_{v \in K(w)} \{ \inf_{u^* \in T(u)} \langle u^* + B(w), v - u \rangle + f(u,v) + J^0(\gamma(u); \gamma(v) - \gamma(u) \},$$

and for $t \in \mathbb{R}$, we define the following associated set:

$$\mathbb{H}_w(t) = \{ u \in K(w) : h_w(u) \geq t \}.$$

Note that

$$h_w(u) \leq 0, \text{ for all } u \in K(w).$$

It follows that $h_w(u) = 0$ for all $u \in K(w)$. In addition, we have

$$\mathbb{H}_w(0) = \mathbb{S}(w). \tag{12.3}$$

Let us consider the perturbation functions $\tilde{\beta}(\cdot)$ defined, for $t \in \mathbb{R}$ by

$$\tilde{\beta}(t) = \inf_{w \in U_{ad},\ u \in \mathbb{H}_w(t)} \mathcal{J}(w,u).$$

It is easy to see that $\tilde{\beta}(0)$ is the optimal value of the problem (12.2).

Definition 12.2.1 *Let $P : \mathbb{R} \times \mathbb{R}_- \to \mathbb{R}$ be a function. The nonlinear Lagrangian function $\tilde{\mathcal{L}}_P : U_{ad} \times K(U_{ad}) \times \mathbb{R}_+ \to \mathbb{R}$ for the problems (12.2) is defined as*

$$\tilde{\mathcal{L}}_P(w,u,d) = P(\mathcal{J}(w,u), d h_w(u)).$$

The function $\tilde{\mathcal{F}}_P(d) = \inf_{w \in U_{ad},\ u \in K(w)} \tilde{\mathcal{L}}_P(w,u,d)$ is called the nonlinear Lagrangian dual functions of the problem (12.2). The equality

$$\tilde{\beta}(0) = \sup_{d \in \mathbb{R}_+} \tilde{\mathcal{F}}_P(d) \tag{12.4}$$

is called the zero duality gap property of the problem (12.2).

We consider the following assumption:

[A1] The function $P : \mathbb{R} \times \mathbb{R}_- \to \mathbb{R}$ satisfies the following properties:

(**P**$_i$) If $s_1 \leq s_2$, then $P(s_1,t) \leq P(s_2,t)$, for all $t \in \mathbb{R}_-$;

(**P**$_{ii}$) $P(s,0) = s$, for all $s \in \mathbb{R}_+$;

(**P**$_{iii}$) There exists a number $\tau < 0$, such that

$$P(s,t) \geq \max\{s, \tau t\}, \text{ for all } (s,t) \in \mathbb{R}_+ \times \mathbb{R}_-.$$

In all the rest of the paper, we assume, without loss of generality, that $\mathcal{J}(w,u) \geq m_0$, for all $w \in U_{ad}$ and $u \in K(w)$ for some $m_0 \geq 0$.

Similarly as in [33], we have the following sufficient and necessary conditions for the zero duality gap properties (12.4). For completeness, we include their proofs.

Proposition 12.2.2 *Suppose that $P : \mathbb{R} \times \mathbb{R}_- \to \mathbb{R}$ is continuous and satisfies* (**P**$_i$) *and* (**P**$_{ii}$) *of* **[A1]**. *If the zero duality gap property (12.4) is satisfied, then the perturbation function $\tilde{\beta}(\cdot)$ is lower semicontinous at 0.*

Proof. Suppose on the contrary that the perturbation function $\tilde{\beta}(\cdot)$ is not lower semicontinous at 0. Hence, there exists $r > 0$ and $\{t_k\}_{k\in\mathbb{N}}$ such that $t_k \to 0$ and

$$\tilde{\beta}(t_k) < \tilde{\beta}(0) - r. \tag{12.5}$$

As $\tilde{\beta}(t_k) = \inf\limits_{w\in U_{ad},\ u\in\mathbb{H}_w(t_k)} \mathcal{J}(w,u)$, there exists $w_k \in U_{ad}$ and $u_k \in \mathbb{H}_{w_k}(t_k)$ such that

$$\mathcal{J}(w_k,u_k) < \tilde{\beta}(t_k) + \frac{r}{4}.$$

Using (12.5), we get

$$\mathcal{J}(w_k,u_k) < \tilde{\beta}(0) - \frac{3r}{4}. \tag{12.6}$$

On the other hand, the zero duality gap property (12.4) implies that there exists $d \in \mathbb{R}_+$ such that

$$\tilde{\beta}(0) - \frac{r}{2} < \tilde{\mathcal{F}}_P(d) \leq \inf_{w\in U_{ad},\ u\in\mathbb{H}_w(t_k)} P(\mathcal{J}(w,u), dh_w(u)) \leq P(\mathcal{J}(w_k,u_k), dh_{w_k}(u_k)). \tag{12.7}$$

By using (**P**$_i$) and (12.6), we obtain

$$\tilde{\beta}(0) - \frac{r}{2} < P(\tilde{\beta}(0) - \frac{3r}{4}, dh_{w_k}(u_k)).$$

Since $t_k \leq h_{w_k}(u_k) \leq 0$ and $t_k \to 0$, it follows that $h_{w_k}(u_k) \to 0$. Hence, from (12.7) and the continuity of P, we deduce that $\tilde{\beta}(0) - \frac{r}{2} \leq P(\tilde{\beta}(0) - \frac{3r}{4}, 0)$. By using (**P**$_{ii}$), we derive that $\tilde{\beta}(0) - \frac{r}{2} \leq \tilde{\beta}(0) - \frac{3r}{4}$ or equivalently $\tilde{\beta}(0) \leq \tilde{\beta}(0) - \frac{r}{4}$, which is a absurd. □

Proposition 12.2.3 *Suppose that the function $P : \mathbb{R} \times \mathbb{R}_- \to \mathbb{R}$ satisfies* **[A1]**. *If $-\infty < \tilde{\beta}(0) < +\infty$ and the perturbation function $\tilde{\beta}(\cdot)$ is lower semicontinous at 0, then the zero duality gap property (12.4) holds.*

Proof. We shall proof that the duality gap property (12.4) holds. Note that for any $d \in \mathbb{R}_+$ we have

$$\tilde{\mathcal{F}}_P(d) = \inf_{w \in U_{ad},\ u \in K(w)} P(\mathcal{J}(w,u), dh_w(u)) \leq \inf_{w \in U_{ad},\ u \in \mathbb{H}_w(0)} P(\mathcal{J}(w,u), dh_w(u)).$$

Since $h_w(u) = 0$ for any $u \in \mathbb{H}_w(0)$, it follows, thanks to $(\mathbf{P}_{ii})$, that

$$\tilde{\mathcal{F}}_P(d) \leq \inf_{w \in U_{ad},\ u \in \mathbb{H}_w(0)} P(\mathcal{J}(w,u), 0) = \inf_{u \in U_{ad},\ u \in \mathbb{H}_w(0)} \mathcal{J}(w,u) = \tilde{\beta}(0), \ \ \forall d \in \mathbb{R}_+. \tag{12.8}$$

Suppose by contradiction that the zero duality gap property (12.4) is not satisfied. Then, from (12.8) we deduce that there exists $r > 0$ such that

$$\tilde{\beta}(0) \geq \sup_{d \in \mathbb{R}_+} \tilde{\mathcal{F}}_P(d) + r.$$

That is

$$\tilde{\beta}(0) \geq \inf_{w \in U_{ad},\ u \in K(w)} P(\mathcal{J}(w,u), dh_w(u)) + r, \ \ \forall d \in \mathbb{R}_+.$$

As by hypothesis $\tilde{\beta}(0)$ is a finite real number, we derive from the previous inequality that for each $k \in \mathbb{N}^*$ there exists $w_k \in U_{ad}$ and $u_k \in K(w_k)$ such that

$$\tilde{\beta}(0) \geq P(\mathcal{J}(w_k,u_k), kh_{w_k}(u_k)) + \frac{r}{2}. \tag{12.9}$$

On the other hand, from $(\mathbf{P}_{ii})$ we have that

$$\begin{aligned} P(\mathcal{J}(w_k,u_k), kh_{w_k}(u_k)) &\geq \max\{\mathcal{J}(w_k,u_k), \tau kh_{w_k}(u_k)\} \\ &\geq \tau kh_{w_k}(u_k). \end{aligned} \tag{12.10}$$

Hence, from (12.9), we get

$$\tilde{\beta}(0) \geq \tau kh_{w_k}(u_k).$$

It follows that $h_{w_k}(u_k) \geq t_k$, where $t_k := \frac{\tilde{\beta}(0)}{\tau k}$. This implies that $u_k \in \mathbb{H}_{w_k}(t_k)$ with $t_k \to 0$.
Therefore, by using (12.9) and (12.10), we have

$$\tilde{\beta}(0) \geq \mathcal{J}(w_k,u_k) + \frac{r}{2} \geq \inf_{w \in U_{ad},\ u \in \mathbb{H}_w(t_k)} \mathcal{J}(w,u) + \frac{r}{2} = \tilde{\beta}(t_k) + \frac{r}{2}.$$

By using the lower semicontinuity of $\tilde{\beta}(\cdot)$ at 0, we obtain that $\tilde{\beta}(0) \geq \tilde{\beta}(0) + \frac{r}{2}$, which is a absurd. □

Recall first some definitions and basic results for our later use.

Definition 12.2.4 *A set-valued mapping $T : X \to 2^{X^*}$ is said to be monotone, iff for any $x, y \in \mathcal{D}(T)$, the inequality $\langle x^* - y^*, x - y\rangle \geq 0$ holds for all $x^* \in T(x)$ and $y^* \in T(y)$.*

Definition 12.2.5 *A single-valued mapping $T : X \to X^*$ is said to be*

(a) pseudomonotone in the sense of Brézis, if for any sequence $\{x_n\}_{n\in\mathbb{N}} \subset \mathcal{D}(A)$ with $x_n \rightharpoonup x$ in X and $\limsup\langle T(x_n), x_n - x\rangle \leq 0$, we have

$$\liminf\langle T(x_n), x_n - y\rangle \geq \langle T(x), x - y\rangle, \quad \text{for all } y \in X;$$

(b) hemicontinuous (respectively, upper hemicontinuous) iff for all $x, y, z \in X$, the functional $t \mapsto \langle T(x + ty), z\rangle$ is continuous (respectively, upper semicontinuous) on [0,1].

Now, we recall the concepts mentioned above for real-valued bifunction considered within the literature in the recent years. Most of these notions were inspired by similar monotonicity/continuity concepts defined for operators acting from a topological vector space to its dual space, see for instance [5, 11].

Definition 12.2.6 *A real-valued bifunction $\Phi : X \times X \longrightarrow \mathbb{R}$ is said to be*

(i) monotone, if $\Phi(x, y) + \Phi(y, x) \leq 0$, for all $x, y \in X$;

(ii) pseudomonotone in the sense of Brézis, for short B*-pseudomonotone, if for any sequence $\{x_n\}_{n\in\mathbb{N}}$ in X such that $x_n \rightharpoonup x$ in X and $\liminf \Phi(x_n, x) \geq 0$, we have*

$$\limsup \Phi(x_n, y) \leq \Phi(x, y), \ \ \forall y \in X;$$

(iii) hemicontinuous (respectively, upper hemicontinuous) if for all $x, y \in X$, the functional $t \mapsto \Phi(tx + (1 - t)y, x)$ is continuous (respectively, upper semicontinuous) on [0,1].

Remark 12.2.7 *(a) It is easy to see that if $T : X \to X^*$ is pseudomonotone in the sense of Brézis, then the bifunction Φ defined by $\Phi(x, y) = \langle T(x), y - x\rangle$ is* B*-pseudomonotone.*

(b) If the bifunction Φ is upper semicontinuous with respect to the first argument for the weak topology $\sigma(X, X^*)$, then it is B*-pseudomonotone.*

(c) If $\Phi, \Psi : X \times X \to \mathbb{R}$ are B*-pseudomonotone such that $\Phi(x, x) \leq 0$ and $\Psi(x, x) \leq 0$ for all $x \in X$, then $\Phi + \Psi$ is also* B*-pseudomonotone, see [8].*

We give the following definition.

Definition 12.2.8 *Let $T : X \to 2^{X^*}$ be a set-valued mapping and $g : X \times X \to \mathbb{R}$ be a bifunction. Then T is said to be*

(i) *g-pseudomonotone ([18, 41, 38]), if for each $x, y \in X$ and all $x^* \in T(x)$ and $y^* \in T(y)$,*

$$\langle x^*, y-x\rangle + g(x,y) \geq 0 \Longrightarrow \langle y^*, y-x\rangle + g(x,y) \geq 0;$$

(ii) *stably g-pseudomonotone with respect to a set $M \subset X^*$ ([18, 41, 38]), if $T(\cdot)+x^*$ is g-pseudomonotone for every $x^* \in M$;*

(iii) *weakly stable g-pseudomonotone, if for $\varepsilon \leq 0$ and $x, y \in X$ such that $\langle x^*, y-x\rangle + g(x,y) \geq \varepsilon$ for all $x^* \in T(x)$, then $\langle y^*, y-x\rangle + g(x,y) \geq \varepsilon$ for all $y^* \in T(y)$;*

(iv) *weakly stable g-pseudomonotone with respect to a set $M \subset X^*$, if $T(\cdot)+x^*$ is weakly g-pseudomonotone for every $x^* \in M$.*

Remark 12.2.9 *Let $T : X \to 2^{X^*}$ be a set-valued mapping and $g : X \times X \to \mathbb{R}$ be a bifunction, then*

T is monotone ⇒ *T is weakly stable g-pseudomonotone with respect to $M \subset X^*$*

⇓

T is stably g-pseudomonotone with respect to $M \subset X^*$

⇓

T is g-pseudomonotone.

Definition 12.2.10 *Let E, G be two Banach spaces. A set-valued mapping $F : E \to 2^G$ is said to be lower semicontinuous at a point $x_0 \in E$ (for short, l.s.c. at x_0), if and only if, for any open set $\mathcal{O} \subset G$ such that $F(x_0) \cap \mathcal{O} \neq \emptyset$, there exists a neighborhood U of x_0 such that $F(x) \cap \mathcal{O} \neq \emptyset$ for every $x \in U$. We say that F is lower semicontinuous (for short, l.s.c.) if F is l.s.c. for every $x_0 \in E$.*

The following proposition gives a characterization of the lower semicontinuity of a set-valued mapping in terms of sequences.

Proposition 12.2.11 *[30, Proposition 6.1.4.] Let E, G be two Banach spaces and $F : E \to 2^G$ a set-valued map. Then, F is l.s.c., if and only if for any pair $(x,y) \in \mathcal{G}(F)$ and any sequence $\{x_n\}_{n\in\mathbb{N}} \subset E$ converging to x, we can determine, for each $n \in \mathbb{N}$, an element $y_n \in F(x_n)$ such that $y_n \to y$.*

We recall the following continuity property introduced by Mosco [26].

Definition 12.2.12 *Let C and D be nonempty closed and convex subsets of Banach spaces X and Y, respectively. A set-valued mapping $F : C \to 2^D$ is said to be M-continuous if the following conditions hold:*

(i) *For any sequence $\{x_n\}_{n\in\mathbb{N}} \subset C$ with $x_n \rightharpoonup x$, and for each $y \in F(x)$, there exists $\{y_n\}_{n\in\mathbb{N}}$ such that $y_n \in F(x_n)$ and $y_n \to y$.*

(ii) *For $y_n \in F(x_n)$ with $x_n \rightharpoonup x$ and $y_n \rightharpoonup y$, we have $y \in F(x)$.*

Below, we recall the fixed point theorem for set-valued maps of Q.H. Ansari and J-C. Yao [1] that will be needed in the sequel.

Theorem 12.2.13 *Let C be a nonempty, closed, and convex subset of a Hausdorff topological vector space E and let $S,T : C \rightrightarrows C$ be two set-valued maps. Assume that*

(i) *For each $x \in C$, $co(S(x)) \subset T(x)$ and $S(x)$ is nonempty;*

(ii) $C = \bigcup\{int_C(S^{-1}(y)) : y \in C\}$;

(iii) *If C is not compact, there exists a nonempty compact convex subset C_0 of C and a nonempty compact subset C_1 of C such that for each $x \in C \setminus C_1$, there exists $\tilde{y} \in C_0$ satisfying $x \in int_C(S^{-1}(\tilde{y}))$.*

Then there exists $\bar{x} \in C$ such that $\bar{x} \in T(\bar{x})$.

For the convenience of the reader, we end this section by recalling some notations and results from nonsmooth analysis, which will be used in the sequel. A functional $\varphi : X \to \mathbb{R}$ is said to be *locally Lipschitz* if for every $x \in X$ there exists a neighbourhood $\mathcal{N}$ of x and a constant $k_x > 0$ such that $|\varphi(z) - \varphi(y)| \leq k_x\|z-y\|_X$, for all $z, y \in \mathcal{N}$. The Clarke's generalized directional derivative of the locally Lipschitz mapping $\varphi : X \to \mathbb{R}$ at the point $x \in X$ in the direction $v \in X$ is defined by (see [9])

$$\varphi^0(x;v) := \limsup_{y \to x,\ t \downarrow 0} \frac{\varphi(y+tv) - \varphi(y)}{t}.$$

The Clarke's generalized gradient of φ at $x \in X$ is defined by $\partial\varphi(x) = \{x^* \in X^* : \varphi^0(x;v) \geq \langle x^*, v\rangle,\ \forall v \in X\}$. Note that by using the Hahn-Banach Theorem, we can verify that $\partial\varphi(x) \neq \emptyset$ for each $x \in X$. The next two propositions give important properties of the Clarke's generalized directional derivative and the Clarke's generalized gradient.

Proposition 12.2.14 *[9, Proposition 2.1.1] Let $\varphi : X \to \mathbb{R}$ be a locally Lipschitz functional of constant k_x near the point $x \in X$. Then,*

(i) The function $v \in E \mapsto \varphi^0(x;v)$ is finite, positively homogeneous, subadditive and satisfies $|\varphi^0(x;v)| \leq k_x\|v\|_X$;

(ii) $\varphi^0(x;v)$ is upper semicontinuous as a function of (x,v).

Proposition 12.2.15 *[9, Proposition 2.1.2] Let $\varphi : X \to \mathbb{R}$ be a locally Lipschitz functional of constant k_x near the point $x \in X$. Then,*

(i) $\partial\varphi(x)$ is a convex, weak compact subset of X^* and $\|x^*\|_{X^*} \leq k_x$, for all $x^* \in \partial\varphi(x)$;*

(ii) For each $v \in X$, one has $\varphi^0(x;v) = \max\{\langle x^*, v\rangle : x^* \in \partial f(x)\}$.

12.3 Existence Results for Solutions

In this section, we study the existence of solutions for the state control systems (12.1) under some monotonicity type conditions.

Let X be a reflexive Banach space and X^* its topological dual. Let E and W be reflexive Banach spaces, $U_{ad} \subset W$ be the set of admissible controls and $K : U_{ad} \to 2^X$ be a set-valued mapping with nonempty values. We suppose throughout this paper that U_{ad} is a nonempty, closed and convex subset of W. Let $T : K(U_{ad}) \to 2^{X^*}$, $B : U_{ad} \to X^*$ and $\gamma : X \to E$ be given mappings, and $f : X \times X \to \mathbb{R}$ be a bifunction such that $f(u,u) = 0$ for every $u \in X$. Let $J : E \to \mathbb{R}$ be a locally Lipschitz function, we denote by $J^0(x;y)$ the generalized directional derivative of J at the point $x \in E$ in the direction $y \in E$.

We consider the following assumptions:

[H$_K$] $K : U_{ad} \to 2^X$ is such that for each $w \in U_{ad}$, $K(w)$ is nonempty, closed and convex subset of X.

[H$_T^1$] $T : X \to 2^{X^*}$ is lower semicontinuous.

[H$_T^2$] $T : K(U_{ad}) \to 2^{X^*}$ is a set-valued mapping such that for any $w \in U_{ad}$ and $A \in \mathcal{F}(K(w))$, the restriction of T to conv(A) is lower semicontinuous with respect to the weak*-topology of X^*.

[H$_f$] $f : X \times X \to \mathbb{R}$ satisfies the following properties:

- **(i)** f is B-pseudomonotone;
- **(ii)** For all $u \in K(U_{ad})$, $f(u,\cdot)$ is convex;
- **(iii)** For each $w \in U_{ad}$, $v \in K(w)$ and $A \in \mathcal{F}(K(w))$, the functions $f(\cdot, v)$ is upper semicontinuous on conv(A).

[H$_\gamma$] $\gamma : X \to E$ is linear, bounded and compact.

[H$_c$] (Coercivity) For each $w \in U_{ad}$, there exists a nonempty weakly compact set $D_w \subset K(w)$ and a nonempty, convex and weakly compact subset $C_w \subset K(w)$, such that for each $u \in K(w) \setminus D_w$, there exists $v \in C_w$ satisfying

$$\langle u^* + B(w), v - u\rangle + f(u,v) + J^0(\gamma(u); \gamma(v) - \gamma(u)) < 0, \text{ for each } u^* \in T(u).$$

Remark 12.3.1 *Note that [H$_T^1$] implies [H$_T^2$].*

From Lemma 12.2.15, for each $u \in X$ there exists $e_u^* \in \partial J(\gamma(u))$ such that for each $e \in E$,

$$J^0(\gamma(u); e) = \langle e_u^*, e\rangle = \max\{\langle e^*, e\rangle : e^* \in \partial J(\gamma(u))\}.$$

Let $\gamma^* : E^* \to X^*$ be the adjoint operator of γ. We consider the subset $U(\gamma, J)$ of X^* defined as the following

$$U(\gamma, J) = \{-\xi_u^* : u \in X \text{ and } \xi_u^* = \gamma^*(e_u^*)\}. \tag{12.11}$$

We start, first, by showing the following lemma.

Lemma 12.3.2 *Let $T : K(U_{ad}) \to 2^{X^*}$ be a set-valued mapping satisfying* $[\mathbf{H}_T^2]$ *and $g : X \times X \to \mathbb{R}$ be a bifunction such that $g(u,\cdot)$ is convex and $g(u,u) \geq 0$, for all $u \in X$. Suppose that for each $w \in U_{ad}$, $A \in \mathcal{F}(K(w))$ and $v \in K(w)$, $g(\cdot,v)$ is upper semicontinuous on* $\mathrm{conv}(A)$. *Then, for each $w \in U_{ad}$ and $Z \in \mathcal{F}(K(w))$, there exists $u \in \mathrm{conv}(Z)$ such that for all $u^* \in T(u)$, we have $\langle u^*, v-u\rangle + g(u,v) \geq 0$, for all $v \in \mathrm{conv}(Z)$.*

Proof. We proceed by contradiction. Suppose that there exists $w \in U_{ad}$ and $Z \in \mathcal{F}(K(w))$ such that for all $u \in \mathrm{conv}(Z)$, there exists $u^* \in T(u)$ and $v \in \mathrm{conv}(Z)$ satisfying

$$\langle u^*, v-u\rangle + g(u,v) < 0. \tag{12.12}$$

Let us consider the set-valued mapping $F : \mathrm{conv}(Z) \to 2^{\mathrm{conv}(Z)}$ defined for $u \in \mathrm{conv}(Z)$ by

$$F(u) = \{v \in \mathrm{conv}(Z) : \inf_{u^* \in T(u)} \langle u^*, v-u\rangle + g(u,v) < 0\},$$

From (12.12), we have that $F(u) \neq \emptyset$ for all $u \in \mathrm{conv}(Z)$. Furthermore, $F(u)$ is convex for each $u \in \mathrm{conv}(Z)$. Now, let us verify that $F^{-1}(v) = \{u \in \mathrm{conv}(Z) : v \in F(u)\}$ is open in $\mathrm{conv}(Z)$ for any $v \in \mathrm{conv}(Z)$. Indeed, we verify that for each $v \in \mathrm{conv}(Z)$, $[F^{-1}(v)]^c$ is closed in $\mathrm{conv}(Z)$, where the complementary is considered with respect to $\mathrm{conv}(Z)$. Let $\{u_n\}_{n\in\mathbb{N}} \subset [F^{-1}(v)]^c$ such that $u_n \to u \in \mathrm{conv}(Z)$. We verify that $u \in [F^{-1}(v)]^c$. Note that on $\mathrm{conv}(Z)$ the weak and strong topologies coincides. Since $u_n \in [F^{-1}(v)]^c$, it follows that

$$\langle u_n^*, v-u_n\rangle + g(u_n,v) \geq 0, \;\; \forall u_n^* \in T(u_n). \tag{12.13}$$

Now, let $u^* \in T(u)$ be an arbitrary element. As the restriction of T to $\mathrm{conv}(Z)$ is lower semicontinuous with respect to the weak*-topology of X^*, there exists $\xi_n^* \in T(u_n)$ such that $\xi_n^* \rightharpoonup u^*$. Hence, from (12.13) we get

$$\langle \xi_n^*, v-u_n\rangle + g(u_n,v) \geq 0. \tag{12.14}$$

Since $g(\cdot,v)$ is upper semicontinous on $\mathrm{conv}(Z)$ and $\xi_n^* \rightharpoonup u^*$, we derive from (12.14) that $\langle u^*, v-u\rangle + g(u,v) \geq 0$. This implies that $u \in [F^{-1}(v)]^c$ since u^* is considered as an arbitrary element in $T(u)$. Thus, $u \in [F^{-1}(v)]^c$. Therefore, $F^{-1}(v)$ is open for each $v \in \mathrm{conv}(Z)$.
Now, we verify that $\mathrm{conv}(Z) = \bigcup_{v\in\mathrm{conv}(Z)} F^{-1}(v)$. Since, $F^{-1}(v) \subset \mathrm{conv}(Z)$ for each $v \in \mathrm{conv}(Z)$ it follows that $\bigcup_{v\in\mathrm{conv}(Z)} F^{-1}(v) \subset \mathrm{conv}(Z)$. Let $u \in \mathrm{conv}(Z)$, by using relation (12.12) we deduce that there exists $v \in \mathrm{conv}(Z)$ such that $u \in F^{-1}(v)$. Hence, $\mathrm{conv}(Z) \subset \bigcup_{v\in\mathrm{conv}(Z)} F^{-1}(v)$ and therefore $\mathrm{conv}(Z) = \bigcup_{v\in\mathrm{conv}(Z)} F^{-1}(v)$. Consequently, we have shown that all the conditions of Theorem 12.2.13 are satisfied with $S = F$ and $C = \mathrm{conv}(Z)$. Thus, there exists

$\bar{u} \in \text{conv}(Z)$ such that $\bar{u} \in F(\bar{u})$. Hence, $0 \leq \inf_{u^* \in T(u)} \langle u^*, \bar{u} - \bar{u} \rangle + g(\bar{u}, \bar{u}) < 0$, which is impossible. □

Next, we establish some results on the existence of solutions of the problem (12.1).

Theorem 12.3.3 *Assume that* $[\mathbf{H}_K]$, $[\mathbf{H}_T^2]$, $[\mathbf{H}_f]$, $[\mathbf{H}_\gamma]$ *and* $[\mathbf{H}_c]$ *are satisfied. In addition, suppose that T is stably f-pseudomonotone with respect to $\mathcal{R}(B) + U(\gamma, J)$, where $U(\gamma, J)$ is defined in (12.11). Then for each $w \in U_{ad}$, $\mathbb{S}(w)$ is nonempty and bounded.*

Proof. We will proceed in two steps. Before that, for simplicity, let us consider the bifunctions $h, g : X \times X \to \mathbb{R}$ defined by

$$h(u,v) := J^0(\gamma(u); \gamma(v) - \gamma(u)) + \langle B(w), v - u \rangle \quad \text{and} \quad g(u,v) := f(u,v) + h(u,v),$$

where w is a fixed element in U_{ad}. By using $[\mathbf{H}_\gamma]$ and Proposition 12.2.14, we obtain that h is weakly upper semicontinuous with respect to the first argument. Hence, from Remark 12.2.7 (b), we deduce that h is B-pseudomonotone. It follows, thanks to Remark 12.2.7 (c), that g is B-pseudomonotone since f is B-pseudomonotone by assumptions. In addition, from $[\mathbf{H}_\gamma]$ and Proposition 12.2.14 (i), we deduce that $h(u, \cdot)$ is convex. It follows that the function $g(u, \cdot)$ is convex.
Step 1: Let E_w be a nonempty, convex and weakly compact subset of $K(w)$. For $A \in \mathcal{F}(E_w)$, let

$$\mathbb{M}_A := \{u \in E_w : \langle u^*, v - u \rangle + g(u,v) \geq 0, \ \forall u^* \in T(u), \ \forall v \in \text{conv}(A)\}.$$

From Lemma 12.3.2, we obtain that $\mathbb{M}_A$ is a nonempty. Moreover, we can easily verify that the family of sets $\{\mathbb{M}_A\}_{A \in \mathcal{F}(E_w)}$ has the finite intersection property. Since E_w is weakly compact, it follows that $\bigcap_{A \in \mathcal{F}(E_w)} cl(\mathbb{M}_A) \neq \emptyset$, where the closure is considered with respect to the weak topology of X. Let $\bar{u} \in \bigcap_{A \in \mathcal{F}(E_w)} cl(\mathbb{M}_A)$ and $v \in E_w$ be an arbitrary element. As $\bar{u} \in cl(\mathbb{E}_{\{\bar{u}, v\}})$, there exists $\{u_n\}_{n \in \mathbb{N}} \subset \mathbb{M}_{\{\bar{u}, v\}}$ such that $u_n \rightharpoonup \bar{u}$. Hence, for each $n \in \mathbb{N}$ we have

$$\langle u_n^* + B(w), z - u_n \rangle + f(u_n, z) + J^0(\gamma(u_n); \gamma(z) - \gamma(u_n)) \geq 0, \qquad (12.15)$$

for all $u_n^* \in T(u_n)$, for all $z \in \text{co}(\{v, \bar{u}\})$.
By considering $z = \bar{u}$ in (12.15), we obtain

$$\langle u_n^* + B(w), \bar{u} - u_n \rangle + f(u_n, \bar{u}) + J^0(\gamma(u_n); \gamma(\bar{u}) - \gamma(u_n)) \geq 0, \qquad (12.16)$$

for all $u_n^* \in T(u_n)$.
On the other hand, as $J^0(\gamma(u_n); \gamma(\bar{u}) - \gamma(u_n)) = \langle e_{u_n}^*, \gamma(\bar{u}) - \gamma(u_n) \rangle$ for some $e_{u_n}^* \in \partial J(\gamma(u_n))$, we deduce that $J^0(\gamma(u_n); \gamma(\bar{u}) - \gamma(u_n)) = \langle \gamma^*(e_{u_n}^*), \bar{u} - u_n \rangle = \langle \xi_{u_n}^*, \bar{u} - u_n \rangle$, where $\xi_{u_n}^* := \gamma^*(e_{u_n}^*) \in U(\gamma, J)$. Hence, relation (12.16) becomes

$$\langle u_n^* + B(w) + \xi_{u_n}^*, \bar{u} - u_n \rangle + f(u_n, \bar{u}) \geq 0, \quad \text{for all } u_n^* \in T(u_n).$$

As T is stably f-pseudomonotone with respect to $\mathcal{R}(B)+U(\gamma,J)$, we deduce that

$$\langle u^*+B(w)+\xi^*_{u_n},\bar{u}-u_n\rangle+f(u_n,\bar{u})\geq 0,\ \text{for all } u^*\in T(\bar{u}),$$

or equivalently,

$$\langle u^*+B(w),\bar{u}-u_n\rangle+f(u_n,\bar{u})+J^0(\gamma(u_n);\gamma(\bar{u})-\gamma(u_n))\geq 0, \tag{12.17}$$

for all $u^*\in T(\bar{u})$.

From Proposition 12.2.14 (ii) and condition $[\mathbf{H}_\gamma]$, we obtain that

$$\limsup J^0(\gamma(u_n);\gamma(\bar{u})-\gamma(u_n))\leq 0.$$

Hence, by considering the lower limit in (12.17), we get that $\liminf f(u_n,\bar{u})\geq 0$. It follows, thanks to the B-pseudomonotonicity of f, that $\limsup f(u_n,z)\leq f(\bar{u},z)$, for all $v\in X$. This implies, particularly for $z=v$, that

$$\limsup f(u_n,v)\leq f(\bar{u},v). \tag{12.18}$$

Now, by considering $z=v$ in (12.15), we obtain

$$\langle u_n^*+B(w),v-u_n\rangle+f(u_n,v)+J^0(\gamma(u_n);\gamma(v)-\gamma(u_n))\geq 0,\ \forall u_n^*\in T(u_n).$$

By using the fact that T is stably f-pseudomonotone with respect to $\mathcal{R}(B)+U(\gamma,J)$, we get

$$\langle v^*+B(w),v-u_n\rangle+f(u_n,v)+J^0(\gamma(u_n);\gamma(v)-\gamma(u_n))\geq 0,\ \forall v^*\in T(v). \tag{12.19}$$

On the other hand, Proposition 12.2.14 (ii) and condition $[\mathbf{H}_\gamma]$ imply that

$$\limsup J^0(\gamma(u_n);\gamma(v)-\gamma(u_n))\leq J^0(\gamma(\bar{u});\gamma(v)-\gamma(\bar{u})). \tag{12.20}$$

By passing to the upper limit in (12.19), we obtain, by using (12.18) and (12.20), that

$$\langle v^*+B(w),v-\bar{u}\rangle+f(\bar{u},v)+J^0(\gamma(\bar{u});\gamma(v)-\gamma(\bar{u}))\geq 0, \tag{12.21}$$

for all $v^*\in T(v)$, for all $v\in E_w$.

Let z be an arbitrary element in E_w and $z_n:=\frac{1}{n}z+(1-\frac{1}{n})\bar{u}\in E_w$, for $n\in\mathbb{N}\setminus\{0\}$. Note that $z_n\to\bar{u}$ and from (12.21) we have

$$\langle z_n^*+B(w),z_n-\bar{u}\rangle+f(\bar{u},z_n)+J^0(\gamma(\bar{u});\gamma(z_n)-\gamma(\bar{u}))\geq 0, \tag{12.22}$$

for all $z_n^*\in T(z_n)$.

It follows, by using $[\mathbf{H}_f]$ (ii) and Proposition 12.2.14 (i), that

$$\langle z_n^*+B(w),z-\bar{u}\rangle+f(\bar{u},z)+J^0(\gamma(\bar{u});\gamma(z)-\gamma(\bar{u}))\geq 0,\quad \text{for all } z_n^*\in T(z_n). \tag{12.23}$$

Now, consider $u^* \in T(\bar{u})$. As $z_n \to \bar{u}$, then from **[$\mathbf{H}_T^2$]** and Proposition 12.2.11 we deduce that there exists $x_n^* \in T(z_n)$ such that $x_n^* \rightharpoonup u^*$. Hence, using (12.23) we get

$$\langle x_n^* + B(w), z - \bar{u}\rangle + f(\bar{u}, z) + J^0(\gamma(\bar{u}); \gamma(z) - \gamma(\bar{u})) \geq 0. \tag{12.24}$$

By considering the limit when $n \to +\infty$ in (12.24), we obtain as a conclusion of this first step: For any nonempty, convex and weakly compact subset E_w of $K(w)$, there exists $\bar{u} \in E_w$ such that

$$\langle u^* + B(w), z - \bar{u}\rangle + f(\bar{u}, z) + J^0(\gamma(\bar{u}); \gamma(z) - \gamma(\bar{u})) \geq 0, \ \forall u^* \in T(\bar{u}), \ \forall z \in E_w.$$

Step 2: Let $A \in \mathcal{F}(K(w))$ and consider $\widetilde{E}_w := \text{conv}(A \cup C_w)$, which is a convex and weakly compact subset of X. From Step 1, there exists $\tilde{u} \in \widetilde{E}_w$ such that

$$\langle u^* + B(w), z - \tilde{u}\rangle + f(\tilde{u}, z) + J^0(\gamma(\tilde{u}); \gamma(z) - \gamma(\tilde{u})) \geq 0, \ \forall u^* \in T(\tilde{u}), \ \forall z \in \tilde{E}_w.$$

Moreover, assumption **[$\mathbf{H}_c$]** implies that $\tilde{u} \in D_w$. For $A \in \mathcal{F}(K(w))$, let us consider $\widetilde{\mathbb{M}}_A := \{u \in D_w : \forall u^* \in T(u), \langle u^* - B(w), z - u\rangle + f(u, z) + J^0(\gamma(u); \gamma(z) - \gamma(u)) \geq 0, \ \forall z \in \text{conv}(A \cup C_w)\}$, which is, given the above, a nonempty subset of X. It is easy to verify that the family of sets $\{\widetilde{\mathbb{M}}_A\}_{A \in \mathcal{F}(K(w))}$ has the finite intersection property. As D_w is compact, it follows that $\bigcap_{A \in \mathcal{F}(K(w))} cl(\widetilde{\mathbb{M}}_A) \neq \emptyset$, where the closure is considered with respect to the weak topology of X. Let $\bar{u} \in \bigcap_{A \in \mathcal{F}(K(w))} cl(\widetilde{\mathbb{M}}_A)$ and v be an arbitrary element in $K(w)$. Since $\bar{u} \in cl(\widetilde{\mathbb{M}}_{\{\bar{u}, v\}})$, there exists $\{u_n\}_{n \in \mathbb{N}} \subset \widetilde{\mathbb{M}}_{\{\bar{u}, v\}}$ such that $u_n \rightharpoonup \bar{u}$. From $u_n \in \widetilde{\mathbb{M}}_{\{\bar{u}, v\}}$, we obtain for all $u_n^* \in T(u_n)$

$$\langle u_n^* + B(w), z - u_n\rangle + f(u_n, z) + J^0(\gamma(u_n); \gamma(z) - \gamma(u_n)) \geq 0, \tag{12.25}$$

for all $z \in \text{conv}(\{v, \bar{u}\} \cup C_w)$.

By following the same approach used in Step 1 by considering, respectively $z = \bar{u}$ and $z = v$ in (12.25), we obtain

$$\langle v^* + B(w), y - \bar{u}\rangle + f(\bar{u}, z) + J^0(\gamma(\bar{u}); \gamma(z) - \gamma(\bar{u})) \geq 0, \tag{12.26}$$

for all $v^* \in T(v), \forall v \in K(w)$.

Finally, by proceeding similarly as in Step 1, we show that

$$\langle u^* + B(w), v - \bar{u}\rangle + f(\bar{u}, v) + J^0(\gamma(\bar{u}); \gamma(v) - \gamma(\bar{u})) \geq 0, \ \forall u^* \in T(\bar{u}), \ \forall v \in K(w).$$

Hence, $\bar{u}$ is a solution of the problem (12.1). Moreover, from the coercivity condition **[$\mathbf{H}_c$]** we deduce that $\mathbb{S}(w) \subset D_w$. Which completes the proof. □

Remark 12.3.4 *If $K(w)$ is compact, then the coercivity conditions* **[$\mathbf{H}_c$]** *in Theorem 12.3.3 can be removed.*

Theorem 12.3.5 *Assume that* $[\mathbf{H}_K]$, $[\mathbf{H}_T^2]$, $[\mathbf{H}_f]$ *and* $[\mathbf{H}_\gamma]$ *are satisfied. In addition, suppose that the following conditions hold:*

(i) *T is stably f-pseudomonotone with respect to $\mathcal{R}(B)+U(\gamma,J)$, where $U(\gamma,J)$ is defined in (12.11);*

(ii) *(coercivity) For each $w \in U_{ad}$, there exists $n_w \in \mathbb{N}$ such that for each $u \in K(w)\setminus B_{n_w}(\mathbf{0})$, there exists some $v \in K(w)$ with $\|v\| < \|u\|$ such that*

$$\sup_{u^* \in T(u)} \langle u^* + B(w), v-u\rangle + f(u,v) + J^0(\gamma(u);\gamma(v)-\gamma(u)) \le 0.$$

Then for each $w \in U_{ad}$, $\mathbb{S}(w)$ is nonempty and bounded.

Proof. Consider $p \in \mathbb{N}$ such that $p > n_w$. As $B_p(\mathbf{0})$ is convex and weakly compact, then from Theorem 12.3.3 and Remark 12.3.4 we deduce that there exists $u_p \in K(w)\cap B_p(\mathbf{0})$ such that

$$\langle u_p^* + B(w), z-u_p\rangle + f(u_p,z) + J^0(\gamma(u_p);\gamma(z)-\gamma(u_p)) \ge 0, \tag{12.27}$$

for all $u_p^* \in T(u_p)$ and all $z \in K(w)\cap B_p(\mathbf{0})$. We distinguish the following cases:

1- If $\|u_p\| = p$, then $\|u_p\| > n_w$. From condition (ii), we deduce that there exists $v_p \in K(w)$ such that $\|v_p\| < \|u_p\| = p$ and

$$\langle u_p^* + B(w), v_p-u_p\rangle + f(u_p,v_p) + J^0(\gamma(u_p);\gamma(v_p)-\gamma(u_p)) \le 0,\ \forall u_p^* \in T(u_p). \tag{12.28}$$

Let v be an arbitrary element in $K(w)$. As $\|v_p\| < p$, then there exists $t \in (0,1)$ such that $v_t = tv + (1-t)v_p \in K(w)\cap B_p(\mathbf{0})$. Let us take $z = v_t$ in (12.27), it follows, thanks to Proposition 12.2.14 (i), condition $[\mathbf{H}_f]$ (ii) and relation (12.28), that

$$\langle u_p^* + B(w), v-u_p\rangle + f(u_p,v) + J^0(\gamma(u_p);\gamma(v)-\gamma(u_p)) \ge 0,\ \forall u_p^* \in T(u_p). \tag{12.29}$$

Hence, u_p is a solution of the problem (12.1).

2- If $\|u_p\| < p$, then for an arbitrary element $v \in K(w)$, there exists $t \in (0,1)$ such that $v_t = tv + (1-t)v_p \in K(w)\cap B_p(\mathbf{0})$. Hence, by considering $z = v_t$ in (12.27), we obtain, thanks to Proposition 12.2.14 (i) and condition $[\mathbf{H}_f]$ (ii), that the inequality (12.29) holds. Thus, u_p is a solution of the problem (12.1).

On the other hand, the coercivity condition (ii) implies that $\mathbb{S}(w) \subset B_{n_w}(\mathbf{0})$, for each $w \in U_{ad}$. Hence, $\mathbb{S}(w)$ is bounded. □

12.4 Optimal Control

In this section, we study the existence of solutions of the optimal control problems (12.2). We establish several sufficient conditions for the zero duality gap property between the optimal control problem considered and its dual problem by using the nonlinear Lagrangian function introduced in Definition 12.2.1.

In the next results, we establish existence of solutions of the optimal control problem (12.2) under some coercivity conditions on the cost function $\mathcal{J}$ and the state control system (12.1).

Theorem 12.4.1 *Assume that* $[\mathbf{H}_K]$, $[\mathbf{H}_T^1]$, $[\mathbf{H}_f]$ *(ii)-(iii),* $[\mathbf{H}_\gamma]$ *are satisfied, and that* $K : U_{ad} \to 2^X$ *is M-continuous. In addition, suppose that the following conditions hold:*

(i) *The cost function* $\mathcal{J} : U_{ad} \times X \to \mathbb{R}$ *is weakly lower semicontinuous and for any* $w \in U_{ad}$, $u \in K(w)$, $\lim_{\|w\| \to +\infty} \mathcal{J}(w,u) = +\infty$;

(ii) T *is stably* f*-pseudomonotone with respect to* $\mathcal{R}(B) + U(\gamma, J)$*, where* $U(\gamma, J)$ *is defined in (12.11);*

(iii) *The operators* $B : U_{ad} \to X^*$ *is strongly continuous from the weak topology of* W *to the topology of* X^*;

(iv) *If* $\{u_n\}_{n\in\mathbb{N}}$ *and* $\{\tilde{u}_n\}_{n\in\mathbb{N}}$ *are two sequences in* X *with* $u_n \rightharpoonup u$ *and* $\tilde{u}_n \to u$ *such that* $\liminf f(u_n, \tilde{u}_n) \geq 0$*, then* $\limsup f(u_n, v_n) \leq f(u, v)$ *for all* $v \in X$ *and* $\{v_n\}_{n\in\mathbb{N}} \subset X$ *such that* $v_n \to v$;

(v) *(Coercivity) There exists a nonempty weakly compact subset* D *of* X *and for any* $w \in U_{ad}$ *there exists a weakly compact convex subset* C_w *of* $K(w)$ *such that for each* $u \in K(w) \setminus D$*, there exists* $v \in C_w$ *satisfying*

$$\sup_{u^* \in T(u)} \langle u^* + B(w), v - u \rangle + f(u, v) + J^0(\gamma(u); \gamma(v) - \gamma(u)) \leq 0.$$

Then, $-\infty < \tilde{\beta}(0) < +\infty$.

Proof. Observe that condition (iv) implies that f is B-pseudomonotone, and condition (v) implies that $[\mathbf{H}_c]$ is satisfied. Therefore, from Theorem 12.3.3 we deduce that $\mathbb{S}(w) \neq \emptyset$ for each $w \in U_{ad}$. By relation (12.3), we have $\mathbb{H}_w(0) = \mathbb{S}(w)$ and hence $\tilde{\beta}(0) = \inf_{w\in U_{ad},\, u\in\mathbb{S}(w)} \mathcal{J}(w,u)$. Let $\{(w_n, u_n)\}_{n\in\mathbb{N}} \subset U_{ad} \times K(U_{ad})$ be a sequence such that $u_n \in \mathbb{S}(w_n)$ and

$$\mathcal{J}(w_n, u_n) \leq \tilde{\beta}(0) + \frac{1}{1+n}, \quad \text{for } n \in \mathbb{N}. \tag{12.30}$$

Condition (i) implies that $\{w_n\}_{n\in\mathbb{N}}$ is bounded in W, and hence, for a subsequence, we have $w_n \rightharpoonup \bar{w} \in U_{ad}$ since U_{ad} is a convex and closed subset of W.

On the other part, the coercivity condition (v) implies that $\mathbb{S}(w_n) \subset D$ for each $n \in \mathbb{N}$. It follows that the sequence $\{u_n\}_{n\in\mathbb{N}}$ is bounded in X, and hence, for a subsequence, we have $u_n \rightharpoonup \bar{u} \in X$. By using the M-continuity of $K(\cdot)$, we deduce that $\bar{u} \in K(\bar{w})$. Let us verify that $\bar{u} \in \mathbb{S}(\bar{w})$. As $\bar{u} \in K(\bar{w})$ and $w_n \rightharpoonup \bar{w}$, then from Definition 12.2.12 (ii), there exists $\tilde{u}_n \in K(w_n)$ such that $\tilde{u}_n \to \bar{u}$. As $u_n \in \mathbb{S}(w_n)$, it follows that

$$\langle z_n^* + B(w_n), \tilde{u}_n - u_n\rangle + f(u_n, \tilde{u}_n) + J^0(\gamma(u_n); \gamma(\tilde{u}_n) - \gamma(u_n)) \geq 0, \forall z_n^* \in T(u_n). \tag{12.31}$$

As $J^0(\gamma(u_n); \gamma(\tilde{u}_n) - \gamma(u_n)) = \langle \gamma^*(e_{u_n}^*), \tilde{u}_n - u_n\rangle = \langle \xi_{u_n}^*, \tilde{u}_n - u_n\rangle$, where $\xi_{u_n}^* := \gamma^*(e_{u_n}^*) \in U(\gamma, J)$ and $e_{u_n}^* \in \partial J(\gamma(u_n))$, then relation (12.31) becomes

$$\langle z_n^* + \xi_{u_n}^* + B(w_n), \tilde{u}_n - u_n\rangle + f(u_n, \tilde{u}_n) \geq 0, \text{ for all } z_n^* \in T(u_n).$$

Since T is stably f-pseudomonotone with respect to $\mathcal{R}(B) + U(\gamma, J)$, it follows

$$\langle y_n^* + \xi_{u_n}^* + B(w_n), \tilde{u}_n - u_n\rangle + f(u_n, \tilde{u}_n) \geq 0, \text{ for all } y_n^* \in T(\tilde{u}_n),$$

or equivalently

$$\langle y_n^* + B(w_n), \tilde{u}_n - u_n\rangle + f(u_n, \tilde{u}_n) + J^0(\gamma(u_n); \gamma(\tilde{u}_n) - \gamma(u_n)) \geq 0, \text{ for all } y_n^* \in T(\tilde{u}_n). \tag{12.32}$$

Let $z^* \in T(\bar{u})$. As $\tilde{u}_n \to \bar{u}$ and T is lower semicontinuous at $\bar{u}$ (condition $[\mathbf{H}_T^1]$), then from Proposition 12.2.11 we deduce that there exists $\theta_n^* \in T(\tilde{u}_n)$ such that $\theta_n^* \to z^*$. Hence, from (12.32) we get

$$\langle \theta_n^* + B(w_n), \tilde{u}_n - u_n\rangle + f(u_n, \tilde{u}_n) + J^0(\gamma(u_n); \gamma(\tilde{u}_n) - \gamma(u_n)) \geq 0. \tag{12.33}$$

Taking the lower limit in (12.33) as $n \to +\infty$, we obtain, thanks to Proposition 12.2.14 (ii) and condition $[\mathbf{H}_\gamma]$, that

$$\liminf f(u_n, \tilde{u}_n) \geq 0.$$

Thus, from condition (iv) we derive that

$$\limsup f(u_n, v_n) \leq f(u, v), \text{ for all } v \in X \text{ and } v_n \to v. \tag{12.34}$$

On the other hand, it follows from $u_n \in \mathbb{S}(w_n)$ that

$$\langle z_n^* + B(w_n), v - u_n\rangle + f(u_n, v) + J^0(\gamma(u_n); \gamma(v) - \gamma(u_n)) \geq 0, \tag{12.35}$$

for all $z_n^* \in T(u_n)$, for all $v \in K(w_n)$.

Let v be an arbitrary element in $K(\bar{w})$. As $w_n \rightharpoonup \bar{w}$, then from Definition 12.2.12 (i) we deduce that there exists $v_n \in K(w_n)$ such that $v_n \to v$. Using (12.35), we obtain

$$\langle z_n^* + B(w_n), v_n - u_n\rangle + f(u_n, v_n) + J^0(\gamma(u_n); \gamma(v_n) - \gamma(u_n)) \geq 0, \ \forall z_n^* \in T(u_n).$$

In a similar way as before, using the fact that T is stably f-pseudomonotone with respect to $\mathcal{R}(B)+U(\gamma,J)$, we obtain

$$\langle \delta_n^* + B(w_n), v_n - u_n\rangle + f(u_n, v_n) + J^0(\gamma(u_n); \gamma(v_n) - \gamma(u_n)) \geq 0, \ \ \forall \delta_n^* \in T(v_n). \tag{12.36}$$

Let v^* be an arbitrary element in $T(v)$, then by using the fact that $v_n \to v$ and T is lower semicontinuous at v, we deduce, thanks to Proposition 12.2.11, that there exists $v_n^* \in T(v_n)$ such that $v_n^* \to v^*$. Hence, using (12.36) we obtain that

$$\langle v_n^* + B(w_n), v_n - u_n\rangle + f(u_n, v_n) + J^0(\gamma(u_n); \gamma(v_n) - \gamma(u_n)) \geq 0. \tag{12.37}$$

Therefore, taking the upper limit when $n \to +\infty$ in (12.37), we get, thanks to (12.34), condition $[\mathbf{H}_\gamma]$ and Proposition 12.2.14 (ii), that

$$\langle v^* + B(\bar{w}), v - \bar{u}\rangle + f(\bar{u}, v) + J^0(\gamma(\bar{u}); \gamma(v) - \gamma(\bar{u})) \geq 0, \ \forall v^* \in T(v), \ \forall v \in K(\bar{w}).$$

Now, let z be an arbitrary element in $K(\bar{w})$ and let us set $z_n := \frac{1}{n}z + (1-\frac{1}{n})\bar{u} \in K(\bar{w})$, with $n \in \mathbb{N}\setminus\{0\}$. Note that $z_n \to \bar{u}$ and from (12.37) we have

$$\langle z_n^* + B(\bar{w}), z_n - \bar{u}\rangle + f(\bar{u}, z_n) + J^0(\gamma(\bar{u}); \gamma(z_n) - \gamma(\bar{u})) \geq 0, \ \ \forall\, z_n^* \in T(z_n).$$

It follows, by using $[\mathbf{H}_f]$ (ii) and Proposition 12.2.14 (i), that

$$\langle z_n^* + B(\bar{w}), z - \bar{u}\rangle + f(\bar{u}, z) + J^0(\gamma(\bar{u}); \gamma(z) - \gamma(\bar{u})) \geq 0, \quad \text{for all } z_n^* \in T(z_n). \tag{12.38}$$

Let u^* be an arbitrary element in $T(\bar{u})$. As $z_n \to \bar{u}$, then from $[\mathbf{H}_T^1]$ and Proposition 12.2.11 we deduce that there exists $x_n^* \in T(z_n)$ such that $x_n^* \to u^*$. Hence, using (12.38) we get

$$\langle x_n^* + B(w), z - \bar{u}\rangle + f(\bar{u}, z) + J^0(\gamma(\bar{u}); \gamma(z) - \gamma(\bar{u})) \geq 0. \tag{12.39}$$

By considering the limit when $n \to +\infty$ in (12.39), we obtain

$$\langle u^* + B(\bar{w}), z - \bar{u}\rangle + f(\bar{u}, z) + J^0(\gamma(\bar{u}); \gamma(z) - \gamma(\bar{u})) \geq 0, \ \forall u^* \in T(\bar{u}), \ \forall z \in K(\bar{w}).$$

This implies that $\bar{u} \in \mathbb{S}(\bar{w})$. The conclusion follows from the weak lower semicontinuity of the functional $\mathcal{J}$ and relation (12.30). □

Theorem 12.4.2 *Assume that* $[\mathbf{H}_K]$, $[\mathbf{H}_T^1]$, $[\mathbf{H}_f]$ *(ii)-(iii),* $[\mathbf{H}_\gamma]$ *are satisfied, and that* $K : U_{ad} \to 2^X$ *is M-continuous. In addition, suppose that the following conditions hold:*

(i) *The cost function* $\mathcal{J} : U_{ad} \times X \to \mathbb{R}$ *is weakly lower semicontinuous and for any* $w \in U_{ad}$, $u \in K(w)$, $\lim_{\|w\| \to +\infty} \mathcal{J}(w,u) = +\infty$;

(ii) T *is stably* f*-pseudomonotone with respect to* $\mathcal{R}(B)+U(\gamma,J)$*, where* $U(\gamma,J)$ *is defined in (12.11);*

(iii) *The operators $B : U_{ad} \to X^*$ is strongly continuous from the weak topology of W to the topology of X^*;*

(iv) *If $\{u_n\}_{n\in\mathbb{N}}$ and $\{\tilde{u}_n\}_{n\in\mathbb{N}}$ are two sequences in X with $u_n \rightharpoonup u$ and $\tilde{u}_n \to u$ such that* $\liminf f(u_n, \tilde{u}_n) \geq 0$, *then* $\limsup f(u_n, v_n) \leq f(u,v)$ *for all $v \in X$ and $\{v_n\}_{n\in\mathbb{N}} \subset X$ such that $v_n \to v$;*

(v) *(Coercivity) there exists $n_0 \in \mathbb{N}$ such that for each $w \in U_{ad}$ and $u \in K(w) \setminus B_{n_0}(\mathbf{0})$, there exists some $v \in K(w)$ with $\|v\| < \|u\|$ satisfying*

$$\sup_{u^* \in T(u)} \langle u^* + B(w), v - u\rangle + f(u,v) + J^0(\gamma(u);\gamma(v) - \gamma(u)) \leq 0.$$

Then, $-\infty < \tilde{\beta}(0) < +\infty$.

Proof. We can see that condition (iv) implies that f is B-pseudomonotone, and that condition (ii) of Theorem 12.3.5 is a direct consequence of the coercivity condition (v). Hence, by Theorem 12.3.5 we deduce that $\emptyset \neq \mathbb{S}(w) \subset B_{n_0}$ for any $w \in U_{ad}$. As $\mathbb{H}_w(0) = \mathbb{S}(w)$, it follows that

$$\tilde{\beta}(0) = \inf_{w\in U_{ad},\ u\in\mathbb{S}(w)} \mathcal{J}(w,u).$$

Let $\{(w_n, u_n)\}_{n\in\mathbb{N}} \subset U_{ad} \times K(U_{ad})$ be a sequence such that $u_n \in \mathbb{S}(w_n)$ and

$$\mathcal{J}(w_n, u_n) \leq \tilde{\beta}(0) + \frac{1}{1+n}, \quad \text{for } n \in \mathbb{N}. \tag{12.40}$$

Condition (i) implies that $\{w_n\}_{n\in\mathbb{N}}$ is bounded in W, and hence, for a subsequence, we have $w_n \rightharpoonup \bar{w} \in U_{ad}$. On the other hand, since $\mathbb{S}(w_n) \subset B_{n_0}$ for each $n \in \mathbb{N}$, it follows that the sequence $\{u_n\}_{n\in\mathbb{N}}$ is bounded in X, and hence, for a subsequence, we have $u_n \rightharpoonup \bar{u} \in X$. By using the M-continuity of $K(\cdot)$, we deduce that $\bar{u} \in K(\bar{w})$. To complete the proof, it suffices to verify that $\bar{u} \in \mathbb{S}(\bar{w})$. This is obtained by proceeding similarly as in the proof of Theorem 12.4.1. □

In the following result, we establish existence of solutions of the optimal control problem (12.2) without any coercivity condition on the cost function $\mathcal{J}$.

Theorem 12.4.3 *Assume that* $[\mathbf{H}_K]$, $[\mathbf{H}_T^1]$, $[\mathbf{H}_f]$ *(ii)-(iii),* $[\mathbf{H}_\gamma]$ *are satisfied, and that $K : U_{ad} \to 2^X$ is M-continuous. In addition, suppose that the conditions (ii), (iii) and (iv) of Theorem 12.4.1 are satisfied, the cost function $\mathcal{J} : U_{ad} \times X \to \mathbb{R}$ is weakly lower semicontinuous and the following coercivity condition holds:*

($\mathcal{C}$) *There exists $v_0 \in \bigcap_{w\in U_{ad}} K(w)$ such that*

$$\lim_{\|(w,u)\|\to+\infty} \Big[\sup_{u^*\in T(u)} \langle u^* + B(w), v_0 - u\rangle + f(u,v_0) + J^0(\gamma(u);\gamma(v_0) - \gamma(u))\Big] = -\infty.$$

Then, $-\infty < \tilde{\beta}(0) < +\infty$.

Proof. As in the proof of Theorem 12.4.1, we have that f is B-pseudomonotone. Moreover, we can verify that the condition $(\mathcal{C})$ implies $[\mathbf{H}_c]$. By using Theorem 12.3.3, we get $\mathbb{S}(w) \neq \emptyset$ for each $w \in U_{ad}$. By relation (12.3), we have $\mathbb{H}_w(0) = \mathbb{S}(w)$ and hence

$$\tilde{\beta}(0) = \inf_{w \in U_{ad},\ u \in \mathbb{S}(w)} \mathcal{J}(w,u) \tag{12.41}$$

Let $\{(w_n,u_n)\}_{n\in\mathbb{N}}$ be a minimizing sequence of the problem (12.41), that is $u_n \in \mathbb{S}(w_n)$ and

$$\lim_{n\to+\infty} \mathcal{J}(w_n,u_n) = \inf_{w \in U_{ad},\ u \in \mathbb{S}(w)} \mathcal{J}(w,u). \tag{12.42}$$

Let us verify that the sequence $\{(w_n,u_n)\}_{n\in\mathbb{N}}$ is bounded. On the contrary, suppose that for a subsequence one has $\|(w_n,u_n)\| \to +\infty$. It follows from the coercivity condition $(\mathcal{C})$ that

$$\lim_{\|(w_n,u_n)\|\to+\infty} [\sup_{u^*\in T(u_n)} \langle u^* + B(w_n), v_0 - u_n\rangle + f(u_n,v_0) + J^0(\gamma(u_n);\gamma(v_0)-\gamma(u_n))] = -\infty. \tag{12.43}$$

As $u_n \in \mathbb{S}(w_n)$ and $v_0 \in K(w_n)$, we get

$$\sup_{u^*\in T(u_n)} \langle u^* + B(w_n), v_0 - u_n\rangle + f(u_n,v_0) + J^0(\gamma(u_n);\gamma(v_0)-\gamma(u_n)) \geq 0.$$

Hence, we obtain a contradiction with (12.43) by considering the limit in the previous inequality. Thus, the sequence $\{(w_n,u_n)\}_{n\in\mathbb{N}}$ is bounded. Therefore, there exists a subsequence $\{(w_{n_k},u_{n_k})\}_{k\in\mathbb{N}}$ of $\{(w_n,u_n)\}_{n\in\mathbb{N}}$, such that $(w_{n_k},u_{n_k}) \rightharpoonup (\bar{w},\bar{u})$. Since $\mathcal{J}$ is weakly lower semicontinuous, we have

$$\mathcal{J}(\bar{w},\bar{u}) \leq \liminf \mathcal{J}(w_{n_k},u_{n_k}).$$

In order to conclude, we need to verify that $\bar{u} \in \mathbb{S}(\bar{w})$. This is obtained by proceeding similarly as in the proof of Theorem 12.4.1. □

In the following, we give several sufficient conditions for the zero duality gap between the optimal control problem and its nonlinear dual problem.

Theorem 12.4.4 *Assume that* $[\mathbf{H}_K]$, $[\mathbf{H}_T^1]$, $[\mathbf{H}_f]$ *(ii)-(iii),* $[\mathbf{H}_\gamma]$ *are satisfied, and that* $K : U_{ad} \to 2^X$ *is M-continuous. Suppose that conditions (i), (iii), (iv) and (v) of Theorem 12.4.1 are satisfied and* T *is weakly stable* f*-pseudomonotone with respect to* $\mathcal{R}(B) + U(\gamma,J)$*, where* $U(\gamma,J)$ *is defined in (12.11). If the function* $P : \mathbb{R}\times\mathbb{R}_- \to \mathbb{R}$ *satisfies* **[A1]**, *then the zero duality gap property (12.4) holds.*

Proof. Theorem 12.4.1 implies that $-\infty < \tilde{\beta}(0) < +\infty$, and by Proposition 12.2.3 we only need to verify that the perturbation function $\tilde{\beta}(\cdot)$ is lower semi-continuous at 0. By contradiction, suppose that there exists $r_0 > 0$ such that

$$\liminf_{t\to 0} \tilde{\beta}(t) \leq \tilde{\beta}(0) - r_0.$$

Hence, there exists $t_n \to 0$, $w_n \in U_{ad}$ and $u_n \in \mathbb{H}_{w_n}(t_n)$ such that

$$\mathcal{J}(w_n, u_n) \leq \tilde{\beta}(0) - \frac{1}{2} r_0, \text{ for all } n \in \mathbb{N}. \tag{12.44}$$

From condition (i) of Theorem 12.4.1 and relation (12.44), we get that $\{w_n\}_{n\in\mathbb{N}}$ is bounded. Therefore, for a subsequence we have $w_n \rightharpoonup \bar{w} \in U_{ad}$. On the other hand, from the proof of Theorem 12.4.1, we have that $\mathbb{S}(w_n) \subset D$ for each $n \in \mathbb{N}$, where D is the weakly compact subset of X given in the coercivity condition (v) of Theorem 12.4.1. It follows that the sequence $\{u_n\}_{n\in\mathbb{N}}$ is bounded in X, hence for a subsequence we have $u_n \rightharpoonup \bar{u} \in X$. Since $K(\cdot)$ is M-continuous, we obtain that $\bar{u} \in K(\bar{w})$. We claim that $\bar{u} \in S(\bar{w})$. Indeed, as $u_n \in \mathbb{H}_{w_n}(t_n)$, then $u_n \in K(w_n)$ and $h_{w_n}(u_n) \geq t_n$. It follows that $t_n \leq 0$ and

$$\langle u_n^* + B(w_n), z_n - u_n\rangle + f(u_n, z_n) + J^0(\gamma(u_n); \gamma(z_n) - \gamma(u_n)) \geq t_n, \tag{12.45}$$

for all $z_n \in K(w_n)$, for all $u_n^* \in T(u_n)$.

Since $\bar{u} \in K(\bar{w})$ and $w_n \rightharpoonup \bar{w}$, then from Definition 12.2.12 (i) we deduce that there exists $\tilde{u}_n \in K(w_n)$ such that $\tilde{u}_n \to \bar{u}$. Hence, from (12.45) we get

$$\langle u_n^* + B(w_n), \tilde{u}_n - u_n\rangle + f(u_n, \tilde{u}_n) + J^0(\gamma(u_n); \gamma(\tilde{u}_n) - \gamma(u_n)) \geq t_n,\ \forall u_n^* \in T(u_n). \tag{12.46}$$

As $J^0(\gamma(u_n); \gamma(\tilde{u}_n) - \gamma(u_n)) = \langle \gamma^*(e_{u_n}^*), \tilde{u}_n - u_n\rangle = \langle \xi_{u_n}^*, \tilde{u}_n - u_n\rangle$, where $\xi_{u_n}^* := \gamma^*(e_{u_n}^*) \in U(\gamma, J)$ and $e_{u_n}^* \in \partial J(\gamma(u_n))$, then relation (12.46) becomes

$$\langle u_n^* + \xi_{u_n}^* + B(w_n), \tilde{u}_n - u_n\rangle + f(u_n, \tilde{u}_n) \geq t_n,\ \ \forall u_n^* \in T(u_n). \tag{12.47}$$

Since T is weakly stable f-pseudomonotone with respect to $\mathcal{R}(B) + U(\gamma, J)$, it follows that

$$\langle z_n^* + \xi_{u_n}^* + B(w_n), \tilde{u}_n - u_n\rangle + f(u_n, \tilde{u}_n) \geq t_n,\ \forall z_n^* \in T(\tilde{u}_n), \tag{12.48}$$

which is equivalent to

$$\langle z_n^* + B(w_n), \tilde{u}_n - u_n\rangle + f(u_n, \tilde{u}_n) + J^0(\gamma(u_n); \gamma(\tilde{u}_n) - \gamma(u_n)) \geq t_n,\ \forall z_n^* \in T(\tilde{u}_n). \tag{12.49}$$

Let $z^* \in T(\bar{u})$. As $\tilde{u}_n \to \bar{u}$ and T is lower semicontinuous at $\bar{u}$ (condition $[\mathbf{H}_T^1]$), then from Proposition 12.2.11 we deduce that there exists $\varpi_n^* \in T(\tilde{u}_n)$ such that $\varpi_n^* \to z^*$. Hence, from (12.49) we get

$$\langle \varpi_n^* + B(w_n), \tilde{u}_n - u_n\rangle + f(u_n, \tilde{u}_n) + J^0(\gamma(u_n); \gamma(\tilde{u}_n) - \gamma(u_n)) \geq t_n. \tag{12.50}$$

Taking the lower limit when $n \to +\infty$ in both sides of (12.50), we obtain, thanks to $[\mathbf{H}_\gamma]$ and Proposition 12.2.14 (ii), that

$$\liminf f(u_n, \tilde{u}_n) \geq 0. \tag{12.51}$$

Hence, from condition (iv) of Theorem 12.4.1 we obtain that

$$\limsup f(u_n, z_n) \leq f(u, z), \text{ for all } z \in X \text{ and } z_n \to z. \tag{12.52}$$

Let y be an arbitrary element in $K(\bar{w})$. As $w_n \rightharpoonup \bar{w}$, then from Definition 12.2.12 (i) we deduce that there exists $y_n \in K(w_n)$ such that $y_n \to y$. From (12.45), we obtain

$$\langle u_n^* + B(w_n), y_n - u_n \rangle + f(u_n, y_n) + J^0(\gamma(u_n); \gamma(y_n) - \gamma(u_n)) \geq t_n, \ \forall u_n^* \in T(u_n). \tag{12.53}$$

Using the fact that T is weakly stable f-pseudomonotone with respect to $\mathcal{R}(B) + U(\gamma, J)$, we obtain

$$\langle y_n^* + B(w_n), y_n - u_n \rangle + f(u_n, y_n) + J^0(\gamma(u_n); \gamma(y_n) - \gamma(u_n)) \geq t_n, \ \forall y_n^* \in T(y_n). \tag{12.54}$$

Let y^* be an arbitrary element in $T(y)$, then by using the fact that $y_n \to y$ and T is lower semicontinuous at y, we deduce, thanks to Proposition 12.2.11, that there exists $s_n^* \in T(y_n)$ such that $s_n^* \to y^*$. By (12.54) we obtain that

$$\langle s_n^* + B(w_n), y_n - u_n \rangle + f(u_n, y_n) + J^0(\gamma(u_n); \gamma(y_n) - \gamma(u_n)) \geq t_n. \tag{12.55}$$

Therefore, taking the upper limit when $n \to +\infty$ in both sides of (12.55), we get thanks to condition $[\mathbf{H}_\gamma]$, Proposition 12.2.14 (ii) and relation (12.52), that

$$\langle y^* + B(\bar{w}), y - \bar{u} \rangle + f(\bar{u}, y) + J^0(\gamma(\bar{u}); \gamma(y) - \gamma(\bar{u})) \geq 0, \ \forall y \in K(\bar{w}), \ \forall y^* \in T(y). \tag{12.56}$$

Let v be an arbitrary element in $K(\bar{w})$ and let us set $v_n := \frac{1}{n}v + (1 - \frac{1}{n})\bar{u} \in K(\bar{w})$, with $n \in \mathbb{N} \setminus \{0\}$. Note that $v_n \to \bar{u}$ and from (12.56) we have

$$\langle v_n^* + B(\bar{w}), v_n - \bar{u} \rangle + f(\bar{u}, v_n) + J^0(\gamma(\bar{u}); \gamma(v_n) - \gamma(\bar{u})) \geq 0, \quad \text{for all } v_n^* \in T(v_n). \tag{12.57}$$

It follows, by using $[\mathbf{H}_f]$ (ii) and Proposition 12.2.14 (i), that

$$\langle v_n^* + B(\bar{w}), v - \bar{u} \rangle + f(\bar{u}, v) + J^0(\gamma(\bar{u}); \gamma(v) - \gamma(\bar{u})) \geq 0, \quad \text{for all } v_n^* \in T(v_n). \tag{12.58}$$

Let u^* be an arbitrary element in $T(\bar{u})$. As $v_n \to \bar{u}$, then from $[\mathbf{H}_T^1]$ and Proposition 12.2.11 we deduce that there exists $l_n^* \in T(v_n)$ such that $l_n^* \to u^*$. Hence, from (12.58) we get

$$\langle l_n^* + B(\bar{w}), v - \bar{u} \rangle + f(\bar{u}, v) + J^0(\gamma(\bar{u}); \gamma(v) - \gamma(\bar{u})) \geq 0. \tag{12.59}$$

By considering the limit when $n \to +\infty$ in (12.59), we obtain

$$\langle u^* + B(\bar{w}), v - \bar{u}\rangle + f(\bar{u}, v) + J^0(\gamma(\bar{u}); \gamma(v) - \gamma(\bar{u})) \geq 0, \ \forall u^* \in T(\bar{u}), \ \forall v \in K(\bar{w}).$$

Thus, $\bar{u} \in \mathbb{S}(\bar{w})$. Consequently, as the functional $\mathcal{J}$ is weakly lower semicontinuous, then from (12.44) we get

$$\tilde{\beta}(0) \leq \mathcal{J}(\bar{w}, \bar{u}) \leq \liminf \mathcal{J}(w_n, u_n) \leq \tilde{\beta}(0) - \frac{1}{2} r_0,$$

which is impossible since $r_0 > 0$. Which completes the proof. □

Theorem 12.4.5 *Assume that* $[\mathbf{H}_K]$, $[\mathbf{H}_T^1]$, $[\mathbf{H}_f]$ *(ii)-(iii),* $[\mathbf{H}_\gamma]$ *are satisfied, and that* $K : U_{ad} \to 2^X$ *is M-continuous. Suppose that conditions (i), (iii), (iv) and (v) of Theorem 12.4.2 are satisfied and T is weakly stable f-pseudomonotone with respect to* $\mathcal{R}(B) + U(\gamma, J)$*, where* $U(\gamma, J)$ *is defined in (12.11). If the function* $P : \mathbb{R} \times \mathbb{R}_- \to \mathbb{R}$ *satisfies* **[A1]**, *then the zero duality gap property (12.4) holds.*

Proof. The proof is similar to the one of Theorem 12.4.4. □

Theorem 12.4.6 *Assume that* $[\mathbf{H}_K]$, $[\mathbf{H}_T^1]$, $[\mathbf{H}_f]$ *(ii)-(iii),* $[\mathbf{H}_\gamma]$ *are satisfied, and that* $K : U_{ad} \to 2^X$ *is M-continuous. In addition, suppose that the conditions (iii) and (iv) of Theorem 12.4.1 are satisfied, the cost function* $\mathcal{J} : U_{ad} \times X \to \mathbb{R}$ *is weakly lower semicontinuous, T is weakly stable f-pseudomonotone with respect to* $\mathcal{R}(B) + U(\gamma, J)$*, where* $U(\gamma, J)$ *is defined in (12.11) and the following coercivity condition holds:*

$(\mathcal{C})$ *There exists* $v_0 \in \bigcap_{w \in U_{ad}} K(w)$ *such that*

$$\lim_{\|(w,u)\| \to +\infty} \Big[\sup_{u^* \in T(u)} \langle u^* + B(w), v_0 - u\rangle + f(u, v_0) + J^0(\gamma(u); \gamma(v_0) - \gamma(u))\Big] = -\infty.$$

If the function $P : \mathbb{R} \times \mathbb{R}_- \to \mathbb{R}$ *satisfies* **[A1]**, *then the zero duality gap property (12.4) holds.*

Proof. By using Theorem 12.4.3 we obtain that $-\infty < \tilde{\beta}(0) < +\infty$. Thanks to Proposition 12.2.3, it sufficient to verify that the perturbation function $\tilde{\beta}(\cdot)$ is lower semicontinuous at 0. By contradiction suppose that there exists $r_0 > 0$ such that

$$\liminf_{t \to 0} \tilde{\beta}(t) \leq \tilde{\beta}(0) - r_0.$$

Hence, there exists $t_n \to 0$, $w_n \in U_{ad}$ and $u_n \in \mathbb{H}_{w_n}(t_n)$ such that

$$\mathcal{J}(w_n, u_n) \leq \tilde{\beta}(0) - \frac{1}{2} r_0, \text{ for all } n \in \mathbb{N}. \tag{12.60}$$

Let us verify that the sequence $\{(w_n,u_n)\}_{n\in\mathbb{N}}$ is bounded. Suppose the contrary, then for a subsequence we have $\|(w_n,u_n)\|\to+\infty$. As $u_n\in\mathbb{H}_{w_n}(t_n)$, then $u_n\in K(w_n)$ and $h_{w_n}(u_n)\geq t_n$. It follows that $t_n\leq 0$ and

$$\langle u_n^*+B(w_n),v-u_n\rangle+f(u_n,v)+J^0(\gamma(u_n);\gamma(v)-\gamma(u_n))\geq t_n, \qquad (12.61)$$

for all $v\in K(w_n)$, for all $u_n^*\in T(u_n)$.

By taking $v=v_0$ in the previous inequality, we obtain

$$\sup_{u^*\in T(u_n)}\left[\langle u_n^*+B(w_n),v_0-u_n\rangle+f(u_n,v_0)+J^0(\gamma(u_n);\gamma(v_0)-\gamma(u_n))\right]\geq t_n. \qquad (12.62)$$

By taking the limit when $n\to+\infty$ in both sides of (12.62) and since $t_n\to 0$, we get

$$\lim_{n\to+\infty}\left[\sup_{u^*\in T(u_n)}\langle u_n^*+B(w_n),v_0-u_n\rangle+f(u_n,v_0)+J^0(\gamma(u_n);\gamma(v_0)-\gamma(u_n))\right]\geq 0,$$

which is in contradiction with the coercivity condition $(\mathcal{C})$. Therefore, the sequence $\{(w_n,u_n)\}_{n\in\mathbb{N}}$ is bounded. Hence, for a subsequence we have $w_n\rightharpoonup\bar{w}\in U_{ad}$ and $u_n\rightharpoonup\bar{u}$. Since $u_n\in K(w_n)$ and $K(\cdot)$ is M-continuous, we obtain that $\bar{u}\in K(\bar{w})$. For the rest of the proof, we proceed similarly as in the proof of Theorem 12.4.4 by showing that $\bar{u}\in\mathbb{S}(\bar{w})$. □

12.5 Application to Optimal Control of a Frictional Contact Problem

In this section, we give a physical application to which our main results of the previous section can be applied. We consider the optimal control of a frictional contact problem from theory of elasticity with subdifferential boundary conditions.

We consider the following physical setting. A deformable body occupies an open bounded connected set $\Omega\subset\mathbb{R}^d$ $(d=1,2,3)$ with boundary $\partial\Omega=\Gamma$ assumed to be Lipschitz continuous. We denote by $\nu=(\nu_i)$ the outward normal vector. Here and below, the indices i,j,k,l run from 1 to d; an index that follows a comma indicates a derivative with respect to the corresponding component of the spatial variable $\mathbf{x}=(x_i)\in\bar{\Omega}=\Omega\cup\Gamma$ describing the position vector, and the summation convention over repeated indices is adopted. We suppose that Γ consists of three mutually disjoint and measurable parts Γ_D, Γ_N and Γ_C such that $meas(\Gamma_D)>0$. We denote by $\mathbb{S}^d$ the space of second order symmetric tensors on $\mathbb{R}^d$ or, equivalently, the space of symmetric matrices of order d. On $\mathbb{R}^d$ and $\mathbb{S}^d$ we use the inner products and the Euclidean norms defined by

$$\mathbf{u}\cdot\mathbf{v}=u_iv_i,\quad \|\mathbf{u}\|=(\mathbf{u}\cdot\mathbf{u})^{1/2}\quad \text{for all } \mathbf{u}=(u_i),\mathbf{v}=(v_i)\in\mathbb{R}^d,$$
$$\sigma\cdot\tau=\sigma_i\tau_i,\quad \|\sigma\|=(\sigma\cdot\sigma)^{1/2}\quad \text{for all } \sigma=(\sigma_{ij}),\tau=(\tau_{ij})\in\mathbb{S}^d.$$

We denote by u_ν and $\mathbf{u}_\tau$ the normal and tangential components of the displacement field $\mathbf{u}$ on the boundary, give by

$$u_\nu = \mathbf{u}\cdot\nu, \quad \mathbf{u}_\tau = \mathbf{u} - u_\nu \nu.$$

We also denote by σ_ν and σ_τ the normal and tangential components of the tensor σ on the boundary, i.e.,

$$\sigma_\nu = (\sigma\nu)\cdot\nu, \ \sigma_\tau = \sigma\nu - \sigma_\nu\nu.$$

Let $\mathcal{P}$ and $\mathcal{Q}$ be reflexive Banach space and $W = \mathcal{P}\times\mathcal{Q}$. Let $\mathcal{P}_{ad}$ and $\mathcal{Q}_{ad}$ be, respectively, nonempty, closed and convex subsets of $\mathcal{P}$ and $\mathcal{Q}$, and $U_{ad} = \mathcal{P}_{ad}\times\mathcal{Q}_{ad}\subset W$ be the set of admissible controls.

The classical model for the contact process is the following.

Problem $(\mathcal{P}_1)$**:** Given $w=(p,q)\in U_{ad}$, find a displacement field $\mathbf{u}=(u_i):\Omega\to\mathbb{R}^d$, a stress field $\sigma=(\sigma_{ij}):\Omega\to\mathbb{S}^d$ and an interface force $\xi_\nu:\Gamma_C\to\mathbb{R}$ such that

$$\sigma(\mathbf{u}) = \mathcal{A}(\varepsilon(\mathbf{u})) \quad \text{in } \Omega, \tag{12.63}$$

$$\mathrm{Div}\,\sigma(\mathbf{u}) + \mathbf{f}_0 = \mathbf{0} \quad \text{in } \Omega, \tag{12.64}$$

$$\mathbf{u} = \mathbf{0} \quad \text{on } \Gamma_D, \tag{12.65}$$

$$\sigma(\mathbf{u})\nu = \mathbf{f}_N + B(q) \quad \text{on } \Gamma_N, \tag{12.66}$$

$$u_\nu \le g(p), \sigma_\nu(\mathbf{u}) + \xi_\nu \le 0, (\sigma_\nu(\mathbf{u})+\xi_\nu)(u_\nu+\xi_\nu) = 0, \xi_\nu \in \partial j_\nu(u_\nu) \quad \text{on } \Gamma_C, \tag{12.67}$$

$$\|\sigma_\tau(\mathbf{u})\| \le F_b(u_\nu), -\sigma_\tau(\mathbf{u}) = F_b(u_\nu)\frac{\mathbf{u}_\tau}{\|\mathbf{u}_\tau\|} \ \text{ if } \|\mathbf{u}_\tau\| \ne 0 \quad \text{on } \Gamma_C. \tag{12.68}$$

Problem $(\mathcal{P}_1)$ was first introduced and studied in [24], see also [12].

A description of the equations and conditions in Problem $(\mathcal{P}_1)$ is the following. Equation (12.63) represents a general elastic constitutive law, where $\mathcal{A}$ is the elasticity operator, assumed to be nonlinear, and $\varepsilon(\mathbf{u})$ denotes the linearized strain tensor defined by

$$\varepsilon(\mathbf{u}) = (\varepsilon_{ij}(\mathbf{u})), \ \ \varepsilon_{ij}(\mathbf{u}) = \frac{1}{2}(u_{i,j}+u_{j,i}) \quad \text{in } \Omega.$$

Equation (12.64) is the equation of equilibrium, where $\mathbf{f}_0$ denotes the density of the body forces. As the process is assumed to be static, then the inertial term in the equation of motion is neglected. Here "Div" is the divergence operator, i.e., $\mathrm{Div}\,\sigma = (\sigma_{ij,j})$ where $\sigma_{ij,j} = \frac{\partial\sigma_{ij}}{\partial x_j}$. Relation (12.65) represents the displacement homogeneous boundary condition, which means that the body is fixed on Γ_D. Equation (12.66) is the traction boundary condition with surface traction of density $\mathbf{f}_N + B(q)$ acting on Γ_N, where q is the control parameter. Conditions (12.67) and (12.68), formulated on the contact surface Γ_C, represent the contact and the friction law, respectively. Here $g > 0$ denotes the thickness of the elastic layer which depends on the control parameter p, F_b is the frictional bound which is a positive function and $\partial j_\nu(\cdot)$ represents the Clarke subdifferential of a given function j_ν. To give a brief comment on the contact and the friction law, condition (12.67) represents the multi-valued normal compliance contact condition with unilateral constraints of Signorini type and the friction law (12.68) is a variant of the Coulomb law of dry friction in which the friction bound F_b depends on the normal displacement u_ν. We refer to [24] for more detailed description of these conditions with mechanical interpretations. More details on static contact models with elastic materials can be found in [23, 25, 36].

For the variational formulation of the problem $(\mathcal{P}_1)$, we use the spaces

$$H = L^2(\Omega;\mathbb{R}^d),\ \mathcal{H} = L^2(\Omega;\mathbb{S}^d),\ V = \{\mathbf{v} \in H^1(\Omega;\mathbb{R}^d) : \mathbf{v} = \mathbf{0} \text{ on } \Gamma_D\}.$$

In the sequel, we still denote by $\mathbf{v}$ the trace of an element $\mathbf{v} \in H^1(\Omega;\mathbb{R}^d)$. On the space V we consider the inner product and the associated norm given by

$$\langle \mathbf{u},\mathbf{v}\rangle_V = \langle \varepsilon(\mathbf{u}),\varepsilon(\mathbf{v})\rangle_{\mathcal{H}},\ \ \|\mathbf{u}\|_V = \|\varepsilon(\mathbf{u})\|_{\mathcal{H}} \quad \text{for all } \mathbf{u},\mathbf{v} \in V.$$

As $meas(\Gamma_D) > 0$, then V is a Hilbert space, see, e.g., [23]. Furthermore, by the Sobolev trace theorem, we have

$$\|\mathbf{v}\|_{L^2(\Gamma;\mathbb{R}^d)} \le \|\gamma\|\,\|\mathbf{v}\|_V, \text{ for all } \mathbf{v} \in V,$$

where $\|\gamma\|$ is the norm of the trace operator $\gamma : V \to L^2(\Gamma;\mathbb{R}^d)$. The space $\mathcal{H}$ will be endowed with the Hilbertian structure given by the inner product

$$\langle \sigma,\tau\rangle_{\mathcal{H}} = \int_\Omega \sigma_{ij}(x)\,\tau_{ij}(x)\,dx, \quad \sigma,\tau \in \mathcal{H}$$

and the associated norm $\|\cdot\|_{\mathcal{H}}$.

In our study of the optimal control problem $(\mathcal{P}_1)$, we assume that the elastic operator $\mathcal{F}$, the potential function j_ν and the friction coefficient bound F_b verify the following hypotheses:

[$\mathbf{H}_{\mathcal{F}}$] $\mathcal{F} : \Omega \times \mathbb{S}^d \to \mathbb{S}^d$ satisfies

(1) $\mathcal{F}(\cdot,\varpi)$ is measurable on Ω for all $\varpi \in \mathbb{S}^d$;

(2) $\mathcal{F}(x,\cdot)$ is continuous on $\text{conv}(N)$ for each finite subset N of $\mathbb{S}^d$ and a.e. $x \in \Omega$;

(3) There exists $\alpha_0 \in L^2(\Omega)$, $\alpha_0 \ge 0$, and a constant $\alpha_1 > 0$ such that

$$\|\mathcal{F}(x,\varpi)\| \le \alpha_0(x) + \alpha_1\|\varpi\|, \text{ for all } \varpi \in \mathbb{S}^d, \text{ a.e. } x \in \Omega;$$

(4) For all $\varepsilon_1,\varepsilon_2 \in \mathbb{S}^d$ and a.e. $x \in \Omega$

$$(\mathcal{F}(x,\varepsilon_1) - \mathcal{F}(x,\varepsilon_2))\cdot(\varepsilon_1 - \varepsilon_2) \ge 0;$$

(5) $\mathcal{F}(x, \mathbf{0}_{\mathbb{S}^d}) = \mathbf{0}_{\mathbb{S}^d}$ for a.e. $x \in \Omega$.

[H$_{j_\nu}$] $j_\nu : \Gamma_C \times \mathbb{R}^d \to \mathbb{R}$ is such that

(1) $j_\nu(x, \cdot)$ is locally Lipschitz on $\mathbb{R}^d$ for a.e. $x \in \Gamma_C$;

(2) $j_\nu(\cdot, \xi)$ is measurable on Γ_C for all $\xi \in \mathbb{R}^d$;

(3) $|\eta| \le a(1 + |\xi|)$ for all $\eta \in \partial j_\nu(x, \xi)$, $\xi \in \mathbb{R}^d$ and a.e. $x \in \Gamma_C$ with $a > 0$.

[H$_{F_b}$] $F_b : \Gamma_C \times \mathbb{R}_+ \to \mathbb{R}_+$ is such that

(1) $F_b(\cdot, s)$ is measurable on Γ_C for all $s \in \mathbb{R}_+$;

(2) There exists $L_{F_b} > 0$ such that

$$|F_b(x, s_1) - F_b(x, s_2)| \le L_{F_b}|s_1 - s_2|, \text{ for all } s_1, s_2 \in \mathbb{R}_+, \text{ a.e. } x \in \Gamma_C;$$

(3) $F_b(x, s) = 0$ for all $s \le 0$, $F_b(x, s) \ge 0$ for all $s \ge 0$, for a.e. $x \in \Gamma_C$.

Moreover, we suppose that the following regularity conditions are satisfied by the densities of the body forces and surface traction:

$$\mathbf{f}_0 \in H, \ \ \mathbf{f}_N \in L^2(\Gamma_N; \mathbb{R}^d), \tag{12.69}$$

and that

$$g \in C(\Gamma_C \times \mathcal{P}; \mathbb{R}_+), \ \ B \in \mathcal{L}(\mathcal{Q}; L^2(\Gamma_N; \mathbb{R}^d)). \tag{12.70}$$

We consider the set of admissible displacement field defined for $w = (p, q) \in U_{ad}$ by

$$K(w) = \{\mathbf{u} \in V : u_\nu \le g(p) \text{ on } \Gamma_C\}. \tag{12.71}$$

Furthermore, we define an element $\mathbf{f} \in V^*$ by

$$\langle \mathbf{f}, \mathbf{v} \rangle = \langle \mathbf{f}_0, \mathbf{v} \rangle_H + \langle \mathbf{f}_N, \mathbf{v} \rangle_{L^2(\Gamma_N; \mathbb{R}^d)}, \text{ for all } \mathbf{v} \in V, \tag{12.72}$$

and an operator $\mathcal{B} \in \mathcal{L}(W; V^*)$ defined for $w = (p, q) \in W$ by

$$\langle \mathcal{B}(w), v \rangle_V = \langle B(q), v \rangle_{L^2(\Gamma_N; \mathbb{R}^d)}, \text{ for all } \mathbf{v} \in V. \tag{12.73}$$

From (12.63)–(12.68) and (12.69)–(12.73), using integration by part and standard argument we derive the following variational formulation of Problem $(\mathcal{P}_1)$:

Problem $(\mathcal{P}_2)$**:** Given $w \in U_{ad}$, find $\mathbf{u} \in K(w)$ such that

$$\begin{aligned} &\langle \mathcal{F}(\varepsilon(\mathbf{u})), \varepsilon(\mathbf{v}) - \varepsilon(\mathbf{u}) \rangle_{\mathcal{H}} + \int_{\Gamma_C} F_b(u_\nu)(\|\mathbf{v}_\tau\| - \|\mathbf{u}_\tau\|)d\Gamma \\ &+ \int_{\Gamma_C} j_\nu^0(\mathbf{u}_\nu; \mathbf{v}_\nu - \mathbf{u}_\nu)d\Gamma \ge \langle \mathbf{f} + \mathcal{B}(w), \mathbf{v} - \mathbf{u} \rangle, \ \forall \mathbf{v} \in K(w). \end{aligned} \tag{12.74}$$

We shall apply the results obtained in Section 3 in the following functional framework: $X = V$, $K : U_{ad} \to 2^V$ given by relation (12.71),

$$T : V \to V^*, \qquad \langle T(\mathbf{u}), \mathbf{v}\rangle_V = \langle \mathcal{F}(\varepsilon(\mathbf{u})), \varepsilon(\mathbf{v})\rangle_{\mathcal{H}}, \quad \text{for } \mathbf{u}, \mathbf{v} \in V,$$

$$f : V \times V \to \mathbb{R}, \qquad f(\mathbf{u}, \mathbf{v}) = \int_{\Gamma_C} F_b(u_\nu)(\|\mathbf{v}_\tau\| - \|\mathbf{u}_\tau\|)d\Gamma, \quad \text{for } \mathbf{u}, \mathbf{v} \in V,$$

$$\mathbf{B} : U_{ad} \to V^*, \qquad \langle \mathbf{B}(w), \mathbf{v}\rangle_V = \langle -\mathbf{f} - \mathcal{B}(w), \mathbf{v}\rangle_V, \quad \text{for } w \in U_{ad}, \mathbf{v} \in V,$$

$$J : V \to \mathbb{R}, \qquad J(\mathbf{v}) = \int_{\Gamma_C} j_\nu(\mathbf{v}_\nu)d\Gamma, \quad \text{for } \mathbf{v} \in V.$$

Hypothesis $[\mathbf{H}_{j_\nu}]$ guaranty that the function $J(\cdot)$ is well defined and locally Lipschitz, and by Theorem 3.47 in [23] we obtain

$$J^0(\mathbf{u}; \mathbf{v}) \le \int_{\Gamma_C} j_\nu^0(\mathbf{u}_\nu; \mathbf{v}_\nu)d\Gamma, \quad \text{for } \mathbf{u}, \mathbf{v} \in V.$$

The cost function $\mathcal{J} : U_{ad} \times K(U_{ad}) \to \mathbb{R}$ of the optimal control problem governed by the problem $(\mathcal{P}_2)$ is given by

$$\mathcal{J}(w, u) := \|\Lambda(u) - \Upsilon\|_Z^2 + \varepsilon\|w\|_W^2,$$

where Z is a given Banach space, $\Lambda : W \to Z$ is a compact mapping and $\Upsilon \in Z$ is a target. We pose the following optimal control problem: Find $w^* = (p^*, q^*) \in U_{ad}$ (optimal control), $\mathbf{u}^* \in K(w^*)$ and $\mathbf{u}^* \in \mathbb{S}(w^*)$ such that

$$\mathcal{J}(w^*, \mathbf{u}^*) = \min_{w \in U_{ad},\ \mathbf{u} \in \mathbb{S}(w)} \mathcal{J}(w, \mathbf{u}), \tag{12.75}$$

where $\mathbb{S}(w)$ is the solution set of Problem $(\mathcal{P}_2)$.

Our results in Section 3 can be applied to ensure, by adding some appropriate smallness conditions, the existence of an optimal control of the problem (12.75) as well as to establish a zero duality gap property between the primal problem and its augmented Lagrangian dual problem.

12.6 Remarks and Comments

In comparison with recent results in literature on Lagrangian methods for optimal control problems governed by mixed hemivariational inequalities, we would like to mention that our results improve considerably the ones in [20] and [18, Theorem 4.2] where it has been assumed that the bifunction f in the state control system (12.1) is weakly upper semicontinuous with respect to the first argument and antimonotone, i.e., $f(u, v) + f(v, u) \ge 0$. In our approach, we have avoided

the antimonotonicity assumption on f and we have relaxed the weak upper semi-continuity of f with respect to the first argument by using the pseudomonotonicity of f in the sense of Brézis, which is a strictly weaker condition as pointed out by Steck in his recent paper [37]. We would like also to mention that our results improve also the ones in [39], where the state control system takes a particular form of the inequality (12.1).
On the other hand, it is important to underline that some ambiguities have been pointed out in [20, 39], they are as the following:

- Condition (H_P) in [20] seems to be not well defined: Take for instance in $(H_P)(iii)$, $z=0$ and $y<0$, then we obtain, by using $(H_P)(i)$, that

  $$y = P(y,0) \geq \max\{y, a0\} = 0,$$

  which is impossible. The same remark still holds for Assumption 2.1 in [39] and Assumption 1 in [21].

- In [20], the authors considered in relation (2.4) the function $g_w(\cdot)$ defined on $K(w)$ by

  $$g_w(u) = \sup_{v\in K(w)} \sup_{u^*\in A(u)} \langle u^* + Bw, v-u\rangle_X + f(u,v) + J^0(\gamma u; \gamma v - \gamma u), \quad u \in K(w),$$

  and the set $K_w(y)$ defined for $y>0$ by

  $$K_w(y) = \{u \in K(w) : g_w(u) \leq y\}.$$

  The authors affirmed that "$K_w(0) = S(w)$", where $S(w)$ is the solution set of the state control system (2.3) considered in [20], but this affirmation seems to be not valid. Hence, in [20] it is not clear why $\beta(0)$ is the optimal value of the considered optimal control problem (2.2), where $\beta(\cdot)$ is perturbation function given by relation (2.6) in this paper.

- Theorems 3.3 and 3.4 in [20] and their proofs need to be deeply revised since the assumption (H_A) is not enough to guaranty the validity of the results given in those theorems.

Therefore, the results given in our chapter represent an alternative to the ambiguities present in the papers listed above.

References

[1] Q.H. Ansari and J.-C. Yao. A fixed point theorem and its applications to a system of variational inequalities. Bull. Aust. Math. Soc., 59: 433–442, 1999.

[2] C. Baiocchi and A. Capelo. *Variational and Quasivariational Inequalities: Applications to Free-Boundary Problems*. Wiley, Chichester, 1984.

[3] M. Bergounioux. Optimal control of problems governed by abstract elliptic variational inequalities with state constraints. SIAM J. Control. Optim., 36: 273–289, 1998.

[4] M. Bergounioux and H. Dietrich. Optimal control of problems governed by obstacle type variational inequalities: A dual regularization-penalization approach. Journal of Convex Analysis, 5: 329–352, 1998.

[5] E. Blum and W. Oettli. From optimization and variational inequalities to equilibrium problems. The Mathematics Student, 63: 123–145, 1994.

[6] H. Brézis. Equations et inéquations non linéaires dans les espaces vectoriels en dualité. Ann. Inst. Fourier (Grenoble), 18: 115–175, 1968.

[7] H. Brézis. Problèmes unilatéraux. J. Math. Pures Appl., 51: 1–168, 1972.

[8] O. Chadli, S. Schaible and J.-C. Yao. Regularized equilibrium problems with application to noncoercive hemivariational inequalities. J. Optim. Theory Appl., 121: 571–596, 2004.

[9] FH. Clarke. *Optimization and Nonsmooth Analysis*. John Wiley, New York, 1983.

[10] J. Gwinner. *Nichtlineare Variationsungleichungen mit Anwendungen*. PhD Thesis, Universität Mannheim, 1978.

[11] J. Gwinner. A note on pseudomonotone functions, regularization, and relaxed coerciveness. Nonlinear Anal., 30: 4217–4227, 1997.

[12] C. Jiang and B. Zeng. Continuous dependence and optimal control for a class of variational–hemivariational inequalities. Appl. Math. Optim., 82: 637–656, 2020.

[13] A.A. Khan, S. Migórski and M. Sama. Inverse problems for multi-valued quasi variational inequalities and noncoercive variational inequalities with noisy data. Optimization, 68: 1897–1931, 2019.

[14] D. Kinderlehrer and G. Stampacchia. *An Introduction to Variational Inequalities and their Applications*. Classics in Applied Mathematics, Vol. 31. SIAM, Philadelphia, 2000.

[15] A.A. Khan and M. Sama. Optimal control of multivalued quasi variational inequalities. Nonlinear Anal., 75: 1419–1428, 2012.

[16] F. Liu and M.Z. Nashed. Regularization of nonlinear Ill-posed variational inequalities and convergence rates. Set-Valued Analysis, 6: 313–344, 1998.

[17] Z.H. Liu and B. Zeng. Optimal control of generalized quasi-variational hemivariational inequalities and its applications. Appl. Math. Optim., 72: 305–323, 2015.

[18] Z.H. Liu, S. Migórski and B. Zeng. Existence results and optimal control for a class of quasi mixed equilibrium problems involving the (f,g,h)-quasimonotonicity. Appl. Math. Optim., 79: 257–277, 2019.

[19] O.A. Liskovets. Discrete regularization of optimal control problems on Ill-posed monotone variational inequalities. Math. USSR Izvestiya, 37: 321–335, 1991.

[20] F. Long and B. Zeng. The zero duality gap property for an optimal control problem governed by a multivalued hemivariational inequality. Appl. Math. Optim., 2020.

[21] F. Long and B. Zeng. Lagrangian methods for optimal control problems governed by quasi-hemivariational inequalities. Miskolc Mathematical Notes, 21(2): 969–982, 2020.

[22] S. Migórski, A.A. Khan and S.D. Zeng. Inverse problems for nonlinear quasi-hemivariational inequalities with application to mixed boundary value problems. Inverse Problems, 36: 024006, 2020.

[23] S. Migórski, A. Ochal and M. Sofonea. *Nonlinear Inclusions and Hemivariational Inequalities. Models and Analysis of Contact Problems*. Advances in Mechanics and Mathematics, Vol. 26. Springer, New York, 2013.

[24] S. Migórski, A. Ochal and M. Sofonea. A class of variational-hemivariational inequalities in reflexive Banach spaces. J. Elast., 127: 151–178, 2017.

[25] D. Motreanu and M. Sofonea. Quasivariational inequalities and applications in frictional contact problems with normal compliance. Adv. Math. Sci. Appl., 10: 103–118, 2000.

[26] U. Mosco. Convergence of convex sets and of solutions of variational inequalities. Adv. Math., 3: 512–585, 1969.

[27] Z. Naniewicz and P.D. Panagiotopoulos. *Mathematical Theory of Hemivariational Inequalities and Applications*. Marcel Dekker Basel, New York, Hong Kong, 1995.

[28] M.Z. Nashed and O. Scherzer. Stable approximation of nondifferentiable optimization problems with variational inequalities. pp. 155–207. *In*: Y. Censor and S. Reich (eds.). *Recent Developments in Optimization Theory and Nonlinear Analysis, Contemp. Math., Vol. 204*. Amer. Math. Soc., Providence, 1997.

[29] P.D. Panagiotopoulos. *Inequality Problems in Mechanics and Applications*. Birkhäuser, Boston, 1985.

[30] N.S. Papageorgiou and S.T.H. Kyritsi-Yiallourou. *Handbook of Applied Analysis*. Advances in Mechanics and Mathematics, Vol. 19. Springer, Dordrecht, 2009.

[31] F. Patrone. On the optimal control for variational inequalities. J. Optim. Theory Appl., 22(3): 373–388, 1977.

[32] Z. Peng and K. Kunisch. Optimal control of elliptic variational–hemivariational inequalities. J. Optim. Theory Appl., 178: 1–25, 2018.

[33] A.M. Rubinov, X.X. Huang and X.Q. Yang. The zero duality gap property and lower-semi continuity of the perturbation function. Math. Oper. Res., 27: 775–791, 2001.

[34] Shuzhong Shi. Optimal control of strongly monotone variational inequalities. SIAM J. Control. Optim., 26: 274–290, 1988.

[35] M. Sofonea. Optimal control of a class of variational-hemivariational inequalities in reflexive Banach spaces. Appl. Math. Optim., 79: 621–646, 2019.

[36] M. Sofonea and A. Matei. *Mathematical Models in Contact Mechanics*. London Mathematical Society Lecture Note Series, Vol. 398. Cambridge University Press, Cambridge, 2012.

[37] D. Steck. Brezis pseudomonotonicity is strictly weaker than Ky-Fan hemicontinuity. J. Optim. Theory Appl., 181: 318–323, 2019.

[38] G.J. Tang and N.J. Huang. Existence theorems of the variational-hemivariational inequalities. J. Glob. Optim., 56: 605–622, 2013.

[39] Z.B. Wang, Z.L. Chen, Z.Y. Chen and S.S. Yao. Lagrangian methods for optimal control problems governed by a mixed quasi-variational inequality. Optim. Lett., 12: 1357–1371, 2018.

[40] Z.B. Wang and N.J. Huang. The existence results for optimal control problems governed by quasivariational inequalities in reflexive Banach spaces. Taiwanese J. Math., 16(4): 1221–1243, 2012.

[41] R. Wangkeeree and P. Preechasilp. Existence theorems of the hemivariational inequality governed by a multi-valued map perturbed with a nonlinear term in Banach spaces. J. Glob. Optim., 57: 1447–1464, 2013.

[42] Y.-Y. Zhou, X.-Q. Yang and K.-L. Teo. The existence results for optimal control problems governed by a variational inequality. J. Math. Anal. Appl., 321: 595–608, 2006.

[43] Y.-Y. Zhou, X.-Q. Yang and K.-L. Teo. Optimal control problems governed by a variational inequality via nonlinear Lagrangian methods. Optimization, 55: 187–203, 2006.

Chapter 13

Data Driven Reconstruction Using Frames and Riesz Bases

Andrea Aspri[a], *Leon Frischauf*[b,*], *Yury Korolev*[c] and *Otmar Scherzer*[b,d]

2000 Mathematics Subject Classification. 65J22, 47A52, 42C15

The authors dedicate this chapter to Zuhair Nashed. Otmar Scherzer is grateful for Zuhair's long lasting mentorship, his friendship, and the personal and professional exchange with him.

13.1 Introduction

Inverse problems are concerned with the reconstruction of an unknown quantity $u \in \mathcal{U}$ from its indirect measurements $y \in \mathcal{Y}$ which are related by the *forward model* $T : \mathcal{U} \to \mathcal{Y}$ that describes the relationship between the quantities of interest and the measurements. The forward operator T models the physics of data acquisition and may involve, for instance, integral transforms (such as the Radon

[a] Department of Mathematics, University of Pavia, Via Ferrata, 5 - 27100 Pavia.

[b] Faculty of Mathematics, University of Vienna, Oskar-Morgenstern-Platz 1, A-1090 Vienna, Austria.

[c] Department of Applied Mathematics and Theoretical Physics, University of Cambridge, Wilberforce Road, Cambridge CB3 0WA, United Kingdom.

[d] Johann Radon Institute for Computational and Applied Mathematics (RICAM), Altenbergerstraße 69, A-4040 Linz, Austria.

Emails: andrea.aspri@unipv.it; y.korolev@maths.cam.ac.uk; otmar.scherzer@univie.ac.at

* Corresponding author: leon.frischauf@univie.ac.at

transform, see for instance [12, 13, 9]) and partial differential equations (PDEs) (see for instance [8, 16]).

Previously inverse problems were considered *model driven*, meaning that the physics and chemistry of the acquisition process were expressed as accurately as possible with mathematical formulas. Typically this allows to write the inverse problem as an operator equation

$$Tu = y\,. \tag{13.1}$$

With the rise of the area of big data, *data driven* approaches (that means *avoiding* modeling of the operator T) have emerged (see [2]). They are attractive because they do not require the forward operator explicitly, and often yield superior visual quality of the reconstruction. Instead these approaches require a series of training data.

Currently there is no adequate theory for purely data driven regularisation in inverse problems, i.e., a theory in the setting when the forward operator is given only via n *training pairs*

$$\{u_i, y_i\} \quad \text{such that} \quad Tu_i = y_i \quad \text{for all} \quad i = 1, \dots, n. \tag{13.2}$$

We call $\{u_i\}$ *training inputs* and $\{y_i\}$ *training outputs*, respectively. In [3] we made a first step of an analysis for purely data driven regularization by utilizing the similarity to the concept of *regularization by projection*. We demonstrated that regularisation by projection [15, 6] and variational regularisation [14] can be formulated in a data driven setting and usual results such as convergence and stability can be obtained.

As mentioned above, the proposed method in [3] does not require the explicit knowledge of the operator T but only information on training pairs. For practical applications and in theoretical considerations the training pairs need to be orthonormalized, which we implemented via Gram-Schmidt in [3]. This chapter evaluates alternatives to the Gram-Schmidt orthonormalization, such as Householder reflections, QR decomposition, and in particular *frame decompositions*. The latter can be analyzed along the lines of [3] when the frame forms a *Riesz basis*.

The chapter is organized as follows. In Section 13.2 we review basic results from [3]. In Section 13.3 we review basic facts on *frames* and *Riesz bases*, which are applied in Section 13.4 to data driven regularization. Finally we present numerical results in Section 13.5.

13.2 Gram-Schmidt Orthonormalization

In this section, we recall the main idea used in [3] of data-driven projection methods for reconstructions.

Let T be an operator acting between Hilbert spaces, i.e., $T : \mathcal{U} \to \mathcal{Y}$. The operator T is assumed to be linear, bounded and injective. We consider (13.1) from the introduction.

Let $\mathcal{U}_n$ and $\mathcal{Y}_n$ be finite-dimensional subspaces (of dimension n) of the Hilbert spaces $\mathcal{U}$ and $\mathcal{Y}$, respectively. Let P_{H_n} represents the orthogonal projection operator onto H_n, which is either $H_n = \mathcal{U}_n$ or $H_n = \mathcal{Y}_n$.

In the sequel we denote by $u^\dagger$ the solution of (13.1) and we assume that the *training inputs* $\{u_i\}$ from (13.2) are linearly independent and consequently, due to the injectivity of the operator T, the same holds for $\{y_i\}$.

Finally, it is assumed that $\mathcal{U}_n \subset \mathcal{U}_{n+1}$ and $\mathcal{Y}_n \subset \mathcal{Y}_{n+1}$, for all n and

$$\overline{\bigcup_{n\in\mathbb{N}} \mathcal{U}_n} = \mathcal{U}, \qquad \overline{\bigcup_{n\in\mathbb{N}} \mathcal{Y}_n} = \overline{R(T)}. \tag{13.3}$$

Regularization by projection consists in approximating the solution $u^\dagger$ of (13.1) by the *minimum norm solution* of the projected equation

$$TP_{\mathcal{U}_n} u = y, \tag{13.4}$$

where $P_{\mathcal{U}_n}$ is the orthogonal projection operator onto $\mathcal{U}_n$. The minimum norm solution of this equation is unique and is given by

$$u_n^{\mathcal{U}} = (TP_{\mathcal{U}_n})^\dagger y,$$

where $(TP_{\mathcal{U}_n})^\dagger$ denotes the Moore-Penrose inverse of the operator $TP_{\mathcal{U}_n}$ ([11]). The projection takes place in the space $\mathcal{U}$, hence the superscript in our notation $u_n^{\mathcal{U}}$.

The topic of [3] was to find $u_n^{\mathcal{U}}$ by making use of the training pairs (13.2) without explicit knowledge of the operator T.

This was numerically realized by application of the Gram-Schmidt orthonormalization procedure to the training outputs $\{y_i\}_{i=1}^\infty$, resulting in an orthonormal basis $\{\underline{y_i}\}_{i=1}^\infty$. That is

$$\underline{y_i} = \frac{y_i - \sum_{k=1}^{i-1} \langle y_i, \underline{y_k}\rangle \underline{y_k}}{\|y_i - P_{\mathcal{Y}_{i-1}} y_i\|} \quad \text{for all} \quad i \in \mathbb{N},$$

and consequently with $T\underline{u_i} = \underline{y_i}$ we get

$$\underline{u_i} = \frac{u_i - \sum_{k=1}^{i-1} \langle y_i, \underline{y_k}\rangle \underline{u_k}}{\|y_i - P_{\mathcal{Y}_{i-1}} y_i\|} \quad \text{for all} \quad i \in \mathbb{N};$$

As shown in [3], $(TP_{\mathcal{U}_n})^\dagger = T^{-1}P_{\mathcal{Y}_n}$, hence we get the following reconstruction formula

$$\boxed{u_n^{\mathcal{U}} = T^{-1}P_{\mathcal{Y}_n} y = \sum_{i=1}^{n} \langle y, \underline{y_i}\rangle \underline{u_i} \quad \text{and} \quad Tu_n^{\mathcal{U}} = \sum_{i=1}^{n} \langle y, \underline{y_i}\rangle \underline{y_i}.} \tag{13.5}$$

Remark 13.2.1 *We stress that this algorithm doesn't require the explicit knowledge of the operator T.*

13.2.1 Weak Convergence

We recall a weak convergence result from [3], which is actually formulated for the orthonormalized training inputs $\{\overline{u_i}\}$ of $\{u_i\}$ via Gram-Schmidt. Moreover, we define $T\overline{u_i} = \overline{y_i}$. Note the difference in terminology, because previously we orthonormalized the data $\{y_i\}$ resulting in $\underline{y_i}$.

To prove weak convergence of the reconstruction formula (13.5) for $n \to \infty$, we posed in [3] some assumptions on $\{\overline{u_i}, \overline{y_i}\}$. This seems better suited for inverse problems, because if $\{\overline{u_i}\}$ is orthonormal, the sequence $\{\|\overline{y_i}\|\}$ can be expected to converge to 0, or in other words one may expect some decay in the coefficients of the expansions of $\{\overline{y_i}\}$.

Assumption 13.2.2 *Let*

1. $\sum_{i=1}^{\infty} |\langle u^\dagger, \overline{u_i}\rangle| < \infty$;
2. *For every $n \in \mathbb{N}$ and any $i \geq n+1$ consider the following expansion $P_{y_n}\overline{y_i} = \sum_{j=1}^{n} \beta_j^{i,n} \overline{y_j}$. We assume that there exists some $C > 0$ such that for every $n \in \mathbb{N}$ and every $i \geq n+1$, $\sum_{j=1}^{n} (\beta_j^{i,n})^2 \leq C$.*

Theorem 13.2.3 (Theorems 9 and 11 in [3]) *Let y be the exact right-hand side of (13.1) and $\{u_i, y_i\}_{i=1}^{n}$ the training pairs defined in (13.2). Let Assumption 13.2.2 hold, then $u_n^{\mathcal{U}}$ converges weakly to $u^\dagger$.*

The rest of the chapter consists in deriving similar algorithms for frames and Riesz-bases.

13.3 Basics on Frames and Riesz-Bases

This section is devoted to collect some notations, utilized in the rest of the chapter, and useful results on frames' theory.

In this section, H represents a generic Hilbert space. We denote by $\|\cdot\|$ the norm induced by the inner product in H, denoted by $\langle\cdot,\cdot\rangle$.

Definition 13.3.1 *A sequence $\{f_i\}_{i=1}^{\infty}$ of elements in H is a frame for H if there exist constants $A, B > 0$ such that*

$$A\|f\|^2 \leq \sum_{i=1}^{\infty} |\langle f, f_i\rangle|^2 \leq B\|f\|^2 \quad \textit{for all} \quad f \in H, \tag{13.6}$$

where A, B are called frames bounds.

It follows from the definition that if $\{f_i\}_{i=1}^{\infty}$ is a frame for H, then

$$\overline{\operatorname{span}\{f_i\}_{i=1}^{\infty}} = H\,.$$

There exist some operators associated to a frame

- $F : l^2(\mathbb{N}) \to H$, called *synthesis operator*

$$Fc_i = \sum_{i=1}^{\infty} c_i f_i.$$

- $F^* : H \to l^2(\mathbb{N})$, the adjoint operator of F, called *analysis operator*

$$F^* f = \{\langle f, f_i \rangle\}_{i=1}^{\infty}.$$

- $S : H \to H$, called *frame operator*

$$S = FF^*, \quad Sf = FF^* f = \sum_{i=1}^{\infty} \langle f, f_i \rangle f_i.$$

  S is bounded, invertible, self-adjoint and positive and for every $f \in H$

$$Sf = \sum_{i=1}^{\infty} \langle f, f_i \rangle f_i$$

  is unconditionally convergent (see [5]).

The following theorem follows from the properties of S.

Theorem 13.3.2 *Let $\{f_i\}_{i=1}^{\infty}$ be a frame with frame operator S. Then*

$$f = \sum_{i=1}^{\infty} \langle f, S^{-1} f_i \rangle f_i \quad \text{for all} \quad f \in H \tag{13.7}$$

and

$$f = \sum_{i=1}^{\infty} \langle f, f_i \rangle S^{-1} f_i \quad \text{for all} \quad f \in H. \tag{13.8}$$

Both series are unconditionally convergent.

For our purposes we are interested in a special class of frames, that is Riesz bases. For reader's convenience, we recall here their definition, see for more details [5].

Definition 13.3.3 (Riesz's basis) *Let $\{e_i\}_{i=1}^{\infty}$ be an orthonormal basis for H. A Riesz basis $\{f_i\}_{i=1}^{\infty}$ for H is a family of the form $\{f_i\}_{i=1}^{\infty} = \{Le_i\}_{i=1}^{\infty}$ where $L : H \to H$ is a bounded and bijective operator.*

As a consequence of the previous definition, a Riesz basis is ω-independent, that is

$$\sum_{i=1}^{\infty} c_i f_i = 0 \quad \Rightarrow \quad c_i = 0 \quad \text{for all } i.$$

We summarize some of the properties of Riesz basis in the following proposition.

Proposition 13.3.4 *A Riesz basis $\{f_i\}_{i=1}^{\infty}$ for H is a frame for H, i.e., it satisfies (13.6), and the Riesz basis bounds coincide with the frame bounds A and B. Moreover*

1. *$\{f_i\}_{i=1}^{\infty}$ and $\{S^{-1}f_i\}_{i=1}^{\infty}$ are biorthogonal, i.e., $\langle f_i, S^{-1}f_j\rangle = \delta_{ij}$, where δ_{ij} is the Kronecker symbol;*

2. *for each $f \in H$ there exists a unique sequence of scalars $\{c_i\}_{i=1}^{\infty}$ such that $f = \sum_{i=1}^{\infty} c_i f_i$ and $\sum_{i=1}^{\infty} |c_i|^2 < \infty$;*

3. *for every finite scalar sequence $\{c_i\}$, it holds*

$$A\sum_{i=1}^{\infty}|c_i|^2 \leq \left\|\sum_{i=1}^{\infty}c_i f_i\right\|^2 \leq B\sum_{i=1}^{\infty}|c_i|^2. \tag{13.9}$$

Finally, as a consequence of the previous properties for Riesz basis, it holds

Proposition 13.3.5 *Let J be a countable index set. Any subfamily $\{f_i\}_{i\in J}$ is a Riesz basis for its closed linear spanning set $\overline{span\{f_i\}_{i\in J}}$, with bounds A and B.*

We refer to [4, 5] for more details and some literature on the topic.

13.4 Data Driven Regularization by Frames and Riesz Bases

We propose a reconstruction algorithm based on projection methods onto finite-dimensional subspaces, similar to the one discussed in Section 13.2. However, now, compared with Section 13.2, we consider the case when $\{y_i\}_{i=1}^{\infty}$ forms a frame for $\mathcal{Y}$. Associated with the frame is the synthesis operator F and the Frame operator S on $\mathcal{Y}$. We assume that $\{y_i\}_{i=1}^{n}$ is a frame on $\mathcal{Y}_n :=$ Span$\{y_i : i = 1, \ldots, n\}$ as well. The corresponding *restricted frame operator* $S_n : \mathcal{Y}_n \to \mathcal{Y}_n$ is given by $S_n y = \sum_{i=1}^{n}\langle y, y_i\rangle y_i$, and therefore because of Theorem 13.3.2

$$y = \sum_{i=1}^{n}\left\langle y, S_n^{-1}y_i\right\rangle y_i \quad \text{for all } y \in \mathcal{Y}_n. \tag{13.10}$$

Note that for every $y \in \mathcal{Y}$, $P_{\mathcal{Y}_n}y \in \mathcal{Y}_n$ and therefore, because $\langle P_{\mathcal{Y}_n}y, y_j\rangle = \langle y, y_j\rangle$ we get

$$P_{\mathcal{Y}_n}y = \sum_{i=1}^{n}\left\langle P_{\mathcal{Y}_n}y, S_n^{-1}y_i\right\rangle y_i = \sum_{i=1}^{n}\left\langle y, S_n^{-1}y_i\right\rangle y_i \quad \text{for all } y \in \mathcal{Y}. \tag{13.11}$$

Using the injectivity hypothesis on the operator T, we find that

$$\boxed{u_n^{\mathcal{U}} = \sum_{i=1}^{n}\left\langle y, S_n^{-1}y_i\right\rangle u_i \text{ and } Tu_n^{\mathcal{U}} = \sum_{i=1}^{n}\left\langle y, S_n^{-1}y_i\right\rangle y_i.} \tag{13.12}$$

Remark 13.4.1 *This is the comparable formula for the Gram-Schmidt orthonormalization procedure (13.5). In order to identify the unknown coefficients* $\langle y, S_n^{-1} y_i \rangle$, *we proceed as in [1]: It follows from (13.11) that*

$$\begin{aligned} \langle y, y_j \rangle = \langle P_{\mathcal{Y}_n} y, y_j \rangle &= \left\langle \sum_{i=1}^{n} \langle y, S_n^{-1} y_i \rangle y_i, y_j \right\rangle \\ &= \sum_{i=1}^{n} \langle y, S_n^{-1} y_i \rangle \langle y_i, y_j \rangle \quad \textit{for all} \quad y_j \in \mathcal{Y}_n, \end{aligned} \tag{13.13}$$

or in other words

$$G_{\mathcal{U}_n} X = Y \textit{ with } G_{\mathcal{U}_n} = \left(\langle y_i, y_j \rangle \right)_{i,j=1}^{n}, \; X = \left(\langle y, S_n^{-1} y_i \rangle \right)_{i=1}^{n} \textit{ and } Y = \left(\langle y, y_j \rangle \right)_{j=1}^{n}. \tag{13.14}$$

(13.13) can be implemented for reconstruction.

13.4.1 Weak Convergence

Following the analysis in [3] a similar result as Theorem 13.2.3 on weak convergence can be obtained for Riesz bases. In this case Gram-Schmidt orthormalization is replaced by the calculation of dual frame.

Assumption 13.4.2 *Now, we assume that the training inputs*

$$\{u_i\}_{i=1}^{\infty} \textit{ form a Riesz basis for } \mathcal{U}. \tag{13.15}$$

We emphasize that the assumption that the image data form a Riesz basis is only necessary for the theoretical analysis. In practical applications we only require the knowledge of a dual frame to implement (13.12).

As a consequence of (13.8) we see that

$$u^\dagger = \sum_{i=1}^{\infty} \langle u^\dagger, S^{-1} u_i \rangle u_i \quad \text{and therefore also} \quad y = \sum_{i=1}^{\infty} \langle u^\dagger, S^{-1} u_i \rangle y_i.$$

Then, we consider the projection onto $\mathcal{Y}_n$ that is

$$P_{\mathcal{Y}_n} y = \sum_{i=1}^{\infty} \langle u^\dagger, S^{-1} u_i \rangle P_{\mathcal{Y}_n} y_i$$

Note that in comparison with (13.11) here the inverse of the frame operator S on $\mathcal{U}$ is used, and not S_n on $\mathcal{U}_n$.

We investigate weak convergence of the *Riesz bases based approximation*:

Definition 13.4.3 (Riesz bases based approximation) *We define*

$$\widetilde{u_n^{\mathcal{U}}} := T^{-1} P_{\mathcal{Y}_n} y = \sum_{i=1}^{\infty} \langle u^\dagger, S^{-1} u_i \rangle T^{-1} P_{\mathcal{Y}_n} y_i. \tag{13.16}$$

We can represent $T^{-1}P_{\mathcal{Y}_n}y_i$ in terms of the Riesz basis, for all n and i, that is

$$T^{-1}P_{\mathcal{Y}_n}y_i = \sum_{j=1}^{\infty} c_j^{i,n} u_j. \tag{13.17}$$

To study the convergence of the sequence $\widetilde{u}_n^{\mathcal{U}}$, we need some assumptions about the coefficients of the expansion in (13.16) and (13.17).

Lemma 13.4.4 *Let $\{u_i\}_{i=1}^{\infty}$ be a Riesz basis. If $(\langle u^{\dagger}, S^{-1}u_i\rangle)_{i=1}^{\infty} \in l^1$ and, for every i and n, $\sum_{j=1}^{\infty}\left|c_j^{i,n}\right|^2 < C$, where C is independent of i and n, then $\|\widetilde{u}_n^{\mathcal{U}}\|$ is bounded.*

Proof. Apply Hölder inequality to (13.16), i.e.,

$$\|\widetilde{u}_n^{\mathcal{U}}\| \leq \sum_{i=1}^{\infty} |\langle u^{\dagger}, S^{-1}u_i\rangle| \ \ \sup_i \|T^{-1}P_{\mathcal{Y}_n}y_i\|$$

and, thanks to (13.17) and the assumption on $\sum_{j=1}^{\infty}\left|c_j^{i,n}\right|^2$, we have that

$$\|T^{-1}P_{\mathcal{Y}_n}y_i\|^2 = \|\sum_{j=1}^{\infty} c_j^{i,n}u_j\|^2 \leq B\sum_{j=1}^{\infty}\left|c_j^{i,n}\right|^2 < \infty.$$

The assertion follows using the hypothesis on the coefficients $(\langle u^{\dagger}, S^{-1}u_i\rangle)_{i=1}^{\infty}$.
□

Theorem 13.4.5 *Let the hypotheses of Lemma 13.4.4 hold. Then the sequence (13.16) is weakly convergent to $u^{\dagger}$.*

13.5 Numerical Experiments

The goal of this section is to present numerical experiments illustrating the reconstruction with (13.12) and (13.13) and compare it with different orthonormalization procedures, such as Gram-Schmidt originally proposed in [3], Householder reflections and the QR decomposition.

General Structure of the Experiments. For the numerical experiments, the operator $T : L^2(\Omega) \longrightarrow L^2(\mathbb{R}\times[0,\pi))$ is the Radon transform with a parallel beam geometry (see [9]), which is the same example as considered in [3]. The finite-dimensional training pairs are denoted in this section via the notation $\{\vec{u}_i, \vec{y}_i\}_{i=1}^{n}$, where $\vec{u}_i \in \mathbb{R}^k$ and $\vec{y}_i \in \mathbb{R}^h$, for some $h, k \in \mathbb{N}$.

Each data set includes n different pictures, where each picture consists of N pixels represented as N points, with a gray scale intensity in $[0,1]$, which can be represented as linearly independent elements of $\mathbb{R}^N$. They are used as training data and Radon transformed by the built-in MATLAB®-function for K different angles with $\theta_k \in [0, \pi)$. This provides n different elements of $\mathbb{R}^{M \times K} \simeq \mathbb{R}^{M \cdot K}$, where M is the length of a Radon projection at a specific angle. In the case of quadratic pictures with size $\sqrt{N} \times \sqrt{N}$, this implies that $M \approx \sqrt{2 \cdot N}$, which is the length of the diagonal of the square. In order to receive the preimages, the orthonormal system $\{\underline{\vec{y}_1}, \ldots, \underline{\vec{y}_n}\}$ is backtransformed via the exact inverse Radon transform. This makes it possible to investigate the quality of the procedure by comparing these results to the validation data sets.

13.5.1 Orthonormalization Procedures

In this section we compare *Gram-Schmidt orthonormalization procedure*, *QR decomposition* and *Householder reflection* for solving (13.5).

Gram-Schmidt Method. The vectors defined by

$$c_i := \left\{ \vec{y}_i - \sum_{j=1}^{i-1} \langle \vec{y}_i, \vec{y}_j \rangle \vec{y}_j \right\}_{i=1}^{n}$$

are an orthogonal system (see [7]). After normalizing, we get the orthonormal system by $\underline{\vec{y}_i} := \frac{c_i}{\|c_i\|}$. The computational effort of this algorithm is $\mathcal{O}(MKn^2)$. It is possible to rearrange these calculation steps to make the computational procedure more stable of numerical errors, whereas the computational effort stays the same. This algorithm can be found in [7] and is used here for further computations.

QR Decomposition. By writing all vectors $\vec{y}_i$ as columns of a matrix and performing the MATLAB native *QR* decomposition, we receive an orthonormal system with the same span as the columns of the original matrix, since the columns of Q represent an orthonormal system. The computational effort of this algorithm is $\mathcal{O}(M^2K^2n - MKn^2 + n^3/3)$.

Householder Reflection Method. By applying Householder transformations to the set, one receives an orthonormal system of vectors. The computational effort of this algorithm is $\mathcal{O}(M^2K^2n - MKn^2 + n^3/3)$.

Accuracy of the Orthonormalization Procedures

We investigate the stability of the algorithms on the example of our imaging application. We assume the set $\left\{\underline{\vec{y}_i}\right\}_{i=1}^{n}$ being available and analyze the error of the resulting orthonormal system. We first define an appropriate measure of this error, which quantifies the success of the orthonormalization procedure as a numerical value.

Definition 13.5.1 *For a set* $\left\{\underline{\vec{y}_i}\right\}_{i=1}^{n} \subset \mathbb{R}^{M \cdot K}$*, which is assumed to be approximately orthonormal, we define the matrix* $\underline{Y} \in \mathbb{R}^{n \times n}$ *by*

$$(\underline{Y_{ij}}) := \langle \underline{\vec{y}_i}, \underline{\vec{y}_j} \rangle.$$

Furthermore, we define the orthonormality error ε_{ortho} *by*

$$\varepsilon_{ortho} := \|\underline{Y} - I\|,$$

where I *denotes the* $\mathbb{R}^{n\times n}$ *identity matrix and* $\|\cdot\|$ *maximum absolute column sum of the matrix.*

We test the methods on the example of the Sunflower data set from

`www.kaggle.com/alxmamaev/flowers-recognition`

with different numbers of images and plot the error $\varepsilon_{\text{ortho}}$ over the number n. We furthermore investigate the impact of random permutation of the images, before the method is applied. The results can be observed in Figure 13.1–Figure 13.3.

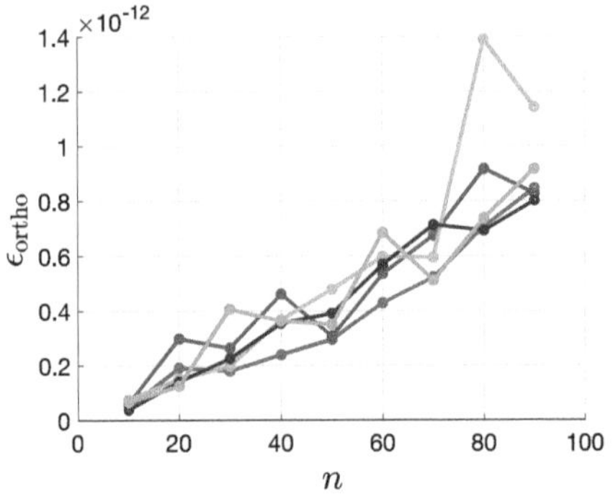

Figure 13.1: Gram-Schmidt method.

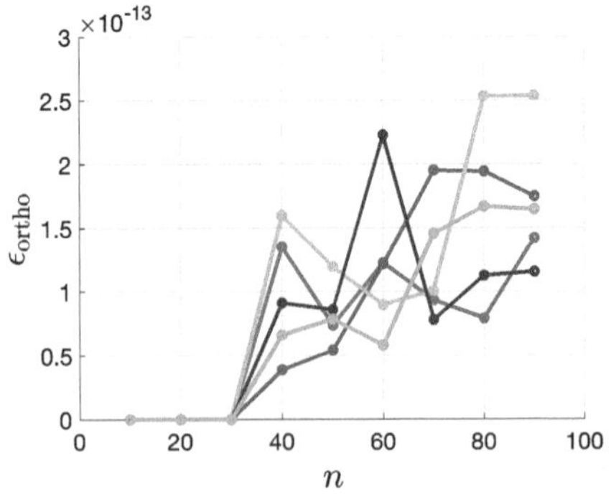

Figure 13.2: Householder reflections.

We see that the error increases with an increased number of images. The sequential order of the images generates slight deviations, but the increasing trend

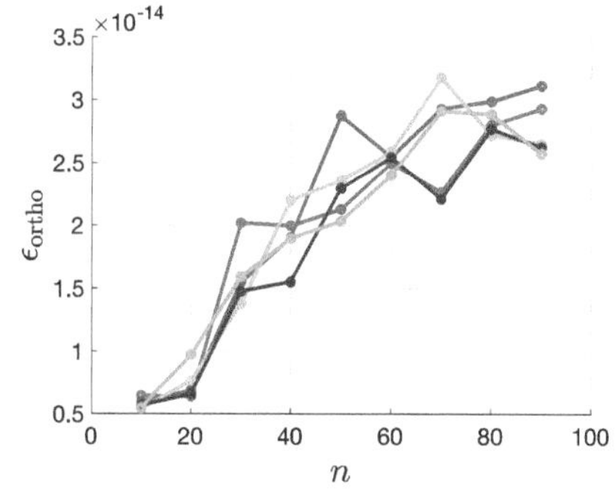

Figure 13.3: QR decomposition in MATLAB.

remains similar. We can furthermore observe that the numerical errors of the Gram-Schmidt method ($\sim 10^{-12}$) are 1 to 2 magnitudes larger that the orthonormalization errors of the Householder reflections ($\sim 10^{-13}$) and the QR decomposition in MATLAB ($\sim 10^{-14}$). So, we choose the QR decomposition for further comparisons.

13.5.2 Comparison Between Frames and Decomposition Algorithms

Our goal now is to compare the "best orthonormalization procedure", namely the QR decomposition, with the reconstruction via (13.14). This comparison is done via the backtransformation of the test data. On the one side, we will compare the two methods in terms of computational efficiency. On the other hand, we will compare the methods in terms of the reconstructed images.

Computational Efficiency

Here we compare the computational efficiency of (13.14) with the computational efficiency of the native QR decomposition. In our case, the reconstruction via (13.14) has clear advantages over the reconstruction via the QR decomposition. For the experiments, a 2,4 GHz 8-Core Intel Core i9 processor is used.

Visual Observations

This section observes the reconstructed images of the methods visually. Applying the method on the Radon transforms of the test images, we can compare the original test image with the output of our algorithm. Additionally, we compare the projected Radon transform $Q_n y$ to the Radon transform of the validation data set.

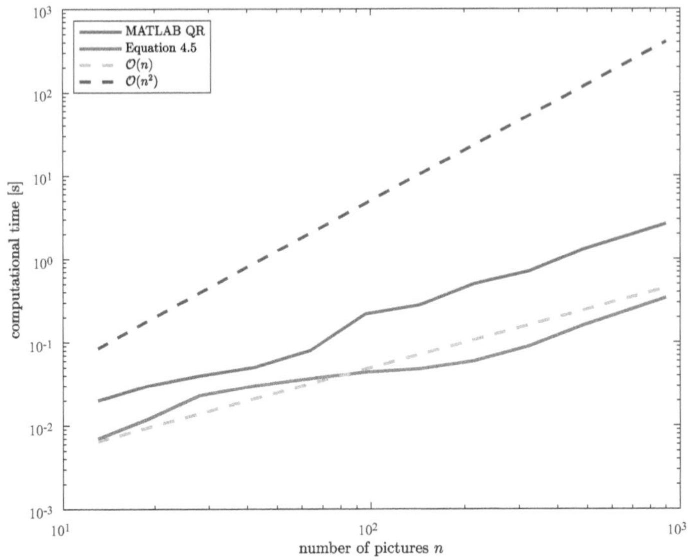

Figure 13.4: Time comparison.

Sunflower data set.

We use $n = 726$ training images (150×150 pixels each) of the sunflower data set. Seven additional images, which are not part of the training images are used as test images. These test images contain 4 images with typical motives of sunflowers, where a good approximation on base of the training data is expected and further 3 images with atypical content. On each test image, the reconstruction procedure is applied individually. The results can be seen in Figures 13.5 and 13.6.

We observe a better similarity of the pictures in Figure 13.5, since due to the similarity of sunflowers, the Radon transformations of sunflower motives can be assumed to be closer to the finite dimensional subspace spanned by the training data, than other arbitrary motives.

Furthermore, we could see that the reconstruction via (13.14) proceeds at a similar level to the reconstruction via the QR decomposition.

Digits data set.

Similar observations are made with a digits data set [10] with $n = 95$ and $n = 995$ training images (28×28 pixels each) and 5 test images in Figures 13.7–13.8. We see that in the case of $n = 995$, the reconstruction via (13.14) works clearly better than the reconstruction via the QR decomposition. The images are much less blurred.

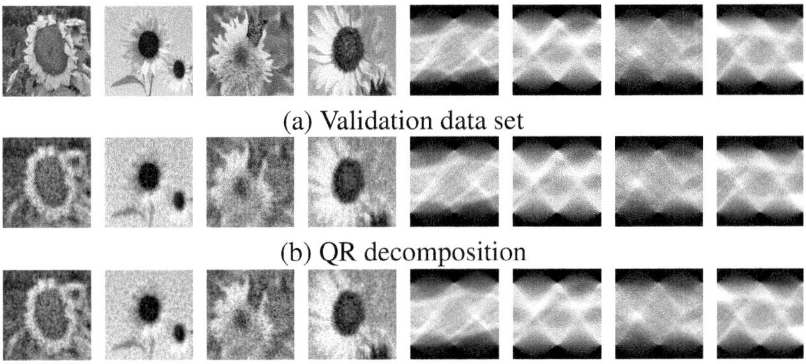

(a) Validation data set

(b) QR decomposition

(c) Reconstruction with (13.14)

Figure 13.5: Reconstructed images via the different methods in comparison to the validation data set for sunflower pictures.

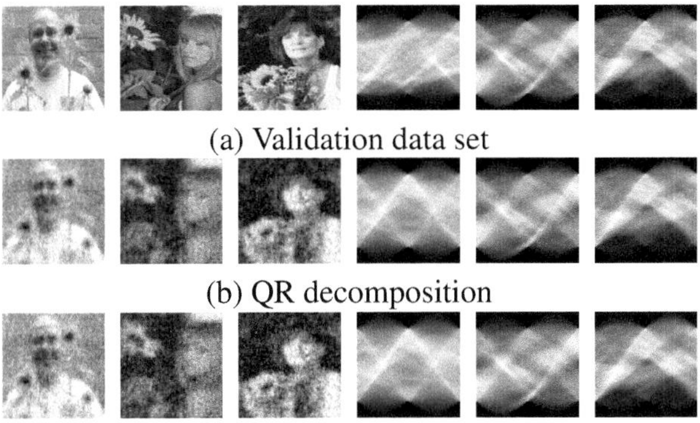

(a) Validation data set

(b) QR decomposition

(c) Reconstruction with (13.14)

Figure 13.6: Reconstructed images via the different methods in comparison to the validation data set for untypical pictures of the data set, which contain a person and where the sunflower motive is only incidental.

13.6 Conclusions

We have adapted the projection method applied in frames theory to a data driven reconstruction algorithm for solving inverse problems. We have shown some numerical experiments comparing the reconstruction formula (13.14) with the one in (13.5), proposed by the authors in [3], which is based on orthonormalization procedures. Numerical results based on the frame method are promising, shown that, with a big amount of training pairs, reconstructions are better than those provided by (13.5), see, for example, Figure 13.8 and with a lower cost in terms

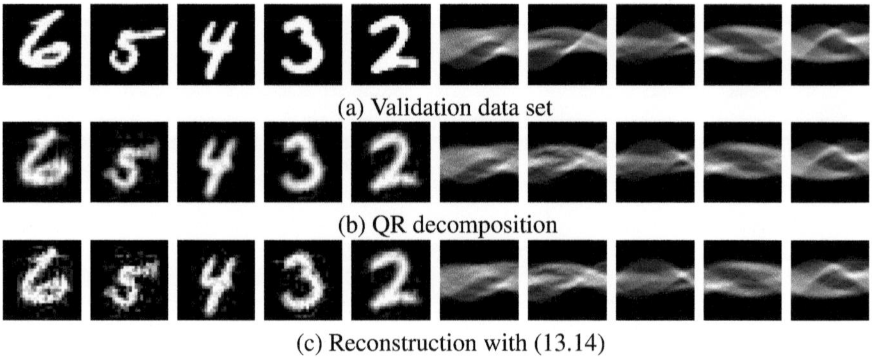

Figure 13.7: Number of training images: 95.

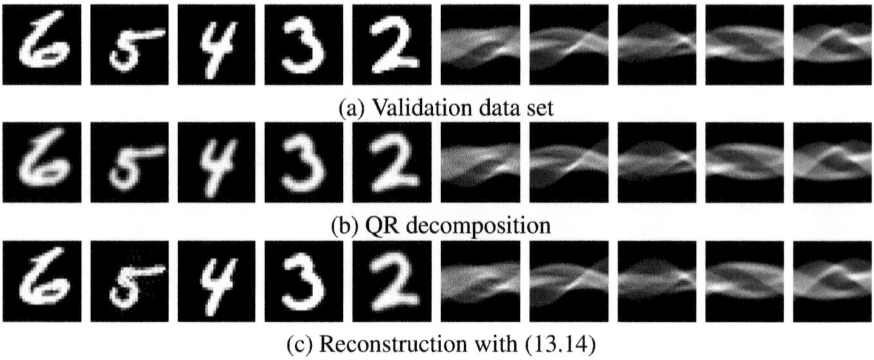

Figure 13.8: Number of training images: 995.

of computational time. Studies on convergence results and rates will be the focus of future works.

Acknowledgments

LF and OS are supported by the FWF via the projects I3661-N27 (Novel Error Measures and Source Conditions of Regularization Methods for Inverse Problems). OS is also supported by FWF via SFB F68, project F6807-N36 (Tomography with Uncertainties). YK acknowledges the support of the EPSRC (Fellowship EP/V003615/1), the Cantab Capital Institute for the Mathematics of Information and the National Physical Laboratory.

References

[1] B. Adcock and D. Huybrechs. Frames and numerical approximation. SIAM Rev., 61(3): 443–473, 2019.

[2] S. Arridge, P. Maass, O. Öktem and C. Schönlieb. Solving inverse problems using data-driven models. Acta Numerica, 28: 1–174, 2019.

[3] A. Aspri, Y. Korolev and O. Scherzer. Data driven regularization by projection. Inverse Problems, 36(12): 125009, 35, 2020.

[4] O. Christensen. Frames containing a Riesz basis and approximation of the frame coefficients using finite-dimensional methods. J. Math. Anal. Appl., 199(1): 256–270, 1996.

[5] O. Christensen. *An Introduction to Frames and Riesz Bases*. Applied and Numerical Harmonic Analysis. Birkhäuser/Springer, second edition, 2016.

[6] H.W. Engl, M. Hanke and A. Neubauer. *Regularization of Inverse Problems*, volume 375 of *Mathematics and its Applications*. Kluwer Academic Publishers Group, Dordrecht, 1996.

[7] G.H. Golub and C.F. Van Loan. *Matrix Computations*. Johns Hopkins Studies in the Mathematical Sciences. Johns Hopkins University Press, Baltimore, MD, third edition, 1996.

[8] V. Isakov. Some inverse problems for elliptic and parabolic equations. pp. 203–214. *In*: *Inverse Problems in Partial Differential Equations (Arcata, CA, 1989)*. SIAM, Philadelphia, PA, 1990.

[9] P. Kuchment. *The Radon Transform and Medical Imaging*. Society for Industrial and Applied Mathematics, Philadelphia, 2014.

[10] Y. Lecun, L. Bottou, Y. Bengio and P. Haffner. Gradient-based learning applied to document recognition. Proceedings of the IEEE, 86(11): 2278–2324, 1998.

[11] M.Z. Nashed (ed.). *Generalized Inverses and Applications*, New York, 1976. Academic Press [Harcourt Brace Jovanovich Publishers].

[12] F. Natterer. *The Mathematics of Computerized Tomography*, volume 32 of *Classics in Applied Mathematics*. Society for Industrial and Applied Mathematics (SIAM), Philadelphia, PA, 2001. Reprint of the 1986 original.

[13] F. Natterer and F. Wübbeling. *Mathematical Methods in Image Reconstruction*. Society for Industrial and Applied Mathematics, 2001.

[14] O. Scherzer, M. Grasmair, H. Grossauer, M. Haltmeier and F. Lenzen. *Variational Methods in Imaging*, volume 167 of *Applied Mathematical Sciences*. Springer, New York, 2009.

[15] T.I. Seidman. Nonconvergence results for the application of least-squares estimation to ill-posed problems. J. Optim. Theory Appl., 30(4): 535–547, 1980.

[16] W.W. Symes. The seismic reflection inverse problem. Inverse Problems, 25(12): 123008, 39, 2009.

Chapter 14

Antenna Problem Induced Regularization and Sampling Strategies

Willi Freeden

2000 AMS Mathematics Subject Classification. 11P21, 35R30, 40A25, 47A52, 62D05, 65B15, 65J20, 65N21.

Dedicated to M. Zuhair Nashed

14.1 Uni-Variate Antenna Problem Induced Recovery Strategies

There is no doubt that the trend setting philosophy to treat ill-posed problems of mathematics was significantly influenced by *M. Zuhair Nashed's understanding of the one-dimensional antenna problem* published in "IEEE Transactions on Antennas and Propagation, Vol. AP-29, No. 2, 220–231, 1981" under the title "Operator-Theoretic and Computational Approaches in Ill-Posed Problems with Applications to Antenna Theory" (cf. [85]).

Department of Mathematics, University of Kaiserslautern, 67663 Kaiserslautern, Germany.
Email: freeden@rhrk.uni-kl.de

M.Z. Nashed's thoughts start from the following situation: Let $F^{\wedge}_{\mathcal{F}_{\sigma\mathbb{Z}}}$ be a function bandlimited to the one-dimensional fundamental cell $\mathcal{F}_{\sigma\mathbb{Z}} = [-\frac{\sigma}{2}, \frac{\sigma}{2})$, $\sigma > 0$, of the 1D lattice $\Lambda = \sigma\mathbb{Z}$, i.e., the Fourier integral

$$F^{\wedge}_{\mathcal{F}_{\sigma\mathbb{Z}}}(t) = \int_{\mathcal{F}_{\sigma\mathbb{Z}}} F(x)\, e^{-2\pi i x \cdot t}\, dx, \quad t \in \mathbb{R}, \tag{14.1}$$

for some square-integrable function F on $\mathcal{F}_{\sigma\mathbb{Z}}$, i.e., $F \in L^2(\mathcal{F}_{\sigma\mathbb{Z}})$.

• **Uni-Variate Antenna Problem in L^2-framework.** Determine the aperture distribution $F \in L^2(\mathcal{F}_{\sigma\mathbb{Z}})$ from the far field $F^{\wedge}_{\mathcal{F}_{\sigma\mathbb{Z}}}$ via the Fredholm integral equation of the first kind

$$AF(t) = \int_{\mathcal{F}_{\sigma\mathbb{Z}}} F(x)\, e^{-2\pi i t \cdot x}\, dx = F^{\wedge}_{\mathcal{F}_{\sigma\mathbb{Z}}}(t) \quad t \in \mathbb{R}. \tag{14.2}$$

Clearly, it is canonical to start with a characterization of the well-posedness of the problem (14.2). Conventionally, a mathematical problem is called well-posed in the sense of Hadamard (cf. [52], [53]), if it satisfies the following properties:

(H1) (Existence) For all (suitable) data, there exists a solution of the problem (in an appropriate sense).

(H2) (Uniqueness) For all (suitable) data, the solution is unique.

(H3) (Stability) The solution depends continuously on the data.

According to this definition, a problem is *ill-posed (or improperly posed) in the sense of Hadamard* if one of these three conditions is violated.

Now, $A : L^2(\mathcal{F}_{\sigma\mathbb{Z}}) \to L^2(\mathbb{R})$, as defined by (14.2), is a compact linear operator mapping the space $L^2(\mathcal{F}_{\sigma\mathbb{Z}})$ to the range $\mathcal{R}(A)$, that understood as subset of $L^2(\mathbb{R})$ is non-closed. Thus, because of the violation of (H3), the integral equation (14.2) represents an ill-posed problem (IPP) in the sense of Hadamard's classification. In other words, the problem (14.2) requires particular solvability procedures.

Ill-posed problems (IPP's) arise in many branches of science, engineering, and mathematics, including computer vision, natural language processing, machine learning, statistics, statistical inference, medical imaging, remote sensing, non-destructive testing, astronomy, geodesy and geophysics, exploration and prospection, and many other fields. It should be noted that J. Hardamard (1865–1963) dismissed ill-posed problems as irrelevant to physics or real world applications, but he was proven wrong four decades after his declaration. It turned out that Hadamard's classification had a tremendous influence on the development of mathematics. Even more, some years ago, starting from Hadamard's properties a more relevant understanding of ill-posedness was provided by a more detailed functional analytical background (cf. [86]) that will be discussed later on.

It should be noted that, during the last century, the *concept of a pseudoinverse (generalized inverse)* found considerable attention in the mathematical as well as geodetic literature (a bibliography, for example, listing over 1700 references on the subject is available in [82]). One of the most significant applications of generalized inverses is to problems of best fit. Therefore one might seek such evidence in the writings of those who laid the foundations of the method of least squares. C.F. Gauss developed the method of least squares in 1794, but he did not publish his results until several years later. Gauss's interest in the subject may be dated back to his considerations of problems in geodesy. One should point out that Gauss [48], [49] did not formally display the pseudoinverse $A^{\dagger}$. However, following D.W. Robinson [102], the ingredients for the construction of a generalized inverse were essentially available to him, but he did not use them. Indeed, there appears to be no evidence that he was inclined to proceed in that direction. On the other hand, his approach to the problem of determining best estimates is certainly in the spirit of generalized inverses. Early interest in the first half of the last century in the subject of generalized inverses was initiated by a paper on matrices by R. Penrose [100]. As a matter of fact, basic elements of this concept had been considered somewhat earlier. For example, E.H. Moore [76] presented a development of the notion (see, e.g., [82] for brief historical sketches of the subject).

The *generalized inverse (or pseudoinverse)* $A^{\dagger}$ is the linear operator which assigns to each element of $\mathcal{D}(A^{\dagger}) = \mathcal{R}(A) + \mathcal{R}(A)^{\perp}$ the unique solution in $\mathcal{N}(A)^{\perp}$ of the *normal equation*. It also follows that $A^{\dagger}$ can be characterized as the linear operator with the function-theoretic properties:

$$\mathcal{D}(A^{\dagger}) = \mathcal{R}(A) + \mathcal{R}(A)^{\perp}, \quad \mathcal{N}(A^{\dagger}) = \mathcal{R}(A)^{\perp} = \mathcal{N}(A^{*}) \tag{14.3}$$

and

$$\mathcal{R}(A^{\dagger}) = \mathcal{N}(A)^{\perp}. \tag{14.4}$$

The equivalence of these characterizations of $A^{\dagger}$ is established and generalized by M. Zuhair Nashed to unbounded operators such as the integral operator A, given in (14.2), in the lucid paper [86].

Following the context [85], the rationale in most methods for resolution (approximate solvability) of an IPP is to construct a "solution" that is acceptable physically as a meaningful approximation and is sufficiently stable from the computational standpoint. The main dilemma of modeling of ill-posed problems is that the closer the mathematical model describes the IPP, the worse is the "condition number" of the associated computational problem (i.e., the more sensitive to errors). It is conventional to use the phrase *"regularization of an ill-posed problem"* to refer to various approaches to circumvent the lack of continuous dependence as well as to bring about existence and uniqueness, if necessary. Roughly speaking, this entails an analysis of an IPP via an analysis of an associated well-posed problem, or a family (usually a sequence or a net) of well-posed problems, provided that this analysis yields a physically meaningful answer to the IPP.

We distinguish different realizations of regularization, which M.Z. Nashed has critically followed over the years and further developed in a sustainable way, when necessary, in a series of papers (see, e.g., [79]–[96] and [19], [20]).
We mention the most important regularization techniques in a rough classification (cf. [39], [42]) without going into the details here:

(i) Regularization methods in function spaces is one category. This includes Tikhonov-type regularization (see, e.g., [82], [113]), the method of quasi-reversibility, the use for certain function spaces such as scale spaces in multi-resolutions, the method of generalized inverses (pseudoinverses) in reproducing kernel Hilbert spaces (cf. [80], [81]), and multi-scale wavelet regularization (see, e.g., [29], [31], [42]).

(ii) Resolution of ill-posed problems by "control of dimensionality" is another category (see, e.g., [42] and the literature therein). This includes projection methods, moment-discretization schemes. The success of these methods hinges on the possibility of obtaining an approximate solution while keeping the dimensionality of the finite dimensional problem within the "range of numerical stability". It also depends on deriving error estimates for the approximate solutions that is crucial to the control of the dimensionality.

(iii) A third category is formed by iterative methods (see, e.g., [64], [65]) which can be applied either to the problem in function spaces or to a discrete version of it. The crucial ingredient in iterative methods is to stop the iteration before instability creeps into the process. Thus iterative methods have to be modified or accelerated so as to provide a desirable accuracy by the time a stopping rule is applied.

(iv) A fourth category constitutes filter methods. Filter methods refer to procedures where, for example, values producing highly oscillatory solutions are eliminated. Various "low pass" filters can, of course, be used. They are also crucial for determination of a stopping rule.

(v) Mollifiers (see, e.g., [21], [22], [40], [41], [46]) are known as smooth functions with special properties to create sequences of smooth functions approximating a non-smooth or singular function. Thus, we compromises by changing the problem into a more well-posed one, namely that of trying to determine a mollified version of the solution. The heuristic motivation is that the trouble usually comes from high frequency components of the data and of the solution, which are damped out by mollification.

(vi) The root of the Backus–Gilbert method (BG method) was geophysical (cf. [4], [5], [6]). The characterization involved in the model is known as moment problem in the mathemetical literature. The BG method can be thought of as resulting from discretizing an integral equation of the first kind. Where other regularization methods, such as the frequently used Tikhonov regularization method, seek to impose smoothness constraints on the solution, the BG method instead realizes stability constraints (cf. [114]). As a consequence, the solution is varying as little as possible if the input data were resampled multiple times. The common feature between the mollifier and the BG method is that an approximate inverse is determined independently from the right hand side of the equation.

The particular interest in the IEEE Transactions on Antennas and Propagation, Vol. AP-29, No. 2, 220–231, 1981 (cf. [85]), however, was the question: Can we endow $\mathcal{R}(A)$ for the operator A, defined by the integral equation (14.2), with a new inner product that would make $\mathcal{R}(A)$ a reproducing kernel Hilbert space (RKHS) with useful properties? In fact, Nashed's concept is as follows: Shrink the image space $L^2(\mathbb{R})$ to the range $\mathcal{R}(A)$ and understand the latter space as the Paley–Wiener space $H_{K_{\mathcal{F}_{\sigma\mathbb{Z}}}}$ with the associated topology to guarantee that the range is closed. Therefore, in answering this question for the antenna problem, M.Z. Nashed [85] was led by a remarkable transition, namely from an ill-posed problem in the sense of Hadamard (in the nomenclature of $L^2(\mathbb{R})$) to a well-posed problem in the Paley–Wiener reproducing kernel Hilbert space $\mathcal{R}(A)$ (in canonically defined topology).

As an evolution of Hadamard's classification, the framework of [82], [85] [86] shows the advantage of adopting a notion of well-posedness that is focused on infinite-dimensional problems (e.g., an inconsistent finite system of linear algebraic equations will not be ill-posed in above sense, while it is ill-posed in the sense of Hadamard). Indeed, it follows immediately from the open mapping theorem in functional analysis that the following statements are equivalent (see [85], [86]):

(N1) IP is well-posed,

(N2) $\mathcal{R}(A)$ is closed,

(N3) $A^{\dagger}$ is bounded.

All in all, we are led to call an IP *well-posed in the sense of Nashed*, if $\mathcal{R}(A)$ is closed. If $\mathcal{R}(A)$ is not closed (such as (14.2) in the L^2-nomenclature), IP is called *ill-posed in the sense of Nashed*.

Today, the discussion of IP's can be found in a huge number of publications, e.g., in the texbooks [21], [50], [51], [66], [73], [74], [77], [101], [113], but the proper understanding of the role of the generalized inverse in a functional analytic context is essentially due to [85], [86].

• **Paley–Wiener Reproducing Kernel Hilbert Space.** The *Paley–Wiener space* $H_{K_{\mathcal{F}_{\sigma\mathbb{Z}}}}$

$$H_{K_{\mathcal{F}_{\sigma\mathbb{Z}}}} = \{\mathbb{R} \ni y \mapsto F^{\wedge}_{\mathcal{F}_{\sigma\mathbb{Z}}}(y) = \int_{\mathcal{F}_{\sigma\mathbb{Z}}} e^{-2\pi i a\cdot y} F(a)\, da : F \in \mathrm{L}^2(\mathcal{F}_{\sigma\mathbb{Z}})\} \tag{14.5}$$

is a reproducing kernel Hilbert space (RKHS) with reproducing kernel (RK)

$$K_{\mathcal{F}_{\sigma\mathbb{Z}}}(x,u) = \int_{\mathcal{F}_{\sigma\mathbb{Z}}} e^{2\pi i t\cdot(x-u)}\, dt = \frac{\sin(\pi(x-u)\sigma)}{\pi(x-u)} = \sigma \text{ sinc}\left(2\pi(x-u)\frac{\sigma}{2}\right). \tag{14.6}$$

$H_{K_{\mathcal{F}_{\sigma\mathbb{Z}}}}$ has many interesting properties collected, for example, in [94]:

(i) The sequence

$$\{K_{\mathcal{F}_{\sigma\mathbb{Z}}}(h,\cdot)\}_{h\in\sigma^{-1}\mathbb{Z}} \tag{14.7}$$

is an orthonormal basis for $H_{K_{\mathcal{F}_{\sigma\mathbb{Z}}}}$.

(ii) The sequence (14.7) shows the discrete orthogonality property:

$$K_{\mathcal{F}_{\sigma\mathbb{Z}}}(h',h) = \delta_{h',h} = \begin{cases} 1, & h' = h, \\ 0, & h' \neq h. \end{cases} \tag{14.8}$$

(iii) $F^{\wedge}_{\mathcal{F}_{\sigma\mathbb{Z}}}(\cdot - c) \in H_{K_{\mathcal{F}_{\sigma\mathbb{Z}}}}$ and $\|F^{\wedge}_{\mathcal{F}_{\sigma\mathbb{Z}}}(\cdot - c)\|_{\mathrm{L}^2(\mathbb{R})} = \|F^{\wedge}_{\mathcal{F}_{\sigma\mathbb{Z}}}\|_{\mathrm{L}^2(\mathbb{R})}$ for all $F \in H_{K_{\mathcal{F}_{\sigma\mathbb{Z}}}}$ and $c \in \mathbb{R}$, such that $H_{K_{\mathcal{F}_{\sigma\mathbb{Z}}}}$ is a unitarily translation-invariant subspace of $\mathrm{L}^2(\mathbb{R})$.

(vi) $H_{K_{\mathcal{F}_{\mathbb{Z}}}}$ is a shift-invariant subspace of $\mathrm{L}^2(\mathbb{R})$

$$H_{K_{\mathcal{F}_{\mathbb{Z}}}} = \left\{ \sum_{h\in\sigma^{-1}\mathbb{Z}} c(h)\, K_{\mathcal{F}_{\sigma\mathbb{Z}}}(h,\cdot) : \sum_{h\in\sigma^{-1}\mathbb{Z}} |c(h)|^2 < \infty \right\}. \tag{14.9}$$

• **Uni-Variate Antenna Problem in $H_{K_{\mathcal{F}_{\Lambda}}}$-Nomenclature.** Under the assumption that $\mathcal{R}(A)$ is the subspace $H_{K_{\mathcal{F}_{\sigma\mathbb{Z}}}}$ of $L^2(\mathbb{R})$, the operator A defined by the integral equation (14.2) becomes *onto and*, hence, by the open mapping theorem, the inverse operator $A^{-1} : H_{K_{\mathcal{F}_{\sigma\mathbb{Z}}}} \to L^2(\mathcal{F}_{\sigma\mathbb{Z}})$ is *bounded*.

The kernel (14.6) also is of central importance in lattice point sampling. The most common form of sampling today is lattice point sampling of a bandlimited signal $F^{\wedge}_{\mathcal{F}_{\sigma\mathbb{Z}}}$ over the fundamental cell $\mathcal{F}_{\sigma\mathbb{Z}} = [-\frac{\sigma}{2}, \frac{\sigma}{2})$, $\sigma > 0$, of the lattice $\sigma\mathbb{Z}$ for a square-integrable function F on $\mathcal{F}_{\sigma\mathbb{Z}}$. Already in the first half of the last century, H. Nyquist [97], [98] was led to the following 1D statement: If a 1D function (signal) $F^{\wedge}_{\mathcal{F}_{\sigma\mathbb{Z}}}$ (dependent on the time variable t) contains no frequencies higher than $\frac{\sigma}{2}$, it is completely determined by its functional values at a series of points spaced $\frac{1}{\sigma}$ apart. Hence, a sufficient rate amounts to σ samples, or anything larger. In fact, a more detailed study in the sampling area due to C.E. Shannon [104], [105] tells that, for a given *sample rate*, perfect reconstruction is guaranteed for any *bandwidth* smaller than the sample rate. If the bandwidth is too high, the reconstruction exhibits imperfections known as *aliasing*.

• **Shannon Sampling Theorem.** Let $\sigma^{-1}\mathbb{Z}$ denote the inverse lattice $(\sigma\mathbb{Z})^{-1}$ of $\sigma\mathbb{Z}$, where $\|\mathcal{F}_{\sigma\mathbb{Z}}\| = \sigma = \|\mathcal{F}_{\sigma^{-1}\mathbb{Z}}\|^{-1}$ is the length of the fundamental cell $\mathcal{F}_{\sigma\mathbb{Z}}$

(note that $\mathbb{Z}^{-1} = \mathbb{Z}$). $\sum_{h\in\sigma^{-1}\mathbb{Z}} \ldots$ means that the sum is extended over all points h of the inverse lattice $\sigma^{-1}\mathbb{Z}$.

The celebrated *1D-Shannon sampling theorem* as expansion of the bandlimited signal $F^{\wedge}_{\mathcal{F}_{\sigma\mathbb{Z}}}$ is given by the *cardinal series*

$$F^{\wedge}_{\mathcal{F}_{\sigma\mathbb{Z}}}(t) = \sum_{h\in\sigma^{-1}\mathbb{Z}} F^{\wedge}_{\mathcal{F}_{\sigma\mathbb{Z}}}(h) \underbrace{\frac{\sin(2\pi(h-t)\frac{\sigma}{2})}{2\pi(h-t)\frac{\sigma}{2}}}_{=\frac{1}{\sigma}\int_{\mathcal{F}_{\sigma\mathbb{Z}}} e^{2\pi i x\cdot(h-t)}\,dx}. \tag{14.10}$$

Equivalently, we find in the standard nomenclature of sampling using the sinc-function that

$$F^{\wedge}_{\mathcal{F}_{\sigma\mathbb{Z}}}(t) = \sum_{n\in\mathbb{Z}} F^{\wedge}_{\mathcal{F}_{\sigma\mathbb{Z}}}\left(\frac{n}{\sigma}\right) \underbrace{\frac{\sin(\pi\sigma(\frac{n}{\sigma}-t))}{\pi\sigma(\frac{n}{\sigma}-t)}}_{=\mathrm{sinc}\left(\pi\sigma(\frac{n}{\sigma}-t)\right)}. \tag{14.11}$$

In the lattice point terminology used in this work, Shannon's sampling result (14.11) can be reformulated as follows: Any function $F^{\wedge}_{\mathcal{F}_{\sigma\mathbb{Z}}}$ bandlimited to the fundamental cell $\mathcal{F}_{\sigma\mathbb{Z}} = \left[-\frac{\sigma}{2}, \frac{\sigma}{2}\right)$ of the lattice $\sigma\mathbb{Z}$, i.e., the Fourier integral (14.1) may be reconstructed from the sequence of samples $\{F^{\wedge}_{\mathcal{F}_{\sigma\mathbb{Z}}}(h)\}_{h\in\sigma^{-1}\mathbb{Z}}$ via the identity

$$F^{\wedge}_{\mathcal{F}_{\sigma\mathbb{Z}}}(t) = \sum_{h\in\sigma^{-1}\mathbb{Z}} F^{\wedge}_{\mathcal{F}_{\sigma\mathbb{Z}}}(h) \frac{1}{\|\mathcal{F}_{\sigma\mathbb{Z}}\|} \int_{\mathcal{F}_{\sigma\mathbb{Z}}} e^{2\pi i x\cdot(h-t)}\,dx, \quad t\in\mathbb{R}, \tag{14.12}$$

where the *cardinal series* on the right side of (14.12) is absolutely and uniformly convergent on any compact set of the real line $\mathbb{R}$. Obviously, the Fourier transform $F^{\wedge}_{\mathcal{F}_{\sigma\mathbb{Z}}}$ (considered as a one-dimensional signal) is an infinitely repeated replication of the samples at points h of the inverse lattice $\sigma^{-1}\mathbb{Z}$. The portion of the Fourier integral between $-\frac{\sigma}{2}$ and $\frac{\sigma}{2}$, i.e., the fundamental cell $\mathcal{F}_{\sigma\mathbb{Z}}$ of the lattice $\sigma\mathbb{Z}$ is called the base band.

In classical Shannon theory, it has been recognized that the space of bandlimited functions is the same as the Paley–Wiener space of entire functions whose restriction to the real line is of exponential growth. This space is a reproducing kernel Hilbert space with (14.6) as a reproducing kernel. For various perspectives and surveys on sampling expansions the reader is referred to [10], [12], [13], [56], [57], [58], [60], [61], [62], [115] and many others.

• **Developments in Sampling Theory.** Many of the basic ideas of sampling are drastically generalized in new directions and applied in diverse fields of sampling, far beyond what anyone could have envisioned in the early days of the sampling theory. So, there have been many advances in the sampling theory and its applications to signal and image processing in the past three decades.

Many authors developed sampling theorems based on the theory of regular and singular boundary value problems and also by use of transforms other than the Fourier transform, including such techniques as the Sturm–Liouville, Legendre, Laguerre, Jacobi transform (see, e.g., [94], [95], [115]) originated by Kramer's approach (see [67]). Another field of research has been in non-uniform sampling for non-bandlimited signals. More recently, methods of functional analysis and harmonic analysis have played a pivotal role to provide major advances in sampling theory and its foundational aspects. In particular, new directions have been proposed involving various function spaces that admit sampling expansions such as Sobolev spaces, Wiener amalgam spaces, shift invariant spaces, translation-invariant spaces, convolution sampling, non-linear sampling and other fundamental issues in sampling theory. Nevertheless, even today, 1D sampling has a number of problems, for example, bandlimiting operation generates Gibb's oscillations, the sinc-function has a very slow decay at infinity which makes computation in the signal domain rather difficult, aso.

M. Z. Nashed and G.G. Walter [88] showed how to construct a reproducing kernel Hilbert space from a function space that admits sampling expansions. In view of the affinity between reproducing kernel spaces and sampling expansions, it is not surprising that in the past 30 years, reproducing kernel Hilbert spaces have played major roles in signal analysis and applications in inverse problems and imaging. For further perspectives on the role of various function spaces in sampling expansions see [94], [96] and also the introductions to [36], [45].

Multi-dimensional sampling can be found in, e.g., [1], [2], [8], [10], [15], [16], [63], [75], [99] and many other contributions. Usually, it is restricted to the fundamental cell of $\mathbb{Z}^q, q \geq 2$, and based on iterated one-dimensional framework.

The close relationship of multi-variate Shannon sampling to lattice point identities of geometric number theory seems to be a new field of interest. W. Freeden, M.Z. Nahed [36], [45] provide the point of departure for a palette of so-called *Shannon-type sampling formulas* and explicit over- and under-sampling characterizations for a diversity of geometries different from the fundamental cell $\mathcal{F}_{\sigma\mathbb{Z}}$ of the chosen lattice $\sigma\mathbb{Z}$, whose practical usefulness, applicability, economy, and efficiency are evident (for example, in geoexploration discussing Fredholm integral equations of the first kind).

• **M. Zuhair Nashed's Synopsis** taken from a lecture given by himself 2013 in the Fraunhofer Center, Kaiserslautern, is as follows (see also [94]): Since the middle of the last century, the rudiments of sampling are covered in almost every engineering textbook on signal analysis, but sampling theory could be found only in rare exceptions in the mathematical literature. Several decades ago the connections among these areas (inverse problems, signal processing, and image analysis) were rather tenuous. Researchers in one of these areas were often unfamiliar with the techniques and relevance of the other areas. Today the situation, however, has changed drastically, not least because of the bridging links of the sampling methodology. With the surge of new techniques in analysis, sampling theory has started to take a new prominent role within the traditional branches of mathematics, thereby leading to discoveries in other areas of mathematics, such as inverse problems, signal processing, and image analysis:

- *Inverse Problems* deal with determining for a given input- output system an input that produces an observed output, or of determining an input that produces a desired output (or comes as close to it as possible), often in the presence of noise. Most inverse problems are ill-posed and demand regularization.
- *Signal Analysis/Processing* deals with digital representations of signals and their analog reconstructions from digital representations. Sampling expansions, filters, reproducing kernel spaces, various function spaces, and techniques of functional analysis, computational and harmonic analysis play pivotal roles in this area.
- *Image Analysis/Processing* deals with image refinement and recovery, and include medical imaging. Moment problems deal with recovery of a function or signal from its moments, and the construction of efficient stable algorithms for determining or approximating the function.

The common thread among inverse problems, signal analysis, and imaging is a canonical problem:

Recovering an object (function, signal, picture) from partial or indirect information about the object.

A substantial amount of the machinery from functional analysis, approximation theory, special function theory, potential theory, optimization, and numerical analysis has been brought to bear on the resolution and understanding of a recovery problem, and the interdisciplinary character of many recovery problems has emerged very clearly. As a consequence, this concept is to provide a new outlook within which technical results can be better motivated and understood. Within this framework, criteria can be given relative to which the scope and limitations of the various methods can be assessed. These aspects are important both in theory and practice since there is no cure-all method for ill-posed problems; therefore it is imperative to be able within the framework of recovery problems to clarify why a certain strategy works in the recovery context as well as when not to use that method.

14.2 Multi-Variate Antenna Problem Induced Recovery Strategies

Following the principles of the 1D approach we are now interested in replacing the results of Chapter 14.1 involving the bandlimited integral (14.1) by multi-variate counterparts

$$F_{\mathcal{G}}^{\wedge}(y) = \int_{\mathcal{G}} F(x)\, e^{-2\pi i x \cdot y}\, dx, \quad y \in \mathbb{R}^q, \tag{14.13}$$

acting within the following context:

• **$\mathcal{G}$ is a regular region in $\mathbb{R}^q$**,, i.e., $\mathcal{G}$ is understood to be an open and connected subset in $\mathbb{R}^q$, $q \geq 2$, for which (i) its boundary $\partial\mathcal{G}$ constitutes an orientable, piecewise smooth Lipschitzian manifold of dimension $q-1$, (ii) the origin is contained in $\mathcal{G}$, and (iii) $\mathcal{G}$ divides $\mathbb{R}^q$ uniquely into the bounded "inner space" $\mathcal{G}$ and the "outer space" $\mathcal{G}^c = \mathbb{R}^q \backslash \overline{\mathcal{G}}$, $\overline{\mathcal{G}} = \mathcal{G} \cup \partial\mathcal{G}$.

• **Lattices in q-dimensional Euclidean Space $\mathbb{R}^q$.** Our further interest is to replace the 1D-lattice $\sigma\mathbb{Z}$ by (general) lattices Λ in $\mathbb{R}^q$, which are defined as follows: Let $g_1, \ldots, g_q$ be linearly independent vectors in the q-dimensional Euclidean space $\mathbb{R}^q$. The set Λ of all points

$$g = n_1 g_1 + \ldots + n_q g_q \tag{14.14}$$

$n_i \in \mathbb{Z}$, $i = 1, \ldots, q$, is called a *lattice in* $\mathbb{R}^q$ *with basis* $g_1, \ldots, g_q$. The half-open parallelotope $\mathcal{F}_\Lambda$ consisting of the points $x \in \mathbb{R}^q$ with

$$x = t_1 g_1 + \ldots + t_q g_q, \quad -\frac{1}{2} \leq t_i < \frac{1}{2}, \tag{14.15}$$

$i = 1, \ldots, q$, is called the *fundamental cell of the lattice* Λ. From linear algebra (see, e.g., [18]), it is well known that the volume $||\mathcal{F}_\Lambda||$ of $\mathcal{F}_\Lambda$ is equal to the quantity

$$||\mathcal{F}_\Lambda|| = \int_{\mathcal{F}_\Lambda} dx = \sqrt{\det\left((g_i \cdot g_j)_{i,j=1,\ldots,q}\right)} \tag{14.16}$$

(dx is the volume element). Since the vectors $g_1, \ldots, g_q$ are assumed to be linearly independent, there exists a system of vectors $h_1, \ldots, h_q$ in $\mathbb{R}^q$ such that

$$h_j \cdot g_i = \delta_{ij} = \begin{cases} 0 & , \quad i \neq j \\ 1 & , \quad i = j \end{cases} \tag{14.17}$$

(δ_{ij} is the Kronecker symbol). The lattice with basis $h_1, \ldots, h_q$ is called the *inverse (or dual) lattice* Λ^{-1} to Λ. The inverse lattice Λ^{-1} consists of all vectors $h \in \mathbb{R}^q$ such that the inner product $h \cdot g$ is an integer for all $g \in \Lambda$. Obviously, $\Lambda = (\Lambda^{-1})^{-1}$. Moreover, for the fundamental cell $\mathcal{F}_{\Lambda^{-1}}$ of the inverse lattice Λ^{-1} we have $||\mathcal{F}_{\Lambda^{-1}}|| = ||\mathcal{F}_\Lambda||^{-1}$.

Let $\Lambda = \sigma\mathbb{Z}^q$ be the lattice generated by the "dilated" basis $\sigma\varepsilon^1, \ldots, \sigma\varepsilon^q$, $\sigma > 0$, where $\varepsilon^1, \ldots, \varepsilon^q$ forms the canonical orthonormal basis in $\mathbb{R}^q$. Then, the volume of the fundamental cell of $\Lambda = \sigma\mathbb{Z}^q$ is $||\mathcal{F}_\Lambda|| = \sigma^q$. Generating vectors of the

inverse lattice Λ^{-1} are $\sigma^{-1}\varepsilon^1,\ldots,\sigma^{-1}\varepsilon^q$. The volume of the fundamental cell of the inverse lattice is given by $\|\mathcal{F}_{\Lambda^{-1}}\| = \sigma^{-q} = \|\mathcal{F}\|^{-1}$.
In particular, for $\sigma = 1$, i.e., the lattice $\Lambda = \mathbb{Z}^q$, we have $\Lambda^{-1} = \mathbb{Z}^q = \Lambda$ such that $\|\mathcal{F}_{\Lambda^{-1}}\| = 1 = \|\mathcal{F}_\Lambda\|$.

From an historic point of view (see [33], [38], [43], [45] for more details) it is helpful to start our multi-variate concepts from the bi-variate case with the *Hardy–Landau identity of geometric number theory* dealing in its classical form (cf. [47]) with the total number of lattice points of $\mathbb{Z}^2$ inside and on the boundary of disks $\overline{\mathbb{B}^2_N} = \{x \in \mathbb{R}^2 : |x| \le N\}$, i.e.,

$$\#_{\mathbb{Z}^2}\left(\overline{\mathbb{B}^2_N}\right) = \#\left\{(n_1,n_2)^T \in \mathbb{Z}^2 : n_1^2 + n_2^2 \le N^2\right\}. \tag{14.18}$$

• **Hardy–Landau Identity for Circle and Unit Lattice.** G.H. Hardy and E. Landau [54], [55], [68], [69], [70] (see also C. Müller [78]) showed that

$$\sum_{\substack{|g|\le N\\ g\in\mathbb{Z}^2}}{}' \, 1 = \lim_{R\to\infty} \sum_{\substack{|h|\le R\\ h\in\mathbb{Z}^2}} \int_{\substack{|x|\le N\\ x\in\mathbb{R}^2}} e^{-2\pi i x\cdot h}\, dx, \tag{14.19}$$

where we follow the convention

$$\sum_{\substack{|g|\le N\\ g\in\Lambda}}{}' \, 1 = \sum_{\substack{|g|<N\\ g\in\Lambda}} 1 + \frac{1}{2}\sum_{\substack{|g|=N\\ g\in\Lambda}} 1 \tag{14.20}$$

So, the Hardy–Landau identity provides a bi-variate result for the integral (14.13), however, for constant weight and circle geometry in $\mathbb{R}^2$. It is a special manifestation of the two-dimensional Poisson summation formula (see [33]).

• From the theory of Bessel functions (see, e,g, [34]) we know that the *remainder term*, i.e., the 2D sum on the right side of (14.19), can be represented as an alternating series, called *Hardy–Landau series*. More explicitly, we have (in terms of the specific nomenclature of Bessel functions in [34])

$$\sum_{\substack{|g|\le N\\ g\in\Lambda}}{}' \, 1 = \frac{\pi N^2}{\|\mathcal{F}_\Lambda\|} + \lim_{R\to\infty} \frac{\pi N^2}{\|\mathcal{F}_\Lambda\|} \sum_{\substack{0<|h|\le R\\ h\in\Lambda^{-1}}} \frac{J_1(2;2\pi|h|N)}{\pi|h|N}. \tag{14.21}$$

• **Hardy–Landau Identity for Circles, Arbitrary Lattices, and General Weight Functions.** W. Freeden [23] proved that the lattice points can be affected by non–constant weights

$$\begin{aligned} &\sum_{\substack{|a+g|\le N\\ g\in\Lambda}}{}' \, e^{2\pi i y\cdot(a+g)} F(a+g) \\ &= \lim_{R\to\infty} \frac{1}{\|\mathcal{F}_\Lambda\|} \sum_{\substack{|h-y|\le R\\ h\in\Lambda^{-1}}} e^{2\pi i a\cdot h} \int_{\substack{|x|\le N\\ x\in\mathbb{R}^2}} F(x)\, e^{-2\pi i x\cdot(h-y)}\, dy, \end{aligned} \tag{14.22}$$

where $a, y \in \mathbb{R}^2$, F is twice continuously differentiable in $\overline{\mathbb{B}^2_N}$, $N > 0$. Note that, for $F = 1$, this formula leads back to

$$e^{2\pi i a\cdot y} \sum_{\substack{|g+a|\leq N \\ g\in\Lambda}}{}' e^{2\pi i g\cdot y} = \lim_{R\to\infty} \frac{\pi N^2}{\|\mathcal{F}_\Lambda\|} \sum_{\substack{|h-y|\leq R \\ h\in\Lambda^{-1}}} e^{2\pi i a\cdot h} \frac{J_1(2; 2\pi|h-y|N)}{\pi|h-y|N}. \tag{14.23}$$

For $a = y = 0$ we indeed obtain the *classical Hardy–Landau identity*, i.e.,

$$\sum_{\substack{|g|\leq N \\ g\in\Lambda}}{}' 1 = \lim_{R\to\infty} \frac{\pi N^2}{\|\mathcal{F}_\Lambda\|} \sum_{\substack{|h|\leq R \\ h\in\Lambda^{-1}}} \frac{J_1(2; 2\pi|h|N)}{\pi|h|N}. \tag{14.24}$$

Observe that $J_1(2;\cdot)$ satisfies the asymptotic relation $J_1(2;r) = \frac{r}{2} + \ldots$, so that (14.21) and (14.24) are equivalent.

• **Hardy–Landau Identities for Certain Regular Regions in $\mathbb{R}^2$.** V.K. Ivanow [59] noticed that lattice points can be extended over particular 2D regular regions in Euclidean space $\mathbb{R}^2$, however, for the case of constant weight. W. Freeden [33] extended these 2D results to general weights F. More explicitly, let Λ be an arbitrary lattice in $\mathbb{R}^2$. Let $\mathcal{G} \subset \mathbb{R}^2$ be a convex region containing the origin and possessing a boundary curve ∂G such that its normal field ν is continuously differentiable and its curvature is non–vanishing. Suppose that F is of class $\mathrm{C}^{(2)}(\overline{\mathcal{G}})$. Then, for all $a, y \in \mathbb{R}^2$, the series

$$\sum_{g\in\Lambda} e^{2\pi i a\cdot g} \underbrace{\int_{\mathcal{G}} F(x)\, e^{-2\pi i x\cdot(g-y)}\, dx}_{=F^\wedge_{\mathcal{G}}(g-y)} \tag{14.25}$$

converges in the spherical sense, and we have

$$\begin{aligned} &\frac{1}{\|\mathcal{F}_\Lambda\|} \sum_{\substack{a+h\in\overline{\mathcal{G}} \\ h\in\Lambda^{-1}}}{}' e^{2\pi i y\cdot(a+h)} F(a+h) \\ &= \lim_{N\to\infty} \sum_{\substack{|g-y|\leq N \\ g\in\Lambda}} e^{2\pi i a\cdot g} \int_{\mathcal{G}} F(x) e^{-2\pi i x\cdot(g-y)} dx. \end{aligned} \tag{14.26}$$

• **Hardy–Landau Identities for Regular Regions in $\mathbb{R}^q, q \geq 2$, Arbitrary Lattices, and General Weight Functions in Gaussian Summability.** W. Freeden [33] guarantees qD formulations for general lattices $\Lambda \subset \mathbb{R}^q$ and general regular regions $\mathcal{G} \subset \mathbb{R}^q, q \geq 2$, and continuous functions on $\overline{\mathcal{G}} = \mathcal{G} \cup \partial\mathcal{G}$, however, in

Gaussian summability

$$\sum_{\substack{a+g\in\overline{\mathcal{G}}\\ g\in\Lambda}}{}' e^{2\pi iy\cdot(a+g)}F(a+g) \tag{14.27}$$
$$= \lim_{\substack{\tau\to 0\\ \tau>0}} \frac{1}{\|\mathcal{F}_\Lambda\|} \sum_{h\in\Lambda^{-1}} e^{-\tau\pi^2h^2} e^{2\pi ih\cdot a} \int_{\mathcal{G}} F(x)e^{-2\pi ix\cdot(h-y)}\,dx, \; a,y\in\mathbb{R}^q.$$

In fact, we have

$$\sum_{\substack{a+g\in\overline{\mathcal{G}}\\ g\in\Lambda}}{}' e^{2\pi iy\cdot(a+g)}F(a+g) \tag{14.28}$$
$$= \frac{1}{\|\mathcal{F}_\Lambda\|}\int_{\mathcal{G}} F(x)e^{2\pi ix\cdot y}\,dx$$
$$+ \lim_{\substack{\tau\to 0\\ \tau>0}} \frac{1}{\|\mathcal{F}_\Lambda\|} \sum_{\substack{0<|h|\le R\\ h\in\Lambda^{-1}}} e^{-\tau\pi^2h^2} e^{2\pi ih\cdot a} \int_{\mathcal{G}} F(x)e^{-2\pi ix\cdot(h-y)}\,dx, \; a,y\in\mathbb{R}^q,$$

where the following abbreviation has been used consistently

$$\sum_{\substack{a+g\in\overline{\mathcal{G}}\\ g\in\Lambda}}{}' \ldots = \sum_{\substack{a+g\in\mathcal{G}\\ g\in\Lambda}} \ldots + \sum_{\substack{a+g\in\partial\mathcal{G}\\ g\in\Lambda}} \alpha(a+g)\ldots \tag{14.29}$$

with $\alpha(a+g)$ denoting the *solid angle* subtended by $\partial\mathcal{G}$ at $a+g$ (note that, as geoscientifically relevant regular regions (cf. [35]), we may choose the interior of the (actual) Earth's body or parts of it, the interior of geoscientifically relevant surfaces such as the geoid, telluroid, etc., but also ball, ellipsoid, cube, polyhedral bodies, etc. are included in accordance with the definition of a regular region).

• **Shannon-Type Sampling Theorem.** As a consequence, W. Freeden, M.Z. Nashed [36], [45] obtained qD Shannon-type sampling procedures by formal integration of the lattice point identity (14.27) over a general regular region $\mathcal{H}\subset\mathbb{R}^q$ that is not-necessarily equal to the regular region $\mathcal{G}\subset\mathbb{R}^q$

$$\int_{\mathcal{H}} \sum_{\substack{a+g\in\overline{\mathcal{G}}\\ g\in\Lambda}}{}' e^{-2\pi iy\cdot(a+g)}F(a+g)\,da \tag{14.30}$$
$$= \sum_{\substack{(\mathcal{F}_\Lambda+\{g'\})\cap\overline{\mathcal{H}}\neq\emptyset\\ g'\in\Lambda}} \underbrace{\int_{\mathcal{G}\cap\bigcup_{g\in\Lambda}(((\overline{\mathcal{H}}\cap(\mathcal{F}_\Lambda+\{g'\}))-\{g'\})+\{g\})} F(x)e^{-2\pi iy\cdot x}\,dx}_{=F^\wedge_{\mathcal{G}\cap\bigcup_{g\in\Lambda}(((\overline{\mathcal{H}}\cap(\mathcal{F}_\Lambda+\{g'\}))-\{g'\})+\{g\})}(y)}$$
$$= \lim_{\substack{\tau\to 0\\ \tau>0}} \frac{1}{\|\mathcal{F}_\Lambda\|} \sum_{h\in\Lambda^{-1}} e^{-\tau\pi^2h^2} \underbrace{\int_{\mathcal{G}} F(x)e^{-2\pi ih\cdot x}\,dx}_{=F^\wedge_{\mathcal{G}}(h)} \underbrace{\int_{\mathcal{H}} e^{2\pi ia\cdot(h-y)}\,da}_{=K_{\mathcal{H}}(h-y)}.$$

The identity (14.30) has many interesting properties. For example, by virtue of the Gaussian summability, the convergence of the cardinal-type series on the right hand side of (14.30) is exponentially accelerated. Furthermore, all manifestations of over- and under-sampling can be explicitly analyzed by the finite sum of Fourier transforms on the left side of the identity, dependent on the geometric configurations of the chosen regular regions $\mathcal{G}, \mathcal{H}$.

• **Over- and Under-Sampling by Special Choices of the Regular Regions** $\mathcal{G}, \mathcal{H}$ can be studied in more detail, where we almost literally follow [36]: We begin with $\overline{\mathcal{H}} \subset \overline{\mathcal{F}_\Lambda}$ and $\mathcal{G}$ arbitrary. In this case we have

$$\begin{aligned}
&\sum_{\substack{(\mathcal{F}_\Lambda+\{g'\})\cap\mathcal{H}\neq\emptyset \\ g'\in\Lambda}} F^{\wedge}_{\mathcal{G}\cap\bigcup_{g\in\Lambda}(((\mathcal{H}\cap(\mathcal{F}_\Lambda+\{g'\}))-\{g'\})+\{g\})}(y) \qquad (14.31)\\
&= F^{\wedge}_{\mathcal{G}\cap\bigcup_{g\in\Lambda}(\mathcal{H}+\{g\})}(y)\\
&= \frac{1}{\|\mathcal{F}_\Lambda\|} \lim_{\substack{\tau\to 0\\ \tau>0}} \sum_{h\in\Lambda^{-1}} e^{-\tau\pi^2 h^2} \underbrace{\int_{\mathcal{G}} F(x) e^{-2\pi i y\cdot x}\, dx}_{=F^{\wedge}_{\mathcal{G}}(h)} \underbrace{\int_{\mathcal{H}} e^{2\pi i a\cdot(h-y)}\, da}_{=K_{\mathcal{H}}(h-y)}.
\end{aligned}$$

As a consequence, for $\overline{\mathcal{H}} = \overline{\mathcal{F}_\Lambda}$ and $\mathcal{G}$ arbitrary, we obtain

$$\begin{aligned}
&\sum_{\substack{(\mathcal{F}_\Lambda+\{g'\})\cap\mathcal{H}\neq\emptyset \\ g'\in\Lambda}} F^{\wedge}_{\mathcal{G}\cap\bigcup_{g\in\Lambda}(((\mathcal{H}\cap(\mathcal{F}_\Lambda+\{g'\}))-\{g'\})+\{g\})}(y) \qquad (14.32)\\
&= F^{\wedge}_{\mathcal{G}}(y)\\
&= \frac{1}{\|\mathcal{F}_\Lambda\|} \lim_{\substack{\tau\to 0\\ \tau>0}} \sum_{h\in\Lambda^{-1}} e^{-\tau\pi^2 h^2} \underbrace{\int_{\mathcal{G}} F(x) e^{-2\pi i h\cdot x}\, dx}_{=F^{\wedge}_{\mathcal{G}}(h)} \underbrace{\int_{\mathcal{F}_\Lambda} e^{2\pi i a\cdot(h-y)}\, da}_{=K_{\mathcal{F}_\Lambda}(h-y)}.
\end{aligned}$$

We continue with $\overline{\mathcal{G}} \subset \overline{\mathcal{F}_\Lambda}$ and $\mathcal{H}$ arbitrary. This yields the identity

$$\begin{aligned}
&\sum_{\substack{(\mathcal{F}_\Lambda+\{g'\})\cap\mathcal{H}\neq\emptyset \\ g'\in\Lambda}} F^{\wedge}_{\mathcal{G}\cap\bigcup_{g\in\Lambda}(((\mathcal{H}\cap(\mathcal{F}_\Lambda+\{g'\}))-\{g'\})+\{g\})}(y) \qquad (14.33)\\
&= \sum_{\substack{(\mathcal{F}_\Lambda+\{g'\}\cap\mathcal{H}\neq\emptyset) \\ g'\in\Lambda}} F^{\wedge}_{\mathcal{G}\cap((\mathcal{H}\cap(\mathcal{F}_\Lambda+\{g'\}))-\{g'\})}(y)\\
&= \frac{1}{\|\mathcal{F}_\Lambda\|} \lim_{\substack{\tau\to 0\\ \tau>0}} \sum_{h\in\Lambda^{-1}} e^{-\tau\pi^2 h^2} \underbrace{\int_{\mathcal{G}} F(x) e^{-2\pi i h\cdot x}\, dx}_{=F^{\wedge}_{\mathcal{G}}(h)} \underbrace{\int_{\mathcal{H}} e^{2\pi i a\cdot(h-y)}\, da}_{=K_{\mathcal{H}}(h-y)}.
\end{aligned}$$

For $\overline{\mathcal{G}}, \overline{\mathcal{H}} \subset \overline{\mathcal{F}_\Lambda}$ we have

$$\begin{aligned} &\sum_{\substack{(\mathcal{F}_\Lambda+\{g'\})\cap\mathcal{H}\neq\emptyset \\ g'\in\Lambda}} F^{\wedge}_{\mathcal{G}\cap\bigcup_{g\in\Lambda}(((\mathcal{H}\cap(\mathcal{F}_\Lambda+\{g'\}))-\{g'\})+\{g\})}(y) \qquad (14.34) \\ &= F^{\wedge}_{\mathcal{G}\cap\mathcal{H}}(y) \\ &= \frac{1}{\|\mathcal{F}_\Lambda\|} \lim_{\substack{\tau\to 0\\ \tau>0}} \sum_{h\in\Lambda^{-1}} e^{-\tau\pi^2 h^2} F^{\wedge}_{\mathcal{G}}(h)\ K_{\mathcal{H}}(h-y). \end{aligned}$$

For $\overline{\mathcal{G}} \subset \overline{\mathcal{H}} \subset \overline{\mathcal{F}_\Lambda}$ we have

$$F^{\wedge}_{\mathcal{G}}(y) = \frac{1}{\|\mathcal{F}_\Lambda\|} \lim_{\substack{\tau\to 0\\ \tau>0}} \sum_{h\in\Lambda^{-1}} e^{-\tau\pi^2 h^2} F^{\wedge}_{\mathcal{G}}(h)\ K_{\mathcal{H}}(h-y), \qquad (14.35)$$

whereas, for $\overline{\mathcal{H}} \subset \overline{\mathcal{G}} \subset \overline{\mathcal{F}_\Lambda}$,

$$F^{\wedge}_{\mathcal{H}}(y) = \frac{1}{\|\mathcal{F}_\Lambda\|} \lim_{\substack{\tau\to 0\\ \tau>0}} \sum_{h\in\Lambda^{-1}} e^{-\tau\pi^2 h^2} F^{\wedge}_{\mathcal{G}}(h)\ K_{\mathcal{H}}(h-y). \qquad (14.36)$$

In particular, for $\overline{\mathcal{G}} = \overline{\mathcal{H}} \subset \overline{\mathcal{F}_\Lambda}$, we are able to formulate the following identity

$$F^{\wedge}_{\mathcal{G}}(y) = \frac{1}{\|\mathcal{F}_\Lambda\|} \lim_{\substack{\tau\to 0\\ \tau>0}} \sum_{h\in\Lambda^{-1}} e^{-\tau\pi^2 h^2} F^{\wedge}_{\mathcal{G}}(h)\, K_{\mathcal{G}}(h-y),\ y\in\mathbb{R}^q. \qquad (14.37)$$

Especially, for a qD ball $\mathbb{B}^q_N$ with radius N around the origin satisfying $\overline{\mathbb{B}^q_N} \subset \overline{\mathcal{F}_\Lambda}$, it follows that

$$F^{\wedge}_{\mathbb{B}^q_N}(y) = \frac{\|\mathbb{S}^{q-1}\|\, N^q}{\|\mathcal{F}_\Lambda\|} \lim_{\substack{\tau\to 0\\ \tau>0}} \sum_{h\in\Lambda^{-1}} e^{-\tau\pi^2 h^2} F^{\wedge}_{\mathbb{B}^q_N}(h)\, \frac{J_1(q; 2\pi|h-y|N)}{2\pi|h-y|N},\ y\in\mathbb{R}^q, \qquad (14.38)$$

where $\|\mathbb{S}^{q-1}\| = 2\frac{\pi^{\frac{q}{2}}}{\Gamma(\frac{q}{2})}$ is the area of the unit sphere $\mathbb{S}^{q-1}$ in $\mathbb{R}^q$.
Obviously, by choosing a small sampling density such that $\overline{\mathcal{F}_\Lambda}$ covers the compact support $\overline{\mathcal{G}}$ of the original signal $F^{\wedge}_{\mathcal{G}}$, the number of samples $F^{\wedge}_{\mathcal{G}}(h), h\in\Lambda^{-1}$, for reconstruction is high, and vice versa. In practice, we are therefore required to find a compromise between sampling density and total number of samples. This can be achieved by a choice of Λ such that $\overline{\mathcal{F}_\Lambda}$ covers $\overline{\mathcal{G}}$ tightly.

For $\overline{\mathcal{G}} \subset \overline{\mathcal{F}_\Lambda} = \overline{\mathcal{H}}$ and the lattice Λ generated by the vectors $g_1,\ldots,g_q \in \mathbb{R}^q$ we have using sinc-functions in explicitly written form

$$F^{\wedge}_{\mathcal{G}}(y) = \lim_{\substack{\tau\to 0\\ \tau>0}} \sum_{h\in\Lambda^{-1}} e^{-\tau\pi^2 h^2} F^{\wedge}_{\mathcal{G}}(h) \frac{\sin(\pi(g_1\cdot(h-y)))}{\pi(g_1\cdot(h-y))} \cdot \ldots \cdot \frac{\sin(\pi g_q\cdot(h-y))}{\pi(g_q\cdot(h-y))}. \qquad (14.39)$$

In other words, for sufficiently small $\tau > 0$, $F_{\mathcal{G}}^{\wedge}$ can be expressed by the series on the right side of (14.39) in exponential convergence, i.e.,

$$(F^{(\tau)})_{\mathcal{G}}^{\wedge}(y) \simeq \sum_{h\in\Lambda^{-1}} e^{-\tau\pi^2 h^2} F_{\mathcal{G}}^{\wedge}(h) \frac{\sin(\pi(g_1\cdot(h-y)))}{\pi(g_1\cdot(h-y))} \cdot \ldots \cdot \frac{\sin(\pi g_q\cdot(h-y))}{\pi(g_q\cdot(h-y))}. \tag{14.40}$$

Replacing the lattice Λ by its dilated lattice $\sigma\Lambda$, $\sigma > 1$, we get

$$F_{\mathcal{G}}^{\wedge}(y) = \lim_{\substack{\tau\to 0\\ \tau>0}} \sigma^q \sum_{h\in\Lambda^{-1}} e^{-\tau\pi^2\left(\frac{h}{\sigma}\right)^2} F_{\mathcal{G}}^{\wedge}\left(\frac{h}{\sigma}\right) \frac{\sin(\pi(\sigma g_1\cdot(\frac{h}{\sigma}-y)))}{\pi(\sigma g_1\cdot(\frac{h}{\sigma}-y))} \cdot \ldots \cdot \frac{\sin(\pi(\sigma g_q\cdot(\frac{h}{\sigma}-y)))}{\pi(\sigma g_q\cdot(\frac{h}{\sigma}-y))}. \tag{14.41}$$

• **The Standard Form of Sampling in Gauß–Weierstraß Summability** is provided by taking $\overline{\mathcal{G}} = \overline{\mathcal{H}} = \overline{\mathcal{F}_\Lambda}$, i.e.,

$$F_{\mathcal{F}_\Lambda}^{\wedge}(y) = \frac{1}{\|\mathcal{F}_\Lambda\|} \lim_{\substack{\tau\to 0\\ \tau>0}} \sum_{h\in\Lambda^{-1}} e^{-\tau\pi^2 h^2} F_{\mathcal{F}_\Lambda}^{\wedge}(h)\, K_{\mathcal{F}_\Lambda}(h-y),\ y\in\mathbb{R}^q. \tag{14.42}$$

Given an arbitrary lattice $\Lambda\subset\mathbb{R}^q$ and an arbitrary regular region $\mathcal{H}\subset\mathbb{R}^q$, we are able to find a constant $\sigma\in\mathbb{R}$ such that $\overline{\mathcal{H}}\subset\overline{\mathcal{F}_{\sigma\Lambda}}$ as tightly as possible. Under these circumstances we obtain

$$\begin{aligned} &F_{\mathcal{G}\cap\bigcup_{g\in\sigma\Lambda}(\mathcal{H}+\{g\})}^{\wedge}(y) \\ &= \frac{1}{\|\mathcal{F}_{\sigma\Lambda}\|} \lim_{\substack{\tau\to 0\\ \tau>0}} \sum_{h\in(\sigma\Lambda)^{-1}} e^{-2\tau\pi^2 h^2} F_{\mathcal{G}}^{\wedge}(h) K_{\mathcal{H}}(h-y) \\ &= \frac{1}{\|\mathcal{F}_{\Lambda}\|} \lim_{\substack{\tau\to 0\\ \tau>0}} \frac{1}{\sigma^q} \sum_{h\in\Lambda^{-1}} e^{-\tau\pi^2\left(\frac{h}{\sigma}\right)^2} F_{\mathcal{G}}^{\wedge}\left(\frac{h}{\sigma}\right) K_{\mathcal{H}}\left(\frac{h}{\sigma}-y\right). \end{aligned} \tag{14.43}$$

In comparison to sampling with respect to the lattice Λ the identity (14.43) related to $\sigma\Lambda$ provides *up–sampling* for values $\sigma > 1$ or *down–sampling* for values $\sigma < 1$, respectively. Of particular significance are choices of σ, such that Λ is a sublattice of $\sigma\Lambda, \sigma > 1$, or $\sigma\Lambda, \sigma < 1$, is a sublattice of Λ.

The Gaussian summability of the cardinal series on the right hand side of (14.30) is of great importance seen from the numerical point of view; it enables a fast computation of the cardinal series. Nonetheless, W. Freeden, M.Z. Nashed [36] show that the identity (14.30) and all subsequent identities additionally hold true in ordinary pointwise sense.

• **Shannon-Type Sampling Theorem.** Let $\mathcal{G}, \mathcal{H}$ be regular regions in $\mathbb{R}^q$. Suppose that F is a member of the class $\mathrm{C}^{(0)}(\overline{\mathcal{G}})$. Then

$$\int_{\mathcal{H}} \sum_{\substack{a+g\in\overline{\mathcal{G}}\\ g\in\Lambda}}{}' e^{-2\pi i y\cdot(a+g)} F(a+g)\, da \tag{14.44}$$

$$= \sum_{\substack{(\mathcal{F}_\Lambda+\{g'\})\cap\mathcal{H}\neq\emptyset\\ g'\in\Lambda}} F^{\wedge}_{\mathcal{G}\cap\bigcup\limits_{g\in\Lambda}(((\mathcal{H}\cap(\mathcal{F}_\Lambda+\{g'\}))-\{g'\})+\{g\})}(y)$$

$$= \frac{1}{\|\mathcal{F}_\Lambda\|} \sum_{h\in\Lambda^{-1}} F^{\wedge}_{\mathcal{G}}(h)\, K_{\mathcal{H}}(h-y) \tag{14.45}$$

is valid for all $y \in \mathbb{R}^q$. For $\overline{\mathcal{G}} \subset \overline{\mathcal{H}} \subset \overline{\mathcal{F}_\Lambda}$, we have

$$F^{\wedge}_{\mathcal{G}}(y) = \frac{1}{\|\mathcal{F}_\Lambda\|} \sum_{h\in\Lambda^{-1}} F^{\wedge}_{\mathcal{G}}(h)\ K_{\mathcal{H}}(h-y),\ y\in\mathbb{R}^q. \tag{14.46}$$

Finally, under the assumption $\overline{\mathcal{G}} = \overline{\mathcal{H}} \subset \overline{\mathcal{F}_\Lambda}$, the identity (14.46) implies that

$$F^{\wedge}_{\mathcal{G}}(y) = \frac{1}{\|\mathcal{F}_\Lambda\|} \sum_{h\in\Lambda^{-1}} F^{\wedge}_{\mathcal{G}}(h)\ K_{\mathcal{G}}(h-y),\ y\in\mathbb{R}^q, \tag{14.47}$$

so that, especially for a qD ball $\mathbb{B}^q_N$ with radius N around the origin satisfying $\mathbb{B}^q_N \subset \overline{\mathcal{F}_\Lambda}$, we have

$$F^{\wedge}_{\mathbb{B}^q_N}(y) = \frac{\|\mathbb{S}^{q-1}\|\ N^q}{\|\mathcal{F}_\Lambda\|} \sum_{h\in\Lambda^{-1}} F^{\wedge}_{\mathbb{B}^q_N}(h)\ \frac{J_1(q;2\pi|h-y|N)}{2\pi|h-y|N},\ y\in\mathbb{R}^q. \tag{14.48}$$

Furthermore, for $\overline{\mathcal{G}} \subset \overline{\mathcal{H}} = \overline{\mathcal{F}_\Lambda}$, we obtain

$$F^{\wedge}_{\mathcal{G}}(y) = \frac{1}{\|\mathcal{F}_\Lambda\|} \sum_{h\in\Lambda^{-1}} F^{\wedge}_{\mathcal{G}}(h)\, K_{\mathcal{F}_\Lambda}(h-y),\ y\in\mathbb{R}^q. \tag{14.49}$$

Explicitly written out (see, e.g., [99], [75]) we obtain for $\overline{\mathcal{G}} \subset \overline{\mathcal{H}} = \overline{\mathcal{F}_\Lambda}$ and the lattice Λ generated by the vectors $g_1,\ldots,g_q \in \mathbb{R}^q$

$$F^{\wedge}_{\mathcal{G}}(y) = \sum_{h\in\Lambda^{-1}} F^{\wedge}_{\mathcal{G}}(h) \frac{\sin(\pi(g_1\cdot(h-y)))}{\pi(g_1\cdot(h-y))} \cdot \ldots \cdot \frac{\sin(\pi g_q\cdot(h-y))}{\pi(g_q\cdot(h-y))},\ y\in\mathbb{R}^q. \tag{14.50}$$

In fact, the identity

$$F^{\wedge}_{\mathcal{G}}(y) = \frac{1}{\|\mathcal{F}_\Lambda\|} \sum_{h\in\Lambda^{-1}} F^{\wedge}_{\mathcal{G}}(h)\ K_{\mathcal{G}}(h-y). \tag{14.51}$$

is a multi-variate variant of the Shannon sampling theorem (cf. [104]) in ordinary pointwise sense, but now for multi-variate regular regions $\mathcal{G}$. The principal impact of Shannon sampling on information theory is that it allows the replacement of a bandlimited signal $F_{\mathcal{G}}^{\wedge}$ related to $\mathcal{G}$ by a discrete sequence of its samples without loss of any information. Also it specifies the lowest rate, i.e., the Nyquist rate (cf. [36]), that enables to reproduce the original signal. In other words, Shannon sampling provides the bridge between continuous and discrete versions of a bandlimited function.

The extensions of the Shannon sampling theorem as presented here has many applications in engineering and physics, for example, in signal processing, data transmission, cryptography, constructive approximation, and inverse problems such as, e.g., the antenna problem.

First, some of the aspects leading to Paley–Wiener spaces will be explained (see also [36]).

• **Paley–Wiener Reproducing Kernel Hilbert Space.** For simplicity we restrict ourselves to regular regions $\mathcal{G} \subset \mathbb{R}^q$ with $\overline{\mathcal{G}} \subset \overline{\mathcal{F}_\Lambda}$. Then the continuous signal

$$F_{\mathcal{G}}^{\wedge}(y) = \int_{\mathcal{G}} F(a) e^{-2\pi i a \cdot y} \, da, \; y \in \mathbb{R}^q \tag{14.52}$$

is recovered from the sampled signal over lattice points of the inverse lattice $F_{\mathcal{G}}^{\wedge}(h), h \in \Lambda^{-1}$, i.e.,

$$F_{\mathcal{G}}^{\wedge}(y) = \frac{1}{\|\mathcal{F}_\Lambda\|} \sum_{h \in \Lambda^{-1}} F_{\mathcal{G}}^{\wedge}(h) \, K_{\mathcal{G}}(h-y), \; y \in \mathbb{R}^q \tag{14.53}$$

with

$$K_{\mathcal{G}}(x-y) = \int_{\mathcal{G}} e^{-2\pi i a \cdot (x-y)} \, da, \quad x, y \in \mathbb{R}^q. \tag{14.54}$$

Indeed, we are able to deduce some interesting results in the area of *approximate integration* (see also [37]): The bandlimited function $F_{\mathcal{G}}^{\wedge}$ allows to express its integral over the Euclidean space $\mathbb{R}^q$ by the product of the lattice density and the sum over all samples in points of the inverse lattice

$$\lim_{N \to \infty} \int_{\substack{|x| \le N \\ x \in \mathbb{R}^q}} F_{\mathcal{G}}^{\wedge}(x) \, dx = \frac{1}{\|\mathcal{F}_\Lambda\|} \sum_{h \in \Lambda^{-1}} F_{\mathcal{G}}^{\wedge}(h). \tag{14.55}$$

Furthermore, the Parseval identity (see [36], [37]) is valid:

$$\frac{1}{\|\mathcal{F}_\Lambda\|} \sum_{h \in \Lambda^{-1}} |F_{\mathcal{G}}^{\wedge}(h)|^2 = \int_{\mathcal{G}} |F(a)|^2 \, da. \tag{14.56}$$

From the Fourier theory it follows that

$$\int_{\mathcal{G}} |F(a)|^2 \, da = \int_{\mathbb{R}^q} \left|F_{\mathcal{G}}^{\wedge}(y)\right|^2 \, dy. \tag{14.57}$$

In other words, if $F_{\mathcal{G}}^{\wedge}$, $\overline{\mathcal{G}} \subset \overline{\mathcal{F}_\Lambda}$, belongs to the inner product space

$$\mathrm{H}_{K_{\mathcal{G}}}^{(0)} = \left\{ y \mapsto \underbrace{\int_{\mathcal{G}} e^{-2\pi i a y} F(a)\, da}_{=F_{\mathcal{G}}^{\wedge}(y)} : F \in \mathrm{C}^{(0)}(\overline{\mathcal{G}}) \right\}, \tag{14.58}$$

then

$$\int_{\mathbb{R}^q} |F_{\mathcal{G}}^{\wedge}(y)|^2\, dy = \frac{1}{\|\mathcal{F}_\Lambda\|} \sum_{h \in \Lambda^{-1}} |F_{\mathcal{G}}^{\wedge}(h)|^2. \tag{14.59}$$

Replacing Λ by its inverse lattice Λ^{-1} we find

$$\int_{\mathbb{R}^q} |F_{\mathcal{G}}^{\wedge}(y)|^2\, dy = \|\mathcal{F}_\Lambda\| \sum_{g \in \Lambda} |F_{\mathcal{G}}^{\wedge}(g)|^2. \tag{14.60}$$

Looking at our approach critically we notice that Shannon sampling is formulated on the reference set $\mathrm{H}_{K_{\mathcal{G}}}^{(0)}$, that is a strict subset of the associated Paley–Wiener space

$$\mathrm{H}_{K_{\mathcal{G}}} = \left\{ y \mapsto \int_{\mathcal{G}} e^{-2\pi i a \cdot y} F(a)\, da,\ y \in \mathbb{R}^q : F \in \mathrm{L}^2(\mathcal{G}) \right\}. \tag{14.61}$$

Now, every $F \in \mathrm{L}^2(\mathcal{G})$ can be approximated (in $\mathrm{L}^2(\mathcal{G})$–sense) by a function $F_\varepsilon \in \mathrm{C}^{(0)}(\overline{\mathcal{G}})$ in ε-accuracy such that

$$\begin{aligned} & \sup_{y \in \mathbb{R}^q} \left| F_{\mathcal{G}}^{\wedge}(y) - (F_\varepsilon)_{\mathcal{G}}^{\wedge}(y) \right| \\ \leq\ & \sup_{y \in \mathbb{R}^q} \left| \int_{\mathcal{G}} e^{-2\pi i a \cdot y} (F(a) - F_\varepsilon(a))\, da \right| \\ \leq\ & \left(\int_{\mathcal{G}} |F(a) - F_\varepsilon(a)|^2\, da \right)^{1/2} \left(\int_{\mathcal{G}} |e^{-2\pi i a \cdot y}|^2\, da \right)^{1/2} \\ \leq\ & \left(\int_{\mathbb{R}^q} \left| F_{\mathcal{G}}^{\wedge}(a) - (F_\varepsilon)_{\mathcal{G}}^{\wedge}(a) \right|^2 da \right)^{1/2} \left(\int_{\mathcal{G}} |e^{-2\pi i a \cdot y}|^2\, da \right)^{1/2} \\ =\ & \sqrt{\|\mathcal{G}\|}\ \varepsilon. \end{aligned} \tag{14.62}$$

Thus, if $\mathcal{G} \subset \mathbb{R}^q$ is a regular region with $\overline{\mathcal{G}} \subset \overline{\mathcal{F}_\Lambda}$, then the *Paley–Wiener space* $\mathrm{H}_{K_{\mathcal{G}}}$ is the completion of the space $\mathrm{H}_{K_{\mathcal{G}}}^{(0)}$ under the $\mathrm{L}^2(\mathbb{R}^q)$–topology:

$$\mathrm{H}_{K_{\mathcal{G}}} = \overline{\mathrm{H}_{K_{\mathcal{G}}}^{(0)}}^{\|\cdot\|_{\mathrm{L}^2(\mathbb{R}^q)}}. \tag{14.63}$$

Note that, by virtue of (14.57), we see that

$$|F_{\mathcal{G}}^{\wedge}(y)| \leq \sqrt{\|\mathcal{G}\|} \sqrt{\int_{\mathcal{G}} |F(a)|^2 \, da} = \sqrt{\|\mathcal{G}\|} \sqrt{\int_{\mathbb{R}^q} |F_{\mathcal{G}}^{\wedge}(w)|^2 \, dw}. \tag{14.64}$$

Moreover, standard Fourier inversion (see, e.g., [111]) yields

$$\begin{aligned} F_{\mathcal{G}}^{\wedge}(y) &= \int_{\mathbb{R}^q} F_{\mathcal{G}}^{\wedge}(x) \left(\int_{\mathcal{G}} e^{2\pi i a\cdot(x-y)} \, da \right) dx \\ &= \int_{\mathbb{R}^q} F_{\mathcal{G}}^{\wedge}(x) \, K_{\mathcal{G}}(x-y) \, dx \end{aligned} \tag{14.65}$$

for all $y \in \mathbb{R}^q$, where

$$\int_{\mathbb{R}^q} \cdots = \lim_{N\to\infty} \int_{\substack{|x|\leq N \\ x\in\mathbb{R}^q}} \cdots . \tag{14.66}$$

Hence, by standard arguments of the theory of reproducing kernels (see, e.g., [3], [103]), it follows that $\mathrm{H}_{K_{\mathcal{G}}}$ *is a reproducing kernel Hilbert space.*

Summarizing our considerations we are able to formulate the following result: $\mathrm{H}_{K_{\mathcal{G}}}$ given by

$$\mathrm{H}_{K_{\mathcal{G}}} = \left\{ y \mapsto \int_{\mathcal{G}} F(a) \, e^{-2\pi i a\cdot y} \, da, \ y \in \mathbb{R}^q : F \in \mathrm{L}^2(\mathcal{G}) \right\} \tag{14.67}$$

is a reproducing kernel Hilbert space with reproducing kernel (14.54). The system $\{K_{\mathcal{H}}(h-\cdot)\}_{h\in\Lambda^{-1}}$ is closed and complete in $\mathrm{H}_{K_{\mathcal{G}}}$, i.e.,

$$\overline{\mathrm{span}_{h\in\Lambda^{-1}} K_{\mathcal{H}}(h-\cdot)} = \mathrm{H}_{K_{\mathcal{G}}}, \tag{14.68}$$

where the completion is understood in the sense of $\|\cdot\|_{\mathrm{L}^2(\mathbb{R}^q)}$.

Following [36] we are therefore allowed to come to the following conclusions:

- All routes to sampling expansions lead to reproducing kernels.
- Seminal ideas are often triggered by amazing insights. Many of such ideas are drastically generalized in new directions and applied in diverse fields, far beyond what anyone could have envisioned. The developments in sampling theory and the theory of ill-posed problems represent such examples.

• **Multi-Variate Antenna Problem.** Finally, we are interested in the *qD antenna problem*

$$AF(y) = \int_{\mathcal{G}} F(a) \, e^{-2\pi i a\cdot y} \, da = F_{\mathcal{G}}^{\wedge}(y), \quad y \in \mathbb{R}^q, \tag{14.69}$$

where $F \in L^2(\mathcal{G})$ represents the aperture distribution, $F_{\mathcal{G}}^{\wedge}$ represents the far-field pattern, and A is the operator which relates these two functions, characterizing the antenna structure.

The treatment of the well/ill-posedness of the multi-variate qD antenna problem is analogous to the already known uni-variate case. We omit the details.

Suppose that the far-field pattern $F_{\mathcal{G}}^{\wedge}$ is given, specified through samples at a finite number of lattice points, and we wish to determine a source F, whose far-field radiation pattern approximates the desired pattern in some acceptable manner. Then we are immediately led to a representation of the far field $F_{\mathcal{G}}^{\wedge}$ as linear combination in terms of Paley–Wiener reproducing kernels, so that the aparture distribution F is available by Fourier inversion as a linear combination of exponential functions. Nontheless, we are left with the problem to determine the weight coefficients in the linear combinations, which will be done here within a Paley–Wiener spline framework.

• **Spline Interpolation in Paley–Wiener Spaces.** There are diverse important spline concepts in the context of lattice point sampling, for example, [1], [9], [11], [14], [112], mostly based on (iterated) univariate approaches.

In the line of the spline concepts [24], [25],[27], [28], [30] we propose a specific spline procedure resulting from the reproducing kernel structure of the Paley–Wiener space $\mathrm{H}_{K_{\mathcal{G}}}$. More concretely, let $\mathcal{G}$ be a regular region in $\mathbb{R}^q$ with $\overline{\mathcal{G}} \subset \overline{\mathcal{F}_\Lambda}$. Suppose that $\mathfrak{Q} \subset \mathbb{R}^q$ is a regular region such that the total number $\#_{\Lambda^{-1}}(\mathfrak{Q})$ of lattice points $h' \in \Lambda^{-1}$ in $\mathfrak{Q}$ is positive. Assume that the set of samples $\{F_{\mathcal{G}}^{\wedge}(h')\}_{h' \in \mathfrak{Q}}$ corresponding to the finite set of lattice points $h' \in \mathfrak{Q}$ is known.

Our purpose is to deal with spline interpolation, i.e., minimum norm interpolation in the Paley–Wiener space $\mathrm{H}_{K_{\mathcal{G}}}$. To be more specific, we determine the spline interpolant of $F_{\mathcal{G}}^{\wedge}$ from the known values $F_{\mathcal{G}}^{\wedge}(h'), h' \in \mathfrak{Q}$, in the following way: Suppose that the matrix

$$\mathbf{k}_{\mathfrak{Q}} = (K_{\mathcal{G}}(h'-h))_{h',h \in \mathfrak{Q}} \tag{14.70}$$

is non-singular (note that $\mathbf{k}_{\mathfrak{Q}}$ is a Gram matrix). Then, any function $S_{\mathfrak{Q}}$ of the form

$$S_{\mathfrak{Q}}(y) = \sum_{h' \in \mathfrak{Q}} a_{h'} \underbrace{\int_{\mathcal{G}} e^{2\pi i a \cdot (h'-y)} da}_{=K_{\mathcal{G}}(h'-y)}, \quad y \in \mathbb{R}^q, \tag{14.71}$$

is called a $\mathrm{H}_{K_{\mathcal{G}}}$*-spline function relative to* $\mathfrak{Q}$. The class of all $\mathrm{H}_{K_{\mathcal{G}}}$-splines relative to $\mathfrak{Q}$ is denoted by $\mathrm{Spline}_{\mathrm{H}_{K_{\mathcal{G}}}}(\mathfrak{Q})$. Obviously, $\mathrm{Spline}_{\mathrm{H}_{K_{\mathcal{G}}}}(\mathfrak{Q})$ is a finite subset of $\mathrm{H}_{K_{\mathcal{G}}}$.

By virtue of the reproducing kernel structure it is easy to verify that the so-called *spline interpolation formula*

$$\sum_{h'\in\Omega} a_{h'} P(h') = \sum_{h'\in\Omega} a_{h'} \int_{\mathbb{R}^q} K_{\mathcal{G}}(h'-y)\, \overline{P(y)}\, dy = \int_{\mathbb{R}^q} S_\Omega(y)\, \overline{P(y)}\, dy \quad (14.72)$$

holds true for all $P \in \mathrm{H}_{K_{\mathcal{G}}}$. Under the regularity assumption (14.70) there exists one and only one spline function $S_\Omega^{\hat{F}} \in \mathrm{Spline}_{\mathrm{H}_{K_{\mathcal{G}}}}(\Omega)$ of the form

$$S_\Omega^{\hat{F}}(y) = \sum_{h'\in\Omega} \hat{a}_{h'}^F \int_{\mathcal{G}} e^{2\pi i a\cdot(h'-y)} da, \quad y \in \mathbb{R}^q, \quad (14.73)$$

satisfying the linear equations

$$S_\Omega^{\hat{F}}(h) = F_{\mathcal{G}}^{\wedge}(h), \ \ h \in \Omega, \quad (14.74)$$

i.e.,

$$\sum_{h'\in\Omega} \hat{a}_{h'}^F \int_{\mathcal{G}} e^{2\pi i a\cdot(h'-h)} da \ = \ F_{\mathcal{G}}^{\wedge}(h), \ \ h \in \Omega. \quad (14.75)$$

From (14.74) it follows that

$$\int_{\mathbb{R}^q} S_\Omega^{\hat{F}}(y)\, \overline{(S_\Omega^{\hat{F}}(y) - P(y))}\, dy = \sum_{h'\in\Omega} \hat{a}_{h'}^F S_\Omega^{\hat{F}}(h) - \sum_{h'\in\Omega} \hat{a}_{h'}^F P(h') \ = 0 \quad (14.76)$$

holds for all $P \in \mathrm{H}_{K_{\mathcal{G}}}$ with $P(h) = F_{\mathcal{G}}^{\wedge}(h)$, $h \in \Omega$. This implies that

$$\begin{aligned} \int_{\mathbb{R}^q} P(y)\, \overline{P(y)}\, dy \ &= \ \int_{\mathbb{R}^q} S_\Omega^{\hat{F}}(y)\, \overline{S_\Omega^{\hat{F}}(y)}\, dy \\ &+ \ \int_{\mathbb{R}^q} \left(S_\Omega^{\hat{F}}(y) - P(y)\right) \overline{(S_\Omega^{\hat{F}}(y) - P(y))}\, dy. \end{aligned} \quad (14.77)$$

Summarizing our results we obtain the *minimum norm characterization of an interpolating spline function in the Paley–Wiener space* $\mathrm{H}_{K_{\mathcal{G}}}$ *-framework* (variational formulation of Paley–Wiener spline interpolation): Suppose that a finite discrete dataset $\{F_{\mathcal{G}}^{\wedge}(h), h \in \Omega\}$ is known. Then, the spline function given by

$$S_\Omega^{\hat{F}}(y) = \sum_{h'\in\Omega} \hat{a}_{h'}^F \int_{\mathcal{G}} e^{2\pi i a\cdot(h'-y)}\, da, \ y \in \mathbb{R}^q, \quad (14.78)$$

with coefficients $\hat{a}_{h'}^F$ determined by the linear equations (14.75) fulfills the *minimum norm property*

$$\left(\int_{\mathcal{G}} \left|S_\Omega^{\hat{F}}(y)\right|^2 dy\right)^{1/2} \ = \ \min_{\substack{P\in \mathrm{H}_{K_{\mathcal{G}}} \\ P(h)=F_{\mathcal{G}}^{\wedge}(h) \\ h\in\Lambda^{-1}\cap\Omega}} \left(\int_{\mathcal{G}} |P(y)|^2\, dy\right)^{1/2}. \quad (14.79)$$

In addition, the *Paley–Wiener spline interpolatory convergence* is guaranteed. More explicitly (see [43]), let $F_{\mathcal{G}}^{\wedge}$ be of class $\mathrm{H}_{K_{\mathcal{G}}}$. Suppose that $\{\Lambda_N^{-1}\}$ is a sequence of lattices Λ_N^{-1} such that

$$\Theta_{\Omega}^{\Lambda_N^{-1}} = \sup_{y \in \mathbb{R}^q} \left(\min_{\substack{h \in \Omega \\ h \in \Lambda^{-1}}} |y-h| \right) \to 0 \tag{14.80}$$

as $N \to \infty$. Then the sequence $\{(\hat{S}_{\Omega}^F)^{\Lambda_N^{-1}}\}$ of the uniquely determined solutions $(\hat{S}_{\Omega}^F)^{\Lambda_N^{-1}}$ of the variational problems

$$\left(\int_{\mathcal{G}} \left| (\hat{S}_{\Omega}^F)^{\Lambda_N^{-1}}(y) \right|^2 dy \right)^{1/2} = \min_{\substack{P \in \mathrm{H}_{K_{\mathcal{G}}} \\ P(h) = F_{\mathcal{G}}^{\wedge}(h) \\ h \in \Lambda_N^{-1} \cap \Omega}} \left(\int_{\mathcal{G}} |P(y)|^2 \, dy \right)^{1/2} \tag{14.81}$$

satisfies the limit relation

$$\lim_{N \to \infty} \sup_{y \in \Omega} \mid (\hat{S}_{\Omega}^F)^{\Lambda_N^{-1}}(y) - F_{\mathcal{G}}^{\wedge}(y) \mid = 0. \tag{14.82}$$

This means that we are able to approximate any function $F_{\mathcal{G}}^{\wedge} \in \mathrm{H}_{K_{\mathcal{G}}}$ in a constructive way using Paley–Wiener spline interpolation provided that $\Theta_{\Omega}^{\Lambda_N^{-1}} \to 0$ as $N \to \infty$.

Further spline methods (such as Sard's Theorem, Schönberg's Theorem, spline smoothing of noisy data, best approximation of linear functionals, etc.) can be realized in a canonical way (see, e.g., [24, 28] for the methodology in the multi-periodic case) by use of the reproducing property of the kernel (14.54). The details are omitted here. Moreover, combined spline interpolation/smoothing (as proposed in [26]) can be used instead of spline interpolation if the data are only (partially) noisy.

For a more detailed information about sampling in reproducing kernel Hilbert spaces the reader is referred to [36], [88], [94].

• **Paley–Wiener Spline Solution of the** qD **Antenna Problem.** Suppose that the far-field pattern $F_{\mathcal{G}}^{\wedge}$ is given, specified through samples at a finite number of lattice points, and we wish to determine a source F, whose far-field radiation pattern approximates the desired pattern by Paley–Wiener splines in some acceptable manner.

A spline solution method of the *qD antenna problem* (14.69) should be explained briefly: Consider the problem (14.69) of a linear aperture on $\mathcal{G}$, so that the aperture distribution F is related to the far field $F_{\mathcal{G}}^{\wedge} \in \mathrm{H}_{K_{\mathcal{G}}}$ by means of the integral equation $AF = F_{\mathcal{G}}^{\wedge}$, the pattern being limited to a visible range Ω containing the lattice points $h \in \mathfrak{Q} \cap \Lambda^{-1}$. In fact, assuming that $F_{\mathcal{G}}^{\wedge}(h)$ is known for the lattice points $h \in \mathfrak{Q} \cap \Lambda^{-1}$ we are led back to a spline interpolant

$$S_{\mathfrak{Q}}^{\hat{F}}(y) = \sum_{h' \in \mathfrak{Q}} a_{h'}^F \int_{\mathcal{G}} e^{2\pi i a \cdot (h'-y)} dy, \quad y \in \mathbb{R}^q, \tag{14.83}$$

that should be "close" to $F_{\mathcal{G}}^{\wedge}$ in $\mathcal{G}$. Then, for points $x \in \mathcal{G}$, the Fourier inversion formula yields the identity

$$F(x) \approx \int_{\mathbb{R}^q} e^{2\pi i x \cdot y} \, S_{\mathfrak{Q}}^{\hat{F}}(y) \, dy \tag{14.84}$$

$$= \sum_{h' \in \mathfrak{Q}} \hat{a}_{h'}^F \int_{\mathbb{R}^q} e^{2\pi i x \cdot y} \int_{\mathcal{G}} e^{2\pi i a \cdot (h'-y)} \, da \, dy$$

$$= \sum_{h' \in \mathfrak{Q}} \hat{a}_{h'}^F \, e^{2\pi i x \cdot h'}$$

with coefficients $\hat{a}_{h'}^F$ determined from the already known linear (spline) equations (14.75). Thus, our spline interpolation technique approximately solves the multivariate inversion problem of determining the function $F \in L^2(\mathcal{G})$ from a finite set of discrete values of $F_{\mathcal{G}}^{\wedge}$, and an approximation to the aperture distribution is known from the formula (14.84).

Altogether, our Shannon-type sampling procedure enables Paley–Wiener spline interpolation of Fourier transforms from discrete data, located in lattice points.

● **Paley–Wiener Solution of the qD Antenna Problem by Slepian Functions.** Functions cannot be space- and bandlimited at the same time (see, e.g., [44]). Finding signals that are optimally concentrated in both is a fundamental problem in information theory, for which fundamental results were given in the early 1960s by D. Slepian, H.J. Landau, and H.O. Pollak [108], [71], [72], [109], [110]. The concentration problem has strong connections to the role of the uncertainty principle in the concept of wavelets and multi-scale approximation (see, e.g., [17], [30], [31], [32], [44]). Our interest, however, is in what is referred to as Slepian functions (see, e.g., [106], [107], [44] and the references therein).

In fact, the ideas of Slepian functions can be applied to the function systems

$$\{K_{\mathcal{G}}(h' - \cdot)\}_{h' \in \mathfrak{Q}}. \tag{14.85}$$

To this end we consider $H_{K_{\mathcal{G}}}$-spline function relative to $\mathfrak{Q}$ of the form

$$S(x) = \sum_{h' \in \mathfrak{Q}} b_{h'} K_{\mathcal{G}}(h' - x), \quad x \in \mathbb{R}^q, \tag{14.86}$$

with the aim that they maximize the spatial concentration

$$0 < \gamma_{\mathcal{G}}(S) = \frac{\displaystyle\int_{\mathcal{G}} |S(x)|^2 \, dx}{\displaystyle\int_{\mathbb{R}^q} |S(x)|^2 \, dx} < 1. \tag{14.87}$$

In antenna theory, the value $\gamma_{\mathcal{G}}(S)$ may be also interpreted as a *superdirective ratio*, i.e., a measure of the difficulty in realizing the aparture distribution from discrete far field knowledge, since the aparture distribution may have rapid oscillation (which imply that a portion of the input power would be radiated). With the realization condition in mind, the requirement (14.87) means a restriction of the aparture distribution (especially by the prescribed value 1).

The condition (14.87) leads to a generalized eigenvalue problem

$$\sum_{h'\in\mathfrak{Q}} \langle K_{\mathcal{G}}(h-\cdot), K_{\mathcal{G}}(h'-\cdot)\rangle_{L^2(\mathcal{G})} b_{h'} = \lambda \sum_{h'\in\mathfrak{Q}} \langle K_{\mathcal{G}}(h-\cdot), K_{\mathcal{G}}(h'-\cdot)\rangle_{L^2(\mathbb{R}^3)} b_{h'},$$

$$\tag{14.88}$$

$h \in \mathfrak{Q}.$

We assume that the eigenvalues are ordered in a way that

$$1 \ge \lambda_{\mathcal{G}}^{(1)} \ge \ldots \ge \lambda_{\mathcal{G}}^{\#_{\Lambda^{-1}}\mathfrak{Q}} \ge 0. \tag{14.89}$$

The corresponding eigenvectors $b_{h'}^{(j)}$, $h' \in \mathfrak{Q}$, $j = 1, \ldots, \#_{\Lambda^{-1}}\mathfrak{Q}$, generate the *spline-type Slepian functions*

$$K^{(j)}(x) = \sum_{h'\in\mathfrak{Q}} b_{h'}^{(j)} K_{\mathcal{G}}(h'-x), \quad j = 1, \ldots, \#_{\Lambda^{-1}}\mathfrak{Q}. \tag{14.90}$$

They form an orthogonal system of functions represented by a linear combination of $\{K_{\mathcal{G}}(h'-\cdot)\}_{h'\in\mathfrak{Q}}$. The smaller the index j is, the more concentrated is the function $K^{(j)}$ in the region $\mathcal{G}$.

Constructive approximation using Slepian functions (including noise) has enjoyed increasing popularity over the last 20 years (see, e.g., the (geomathematical) strategies explained by F.J. Simons [106] and also the references therein). This is the reason why we do not go into detail to specify coefficients c_j, $j = 1, \ldots, \#_{\Lambda^{-1}}\mathfrak{Q}$, such that a linear combination

$$\sum_{j=1}^{\#_{\Lambda^{-1}}\mathfrak{Q}} c_j \, K^{(j)} \tag{14.91}$$

is "close to" the far field $F_{\mathcal{G}}^{\wedge} \in \mathrm{H}_{K_{\mathcal{G}}}$, so that

$$F_{\mathcal{G}}^{\wedge}(x) \approx \sum_{j=1}^{\#_{\Lambda^{-1}}\Omega} c_j\, K^{(j)}(x) = \sum_{j=1}^{\#_{\Lambda^{-1}}\Omega} c_j \sum_{h'\in\Omega} b_{h'}^{(j)}\, K_{\mathcal{G}}(h'-x), \quad (14.92)$$

$$= \sum_{h'\in\Omega} \underbrace{\sum_{j=1}^{\#_{\Lambda^{-1}}\Omega} c_j\, b_{h'}^{(j)}}_{=d_{h'}} K_{\mathcal{G}}(h'-x).$$

As a consequence, the aperture distribution F admits an approximation of the form

$$F(x) \approx \sum_{h'\in\Omega} d_{h'}\, e^{2\pi i x\cdot h'}, \quad (14.93)$$

where

$$d_{h'} = \sum_{j=1}^{\#_{\Lambda^{-1}}\Omega} c_j\, b_{h'}^{(j)}. \quad (14.94)$$

All in all, the antenna problem induced extensions of the Shannon-type sampling theorem as presented here allow many applications in engineering and physics, for example, in signal processing, inverse problems, and constructive approximation.

References

[1] A. Aldroubi and K. Gröchenig. Non-uniform sampling and reconstruction in shift invariant spaces. SIAM Rev., 43: 585–620, 2001.

[2] A. Aldroubi, Q. Sun and W.-S. Tang. Convolution, average sampling and a calderon resolution of the identity for shift-invariant spaces. J. Fourier Anal. Appl., 22: 215–244, 2005.

[3] N. Aronszajn. Theory of reproducing kernels. Trans. Am. Math. Soc., 68: 337–404, 1950.

[4] G.E. Backus and F. Gilbert. Numerical applications of a formalism for geophysical inverse problems. Geophys. J.R. Astron. Soc., 13: 247–276, 1967.

[5] G.E. Backus and F. Gilbert. The resolving power of gross Earth data. Geophys. J.R. Astron. Soc., 16: 169–205, 1968.

[6] G.E. Backus and F. Gilbert. Uniqueness of the inversion of inaccurate gross Earth data. Philos. Trans. R. Soc. London, 226: 123–197, 1970.

[7] G.E. Backus. Poloidal and toroidal fields in geomagnetic field modeling. Rev. Geophysics, 24: 75–109, 1986.

[8] H. Behmard and A. Faridani. Sampling of bandlimited functions on union of shifted lattices. J. Fourier Anal. Appl., 8: 43–58, 2001.

[9] C. de Boor, K. Höllig and S. Riemenschneider. Bivariate cardinal interpolation by splines on a three-direction Mesh. Ill. J. Math., 29: 533–566, 1985.

[10] P.L. Butzer. A Survey of the Whittaker Shannon sampling theorem and some of its extensions. J. Math. Res. Exposition, 3: 185–212, 1983.

[11] P.L. Butzer, W. Engels, S. Ries and R.L. Stens. The Shannon sampling series and the reconstruction of signals in terms of linear, quadratic, and cubic splines. SIAM J. Appl. Math., 46: 299–323, 1986.

[12] P.L. Butzer, W. Splettstösser and R.L. Stens. The sampling theorem and linear prediction in signal analysis. Jahresber. Deutsch. Math. Verein, 90: 1–60, 1988.

[13] P.L. Butzer and R.L. Stens. Sampling theory for not necessarily band-limited functions: A historical overview. SIAM Rev., 34: 40–53, 1992.

[14] C.K. Chui, K. Jetter and J.D. Ward. Cardinal interpolation by multivariate splines. Math. Comput., 48: 711–724, 1987.

[15] D. Costarelli and G. Vinti. Approximation by nonlinear multivariate sampling Kontorovich type operators and applications to image processing. Numer. Funct. Anal. Optimization, 34: 819–844, 2013.

[16] F. Cluny, D. Costarelli, A. Minotti and G. Vinti. Enhancement of thermographic images as tool for structural analysis in Earthquake engineering. NDT & E International, 70: 60–72, 2015.

[17] I. Daubechies. Time-frequency localization operators: A geometric phase space approach. IEEE Transactions on Informat. Theory, 34: 961–1005, 1988.

[18] P.J. Davis. *Interpolation and Approximation*. Blaisdell, New York, 1963.

[19] H.W. Engl and M.Z. Nashed. Stochastic projectional schemes for random linear operator equations of the first and second kinds. Numer. Funct. Anal. and Optimiz., 1: 451–473, 1979.

[20] H.W. Engl and M.Z. Nashed. New extremal characterizations of generalized inverses of linear operators. J. Math. Anal. Appl., 82: 566–586, 1981.

[21] H.W. Engl, M. Hanke and A. Neubauer. *Regularization of Inverse Problems*. Kluwer Academic Publisher, Dordrecht, 1996.

[22] H.W. Engl. *Integralgleichungen*. Springer Lehrbuch Mathematik, Wien, 1997.

[23] W. Freeden. Über eine Verallgemeinerung der Hardy–Landauschen Identität. Manuscr. Math., 24: 205–216, 1978.

[24] W. Freeden. On spherical spline interpolation and approximation. Math. Meth. in the Appl. Sci., 3: 551–575, 1981a.

[25] W. Freeden. On approximation by harmonic splines. Manuscr. Geod., 6: 193–244, 1981b.

[26] W. Freeden and B. Witte. A combined (spline-)interpolation and smoothing method for the determination of the gravitational potential from heterogeneous data. Bull. Géod., 56: 53–62, 1982.

[27] W. Freeden. Spherical spline interpolation: basic theory and computational aspects. J. Comput. Appl. Math., 11: 367–375, 1984.

[28] W. Freeden. Interpolation by multidimensional periodic splines. J. Approx. Theory, 55: 104–117, 1988.

[29] W. Freeden and F. Schneider. Regularization wavelets and multiresolution. Inverse Probl., 14: 493–515, 1998.

[30] W. Freeden, T. Gervens and M. Schreiner. *Constructive Approximation on the Sphere (With Applications to Geomathematics)*. Oxford Science Publications, Clarendon, Oxford, 1998.

[31] W. Freeden. *Multiscale Modelling of Spaceborne Geodata*. B.G. Teubner, Stuttgart, Leipzig, 1999.

[32] W. Freeden and M. Schreiner. *Spherical Functions of Mathematical Geosciences: A Scalar, Vectorial, and Tensorial Setup*. Springer, Heidelberg, 2009.

[33] W. Freeden. *Metaharmonic Lattice Point Theory*. CRC Press, Taylor & Francis Group, Boca Raton, 2011.

[34] W. Freeden and M. Gutting. *Special Functions of Mathematical (Geo)Physics*. Birkhäuser, Basel, 2013.

[35] W. Freeden. Geomathematics: its role, its aim, and its potential. pp. 3–79. *In*: W. Freeden, M.Z. Nashed and T. Sonar (eds.). *Handbook of Geomathematics, Vol. 1, 2nd Edition*. Springer, New York, Berlin, Heidelberg, 2015.

[36] W. Freeden and M.Z. Nashed. Multi-variate Hardy-type lattice point summation and Shannon-type sampling. GEM Int. J. Geomath., 6: 163–249, 2015.

[37] W. Freeden and M. Gutting. *Integration and Cubature Methods*. CRC Press, Taylor & Francis Group, Boca Raton, 2017.

[38] W. Freeden, T. Sonar and B. Witte. Gauss as scientific mediator between mathematics and Geodesy from the past to the present. *In*: W. Freeden and M.Z. Nashed (eds.). *Handbook of Mathematical Geodesy*. Birkhäuser, Basel, 2017.

[39] W. Freeden and M.Z. Nashed. Ill-Posed problems: Operator methodologies of resolution and regularization approaches. pp. 201–314. *In*: W. Freeden and M.Z. Nashed (eds.). *Handbook of Mathematical Geodesy*. Geosystems Mathematics, Springer International Publishing, Birkhäuser, Basel, New York, Heidelberg, 2018a.

[40] W. Freeden and M.Z. Nashed. Inverse gravimetry as an Ill-posed problem in mathematical geodesy. pp. 641–685. *In*: W. Freeden and M.Z. Nashed (eds.). *Handbook of Mathematical Geodesy*. Geosystems Mathematics, Springer, Basel, New York, Heidelberg, 2018b.

[41] W. Freeden and M.Z. Nashed. Inverse gravimetry: Background material and multiscale mollifier approaches. GEM Int. J. Geomath., 9: 199–264, 2018c.

[42] W. Freeden and M.Z. Nashed. Operator-theoretic and regularization approaches to Ill-posed problems. GEM Int. J. Geomath., 9: 1–115, 2018d.

[43] W. Freeden and M.Z. Nashed. From Gaussian circle problem to multivariate Shannon sampling. pp. 213–238. *In*: M.Z. Nashed and X. Li (eds.). *Frontiers in Orthogonal Polynomials and q-Series*. World Scientific, 2018e.

[44] W. Freeden, M.Z. Nashed and M. Schreiner. *Spherical Sampling. Geosystems Mathematics*. Springer International Publishing, Basel, New-York, Heidelberg, 2018.

[45] W. Freeden and M.Z. Nashed. *Lattice Point Identities and Shannon-Type Sampling*. CRC Press, Taylor & Francis, Boca Raton, 2020.

[46] W. Freeden. *Decorrelative Mollifier Gravimetry—Basics, Concepts, Examples and Perspectives*. Birkhäuser, Springer Nature, Switzerland, 2021.

[47] F. Fricker. *Einführung in die Gitterpunktlehre*. Birkhäuser, Basel, Boston, Stuttgart, 1981.

[48] C.F. Gauss. *Theoria motus corporum coelestium in sectionibus conicis solem ambientium*. Hamburg, 1809, Werke 7. Translated into English by C.H. Davis, 1963.

[49] C.F. Gauss. *Theoria combinationis observationum erroribus minimis obnoxiae*. 1. Teil, Göttingen, 1821.

[50] C.W. Groetsch. *Generalized Inverses of Linear Operators*. Marcel Dekker. Inc., New York, 1977.

[51] C.W. Groetsch. *Inverse Problems in the Mathematical Science*. Vieweg, Braunschweig, 1993.

[52] J. Hadamard. Sur les problémes aux dérivés partielles et leur signification physique. Princeton Univ. Bull., 13: 49–52, 1902.

[53] J. Hadamard. *Lectures on the Cauchy Problem in Linear Partial Differential Equations*. Yale University Press, New Haven, 1923.

[54] G.H. Hardy. On the expression of a number as the sum of two squares. Quart. J. Math. (Oxford), 46: 263–283, 1915.

[55] G.H. Hardy and E. Landau. The lattice points of a circle. Proceedings of the Royal Society, A., 105: 244–258, 1924.

[56] J.R. Higgins. Five short stories about the cardinal series. Bull. Am. Math. Soc., 12: 45–89, 1985.

[57] J.R. Higgins. *Sampling Theory in Fourier and Signal Analysis. Volume 1: Foundations*. Oxford University Press, Oxford, 1996.

[58] J.R. Higgins and R.L. Stens. *Sampling Theory in Fourier and Signal Analysis: Volume 2: Advanced Topics*. Oxford Science Publications, Oxford, 2000.

[59] V.K. Ivanow. A generalization of the Voronoi-Hardy identity. Sibirsk. Math. Z., 3: 195–212, 1962.

[60] J.A. Jerri. On the application of some interpolating functions in physics. J. Res. Nat. Bur. Standards, Sec. B, 73B: 241–245, 1969.

[61] J.A. Jerri. Sampling expansion for Laguerre—L^2 transforms. J. Res. Nat. Bur. Standards, Sect B, 80B: 415–418, 1976.

[62] J.A. Jerri. The Shannon sampling theorem—its various extensions and applications: A tutorial review. Proc. IEEE, 65: 1565–1596, 1977.

[63] T. Kalker. On multidimensional sampling. *In*: V.K. Madisetti and D.B. Williams (eds.). *Digital Signal Processing Handbook*. CRC Press, Boca Raton, 1999.

[64] W.J. Kammerer and M.Z. Nashed. The convergence of the conjugate gradient method for singular linear operator equations. SIAM J. Numer. Anal., 9: 165–181, 1972a.

[65] W.J. Kammerer and M.Z. Nashed. Iterative methods for best approximate solutions of linear integral equations of the first and second kind. J. Math. Anal. Appl., 40: 547–573, 1972b.

[66] A. Kirsch. *An Introduction to the Mathematical Theory of Inverse Problems*. 2nd ed., Springer, Heidelberg, 1996.

[67] H.P. Kramer. A generalized sampling theorem. J. Mat. Phys., 38: 68–72, 1959.

[68] E. Landau. Über die Gitterpunkte in einem Kreis (Erste Mitteilung). Gött. Nachr., 148–160, 1915.

[69] E. Landau. Über die Gitterpunkte in einem Kreis IV. Gött. Nachr., 58–65, 1924.

[70] E. Landau. Vorlesungen über Zahlentheorie, Chelsea Publishing Compagny, New York, 1969 (reprint from the orignal version published by S. Hirzel, Leipzig, 1927).

[71] H.J. Landau and H.O. Pollak. Prolate spheroidal wave functions, Fourier analysis and uncertainty—II. Bell Syst. Tech. J., 40: 65–84, 1961.

[72] H.J. Landau and H.O. Pollak. Prolate spheroidal wave functions, Fourier analysis and uncertainty—III. Bell Syst. Tech. J., 41: 1295–1336, 1962.

[73] M.M. Lavrentiev. *Some Improperly Posed Problems of Mathematicsl Physics*. Izdat. Sibirsk. Otdel, Akad. Nauk. SSSR, Novosibirsk, 1962, Englisch Transl., Springer Tracts in Natural Philosophy, Vol. 11, Springer-Verlag, Berlin, 1967.

[74] A.K. Louis. *Inverse und schlecht gestellte Probleme*. Teubner, Stuttgart, 1989.

[75] R.J. Marks II. *Introduction to Shannon Sampling and Interpolation Theory*. Springer, Berlin, 1991.

[76] E.H. Moore. On the reciprocal of the general algebraic matrix. Bull. Americ. Math. Soc., 26: 394–395, 1920.

[77] V.A. Morozov. *Methods for Solving Incorrectly Posed Problems*. Springer-Verlag, New York, 1984.

[78] C. Müller. Eine Erweiterung der Hardyschen Identität, Abh. Math. Sem. Univ. Hamburg, 19: 66–76, 1954.

[79] M.Z. Nashed. Generalized inverses, normal solvability and iteration for singular operator equations. pp. 311–359. *In*: L.B. Rall (ed.). *Nonlinear Functional Analysis and Applications*. Academic, New York, 1971.

[80] M.Z. Nashed and G. Wahba. Regularization and approximation of linear operator equations in reproducing kernel spaces. Bull. Am. Math. Soc., 80: 1213–1218, 1974a.

[81] M.Z. Nashed and G. Wahba. Generalized inverses in reproducing kernel spaces: An approach to regularization of linear operator equations. SIAM J. Math. Anal., 5: 974–987, 1974b.

[82] M.Z. Nashed. Aspects of generalized inverses in analysis and regularization. pp. 193–244. *In*: *Generalized Inverses and Applications*. Academic Press, New York, 1976.

[83] M.Z. Nashed and F.G. Votruba. A unified operator theory of generalized inverses. pp. 1–109. *In*: M.Z. Nashed (ed.). *Generalized Inverses and Applications*. Academic Press, New York, 1976.

[84] M.Z. Nashed and H.W. Engl. Random generalized inverses and approximate solution of random operator equations. pp. 149–210. *In*: A.T. Bharucha-Reid (ed.). *Approximate Solution of Random Equations*. North Holland, New York, 1979.

[85] M.Z. Nashed. Operator-theoretic and computational approaches to ill-posed problems with applications to antenna theory. IEEE Trans. Antennas Propagation, 29: 220–231, 1981.

[86] M.Z. Nashed. Inner, outer, and generalized inverses in Banach and Hilbert spaces. Numer. Funct. Anal. Optim., 9: 261–326, 1987.

[87] M.Z. Nashed and G.G. Walter. General sampling theorems for functions in reproducing kernel Hilbert spaces. Math. Control Signals Systems, 4: 363–390, 1991.

[88] M.Z. Nashed and G.G. Walter. Reproducing kernel Hilbert space from sampling expansions. Contemp. Math., 190: 221–226, 1995.

[89] M.Z. Nashed and F. Liu. On nonlinear ill-posed problems II: Monotone operator equations and monotone variational inequalities. pp. 223–240. *In*: A. Kartsatos (ed.). *Theory and Applications of Nonlinear Operators of Monotone and Assertive Type*. Marcel Dekker, New York, 1996.

[90] M.Z. Nashed and O. Scherzer. Stable approximation of nondifferentiable optimization problems with variational inequalities. Contemp. Math., 204: 155–170, 1997a.

[91] M.Z. Nashed and O. Scherzer. Stable approximation of a minimal surface problem with variational inequalities. Appl. Anal., 2: 137–161, 1997b.

[92] M.Z. Nashed and O. Scherzer (eds.). *Inverse Problems, Image Analysis and Medical Imaging*. Contemp. Math., Vol. 313, American Mathematical Socienty, Providence, R.I., 2002.

[93] M.Z. Nashed, Q. Sun and W.S. Tang. Average sampling in L^2. Can. Acad. Sci., Ser. 1(347): 1007–1010, 2009.

[94] M.Z. Nashed. Inverse problems, moment problems and signal processing: Un Menage a Trois. pp. 1–19. *In*: A.H. Siddiqi, R.C. Singh and P. Manchanda (eds.). *Mathematics in Science and Technology*. World Scientific, New Jersey, 2010.

[95] M.Z. Nashed and Q. Sun. Sampling and reconstruction of signals in a reproducing kernel subspace of $L^p(\mathbb{R}^d)$. J. Function Anal., 258: 2422–2452, 2010.

[96] M.Z. Nashed and Q. Sun. Function spaces for sampling expansions. Multiscale Signal Analysis and Modeling. X. Shen, A.I. Zayed (Eds.), 81–104, 2013.

[97] H. Nyquist. Certain factors affecting telegraph speed. Bell Syst. Tech. J., 3: 324–346, 1924.

[98] H. Nyquist. Certain topics in telegraph transmission theory. Trans. AIEE., 47: 617–644, 1928.

[99] E. Parzen. *A Simple Proof and Some Extensions of the Sampling Theorem*. Technical Report No. 7, Department of Statistics, Stanford University, 1–10, 1956.

[100] R. Penrose. A generalized inverse for matrices. Proceedings Cambridge Philosophical Soc., 51: 406–413, 1955.

[101] A. Rieder. *Keine Probleme mit Inversen Problemen*. Springer-Vieweg, Wiesbaden, 2003.

[102] D.W. Robinson. Gauss and generalized inverses. Historia Mathematics, 7: 118–125, 1980.

[103] S. Saitoh. *Theory of Reproducing Kernels and its Applications*. Longman, New York, 1988.

[104] C.E. Shannon. Communication in the presence of noise. Proc. Institute of Radio Engineers, 37: 10–21, 1949a.

[105] C.E. Shannon. *The Mathematical Theory of Communication*. University of Illinois Press, Urbana, Ill., 1949b

[106] F.J. Simons. Slepian functions and their use in signal estimation and spectral analysis. pp. 891–923. *In*: W. Freeden, M.Z. Nashed and T. Sonar (eds.). *Handbook of Geomathematics*. 1st Ed., Vol. 1, Springer, Heidelberg, 2010.

[107] F.J. Simons and A. Plattner. Scalar and vector Slepian functions, spherical signal estimation and spectral analysis. pp. 2563–2608. *In*: W. Freeden, M.Z. Nashed and T. Sonar (eds.). *Handbook of Geomathematics*. 2nd Edition, Vol. 3, 2015.

[108] D. Slepian and H.O. Pollak. Prolate spheroidal wave functions, Fourier analysis and Uncertainty—I. Bell Syst. Tech. J., 40: 43–64, 1961.

[109] D. Slepian. Prolate spheroidal wave functions, Fourier analysis and Uncertainty—IV. Extensions to Many Dimensions; Generalized Prolate Spheroidal Functions. Bell System Tech. J., 43: 3009–3057, 1964.

[110] D. Slepian. Some comments on Fourier analysis, uncertainty and modeling. SIAM Rev., 25: 379–393, 1983.

[111] E.M. Stein and G. Weiss. *Introduction to Fourier Analysis on Euclidean Spaces*. Princeton University Press, Princeton, NJ, 1971.

[112] W. Sun and X. Zhou. Average sampling in spline subspaces. Appl. Math. Letters, 15: 233–237, 2002.

[113] A.N. Tikhonov and V.Y. Arsenin. *Solutions of Ill-Posed Problems*. Wiley, New York, 1977.

[114] X.G. Xia and M.Z. Nashed. The Backus-Gilbert method for signals in reproducing Hilbert spaces and wavelet subspaces. Inverse Probl., 10: 785–804, 1994.

[115] A. Zayed. *Advances in Shannon's Sampling Theory*. CRC Press, Taylor & Francis Group, Boca Raton, 1993.

Chapter 15

An Equation Error Approach for Identifying a Random Parameter in a Stochastic Partial Differential Equation

Baasansuren Jadamba[a,*], *Akhtar A Khan*[a], *Quinn T Kolt*[a] and *Miguel Sama*[b]

2000 Mathematics Subject Classification. 35R30, 49N45, 65J22, 65M30.

15.1 Introduction

Stochastic partial differential equations (SPDEs) involving random variables parameters appear in abundance in applied models. The typical examples include the stochastic diffusion coefficient in the diffusion equation, the flexural rigidity coefficient in the Cauchy-Euler beam and plate models, the stochastic Láme parameters in the linear elasticity system equations, and the stochastic viscosity

[a] School of Mathematical Sciences, Rochester Institute of Technology, 85 Lomb Memorial Drive, Rochester, New York, 14623, USA.

[b] Departamento de Matemática Aplicada, Universidad Nacional de Educación a Distancia, Calle Juan del Rosal, 12, 28040 Madrid, Spain.

Emails: aaksma@rit.edu; ahk1190@rit.edu; msama@ind.uned.es

* Corresponding author: bxjsma@rit.edu

in the Stokes's equations. The significance of stochastic equations, differential and integral, was evident long ago; see the fundamental contributions by Engl and Nashed [21, 22], Nashed and Engl [40], and Nashed and Salehi [41], and the monograph by Bharucha-Reid [12]. Earlier research on SPDEs, besides establishing useful theoretical results, also developed some computational schemes. However, it is only in recent years when concentrated research efforts on the systematic numerical treatment of SPDEs have been made. See the basic results developed by Ghanem and Spanos [25], Deb, Babuvska, and Oden [20], Babuvska and Chatzipantelidis [5], Babuvska, Tempone, and Zouraris [7, 8], Babuvska, Nobile, and Tempone [6], and the cited references.

Assume that $(\Omega, \mathcal{F}, \mu)$ is a probability space, and $D \subset \mathbb{R}^m$ is a sufficiently smooth bounded domain and ∂D is its boundary. Given random fields $a : \Omega \times D \to \mathbb{R}$ and $f : \Omega \times D \to \mathbb{R}$, the direct problem in this work seeks a random field $u : \Omega \times D \to \mathbb{R}$ that almost surely satisfies the following boundary value problem (BVP) with random data:

$$-\nabla \cdot (a(\omega,x)\nabla u(\omega,x)) = f(\omega,x), \text{ in } D, \tag{15.1a}$$

$$u(\omega,x) = 0, \text{ on } \partial D. \tag{15.1b}$$

SPDE (15.1) appears in many applied models and has been extensively studied. SPDE (15.1) constitutes the direct problems in this study, and there are two associated inverse problems. The first inverse problem seeks, from some statistical information of $u(x,\omega)$, the statistical information of the random coefficient $a(x,\omega)$. This inverse problem is commonly referred to as the parameter identification problem. The second inverse problem seeks the right-hand side f, again from some information concerning the solution u. This inverse problem is the source identification problem. The latter problem is closely connected to the optimal control problem of finding the control $\theta(\omega,x)$ when the source term has the form $f(\omega,x) \equiv f(\omega,x) + \theta(\omega,x)$. In this work, we will focus on the inverse problem of parameter identification.

The problem of estimating stochastic or deterministic parameters in stochastic PDEs from a measurement of the solution of the SPDE has been widely studied in the last few years. We note that a common approach for inverse problems with data uncertainty is the Bayesian approach (see [23, 24, 45, 43]). The so-called variational approach attracted quite a bit of attention in recent years due to some of the shortcomings of the Bayesian approach. The variational approach is suitable for identifying distributed and spatially correlated parameters in SPDEs. It involves posing an optimization problem whose solution can provide information on statistical quantities associated with an unknown parameter. The key advantages of the variational approach include access to an array of efficient and reliable optimization algorithms, a theoretical framework for convergence analysis, and the ability to embed the parameter structure into the inversion framework. For some of the recent developments in stochastic control problems and stochastic inverse problems, we refer the reader to [1, 4, 10, 13, 14, 15, 16, 17, 18, 32, 34, 35, 36, 37, 39, 42, 44, 46, 47, 48, 49, 50] and the cited references.

The most commonly used optimization formulation for the stochastic inverse problem of parameter identification is the following output least-squares:

$$J_0(a) := \frac{1}{2}\mathbb{E}\left[\|u_a(\omega,x) - z(\omega,x)\|^2\right], \tag{15.2}$$

where $u_a(\omega,x)$ is the solution of (15.1) for $a(\omega,x)$, $z(\omega,x) \in L^2(\Omega;L^2(D))$ is the measured data, and $\|\cdot\|$ is a suitable norm, For example, $L_2(D)$-norm was considered in [1], whereas Wyk [48] employed $H_1(D)$-norm; $H_1(D)$-seminorm is another possibility. Here $\mathbb{E}[\cdot]$ is the expectation.

Recently, in the context of (15.1), the following modified output least-squares (MOLS) objective functional was introduced in [33]:

$$J(a) = \frac{1}{2}\mathbb{E}\left[\int_D a(\omega,x)\nabla(u_a(\omega,x) - z(\omega,x))\cdot\nabla(u_a(\omega,x) - z(\omega,x))dx\right],$$

where $u_a(\omega,x)$ is the weak solution of (15.1) for $a(\omega,x)$ and $z(\omega,x)$ is the measured data.

In [33], it was shown that the MOLS functional given above is convex. Similar results for the inverse problem of identifying a stochastic flexural rigidity coefficient in a fourth-order plate model are available in [30].

The primary objective of this work is to propose an equation error approach for solving the inverse problem of parameter identification in stochastic PDE (15.1). Besides advocating for the usefulness of the equation error approach for inverse problems, the developed framework also pitches it as a reliable and efficient fast alternative to other optimization formulations.

We divide the contents of this chapter into seven sections. In Section 2, we collect preliminary results related to the stochastic PDE and discuss the solvability of the associated variational form. Section 3 presents an overview of some of the most commonly used techniques for solving stochastic PDEs. Section 4 is devoted to the study of the new equation error formulation for the considered stochastic inverse problem. We give the unique solvability of the regularized stochastic optimization problem emerging from the equation error approach. We provide discrete formulas in Section 5. Section 6 gives preliminary numerical results. The chapter concludes with some general remarks.

15.2 Solvability of the Direct Problem

We begin with an overview of SPDEs and common computational techniques, noting that a majority of the available literature focused on (15.1). Before discussing the solvability of (15.1) and the associated inverse problem, we first recall some function spaces. Given the domain D, for $1 \leq p < \infty$, by $L^p(D)$, we represent the space of pth Lebesgue integrable functions, that is

$$L^p(D) = \left\{ y : D \mapsto \mathbb{R} \text{ is measurable, and } \int_D |y|^p \, dx < +\infty \right\}.$$

The space $L^\infty(D)$ consists of measurable functions that are bounded almost everywhere (a.e.) on D. We also recall that the Sobolev spaces are given by

$$\begin{aligned} H^1(D) &= \left\{ y \in L^2(D), \ \partial_{x_i} y \in L^2(D), \ i = 1, \ldots, n \right\}, \\ H_0^1(D) &= \left\{ y \in H^1(D), \ y|_{\partial D} = 0 \right\}, \end{aligned}$$

and $H^{-1}(D) = (H_0^1(D))^*$ is the topological dual of $H_0^1(D)$. For $m \in \mathbb{N}$, higher-order Sobolev spaces $H^m(D)$ consist of $L^2(D)$ functions with all partial derivatives up to order m reside in $L^2(D)$.

Moreover, we recall that given a real Banach space X, a probability space $(\Omega, \mathcal{F}, \mu)$, and an integer $p \in [1, \infty)$, the Bochner space $L^p(\Omega; X)$ consists of Bochner integrable functions $u : \Omega \to X$ with finite p-th moment, that is,

$$\|u\|_{L^p(\Omega;X)} := \left(\int_\Omega \|u(\omega)\|_X^p d\mu(\omega) \right)^{1/p} = \mathbb{E}\left[\|u(\omega)\|_X^p \right]^{1/p} < \infty,$$

where $\mathbb{E}[\cdot]$ is the expectation. For details and properties of these spaces, see [38].

If $p = \infty$, then $L^\infty(\Omega; X)$ is the space of Bochner measurable functions $u : \Omega \to X$ such that

$$\text{ess sup}_{\omega \in \Omega} \|u(\omega)\|_X < \infty.$$

Many useful features of $L^p(D)$ spaces of Lebesgue integrable functions translate naturally to Bochner spaces $L^p(\Omega; X)$. Moreover, it is known that $L^\infty(\Omega; L^\infty(D)) \subset L^\infty(\Omega \times D)$, but $L^\infty(\Omega; L^\infty(D)) \neq L^\infty(\Omega \times D)$, in general. Furthermore, the space $L^p(\Omega; L^q(D))$, for $p, q \in [1, \infty)$, is isomorphic to

$$\left\{ v : \Omega \times D \to \mathbb{R}^n | \int_\Omega \left(\int_D |v(\omega, x)|^q \, dx \right)^{p/q} d\mu(\omega) < \infty \right\}.$$

A critical part of the study of SPDEs is the **finite-dimensional noise** representation of the random fields by a finite number of mutually independent random variables (see [7, 38]): Given M random variables $\xi_k : \Omega \mapsto \Gamma_k$, for $k = 1, \ldots, M$, a function $v \in L^2(\Omega; L^2(D))$ of the form $v(\xi(\omega), x)$ for $x \in D$ and $\omega \in \Omega$, where $\xi = (\xi_1, \xi_2, \ldots, \xi_M) : \Omega \mapsto \Gamma \subset \mathbb{R}^M$ and $\Gamma := \Gamma_1 \times \Gamma_2 \cdots \times \Gamma_M$, is called a finite-dimensional noise.

If a random field $v(\omega, x)$ is finite-dimensional noise, a change of variables can be performed for computing expectations. To be specific, denoting by σ, the joint density of ξ, we have

$$\|v\|_{L^2(\Omega;L^2(D))}^2 = \mathbb{E}\left[\|v\|_{L^2(D)}^2 \right] = \int_\Gamma \sigma(y) \|v(y, \cdot)\|_{L^2(D)}^2 dy.$$

Therefore, by defining $y_k := \xi_k(\omega)$ and setting $y = (y_1, y_2, \ldots, y_M)$, we associate a random field $v(\omega, x)$ with a finite-dimensional noise by a function $v(x,y)$ in the weighted L^2 space:

$$L^2_\sigma(\Gamma; L^2(D)) := \left\{ v : \Gamma \times D \to \mathbb{R} : \int_\Gamma \sigma(y) \|v(\cdot, y)\|^2_{L^2(D)} dy < \infty \right\}.$$

Assume that $a(\omega, x)$ and $f(\omega, x)$ are finite-dimensional noises and given by

$$a(\omega, x) = a_0(x) + \sum_{k=1}^{P} a_k(x) \xi_k(\omega), \tag{15.3}$$

$$f(\omega, x) = f_0(x) + \sum_{k=1}^{L} f_k(x) \xi_k(\omega), \tag{15.4}$$

where the real-valued functions a_k and f_k are uniformly bounded. Then, as a consequence of the celebrated Doob-Dynkin lemma, a solution of (15.6) is finite-dimensional noise and u is a function of ξ where $\xi = (\xi_1, \xi_2, \ldots, \xi_M) : \Omega \mapsto \Gamma$ and $M := \max\{P, L\}$, see [38].

For the solvability of the variational problem (15.6), in the following we assume that there are constants k_0 and k_1 with

$$0 < k_0 \le a(\omega, x) \le k_1 < \infty, \text{ almost everywhere in } \Omega \times D. \tag{15.5}$$

For the variational form of BVP (15.1), we will use $\widehat{V} := L^2(\Omega; H^1(D))$ which is a Hilbert space with the inner product defined by

$$\langle u, v \rangle = \int_\Omega \langle u(\omega, x), v(\omega, x) \rangle_{H^1(\Omega)} \, d\mu(\omega).$$

To impose the boundary conditions, we will use $V = L^2(\Omega; H^1_0(\Omega)) \subset \widehat{V}$.

To derive the variational formulation, we take $u \in L^2(\Omega; H^2(D))$ and multiply (15.1) by a test function $v \in V$ and by integrating the product on both sides, invoking the Green's identity, and using the boundary conditions, we obtain

$$\begin{aligned} &\int_\Omega \int_D a(\omega, x) \nabla u(\omega, x) \cdot \nabla v(\omega, x) dx d\mu(\omega) \\ &\quad = \int_\Omega \int_D f(\omega, x) v(\omega, x) \, dx d\mu(\omega), \text{ for every } v \in V. \end{aligned} \tag{15.6}$$

Therefore, we are looking for elements $u \in V$ such that (15.6) holds for all $v \in V$.

For the solvability of (15.6), we introduce the following notation

$$s(u, v) = \int_\Omega \int_D a(\omega, x) \nabla u(\omega, x) \nabla v(\omega, x) \, dx d\mu(\omega), \tag{15.7}$$

$$m(v) = \int_\Omega \int_D f(\omega, x) v(\omega, x) \, dx d\mu(\omega), \tag{15.8}$$

and, for a fixed $a(\omega,x)$, write (15.6) as the problem of finding $u \in V$ with

$$s(u,v) = m(v), \quad \text{for every } v \in V. \tag{15.9}$$

Since $a(\omega,x) \in L^\infty(\Omega \times D)$ and $V \subset L^2(\Omega; L^2(D)) \cong L^2(\Omega \times D)$, we can show that

$$|s(u,v)| \leq \|a(\omega,x)\|_{L^\infty(\Omega\times D)} \|u(\omega,x)\|_V \|v(\omega,x)\|_V,$$

which proves that the bilinear form s is continuous.

Furthermore, the bilinear form $s(\cdot,\cdot)$ is coercive as well because

$$s(u,v) = \mathbb{E}\left[\int_D a(\omega,x)\nabla v(\omega,x)\cdot\nabla v(\omega,x)dx\right] \geq \alpha\|v(\omega,x)\|_V^2,$$

where α is a positive constant involving the Poincare's constant.

For the given $f \in L^2(\Omega; H^1(D)^*)$ and for any $v \in V$, for the functional $m(\cdot)$, we have

$$|m(v)| = \left|\mathbb{E}\left[\int_D f(\omega,x)v(\omega,x)\,dx\right]\right| \leq \|f(\omega,x)\|_{H^1(\Omega;H^1(D)^*)}\|v(\omega,x)\|_V,$$

which proves the continuity of m. Hence, the unique solvability of (15.6) ensues from the Lax-Milgram lemma.

For the inverse problem of parameter identification, analytic properties of the parameter-to-solution map $a \mapsto u_a(\omega,x)$, that assigns to a, the unique solution $u_a(\omega,x)$ of (15.6), are crucial. For this, we define $K \subset B := L^\infty(\Omega; L^\infty(D))$ to be the set of feasible parameters with a nonempty interior. We emphasize that the feasible parameters in K must satisfy (15.5). We recall the following result that gives the Lipschitz continuity of the parameter-to-solution map.

Proposition 15.2.1 [33] *The map $K \ni a(\omega,x) \mapsto u_a(\omega,x)$ is Lipschitz continuous.*

We next recall the following result that gives a derivative characterization of the parameter-to-solution map:

Theorem 15.2.2 [33] *Let $a(\omega,x)$ be in the interior of K. Then, the derivative $\delta u_a(\omega,x) := Du_a(\delta a(\omega,x))$ of $u_a(\omega,x)$ in the direction $\delta a(\omega,x)$ is the unique solution of the stochastic variational problem: Find $\delta u_a(\omega,x) \in V$ such that*

$$\begin{aligned}\int_\Omega\int_D & a(\omega,x)\nabla\delta u_a(\omega,x)\cdot\nabla v(\omega,x)dx\,d\mu(\omega) \\ &= -\int_\Omega\int_D \delta a\nabla u_a(\omega,x)\cdot\nabla v(\omega,x)\,dx\,d\mu(\omega), \quad \textit{for every } v \in V.\end{aligned} \tag{15.10}$$

The above derivative characterization plays a central role in developing a gradient-based optimization framework for solving the inverse problem and is instrumental in obtaining discrete formulas for the gradient of various objective functionals.

We note that under (15.3) and (15.4), the variational problem (15.6) reduces to the following parametric variational problem, which is commonly used for numerical simulations: Find $u(y,x) \in V_\sigma := L^2_\sigma(\Gamma; H^1_0(D))$ such that

$$\int_\Gamma \sigma(y) \int_D a(y,x)\nabla u(y,x) \cdot \nabla v(y,x) dx dy \\ = \int_\Gamma \sigma(y) \int_D f(y,x)v(y,x)\, dx dy, \quad \text{for all } v(y,x) \in V_\sigma. \tag{15.11}$$

15.3 Numerical Techniques for Stochastic PDEs

In the following, we briefly describe three of the commonly used numerical methods for solving SPDEs.

15.3.1 *Monte Carlo Finite Element Type Methods*

A heavily used approach for the numerical treatment of (15.11) is the sampling-based Monte Carlo Finite Element Method (MC-FE) approach, where for the deterministic component, a finite element discretization scheme is used. For the MC-FE method, s realizations of the random variable $y_j := (y^1_j, \ldots, y^m_j)$, $j = 1, \ldots, s$, are generated, and for each realization y_j, a solution of $u_j = u(y_j, x)$ of (15.11) is obtained involving the realizations of $a(y,x)$ and $f(y,x)$. From the solution samples, the desired statistics ensues. For instance, the ℓ-th moment of the solution $u(y,x)$ is obtained by

$$\mathbb{E}\left[u(\cdot,x)^\ell\right] \approx \frac{1}{s}\sum_{j=1}^{s} u(y_j,x)^\ell.$$

The MC-FE approach is robust, easily implementable, uses existing finite element solvers, and does not impose regularity restrictions on the data. However, a glaring pitfall is a slow convergence, with asymptotic order $\frac{1}{\sqrt{s}}$, requiring a large sample size for an acceptable approximation.

One of the many generalization of the MC-FE method, the **Multilevel Monte Carlo Finite Element** (MLMC-FE) method (see Giles [27], Barth et al. [11]), significantly reduces its computational cost. The key idea of the MLMC-FE is to employ hierarchical finite element spaces, acquiring sample solution on varying mesh-sizes and gradually decreasing the sample size on each finer mesh, finding a fine compromise between the convergence and discretization error.

15.3.2 The Stochastic Collocation Method

The stochastic collocation method (see [7]) is based on combining collocation on Γ and finite element discretization of D. It is similar to the MC-FE method in that it samples the random data, but without choosing the sampling point randomly. Given collocation points, $\{y_j\}_{j=1}^s$ in Γ, the collocation scheme defines an approximate solution as the Lagrangian interpolant

$$u_P(y,x) = \sum_{k=1}^{s} u(y_k,x)L_k(y),$$

where $L_k : \Gamma \mapsto \mathbb{R}$ is the Lagrange polynomial satisfying $L_k(y_s) = \delta_{ks}$, and $u(y_k,x)$ is the solution of the parametric PDE (15.11) at y_k.

Employing the Galerkin finite element discretization for the spatial component and denoting the finite element basis by $\{\phi_1,\ldots,\phi_N\}$, the complete approximate solution is given by

$$u_{hP}(y,x) = \sum_{k=1}^{s}\sum_{l=1}^{N} u_l^k \phi_l(x)L_k(y).$$

The commonly used collocation points are those generated by Smolyak's algorithm and lie on a sparse grid. For high stochastic dimension, Smolyak sparse grids have fewer points than the full tensor product, but only a slightly slow order of convergence. There are many variants of the stochastic collocation method. Bäck et al. [9] presented a comprehensive comparison of the stochastic Galerkin and stochastic collocation methods.

15.3.3 The Stochastic Galerkin Method

The stochastic Galerkin method (see [38]) builds around the parametric variational problem (15.11). Let V_h be an N-dimensional subspace of $H_0^1(D)$ and S_k be a Q-dimensional subspace of $L_\sigma^2(\Gamma)$ with

$$V_h = \text{span}\{\phi_1,\phi_2,\ldots,\phi_N\},$$
$$S_k = \text{span}\{\psi_1,\psi_2,\ldots,\psi_Q\},$$

where we assume that the basis $\{\psi_1,\psi_2,\ldots,\psi_Q\}$ is orthonormal with respect to σ. In stochastic Galerkin, the NQ-dimensional subspace V_σ can be constructed by tensorising the basis functions ϕ_i and ψ_j:

$$V_{hk} := V_h \otimes S_k := \text{span}\{\phi_i\psi_j \,|\, i=1,\ldots,N,\ j=1,\ldots,Q\}.$$

The **stochastic Galerkin solution** $u_{hk} \in V_{hk}$ then satisfies for all $v \in V_{hk}$:

$$\int_\Gamma \sigma(y)\int_D a(y,x)\nabla u_{hk}(y,x)\cdot\nabla v(y,x)dx\,dy = \int_\Gamma \sigma(y)\int_D f(y,x)v(y,x)dx\,dy.$$

In the above variational equations, taking the representation

$$u_{hk} = \sum_{k=1}^{N} \sum_{m=1}^{Q} U_{km} \phi_k(x) \psi_m(y),$$

a sparse linear system emerges which gives an approximate solution.

15.4 An Equation Error Approach

For inverse problems of identifying deterministic parameters, the extensively studied equation error approach is considered a compromise between an optimization-based iterative scheme and a direct solution method for finding the unknown parameter. Although the equation error approach is an optimization formulation, it bears no connection to the underlying PDE while solving the optimization problem. The OLS-based or MOLS-based optimization problems need to solve the underlying PDEs at every update, a strategy that makes these methods computationally demanding. In contrast, the equation error approach results in a speedy process for inverse problems. Moreover, being an optimization problem, the equation error approach allows for the natural inclusion of the regularization for stability. However, a drawback of not being related to the PDEs is that it heavily relies on the supplied data quality and performs poorly under high data contamination. For details on the equation error approach, see [2, 3, 19, 26, 28, 29].

For the stochastic inverse problem of estimating $a(\omega,x)$ from the data $z(\omega,x) \in L^2(\Omega; H_0^1(D))$, we propose the following equation error formulation:

$$J_{\mathcal{E}}(a(\omega,x)) := \frac{1}{2}\mathbb{E}\left[\|e(a,z)\|^2_{H^1(D)}\right] = \frac{1}{2}\int_{\Omega} \|e(a,z)\|^2_{H^1(D)}\, d\mu(\omega), \tag{15.12}$$

where $e(\cdot,\cdot) \in L^2(\Omega; H_0^1(D))$ is such that for every $v \in L^2(\Omega; H_0^1(D))$, we have

$$\begin{aligned}&\langle e(a,u), v\rangle_{L^2(\Omega;H_0^1(D))}\\ &= \int_{\Omega}\int_{D} [a(\omega,x)\nabla u(\omega,x)\cdot\nabla v(\omega,x) - f(\omega,x)v(\omega,x)]\, dx\, d\mu(\omega).\end{aligned} \tag{15.13}$$

For regularizing the equation error objective, we define the following admissible set

$$A := \left\{a \in H := L^2(\Omega; H(D)) :\ 0 < k_0 \le a(\omega,x) \le k_1 \text{ a.s. } \Omega \times D\right\},$$

where the regularization space H, a separable Hilbert space, is compactly embedded into $B := L^\infty(\Omega; L^\infty(D))$, and $H(D)$ is continuously embedded in $L^\infty(\Omega)$.

We now propose the following regularized equation error problem:

$$\min_{a\in A} J^{\kappa}_{\mathcal{E}}(a) := \frac{1}{2}\mathbb{E}\left[\|e(a,z)\|^2_{H^1(D)}\right] + \frac{\kappa}{2}\|a(\omega,x)\|^2_{H}, \tag{15.14}$$

where $z(\omega,x) \in L^2(\Omega;H_0^1(D))$ is the measured data, $\kappa > 0$ is a fixed regularization parameter, and $\|\cdot\|_H^2$ is the quadratic regularizer.

We have the following existence result:

Theorem 15.4.1 *For each $\kappa > 0$, the equation error based optimization problem (15.14) has a unique solution.*

Proof. Since $J_\varepsilon^\kappa(a) \geq 0$ for all $a \in A$, there exists a minimizing sequence $\{a_n\}$ in A, such that $\lim_{n\to\infty} J_\varepsilon^\kappa(a_n) = \inf_{a\in A} J_\varepsilon^\kappa(a)$. By the definition of the regularized equation error functional, the sequence $\{a_n\}$ is bounded in the H-norm. This, however, implies the existence of a subsequence, still denoted by $\{a_n\}$, that converges to some $\bar{a} \in A$ in the B-norm. In view of the definition of $e(\cdot,\cdot)$, for every $v \in L^2(\Omega;H_0^1(D))$, we have

$$\langle e(a_n,z),v\rangle_{L^2(\Omega;H_0^1(D))} = \mathbb{E}\left[\int_D [a_n\nabla z(\omega,x)\cdot\nabla v(\omega,x) - f(\omega,x)v(\omega,x)]\,dx\right],$$

$$\langle e(\bar{a},z),v\rangle_{L^2(\Omega;H_0^1(D))} = \mathbb{E}\left[\int_D [\bar{a}\nabla z(\omega,x)\cdot\nabla v(\omega,x) - f(\omega,x)v(\omega,x)]\,dx\right].$$

Subtracting the above two equations and setting $v = e(a_n,z) - e(\bar{a},z)$, we get

$$\begin{aligned}\|e(a_n,z)-e(\bar{a},z)\|^2_{L^2(\Omega;H_0^1(D))} &= \mathbb{E}\left[\int_D (a_n-\bar{a})\nabla z\cdot\nabla(e(a_n,z)-e(\bar{a},z))\,dx\right]\\ &\leq \|a_n-\bar{a}\|_{L^\infty(\Omega;L^\infty(D))}\|e(a_n,z)-e(\bar{a},z)\|_{L^2(\Omega;H_0^1(D))}\|z\|_{L^2(\Omega;H_0^1(D))},\end{aligned}$$

which confirms that $\|e(a_n,z)-e(\bar{a},z)\|^2_{L^2(\Omega;H_0^1(D))} \to 0$.

Consequently,

$$\begin{aligned}J_\varepsilon^\kappa(\bar{a}) &= \frac{1}{2}\mathbb{E}\left[\|e(\bar{a},z)\|^2_{H^1(D)}\right] + \frac{\kappa}{2}\|\bar{a}(\omega,x)\|_H^2\\ &\leq \lim_{n\to\infty}\frac{1}{2}\mathbb{E}\left[\|e(a_n,z)\|^2_{H^1(D)}\right] + \liminf_{n\to\infty}\frac{\kappa}{2}\|a_n(\omega,x)\|_H^2\\ &\leq \liminf_{n\to\infty}\left\{\frac{1}{2}\mathbb{E}\left[\|e(\bar{a},z)\|^2_{H^1(D)}\right] + \frac{\kappa}{2}\|a_n(\omega,x)\|_H^2\right\}\\ &= \inf\left\{J_\varepsilon^\kappa(a) \mid a(\omega,x)\in A\right\},\end{aligned}$$

confirming that $\bar{a}(\omega,x)$ is a solution of (15.14). The uniqueness follows from the strong convexity of the regularizer and convexity of the equation error objective. The proof is complete. □

15.5 Discrete Formulae

We will now give some discrete formulas for numerical simulations. Recall that the parametric variational problem seeks $u \in V_\sigma := L^2_\sigma(\Gamma, H^1_0(D))$ such that

$$\int_\Gamma \sigma(y) \int_D a(y,x)\nabla u(y,x) \cdot \nabla v(y,x)dxdy = \int_\Gamma \sigma(y) \int_D f(y,x)v(y,x)dxdy,$$

for all $v \in V_\sigma$.

Given a finite-dimensional subspace V_{hk} of V_σ, an element $u_{hk} \in V_{hk}$ is the stochastic Galerkin solution if

$$\int_\Gamma \sigma(y) \int_D a(y,x)\nabla u_{hk}(y,x) \cdot \nabla v(y,x)dxdy$$
$$= \int_\Gamma \sigma(y) \int_D f(y,x)v(y,x)dxdy, \text{ for all } v \in V_{hk}.$$

Assume that V_h is an N-dimensional subspace of $H^1_0(D)$ and S_k is a Q-dimensional subspace of $L^2_\sigma(\Gamma)$ such that

$$V_h = \text{span}\{\phi_1, \phi_2, \dots, \phi_N\},$$
$$S_k = \text{span}\{\psi_1, \psi_2, \dots, \psi_Q\}.$$

We assume that the basis $\{\psi_1, \psi_2, \dots, \psi_Q\}$ is orthonormal with respect to σ, that is,

$$\int_\Gamma \sigma(y)\psi_n(y)\psi_m(y)dy = \delta_{nm},$$

where δ_{nm} is the Kronecker delta: $\delta_{nm} = 1$ for $n = m$, $\delta_{nm} = 0$ for $n \neq m$. To obtain a finite-dimensional subspace of V_σ, we use the commonly used process of tensorising the basic functions ϕ_i and ψ_j. That is, we define the following NQ-dimensional subspace for solving the discrete variational problem:

$$V_{hk} = V_h \otimes S_k := \text{span}\{\phi_i\psi_j | \, i = 1, \dots, N, \; j = 1, \dots, Q\}.$$

Therefore, any $v \in V_h \otimes S_k$ has the representation

$$v(y,x) = \sum_{i=1}^{N}\sum_{j=1}^{Q} V_{ij}\phi_i(x)\psi_j(y) = \sum_{j=1}^{Q}\left[\sum_{i=1}^{N} V_{ij}\phi_i(x)\right]\psi_j(y) = \sum_{j=1}^{Q} V_j(x)\psi_j(y),$$

where

$$V_j(x) \equiv \sum_{i=1}^{N} V_{ij}\phi_i(x).$$

Setting, $V_j := \left[V_{1j}, \cdots, V_{Nj}\right]^\top \in \mathbb{R}^N$, we introduce the following vectorized notation:

$$\begin{aligned} V &= \mathrm{vec}(V_{ij}) \\ &= \left[V_{11}, \cdots, V_{N1}, V_{12}, \cdots, V_{N2}, \cdots, V_{1Q}, \cdots, V_{NQ}\right]^\top \\ &= \left[V_1, V_2, \cdots, V_Q\right]^\top \in \mathbb{R}^{QN\times 1}. \end{aligned}$$

Inspired by the use of the KL expansion (see [38]), we assume that the unknown random field $a(\cdot,\cdot)$ admits a finite linear expansion:

$$a(y,x) = a_0(x) + \sum_{s=1}^{M} y_s a_s(x) = \sum_{s=0}^{M} y_s a_s(x), \tag{15.15}$$

where, by convention, we take $y_0 = 1$. We discretize the spatial components a_s by using a P-dimensional space

$$A_h = \mathrm{span}\{\varphi_1, ..., \varphi_P\}.$$

Using the vector notation once again, we have

$$a(y,x) = \sum_{i=1}^{P} A_{i0}\varphi_i(x) + \sum_{s=1}^{M}\left(\sum_{i=1}^{P} A_{is}\varphi_i(x)\right) y_s = \sum_{s=0}^{M} A_s y_s \tag{15.16}$$

where the vectors $A_s(x) \equiv (A_{is}) \in \mathbb{R}^P$ for $s = 0\ldots, M$, and

$$A = \left[A_0, A_1, \cdots, A_M\right]^\top \in \mathbb{R}^{P(M+1)\times 1}.$$

Recall that the discrete variational problem seeks $u_{hk}(y,x) \in V_h \otimes S_Q$ such that

$$\int_\Gamma \sigma(y)\psi_n(y)\left(\int_D a(y,x)\nabla u_{hk}(y,x)\nabla\phi_i(x)dx\right)dy = \int_\Gamma \sigma(y)\psi_n(y)\left(\int_D f(y,x)\phi_i(x)dx\right)dy,$$

for every $i = 1,\ldots,N$, $n = 1,\ldots,Q$.

Then using in the above variational problem the representation

$$u_{hk} = \sum_{k=1}^{N}\sum_{m=1}^{Q} U_{km}\phi_k(x)\psi_m(y),$$

we obtain

$$\int_\Gamma \sigma(y)\psi_n(y)\left(\int_D a(y,x)\nabla\left(\sum_{k=1}^{N}\sum_{m=1}^{Q} U_{km}\phi_k(x)\psi_m(y)\right)\nabla\phi_i(x)dx\right)dy = \int_\Gamma \sigma(y)\psi_n(y)\left(\int_D f(y,x)\phi_i(x)dx\right)dy.$$

By substituting the expansion (15.16) in the above identity, and performing a simple calculation, we obtain, for every $i = 1,\ldots,N$, $n = 1,\ldots,Q$:

$$\sum_{k=1}^{N}\sum_{m=1}^{Q} U_{km}\int_{\Gamma}\sigma(y)\psi_n(y)\psi_m(y)\left(\int_D a(y,x)\nabla\phi_k(x)\nabla\phi_i(x)dx\right)dy$$
$$= \left(K(A_0)+\sum_{s=1}^{M} g_{nn}^{s}K(A_s)\right)U_n + \sum_{N\neq N}\sum_{s=1}^{M} g_{nm}^{s}K(A_s)U_m$$

where for every $s \in \{0,\ldots,M\}$, we define $K(A_s) \in \mathbb{R}^{n\times n}$ and $g_{nm}^{s} \in \mathbb{R}$ by

$$K(A_s)_{i,k} = \int_D A_s(x)\nabla\phi_k(x)\nabla\phi_i(x)dx,$$
$$g_{nm}^{s} = \int_{\Gamma}\sigma(y)\psi_n(y)\psi_m(y)y_s dy.$$

Now, for $s \in \{0,\ldots,M\}$, we set

$$G^s = (g_{nm}^{s}) \in \mathbb{R}^{Q\times Q},$$

where, the case $s = 0$, by orthonormality, corresponds to the unit matrix as follows

$$G^0 = \left(\int_{\Gamma}\sigma(y)\psi_n(y)\psi_m(y)dy\right) = I.$$

On the other hand, we discretize the right-hand side as follows

$$(F_n)_i = \int_{\Gamma}\sigma(y)\psi_n(y)\int_D f(y,x)\phi_i(x)dxdy, \quad \text{for every } n \in \{1,...,Q\}.$$

Summarizing, the discrete variational problem reads

$$\left(K(A_0)+\sum_{s=1}^{M} g_{nn}^{s}K(A_s)\right)U_n+\sum_{m\neq n}\sum_{s=1}^{M} g_{nm}^{s}K(A_s)U_m = F_n, \text{ for every } n = 1,\ldots,Q,$$

which corresponds to solving the linear system $K(A)U = F$ for $U = [U_1,U_2,\cdots,U_Q]^{\top}$, where $F = [F_1,F_2,\cdots,F_Q]^{\top}$ and the matrix $K(A)$ is given by:

$$K(A) := \left[\sum_{s=0}^{M} G^s \otimes K(A_s)\right],$$

where $\otimes$ is the Kronecker product.

The parametric analogue of (15.13) defining $e_{hk}(\cdot,\cdot) \in V_\sigma$ satisfies, for every $v \in V_\sigma$,

$$\langle e_{hk}(a,u),v\rangle_{V_\sigma} = \int_{\Gamma}\int_D [a(\omega,x)\nabla u(\omega,x)\cdot\nabla v(\omega,x) - f(\omega,x)v(\omega,x)]\, dx d\mu(\omega). \tag{15.17}$$

For a discrete form of the regularized equation error functional, we first obtain a discrete form of three inner products in V_σ. For $v_{hk}, w_{hk} \in V_\sigma$ with the following representations

$$v_{hk} = \sum_{k=1}^{N}\sum_{m=1}^{Q} V_{km}\phi_k(x)\psi_m(y),$$

$$w_{hk} = \sum_{k=1}^{N}\sum_{m=1}^{Q} W_{km}\phi_k(x)\psi_m(y),$$

we have

$$\begin{aligned}
\langle v_{hk}, w_{hk}\rangle_0 &:= \int_\Gamma \sigma(y)\int_D v_{hk}w_{hk}dxdy \\
&= \int_\Gamma\int_D \left(\sum_{i_1=1}^{N}\sum_{j_1=1}^{Q} V_{i_1j_1}\phi_{i_1}(x)\psi_{j_1}(y)\right)\left(\sum_{i_2=1}^{N}\sum_{j_2=1}^{Q} W_{i_2j_2}\phi_{i_2}(x)\psi_{j_2}(y)\right)\sigma(y)dxdy \\
&= \sum_{i_1,i_2=1}^{N}\sum_{j_1,j_2=1}^{Q} V_{i_1j_1}W_{i_2j_2}\left(\int_D \phi_{i_1}(x)\phi_{i_2}(x)dx\right)\left(\int_\Gamma \psi_{j_1}(y)\psi_{j_2}(y)\sigma(y)dy\right) \\
&= \sum_{j_1,j_2=1}^{Q} \widehat{V}_{j_1}^\top M_u\widehat{W}_{j_2}\left(\int_\Gamma \psi_{j_1}(y)\psi_{j_2}\sigma(y)dy\right) \\
&= V^\top(I\otimes M_u)W, \qquad (15.18)
\end{aligned}$$

where $\widehat{V}_{j_1} = [V_{1j_1},\ldots,V_{N,j_1}]^\top \in \mathbb{R}^N$, $V = [\widehat{V}_1,\ldots,\widehat{V}_Q]^\top \in \mathbb{R}^{NQ}$, $I \in \mathbb{R}^{Q\times Q}$ is the identity matrix, and $M_u \in \mathbb{R}^{N\times N}$ are given by

$$(M_u)_{i_1i_2} = \int_D \phi_{i_1}(x)\phi_{i_2}(x)dx.$$

Analogously, for computing semi-norms, we have

$$\begin{aligned}
\langle v_{hk}, w_{hk}\rangle_1 &:= \int_\Gamma\int_D \nabla v_{hk}\cdot\nabla w_{hk}\sigma(y)dxdy \\
&= \int_\Gamma\int_D \nabla\left(\sum_{i_1=1}^{N}\sum_{j_1=1}^{Q} V_{i_1j_1}\phi_{i_1}(x)\psi_{j_1}(y)\right)\cdot\nabla\left(\sum_{i_2=1}^{N}\sum_{j_2=1}^{Q} W_{i_2j_2}\phi_{i_2}(x)\psi_{j_2}(y)\right)\sigma(y)dxdy \\
&= \sum_{i_1,i_2=1}^{N}\sum_{j_1,j_2=1}^{Q} V_{i_1j_1}W_{i_2j_2}\left(\int_D \nabla\phi_{i_1}(x)\cdot\nabla\phi_{i_2}(x)dx\right)\left(\int_\Gamma \psi_{j_1}(y)\psi_{j_2}(y)\sigma(y)dy\right) \\
&= \sum_{j_1,j_2=1}^{Q} \widehat{V}_{j_1}^\top K\widehat{W}_{j_2}\left(\int_\Gamma \psi_{j_1}(y)\psi_{j_2}\sigma(y)dy\right) \\
&= V^\top(I\otimes K_u)W, \qquad (15.19)
\end{aligned}$$

where $K_u \in \mathbb{R}^{N\times N}$ is given by

$$(K_u)_{i_1 i_2} = \int_D \nabla\phi_{i_1}(x)\cdot\nabla\phi_{i_2}(x)dx.$$

Finally, combining the above two estimates, we have the following form:

$$\begin{aligned}\langle v_{hk}, w_{hk}\rangle_{V_\sigma} &= \int_\Gamma \sigma(y)\int_D [v_{hk}w_{hk} + \nabla v_{hk}\cdot\nabla w_{hk}]\, dxdy \\ &= V^\top (I\otimes(K_u+M_u))\,W.\end{aligned}$$

Assume that the discrete $e_{hk}(a,z)$ and the data z_{hk} have the representations:

$$\begin{aligned} e_{hk} &= \sum_{k=1}^{N}\sum_{m=1}^{Q} E_{km}(A,Z)\phi_k(x)\psi_m(y), \\ z_{hk} &= \sum_{k=1}^{N}\sum_{m=1}^{Q} Z_{km}\phi_k(x)\psi_m(y),\end{aligned}$$

where $E(A,Z), Z \in \mathbb{R}^{NQ}$.

Then, in view of the above calculations, we obtain from (15.17) that

$$(I\otimes(K_u+M_u))\,E(A,Z) = K(A)Z - F = \left[\sum_{s=0}^{M} G^s\otimes K(A_s)\right] Z - F,$$

or equivalently,

$$\begin{aligned} E(A,Z) &= (I\otimes(K_u+M_u))^{-1}\left[\left[\sum_{s=0}^{M} G^s\otimes K(A_s)\right] Z - F\right] \\ &= I\otimes(K_u+M_u)^{-1}\left[\left[\sum_{s=0}^{M} G^s\otimes K(A_s)\right] Z - F\right]. \end{aligned} \tag{15.20}$$

The above expression at once gives the discrete formula for the equation error formulation (without the regularization term):

$$J_{\mathcal{E}}(A) = \frac{1}{2}\|E(A,Z)\|^2 = \left\langle K(A)Z - F, (I\otimes(K_u+M_u))^{-1}(K(A)Z-F)\right\rangle,$$

where $K(A) = \left[\sum_{s=0}^{M} G^s\otimes K(A_s)\right]$.

A formula for the gradient of $J_{\mathcal{E}}$ can be computed using the linearity of E with respect to A. Moreover, a discrete formula for a norm regularizer can also be easily obtained by the formulas given above for various inner products.

15.6 Computational Experiments

In this section, we present results of some numerical experiments for one-dimensional problems where we use the equation error method with stochastic Galerkin. We assume that the desired parameter is in form of a finite linear combination:

$$a(\omega,x) = a_0(x) + \sum_{\ell=1}^{M} a_\ell(x) Y_\ell(\omega),$$

and that the joint distribution of $(Y_1, Y_2, \ldots, Y_M)$ is known a priori. Piecewise linear finite elements are used and we use the H^1 semi-norm regularization for the objective functional. Relative errors in the mean and variance of a and u are computed by the error functional defined below. For the mean and variance of the coefficient a, we use

$$\varepsilon_{\text{mean}}^{SG}(a) = \frac{\sqrt{\int_D \left(\mathbb{E}[\bar{a}(\cdot,x)] - \mathbb{E}[a^{SG}(\cdot,x)]\right)^2 dx}}{\sqrt{\int_D \mathbb{E}[\bar{a}(\cdot,x)]^2 dx}},$$

$$\varepsilon_{\text{var}}^{SG}(a) = \frac{\sqrt{\int_D \left(\mathbb{V}\text{ar}[\bar{a}(\cdot,x)] - \mathbb{V}\text{ar}[a^{SG}(\cdot,x)]\right)^2 dx}}{\sqrt{\int_D \mathbb{V}\text{ar}[\bar{a}(\cdot,x)]^2 dx}}.$$

Similarly, the relative error functional for the mean and variance of u are defined by

$$\varepsilon_{\text{mean}}^{SG}(u) = \frac{\sqrt{\int_D \left(\mathbb{E}[\bar{u}(\cdot,x)] - \mathbb{E}[u(a^{SG})(\cdot,x)]\right)^2 dx}}{\sqrt{\int_D \mathbb{E}[\bar{u}(\cdot,x)]^2 dx}},$$

$$\varepsilon_{\text{var}}^{SG}(u) = \frac{\sqrt{\int_D \left(\mathbb{V}\text{ar}[\bar{a}(\cdot,x)] - \mathbb{V}\text{ar}[u(a^{SG})(\cdot,x)]\right)^2 dx}}{\sqrt{\int_D \mathbb{V}\text{ar}[\bar{u}(\cdot,x)]^2 dx}}.$$

Example 15.6.1 This example has a single random variable Y_1 and we assume that $Y_1 \sim U[0,1]$ (i.e., Y_1 is uniformly distributed on $[0,1]$). Moreover, SPDE (15.1) is satisfied by the following data set on the domain $D = (0,1)$:

$$\begin{aligned}
\bar{a}(\omega,x) &= 1 + Y_1(\omega), \\
\bar{u}(\omega,x) &= x(1-x) + Y_1(\omega)\sin(\pi x), \\
f(\omega,x) &= (1 + Y_1(\omega))\left(2 + \pi^2 Y_1(\omega)\sin(\pi x)\right).
\end{aligned}$$

Figure 15.1 shows realizations of the exact and the estimated coefficients $a(\omega,x)$, and corresponding point-wise errors in the coefficient in the top row. The second row figures are realizations of the simulated solution $u = u(a)$ (each curve shows

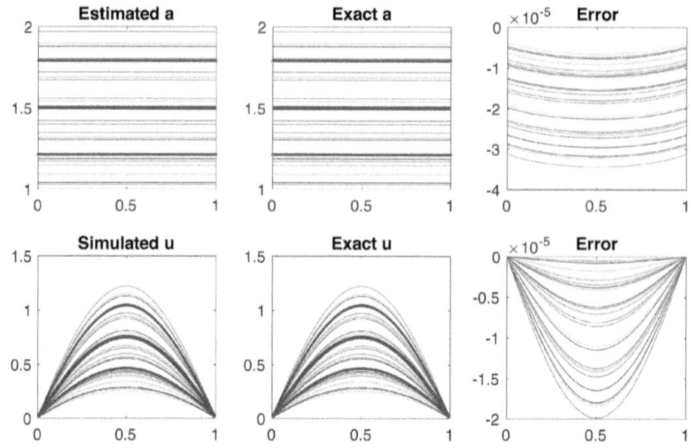

Figure 15.1: A comparison of 30 realizations of the coefficient a and the solution u in the inverse problem of identifying a in Example 15.6.1. Mesh size is $h = 1/50$ and the regularization parameter is $\kappa = 10^{-6}$. The thick red line represents the mean of the random fields a and u, and the red dotted lines represent ± 1 standard deviation from the mean.

a solution of the direct problem using the estimated coefficient a for a fixed value of ω) along with the exact solution u and corresponding point-wise errors. Relative errors for the mean and variance of a and u for various values of the $R = \dim(V_h)$ (mesh size is $h = 1/(R+1)$) are shown in the Table 15.1.

Table 15.1: Relative errors for the equation error method with stochastic Galerkin for Example 15.6.1. The numbers correspond to the case where the regularization parameter κ is fixed at 10^{-6}.

$\dim(V_h)$	$\varepsilon^{SG}_{\text{mean}}(a)$	$\varepsilon^{SG}_{\text{var}}(a)$	$\varepsilon^{SG}_{\text{mean}}(u)$	$\varepsilon^{SG}_{\text{var}}(u)$
50	2.1425e−4	9.1465e−4	7.7522e−5	6.5774e−4
100	5.3570e−5	2.2874e−4	1.9385e−5	1.6448e−4
150	2.3810e−5	1.0167e−4	8.6157e−6	7.3105e−5
200	1.3393e−5	5.7189e−5	4.8464e−6	4.1122e−5

Example 15.6.2 We take $D = (0,1)$, and assume that the two random variables involved are independent from each other and $Y_1, Y_2 \sim U[0,1]$. Moreover, SPDE (15.1) is satisfied by the following data set:

$$\bar{a}(\omega,x) = 3 + x^2 + Y_1(\omega)\cos(\pi x) + Y_2(\omega)\sin(2\pi x),$$
$$\bar{u}(\omega,x) = x(1-x)Y_1(\omega).$$

Realizations of the exact coefficient, the identified coefficient, the exact solution, and the simulated solution are shown in Figure 15.2 along with the corresponding errors. Relative errors for the mean and variance of a and u for various values of the $Q = \dim(V_h)$ are shown in the Table 15.2.

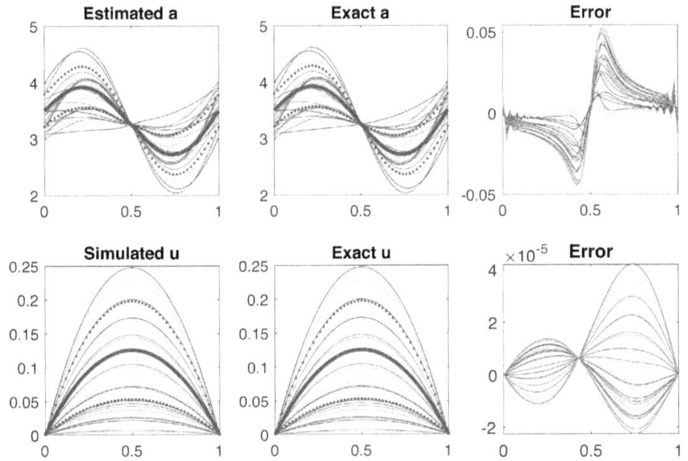

Figure 15.2: A comparison of 30 realizations of a and u in the inverse problem of identifying a in Example 15.6.2. Mesh size is $h = 1/200$ and the regularization parameter is $\kappa = 10^{-5}$. The thick red line represents the mean of the random fields a and u, and the red dotted lines represent ± 1 standard deviation from the mean.

Table 15.2: Relative errors for the equation error method with stochastic Galerkin for Example 15.6.2. The numbers correspond to the case where the regularization parameter κ is 10^{-6}.

$\dim(V_h)$	$\varepsilon_{\text{mean}}^{SG}(a)$	$\varepsilon_{\text{var}}^{SG}(a)$	$\varepsilon_{\text{mean}}^{SG}(u)$	$\varepsilon_{\text{var}}^{SG}(u)$
50	0.0036	0.0096	1.7321e−4	3.4020e−4
100	0.0034	0.0098	4.3343e−5	8.5117e−5
150	0.0033	0.0097	1.9267e−5	3.7835e−5
200	0.0033	0.0095	1.0838e−5	2.1283e−5

Example 15.6.3 We consider an example from [31]. In the example, we have $D = (0,1)$ and the coefficient and the solution have the following expansions:

$$\bar{u}(\omega, x) = x\left(1 - x^2\right) + \sum_{n=1}^{M} \sin(2n\pi x) Y_n,$$

$$\bar{a}(\omega, x) = \left(1 + x^3\right) + \sum_{n=1}^{M} \cos\left(\frac{n\pi x}{2M}\right) Y_n.$$

Here, $Y_1, Y_2, \ldots, Y_M$ are independent and uniformly distributed on $[0,1]$.

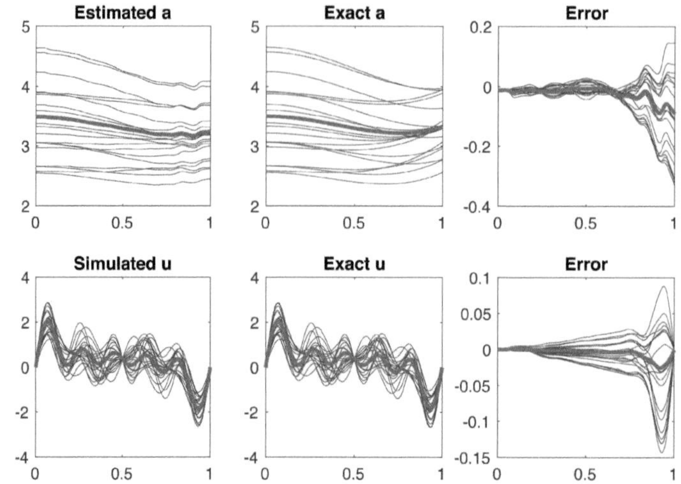

Figure 15.3: A comparison of 20 realizations of a and u in the inverse problem of identifying a in Example 15.6.3. The thick bold lines represent the means of the random fields a and u.

Results of the numerical experiments with 5 random variables ($M = 5$ case) are shown in Figure 15.3. We note that the computational time is dependent on the number of random variables present in the problem (for stochastic Galerkin method, stiffness matrices are assembled for each term a_ℓ in the finite linear expansion of the coefficient a). Equation error method is very efficient in solving the inverse problem compared to other traditional methods such as output least squares (OLS) since the direct problem is not solved at every optimization iteration. For Example 15.6.2 (two random variables), the method takes less than a minute in MATLAB for any reasonable mesh size h that gives a good resolution of both the solution u and the coefficient a (for example, $h = 1/100$ or $1/200$). Computational efforts are scaled proportionally for problems with more random variables (see Example 15.6.3) in one-dimensional case.

15.7 Concluding Remarks

We presented an overview of the recent developments in a stochastic inverse problem and proposed a new approach using equation error method in this work. Preliminary numerical results we obtained demonstrate that the equation error approach is very efficient and delivers good quality identifications for the coefficient. However, a thorough comparison with other methods that use optimization formulations (especially for problems in two- or three-dimensions) is necessary. Sensitivity of the method for data with noise should be also studied carefully. Convergent behavior of the method is observed numerically, and we note that any advance towards developing a rigorous error estimate for the identified coefficient would be of particular importance.

Acknowledgments

B. Jadamba and A. Khan are supported by the NSF (DMS 1720067). M. Sama is supported by Ministerio de Ciencia, Innovación y Universidades (MCIU), Agencia Estatal de Investigación (AEI) (Spain) and Fondo Europeo de Desarrollo Regional (FEDER) under project PGC2018-096899-B-I00 (MCIU/AEI/FEDER, UE) and and [grant number 2021-MAT11] (ETSI Industriales, UNED).

References

[1] R. Aboulaich, N. Fikal, E. El Guarmah and N. Zemzemi. Stochastic finite element method for torso conductivity uncertainties quantification in electrocardiography inverse problem. Math. Model. Nat. Phenom., 11(2): 1–19, 2016.

[2] R. Acar. Identification of the coefficient in elliptic equations. SIAM J. Control Optim., 31(5): 1221–1244, 1993.

[3] M.F. Al-Jamal and M.S. Gockenbach. Stability and error estimates for an equation error method for elliptic equations. Inverse Problems, 28(9): 095006, 15, 2012.

[4] A. Alexanderian, N. Petra, G. Stadler and O. Ghattas. Mean-variance riskaverse optimal control of systems governed by PDEs with random parameter fields using quadratic approximations. SIAM/ASA J. Uncertain. Quantif., 5(1): 1166–1192, 2017.

[5] I. Babuvska and P. Chatzipantelidis. On solving elliptic stochastic partial differential equations. Comput. Methods Appl. Mech. Engrg., 191(37-38): 4093–4122, 2002.

[6] I. Babuvska, F. Nobile and R. Tempone. A stochastic collocation method for elliptic partial differential equations with random input data. SIAM J. Numer. Anal., 45(3): 1005–1034, 2007.

[7] I. Babuvska, R. Tempone and G.E. Zouraris. Galerkin finite element approximations of stochastic elliptic partial differential equations. SIAM J. Numer. Anal., 42(2): 800–825, 2004.

[8] I. Babuvska, R. Tempone and G.E. Zouraris. Solving elliptic boundary value problems with uncertain coefficients by the finite element method: The stochastic formulation. Comput. Methods Appl. Mech. Engrg., 194(12-16): 1251–1294, 2005.

[9] J. Bäck, F. Nobile, L. Tamellini and R. Tempone. Stochastic spectral Galerkin and collocation methods for PDEs with random coefficients: a numerical comparison. pp. 43–62. *In*: *Spectral and High Order Methods for Partial Differential Equations*, volume 76 of *Lect. Notes Comput. Sci. Eng.*Springer, Heidelberg, 2011.

[10] V.A. Badrinarayanan and N. Zabaras. Stochastic inverse heat conduction using a spectral approach. Internat. J. Numer. Methods Engrg., 60(9): 1569–1593, 2004.

[11] A. Barth, C. Schwab and N. Zollinger. Multi-level Monte Carlo finite element method for elliptic PDEs with stochastic coefficients. Numer. Math., 119(1): 123–161, 2011.

[12] A.T. Bharucha-Reid. *Random Integral Equations*. Academic Press, New York-London, 1972. Mathematics in Science and Engineering, Vol. 96.

[13] J. Borggaard and H.-W. van Wyk. Gradient-based estimation of uncertain parameters for elliptic partial differential equations. Inverse Problems, 31(6): 065008, 33, 2015.

[14] A. Borzi. Multigrid and sparse-grid schemes for elliptic control problems with random coefficients. Comput. Vis. Sci., 13(4): 153–160, 2010.

[15] P. Chen, A. Quarteroni and G. Rozza. A weighted reduced basis method for elliptic partial differential equations with random input data. SIAM J. Numer. Anal., 51(6): 3163–3185, 2013.

[16] P. Chen, A. Quarteroni and G. Rozza. Comparison between reduced basis and stochastic collocation methods for elliptic problems. J. Sci. Comput., 59(1): 187–216, 2014.

[17] P. Chen, A. Quarteroni and G. Rozza. Multilevel and weighted reduced basis method for stochastic optimal control problems constrained by Stokes equations. Numer. Math., 133(1): 67–102, 2016.

[18] P. Chen, A. Quarteroni and G. Rozza. Reduced basis methods for uncertainty quantification. SIAM/ASA J. Uncertain. Quantif., 5(1): 813–869, 2017.

[19] E. Crossen, M.S. Gockenbach, B. Jadamba, A.A. Khan and B. Winkler. An equation error approach for the elasticity imaging inverse problem for predicting tumor location. Comput. Math. Appl., 67(1): 122–135, 2014.

[20] M.K. Deb, I.M. Babuvska and J.T. Oden. Solution of stochastic partial differential equations using Galerkin finite element techniques. Comput. Methods Appl. Mech. Engrg., 190(48): 6359–6372, 2001.

[21] H.W. Engl and M.Z. Nashed. Stochastic projectional schemes for random linear operator equations of the first and second kinds. Numer. Funct. Anal. Optim., 1(5): 451–473, 1979.

[22] H.W. Engl and M.Z. Nashed. Generalized inverses of random linear operators in Banach spaces. J. Math. Anal. Appl., 83(2): 582–610, 1981.

[23] O.G. Ernst, B. Sprungk and H.-J. Starkloff. Bayesian inverse problems and Kalman filters. pp. 133–159. *In: Extraction of Quantifiable Information from Complex Systems*, volume 102 of *Lect. Notes Comput. Sci. Eng.* Springer, Cham, 2014.

[24] O.G. Ernst, B. Sprungk and H.-J. Starkloff. Analysis of the ensemble and polynomial chaos Kalman filters in Bayesian inverse problems. SIAM/ASA J. Uncertain. Quantif., 3(1): 823–851, 2015.

[25] R.G. Ghanem and P.D. Spanos. *Stochastic Finite Elements: A Spectral Approach.* Springer-Verlag, New York, 1991.

[26] A. Gibali, B. Jadamba, A.A. Khan, F. Raciti and B. Winkler. Gradient and extragradient methods for the elasticity imaging inverse problem using an equation error formulation: a comparative numerical study. pp. 65–89. *In*: *Nonlinear Analysis and Optimization*, volume 659 of *Contemp. Math.* Amer. Math. Soc., Providence, RI, 2016.

[27] M.B. Giles. Multilevel Monte Carlo path simulation. Oper. Res., 56(3): 607–617, 2008.

[28] M.S. Gockenbach, B. Jadamba and A.A. Khan. Numerical estimation of discontinuous coefficients by the method of equation error. Int. J. Math. Comput. Sci., 1(3): 343–359, 2006.

[29] M.S. Gockenbach, B. Jadamba, A.A. Khan, C. Tammer and B. Winkler. Proximal methods for the elastography inverse problem of tumor identification using an equation error approach. pp. 173–197. *In*: *Advances in Variational and Hemivariational Inequalities*, volume 33 of *Adv. Mech. Math.* Springer, Cham, 2015.

[30] W. Grecksch, B. Jadamba, A.A. Khan, M. Sama and Chr. Tammer. Inverse problem of estimating the stochastic flexural rigidity in fourth-order models. Pure and Applied Functional Analysis. Accepted, at press, 1–27, 2021.

[31] M. Gunzburger, C. Trenchea and C.G. Webster. Error estimates for a stochastic collocation approach to identification and control problems for random elliptic pdes, 2008.

[32] M. Heinkenschloss, B. Kramer and T. Takhtaganov. Adaptive reduced-order model construction for conditional value-at-risk estimation. SIAM/ASA J. Uncertain. Quantif., 8(2): 668–692, 2020.

[33] B. Jadamba, A.A. Khan, M. Sama, H.-J. Starkloff and Chr. Tammer. A convex optimization framework for the inverse problem of identifying a random parameter in a stochastic partial differential equation. Revised version under review, 2020.

[34] P. Kolvenbach, O. Lass and S. Ulbrich. An approach for robust PDE constrained optimization with application to shape optimization of electrical engines and of dynamic elastic structures under uncertainty. Optim. Eng., 19(3): 697–731, 2018.

[35] D.P. Kouri, M. Heinkenschloss, D. Ridzal and B.G. van Bloemen Waanders. A trust-region algorithm with adaptive stochastic collocation for PDE optimization under uncertainty. SIAM J. Sci. Comput., 35(4): A1847–A1879, 2013.

[36] H.-C. Lee and M.D. Gunzburger. Comparison of approaches for random PDE optimization problems based on different matching functionals. Comput. Math. Appl., 73(8): 1657–1672, 2017.

[37] C. Li and G. Stadler. Sparse solutions in optimal control of PDEs with uncertain parameters: The linear case. SIAM J. Control Optim., 57(1): 633–658, 2019.

[38] G.J. Lord, C.E. Powell and T. Shardlow. *An Introduction to Computational Stochastic PDEs*. Cambridge Texts in Applied Mathematics. Cambridge University Press, New York, 2014.

[39] J. Martínez-Frutos and F. Periago E. *Optimal Control of PDEs Under Uncertainty*. Springer Briefs in Mathematics. Springer, 2018.

[40] M.Z. Nashed and H.W. Engl. Random generalized inverses and approximate solutions of random operator equations. pp. 149–210. *In*: *Approximate Solution of Random Equations*. North-Holland, New York-Amsterdam, 1979.

[41] M.Z. Nashed and H. Salehi. Measurability of generalized inverses of random linear operators. SIAM J. Appl. Math., 25: 681–692, 1973.

[42] A. Nouy and C. Soize. Random field representations for stochastic elliptic boundary value problems and statistical inverse problems. European J. Appl. Math., 25(3): 339–373, 2014.

[43] B.V. Rosić and H.G. Matthies. Identification of properties of stochastic elastoplastic systems. pp. 237–253. *In: Computational Methods in Stochastic Dynamics*, volume 26. Springer, Dordrecht, 2013.

[44] E. Rosseel and G.N. Wells. Optimal control with stochastic PDE constraints and uncertain controls. Comput. Methods Appl. Mech. Engrg., 213/216: 152–167, 2012.

[45] A.M. Stuart. Inverse problems: A Bayesian perspective. Acta Numer., 19: 451–559, 2010.

[46] R.E. Tanase. *Parameter estimation for partial differential equations using stochastic methods*, 2016. Thesis (Ph.D.)–University of Pittsburgh.

[47] H. Tiesler, R.M. Kirby, D. Xiu and T. Preusser. Stochastic collocation for optimal control problems with stochastic PDE constraints. SIAM J. Control Optim., 50(5): 2659–2682, 2012.

[48] H.-W. Van Wyk. *A variational approach to estimating uncertain parameters in elliptic systems*. PhD thesis, Virginia Tech, 2012.

[49] J.E. Warner, W. Aquino and M.D. Grigoriu. Stochastic reduced order models for inverse problems under uncertainty. Comput. Methods Appl. Mech. Engrg., 285: 488–514, 2015.

[50] N. Zabaras and B. Ganapathysubramanian. A scalable framework for the solution of stochastic inverse problems using a sparse grid collocation approach. J. Comput. Phys., 227(9): 4697–4735, 2008.

Index